PROCEEDINGS OF THE
BRITISH ACADEMY

VOLUME LXIII

1977

LONDON
PUBLISHED FOR THE BRITISH ACADEMY
BY THE OXFORD UNIVERSITY PRESS
1978

The papers contained in this volume are issued as separate booklets and can be obtained from The British Academy, Burlington House, Piccadilly, London W1V 0NS

ISBN 0 19 725983 9

Printed in Great Britain
at the University Press, Oxford
by Eric Buckley
Printer to the University

CONTENTS

OBITUARY NOTICES

LIST OF ILLUSTRATIONS

OBITUARY NOTICES

THE BRITISH ACADEMY

OFFICERS AND COUNCIL

1977–8

PRESIDENT

SIR ISAIAH BERLIN, O.M., C.B.E.

VICE-PRESIDENTS

PROFESSOR H. L. A. HART
PROFESSOR J. LYONS

COUNCIL

[77] PROFESSOR L. J. AUSTIN
[76] THE REVD. PROFESSOR J. BARR
[75] THE VERY REVD. PROFESSOR M. BLACK
[75] SIR ANTHONY BLUNT, K.C.V.O.
[77] PROFESSOR A. J. BROWN, C.B.E.
[76] SIR KENNETH DOVER
[77] PROFESSOR J. D. EVANS
[75] PROFESSOR M. I. FINLEY
[76] SIR JOHN HABAKKUK
[75] PROFESSOR H. L. A. HART
[77] PROFESSOR F. S. L. LYONS
[76] PROFESSOR J. LYONS
[76] DR. G. MARSHALL
[77] PROFESSOR J. H. PLUMB
[75] PROFESSOR B. A. O. WILLIAMS

TREASURER

PROFESSOR W. G. BEASLEY

FOREIGN SECRETARY

PROFESSOR A. G. DICKENS, C.M.G.

PUBLICATIONS SECRETARY

PROFESSOR J. M. WALLACE-HADRILL*

SECRETARY

MR. J. P. CARSWELL, C.B.*

[75] Elected 1975. [76] Elected 1976. [77] Elected 1977.
* From January 1978.

PROCEEDINGS OF THE BRITISH ACADEMY

1977

PRESIDENTIAL ADDRESS

BY SIR ISAIAH BERLIN

30 June 1977

I BEGIN, as is customary, by expressing our sorrow at the death, since we last met here, of nine Fellows: Professor E. M. Carus-Wilson, Professor R. R. Darlington, Dr. M. H. Dobb, Sir Goronwy Edwards, Professor V. H. Galbraith, Professor H. G. Johnson, Lord Radcliffe, Sir Edward Robinson, and, finally, Sir Mortimer Wheeler. Mortimer Wheeler seems to me to have done more for the Academy than any Fellow, living or dead, save perhaps the founders themselves. He was commemorated by Sir Max Mallowan in a vividly expressed and most memorable address at the memorial service for him in November last year, and his principal achievements are recorded in our Annual Report for 1975/6. I hope to say something about what his personality and services to the Academy meant to us at our Dinner this evening, so I shall say no more about them here; they will surely be remembered so long as this institution is in being. A full obituary account will, of course, be published in our *Proceedings*. The shadow that had been cast by the death of his successor, Derek Allen, whose passing we mourned last year, was deepened by his own death which followed so soon afterwards. In the course of this year, too, we have suffered the tragic death of Allen's successor, Neville Williams, who died before his time in January in Nairobi while engaged upon work for the Academy. There is very little that I can add to the full and memorable tribute paid to him by his life-long friend, the Foreign Secretary, Professor Geoffrey Dickens; but I should like to put on record what every Fellow of the Academy, I am sure, knows—that no better or nicer man, nor one more deeply devoted to our interests, more effective in promoting them and in encouraging others to do so, can ever have rendered service to the Academy. His death was a terrible blow to us all, and particularly to those who worked closely with him, as I, most happily, did. His wisdom, sagacity, tact, and humanity were unique assets to the Academy, and saved me, and perhaps others, from errors and oversights which we might otherwise easily have perpetrated. I know that these qualities, as well as his lively imagination, his charm, his friendliness, and his generous heart found a sympathetic response far outside the walls of the Academy—among the members of the learned bodies, and government departments, with which he dealt; the tributes to him, both from institutions and individuals, sent to us here, were singularly warm and heart-felt—far beyond the conventional condolences it is usual to extend on such occasions. He was the first Secretary not to have been a Fellow of the Academy, and more than justified his choice by my predecessor, Sir Denys Page, and the Council. I am glad to report that Professor Dickens has agreed to write his obituary for our *Proceedings*.

The death of Neville Williams imposed a heavy burden upon our administrative staff. The Academy owes every one of them a debt of gratitude for their devotion and efficiency. It has been a hard time for everyone, for none more so than the Acting Secretary, Mr. Peter Brown. He rose to the occasion wonderfully. His qualities of understanding, tact, unflappable good humour, and excellent judgement have proved of immense value during a difficult time, and have earned him the admiration of us all. It is a source of great personal pleasure to me to be able to say this, and to offer our thanks to him—to Molly Myers, to Michael Evans—to all who have worked with them so well.

II. *Finance*

I now come to one of the centres of our concern, the crucial topic of finance. This year is the first of a new triennium, and we have been waiting with the usual mixture of hope and fear for the announcement of the government grant. I am glad to say that the triennial system under which the Academy's needs are assessed and which is essential for our future planning, although it is under considerable strain, has not—at any rate as yet—collapsed, unlike the quinquennial system for financing universities. After some, probably unavoidable, delay, the Academy was informed that its grant for current expenditure in the coming year was to be £1,590,000, with 'indicative figures' for the rest of the triennium. It is clear that this will provide for virtually no significant expansion of our activities, and that we shall consequently have some difficult decisions to take in determining future priorities. Even with the increase, in monetary terms, in the grant over that of last year, we shall, I fear, have to postpone, or even abandon, for a time at any rate, some important developments which we had hoped to finance. But it would be wrong to end on a gloomy note. The fact that, in these hard times, we can record an increase in our grant, is a cause for gratitude, and I should like to pay a warm tribute to the sympathy and understanding shown by the officials of the Department of Education and Science to the Academy and its activities throughout the long period of detailed and complicated negotiations.

Of our new grant, £772,000 is for the Academy's own needs. The increase over the grant for the previous year is more apparent than real: it is partly accounted for by inflation, partly by different methods of bookkeeping. For example, the arrangement by which the British Council funded certain of the Academy's exchange programmes, principally with Eastern European academies, has been brought to an end; and from this year we assume financial responsibility for all our activities in this area. The grant also includes the Small Grant Research Fund in the Humanities, which in 1976/7 had been provided by the University Grants Committee, but which is now to be transmitted through the Department of Education and Science. Nevertheless, the government grant does enable us to continue with our proper activities; there are no crippling cuts, and this is surely a source of deep satisfaction. Council has accepted the advice of Sir Jeremy Morse, our honorary financial adviser, to entrust the management of our investments to Lloyds Bank, of which he is the Chairman, and this, we hope, will achieve a higher level of income, and maintain the capital values of our funds.

£818,000 is provided for the current needs of the overseas Schools and Institutes (and sponsored societies). This represents an increase of 40 per cent over the comparable figures for 1976/7. The Department of Education and Science has, I am glad to say, accepted the argument that the Schools have been under-compensated in the past few years for the disastrous fall in the value of sterling and for abnormally high rates of local inflation in some of the countries in which they work. I am glad to say that the Department has been able to find some money designed to reverse the trend. However, in view of the prevailing financial stringency our plans for creating a new Institute in Amman have had to be shelved, for, at any rate, one more year. The DES has, however, agreed to look again at this scheme, and to review the whole level of the funding of the Schools in the light of the guidance they receive from the Academy's own Standing Committee on the Schools and Institutes; the need and importance of the task performed by this Committee seems to me to be clearly demonstrated by the Academy's responsibilities in this field.

III. *The British Institute in South-East Asia*

In this connection, I am happy to report that a very well-attended meeting was held in Burlington House to mark the first complete year of operations of our Institute in South-East Asia, in Singapore. This is the only one of our overseas Institutes to be directly administered by the Academy. The Institute has a vital role to play in advising research workers of the opportunities open to them and the correct procedures to be followed in South-East Asia. The Director, Dr. Milton Osborne, has successfully overcome the initial difficulties with which such beginnings are often attended, and we ought once again to record our appreciation of the help he has received from the British High Commission, the Government of Singapore, and local institutions. His recent experience underlines the need, the increasing need, for foreign scholars to think in terms of cooperative research with an institution, or an individual scholar, working in the territory of his interests. I should like to acknowledge with gratitude the contribution to the running expenses of the Institute made by the Academy of the Social Sciences of Australia, in addition to that made earlier by the Australian Academy of the Humanities. Our gratitude is also due to the William Waldorf Astor Foundation for a most generous grant towards visits by British scholars to the Institute.

IV. *Academic Publications*

I reported last year that in our submission to the Government we included an urgent plea for substantial support for academic publications, and suggested that one of the ways of doing this might be interest-free loans for individual works of scholarship, repayable over a period of years. The Department of Education and Science made it clear to us, however, that at present they were in no position to support a major activity of this type, and therefore that it would be best if we tried to mount a separate exercise, parallel to that for help to the learned societies. While these discussions were in progress, the Academy was approached by Mr. George Watson, Fellow of St. John's

College, Cambridge, who felt concern about the difficulties faced, in particular by younger authors, in securing publication of their work. He generously offered to make available a substantial sum of money, if the Academy would agree to encourage literary scholarship by means of a fund for the subvention of publication. This fitted admirably with our own lines of thought about this problem. The Academy accordingly accepted his offer with gratitude, and made a matching grant from its own funds to set up this scheme. In view of Mr. Watson's own scholarly interests, there is a clear preference for literary work, but the new fund is not confined to it. The Publications Committee, acting on the advice of Section sub-committees, has made the first awards from this fund. We look on this as a pilot scheme, and hope to use the experience so gained as evidence for the best way to meet a crying need, since sooner or later we shall again have to return to the Government for help in overcoming the steeply rising obstacles to the publication of scholarly work.

In this connection, I must report that Dr. Robert Shackleton, who has given a great deal of time and labour to the work of the Publications Committee, of which he has been chairman, has found it necessary to resign this post owing to other scholarly commitments; he is to be succeeded in December by Professor Michael Wallace-Hadrill. I need not remind you that this Committee is one of critical importance, since its work lies at the heart of the Academy's interests and those of the entire world of British learning.

V. *Learned Societies*

In the autumn of last year the *Survey of Learned Societies*, commissioned by the Royal Society and the British Academy, and undertaken by Mr. J. F. Embling, was published and circulated. It contained an analysis of the responses to a questionnaire circulated to 315 societies, together with recommendations for assisting the societies with some of the more acute problems confronting them in their activities. In the Survey three areas of concern were singled out for special attention: publication, accommodation, and libraries. Basing themselves on this report, the Presidents of the Royal Society and the Academy addressed an appeal to the Secretary of State for Education and Science for additional government resources designed to help these societies, and in particular to enable earmarked grants to be made where the need seemed greatest, and to provide professional advice on technical matters such as VAT, printing methods, costing and sales promotion of journals and publications which some of the societies plainly needed. The reply of the Secretary of State, although sympathetic, made it plain that in these hard times there was little hope of additional government funds. Discussions with the DES continue, but in the meanwhile approaches are being made to private foundations for funds which would permit the appointment of a specialist adviser on the kind of technical matters I have mentioned, since, in our view, this would enable some societies to make considerable economies. In order to keep the general situation under review, the Royal Society and the Academy have jointly established a new standing Committee charged with concern for the welfare of the learned societies.

VI. *Research Awards*

The major new task undertaken by the Academy during the past year has been the administration of the Small Grants Research Fund in the Humanities. I believe that the Academy was right to agree to assume this extra burden in response to the University Grants Committee's initiative, and that the importance of this fund within the academic community is out of all proportion to its size. In purely scholarly terms it can be seen to have met a real need in assisting areas of study which have not been strongly enough supported in the past from public funds; nor should its contribution to the morale of hard-pressed scholars be under-estimated.

We have sought to devise a set of administrative procedures which combine efficiency, simplicity, and dispatch, without compromising the high standards that we expect of Academy supported work. In the first year of operation we have received 169 applications and we shall have made awards (one further meeting of the awarding committee is still to come) to some 125 scholars. Each Section whose area of scholarship falls within the terms of the scheme has appointed a sub-committee to consider the applications in its field, and the sub-committees have on four occasions scrutinized and assessed applications. Subsequently the Research Fund Committee, which includes the chairmen of each Section, met to make awards. Its task is to issue guidelines on questions of principle and policy, to ensure that the standards of the applications recommended for awards are reasonably uniform, and to look at the financial costings in a standard way. At each of its meetings the Committee has had the benefit of the presence of observers from the UGC's Arts Sub-Committee.

During this first year, the scheme has been wholly financed by the UGC to the extent of £125,000. As a consequence, applications have had to be restricted to staff in post at university institutions which are in receipt of UGC funds. Next year the scheme is being extended as a result of contributions to the fund by the Department of Education and Science, the Department of Education for Northern Ireland, and the Scottish Education Department, which bring the total fund up to *c.* £200,000. This important development means that from now on all staff in polytechnics and other institutions of higher education throughout the UK come within the fund's orbit. The essence of this scheme—to make non-renewable grants of up to £1,000 to support particular pieces of research in the humanities by individual scholars—remains unchanged. Building on experience we have gained from the first year of operation we have now set about attracting a greatly increased number of applications.

The addition of these new funds makes the total sums available to the Academy this year for the direct support of advanced study by means of research awards above £500,000. From our own funds and from our Special Funds we have been able to make grants to 112 applicants. As for our own Academy research projects and committees, following the report of the Major Projects Review Committee, they were asked last year to submit much more detailed reports and estimates so that their work and progress could be more effectively monitored by the Sections. For the first time for some years, the total financial requirement for the Major Projects was less than in the previous year. We have, I am particularly glad to report, been able to increase both the size and the number of grants made in support of Learned Journals, and thereby to give a measure of assistance to the learned societies, since (as was shown by the Survey of Learned Societies) this is one of those areas where help is most urgently needed.

VII. *The Wolfson Fund*

Last year I reported on the first elections to British Academy Wolfson Fellowships in history, law, economics, and political studies. Our intention has always been to allocate the generous grant from the Wolfson Foundation in roughly equal proportions between British scholars wishing to undertake research on the Continent, and continental scholars anxious to study in this country, for periods between three and nine months, the main emphasis being placed on younger scholars. We recognized that during the first year of operation it might prove easier to appoint British scholars of high quality than to identify and attract their continental peers; and, of the eighteen Fellowships offered last year, twelve were to British scholars. This year the scheme was extended, so that it now covers ten Western European countries, and in making awards we have deliberately reversed last year's imbalance, with the result that of twenty-four Fellowships offered, seventeen have been to continental scholars. I should add that it has not always been easy to make adequate arrangements for the reception of these visitors to Britain, in particular to find accommodation, appropriate academic surroundings, useful academic contacts, and the like. This has placed a considerable strain on existing administrative resources. I wish I could anticipate alleviation of this situation. It is not desperate, or even serious, but it still tends to create awkward problems.

VIII. *Overseas*

I now turn to our foreign relations. It is perhaps not generally appreciated how great is the burden placed upon our Foreign Secretary, Professor Geoffrey Dickens, and how devotedly and scrupulously he watches over the development of our foreign programmes. The past year, for example, has seen the conclusion of an important new agreement with the Academy of Sciences of the USSR. The agreement, which is the most detailed and extensive of all our agreements with the academies of Eastern Europe, provides for exchange visits of ten scholars per annum in the humanities and the social sciences, for varying periods of study and research, to a total of fifteen man-months. The new arrangements came into effect in April, together with expanded agreements with the Romanian, Polish, Bulgarian, and Japanese Academies. We have also set about placing our relations with French scholarly institutions on a more satisfactory basis.

IX. *Award Procedures*

Like most human arrangements which pursue a particular purpose, but at the same time remain responsive to changed conditions, new demands and new opportunities, the Academy's methods of providing research grants have, over the years, developed in various directions, in part owing to different rules which govern different types of funds. Such historical development by unpredicted accretion and adaptation to new needs, is not, indeed, at all haphazard, but does, at times, generate anomalies, and needs periodic re-examination, co-ordination, and rationalization. Thus, at present, most applications for research grants are submitted to the Sections which make recommendations to the Research Fund Committee, which, as I have reminded you, includes the heads of all Sections. These recommendations are made at the Spring meetings of the Sections, that is, once a year. Grants for research overseas are decided upon by the Overseas Policy Committee, which is differently constituted; it co-opts its own members and meets under the chairmanship of the Foreign Secretary, four times a year. The applications for Small Grants in the Humanities are scrutinized in the first place by Sectional sub-committees, set up by the Sections concerned with the humanities, and their recommendations go to the Research Fund Committee, which, in consequence, is, like the sub-committees, required to meet four times a year if the reasonable needs of university teachers are to be satisfied. Grants made from funds earmarked for specific purposes, are administered by *ad hoc* committees created for the purpose; so are the grants from funds dedicated to broader purposes, e.g. those made by the Thank-Offering to Britain Fund or the Wolfson Fund. A degree of diversity is made inevitable if only by the fact that in the case of special grants by Foundations or societies, made to the Academy for specific purposes, representatives of the donors are, it seems to me quite rightly, made members of the grant-giving committees, a requirement which does not apply to the allocation of funds to which no special considerations apply. Moreover, qualifications for the eligibility of candidates for various types of grants differ: thus the UGC, in accordance with its rules, has had to impose criteria narrower than those normally applied by the Academy, while the Wolfson Foundation requires some limitation of subject and of countries in which research is to be conducted. In this connection I must report one change which the Council has recently adopted: to apply the same formula for eligibility for research awards as that which now determines eligibility for the Ordinary Fellowship. Henceforth, applicants for research awards will be expected to be normally resident in this country; there will be no reference to nationality or citizenship.

While some differences in the rules of award are therefore to some degree unavoidable, it seems to me that we need a clear account of our award-giving procedures, both for our own benefit and that of the applicants and their sponsors, if our policy is to be—and to be seen to be—consistent, just, well administered, and making the fullest use of the expert knowledge of the Academy. Consequently, I have requested the Acting Secretary, Mr. Peter Brown, to prepare a memorandum on our grant-giving arrangements, which can then be considered by Council and all the Sections.

X. *Union Académique Internationale*

In June this year the 51st Session of the Union Académique Internationale was held in Greece in the Academy of Athens. The British Academy participates actively, through established Academy Committees, in seven of the enterprises of the UAI: the *Corpus Vasorum Antiquorum*, the *Corpus Vitrearum Medii Aevi*, the Medieval Latin Dictionary, the *Sylloge Nummorum Graecorum*, the *Lexicon Iconographicum Mythologiae Classicae*, the *Tabula Imperii Romani*, and the *Fontes Historiae Africanae*. This year the Academy recommended the adoption of a new enterprise—the Critical Edition of the Complete Works of Voltaire—as a project under the patronage of the UAI. The Academy also played its part, through Professor Turner, in the revival of the *Supplementum Epigraphicum Graecum* now to be based at the University of Leiden under the direction of Professor H. W. Pleket.

The Session brought to a close Professor Eric Turner's three-year tenure of the Presidency of the Union. He has filled this office with great distinction, as anyone who has seen him in action in this forum will readily testify. The President of such an international body is called upon to display very considerable gifts of leadership, tact, and diplomacy, both in giving firm guidance in matters of scholarship and also in representing and, where necessary, reconciling differing national approaches and points of view. The UAI (to say nothing of the Academy) owes a great debt of gratitude to Eric Turner for the energy and the wisdom that he has brought to the direction of its affairs, a debt which, I am happy to say, was handsomely acknowledged, both in the public proceedings of the General

Assembly and in the expressions of tribute paid privately by the delegates.

XI. *Secretaryship of the Academy*

I should like to end this account by extending a most warm welcome to our new Secretary-to-be, Mr. J. P. Carswell, who is about to leave the public service after a very distinguished career in the Department of Education and Science and the University Grants Committee, whose chief executive officer he is. Like his predecessor, he has found time to write works of history, highly admired by professional experts in his field. He will, I believe and hope, find this institution to be in a very reasonable state of health and vigour. We all wish him—and ourselves—much happiness and success in his work with us and for us in the coming years.

MORTIMER WHEELER ARCHAEOLOGICAL LECTURE

ROME BEYOND THE SOUTHERN EGYPTIAN FRONTIER

By L. P. KIRWAN

Read 26 January 1977

THE title of this lecture, on a theme inspired by one of Sir Mortimer Wheeler's many books, calls for some explanation. Rome here means Roman ventures, particularly trading ventures, under the earlier Empire. And I use the term 'Roman' in the same loose and general way that Wheeler used it in his *Rome Beyond the Imperial Frontiers*. As he declared in that book, in characteristically robust and ebullient fashion, 'There shall be no great pedantry here in the matter of race or colour or even citizenship.'

Then there is the frontier, or rather frontiers. There are two frontiers to be crossed, not one. When the Roman Army, under Cornelius Gallus, first Prefect of Egypt—no general but a poet admired by Ovid and a friend of Virgil's—arrived at the First Cataract of the Nile in 29 B.C., Egypt's frontier, for all practical purposes, lay close to the island of Philae, on an ancient boundary line which divided Egypt proper from Lower Nubia, the Wawat of the Pharaohs. Under Augustus, however, the frontier was advanced twelve schoinoi, 130 km., to the south as far as Hierasykaminos (el-Maḥarraqa), thereby enclosing a stretch of the Nile valley known from Ptolemaic times as the Dodekaschoinos. In A.D. 297, so Procopius says,[1] it was withdrawn, back to the vicinity of the First Cataract, by Diocletian (Map I).

As far as the regions beyond Egypt are concerned, I will concentrate primarily on the Nubian Nile valley, now submerged as far south as the Dal Cataract under the waters of the High Dam. This Nubian stretch of the valley and beyond, as far probably as the latitude of Sennar on the Blue Nile, comprised the Sudanese kingdom of Meroe during the early Empire. The site of the capital, Meroe, with its remnant temples, its

[1] *History of the Wars*, I, 19.

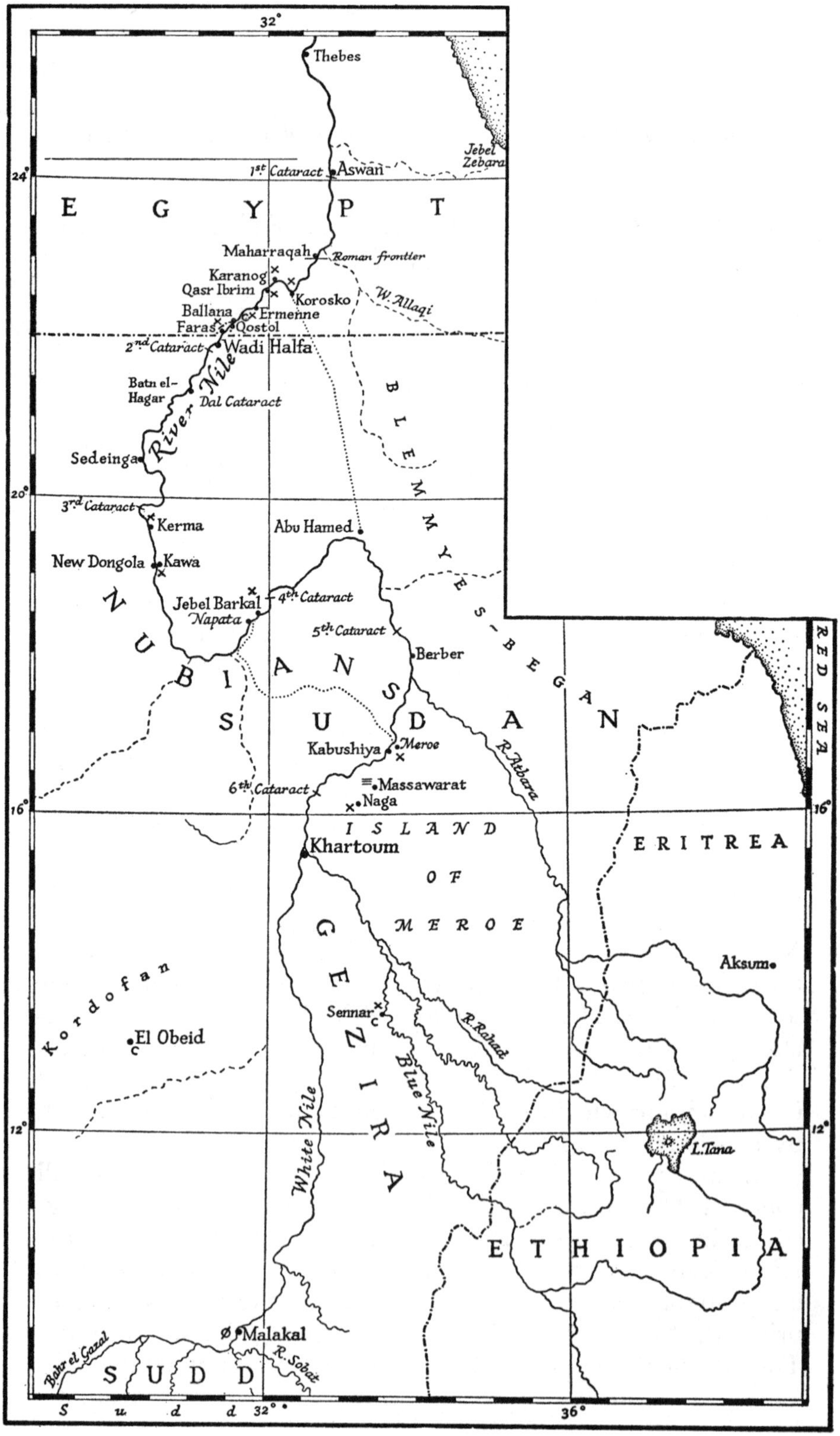
32°
Thebes
Jebel Zebara
1st Cataract
Aswan
24°
EGYPT
Maharraqah
Roman frontier
Karanog
Qasr Ibrim
Korosko
W. Allaqi
Ballana
Ermenne
Faras
Qostol
2nd Cataract
Wadi Halfa
Batn el-Hagar
Dal Cataract
River Nile
BLEMMYES-BEGA
Sedeinga
20°
3rd Cataract
Kerma
Abu Hamed
New Dongola
Kawa
Jebel Barkal
Napata
4th Cataract
5th Cataract
Berber
RED SEA
NUBIA
ANGLO-EGYPTIAN SUDAN
Kabushiya
Meroe
R. Atbara
6th Cataract
Massawarat
Naga
16°
ISLAND OF MEROE
Khartoum
ERITREA
GEZIRA
Kordofan
Aksum
Sennar
R. Rahad
El Obeid
Blue Nile
White Nile
12°
L. Tana
ETHIOPIA
Malakal
Bahr el Gazal
R. Sobat
SUDD
Sudd
36°

Map I.

palace enclosure, and its pyramid tombs, can be seen today on the east bank of the Nile some 200 km. north of Khartoum. But I will touch on modern Ethiopia's ancient kingdom of Aksum, in the highlands of Eritrea and Tigrai, as well, and on the coastlands of Somalia, Kenya, and Tanzania. Aksum is essential. The course of Rome's relations with Meroe and of her trading activities up the Nile can hardly be seen in proper perspective without some reference to the rising power and counter-attractions of Aksum and to the steady growth of Roman trade through the Red Sea and beyond to the incense-bearing lands and coastal slave-markets in the Horn of Africa.

Meroe and Aksum were the principal powers with which Rome had to do in eastern Africa south of Egypt. In origin, in cultural orientation, in their sharply contrasting physical environments, they could hardly have been more different. Aksumite civilization, emerging on a mountain plateau geologically, biologically, and climatically affiliated to the highlands of south-west Arabia, had from the fifth century B.C. been influenced by Sabaean immigrants from across the Red Sea and Arabian influences there became dominant. We know little of this Arabian-orientated kingdom during the first two centuries A.D. or of Rome's relations with it beyond a passing mention of Aksum in *The Periplus of the Erythraean Sea.*[1] But an imposing rock-cut tomb recently discovered by the British Institute in Eastern Africa below the giant monoliths at Aksum included architecture in burnt brick, with horseshoe arches (Fig. 1), quite un-Aksumite and probably Romano-Syrian in origin, and imported Roman glass of the third–fourth century. The tomb has since yielded a radio-carbon date of A.D. 280$\pm$80.[2]

By contrast with this highland civilization, Meroe was a lowland, essentially riverain, kingdom which emerged in the rainlands between the Atbara and the Nile—'the Island of Meroe'—from the sixth century B.C. There it developed as an African civilization. But its roots lay further north, in an earlier, highly Egyptianized kingdom centred on Napata near

[1] W. H. Schoff (ed.), 23, 40 'della raccolta milanese' might refer to a late first-century desert battle between Troglodytes of the coast and Aksumites, and the Romans. See E. G. Turner in *Journal of Roman Studies*, 40 (1950), 57–9, where 'Ethiopia' is interpreted as meaning Meroitic peoples who were essentially riverain.

[2] H. N. Chittick in *Azania IX* (1974), 159–205; and for date *Azania XI* (1976), 180.

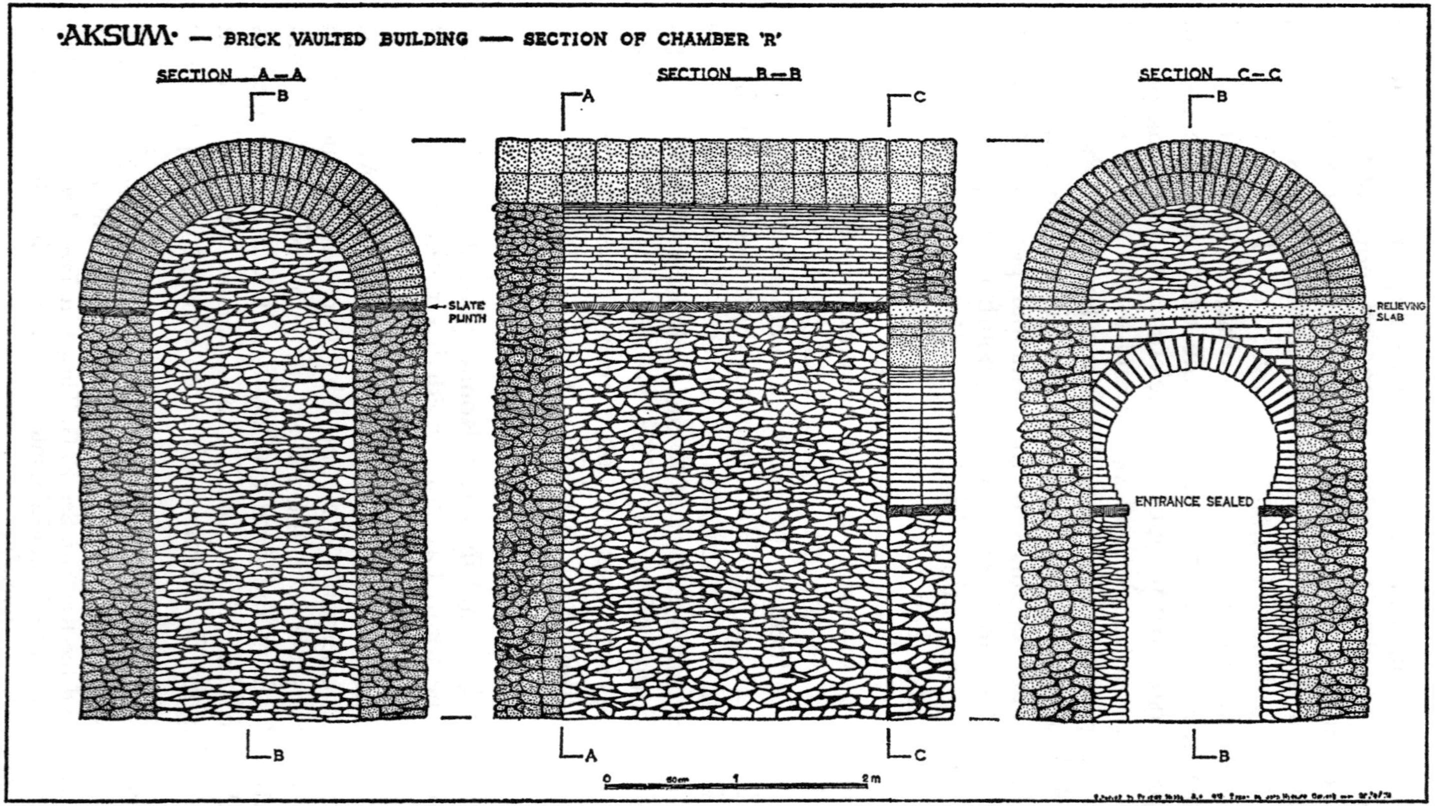

FIG. 1. Redbrick vaulted chamber in tomb at Aksum, third to mid-fourth century A.D.

From *Azania* IX (1974)

the Fourth Cataract. One aspect of Meroe's pervasive and persistent Egyptian inheritance which appealed to Rome was her devotion to Isis. Indeed, Meroe's fame as an antique centre of Isis worship, remote, mysterious, beyond the deserts and the turbulent cataracts of the Nile reached Rome itself, and Juvenal wrote of one ecstatic female devotee who was prepared to travel even 'to the confines of Egypt and fetch water from Hot Meroe with which to sprinkle the temple of Isis' in the Campus Martius.[1]

These two kingdoms, however, had one attribute in common from Rome's point of view, the contribution they could make to her wealth through trade. Aksum had its Red Sea port of Adulis, in the Gulf of Zula (Map II), a port from which elephants, 'Troglodytic' and 'Ethiopian', captured by the Egyptians, had been shipped north for use in the armies of Ptolemy II and III.[2] Pliny, who recalls the port's close links with Egypt, describes it as a part used by both Troglodytes and Ethiopians, by the coastal people and, here probably, the people of the highlands.[3] It was one of those 'established marts' listed in *The Periplus* which served both coast and hinterland.

Meroe for her part held the key to the Nile valley trade route linking Egypt with the resources of the southern Sudan. Her geographical position and her association with friendly tribes far beyond the boundaries of the kingdom which Seneca mentions[4] gave her direct access to the resources and the man-power of inner Africa. The southernmost Meroitic settlement known,[5] near Sennar, a trading outpost yielding first- to second-century bronze vessels imported from Roman Egypt, lay within the perimeter of a primitive, purely African, culture centred on near-by Jebel Moya, in the Gezira. Excavations carried out there before the First World War—by a disappointed Sir Henry Wellcome who had hoped to find the burial ground of a lost white race—produced clear evidence of trade with Meroe.[6]

But this Nile route had severe disadvantages; long desert journeys to bypass the cataracts and the two great bends in the river, journeys across the territory of two tribal confederations of nomads, both independent of Meroe, both a potential

[1] *Sat*, 6, 528.

[2] W. Wolska-Conus (ed.), *Cosmas Indicopleustès, topographie chrétienne*, i, 370.

[3] *HN* 6, 172–3, 181.

[4] *Nat. Qu.* 6, 8, 3–5.

[5] D. M. Dixon in *Kush*, xi (1963), 227 ff.

[6] F. Addison in *Kush*, iv (1956), 4 ff.

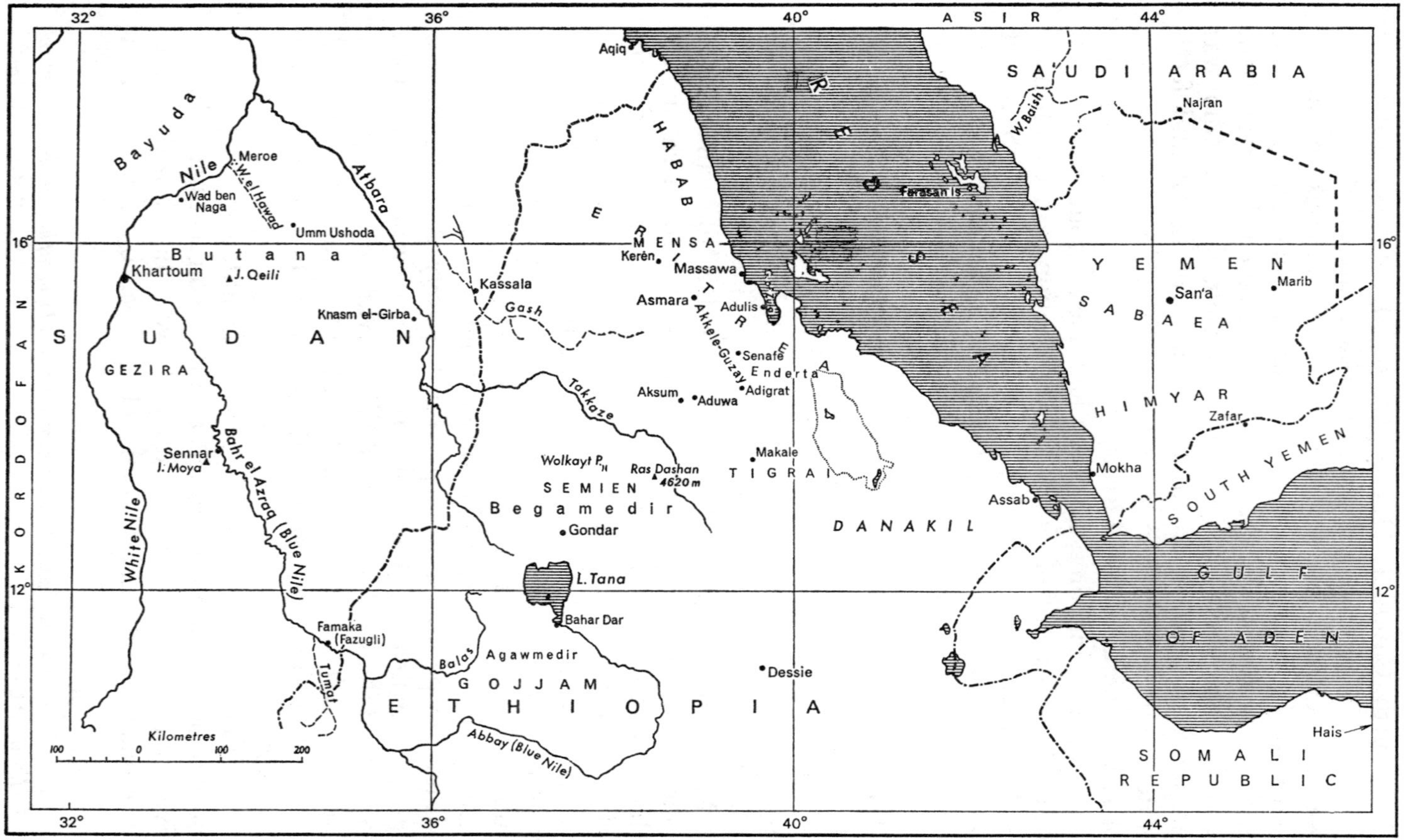

SAUDI ARABIA
ASIR
W. Baish
Najran
YEMEN
SABAEA
Marib
San'a
HIMYAR
Zafar
SOUTH YEMEN
Mokha
RED SEA
Farasan Is
GULF OF ADEN
SOMALI REPUBLIC
Hais
Aqiq
HABAB
MENSA
ERITREA
Kerèn
Massawa
Asmara
Adulis
Akkele-Guzay
Senafe
Enderta
Adigrat
Aksum
Aduwa
Makale
TIGRAI
DANAKIL
Assab
Dessie
Kassala
Gash
Takkaze
Wolkayt P.
Ras Dashan 4620 m
SEMIEN
Begamedir
Gondar
L. Tana
Bahar Dar
Agawmedir
GOJJAM
Balas
ETHIOPIA
Abbay (Blue Nile)
Famaka (Fazugli)
Tumat
Bayuda
Nile
Meroe
W. el Hawad
Wad ben Naga
Umm Ushoda
Atbara
Butana
Khartoum
J. Qeili
Knasm el-Girba
SUDAN
GEZIRA
KORDOFAN
Sennar
J. Moya
Bahr el Azraq (Blue Nile)
White Nile
Kilometres
100 0 100 200
32° 36° 40° 44°
16° 12°

MAP II.

menace to trading caravans. These were the Blemmyes in the Eastern Desert and the Nubians in the Bayuda and west of the Nile. The Blemmyes, first mentioned under that name by Theocritus,[1] have been identified with the marauding Bega[2] of fourth-century Aksumite inscriptions and of early Arabic literature. Indeed they were almost as much a menace to Aksum as to Meroe and Egypt. The northern tribes of the confederation, ancestors it seems likely of the notorious ʿAbābda of whom the nineteenth-century Swiss traveller J. L. Burckhardt gives such an unflattering description in his *Travels in Nubia* were those mentioned in classical and Coptic literature and inscriptions. In the late third century they dominated Upper Egypt.

The Nubians, brigands Strabo calls them,[3] were spread across the Bayùda and west of the Nile from the latitude of Meroe to the Third Cataract. Nothing is known of any Nubian encounters with Rome under the early Empire apart from a doubtful reference by Procopius to their enrolment as federates by Diocletian; an event which should probably be dated a century later. But mid-fourth century inscriptions[4] of the Aksumite king Ezana leave no doubt about the part they played in the decline of Meroe and in the kingdom's ultimate disintegration.

But this background sketch of the kingdoms and tribal confederations confronting Rome beyond Egypt's borders is looking too far ahead and I must return to the main story. When Cornelius Gallus arrived at the First Cataract in the spring of 29 B.C., frontier security, not trade and trade routes, was Rome's immediate preoccupation; security on the frontier of a country destined to be the great granary of the Empire, and one all too ready to revolt as Cornelius Gallus had good reason to know from his recent experiences in Upper Egypt. Meroe was the immediate problem. In the course of the century she had pushed north into the Dodekaschoinos, traditional Egyptian territory, the domain of Isis of Philae, which had been administered as a *limes*, a military frontier district, under the Ptolemies. Strabo who was at the First Cataract a few years

[1] *Idylls*, 7, 112.

[2] J. M. Plumley and W. Y. Adams in *Journal of Egyptian Archaeology*, 60 (1974), 238.

[3] *Geography*, 17, 1–2.

[4] E. Littmann, Äthiopischen inschriften in *Miss. Acad. Berol.* ii (1950), 2; 97 ff.

later says that Pselchis (Ed-Dakka) in the Dodekaschoinos was an 'Ethiopian', a Meroitic, city. Cornelius Gallus had not pushed south beyond Philae. Meroe thus had effective control over the whole territory right up to the frontier.

This was the situation when the Prefect of Egypt met delegates from Meroe at Philae. The outcome of this meeting is contained in Cornelius Gallus' trilingual inscription,[1] in Latin, Greek, and Egyptian, found in the temple of Augustus on the island, broken and reused as paving slabs after his exile and suicide. There were three principal stipulations, couched in decidedly less conciliatory terms in the Latin than in the Greek version. The kingdom of Meroe was declared a Roman protectorate. It was to pay an annual tribute. And a tyrant, a governor, answerable to Rome, was to be appointed to take charge of a stretch of the Nile valley, thirty schoinoi, 320 km., in length, called the Triakonteschoinos.

The precise significance of this term has been a source of much misunderstanding affecting even our interpretation of medieval Christian Nubia's geographical history. Monneret de Villard, historian of medieval Nubia, basing himself on an obscure and dubious passage in Ptolemy, argued[2] that the Triakonteschoinos must have been an extension of the Dodekaschoinos which would have carried it well beyond the Second Cataract. But that is surely untenable. Rome obviously must have been concerned about the stability of the valley immediately adjoining the frontier, the Dodekaschoinos in fact. That too had to be brought under control. Lesquier[3] therefore was probably right in thinking that the Triakonteschoinos included the Dodekaschoinos, and that it should also be measured from Philae, the point from which distances in Roman Nubia were measured as a milestone from Kalābsha shows.[4] Measured in this way the Triakonteschoinos would have extended as far south as Serra, within a few kilometres of latitude 22°N, the line of the international frontier between Egypt and the Sudan established under the Anglo-Egyptian Conventions of 1899. The Triakonteschoinos then would have been roughly the equivalent of pre-High Dam Egyptian Nubia, and regarded as a zone of special significance to Egypt. This was probably the case under the Ptolemies. A Ptolemaic inscription of un-

[1] *CIL* 3, 14147; Cagnat-Jouguet 1293.

[2] In *Storia della Nubia cristiana* (Rome, 1938), 133.

[3] *L'Armée romaine d'Égypte* (Cairo, 1918), 462.

[4] Cairo Museum No. 40286; *CIL* 3, 14148.

known origin records the founding of two Egyptian towns in the Triakonteschoinos late in the second century B.C., named after the reigning sovereigns, Philometoris and Cleopatra. It is dedicated to the gods of the First Cataract.[1]

The man appointed to govern this zone appears to have been Akinidad, Crown Prince of Meroe and in a long Meroitic inscription found near Meroe he carries the title of '*Kharpakh*—deputy of the ruler of Cush for Rome',[2] Cush being the Meroitic name for their kingdom. It should be said here that our knowledge of Meroitic, an alphabetic language unlike Egyptian but written in hieroglyphs and an almost cursive script, is still very rudimentary, forty years after F. Ll. Griffith's first breakthrough. It is likely to remain so pending the discovery of another bilingual inscription. If the longer Meroitic texts—one in particular—could be understood, we would learn much about Meroe's relations with Rome.

There was nothing new, of course, in this appointment of a client prince beyond the frontier answerable to Rome. It had been tried long before, on the Eastern Frontier. But it must always have been a risky business and this proved the case in Lower Nubia. There is no need to go into detail. The story has been told many times and Strabo gives a full, virtually a first-hand, account.[3] In 25 B.C., four years after the meeting at Philae, Meroe's warriors—Sudanese and Nubians—swooped down on the Roman frontier. The attack was carefully planned and carefully timed, in the knowledge that the Roman garrisons in Egypt had been heavily depleted to provide troops for Aelius Gallus' ill-conducted campaign in Arabia. The frontier garrisons, three cohorts stationed at Philae, Syene (Aswan) and the neighbouring island of Elephantine, were taken completely by surprise; the towns were ransacked; and statues of Caesar were torn down. The bronze head of one of them, a magnificent portrait head of Augustus now in the British Museum, was found at Meroe early this century during Garstang's excavations. It had been ceremonially and ignominiously buried under the threshold of a temple.[4]

When Roman retribution came in the autumn, it was overwhelming and the campaign, under C. Petronius, second

1 See Lesquier, op. cit., 414.

2 B. G. Haycock in *Meroitica*, 2 (Berlin, 1976), 39.

3 *Geography*, 17, 53–4.

4 J. Garstang in *Liverpool Annals of Archaeology and Anthropology*, 4, 66–71 and pls. 12–14.

Prefect of Egypt, lasted until the spring of 24 B.C., covering the cool months of the Nubian winter. After a sweeping victory at Pselchis (Ed-Dakka) in the Dodekaschoinos, and the capture of the Meroitic hill-city of Primis (Qaṣr Ibrīm) farther up the river, Petronius—using his cavalry, no doubt—set off across the Eastern Desert for Napata where the treacherous Akinidad had taken refuge. This journey of five hundred kilometres across the high desert carried the Roman Army to its farthest south in Africa. After sacking Napata, Petronius returned to Primis, strengthened its defences, and left 400 men there with supplies for two years. But Rome had not finished with this obdurate Sudanese kingdom. Two years later, just as these supplies were running out, he had to rush south again from Alexandria to rescue the garrison. This was Rome's last battle with Meroe. In the winter of 21–20 B.C., envoys from the queen, the Candake, of Meroe had to travel to Samos in the Aegean to submit to Caesar. The tribute, the alleged source of all the trouble, was remitted. It was an indication perhaps of Rome's continuing claims over Meroe.[1]

Thereafter the *Pax Romana* descended on the Nubian Nile. But it was peace backed this time by prudent military insurance. The Dodekaschoinos was incorporated under the civil administration of the Thebaid, possibly as early as the reign of Augustus, certainly by that of Domitian. Augustus built several temples there, one Talmis (Kalābsha) the largest in Lower Nubia after Abu Simbel. It was dedicated to a local god, Mandulis, a god with eastern connections likely also to appeal to the Blemmyes, the Bega, of the Eastern Desert. Such conciliatory gestures were backed by formidable military arrangements. The principal towns were fortified and garrisoned and these military stations, all but one securely identified, are listed in the early third-century *Antonine Itinerary*; a list reasonably well supported for the first two centuries A.D. by military inscriptions and ostraca[2] found in the Dodekaschoinos ranging in date from Tiberius to Caracalla.

Being concerned now with events beyond the new frontier at Hierasykaminos, it is no part of my task to discuss Roman

[1] See S. Jameson, 'Chronology of the campaigns of Aelius Gallus and C. Petronius', in *Journal of Roman Studies*, 58 (1968), 71–84.

[2] See Lesquier, op. cit. For ostraca, U. Wilcken, *Die Griechischen ostraca* nos. 1129–46; 1220–3; 1265. Also Evelyn White in *Classical Review*, 33 (1919), 109 ff. Many found by the Survey of Nubia 1907–11 are unpublished and now missing.

Nubia, an extension of the Empire sadly neglected by pre-First World War survey expeditions which were not much interested in 'late' remains. The turreted and bastioned mud-brick forts there, all on the west bank of the Nile with bridgheads across the river—a precaution probably against surprise attacks by the nomads of the Eastern Desert—were only superficially explored.[1] And of course these Roman sites, farthest north in Lower Nubia and nearest the river, were the first to be damaged and finally be inundated by the old Aswan Dam and its successive heightenings. But I would like to discuss one problem about the frontier. Did it remain at Hierasykaminos, the southernmost station listed in the *Antonine Itinerary*? Or was the frontier pushed still farther south at any time, as far as Qaṣr Ibrīm. This has been suggested and the problem is very relevant to the Egypt Exploration Society's very successful excavations at Ibrīm which are to be resumed next year.

Certainly Olympiodorus, that remarkable Egyptian diplomat and historian, who travelled with a highly talkative parrot which could dance and sing, claims[2] that Primis, 'Prima' he calls it, was once Egypt's southernmost city. He was there in A.D. 423. But it seems very improbable. Against it there is not only the evidence of the Itinerary but some remarks made by Philostratus. In his *Life of Apollonius Tyana*,[3] written early in the third century, he talks of Hierasykaminos as the frontier town. The strongest evidence, however, in favour of Hierasykaminos, and it spans the whole range of Rome's occupation of the Dodekaschoinos, is archaeological; the very sharp differences in burial customs and pottery to north and south of Hierasykaminos. To the north, both are almost exclusively Romano-Egyptian in character, to the south wholly and markedly Meroitic, with Ba statues, offering tables inscribed in Meroitic, and the elegant, painted Meroitic pottery, African in inspiration though clearly influenced by Hellenistic tradition, which was such a characteristic product of Meroe's northern province. Perhaps Olympiodorus was recalling Strabo and his story of Petronius and his garrison.

It is very likely on the other hand that Primis, Qaṣr Ibrīm, was used by the Romans as an outpost, in advance of but in close touch with the frontier rather like one of the forts north of the Antonine Wall in Roman Britain. Qaṣr Ibrīm is a barren island

[1] See U. Monneret de Villard, *La Nubia romana* (Rome, 1941).

[2] R. Henry (ed.), *Photius, bibliothèque* (Paris, 1959), i, 180 ff.

[3] 6. 2.

site now, its ruins a haven for snakes and scorpions. But before the High Dam, it rose high and gaunt above the Nile and gave commanding views over both river and desert approaches. Such a strategic position, almost impregnable except from the north, would never have been neglected by the Romans in planning their defences of Roman Nubia. And indeed there is evidence that it was not, though it is insufficient at present to indicate any permanent or lengthy occupation. Fragments of Greek and Latin military papyri recently discovered by Professor J. M. Plumley's expedition[1] could be several decades later in date than 22 B.C., the year when Petronius withdrew his garrison. Then there is Marichal's reinterpretation[2] of the text on the *recto* of an Oxyrhynchus papyrus (No. 1511). This is now seen to have been a letter written from Ibrīm one February not very long before A.D. 247—the date on the *verso* of the papyrus. It mentions several high ranking officers then present at Primis, including the Prefect of the Legion *Trajana Fortis*.

There can be no doubt about Ibrīm's exceptionally close links with Roman (and Christian) Egypt. These are evident in building styles and techniques, in coin finds (first to the fourth century)—and coins are very rare south of Ibrīm—and in discoveries of early Coptic papyri.[3] Gaston Maspero, in a position to know because of his post in the Egyptian Antiquities Service, claimed[4] that one building at Ibrīm could certainly be attributed to Septimius Severus and this was accepted without question by no less an authority than Lesquier. What this was based on, I have not been able to discover; possibly a lost building inscription. This would be worth investigating.

All this assertion of Roman power—the rout of Meroe's 'Dervish' warriors, the grim forts with their garrisons, including camel-borne units for wide-ranging desert operations—was thought by earlier scholars to have precipitated the decline of Meroe; 'the decayed capital of Nubia', as Wheeler called her in his *Rome Beyond the Imperial Frontiers*. But that was far from the case. The *Pax Romana* brought trade and through trade prosperity to the Nile valley south of Egypt, unevenly distributed though it was. And it reopened the ancient Meroitic kingdom

[1] See M. E. Weinstein and E. G. Turner in *JEA* 62 (1976), 115 ff.

[2] R. Marichal in *Bull. de la Soc. Nat. des antiquaires de France.* Séance of 14 October 1964.

[3] J. M. Plumley in *JEA* 56 (1970), 18; and Plumley and W. Y. Adams in *JEA* 60 (1974), 226.

[4] *Égypte* (Coll. *Ars Una*), 251. Lesquier, op. cit. 466.

PLATE I

Silver goblet, originally gilded, with scene in relief, Roman work, mid-first century A.D.
From Royal tomb at Meroe

Silver plate with figures and emblems in relief from Ballana, Lower Nubia, fifth century A.D.

Transparent blue glass flutes with polychrome and gilded decoration from Northern Nubia, late third century A.D.

Romano-Meroitic kiosk at Naqa, early first century A.D.

Plaster statue from bath building at Meroe

Bronze hanging vase from Faras, second to third century A.D.

to a fresh wave of cultural influence from the Graeco-Roman world. Meroe's links with classical civilization had a long history and extended through Egypt to Greece itself. At least one Meroitic ruler had appreciated Greek art. One of the more remarkable discoveries in Meroe's royal cemetery, made by Reisner's Harvard/Boston expedition fifty years ago, was of an elegant Attic rhyton, made by the Athenian potter Sotades.[1] He was at work in the mid-fifth century B.C., about the time when Herodotus, interrogating the mixed and polyglot population of the old frontier town of Elephantine, heard reports of Meroe, 'a big city . . . and the capital city of the Ethiopians', and of the country far beyond; as far indeed as that east–west flowing tributary of the Nile which once connected that river with the Lake Chad region; a connection substantiated by modern biologists.

But trade then, and later when Pliny's Ptolemaic Greeks (or Hellenized Egyptians)—Dalion, Simonides, and others—visited Meroe, lived there and wrote about it, and journeyed into the far south, did not compare in volume or richness with that of Roman times. Silverware, bronze vessels and lamps, glass, the finest pottery including *terra sigillata* and barbotine wares, flowed south from the great industrial centres and ateliers of Egypt; Thebes, Coptos, and above all Alexandria (Plates I and IV*b*). There were other luxury imports too, such as wines and olive oil. Some came from very far afield such as the Pergamine wares of the late first century B.C. found at Napata, and an amphora, once full of olive oil, from Tiklat in Algeria, dated by its stamp to the reign of Diocletian.[2]

Not much is known for certain about Meroe's exports to Roman Egypt, bartered in return for these luxuries, but ivory was undoubtedly among them. Juvenal writes, early in the second century, of ivory brought to Aswan, ivory destined to adorn the dining tables of Rome's affluent society.[3] Indeed he may quite possibly have seen some tusk-laden caravan arriving at 'the portals of Syene'. A French expedition excavating at Wad ben Naga, on the Nile south of Meroe, discovered a great store of ivory and ebony; a depot perhaps for this export trade.[4]

[1] W. S. Smith, *Ancient Egypt*, 183 and pl. 120. Boston Museum of Fine Arts, 1960.

[2] D. Dunham, *Royal tombs at Meroe and Barkal*, 93, 186. Boston Museum of Fine Arts, 1957.

[3] *Sat.* 11, 120–5.

[4] J. Vercoutter, 'Un palais des "Candaces" contemporain d'Auguste', in *Syria*, 39 (1962), 262 ff.

Then there was gold, Meroitic gold from the Second/Third Cataract region bartered with Rome. Philostratus refers to this in an anecdote about Roman Nubia's frontier market at Hierasykaminos (El-Maḥarraqa). In addition, he says, to ivory, myrrh, spices, and linen 'lying about without anyone to watch them', there was 'uncoined gold'. The Romans never seem to have worked the 'Gold of Wawat', the gold-mines worked by the Pharaohs in the Wādi 'Allāqi, east of Hierasykaminos. But there was ample gold in the Basement Complex in this cataract region. Gold-mining may well account for the wealth of one or two of the Meroitic towns in this eerie and claustrophobic reach of the Nile valley, a tumult of black rocks and rapids and whirlpools; at Sedeinga, for example, the Meroitic Atīye. It was there that the M. S. Giorgini expedition recently discovered the finest glass found south of Egypt; footed flutes of transparent blue glass with polychrome and gilded decoration imported from Alexandria or perhaps made by Egyptian craftsmen working in Nubia.[1] One bears the Greek inscription, 'Drink and may you live', an inscription from a pagan tomb of the late third century which was to be seen often enough in the Christian catacombs of Rome (Plate III*a*).

Gold must have played some part in the greater and more widespread prosperity of this northern part of the Meroitic kingdom compared with the south, beyond the cataracts. There it appears to have been concentrated in the capital and confined to a ruling feudal class. Another, obvious, reason for this widespread distribution was this northern region's accessibility to Egyptian traders. From the third century, and probably before, there was moreover a considerable Egyptian element in Lower Nubia. And the population itself was much Egyptianized. This can be seen in Meroitic funerary inscriptions, from the frequent adoption of Egyptian names.[2] The Triakonteschoinos was, and remained, very much an Egyptian zone, open not only to merchants but to immigrants including craftsmen bringing to cities like Ibrīm the technical skills of Roman Egypt.

Two new technologies, neither specifically Roman in origin, but both introduced beyond the frontier during the early Empire, should be mentioned here. One was the *sāqiya*, the cogged water wheel fitted with scoops (*qādūs*), pottery buckets; Strabo gives what appears to be a description of one which he

[1] J. Leclant in *Journal of Glass Studies*, 15 (1973), 52 ff.

[2] N. B. Millett in *Journées internationales d'études méroitiques*, July 1973, 18.

saw feeding an irrigation channel near the legionary fortress of Babylon (Old Cairo). The *sāqiya* must have revolutionized the agriculture of Meroitic Lower Nubia. Another was the wine-press, of Graeco-Egyptian type like the one pictured in the tomb of Petosiris.[1]

Roman cultural influence, on art, on architecture, even on manners and customs, was far-reaching and nowhere is it better seen than in the Meroitic sites of the Island of Meroe, between the Atbara and the Nile, including the capital itself. Roman influence on architecture is strikingly illustrated in the little kiosk at Naqa out in the Butana (Plate III*b*), in the bath building at Meroe, and in a *tholos* at Wad ben Naga[2] on the Nile only 100 km. north of Khartoum. A relief of a god at Naqa, portrayed full-face and not in traditional Egyptian profile, must have been due to Roman influence. These temples at Naga date from the end of the first century B.C. or the beginning of the first century A.D., an indication of the rapidity with which these influences from Roman Egypt spread.

The bath building at Meroe was found during Garstang's haphazard and largely unpublished excavations there early this century. It contained several statues. One was of an obese Sudanese reclining on a couch in a Roman manner (Plate IV*a*).[3] Others were of musicians, one of an auletes. Some of these wind instruments, auloi or tibiae, ivory tubes encased in bronze, were found by Reisner in a royal tomb at Meroe of the late first century B.C. They closely resemble some from Pompeii. Like so much else imported from the north they probably came from Alexandria which ranked second only to Corinth as a source of auloi.[4]

Such exotic influences, extending even to Meroitic music, must have been greatly strengthened by travel up and down the Nile between the kingdom of Meroe and Roman Egypt; merchants, officials, private individuals perhaps prepared to venture across the deserts and into the rainlands to the heart of this remote and strange civilization where African gods—elephant gods, lion-headed snake gods—were worshipped side by side with relict deities from the ancient Egyptian pantheon. There are no tourist graffiti at Meroe like those at Thebes; there

[1] U. Monneret de Villard, *La Nubia romana*. Figs. 48 and 50. *Geography*, 17, 1, 30.

[2] J. Vercoutter, loc. cit.

[3] P. Shinnie, *Meroe*, pl. 25.

[4] Nicholas B. Bodley in *American Journal of Archaeology*, 50 (1946), 2; 217–39. Also D. M. Dixon and K. P. Wachsman in *Kush*, 12 (1964), pl. 35.

were none even in the Dodekaschoinos. The Emperor Germanicus' antiquarian tour in A.D. 19 reached no farther south than the First Cataract. However, there are several graffiti, in Greek, Meroitic, Demotic, and Latin from Philae and farther south left by travellers on official missions to Roman Egypt and even to Rome itself. The earliest, from Dakka dated 13 B.C., is in Greek; an unpublished column drum from Meroe with the Greek alphabet inscribed on it shows that Greek was taught there. The Latin inscription, identified by Mommsen as more likely to be Meroitic than Roman in origin, was removed by Lepsius from the great Meroitic religious centre at Messawarat es Sufra, south of Meroe, and taken to Berlin where it was destroyed during the Second World War. However, his paper squeeze has been preserved. The inscription commemorates a visit to Rome by an emissary from the queen of Meroe with a scarcely legible Latin name.[1] The only comparable record of a mission in the opposite direction is the graffito left by one Klados, 'ambassador to Ethiopia', in the tomb of Ramses V at Thebes.

Most of these graffiti date from the late third century when Meroe's contacts with Rome seem to have been exceptionally close, possibly because of mutual concern about the safety of the frontier zone and of the Dodekaschoinos at a time when Blemmyan raids had reached their climax. There is no evidence of Roman official activity in the Dodekaschoinos after about the middle of the third century. From then on Meroe's fortunes were on the wane. But this decline was confined almost wholly to the southern parts of the kingdom. In the north, commercial relations with Roman Egypt flourished through the fourth and even more so during the fifth century as the rich finds from the royal cemetery at Ballana in Lower Nubia showed. These tombs, of Nubian kings, discovered by the late W. B. Emery and myself in 1931, contained some fine examples of the art of Alexandria (Plate II).

One reason for Meroe's economic decline, evident in the latest royal tombs at Meroe, may have been Rome's decreasing use of the Nile valley trade route to the far south, a laborious, costly and hazardous route as I have already pointed out. An attempt to exploit this route more profitably may have been one motive behind Nero's well-known exploring expedition to the southern Sudan which Seneca, Nero's tutor, describes.

[1] See F. Hintze's study of Lepsius' paper squeeze in *Kush*, 12 (1964), 296 ff. and pl. 56.

He interviewed the explorers, two centurions, on their return to Rome. The king of Meroe had provided them with an escort and with introductions to friendly tribes beyond his borders. It is clear enough that they reached the Sudd, that vast and restless mass of floating vegetation which spreads across the Albert Nile. They also heard of cataracts far to the south; the Beddan Rapids perhaps, the first cataract met with south of the junction of the Niles. Seneca maintains that geographical exploration was the object, a search for the sources of the Nile. But discovery could have been linked with hopes of commercial exploitation as was to happen so often in African history. This certainly seems a more likely combination of motives than Pliny's highly improbable, and geographically unjustifiable, suggestion that the expedition was a military reconnaissance because Nero was contemplating a war against 'Ethiopia' at the time.[1]

Whatever the immediate outcome of this journey may have been, a journey of discovery unequalled by Europeans until the nineteenth century, Rome was soon to open up an easier route to the resources of the southern Sudan; by way of the Red Sea and the kingdom of Aksum. This brings me to the final part of this lecture.

The *Periplus of the Erythraean Sea*, a report by a Roman trader or more probably a Roman trade official, provides the evidence for this alternative route to the Southern Sudan. It is now no longer to be dated to the late first century but to the early second or possibly even the third century, on Indian and Arabian grounds.[2] According to *The Periplus*, 'all the ivory from beyond the Nile', here the Blue Nile, came from Kueneion (or Sueneion), possibly Sennar. From there it was carried eastwards to Aksum, and thence by way of Coloe (Kohaito), on the eastern edge of the Abyssinian plateau, down through the passes to Adulis. It was a route more likely to have profited Aksum than Meroe. Its use marked a step, the first step perhaps, towards Aksum's domination over Meroe, finally achieved, as we know from two mid fourth-century inscriptions of the Aksumite king Ezana, when Aksum's armies swept across the grassy plain of the Butana and up and down the Nile valley, south to the Blue Nile junction,

[1] Seneca, *Nat. Qu.* 6, 8, 3–5; Pliny, *HN* 6, 181–5.

[2] Gervase Mathew, 'The dating and the significance of the *Periplus of the Erythraean Sea*', in *East Africa and the Orient* (ed. H. N. Chittick and R. I. Rotberg), 147 ff. Africana Publishing Company, New York, 1975.

north to the Fourth, possibly the Third Cataract, in a savage campaign of systematic burning, pillage, and destruction.[1] The burnt shells of temples and other buildings on the latest levels at Meroe provide abundant confirmation of this.

I managed to visit Adulis in 1972, in between the curfews which had been clamped on Massawa and Asmara because of guerrilla activities. It is a most impressive site, 20 hectares in area and only marginally explored. Adulis is inaccessible now. In Roman times it traded with Egypt and Arabia, imported wine from Syria and Italy, iron and cotton from India, and exported ivory, tortoise shell, and rhinoceros horn. Its excavation, if that is ever possible, would add immensely to our knowledge of the ramifications of Rome's sea-borne trade.

The Periplus lists several other marts along this coast, south of Adulis, and east beyond the Bab el Mandeb, 'far-side' marts trading with Egypt, Arabia, and India, some exporting slaves and ivory and thus competing with the Nile Valley trade. Evidence of Roman activity has been found at two of them. G. Révoil, the French traveller who visited Haïs (Mosyllum or possibly Mundus) late in the nineteenth century, dug up sherds from a red gloss *terra sigillata* bowl; 'poteries rouges vernies, communément appellées poteries de Samos'.[2] From his drawing and description they closely resemble Hayes's Çandarli ware, common in the first half of the second century. Révoil also found a large fragment of a ribbed blue glass bowl, of a type popular during the first century and found at Pompeii and, among other places, at Sir Mortimer Wheeler's celebrated site at Arikamedu, South India. One of the most important of these marts was Opone, Ras Hafūn, in the Horn of Africa, south of Cape Guardafui. According to *The Periplus* it had an expanding slave trade with Egypt. Roman sherds and fragments of amphorae handles have recently been found there by Neville Chittick's survey expedition from the British Institute in eastern Africa, working with Somali colleagues.[3]

Whether there were other ports, south of Opone, trading with Egypt, or possibly even a Roman trading settlement, an East African 'Arikamedu', was a question which much exercised

[1] L. P. Kirwan, 'An Ethiopian-Sudanese frontier zone in ancient history', in *Geogr. Jnl.* 138 (1972), 457 ff.

[2] G. Révoil, *La Vallée du Darror* (Paris, 1882), 290 and pl. 19. See J. W. Hayes, *Late Roman Pottery*, 318 and fig. 63b.

[3] H. N. Chittick, 'An archaeological reconnaissance in the Horn; the British Somali Expedition 1975', *Azania II* (1976), 121 and 118 fig. 1.

Sir Mortimer Wheeler. According to *The Periplus*, trade along this coast, the coast of 'Azania' stretching south to Tanzania, was chiefly in Arab hands, in the hands of middlemen, immigrants who remained subject to the south-west Arabian kingdom of Himyar. They spoke the local language and married African wives. But these men traded in Arab ships through Mocha, and not directly with Roman Egypt.

There were several voyagers of Greek or Graeco-Egyptian origin who landed on this Azanian coast, probably during the early Empire; Ptolemy's Diogenes who was blown off course by the north-east monsoon and landed and heard of (or maybe even saw) the snow-capped mountains of East Africa and the great lakes which fed the Nile; and Sarapion and Nikon who are commemorated in *The Periplus* as the first to navigate 'the courses of Azania'. Two hoards including Roman coins moreover have been found on this coast, one in the 1890s by a German engineer working on a sisal plantation near Tanga in northern Tanzania, one in 1912 by a Captain C. W. Haywood at Bur Gavo (Port Durnford), in southern Somalia. But both hoards contained Islamic coins ranging in date from the eighth to the eighteenth century.[1] They must have been buried long after Roman times.

Sir Mortimer Wheeler, naturally, was not at all discouraged by this inescapable conclusion. 'There can be no doubt', he declared, 'that fully authentic deposits of the kind await discovery.' He may well turn out to be right, as he so often was. Meanwhile, the case is not proven. That being so, Ras Hafūn (like the Sudd in the southern Sudan) is as far south as one can go in this pursuit of Rome beyond the southern Egyptian frontier.[2]

[1] See H. N. Chittick, 'Six early coins from near Tanga', in *Azania I* (1966), 156 ff. And H. Mattingly, 'Coins from a site find in British East Africa', in *Numismatic Chronicle*, 42 (1932), 175.

[2] *Rome Beyond the Imperial Frontiers* (Harmondsworth, 1955), 140.

Acknowledgements. I am indebted for permission to reproduce illustrations as follows: Messrs. Thames & Hudson: Plates I, III*b*, IV*a* and *b* from their publication *Meroe* by P. L. Shinnie (1967); Messrs. Methuen: Plate II from their publication *Nubian Treasure* by Walter B. Emery (1948); Madam M. Schiff-Giorgini: Plate III*a*.

SARAH TRYPHENA PHILLIPS LECTURE IN AMERICAN LITERATURE AND HISTORY

THE OUTLAND DART: AMERICAN WRITERS AND EUROPEAN MODERNISM

By MALCOLM BRADBURY

Read 9 February 1977

MY topic in this lecture is a special affinity: the close connection that seems to me to have existed between an old spectacle, the presence of a considerable number of American writers resident in or expatriated to Europe, and a new one—that dramatic disturbance in society, and even more in thought and all the arts, that we roughly date between about 1890 and 1930 and have come to call 'modernism'. One of the things that has struck the literary critics and scholars, and there are now many, who have examined in detail this crucial and experimental change in style, epistemology, and culture is the large part that was played in it by writers who were, in one way or another, expatriates or *émigrés*. 'A rootless affair', Graham Hough has called the entire episode; while George Steiner has identified a large element of the 'unhoused' in modern art. Perhaps the truest way to say it is that a good deal of modernism has been the result of writers taking a cosmopolitan perspective on their national literary traditions. I shall be suggesting that one of the characteristics of American writing has long been to see the arts in just this way, to intersect cosmopolitanism and nationalism; and that as a result Americans, particularly expatriate ones, became significant observers of, important participants in, and finally influential developers of, the western development of modernism.

What do we mean by modernism? It is recognized as one of the most difficult tendencies or movements to define. This is in part because it is a relatively arcane, or *avant-garde*, tendency offering itself, to by no means total consent, as our modern art; and in part because, on inspection, it dissolves into a great plurality of different, often substantially conflicting, movements or tendencies, with many different sources, many different culture-readings and philosophies, many different views of the nature of the modern situation and the deliverances required of the modern arts. Thus, when inspected closely, even its most obvious surface-characteristics—like *vers libre*, or atonalism in music, or stream-of-consciousness or spatialization of form in the novel—turn out to have been explained or justified in very different ways by the artists who chose to explore them. Moreover, modernism has been more than the sequence of movements for which it has become the collective name. Indeed many of the most important 'modernist' writers were not direct subscribers to any single movement, while others were in and out of several of them.

However, that modernism does exist is certain; one proof is that James McFarlane and I have just devoted a very large book in the Pelican Guides to European Literature series to it. There are many other large books; the term or title has become common usage, especially lately. A fair part of *our* large book appropriately perplexes itself about a definition, a who, a where, a what, why and when of it; I direct you there if you enjoy these perplexities. But let us, for our present convenience, say that for many writers and thinkers in the west a nineteenth-century synthesis visibly dissolves or comes to crisis in or around the 1890s—when positivism struggles with intuitionalism, sociology with psychology, naturalism with aestheticism, when there is a sense of perceptual crisis which throws attention on to consciousness, when world-views pluralize, dusks and dawns in consciousness and civilization are much thought of, and ideas are in radical ferment. The result in ideas is a period of outstanding intellectual innovation, a general upheaval of the western world manifest in much of its science and its thought; this has some prophetic or precursory relation both to the cultural dislocation of the Great War and the postwar re-synthesis. It is a disorientation and resynthesizing that is notably manifest in the arts, one which shifted the role of the artist, privatized and specialized him, in some way dislocated him from his familiar culture. It is primarily a European affair; it has social roots in the processes of late nineteenth-century European change, in the political upheavals of growing democratization, secularization, urbanization, and intellectual ones in the changing and evolving art-tendencies of the nineteenth century. It is also an international affair; indeed it is certain that if anything distinguishes modernism it is its international interfusion—by which I mean that, whether because of simultaneous generation, or because of clear and traceable flows of ideas and influence, we find related artistic phenomena occurring right across the western nations, from Oslo to Rome, from Moscow to Chicago. One then has to add that they occur, however, not quite at the same time, not necessarily in the same order, not always with the same aims or underlying philosophies, with different degrees of hope or despair, different historical expectations, and against different socio-cultural contexts.

But, even so, I think we have now come to settle on three central episodes as counting toward a definition and a history. The first is the struggles of naturalism and aestheticism, or of naturalism yielding to aestheticism, in the 1890s, usually taken as the starting-point, the first trembling of the veil. The second is the accelerating events of the years 1908 to 1915 or so, the period of many movements in the European arts, from futurism to expressionism, cubism to imagism, and of display, magazine, manifesto, the phase that Ford Madox Hueffer called the 'opening world', and Wyndham Lewis the era of 'titanic stirrings and snortings' which he saw as the great effort of modern collective advance in the arts, later lost; it is also the period when, in the Anglo-American line, the American contribution starts to take on especial visibility, and the waves from this reach right across to Chicago. The third is the replay of the 1920s, after a war that had seemed both to confirm and extend the sceptical cultural vision of the *avant-garde*, its sense of anarchy and the abyss, its note of withdrawal from romanticism, its ironic despair, its effort to form salvage from chaos; in this phase we find the largest number of English language texts identified with the tendency, including 'The Waste Land', the early *Cantos*, William Carlos Williams's most imagist phase, key Stevens, Marianne Moore, Hart Crane, *Ulysses*, Virginia Woolf's most experimental novels, early Hemingway, Faulkner, Dos Passos. Now, too, the American constituent is yet larger and more central. Indeed if you stand in London, you may feel the whole affair more or less petered out and died; while if you stand in New York you may well see a continuity passing through into a new stylistic epoch, called 'post-modernism'. It is a rough map, not the one you would come up with if you stood in Berlin, or Moscow. But it serves, if with variations, as a version of the international picture, though a German view would strengthen the 1880s and 1890s, and a French one emphasize yet further the period through from 1930.

But, since this is essentially the story as told from London or New York, let me just remind you again how international the affair was, how large and various the funds, how enormous the thought-flow that ran through the range of European capitals, in complex motions, making some of them centres and others provinces at different phases. We might note that Ibsenite Naturalism started out of Scandinavia, went to Germany to happen, and there turned, in late Ibsen and Strindberg, toward Expressionism. Meanwhile in France Zolaesque Naturalism turned toward aestheticism, Symbolism and an art of the soul and the senses; and both traditions seem to cross to feed the German Expressionist explosion of the immediately prewar years. Paris was also giving London much of its 1890s Naturalism and aestheticism (this much helped by injections from Ireland); for London scarcely noticed Germany, though Ibsen and Nietzsche won attention, and D. H. Lawrence had German Expressionist contacts. In Russia, another version of Symbolism was growing. In Vienna, another entrepôt of ideas, various tendencies were merging, from psychologism to new linguistic theories, which were to push ideas in many directions, east and west. In Paris, in addition to local movements like Unanisme, Marinetti was inventing the Futurism that he would take home to Italy; but this reached Germany, and emerged in another and very important form in Russia, whence it cast large radiations that still survive in modern aesthetics. Imagism in London was derived from French Symbolism, crossed with theories of hardness from Worringer; it was largely an American affair, though many English ideas went into it too. Vorticism, on the other hand, was both abstraction from and attack on Futurism, and one of its founding figures, Wyndham Lewis, was aptly if confusingly born at sea, on a ship off the North Atlantic coast. Dada, with German Expressionist antecedents, was synthesized in a Zurich that, as fans of Tom Stoppard know, also contained Lenin and Joyce; the war over, it took off in two directions, one to Berlin, the other to Paris, where it interacted with French Surrealism. If internationalism is the theme, then it would be hard to find a more eclectic setting than 1920s Paris. And, suitably, the Revolution of the Word, accumulating in the 1920s, culminating in the 1930s, could claim derivation from contingents from France, the States, England, Ireland, Germany, and Romania, to name but a few.

So this much we can say; that modernism was an affair of many movements, of commonly *avant-garde* tendency, with international origins, much change of personnel, and a great capacity for transit. It was also an affair largely of cities, especially ones with cultural–bohemian facilities and fluidity of population, usually the large modern capitals at points of cultural intersection, where old values crossed with the speed and race, the street architecture and mechanical innovations, of modern life. In these cities was usually a bohemia; in practical terms an international, cheap-rent enclave or ghetto, where specialists in a thought-system could gather and find others of like disposition, spending ideas they could afford over drinks they could not. These were usually polyglot communities, manifesting many characteristics of modern art: linguistic and formal anxiety, cultural unease, ambiguity of intellectual role and status, apocalyptic sensibility coupled with revolutionary hope. And the contingent, polyglot, and apocalyptic nature of modern capital cities penetrates many of modernism's central texts, as locus or underlying metaphor: so, for example, Conrad's *The Secret Agent*, Stephen Crane's *Maggie*, Doblin's *Berlin Alexanderplatz*, Pound's *Hugh Selwyn Mauberley*, Hesse's *Steppenwulf*, Eliot's 'Waste Land', Joyce's *Ulysses*, Hart Crane's 'The Bridge', Dos Passos's *Manhattan Transfer*, and you can add more. This urban *émigré* sensibility is recurrent in modernist writing. And the emigration is usually not just internal, from province to national capital, but to external capitals as well. Behind modernism is not just metropolis, but cosmopolis. Its roots may reach back into national materials, its sources to specific social changes and tensions, but it is the art of form as distance; hence, then, Graham Hough's 'rootless affair'.

But let me now turn to the American part in all this. Modernism, Al Alvarez once observed, 'has been a predominantly American concern'. It can hardly be said to have started as such. It began in Europe, and it took a considerable time to cross the Atlantic as a stylistic mode; American writers in the 1890s were just becoming newly preoccupied with the Naturalism from Zola that was, in Europe at this point, largely exhausting itself. Indeed, the full impact of the modernist tendency came in America at least a generation later than it did in Europe; we normally date it from the American mental and technical ferments of 1912, when Freud and Cubism, experiment and radical protest, began to cluster on American soil. Modernism was a European movement, but from about that date it started to matter to Americans; much of its modern importance, and the current sanctification it has acquired, come from that fact. But even then it would not do to suggest that this was solely a matter of imports from Europe. One of the signals of the new in America was the starting of the little magazine *Poetry* in Chicago in 1912; it had Ezra Pound in London as foreign editor, posting in the foreign developments. But *Poetry* felt there was an *American* modern art, and it quickly tired of being told by Pound that American bards must study Remy de Gourmont, Henri de Regnier, Francis Jammes and Tristan Corbiere. 'Mr [Vachel] Lindsay did not go to France for *The Congo* or for *General William Booth Enters Into Heaven*. He did not even stay on the eastern side of the Alleghenies . . . ,' it complained. There was an anti-European streak to the American modern, a streak of nativism; some of the major writers, like William Carlos Williams and William Faulkner, scarcely set foot in Europe, and if we now know that they had their European influences, that was not what they felt mattered.

But others did think Europe mattered. Indeed part of the fascination of the episode is the mediating part played by a significant group of Americans from the 1890s to the 1920s who came to Europe, and did much in the way of stimulating European developments, adapting them, bonding them on to the American scene. Over this period, and with a special and famous point of culmination in the 1920s, you could find in certain European capitals, but especially in London and Paris, a good number of American writers up to an old American custom—literary expatriation—in a new form. They had come to look, in their different ways, for what Americans had long understood lay on the further side of the Atlantic, the Old World, an entity polarized against the New World, of course, and with certain well-established associations: it was past tense by contrast to America's future, static to America's process, female to America's male, dense to America's lightness, feudal to America's democratic, artistic to America's bustling commercialism. In fact they found not the Old World but the New Arts, and to some degree they found them by what T. S. Eliot would call 'great labour'; that is to say, by making them happen. Moreover, operating, on the whole, with sensitive antennae, they managed to catch many of the strongest and most relevant signals, to move when there was moving to be done, and in general to act as a convenient line for attention if we want to know what was going on in various capitals at various times. Their version usually started in London, not usually thought of as the most modernist of cities, reached to Paris and finally centred there; it also touched Italy, glanced at Germany, largely ignored Russia. It was very selective, in some ways provincial, and often conducted on the borderline between an old American notion of a European aesthetic adventure and a new American sense that the arts were everywhere on the boil. But their version has now become a very important historical account of modernism. And, as I have said, it signals a primary bifurcation in the American tradition as such, a contention between naturalism and modernism, between redskin and paleface, between the art of the American breath-rhythm and the polyglot or cosmopolitan cadence.

There are, I suppose, two substantial explanations for American literature now familiarly in existence, notions that have been held both by writers and by critics. One, ancestrally rooted in Sydney Smith, who asked in 1818 'Who reads an American book?', assumes American writing to be an appendage or derivative from English writing in particular and European writing in general. We do read American books (how else do we get through an airport?); but are they not just English books with skyscrapers? It is, in the current balance of power, a fading view, but it once had some prominence in university English departments; now, with Oxbridge fallen, these are most likely to be found in the United States themselves. The other, by compensation, asserts the Americanness of American literature; its ancestral roots are in the many declarations of literary independence that America produced in the nineteenth century, reactions to what Melville called 'literary flunkeyism', or Henry Adams saw as the American 'on his literary knees to the European'. It sounds in William Carlos Williams's view that American English was learned from the mouths of Polish mothers. For modern critical versions of this Americanist bias, the real ancestor is probably an Englishman, D. H. Lawrence; we have now, however, a whole lore of readings of American literature which see it as a totally national phenomenon, with distinctive metrics, styles, epistemologies, cadences, breath-speeds, and above all cultural mythologies—those myths of the frontier and the virgin land, of American Adams and paradisial gardens, which are frequently made manifest to us by demonstrating their formal, stylistic, and mythological distinctiveness from the activities of European writers. Such arguments are substantially true, but often want in effective comparison; indeed it is a small embarrassment that many of the techniques, preoccupations, and myths so distinguished—Richard Chase's 'romance' tradition in the novel, Leslie Fiedler's 'gothic', or Richard Poirier's 'self-made style'—have been used by revisionist critics of European writing, to explicate *its* texts, and so to explode the notion that the predominant tradition of European fiction has been a social realist one. Nationalism is rarely a totally good guide to history in literary matters. So perhaps a truer view is that American writing, perhaps more than most writing, has lived in a persistent tension between nativism and cosmopolitanism. The origins of America as a nation, and of American writing, roughly coincided with the emergence of romantic nationalist aesthetics. The post-revolutionary generation, influenced by Herder and Mme de Stael, quickly sought declarations of literary independence; equally quickly, many writers, like Irving and Cooper, went for extended periods to Europe, in order to find romantic sensibility, storied associations, social densities, accumulated customs. Most subsequent generations re-experienced the problem, on the axis of a new aesthetic: neo-classical, romantic, transcendentalist, realist, naturalist, and modernist versions therefore exist. But the list suggests the problem; transcendentalism is the only American brand name here; American writing had its own distinctive motion, preoccupation, thematics, but it was also bonded into the broad stylistic development of the western nations in general. It belonged not just to the nation, but to the international republic of letters, which had its own frontiers and capitals, these, until latterly, largely assumed to be located in Europe.

Inevitably, then, throughout the nineteenth century, many American writers followed this secret artistic chart and took the path to Europe. They established its imaginative existence in the form of a distinctive metaphoric geography, attaching different meanings to different nations, though one large meaning to the Old World in total. Hence a significant, even if partial, area of American literary experience took place in Europe; some of the best declarations of independence were made there; for a wide variety of motives, from a wide variety of origins, the expatriates came. Now most nations of liberal character produce literary expatriates, particularly if they are post-colonial ones with a sense of provincial status. But America produced a significant number, and they were moving against the migrant tide, the motion of history; this became a public issue and in the expatriates a private drama, an inward tension very manifest in their writing itself. This did not stop the traffic. The pattern not only continued but intensified. And toward the end of the century, when old political hostilities had gone, and new anxieties about American monopoly capitalism and its displacement of the arts had increased, American expatriation to Europe peaked. For some of these pilgrims, passionate or otherwise, Europe was a social recourse, a place where the civilization, manners, and deferences dying in America could be recovered: these were the 'old expatriates', usually distinguishable clearly by residence and lifestyle from the newer ones, whose dispositions were more bohemian, whose sought milieu was usually the artistic ghetto, whose model of expatriation was one of atelier instruction. This was often expressed as a choice between London and Paris, capital and anti-capital, though the London of this period had explicit experimental attractions.

So over the significant years, then, successive waves of American writers came, to the London or the Paris or to a lesser extent the Italy, first of aestheticism and Symbolism, then of the Cubist and Imagist phases of the opening world, finally to the twenties of the 'lost generation', when, if you wanted to find the American writers who were lost, you looked in the cafés in Paris. And they came, in part, as a result of an internal oscillation that had grown up in American culture: between that insistent American realism 'on native grounds' which had, by the 1890s, turned toward a systematic, American version of Naturalism, and the aesthetic deliverance, which had been isolated out and identified with the voyage into art and sensibility, which in turn was the voyage to Europe. This meant that their quest still contained within itself something of the American fancy about Europe as culture, and it had a highly aesthetic or abstract character. So it was form and novelty that mattered; the underlying social turmoil that pushed modernism into existence did not affect them so directly, and, if it was interpreted at all, was often interpreted in a distinctively American way, as I think it is in 'The Waste Land' or *The Cantos*; they detached what they found. But they did find it, and indeed helped to ferment what was going on. And they did assimilate it—with such success that today we see the American arts as modern, not just because they explore an advanced or futuristic society, but because they have incorporated into themselves the lore of the modern art forms.

II

It seems appropriate to begin with the transition into this 'new' expatriation, and where better to start than with that insistent explorer of the American complex fate, Henry James. One of the quieter events we celebrated amid last year's Bicentennial fun was the centennial of Henry James's famous 'choice', his decision to settle in London. As you might expect from James, it was a symbolic one. He had looked first at Italy's 'golden air', rich in resonances, and found it stood for the aesthetic sliding into the corrupt; then at the Parisian spectacle, rich in bohemia, Turgenev, Flaubert, and found it stood for the aesthetic as a coterie affair. And so, in 1876, he elected for London, his 'murky Babylon', 'the most possible form of life', 'the biggest aggregation of life', art mitigated by morals, social decor, material substance, human variety, and society hostesses. It was, you might say, the London of the aesthetic realist. The task was to penetrate it in depth rather than in its full range; James's fictional world was substantially an upper middle class one with bohemian fringes. But social complexity was the novel's stuff; around this time, he told Howells that it needed a complex social machinery to set a novelist in motion, that it was on 'manners, customs, usages, habits, forms' that the novelist lives. The theme of the old American romance of Europe being mitigated toward realism fuels his novels of the 1870s and 1880s. But then he dropped his international theme, even, for a time in the early 1890s, the novel form itself. However, in the later 1890s, when the aesthetic and epistemological pressures in European culture, and in James's own evolving sensibility, were increasing, he returned to fiction, and then to the international theme. And, over the turn of the century, he produced his last three great novels, *The Ambassadors*, *The Wings of the Dove*, *The Golden Bowl*. Though these have their detractors ('James the Old Pretender'), they constitute, I think, his greatest achievement, and they certainly constitute the basis of his claim to being a founding father of the modernist novel in the Anglo-American line—as Gertrude Stein (who said of him: 'Henry James never came amiss. He did not come slowly nor did he come to kiss'), Virginia Woolf, and others would later see.

James's transition into modernism is not entirely easy to explain. It certainly has some American sources, in his brother William's pragmatism and psychological curiosity, also to influence Gertrude Stein, who was taught by William James. But one feature of it is a relative dissolution of James's old Europe. Now our apprehension of the strange coming of modernism is surely part-based on our responding to transitions like this, moments when writing moves over the border, beyond the realist or the naturalist synthesis, into something other; it is this sort of thing we find in Ibsen's work, or Strindberg's. In James's case you could define it, crudely, as a shift from being in the apostolic succession from George Eliot to being in a modern force-field. For, in these late novels of James, there occurs some clear solvency of the realistic mode, and also of the moral support that this mode gets from the social fabric. Instead, consciousness and modes of perception become central facets of experience (as a title like *What Maisie Knew* suggests); society and material phenomena become inert or else coherent only in so far as active apprehension and mental ordering make them so; grammar itself has trouble in forming the relation of subject to verb to object. These are also, of course, the distilling years of the famous prefaces for the New York edition of the novels; and James's delight there in 'a deep-breathing economy and organic form' as the novel's essence also displays a symbolist compact. Gertrude Stein explained this too: 'He saw that he could write two ways at once which he did and if he did he did. And there is nothing alike in heard and saw. Not now or even by itself, not now. / Owen Young said that everything should be clear and everything is now clear.' In some ways, in fact, James became more American, and hence more exposed to the mental shifts and motions of the European new arts; it is significant that the same period saw a new preoccupation in him with the nature of expatriation, and a fear that his was a mistake. He attentively watched the spectacle of Americans wandering through the vaunted scene of Europe, their minds and spirits caught up with its aesthetic rewards: Whistler, Millet, Abbey, and Sargent in painting, Berenson, Santayana, Logan Pearsall Smith, Leo Stein in aesthetics, in writing Howard Sturgis, Edith Wharton, Henry Harland, Constance Fenimore Woolson, as well as antecedents like Hawthorne. He wrote a life of the American sculptor expatriate William Wetmore Story, remarking on Story's 'plenitude of feeling—in the fullness of time and on due occasion—that a man always pays, in one way or another, for a detachment from his plain primary heritage, and that this tax is levied in an amusing variety of ways'. We all know about the amusement of being taxed; it has its dark side. The comedy and the anguishes, the rewards and the disillusions, the psychology and the pathology of expatriation thus became obsessions of this phase.

And they were evidently in his mind when he made his trip of 1904 back to the States which he recorded in *The American*

Scene (1907). It is not surprising that James should take occasion to visit Newport, Rhode Island, that social resort which was both manifestation and patrician criticism of Gilded Age America; nor that his eye should light on a group of people—a collection, he said, of the 'detached, the slightly disenchanted, and casually disqualified, and yet of the resigned and contented, of the socially orthodox; a handful of mild, oh delightfully mild, cosmopolites'—whose symptoms he understood. They had been to Europe, not sacrificed to the American 'black ebony god of business', and had formed critical habits. James imagined them, over their winter whist, 'pending constantly their return of the *Revue des Deux Mondes*' and added: 'I find myself tenderly evoking them as special instances of the great—or perhaps I have a right only to say of the small—American complication; the state of having been so pierced, betimes, by the sharp outland dart as to be able ever afterwards but to move about, vaguely and helplessly, with the shaft in one's side.' James came now to specialize in such vignettes of consciousness displaced against social reality, and he saw them as a distinctly American phenomenon, the result of the 'great ebony god' and the unmitigated nature of American life. And so such figures convert into heroes like Strether, in *The Ambassadors*, the man of incompleteness who seeks to redeem from the contingent largeness of experience, represented by Europe, the framed picture, which, in the impressionist way, becomes real by transmitting itself as form and knowledge. They also convert, for the worse, into the 'dispatriate'—which is what James called Henry Harland, who went through a familiar late nineteenth-century motion from writing realistic novels about America, set in the New York Jewish ghetto, to becoming a London aesthete, editor of the *Yellow Book*, author of abstract, fanciful European romances like *The Cardinal's Snuff Box*, books which sacrificed, said James, to aesthetic unreality, to 'the composite spectacle and the polyglot doom'. James thus saw his experiment as a crisis affair in which what was unreconcilable in America should not be simply displaced onto Europe, but actually reconciled there.

It is for this reason that one puts James at the centre of the impressionist axis. There were writers, like Harland and Henry Blake Fuller, who expatriated in order to oscillate between two worlds: the world of American Naturalism and the hard, unmitigated American fact, and a wonderfully aestheticized, mysterious Europe, without depths or anxieties of its own. There were some, like Stephen Crane, who crossed the Atlantic simply to shift in reputation, to have what his American critics identified as Naturalism recognized, by peers like James, Wells, and Conrad, as a novel Impressionism. James attempted to stand at the centre of, and map, a larger situation, to function as a cosmopolitan intelligence relating the evolution of style to the evolution of modern cultural relations. The outland dart could penetrate to varying depths and with varying effects. And, when the century turned, there were to be two kinds of American expatriates: those who inherited some of the cultural concern, and saw modernism as a crisis of perception and tradition, a promise of and a disaster for form in the European tradition, marking its shift into a new condition, and demonstrating the problem of creating significant culture in a fragmented world; and those who took it as pure style, a joyous event detached from historical determination. You could call it the difference, say, between Ezra Pound and Gertrude Stein, or between London and Paris; it was to give two different lines of American modernism.

III

And so, said Gertrude Stein, 'the twentieth century had come, it began with 1901', and it brought a new phase of American expatriation. By 1914 English literary life had deeply changed, and somewhere in the centre of that change was a considerable contingent of Americans. The outstanding figures are, of course, Ezra Pound, who came in 1909, and T. S. Eliot, who came in 1914, but there were more, including Robert Frost, Hilda Doolittle, John Gould Fletcher, Conrad Aiken; along with other expatriate figures like Joseph Conrad and Wyndham Lewis, they helped give London one of its most cosmopolitan phases. In all this Pound and Eliot stand at the centre. They had left America with considerable lore; Pound was a product of comparative literature, a man with words like 'Villon' and 'Lope de Vega' and 'the European mind' much on his lips, who approached England via Spain and Italy; Eliot had emerged from a Harvard where symbolist issues had penetrated deeply, not just from Europe, but, by the western route, from Japan. They came at once for artistic modernity and for the 'tradition', and they identified an affinity with James—most articulately in the special Henry James number of *Little*

Review, organized by Pound in 1918. Here Eliot remarked that it was 'the final consummation of an American to become, not an Englishman, but a European—something which no born European, no person of any European nationality, can become'. He noted the value of being 'everywhere a foreigner', and the American need to know a special and larger Europe, won by his own mind and sensibility. The American had his own potential; still, it needed the sanctification of a central, civilizing metropolis. Pound had said much the same in *Patria Mia*, written for *The New Age* just before the war. Here he had spoken of America as 'the great rich, Western province which has sent one or two notable artists to the capital. And that capital is, needless to say, not Rome, but the double city of London and Paris.' For Pound at this time the task was to report the city back to the province, to induce a Risorgimento there by importing models, for painting, sculpture, writing. 'If we are to have an art capital [in America] it also must be made by conscious effort', he said. For Eliot, the task was to mediate between tradition (which was, roughly speaking, Europe) and the individual talent (who was the modern poet). For both, contemporaneity was a distinct condition, with the tradition lost, words and consciousness gone away. The need was for a new synthesis, a revised poetic, requiring an *avant-garde* posture from the artist, who was, as Pound said in *his* James essay, 'the antennae of the race'.

The expatriate was thus both explorer and mentor, a guide by virtue of his American cosmopolitanism both to those in Europe and back home. Pound started his visit to London in expatriate deference; he had come to be near Yeats, and he told William Carlos Williams: 'There is no town like London to make one feel the vanity of all art except the highest. To make one disbelieve in all but the most careful and conservative presentation of one's stuff.' He attended, at first as willing provincial, the London coteries, notably those around *The English Review*, *The New Age*, and the splinter group from the Poets' Club, centred round T. E. Hulme, which met at the Eiffel Tower restaurant to discuss poetry. He saw himself much as an English man of letters, involved in aesthetics and cultural affairs. He picked up late Symbolist principles and the new classical ones, Hulme's distillation from Bergson, de Gourmont, Husserl, Sorel, and Worringer. F. S. Flint was drawing attention to the new French movements, in which he showed much interest; Ford Madox Hueffer was promoting post-impressionism: this

Pound fed back to America. But at the same time he was gradually inventing a scenario for modernism, devising his own modern poetic. The *avant-garde* and movement model of the arts, which he took from the French, seemed especially congenial, and he set to work to campaign, to make it new. He was a good tactician of the arts, a sound organizer; someone once called him a Baden-Powell, trying to get all the young artists under canvas. He captured magazines, and determined to start a movement; so came Imagism, founded in a Kensington teashop in 1912, partly a tactical ploy, partly a serious attempt to distil an organized poetic from recent developments. It was a version of poetry that clustered elements from various symbolist and post-impressionist theories going back to the 1890s, but in its move toward the 'hard' image and the defeat of abstraction and romantic overspill it took constituents from Cubist and Futurist aesthetics. Much of this came directly out of the London sequence, but there was a substantial American element. It was partly one of personnel, for he drew on his fellow Americans, getting Hilda Doolittle, for example, to sign her poems 'H. D. Imagiste'. It was also one of perception; the concentrated technique, the emphasis on superpositioning, the introduction of *haiku* and *tanka*, seemed to describe best the developing innovations of his American coterie, and it linked not just with Browning but with Whitman. Hence it passed readily on to American poets like Williams and Marianne Moore. Pound later revised the history appropriately: 'All the developments in English verse since 1910 are due almost wholly to Americans', he said in *How to Read*. It was not entirely true; but it was the Americans who were to prove both the largest synthesizers and the most significant exploiters and developers of the cosmopolitan theories of London between 1909 and 1914, first with Pound and soon with Eliot, then with many writers of the 1920s back at home.

By 1914, Pound was taking the affair further, as he grew more and more conscious of the pressure of cultural decline. His cosmopolitanism enlarged, and London itself began to seem less creative and energetic, despite his growing access to magazines, and the arrival of Eliot. He took his theories of hardness further with Vorticism, with its more distinctly futurist dimensions, its mechanistic substitution for old culture. By the end of the war the traditional expatriate appeal of London seemed to him finished—indeed so did the English literary inheritance itself. His sense of cultural despair had started in America, but he carried it over into his vision of England, now equally damaged, provincialized, vulgarized, by a false cultural economy. He needed a global theory of economies and culture; this underlay the new poetic. Expressing his disillusion with Anglo-Saxon civilization—the text is 'Hugh Selwyn Mauberley' —he moved on to Paris in 1921. The contemporary state of French society did not impress him, but that was not now the issue: Paris was 'the laboratory of ideas' and it had an active experimental scene. 'Find Cocteau and Picabia intelligent', he noted. 'Fools abound but are less in one's way here, or at least for the moment.' The paths of Eliot and Pound here distinctly divide; while Eliot stayed in England, to feel his way beyond the apocalyptic modern city he too perceived, disjunct and in fragments, into Classicism, Royalism, Anglo-Catholicism, and British citizenship, Pound formed his alliances differently. He flourished for a while amid the detached experiments of Paris, though the new expatriates coming into Paris who sought him as mentor did not entirely impress him: 'The new lot of American *émigrés* were anything but the Passionate Pilgrims of James's day or the enquirers of my own. *We* came to find something, to learn, possibly to conserve, but this new lot came in disgust', he wrote. The desire to conserve persisted and took him further, to Rapallo in 1924, and then into the new cultural economics and efficiencies of Mussolini's state. Eliot won the Order of Merit; Pound ended after the war in St. Elizabeth's Hospital, Washington, unfit to plead on a charge of treason.

IV

It was the culturally apocalyptic note, the sense of lost coherence and the desire for recovery, which led Pound and Eliot to be identified as the bleak version of modernism, even the fascist version; it is an excessive view, but it explains why Pound's friend William Carlos Williams could regard *The Waste Land* not as a breakthrough but as an event that set modern poetry back twenty years. But no such cultural anxieties bothered Gertrude Stein. The twentieth century came, as she said; but, she also explained, it came in America and then moved across to France to happen. England, she said, was refusing the twentieth century 'knowing full well that they had gloriously created the nineteenth century and perhaps the twentieth century was going to be too many for them . . .', while the

French simply accepted its arrival, since 'what is was and what was is, was their point of view of which they were not very conscious'. The task fell to Americans: 'Of course they all came to France a great many to paint pictures and naturally they could not do that at home, or write they could not do that at home either, they could be dentists at home.' It especially fell to Gertrude Stein: 'I was there to kill what was not dead, the nineteenth century which was so sure of evolution and prayers.' Miss Stein was never greatly troubled by modesty; she once identified herself as one of the three great twentieth-century geniuses. When she and her brother Leo came to Europe, in 1903, looking for 'glory', they inspected London and rejected it ('Gertrude Stein was not very much amused', she said, so summing up the London espisode). They chose Paris, though a different Paris from a fellow expatriate, Edith Wharton, who sought French society; they were atelier expatriates, wanting Montparnasse, and they finally settled at 27 rue de Fleurus. Here they began art-collecting, a family custom, were guided toward Post-Impressionism, collected painters as well as paintings, and so found themselves amid the ferments of cubism. Sitting under a Cézanne, thinking of Flaubert, Gertrude Stein wrote, between 1904 and 1906, *Three Lives*, where, she said, she established the principle of the continuous present, the 'first definite step away from the nineteenth century and into the twentieth century in literature', she said. It was also Picasso's 'long struggle with the portrait of Gertrude Stein' which led him from Harlequinism to cubism, she claimed: a fascinating view of the causalities of that movement. And in turn she applied cubism to fiction, in *The Making of Americans*, her one novel, a massive text of some 1,000 pages based on the proposition that Americans were cubists, products of the new composition. In prose terms, this required the defeat of the realist noun, the principle of composition by paragraph, the elimination of remembering as a source of causality in fiction, and abstraction by collectivity, the history of one being the history of all. But the novel was narrative, and narrative itself was not enough; the task was to produce a spatial or synchronic object, more like a painting. So now she turned to prose still-lives, portraits, collages, abstracts—gnomic objects which she part-collected in the volume *Tender Buttons*, published in 1914. It was this book that sparked off her recognition in America; she was taken up as the literary wing of the Armory Show—the post-impressionist exhibition displaying Matisse,

Picasso and Duchamps which stirred the radical wing of the American arts in the years just before the war.

Miss Stein's was, in a sense, a studio expatriation. She was in Europe to discover new techniques and art-forms, mostly from painters, and make them into literature. The deeper agonies of the outland dart were not for her; she had no great concern with the progress or the crises of European civilization. She denied that she was an expatriate, and, when a reporter called her one, cried: 'I get so mad, all of a sudden.' She said America was her country and Paris was her home town. As for cubism, she held that, though it may have been invented by Frenchmen and Spaniards, it was really an American art, fitting the American sense of time, and prairie space, its skyscraper cities, its filmic speed. Not surprisingly, her tactics of direct takeover were not universally accepted. There was the famous *Testimony Against Gertrude Stein*, produced by *transition* magazine in 1935; here many European cubists rejected her, finding her work modish, superficial, untheoretical, uncaused. Braque, for example, said: 'Miss Stein obviously saw everything from the outside and never the real struggle we were engaged in. For one who poses as an authority on the epoch it is safe to say that she never went beyond the stage of a tourist.' Certainly she perceived in terms of detachable, abstract styles justified by broad reference to twentieth-century needs; nothing of the cultural or perceptual *angst* that inhabits much modernism shows in her work; the aesthetic behind it was largely explained in terms of speech-pattern and Americanness. Modernity was the issue, and modernity was an American speciality; cubism was the progressive art aptly being mastered by a progressive nation. Yet in her way she was right. Americans had a taste for stylistic mobility and fashion, for the forms that suggested a radical conception of man. They found a relevance in the cubist mode, and American modern style became close to *modernist* style. Moreover modernism seemed to pull together the apparently lonely and eccentric history of American artistic endeavour right through the nineteenth century; the modernist affair could appear to be the coming of age of the American arts. Thus, by the 1920, modernism began to seem the spirit of the new American movement. Writers like Faulkner and Dos Passos took both modernist and more traditional modes as part of their stylistic compendium, moving thus not from a sense of crisis or outrage but from intrinsic necessity, the need to distil form out of modern material.

V

You could also polarize America as material, Europe as technique, and journey between the two. This many did: in the early 1920s, when Gertrude Stein became a cult, she was there to receive that striking third wave of American expatriates in Europe, who flooded with the force of a migration into Paris once the war was over. Indeed a significant part of a whole new literary generation attended, for brief or longish periods, at the expatriate ceremonial. They avoided London, which they saw as part of their provincial and Anglo-Saxon bondage, and chose atelier Paris. They associated it with three things: with the new styles and with formal experiment in general, an aesthetic release, therefore, from a naturalist view of literature, which saw the world as an experience to be reported in journalistic or scientific modes, and which needed the qualifications offered by Stein's cubist novel, Joyce's verbal revolution, Pound's redeemed image, Proust's new structures of consciousness; with an alternative or opposite to the new isolationism and provincialism that the United States seemed to have espoused once the war was over and the Red Scare begun; and with a realm of modernized and reordered experience which came not from a new style of art but from a new condition of man, the postwar condition as such, felt especially in Paris or Germany.

These writers were aware of, but did not, on the whole, go directly to, the new movements of Europe—dada, surrealism and late expressionism. They got their instruction rather through the mediating offices of the previous generation of expatriates: Stein, Pound, Joyce, Ford Madox Hueffer, now Ford. 'Begin over again—and concentrate', Gertrude Stein told Hemingway. One striking feature of this phase of expatriation, and a clear evidence of its scale, was that it was built on the importation into Paris of many primary literary institutions: in came the expatriate English-language magazines (*Transatlantic Review*, *transition*, *Broom*, *Secession*, *This Quarter*, etc.); small presses like the Black Sun; bookshops like the Shakespeare. Cafés like the Rotonde and Dôme were commandeered; Montparnasse seemed like an extension of Greenwich Village, except here you could drink openly and at a very favourable rate of exchange. Indeed Malcolm Cowley, in the one good analytical book on the period, *Exile's Return*, identified these writers as *valuta* expatriates, following the advantageous rates offered to the dollar, rather than the radical protesters against American life they sometimes were judged to be. There *was* an element of direct protest, against the confinements and limitations of contemporary American life, which seemed to be dominated by small-town sensibility. The dissent was ambiguous, as we see in the writing. It expresses a new generational coherence, a modernized, postwar sensibility that could not, as Thomas Wolfe puts it, go home again, but must face the racing modernity, the minimalized language, the lost myths, of Twenties experience. Yet the lost home town is also the repeated subject of this writing. And if, on one side, there was the search for the city of modern experience, there was on the other a search for the primitive simplicities for which the small town had once seemed to stand—for the deep woods that drew Hemingway and Faulkner, the dream of the clean green world that drew Fitzgerald. The modernism that was pursued in Paris was largely a way of looking backward—an urban, aesthetic or generationally modernized angle of experience taken on materials that lay back in America, 3,000 miles away.

By the end of the 1920s, the issue was in effect finished. Politics came back in radical form; the Great Crash cut off the cheques; and for many of the writers the last thing they had expected from a provincial America in the hands of its booboisie had been given—they had become successful writers. A modernism of sorts had settled as an accepted American style, just as Freud and Jung, Picabia and Picasso, the skyscraper and the futurist lines of the motor car had. And with the 1930s, when, thanks to Hitler and Fascism, the tide of migration was reversed, and the European modernists came to America, it seemed as if Miss Stein's hope had come true. Modernism had become the twentieth-century American style, the language of its progressivism, pluralism, cultural convergence. In short, if by 1939 you went looking for Modernism, you were likely to look to the States. It also became successful. Pound ended in the asylum, but Eliot, Hemingway and Faulkner won the Nobel Prize, and now in any history of modern literature the American province has come to seem remarkably central. It *was* a selective version, and we have now to struggle to identify and imagine many of the European aspects of the affair that did not enter the American view. But in 1914 what an unpredictable version of it all this must have looked, not only to Russians, Germans and Frenchmen, but to the Americans themselves.

SHAKESPEARE AND BAROQUE ART

By NICHOLAS BROOKE

Read 30 April 1977

THE artistic vitality of Europe around 1600 was remarkable in many centres and in many arts, but two seem to me to have had a decisive pre-eminence: the theatre in London, and the visual arts in Rome. The two are not generally thought of as contemporary because Roman baroque is the distinctive art of the seventeenth century, whereas English drama is vaguely thought of as renaissance and called Elizabethan, although the bulk of it is later. It is true that the greatest of baroque artists was Bernini, whose career very nearly spanned the seventeenth century, prodigious both in his teens and in his seventies; whereas the greatest of English dramatists was of course Shakespeare who died in 1616. There was a slight overlap, but not much. It is more striking that art historians generally see the revival of Roman art as dating from the arrival in Rome in the early 1590s of Caravaggio and Annibale Carracci. Both were dead by 1610, so that the first energies of baroque erupted in Rome between 1590 and 1610—and that almost exactly corresponds with Shakespeare's career in London. The other supreme baroque artist, Rubens, does more to link the two cities: he served as court painter to the Duke of Mantua from 1600 to 1608; he copied some of Caravaggio's paintings and purchased some for his master (they were later sold to Charles I); he also made sketches from Carracci's masterpiece, the ceiling in the Palazzo Farnese. When the grand art collections began to be formed in England by Arundel, Buckingham, and Charles,[1] Rubens was a key figure in their understanding.

For the artists, I have consulted various books and articles, but relied most heavily on: J. Shearman, *Mannerism*, Harmondsworth 1967; M. Kitson, *Caravaggio*, London 1969; J. Summerson, *Inigo Jones*, Harmondsworth 1966; P. Cabanne, *Rubens*, London 1967; H. Hibbard, *Bernini*, Harmondsworth 1965. References to Shakespeare are to the relevant volumes of the Arden Edition, London 1954– .

[1] In the second and third decades of the seventeenth century.

He came to London as ambassador and later painted the magnificent ceiling panels of James I for the banqueting house which Inigo Jones had built in Whitehall in 1619. Jones had been in Italy from 1613 to 1615, and had probably been there before about the turn of the century. His series of court masques with Ben Jonson's texts began in 1605, based on Italian designs from the late sixteenth century.

Jones alone might offer direct influence within Shakespeare's lifetime; but I am not concerned to claim direct influence. An artist, even a great artist, can be influential only in a receptive environment. We are apt to believe that the rapid diffusion of new artists' work nowadays is due to rapid communications; in fact, it is still strangely selective and must relate to the readiness of some societies and the unreadiness of others. Rubens was instantly accepted in early seventeenth century England, which argues that London was waiting for him to happen. Why London and Rome should have seen simultaneous eruptions in different arts is naturally a very obscure question. There are some resemblances in their history during the sixteenth century which may (I do not know enough to be sure) provide hints. Reformation London was artistically barren until the last two decades of the century; so, precisely, was counter-reformation Rome. There was, of course, one major difference: Roman baroque was largely, though not exclusively, religious; English drama was almost exclusively secular, though not necessarily pagan. But even this difference does depend on a similarity, for both were governed by ecclesiastical pressure: in England, the religious drama was finally suppressed, and explicit allusion to God or heaven was forbidden in the profane public theatres; in Rome, the Council of Trent had commanded a public art that was purely Christian. It is familiar (and even exaggerated) that the London theatres were attended by a wide audience, from courtier to relatively low-paid worker. Roman baroque is associated with the Papacy at its most ostentatious; but its public monuments in churches were designed for a universal audience.

What I am concerned with, therefore, is not influence but broad analogy; with changes in the aesthetic structure of Shakespeare's plays which reflect changes in their imaginative substance. I did not arrive at this peculiar study from a theoretical devotion to inter-disciplinary study, but from a personal discovery of Bavarian baroque in Munich about a dozen years ago, which led me back to Bernini. In Bernini I saw unexpected illumination of problems about *Macbeth* which had puzzled me for many years. Bernini eventually took me to Rome, and Rome produced also Carracci and Caravaggio and a far more detailed illumination of some general problems about Shakespeare's career as a whole. I think this can be most clearly expressed in terms of his comedies. The earliest and the latest are equally based on romance themes. Even *The Comedy of Errors* surrounds a Roman farce with a story of long-lost parents and children wandering on journeys and under threat of death in their search for eventual reunion; that is also the plot of *Pericles*. *A Midsummer Night's Dream* is a magic play, animated by the anarchic spirit of Puck, governed by Oberon who was probably doubled with Theseus; *The Tempest* again concentrates on magic under Ariel's anarchic spirit, governed by Prospero who is himself both Duke and magician. Yet, despite these likenesses, the plays are obviously radically different; understanding that difference has continually proved difficult.

We tend to think of baroque art as simply an extension of the renaissance; superficially it appears so, but that is due to a conscious revival of classical forms in early baroque art and architecture. Between the two lies nearly the whole of the sixteenth century, productive of amazingly varied and experimental works, largely anti-classical in effect. The point can be clarified rapidly with some pictures. In *The Coronation of the Virgin* (Plate VI) early Raphael characteristically frames the painting in the shape of a classical arch; the rounded top is reserved for heavenly beings who are not occupying the same space as the human beings below, indeed they are frequently cut off by a horizontal bank of clouds. The human figures have an extraordinary calm but are not otherwise distorted, nor are they notably individualized. The composition is altogether symmetrical. The next picture was painted roughly a hundred years later. In his *Communion of St. Jerome* (Plate VII), Domenichino also uses a classical arch to frame his picture; but this time it is an actual piece of architecture, heavier than Raphael's classicism, and that does establish the cherubim as within the same space as the human figures. They are placed far off centre, and though they roughly balance the off-centre figure of St. Jerome below, the composition is far from symmetry, or even a simple diagonal. It has to move around the group of figures who attract attention by being strongly individualized: the painting relies on the characterization which used to be Shakespeare's chief fame. St. Jerome himself is painted with precise naturalism, and another structure moves backwards in depth from him into the detailed naturalism of the landscape.

It is manifest that there have been dramatic developments between those two paintings. They were, if anything, more astonishing than the contrast conveys. Raphael's later works are less known here because they were mostly grand designs executed by assistants; he became extraordinarily inventive—so did Michelangelo, but he became more and more frustrated of achievement. Both seem to have moved further and further from classical calm into forms that are either contorted with tension or relaxed into elegance, or both at once: battle scenes that seem to be performed as ballets. The result was mannerism. The difference is immediately obvious. In *The Madonna del collo lungo* by Parmigianino (Plate VIII) the central figure dominates with her own version of calm, and her visible body has its own sensuality; but all this is arrived at through the most extraordinary distortions. The long neck by which the painting is known is only one—her thighs must be even more elongated and so, more disturbingly, is her baby. The literal centre of the picture is the Madonna's navel, but light on skin shifts attention from her remote head to the gathering of seductive angels squeezed together in defiance of symmetry on the left-hand side, finally exposing the long and beautiful leg of the nearest angel who, if probably androgynous, is certainly not asexual. The remarkable sensuality is focused in the emblematic objects, the urn on the left (a perfect echo of the thigh below it) and the dominant pillar on the right. Finally, below the pillar in a quite different scale is the strange El Greco-like male in the bottom right-hand corner.

Elegance dominates the image, and its sensuality is largely shifted to off-centre figures and emblematic objects. Mannerist paintings are continually surprising: they tend to insist on the unexpected, to defy symmetry, and to contrive a predominant elegance out of whatever moral or emotional contortions they display. But that is Florentine; later Roman mannerism was characteristically merely pretty and slight. After Barocci's *Rest on the flight into Egypt* (Plate IX), Caravaggio's work is not merely surprising, it is a revolutionary shock. In *The Conversion of Saul* (Plate X) Parmigianino's elegant elongations are aggressively reversed by the dominating rump of a foreshortened cart-horse. The picture has a double composition: as first seen, it is oddly square, governed by the horse's buttocks and the groom's head at the top right, Saul's head at the bottom right, and extended by the red cloak to the bottom left-hand corner. That is parallel to the frame and would seem almost bas-relief if the horse were not so decidedly three-dimensional. The other composition is quite different: it depends on the illusion of depth, a spatial composition which focuses on Saul, somewhere about his solar plexus; for that, the horse acts simply as a frame, excluding the space above and creating depth in the darkness between its legs. The curious thing is that you cannot look at both compositions at once: like many optical illusions, you see either one or the other. In this case, you are almost certain to see the horse first and Saul second. In other words, Caravaggio creates the idea of miracle by exploiting an understanding of illusion. Miracle it is: if you cut off the painting from Saul's hands down the dramatic intensity evaporates and you are left with only a boring domestic study of a horse with a fine old 'character' of a groom. So the miracle is essential, but the dominant impact remains the aggressive actuality.

That brings out what seems to me to have been a problem for Caravaggio, to affirm the miracle without losing the actuality. It is more acute in an earlier painting of St. Mary Magdalene (Plate XI). When I first saw this, I thought it dull. It seemed to be a private study of a quiet girl brooding, or perhaps dozing, on a hard chair in a bare room. Her dress is beautifully painted, and so are the carelessly disposed trivia on the floor. Only the title suggests the holy prostitute. But the dress is a shade too splendid for the bare room: she seems to be Cinderella just after the ball. But she *is* the Magdalene, for she has the red-gold hair and the golden robe of traditional iconography. The broken string of pearls declares her profession, and her relation to it, and the broken chains suggest not only the source of the nice clothes, but also the bondage involved. The flask should be oil, but it looks very much like Roman wine from which she has been drinking, modestly, alone.

In short, it becomes a very interesting and moving painting once it is explored. Its quietude is the very opposite of aggressive, as the very plausible image of a woman is neither aggressive whore nor idealized saint. But its full interest is generated between the actual painting and the myth expressed in traditional iconography; the myth itself is scarcely in the painting at all. Only half the idea can really be said to be represented. In fact, tradition has been inverted, and that is done even more strikingly in Caravaggio's *St. John in the Wilderness* (Plate XII), the painting beside it in the Doria Gallery. The normally ascetic figure of the Baptist has become an erotic youth (wittily borrowed from the Sistine Chapel), and his emblematic lamb is here a full-grown ram returning John's embrace. The startling projection of the figure is made even more disturbing by the leer with which the boy involves us as voyeurs in complicity with his plausible but unorthodox indulgence.

Light is important there, but it is not clear that it is divine. It certainly is in *The Conversion of Saul*, and the idea of grace becomes more explicit in *The Martyrdom of St. Matthew* (Plate XIII). The initial impact here is made by the brutal and disturbingly sensual central figure of the murderer, displacing the elegant courtly figures to the left, and forming a solid triangle with the other two naked figures below. Matthew's hand is raised in futile resistance. But there, as with *Saul*, the picture reconstructs into another composition, as the raised hand meets the palm offered by the very different nakedness of the angel who twists so attractively over his cloud. The violent world still dominates, but by a play on structures, almost a visual pun, a hint of angelic grace descending is made explicit (as it is in the end of *Hamlet*).

Caravaggio's later works, painted in exile, include a number in prison settings, such as the tragically severe *Beheading of John the Baptist*. The most extraordinary is *The Seven Acts of Mercy* in Naples (Plate XIV). Identifying all the merciful works is difficult, but feeding the hungry is the most striking and bizarre image on the right, where the old man leans through the bars to suck the woman's breast. Into the prison from above sweep a group of angels escorting the Virgin Mary. They are emphatically within the same space, the divine is no longer remote from the human, and the whole complex composition finally contains both naturalistic and mythic dimensions in one.

I offer this selective account of the development from mannerism to Caravaggio in order to draw an analogy that begins with Shakespeare's earliest comedies, which are in several obvious respects mannerist. *Love's Labour's Lost* evolves through four acts its fantasy plot of courtiers and ladies playing elegant sexual games in brilliantly elegant language; but towards the end of the fifth act the messenger of death, Mercadé, destroys the jokes that have, in any case, become uncomfortably cruel, and reorientates the play to a level of perception that could hardly have been anticipated. It is a superb ending, but its achievement depends on a startling violation of expected symmetry. *The Two Gentlemen of Verona* is less elegant, but its ending[1] shifts through a whole series of surprises: an extraordinary band of outlaws, a preposterous reunion of friends at the expense of their girl-friends, and finally an even more preposterous *ménage à quatre* of friends and ladies together: 'One feast, one house, one mutual happiness'.[2] Which is highly improbable. Symmetry of a kind is achieved, but probability is flouted. There is, no doubt, a commentary on the natural, but neither play could conceivably be called naturalistic; nor are they seriously disturbing.

Troilus and Cressida, however, notoriously is, both in its effect of demolishing fantasy worlds in favour of an idea of reality which makes any concept of romance absurd, and in the insistence on a brutal sexuality which concludes with Pandarus bequeathing us his venereal diseases and so involving us in a complicity which articulates that disturbing leer on the face of John the Baptist. Technically, too, it is like Caravaggio in making its point by total reversal of traditional representation, in this case the heroic myth of the Trojan War.

All's Well That Ends Well is much closer to the romance world of *Two Gentlemen*, in plot at least, for in treatment it is vastly different. It is almost a fairy story, of the servant girl who magically cures the King and marries the Duke. Helena is a sort of Cinderella, but it is characteristic of the play that the social differences on which it depends are made minimal. Caste snobbery provokes Bertram to reject her, but she is herself a gentlewoman and only slightly beneath him. Similarly, the King is more competent administrator than elevated royalty: 'I fill a place, I know't.'[3] Reticence is characteristic of the play, both in its restrained language, the absence of imagery, and in the self-concealment of its characters. The plot proceeds by traps that successively expose the central figures, Helena, Parolles, Bertram. Its magical core, the curing of the King,[4] is made strangely ambiguous: it may be achieved by herbs which Helena has inherited from her doctor father, or by divine grace, or by pagan magic, or—as Lafew continually hints—by sexual arousal which cures the King of his fears of old age and impotence—a natural magic. All are suggested, none is decisively supported, and in the tone of the play the naturalistic

[1] Acts IV and V (Act V is very brief).
[2] V. iv. 174.
[3] I. ii. 69.
[4] II. i and iii.

explanation appears the most acceptable. In the final scene, Bertram's callow bluster is very sharply exposed in a way which makes his final recognition of Helena as his wife virtually unacceptable. Theoretically, she is restored to him with the magic of a resurrection, but the 'miracle' has no supernatural resonance. *All's Well* cultivates brilliantly a naturalism and a reticence that is very much of the same order as Caravaggio's Magdalene; and, as with Caravaggio, it seems to me that Shakespeare, having devised the linguistic and dramatic means to naturalize his myth, is left with a problem how, at the same time, to articulate it as myth.

That becomes more explicit in *Measure for Measure*, the play which most strongly suggests Caravaggio's later work. Justice and Mercy are announced as its themes; three of its five acts are set in prison; it has a demonstrative structure which could have resembled a morality play, but does not because of the strong individuality with which most of its characters are presented. It is not reticent, but works often by conflicting eloquences: Angelo's, Isabella's, the Duke's, and Claudio's; but they extend also to Lucio and the pimp Pompey, as well as to the drunken murderer Barnardine who confounds the naïvety of romance plotting by merely refusing to repent, or die.[1] The last third of the play is directed towards a romantic reconciliation alluding to New Testament ethics, but whether it arrives is still uncertain. The Duke pronounces universal matrimony, but the final grouping is strikingly ambiguous: Isabella has not responded to his proposal; Angelo has preferred death to marrying Mariana; and Lucio has described marrying a punk as 'pressing to death, / Whipping, and hanging'.[2] Barnardine has no mate, and seems no more reconciled to life than he was to death. It is a superb play, disturbing in its sexuality and in its sense of actuality; but it does also incorporate an idea of grace within the city setting, however uncertain its validity. It has much in common with Caravaggio's *Seven Acts of Mercy*.

With these plays, then, it seems to me that Shakespeare reaches a point directly analogous with Caravaggio's late work. Caravaggio died, and high baroque developed in ways which seem to me intelligible, though scarcely predictable. I have stressed that Rubens studied his work with enthusiasm; so did Bernini. They also studied Carracci, who was generally less startling. Two series of religious paintings seem to me particu-

[1] IV. iii. 52–62. [2] V. i. 520–1.

larly interesting. One is of *The Assumption of the Virgin*, where his several variations on human flight are strange. The other is of *The Pietà*; their chronological sequence is uncertain, but the one I find most interesting is again in the Doria-Pamphilj Gallery (Plate XV). The Virgin is highly formalized, presenting rather than mourning her son, and governing the painting with a statuesque calm at once suggesting Raphael; but she is in complete contrast to the dramatically dead body of Christ which seems almost to slide off her lap and out of the picture. It is as though Carracci has made a composite picture out of two contrasting genres. That is certainly what he did, though out of far more than two, in his exuberant pagan masterpiece, the Farnese ceiling, painted around 1600. The elaborate architecture is supported by Roman herms, and decorated with medallions, nude youths, putti, and many more; it is dominated by a central panel of *The Triumph of Bacchus*, and at each end are huge easel paintings of Polyphemus (Plate XVI). But this is not actually an easel painting at all, nor has it a frame: the entire ceiling is paint on a smooth barrel vault with curved ends, above the cornice there is no sculptural detail of any kind at all. It is, in other words, a fantastic exercise in illusion. Everything here is paint: the herms, the Michelangelo youths, the Raphael Galatea, the pissing putto, the medallion of Hero and Leander, are all on a single plane. But the camera does partly spoil it, because it makes the tricks too successful. They are amazing in fact, but can only be so if they are seen to be illusions, and the wit and delight of the work depends on that awareness.

To call Carracci's ceiling miraculous would be metaphoric; but I suggested that Caravaggio's use of optical illusion in *Saul* and *St. Matthew* was more than that: the hyperbole is the point of the picture. So it is with Bernini. The celebrated Cornaro Chapel in St. Maria della Vittoria (Plates XVII, XVIII) consists of the entire chapel, not simply of the central image of St. Teresa in ecstasy. A classical arch frames the complex, as in Domenichino's *St. Jerome*, but here a secondary illusion creates space in the sky beyond the ceiling. The two pictorial images are executed in radically different media—marble sculpture and painted stucco—so that they are at once totally distinct, and yet extensions of each other.

The resources of architectural perspective are deployed to make a chapel out of a shallow bay; sculpture makes the chapel like a theatre. The side boxes contain groups of Cornaro Cardinals supposed to be regarding the miracle, but actually some are in conversation, some in private thought, none is noticing the central group. It is a witty comment, focusing attention on the illusory nature of the stone vision. The cunning direction of natural light (from a concealed window above) on to the central group generates the illusion of divine light accessible only to imaginative perception. We have, as the Cardinals do not, a miraculous vision; but they are an essential part of the visible mechanics that produce the miracle. There is no ultimate deception: the work of art succeeds in creating miracle only if the technics of illusion are intelligible as well. Baroque is the imaginative art of a rationalist age; it must have owed much to Galileo's work on lenses, and contributed much to Newton's *Optics*.

The Cornaro Chapel depends, of course, on controlling the spectator's viewpoint. The church is so shaped that you are not aware of the chapel until you are right in front of it: the visual brilliance attracts you towards the central group until the altar rail prevents you going too far. From then on the extraordinary tactile quality of Bernini's marble takes over, setting up a tension between the desire to touch and the enforced distance. The counter-reformation ban on nakedness is strictly observed, but the sensuality is overwhelming. It is at first the angel, rather than Teresa, who has a physical body: like Caravaggio's angels, he is at once hermaphroditic and immensely sexual. The vision is literally a realization of St. Teresa's account in her *Life*; Bernini echoes the matter-of-factness of Teresa's prose in the witty detachedness of the Cardinals, and he combines the religious ecstasy with the sexual literalness to extraordinary effect. The angel's delighted and knowing look (a positive version of John the Baptist's complicit leer) directs attention to Teresa and finally on to her face. This is the most perfect representation I know in art of a woman in orgasm. It is also the climax of the Cornaro Chapel: between it and the ceiling above there is no literal death, the assumption into heaven is achieved as an expansion of the experience in that face, the human ecstasy is the miracle that becomes divine.

St. Teresa wrote of actual visionary experience which, as she insisted, was involuntary and not always welcome. In art, the representation is necessarily voluntary. I have described the Chapel in dramatic terms, probably too much so; but it is essentially dramatic, and more than that, it is theatrical. Baroque art is essentially theatrical, just as seventeenth-century theatre became increasingly visual; both tend towards synaesthesia, and the characteristic baroque invention was opera. The rationale of Bernini's art is provided by the *Spiritual Exercises* of St. Ignatius. His writing, even more than Teresa's, seems so bare, dry and practical that its sensational reception can be surprising. But sensational it literally is: the exercitant is directed to a systematic and intense application of his sensory imagination which demands both the contemplation of things as they actually are, and their translation through intensification of each sense in turn into their imaginative, and thus divine, equivalent, the amplification that proceeds from St. Teresa's vision to her translation into heaven. St. Teresa's visions were involuntary, and therefore a subject for art; St. Ignatius's exercises were voluntary and therefore suggested a method for art.

It is certain that Shakespeare, when he wrote *Macbeth*, was interested in the Jesuits, but I know of no evidence that he read St. Ignatius; yet an understanding of the significance of St. Ignatius in the transformation of western art seems to me illuminating about aspects of the play that I have found deeply puzzling. Lady Macbeth voluntarily invokes a contemplation of cruelty in her first scene: 'Come, you Spirits / That tend on mortal thoughts'.[1] The concentration on sensory imagination amplifies those spirits into 'murth'ring ministers', and finally into 'Come, thick Night' palled 'in the dunnest smoke of hell'. It is a deliberate, if inverted, spiritual exercise. The process is even more extraordinary in Macbeth's contemplation of his sin towards Duncan:

Besides, this Duncan
Hath borne his faculties so meek, hath been
So clear in his great office, that his virtues
Will plead like angels, trumpet-tongu'd, against
The deep damnation of his taking-off;
And Pity, like a naked new-born babe,
Striding the blast, or heaven's cherubin, hors'd
Upon the sightless couriers of the air . . .[2]

Macbeth's contemplation, unlike Lady Macbeth's, is involuntary; what I find strange is the rapid amplification from Duncan's abstract virtues, to angels, to naked new-born babe, and so finally to heaven's cherubin hors'd on the sightless couriers of the air. Professor Cleanth Brooks explained the

[1] I. v. 40–1. [2] I. vii. 16–23.

babe in terms of the numerous other babes in the play; that is true enough, but the strangeness here remains irreducible, because it is the process itself, of visionary amplification, which is important. Like Lady Macbeth, his concentration is primarily on sight, and as she ends with 'sightless substances', so his vision becomes finally sightless (beyond sight; either 'invisible', or 'blind'). But whereas she also invoked touch and smell, Macbeth's second sense is sound: Duncan's virtues 'plead' (the legal sense, or 'beg'), becoming like angels 'trumpet-tongu'd' and hence (by a play on the word) the 'blast' which the babe rides. It is an extraordinary process, and the process itself is of central significance. It echoes Lady Macbeth's speech, and thus partly relates to the peculiar closeness of their relationship. The play is at once peculiarly naturalistic, in its unique delineation of the intimacy of a marriage—their anticipation of each other's mind—and unique too in its demands on visual imagining. That is why it was a central text for two critical traditions so alien as Bradley's discussion of 'character' or the concentration on 'imagery' of the 1930s.

To mediate between those two, the play offers a study of illusion: 'nothing is, but what is not'.[1] The visions of those speeches (and others)[2] consist in words alone, literally visible to no one. Macbeth's dagger is seen only by him, and even he knows it is not there.[3] Banquo's ghost can be seen by the audience as well as by Macbeth, but not by anyone else on the stage: Lady Macbeth looks but on a stool.[4] The weird sisters, on the other hand, are vouched for by Banquo's less impressionable sight.[5] Most of these effects can be played in other ways, but that reduces the range of illusory forms which the play explores. It reaches a kind of climax in the apparitions of Act IV, after which, as Macbeth has it, 'no more sights'.[6] For the rest of the play illusion tricks are subjected to instant rational explanation, as with the moving of Birnam Wood, when vision is returned to the light of common day. The play is an extraordinary *tour de force* exploiting the maximum potential for illusion in an open-air theatre with limited mechanical resources, and no lighting tricks; two-thirds of it are to be imagined as taking place in darkness. This must be at least

[1] I. iii. 142.

[2] See, especially, III. ii. 46–53, when Macbeth comes closest to Lady Macbeth's words.

[3] II. i. 33–49.

[4] III. iv.

[5] I. iii.

[6] IV. i. 155.

Apotheosis of James I, Rubens, London, Whitehall Banqueting Suite

Coronation of the Virgin, Raphael, Rome, Pinacoteca

Communion of St. Jerome, Domenichino, Rome, Pinacoteca

PLATE VIII

Madonna del collo lungo, Parmigianino, Florence, Uffizi

Rest on the Flight into Egypt, Barocci, Rome, Pinacoteca

PLATE X

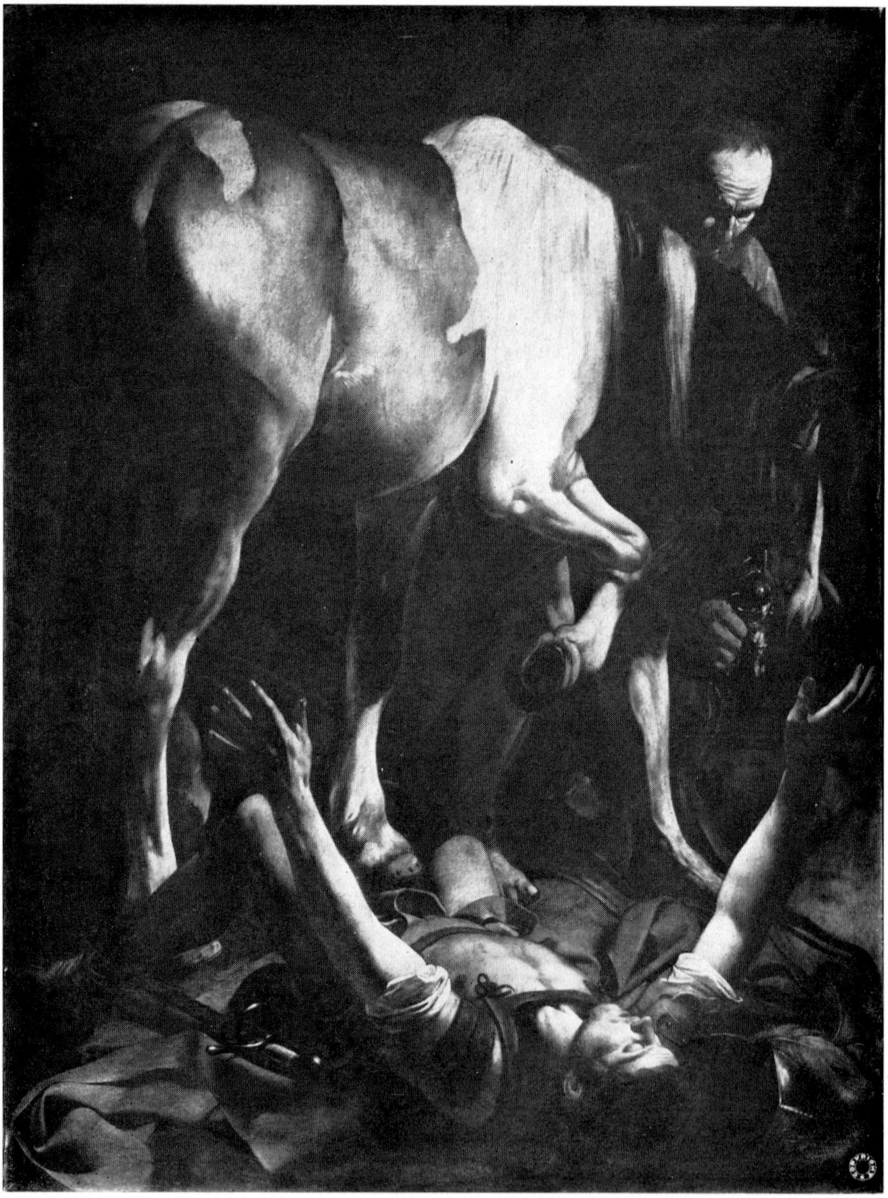

Conversion of Saul, Caravaggio, Rome, St. Maria del Popolo

St. Mary Magdalen, Caravaggio, Rome, Doria-Pamphilj

PLATE XII

St. John in the Wilderness, Caravaggio, Rome, Doria-Pamphilj

Martyrdome of St. Matthew, Caravaggio, Rome, S. Luigi dei Francesi

PLATE XIV

Seven Acts of Mercy, Caravaggio, Naples, Pio Monte della Misericordia

Pietà, Caracci, Rome, Doria-Pamphilj

Polyphemus hurling rocks, Caracci, Rome, Palazzo Farnese

St. Teresa in Ecstasy (Central Group), Bernini, Rome, Cornaro Chapel, St. Maria della Vittoria

PLATE XVIII

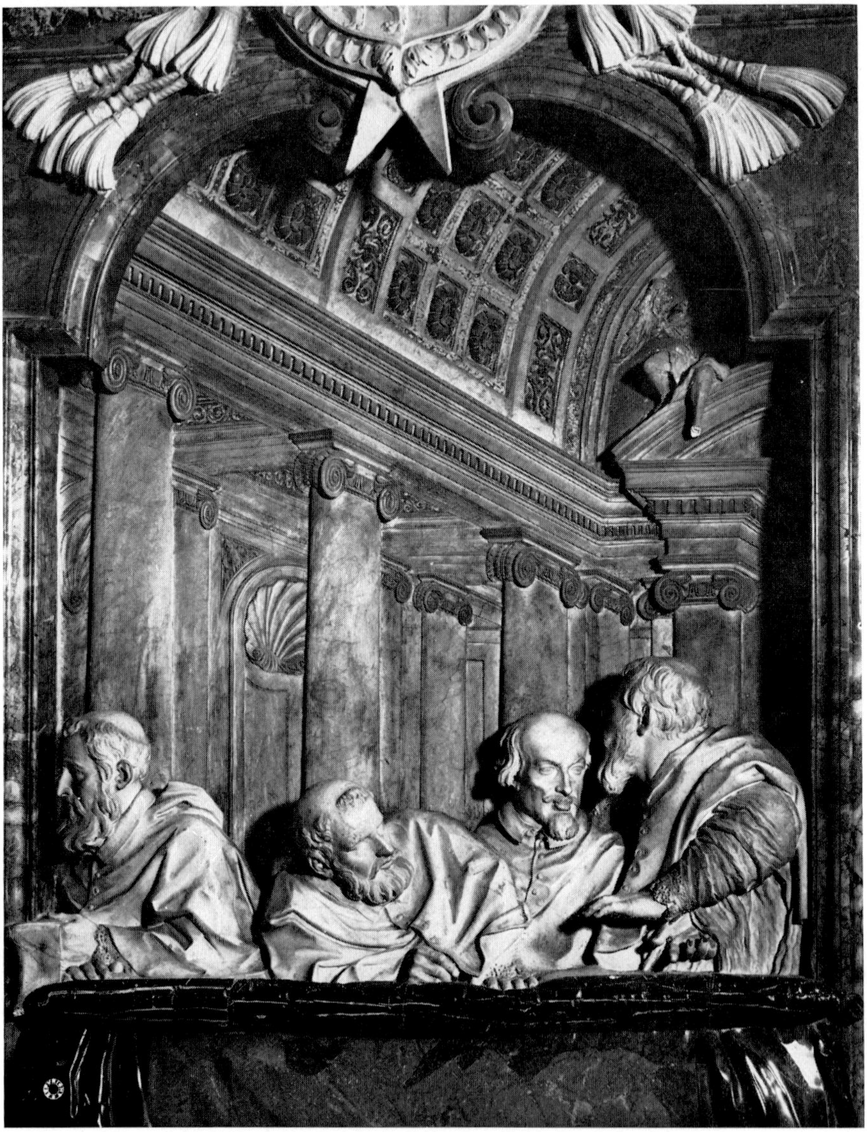

Cornaro Cardinals, Bernini, Rome, Cornaro Chapel

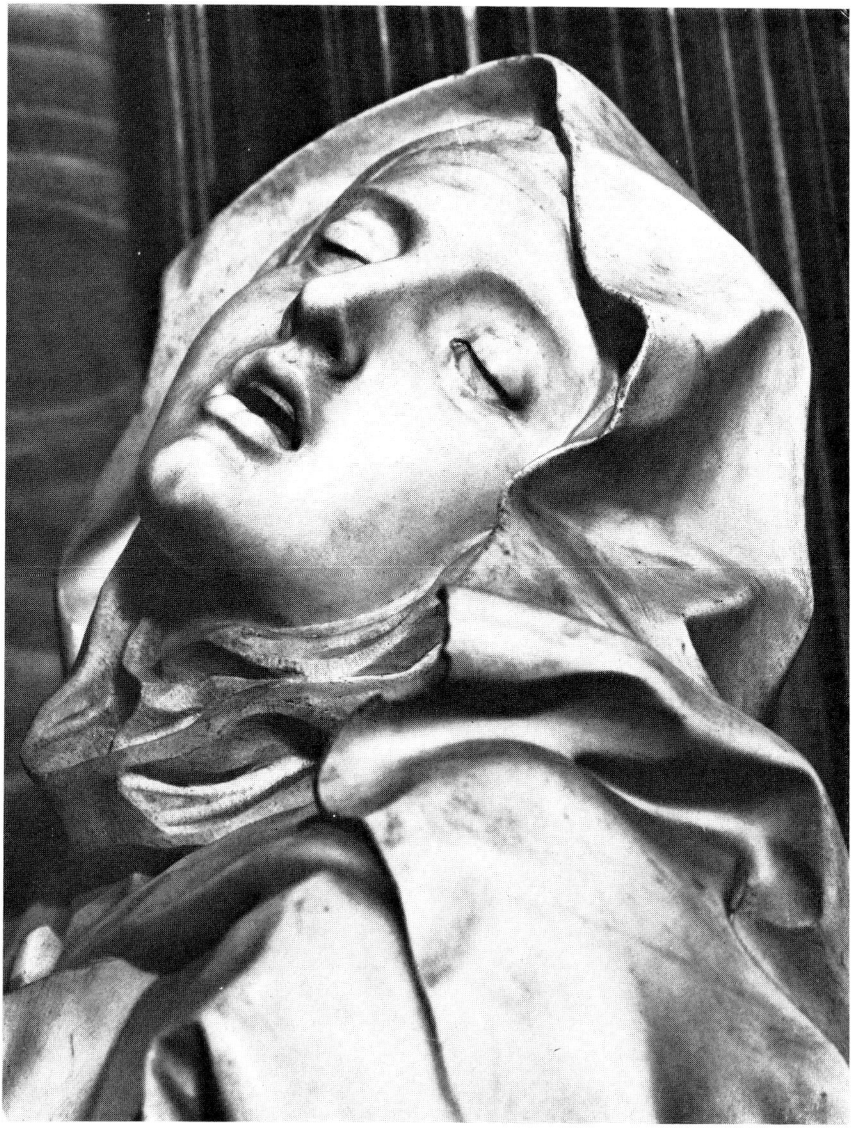

St. Teresa's face, Bernini, Rome, Cornaro Chapel

Marie de Medici's Arrival at Marseilles, Rubens, Paris, Louvre partly why it proves so awkward in the modern theatre where darkness is the natural state.

By being at once the most naturalistic and the most illusionistic of Shakespeare's plays to that time, *Macbeth* clearly solves in its own way the problem of relating naturalistic treatment to mythic structure which I suggested in Caravaggio as well as in *All's Well* and *Measure for Measure*. It leads towards a relationship which is apparently quite unlike theirs. Rubens's *Apotheosis of James I* (Plate V) makes its initial impact as fantastic. The painting, like the vault of the Cornaro Chapel, depends on an illusion that the ceiling has a hole in it through which the heavens above can be seen: James is being wafted up through the clouds by magnificently fleshly angels. But like Bernini, Rubens does not actually deceive: the idea of miracle is proposed by a use of perspective which is designed to be understood. And it needs to be, for such an event for James is indeed miraculous, and that is made clear in the superb portrait of the old man with red-rimmed and boozy eyes turned in intelligent apprehension at his levitation, and dismay at the unfamiliar touch of the opulent lady's arm. In the flamboyant mythologizing, the sense of actuality is also insistent; but it is not primary.

It seems that this was the first representation of the Christian apotheosis of a European King. Shakespeare did not go so far, but he did treat pagan apotheosis in *Antony and Cleopatra*, with a flamboyance close to Rubens. Enobarbus' celebrated 'The barge she sat in'[1] is almost literally illustrated by Rubens's painting of *Marie de Medici's arrival at Marseilles* (Plate XX), which also uses Roman models. The queen's solid features are as naturalistic as James I; the herm-like lady on the barge is as witty as Carracci, and Rubens stresses the dependence of the splendour, not only on the mermaids and tritons, but also on the agony of the galley-slaves. But splendour triumphs as, in the end, it does for Antony and Cleopatra. With them, as with James, the counter-image is very fully displayed, of the ageing drunken lecher and the skittish destructive whore; but they fulfil their mythological destinies superbly. The play, like Rubens's major canvases, has an extraordinary range of political and mythological development; but it centres, as do the paintings, on apotheosis, the translation of sensual glory into divinity.

With Rubens, mythology dominates; but it is meaningless without the insistence on actuality which he derived from Caravaggio, however much he seems to have reversed the

[1] II. ii. 191–218.

proportions. That is what I see in Shakespeare's last comedies: they appear fantastic after *Measure for Measure*, yet compared with the early plays their naturalism is striking. *Cymbeline* has, like *All's Well*, a story from Boccaccio; but where *All's Well* minimized the romance, *Cymbeline* maximizes it. In both *All's Well* and *Measure for Measure*, the wife tricks her way into her husband's bed, and he (who has never before slept with her) is unsuspecting. In *Cymbeline*, the question of sensual identity is astonishingly crossed with beheading (also in *Measure for Measure*) when Imogen mistakes the decapitated body of Cloten, dressed in her husband's clothes, for Posthumus.[1] She feels the limbs and faints, or falls asleep, on it. The possibilities for the grotesque, or offensive, or absurd are all obvious, and they are all developed, as in the Roman Captain's comment:

How? a page?
Or dead, or sleeping on him? But dead rather:
For nature doth abhor to make his bed
With the defunct, or sleep upon the dead.[2]

The event is fantastic, but the responses, like the people, are strikingly natural. The tricks of the celebrated last series of revelations are diverse, absurd, and splendid.[3] Professor Cyrus Hoy, a few years ago, identified the play's rich variety as mannerist.[4] I don't propose to quibble with terms, but would suggest that its marvellous interaction of apparently incompatible genres and its delight in theatrical illusions are far closer to Carracci's Farnese ceiling than to earlier models. Its surprises, however extraordinary, are very firmly organized into its classical five Acts, and so far from averting its natural symmetry in its surprises, as *Love's Labour's Lost* did, it wholeheartedly fulfils it, dream of Jupiter and all.

The Winter's Tale is less complicated, but scarcely less astonishing. Its mixture of genres is notorious, and brilliantly focused in the end of Act III when Antigonus's bleak acceptance of death is translated, not merely by a comic stage direction, but by the clown's amazingly funny description of the bear devouring him just off-stage:

> the men are not yet cold under water, nor the bear half dined on the gentleman: he's at it now.[5]

The direct manipulation of stage illusion there, from one genre to its opposite, is no less remarkable than the supreme demon-

[1] IV. ii. 295–332. [2] IV. ii. 355–8. [3] V. v.
[4] *Shakespeare Survey*, 26, 1973, 49–68. [5] III. iii. 104–5.

stration of illusion in the last Act. Hermione's statue coming to life works by being in actuality the opposite of what it seems: the actor must hold the pose until it can be held no longer, so that inevitable lapses are transformed into miracle:

> See, my lord,
> Would you not deem it breath'd?[1]

Everything Leontes says has one meaning as he understands it, another as we know it to be. The result is a concentration on the technique of illusion that makes the miracle more natural than impossible.

The technical assurance of these plays, almost effrontery as we are made so conscious of it, moves them rapidly towards Bernini. And it is notable how consciously the plays allude to visual arts. In *The Winter's Tale*, of course, there is the celebrated discussion of Giulio Romano which, however misinformed about Raphael's favourite assistant, displays a significant interest in illusionist art, as well as a contempt for mere deception:

> . . . who, had he himself eternity and could put breath into his work, would beguile Nature of her custom, so perfectly he is her ape.[2]

In *Cymbeline*, Iachimo turns from contemplating Imogen's naked beauty to note on his tablets the inventory of her bedroom's delightfully erotic decorations, which he reports to Posthumus:

> Chaste Dian, bathing: never saw I figures
> So likely to report themselves; the cutter
> Was as another Nature, dumb; outwent her,
> Motion and breath left out.[3]

The Tempest, like *Macbeth*, makes the forms of stage illusion its central motif. But where *Macbeth* is essentially written for a daylight theatre, *The Tempest* more strongly suggests the devices of Jones's court masques. It could use all the resources of the Blackfriars, whatever they actually were. It could use them, but rather astonishingly does not need them. The technical skill extends here to the extraordinary feat of writing a play about illusion as miracle which can function equally with or without elaborate resources; equally well, that is, at the Blackfriars or at the Globe. Hence the constant argument as to how it 'ought' to be performed. It arranges its illusions, also, in

[1] v. iii. 63–4. [2] v. ii. 96–9. [3] II. iv. 82–5.

a pattern like *Macbeth*'s: after a sensational opening, relatively simple tricks build up towards the full-scale masque of Juno and Ceres, and after that has been dismissed, the technics of magic are progressively abandoned. The last 'show', of Miranda and Ferdinand playing chess, is at once miraculous to the stage audience (who do not know they are alive) and entirely natural to us (who do); it requires no more machinery than the drawing back of a curtain. It therefore reverses the process of illusion and leads into Miranda's purely 'natural' revelation:

> O, wonder!
> How many goodly creatures are there here!
> How beauteous mankind is! O brave new world,
> That has such people in't!

and Prospero's inevitable rejoinder:

> 'Tis new to thee.[1]

Prospero does not merely drown his books, he finally steps outside his role altogether and speaks as actor to us as audience. The play is balanced very precariously between boredom and magical delight; and the understanding between nature and miracle is entirely in terms of the imaginative grasp of illusion. Its aesthetic structure has precisely the same foundation as Bernini's.

It is as easy to make patterns out of Shakespeare's plays as to shuffle a pack of cards; my hope is that two parallel patterns may be less arbitrary than one. The sequence of Shakespeare's comedies, from elegant fantasy in the early plays to aggressive naturalism in *Troilus*, *All's Well*, and *Measure for Measure*, and then into the flamboyance of the last comedies, may seem like two reversals of direction; but it has a sequential logic that is intelligible in terms of the evolution of Roman baroque from its origins in mannerism, through Caravaggio and Carracci, into Rubens and Bernini. I prefer this to the traditional explanation by conjectured biography and a fictitious 'tragic period', for there is a similar pattern in the tragedies from the mannered *Titus* and *Romeo*, through *Caesar*, *Hamlet*, and *Othello*, to *Lear*, *Macbeth*, and *Antony and Cleopatra*. The Shakespearian tradition has been too insular: his woodnotes were not peculiarly native, nor did he achieve a merely belated renaissance. He was in the mainstream of the radical change in European aesthetics of his day, and he ended (not surprisingly) in its vanguard.

[1] v. i. 181–4.

Pictures make some points more instantly than plays which take longer to see; and I am certain that the art I have shown offers more apt illustration of his work than the crude and often medieval woodcuts that have become standard in our textbooks and theatre programmes. The greatest drama in European history was not a cottage industry, it was one of the seminal points of the baroque aesthetic that dominated Europe for two hundred years.

Acknowledgements. I am indebted for permission to reproduce illustrations as follows: The Department of the Environment: Plate V; The Mansell Collection: Plates VI–XIX; La Réunion des musees nationaux, Paris: Plate XX.

ITALIAN LECTURE

LORENZO DE' MEDICI: THE FORMATION OF HIS STATECRAFT

By NICOLAI RUBINSTEIN

Fellow of the Academy

Read 12 May 1977

WHEN I was asked to choose the topic of this lecture, I was hoping that my lecture would coincide with the publication of the first three volumes of the edition of Lorenzo's letters. I make use in it of some of the letters and the commentary included in these volumes, which cover, roughly, the first ten years of Lorenzo's ascendancy in Florence. This has obviously much facilitated my task, but new evidence, of which there is a great deal, also poses a fresh challenge; and I must admit that Lorenzo's opening words in his *Comento* strike a chord: 'Assai sono stato dubbioso e sospeso se dovevo fare la presente interpretazione'—'I have been in great doubt whether I should undertake the present interpretation.'

Lorenzo's father, Piero di Cosimo de' Medici, died on 2 December 1469, a month before Lorenzo's twenty-first birthday. On the following day, a delegation from a large meeting of leading citizens, which had decided to preserve Lorenzo and his brother Giuliano in 'reputazione e grandezza', 'in prestige and greatness', came to the Medici palace and asked Lorenzo to assume the authority his father and grandfather had exercised in Florence.[1] The vagueness of these terms reflects the indeterminate nature of the Medici regime. Since the days of Cosimo, the political power of the Medici had been exercised, within the framework of the republican constitution, by a variety of controls, primarily of the elections to the Signoria and other high magistracies; and their ascendancy depended

[The following abbreviations will be used: ASF = Florence, Archivio di Stato; ASM, SPE = Milan, Archivio di Stato, Archivio Sforzesco, Potenze Estere; MAP = Florence, Archivio di Stato, Archivio Mediceo avanti il Principato; *Lettere* = Lorenzo de' Medici, *Lettere*, vols. i and ii, ed. R. Fubini (Florence, 1977), vol. iii, ed. N. Rubinstein (Florence, 1977).]

[1] See N. Rubinstein, *The Government of Florence under the Medici, 1434 to 1494* (Oxford, 1968), pp. 174–5.

upon the support of a substantial section of the patriciate. Like the regime itself, succession to its leadership was therefore a matter of political, not of constitutional, arrangement; and like the survival of the regime, it depended on the loyal collaboration of its supporters. The improvised and unofficial character of the meeting of 2 December, which decided the succession of Lorenzo, was entirely in keeping with a situation in which his succession was clearly not felt to be a foregone conclusion. Conditions differed, in fact, from those after the death of Cosimo five years earlier. In 1466 the Medici regime had been seriously threatened by citizens who had hitherto backed it; its electoral controls had been temporarily abolished and statutory elections by lot of the Signoria restored; Piero's death could be the signal for another republican attempt to curb, or even destroy, Medici power. While the apparent unanimity of the decision, to preserve Lorenzo's and Giuliano's 'grandezza', shows their father's success in consolidating and unifying the Medici regime, during the last three years of his life, the question remained of what meaning was to be attached to that 'grandezza'; more precisely, what role the elder of the two sons of Piero was to play within the regime.

The answer depended, above all, on the willingness of Piero's principal supporters to accept the authority of Lorenzo on the same terms as they had accepted that of his father. A Medici could not take their collaboration for granted in the same way as could an Italian prince that of his counsellors, and differences in age and experience could count for a great deal: at the time of Piero's death, his most influential follower, Tommaso Soderini, was 66, while Lorenzo was only twenty. Lorenzo's youth was, moreover, liable to sharpen rivalries within the Medici regime. In fifteenth-century Florence such rivalries were liable to be compounded by conflicting loyalties to foreign states. At the end of 1469, the Duke of Milan and the King of Naples were pursuing different policies in the war Pope Paul II was waging against Roberto Malatesta of Rimini, and both were trying to win over Florence to their side by enlisting the support of leading citizens.[1] Unlike the King of Naples, Galeazzo Maria Sforza was also trying to strengthen Lorenzo's position in Florence.

After the death of Filippo Maria Visconti in 1447, Cosimo de' Medici had persuaded the Florentine government to back

[1] G. Soranzo, 'Lorenzo il Magnifico alla morte del padre e il suo primo balzo verso la Signoria', *Archivio Storico Italiano*, cxi (1953), pp. 50–1.

Francesco Sforza in his bid for the duchy of Milan, and had himself provided the financial means which enabled Francesco to achieve success. Ever since, friendship with the Sforza had been a cornerstone of the foreign policy of the Medici. It had also provided them with an invaluable external insurance of their ascendancy, and indeed security, at home. When Piero had been threatened by his opponents in 1466, Galeazzo Maria Sforza had sent troops to the Florentine frontier; four days after Piero's death, he writes to the Florentine Signoria recommending to them 'Lorenzo and Giuliano . . . whom, owing to the love we have always nourished for that house, we hold . . . dear as if they were our own sons'. And he adds that although he was confident that they would not be required, he had ordered his troops in the territories of Bologna and Parma to obey, if necessary, the orders of the Signoria: 'and we are ready, in such a case, to come in person with the rest of our troops'.[1] But if the close relationship between the Medici and the Sforza benefited the Medici, it was also useful to the Sforza, and not only for reasons of foreign policy. The Sforza court relied heavily on the Milan branch of the Medici Bank; as Raymond de Roover has shown, between 1460 to 1467, the debt of the Sforza to the bank had increased from about 53,000 to no less than 179,000 ducats.[2] Both for political and financial reasons, it was in the interest of Galeazzo Maria Sforza to secure Lorenzo's position in Florence; for political reasons, it was also in his interest to strengthen it. To an autocratic ruler, such as the Duke of Milan, and to his ambassadors, the slowness and complexity of decision-making in a state whose government and administration were still basically republican could be a source of irritation and frustration: it could also affect the reliability of Florence as an ally. Just as the elder statesmen of the Medici regime, whose role had been decisive in securing Lorenzo's succession, could hope to profit from it, so the Duke of Milan might hope to find the inexperienced youth more amenable to his influence and persuasion. What was at stake at the end of 1469 was not only Lorenzo's freedom of action, but also the manner in which the ascendancy of the Medici, which had been gradually and painstakingly established over more than three decades, was to be upheld after his father's death.

[1] R. Magnani, *Relazioni private fra la Corte Sforzesca di Milano e Casa Medici, 1450–1500* (Milan, 1910), doc. 61, pp. xxxviii–xxxix.

[2] *The Rise and Decline of the Medici Bank* (Cambridge, Mass., 1963), pp. 272–3.

Lorenzo was singularly unprepared for the tasks which awaited him. One of the foundations of Medici ascendancy had been, and still remained, the wealth of Giovanni di Bicci's branch of the family; it had helped Cosimo to build up the complex network of personal relationships and loyalties which provided the basis for his rise to power. Lorenzo had received a careful humanist education, but no business training; he also had, in 1469, little practical experience of politics. In 1466 he had been a member of the *Balìa* as a substitute for his father,[1] and Piero had sent him abroad on a few occasions; but his journeys had only incidentally assumed some modest political significance. In 1465 he went to Milan to represent Piero at the ceremony for the marriage between Alfonso of Calabria, the heir to the Neapolitan throne, and Francesco Sforza's daughter Ippolita Maria. In the following year he went to Rome and Naples; in the summer of 1469 he went again to Milan, to act, on Piero's behalf, as godfather at the baptism of Galeazzo Maria Sforza's son. The main purpose of these visits appears to have been to introduce Lorenzo into Italian court society; but Piero may have also wished in this way to acquaint his eldest son, gently, with the organization of the Medici Bank; when Lorenzo went to Rome, in 1466, he was meant to get information about the state of its Roman branch from his uncle Giovanni Tornabuoni, and to agree in Piero's name to a new alum contract.[2] But Piero seems to have been distinctly reluctant to entrust Lorenzo with diplomatic business. When he sent him to Milan for the baptism of Gian Galeazzo Sforza, he explicitly forbade him to get involved in any other matters, 'in cosa alcuna', as he was not going as an ambassador: 'I don't think it is proper', he adds, in his letter to Lucrezia on the eve of their son's departure, 'that the ducklings should teach old ducks to swim'.[3] And when, during the same journey,

[1] In December 1466 the *Balìa* admitted him in the same capacity to the Council of One Hundred, 'non obstante minori etate'. See Rubinstein, *The Government*, p. 221. On Lorenzo's education, see A. Rochon, *La Jeunesse de Laurent de Médicis (1449–1478)* (Paris, 1963), pp. 31–46.

[2] See his letter to Lorenzo of 15 March 1466, in A. Fabroni, *Laurentii Medicis Magnifici vita* (Pisa, 1784), vol. ii, p. 49.

[3] Piero de' Medici to Lucrezia Tornabuoni in Florence, Careggi, 13 July 1469 (ASF, MAP, I, 267): 'Tu sai che malvolentieri decti licentia a Lorenzo, per molti rispecti . . . et pertanto da' modo allo spaccio, et dì a Lorenzo che non esca dello ordine in cosa alcuna, et non faccia tante melarancie, non essendo imbasciadore, ch'io non determino ch'e paperi menino a bere l'oche . . .'

Lorenzo could not help getting involved in a matter concerning the war between Paul II and Roberto Malatesta of Rimini, he humbly apologized to his father: he would not have written to him about it had not the Duke expressly ordered him to do so; but he would keep his letter short, since the resident Florentine ambassador was writing to Piero at length.[1] Lorenzo's letter is dated 29 July 1469, four months before he was asked to succeed his father as head of the Medici regime.

It is not surprising that Lorenzo should write, three years later, in his family memoirs, that he had accepted this invitation reluctantly, 'as it was contrary to my age, and on account of the great responsibility and peril it involved'. He did so, he says, 'per conservazione degli amici', 'for the safety of our supporters', and of our properties: 'perché a Firenze si può mal viver ricco senza lo stato', 'because the rich live badly in Florence outside the political establishment'.[2] (No such hesitations were, incidentally, reported by the foreign ambassadors; and whatever went through Lorenzo's mind during those hours, he appears to have been remarkably in control of himself; so that the Milanese resident could write, hopefully, 'he behaves like an old man'.)[3] Lorenzo's justification of his acceptance is somewhat disingenuous: for the eldest son of Piero de' Medici it was not just a matter of participating in the ruling regime, as it was, for instance, for his sister's father-in-law, Giovanni Rucellai, who writes a year later that he 'had not been accepted by, but suspect to, the regime for twenty-seven years'.[4] What the leading citizens asked Lorenzo to accept was, in his own words, 'la cura della città e dello stato', 'the care of the regime and of the city'. The formulation, certainly not incidental, enshrines the two major aspects of Medici ascendancy.

For 'città' and 'stato' were by no means synonymous; and 'stato' should not be translated by 'state'. It signifies, in this context, as it normally does in the political vocabulary of fifteenth-century Florence, the dominant political regime—in other words, the power structure which, at a given time, formed the foundation of its government. 'Città' and 'stato'

[1] *Lettere*, vol. i, 21, pp. 45–6: 'perché io so m. Luigi ve ne scrive lungamente, non dirò altro, refferendomi a lui. Non harei anche fatto questo, se non per comandamento del Signore . . .'

[2] Fabroni, *Laurentii Medicis vita*, vol. ii, p. 42.

[3] Sacramoro da Rimini to Galeazzo Maria Sforza, Florence, 2 December 1469 (ASM, SPE, Firenze, 277): 'se deporta da vecchio'.

[4] A. Perosa (ed.), *Giovanni Rucellai ed il suo Zibaldone*, vol. i (London, 1960), p. 122: 'sono stato non accetto ma sospetto allo stato anni 27'.

are seen as distinct, yet closely allied: as the Florentine chancellor, Bartolomeo Scala, put it during Lorenzo's peace negotiations in Naples in 1480: 'la città che [è] congiunta collo stato', 'the city and the regime which are joined to one another'.[1] During the war of the Pazzi Conspiracy, Lorenzo once observed: 'la libertà nostra [ne va] con lo stato', 'our liberty goes together with the regime'.[2] The term I have chosen for the title of this lecture, Lorenzo's 'statecraft', is a literal translation of Machiavelli's 'arte dello stato'. The *Shorter Oxford English Dictionary* defines statecraft as 'the art of conducting state affairs', but this definition does not quite render the complex meaning of 'stato' in fifteenth-century Florence. The task which Lorenzo faced in December 1469 was to take charge of the Medici regime, and at the same time to conduct the foreign policy of the republic. In both respects, his actions were subject to considerable restraints. After initial setbacks, he succeeded in consolidating the regime, and his position in it, during the second year of his ascendancy, more precisely between January and July 1471. As far as his domestic policy was concerned, this concludes the first period in the formation of his statecraft. The development of his statesmanship in the conduct of foreign affairs was a lengthier and more gradual process, and there is much to be said for considering its formative period not to be completed until the end of the war of the Pazzi Conspiracy, in March 1480.

Lorenzo proposes 'to follow the methods of his grandfather', writes the Milanese ambassador at the time of Lorenzo's first attempt at internal reform in July 1470, 'which was to do such things as much as possible by constitutional methods', 'di far tal cose cum più civilità si potesse'.[3] These words reflect the constraints under which Lorenzo had to operate if he wanted to preserve the edifice of Medici supremacy, as erected by Cosimo. The cornerstone of that edifice was the office of the *Accoppiatori*, who were in charge of electing the two-monthly Signoria: as the Milanese ambassador put it, on it depended

[1] Bartolomeo Scala to Lorenzo in Naples, 5 January 1480 (ASF, MAP, XXXIV, 412): '. . . a voi et allo stato che è congiunto con voi, et alla città che [è] congiunta collo stato, habbi a venire la sua sicurtà'; cf. Rubinstein, 'Notes on the word *stato* in Florence before Machiavelli', in *Florilegium Historiale. Essays presented to Wallace K. Ferguson*, ed. J. G. Rowe and W. H. Stockdale (Toronto, 1971), pp. 313–26 (319).

[2] Lorenzo to Girolamo Morelli, 24 September 1478, *Lettere*, vol. iii, 332, p. 223.

[3] Quoted in Rubinstein, *The Government*, p. 178, n. 5 (3 July).

Lorenzo's power.[1] At the time of his succession, the *Accoppiatori* were elected annually by the Council of One Hundred; but although that council had been created under Cosimo to serve as a reliable instrument of the regime, its decisions did not always come up to expectation; its members were quite capable of voting against proposals that originated with the head of the regime, and of not toeing the line in the election to offices. The Council of One Hundred, writes the Milanese ambassador in the same letter of 31 July 1470, are in the process of electing the new *Accoppiatori*, and some of its members are known to want to appoint 'men who are not Lorenzo's', 'homini che non fossero de Lorenzo'; but he hopes that they will not succeed: 'one will see to it that those who are elected are Lorenzo's men'. This outcome was clearly not a foregone conclusion; to make it so, was the purpose of Lorenzo's first attempt at constitutional reform. Although this attempt failed, as a result of the opposition of the Council of One Hundred, it is of considerable interest to us, since it shows Lorenzo's earliest reaction, after his succession, to a major problem of Medici rule. According to his design, the *Accoppiatori* were to be chosen from among the 40-odd citizens who had served in this capacity from October 1434 onwards, or at least from among their families. This group would thus have included some of the prominent Medicean families of the time of Cosimo, such as the Guicciardini and Martelli, the Pitti and Ridolfi, as well as elder statesmen such as Tommaso Soderini; in the words of the Milanese ambassador, it would have consisted of 'tutti quisti cavalleri principali', of 'all the leading citizens'; and it was not surprising that Lorenzo's scheme was welcomed by them. Had it been successful, it would have both strengthened the oligarchical strand in Medici government, and provided Lorenzo with a permanent élite group.[2] His proposal pointed to the past as well as to the future. During the years before 1434, preceding the establishment of Medici ascendancy, about sixty-five citizens had formed the core, the inner circle, of the oligarchical regime;[3] in 1480, the Council of Seventy became, for all practical purposes, a permanent senate with life membership. Only a few months after his succession, Lorenzo thus felt the need to

[1] Sacramoro to Galeazzo Maria Sforza, Florence, 31 July, ASM, SPE, Firenze, 279; see Rubinstein, *The Government*, p. 178.

[2] See ibid., pp. 177–9.

[3] See Dale Kent, 'The Florentine *reggimento* in the fifteenth century', *Renaissance Quarterly*, xxviii (1975), pp. 604–10.

establish, at the top of the regime, a group of men on whom he could rely to secure the vital controls of election to the Signoria. His design reflects a hierarchical concept of the structure of the Medici regime, which is neatly spelled out, two years later, by Benedetto Dei in his account of contemporary Florentine society.[1] According to Dei, the innermost circle of the regime was divided into three sections: the top section consisted of twelve citizens, 'principali dello stato', headed by Lorenzo and Tommaso Soderini; below them was a group of eleven citizens, and at the bottom, a 'rearguard' of twenty: in all, the 'uomini del governo' amounted to forty-three citizens.

It was a measure of the limitations of Lorenzo's influence at the beginning of his ascendancy that neither this proposal, nor the alternative one of recruiting the *Accoppiatori* exclusively from those citizens who had previously held that office, was accepted; in the end, in January 1471, the council of One Hundred could be persuaded, though only just, to pass a law by which, during the next five years, the *Accoppiatori* were to be virtually appointed, annually, by their predecessors.[2] The next reform, of July that year, shows that Lorenzo had not given up the substance of his original design. The reform was carried out by one of those short-term commissions with extraordinary powers, *Balìe*, which the Medici and their followers had used from time to time to obtain legislation that the statutory councils could not be expected to pass; the main difficulty consisted in getting these councils to establish such *Balìe*; the alternative of summoning a popular assembly, a *Parlamento*, for this purpose, was too extreme and risky, too contrary to the orderly process of government, to be chosen except on rare occasions. That Lorenzo succeeded in obtaining from the councils the creation of such a *Balìa*—the first for five years—was a remarkable feat and showed consummate timing (he had been advised as early as the summer of 1470 to try this method). The *Balìa* of July 1471 consisted of a first group of forty citizens, who were elected by the Signoria and the *Accoppiatori* and in their turn elected the remaining 200 members of the commission. In order to enhance the reliability of the Council of One Hundred, whose legislative powers were substantially increased, these forty were to remain in office after the *Balìa* had been disbanded as permanent members of that council while the rest of its personnel changed twice a

[1] *Cronaca*, ASF, Manoscritti, 119, fol. 35v.

[2] For this and the following, see Rubinstein, *The Government*, pp. 180–5.

year. Lorenzo had clearly not given up his original design to insert a small élite group of leading citizens as a permanent fixture into the machinery of government. His domestic policy was beginning to show that combination of consistency of design with flexibility of execution which was to mark it in the coming years.

The *Balìa* of July 1471 was also a personal triumph over his rivals and opponents in Florence, and thus reflects the definitive assertion of his authority within the regime, as well as its unification. 'While before, other citizens were honoured and flattered just like him', writes the Milanese ambassador on 5 July, 'now everyone goes to him to recommend himself for election' to the *Balìa*.[1] Rivalries among leading citizens of the regime, and between such citizens and Lorenzo, had overshadowed Lorenzo's political apprenticeship, and had been sharpened by conflicting loyalties to foreign powers. Tommaso Soderini stands out, during this period, both as Lorenzo's principal rival and as the leading figure of the pro-Neapolitan faction in Florence. 'Messer Tommaso seems to believe', writes the Milanese ambassador in November 1470, 'that everyone ought to submit to him, so that he can become great and head' of the regime, 'et cum questo farsi grande e capo': he accordingly wants to diminish Lorenzo's status, 'in order to manage him the way he wants'; in short, he wants to be 'el timone vero de questa barcha', 'the real rudder of this ship'.[2] Two months later, Soderini promised the ambassador, in great secrecy, that he would henceforth back Lorenzo.[3] It was significant of the change in the political climate of Florence after the *Balìa* of July 1471 that in the following month Tommaso Soderini himself should have been sent to Milan, to inform the Duke of the 'consolidation and strengthening of our regime'.[4]

Galeazzo Maria Sforza had previously advised Lorenzo

[1] Sacramoro to Galeazzo Maria Sforza, Florence, 5 July 1471 (ASM, SPE, Firenze, 282): 'hora zaschuno concorre ad ello a recomandarsi per essere de li ellecti'.

[2] Sacramoro to Galeazzo Maria Sforza, Florence, 19 November 1470, quoted in *Lettere*, vol. i, 65, n. 1, p. 209.

[3] Sacramoro to Galeazzo Maria Sforza, 9 January 1471 (ASM, SPE, Firenze, 281): 'io prometto al ducha de Milano . . . che tucto quel ch'esso [i.e. Lorenzo] me accennerà essere el suo bisogno et la voglia de quel Illustrissimo Signore, el consiliarò et favorirò'.

[4] *Lettere*, vol. 1, 90, n. intr., p. 320: 'stabilimento et corroboramento dello stato nostro'.

to achieve this result through a *Balìa*, that is by adopting the kind of measure Lorenzo did in the end adopt in July 1471; Lorenzo could now see, writes his ambassador in that month, 'how good the advice of Your Excellency has been'.[1] The Duke had also sent Tommaso Soderini a gift of 500 ducats to reward him for his change of attitude towards Lorenzo.[2] I have pointed to the advantages the strengthening of Medici power offered to the Duke of Milan. His relations with Lorenzo show his preference for dealing, secretly, with him and, possibly, a small number of his friends, rather than publicly with the Florentine government: this was in keeping with the personal style of diplomacy to which an autocratic Italian ruler was used. Thus, during particularly secret negotiations with the French King, Galeazzo Maria declared that he would confide everything to Lorenzo; matters of lesser importance could be discussed with his principal followers; all that was left to official contacts with the Signoria were 'ordinary and general matters', 'cose vulgare et generale', 'which were anyway public knowledge'.[3] Lorenzo did his best to conform: 'I shall follow the advice of Your Magnificence', he writes to the Sforza ambassador in Florence during the difficult negotiations in 1471 concerning the renewal of the Italian league, 'in keeping everything secret there, for these are matters in which consultation can be of little help', and he expresses the hope that the Florentine ambassador in Milan was writing about the matter 'in private rather than in public; in this way it will be easy to keep it secret'.[4] But there were limits to such secrecy: Florence was not Milan. 'Your Lordship wishes these matters to be very secret', writes Lorenzo, jointly with Tommaso Soderini and Luigi Guicciardini, to the Duke in March 1470, 'but this is difficult to achieve, in view of our methods of government', 'atteso il modo de' governi nostri'.[5] However great Lorenzo's authority in Florence, his diplomacy, like his domestic policy, was subject to manifold restraints, due to the continued functioning of republican

[1] Sacramoro to Galeazzo Maria Sforza, Florence, 5 July 1471 (loc. cit.): 'Possi mo Lorenzo accorgere quanto è stato bono el consiglio de Vostra Excellentia'. Cfr. Soranzo, 'Lorenzo il Magnifico . . .', p. 73.

[2] See *Lettere*, vol. i, 65, n. 1, cit., and Soranzo, 'Lorenzo il Magnifico . . .', p. 71.

[3] Galeazzo Maria Sforza to Filippo Sacramoro, 16 March 1476, quoted in *Lettere*, vol. ii, 219, n. intr., p. 170.

[4] Lorenzo to Sacramoro da Rimini, Bolsena, 28 September 1471, *Lettere*, vol. i, 94, pp. 336–7.

[5] *Lettere*, vol. i, 38, p. 106 (12 March 1470).

institutions. These restraints were, if anything, greater in the field of foreign, than in that of domestic, policy. It must have been difficult for an Italian despot such as the Duke of Milan fully to appreciate this. In monarchical states such as Milan and Ferrara and, for that matter, Naples the ruler alone possessed the ultimate authority to negotiate, conclude treaties, declare war; ambassadors had powers delegated by him alone, as had secret councils, whose function it was to advise the prince and which could take decisions only if authorized to do so by him.[1] In Florence, diplomatic affairs were the competence of the Signoria, which changed every two months, or, in time of war, of the *Dieci di Balìa*, elected for six months at a time. A measure of continuity was provided by advisory committees (*Pratiche*) of the Signoria, in which leading citizens could express their views, and whose advice, though not binding, carried a great deal of weight. But treaties had to be ratified by the councils; and while in a despotic state such as Milan or Ferrara taxes were imposed or regulated by the prince, in Florence it was the councils which had to vote the money that was required to fulfil treaty obligations or to hire troops. As we shall see, this system was modified, to the advantage of Lorenzo, in 1480; at the time of his succession, Florentine foreign policy, like that of Venice, was still essentially based on collective decision-making. Historians of the Medici, following Guicciardini who, writing about sixteen years after Lorenzo's death, telescoped things in retrospect,[2] tend to identify the foreign policy of Florence with that of Lorenzo, but in so doing they oversimplify one of the most intriguing aspects of his ascendancy. What was his role in the making, and in the execution, of decisions, and hence the extent to which he was able, and willing, to take over the conduct of foreign affairs from the official organs of government?

At the time of Piero's death, Florence was in the midst of intense diplomatic activity. Negotiations for the renewal of the Triple Alliance between Florence, Milan, and Naples had been going on for some months; they were meeting with

[1] See *Storia di Milano*, vol. vii (Milan, Fondazione Treccani, 1956), pp. 521–4; F. Valenti, 'I consigli di governo presso gli Estensi dalle origini alla devoluzione di Ferrara', in *Studi in onore di R. Filangieri* (Naples, 1959), vol. ii, pp. 19–33.

[2] F. Guicciardini, *Storie fiorentine*, ed. R. Palmarocchi (Bari, 1931), pp. 72: one of the benefits Florence owed Lorenzo was to have become 'quasi una bilancia di tutta Italia'.

difficulties, largely owing to conflicting policies pursued by the Duke of Milan and the King of Naples in the war between the Pope and Roberto Malatesta of Rimini.[1] After the defeat of the papal army in August 1469 the allies were trying to induce Paul II to conclude peace, but Galeazzo Maria Sforza, apprehensive of a French intervention in his duchy, proved more accommodating than Ferrante of Naples. To settle these differences, a meeting between representatives of the members of the Triple Alliance was arranged to take place in Florence in December; before the ambassadors arrived, Piero had died; and, as a result, it was the young and inexperienced Lorenzo who took his place in the committee of five which was appointed by the Signoria to represent the government of Florence. The meetings, which lasted until March, did not settle the differences between the allies; but they did provide Lorenzo with his apprenticeship in diplomacy. They also provided him with invaluable experience of the way in which in Florence diplomacy could become entangled with domestic politics: the committee of five included partisans of the King of Naples as well as of the Duke of Milan, Tommaso Soderini as well as Lorenzo. Lorenzo, while supporting the Sforza, saw the role of Florence as one of mediation; and Florence badly needed peace and the renewal of the League. These matters, he writes in January 1470 to the Florentine ambassador in Rome, 'seem to me to be among the most troublesome and difficult the city has ever had to face'; but, he adds, this is 'perhaps because, as I have never had to deal with such matters, they are new and therefore more daunting to me';[2] nevertheless, 'as far as I can judge, there is no other way, for our salvation lies entirely in the cohesion and unity of the League'.[3] And when the Triple Alliance was finally renewed, in July 1470, he was jubilant: 'at this moment,' he writes to the Florentine ambassador at the Sforza court, 'we have received letters from Naples . . . They inform us that our league has been renewed, which pleases everyone greatly . . . As to my own personal interests ('spetialità'), I consider it the best news I have ever received.'[4] Later in the same year, during the tortuous negotiations for the renewal of the wider

[1] See Soranzo, 'Lorenzo il Magnifico . . .', pp. 50–9; G. Nebbia, 'La Lega italica . . .', *Archivio Storico Lombardo*, N.S., iv (1939), pp. 125–7.

[2] Lorenzo to Otto Niccolini, 27 January 1470 (*Lettere*, vol. i, 33, p. 88): 'non havendo io mai praticato simili cose, come cose nuove mi dànno magiore admiratione'.

[3] Ibid.

[4] Lorenzo to Angelo della Stufa, 12 July 1470, *Lettere*, vol. i, 58, pp. 172.

Italian League of 1454, Florence appeared once more in the role of mediator between Milan and Naples, and could even be described as 'examen della bilancia', 'the tongue of the balance'.[1] If, after his death, Lorenzo could be praised as the architect of Italian balance of power politics, he owed this to no small extent to his experience of Florentine diplomacy during the formative period of his statecraft.

One of the major problems of that period had been the interaction of domestic and foreign policies; and it was this interaction which was at the root of the gravest crisis his statecraft had to face, the Pazzi conspiracy. On 26 April 1478 Lorenzo and his brother Giuliano were attacked in the Florentine cathedral during High Mass; Giuliano was assassinated, but Lorenzo escaped. The assassination had been planned and organized by the Pope's nephew, Girolamo Riario, and members of the Pazzi family; the Archbishop of Pisa, Francesco Salviati, had participated in the conspiracy. Before he was summarily executed, Francesco Salviati confessed that it had been planned by Francesco Pazzi as long as three years earlier: relations between Lorenzo and the Pazzi had in fact become increasingly strained after 1473.[2] The origins and motives of the conspiracy were complex, and this is not the place to discuss them in detail.[3] I should, however, like to make two points. The events which led to the conspiracy show once more the interaction of Lorenzo's diplomacy and his private interests, his 'spetialità'; they also show how difficult it is to distinguish, in every single case, between his personal diplomacy and that of the republic. Pope Sixtus IV held Lorenzo personally responsible for the unsuccessful attempt by Florence to purchase the Romagna town of Imola from the Duke of Milan in 1473; but Florence had previously exercised a sort of protectorate over this strategically important place beyond her northern frontiers, and it was only natural that she should use the opportunity of its cession to the Duke of Milan by its lord, Taddeo Manfredi, to try to acquire a firm hold over it. In the circumstances, it was not

1 Gentile Becchi to Lorenzo, Rome, 24 November 1470 (ASF, MAP, LXI, 30): 'Sta molto bene hora Firenze vaghegiata da tutta dua, et fia spesso examen della bilancia nel migliore partito se fiano uniti'. Cfr. *Lettere*, vol. i, 70, n. intr., pp. 232–3.

2 Filippo Sacramoro to Bona and Gian Galeazzo Sforza, Florence, 27 April 1478 (ASM, SPE, Firenze, 294): 'erano tri anni che messer Jacobo di Pazzi l'haveva sempre importunato a questo tracto'.

3 On the origins of the conspiracy, see now *Lettere*, vol. ii, docs. xi–xiii, nn. intr., pp. 411–12, 414; 417–18; 430–2, and 270, n. 8, pp. 467–9.

surprising that when the purchase fell through owing to the opposition of the Pope, the Medici Bank decided not to provide the loan to enable his nephew Girolamo Riario to acquire the place; but the refusal to do so led to a further worsening of relations between Sixtus IV and Lorenzo, while the fact that the rival bank of the Pazzi made the loan, in its turn affected relations between that family and Lorenzo.[1] In the following year, the Pope's campaign against Niccolò Vitelli, the lord of Città di Castello, was believed in Florence to pose a threat to the neighbouring Borgo San Sepolcro. Lorenzo was at first in favour of a military demonstration, but he was not alone in this, and later changed his view in favour of a peaceful settlement.[2] Yet it was Lorenzo who was made to suffer through punitive measures against the Medici Bank in Rome. Later in that year, Sixtus IV created Francesco Salviati Archbishop of Pisa, against the express wish of the Signoria, which accepted the advice of a meeting of leading citizens that he should be prevented from taking possession of the see: as one of them declared, they were opposed to his appointment 'not because he is an unworthy person, but because the city wants things to be done differently'.[3] Again, it is difficult to isolate the responsibility of Lorenzo, who had certainly personal reasons for disliking Francesco Salviati; as Lorenzo writes on 7 September 1475 to Galeazzo Maria Sforza, Salviati was 'linked to the Pazzi by family ties as well as obligations of friendship', and was 'molto cosa di costoro', 'very much their man'.[4] '. . . I believe', he writes on 14 December 1474 to Galeazzo Maria, 'that I have been greatly wronged; . . . the offence, if it is one [of having forbidden Francesco Salviati to take possession of the archbishopric of Pisa], . . . has been committed by the whole city, and [the Pope] wants to take revenge for it on me alone'; and on 23 December he sums up, in another letter to the Duke, the events that in his view had led to the present crisis in his relations with Sixtus IV: it is not the affair of Città di Castello,

[1] See *Lettere*, vol. ii, 182, n. intr., pp. 52–3.

[2] Ibid., 171, n. intr., pp. 5–7.

[3] ASF, Consulte e Pratiche, 60, fols. 148^r–149^v (18 October 1474): Giovannozzo Pitti: 'quod preter dignitatem civitatis et petitionem Magistratus archiepiscopus pisanus creatus est molestum esse debere omnibus civibus. Non quod archiepiscopi persona indigna sit, maxime propter familiam, sed quod aliter ac civitas voluerit factum sit . . . Itaque censuit retinendum archiepiscopatum in sua potestate Magistratum, donec archiepiscopus talis sit qualem Magistratus velit . . .' Cfr. also *Lettere*, vol. ii, 182, n. intr., p. 57.

[4] *Lettere*, vol. ii, 201, p. 124.

but that of the archbishopric of Pisa; 'this is the root of everything', 'è quello onde procede tutto questo'. If it is true what the Pope says, Lorenzo continues, that many citizens have written to him in favour of Salviati, this is precisely the reason why he should not be allowed to take possession of his diocese, 'for since the Signoria and the members of the regime', the 'huomini dello stato', do not want him, those who do want him, and have written to this effect, must be men who do not get on with the ruling group, 'con quelli che governano'; and it would be dangerous to leave an unreliable ('sospectosa') city like Pisa in the hands of a man who was acceptable to the former and not to the latter.[1] Lorenzo could have hardly spelled out more forcefully the way in which the policies of the state and of the regime were entwined with one another and with his own personal interests. He certainly had a case for arguing that the Pope did him an injustice in holding him alone responsible for Florence's action.

His case was compounded by the bull of excommunication and interdict, which Sixtus IV issued a little over a month after the attack in the Duomo. Before 1478, the Pope had still observed formal diplomatic procedure by addressing his complaints about Florentine interventions in the Papal State to the Signoria;[2] his bull of 1 June 1478[3] is squarely directed against Lorenzo, the Signoria and other magistrates being implicated solely as his helpers and accomplices. Was Sixtus IV trying to tear down the public façade from the complex structure of Florentine government under the Medici, by placing the full responsibility for its actions on Lorenzo? It may not have been mere coincidence that one of his predecessors, Pius II, had described Lorenzo's grandfather as Signore of Florence in all but name.[4] If the republic handed over Lorenzo and his so-called accomplices for ecclesiastical punishment, Florence would be absolved from guilt by association, for the actions which, according to the bull, deserved punishment—from the interventions in the affairs of Imola and Città di Castello to the hanging of the Archbishop of Pisa, Francesco Salviati, and the detention of the Pope's great-nephew, Cardinal Raffaele

[1] Ibid., 182, pp. 58–9; 184, pp. 69–70.

[2] See the copies of briefs addressed to the Signoria in 1474 and 1475 in ASF, Signori, Carteggi, Responsive, Copiari, 2, fols. 63^v–64^r (28 June 1474), 64^v–65^r (5 July 1474), 92^v–93^r (21 October 1475).

[3] Fabroni, *Laurentii Medicis vita*, vol. ii, pp. 121–9.

[4] *Commentarii* (Rome, 1584), p. 89.

Riario-Sansoni, after the failure of the conspiracy. The point was driven home by the accusation, consistently used from now to the end of the war, that Lorenzo was a tyrant, and by the argument that the Pope was only trying to help the Florentines to free themselves from his tyranny.

For Lorenzo, the aftermath of the conspiracy was the moment of truth in more than one respect; it was also the supreme test of his statecraft, and of the cohesion of the regime. On 26 April the Pazzi had failed to rouse the people of Florence by the ancient republican slogan of 'popolo e libertà', and Sixtus IV's attempt to drive a wedge between Lorenzo and the Florentines proved to be equally counterproductive. That the 'uomini dello stato' would support the head of the regime was a foregone conclusion. Yet the question remained how the complex relationship between Lorenzo and the regime would stand up to the strain of interdict and war. The meeting on 12 June, in which leading citizens discussed, a few days after the publication of the bull, the threat of military action against Florence, provided Lorenzo with an opportunity to test the measure of their support. In a moving speech, he offered to face exile and even death if this could avert war. 'All citizens must place the common before the private good, but I more than anyone else, as one who has received from you and the fatherland more and greater benefits."[1] The reaction of the meeting could have been foreseen; its formulation is not without interest. 'Lorenzo and the house of Medici must be defended in the same way as the fatherland', says one of the speakers, 'Laurentium . . . et Medicam domum non aliter defendendam quam patrie salutem'; while another declares that Lorenzo's safety cannot be distinguished from that of the state, 'ne separari posse eius salutem a salute publica'.[2] And when, a month later, Sixtus IV wrote to the Florentines that he had no quarrel with the Florentine people itself, that, on the contrary, his only aim was to liberate it from the tyranny of Lorenzo, and that once Lorenzo was expelled, the troops he, the Pope, and the King of Naples were moving against Florence, would be used to protect her liberty, the Signoria replied that the man whom the Pope called a tyrant, the Florentines unanimously called 'the defender of our liberty', and that they were prepared, 'what-

[1] ASF, Consulte e Pratiche, 60, fol. 159^{r-v}: 'Cives enim omnes publicam salutem debent suae anteponere; ego vero multo etiam magis quam caeteri omnes, quippe qui a vobis, a patria plura et maiora acceperim beneficia'.

[2] Ibid., fol. 160^{r} (Piero Minerbetti, for the *Otto di Balìa*; Niccolò Berardi).

ever should happen, to stake everything on the safety of Lorenzo de' Medici'.[1]

After the meeting of 12 June Lorenzo must have felt confident that the leading citizens of the regime would stand firmly behind him; on the following day their declaration, that the defence of Florence and that of the Medici were one and the same thing, received an almost symbolic confirmation in Lorenzo's election to the newly appointed *Dieci di Balìa*. The Ten were an office created, with wide powers, in times of war; while it functioned, it took the place of the Signoria in the conduct of the war and of foreign policy. It was the first time that Lorenzo held an office in the government of Florence. From now onwards he was to participate almost continuously in the official conduct of government business in the public world of Palazzo Vecchio, as against the private, or semi-private one of Palazzo Medici. It might be argued that, as far as his actual influence on government was concerned, this would add only little, if anything, to his power. Yet, in the complex and sophisticated system of Medici rule, a great deal depended on the form in which it was exercised. Lorenzo's election to the *Dieci* thus constitutes a landmark in the formation of his statecraft.[2] It may also serve us as an opportunity to examine once more what was, perhaps, its central problem.

Throughout the period of Medici ascendancy, Medicean control of the Signoria was certainly not confined to the election of its members. The Ferrarese ambassador shrewdly observed, when reporting on Lorenzo's succession in December 1469: 'it is understood that the secret business ("le cose secrete"), of the Signoria will now pass through the hands of Lorenzo, as they did through those of his father', because his followers were able to control the elections to that office.[3] Pius II had said of Cosimo that 'affairs of State were debated in his house';[4] the opposition to Piero had demanded that government business be confined to the Palace of the Signoria; and after Piero's

[1] Ed. in L. Pignotti, *Storia della Toscana* (Livorno, 1820), vol. iv, pp. 117–21: 'Eiicere vis nos e civitate Laurentium de Medicis . . . Laurentium de Medicis tyrannum clamitas, at nos populusque noster defensorem nostrae libertatis . . . una omnium voce appellamus' (21 July 1478).

[2] See Rubinstein, *The Government*, pp. 219–21.

[3] Niccolò de' Roberti to Borso d'Este, Florence, 4 December, A. Cappelli (ed.), 'Lettere di Lorenzo de' Medici . . . conservate nell'Archivio Palatino di Modena . . .', *Atti e memorie delle Deputazioni di storia patria per le provincie modenesi e parmensi*, vol. i (1863), p. 250.

[4] Loc. cit.

death there were people in Florence who believed that this was now actually going to happen, but they were wrong.[1] Yet, there were limits to Medici influence on the day-to-day work of the Signoria, due to restraints imposed by ancient political traditions. It was up to the Signoria to summon the citizens they chose for consultation, and they were not bound by their advice; jointly with their two Colleges, they had the last word in the making of decisions; they had their own administrative staff, including, in particular, the chancery. I do not know whether Lorenzo saw, as a rule, all the more important letters addressed to or written by the Signoria, but he would not have had much difficulty in doing so. He had his own sources of information, often more reliable than those of the Signoria, and the Florentine ambassadors would write to him as well as to their government, often at the same time. Alamanno Rinuccini states that during his embassy to the Pope in 1475/6, he had 'as an old friend of Lorenzo's written to him privately, together with his official dispatches, about the weightiest matters'; and he adds that Lorenzo was, on one occasion, annoyed with him because he had reported the Pope's complaints about Lorenzo to the Signoria, as well as to him.[2] Lorenzo expected personal letters from ambassadors to contain more confidential information, not necessarily identical with that included in their official dispatches. They would also serve as channels through which foreign governments could communicate with Lorenzo.[3] This was one of the advantages of Lorenzo's personal diplomacy. Another concerned his own correspondence.

[1] See Rubinstein, *The Government*, p. 173. Cf. the letter of Niccolò de' Roberti, cit.: 'che fra pochi dì si abbia a ridurre ogni cosa al Palazzo'.

[2] *Dialogus de libertate*, ed. F. Adorno, in *Atti e Memorie dell'Accademia Toscana . . . La Colombaria*, xxii (1957), pp. 300–1: 'Quid vero reprehendere in me iure potest, si veteris amicitiae rationem sequutus una cum publicis litteris privatim quoque ad eum de maximis rebus litteras dabam . . .? . . . cum, adstante summorum patrum concilio, Pontifex de ipso verba quaedam graviora contra republicae nostrae decus fecisset, et privatim ad eum et publice ad summum magistratum omnia perscripsi'.

[3] During the secret peace negotiations in June 1479 the Milanese government would even dictate to the Florentine ambassador what he was to write to Lorenzo in his own name: see A. R. Natale (ed.), *Acta in Consilio Secreto in Castello Portae Iovis Mediolani*, vol. iii (Milan, 1969), p. 268 (23 June): Cicco Simonetta 'fecit legere . . . minutam litterarum scribendarum per dictum Magnificum Hieronymum [Morelli], oratorem florentinum, prefato Laurentio . . .' The minute is in ASM, SPE, Firenze, 298, and a copy of it, in Morelli's secretary's hand, in ASF, Carte Strozziane, 2a ser., 96, no. 5.

Owing to his position in Florence, his communications to foreign princes and statesman, whether relayed through ambassadors, his agents, or directly through his letters, were likely to carry more weight than those of the Signoria. His letters had the additional advantage of being technically private. In this sense, what might be broadly called his double diplomacy was really complementary to that of the official organs of government. It rendered Florentine diplomacy more flexible and, if necessary, more secret; among other things, it made it possible for Lorenzo, as it had done earlier for Cosimo, to disclaim ultimate responsibility for government decisions, on the grounds that he was only a private citizen. Lorenzo certainly had also considerable influence on the official correspondence of the Signoria. In this, as in other respects, the head of the chancery, Bartolomeo Scala, provided him with an invaluable link with the Palazzo della Signoria: a Medici client and friend of Lorenzo's, he was, unlike other palace officials, a permanent fixture in Florentine administration, enjoying what in the end amounted to life tenure.[1] At the same time, there were limits to the extent to which Lorenzo could, or would, normally determine the contents of official letters; had this not been the case it would have been hardly necessary, in 1477, explicitly to entrust Lorenzo and a few leading citizens with the drafting of letters for the Signoria, as was the case on several occasions; they formed a small *ad hoc* committee which met in the room of the Gonfalonier of Justice in the Palace of the Signoria.[2] One result of this development was that Lorenzo was now becoming more directly, indeed physically, involved in the official business of government, as transacted in Palazzo Vecchio (apart from being summoned, like other leading citizens, by the Signoria to advisory meetings, in which, moreover, he only spoke rarely).[3] On 1 May 1478 he became a member of the magistracy in charge of public security, the Eight of Ward, having been elected to it, for four months, shortly before the attack in the Duomo; but he resigned from it shortly afterwards, no doubt in order not to be personally implicated in political prosecutions.[4] His election to the *Dieci* in June thus forms yet another step in the same direction: the contrast between Palazzo Vecchio and Palazzo Medici, seen by their opponents as

[1] See Alison Brown's forthcoming *Bartolomeo Scala* (Princeton U.P.).

[2] See *Lettere*, vol. ii, docs. i to xii (24 April to 29 September 1477).

[3] ASF, Consulte e Pratiche, 60, *passim*.

[4] See Rubinstein, *The Government*, p. 220.

symbolic of the system of government of the Medici, was beginning to lose some of its force. The *Dieci* were appointed for six months at a time, but the citizens elected on 13 June were re-elected twice, so that Lorenzo remained continuously in office until 12 December 1479,[1] by which time he had left for Naples to negotiate peace with King Ferrante.

In what ways did this shift of his political activities to Palazzo Vecchio affect the development of his statecraft? He now participated officially in the formulation and execution of the foreign and military policy of the republic, during a war which threatened its very independence. Yet at the same time, he kept up, and if anything intensified, his private diplomacy. It could hardly have been otherwise. Indeed, this diplomacy acquired additional importance during the war, as did his personal relations with foreign rulers, such as the Duchess of Milan and the King of France, and with their ministers—Cicco Simonetta and Philippe de Commynes. The correspondence of the *Dieci* and of Lorenzo shows in great detail how his double diplomacy worked during the war. Their relationship was based on a sort of division of labour, the *Dieci* being in charge of the day-to-day conduct of military operations and diplomatic affairs, Lorenzo more concerned with long-term issues, and, in particular, with secret negotiations. To quote one instance only: in Spring 1479, while official peace negotiations were going on in Rome, Lorenzo was involved in secret talks, conducted partly through his brother-in-law, Rinaldo Orsini, about a peace settlement with the King of Naples. On 11 May he sent the Florentine ambassador in Milan a copy of a letter concerning matters 'di grandissima importantia' which he had received from his colleague in Rome, and asked him to discuss it only with the ducal secretary, Cicco Simonetta, 'as it must be kept very secret': 'To you alone I want to tell my views [on it], according to my free and rough nature', 'secondo la mia natura libera et staglata'.[2] There is no reference to this matter in the dispatch which the Florentine ambassador in Rome sent simultaneously to the *Dieci*; nor in those of the Milanese ambassador in Florence. The incident also illustrates, once more, the role of personal relations in Lorenzo's diplomacy, in this case with the powerful secretary of the Dukes of Milan. It should be added that this type of diplomacy was not without

[1] ASF, Cento, 2, fols. 38^{v}–39^{r}, 43^{v}–44^{r}, 48^{v}–49^{r}.

[2] Lorenzo to Girolamo Morelli, 11 May 1479, ASF, MAP, CXXXVII, 430.

risks: Venice was incensed by the rumours of secret negotiations, and Simonetta's fall from power, after Ludovico Sforza's return to Milan in September 1479, was bound to be a source of embarrassment to Lorenzo. In fact, Ludovico il Moro proved to be much more lukewarm in his attitude to Lorenzo, and to Florence, than Cicco Simonetta had been; and this contributed, in the end, to Lorenzo's decision to follow the Duke of Calabria's advice 'to throw himself into the arms of the King of Naples', on the grounds that 'this is the only way in which I can save the city and myself'.[1] On 6 December, he left Florence for Naples.

Lorenzo's journey to Naples highlights some of the major characteristics and problems of his statecraft, as it had developed over the past ten years. If the aftermath of the Pazzi conspiracy was a moment of truth for his ascendancy in Florence, the setbacks and defeats of the war years provided a new challenge to it. While the leading members of the regime appear to have remained united behind him, there were rumblings of discontent; in Florence too, there were people such as Alamanno Rinuccini who called Lorenzo a tyrant who had deprived the city of her ancient liberty; and they were probably more likely to do so when the war was going badly.[2] Lorenzo's decision to assume personal responsibility for the conclusion of peace thus forms a logical sequel to his offer, in June 1478, to sacrifice himself for the sake of Florence. What was at stake, once more, was, in the widest sense, the relationship between Lorenzo and Florence, but the circumstances were different. In the summer of 1478, the offer might be considered rhetorical; in December 1479, it had a very real meaning. Against the background of defeat, his speech to the meeting which was hastily summoned on the eve of his departure, in order to inform, but not to consult, the leading citizens of his decision, while reminding us of his address to the meeting at the beginning of the war, had a different ring of urgency. As the *Dieci* wrote to the Florentine ambassador in Venice, Lorenzo expressed the belief that, since the Pope and the King of Naples were holding him alone responsible

[1] Lorenzo to Girolamo Morelli, 25 September 1479 (ASF, MAP, L, 11): 'di gittarmi nelle braccia del Re, mostrandone che questa via sola ho da salvare la città et me'.

[2] See his *Dialogus de libertate*, completed in April 1479 (ed. F. Adorno, pp. 270–303). On 14 December, Cardinal Francesco Gonzaga wrote to his brother, the Marquess of Mantua: 'Sonnosi in Firenza trovati scrittarini sparti per la terra che dicevano: L'è pur partito el tyranno' (quoted in G. B. Picotti, *Ricerche umanistiche* (Florence, 1955), p. 58, n. 2).

for the war, he would, by taking this decision, either help to bring about the peace which the city, and the whole of Italy, needed so badly, or find out whether it was really he who was the cause of the war or whether there was some other reason for it; and if it could be shown that 'the cause of the war did not concern him, but the republic, we ought to devote ourselves, unitedly and boldly, to our defence'.[1] By taking the initiative in seeking peace, Lorenzo thus reopened the question of the relationship between his own personal interests, his 'spetialità', and those of the republic—a question which seemed to have been settled and put aside at the beginning of the war. This is spelt out in his outburst after his arrival at Naples, as reported by the Milanese ambassadors there: his journey, he complained, had brought no advantage to his city; even were the King to give him full satisfaction as far as his private interests were concerned, this was not what he wanted if at the same time his fatherland remained dissatisfied; indeed, should this happen, he would, on his return, not be able to open his mouth in Florence.[2] The successful conclusion of the peace negotiations in Naples in March 1480 was therefore not only a diplomatic triumph for Lorenzo; it also decisively strengthened his position at home. The creation of the Council of Seventy, a few weeks after his triumphant return from Naples, must be seen as a further step in the domestic policy Lorenzo had been pursuing from the first year of his political career; but the unprecedented success of this policy, in concentrating power in this all but permanent council, would have hardly been possible without the challenge of peace Lorenzo had met single-handed.

For the journey to Naples was also a supreme test of the other aspect of his statecraft, his personal diplomacy. While the war years had enhanced the judicious blending of public and private diplomacy, they had also shown, once more, the

[1] The *Dieci* to Luigi Guicciardini, 6 December (ASF, Missive interne, 11, fols. 45v–46v): '. . . o veramente potere chiarire se questa cagione o veramente altra cagione è quella che fa questa guerra et perturbatione, a questo fine che, potendosi havere pace . . . , più facilmente si habbi, et non si potendo havere et inteso la cagione della guerra non essere per lui ma per il publico, si venga unitamente et animosamente alla difesa necessaria'.

[2] Pietro da Gallera and Giovanni Angelo Talenti to Galeazzo Maria Sforza, Naples, 22 December, ASMi, SPE, Roma, 86: 'se bene la Maestà del Signore Re nelle particularitate sue gli satisfacesse al tutto, che questo non saria el suo bisogno, restando mal contenta la sua patria, et . . . che'l non potesse parlare in Fiorenza, quando se trovasse che per la sua spetialità el ritornasse ben contento et nelle cose publice la città mal satisfacta'.

value of the latter, in terms of secrecy, initiative, and personal relationships. The journey to Naples epitomizes all this; prepared in well-kept secrecy, as a result of Lorenzo's own initiative, it was greatly facilitated, and incidentally rendered less dangerous than might appear, by his earlier contacts with members of the royal family of Naples. The Duke of Calabria, whom he had known since his visit to Naples in 1466, when informing Lorenzo on 4 December that two Neapolitan galleys were at his disposal, addresses him as 'My dearest and most beloved Lorenzo'[1]—somewhat surprising for a commander of the enemy army; his wife Ippolita Sforza, whose marriage ceremony Lorenzo had attended in Milan, proved a good friend and adviser during the negotiations at Naples—and apparently also good company: at one point, discussions were held up, because Lorenzo could not be found: it turned out that he was visiting her.[2] His refusal to act as official Florentine ambassador was in keeping with the personal style of his diplomacy;[3] his mandate to negotiate and conclude, which was sent to him by the *Dieci*, conferred on him great powers but also implied, by its very nature, that his actions were subject to restraints; and these were fully acknowledged by him, when, for instance, he announced in Naples that he wanted to return to Florence, because he could hope by his presence to persuade the Signoria to make concessions 'to which he did not dare agree on his own'.[4]

[1] ASF, MAP, XLV, 224: 'Lorenzo mio multo caro e multo amato . . .'

[2] The Milanese ambassadors in Naples report on 23 December (ASM, SPE, Napoli, 229) that they had been unable to find Lorenzo in order to deliver a message from the King until late that day, because he had gone to visit the Duchess: 'et non essendo el Magnifico Lorenzo nel suo logiamento, per essere andato a visitare la Illustrissima duchessa de Calabria, ne bisognò expectare insino alla nocte'. A month later, the *Dieci* wrote to her to thank her for having 'prestati grandissimi favori et adoperatovi per noi et durati ogni fatica', as they had been informed by Lorenzo (Florence, Biblioteca Nazionale, MS. Palat. 1091, fol. 45^r, 22 January 1480).

[3] The Milanese ambassador in Florence, Filippo Sacramoro, reports on 30 December 1479 (ASM, SPE, Firenze, 298) that to his question whether Lorenzo 'tenga grado de ambassatore', the *Dieci* had given him to understand that this was not the case, 'né l'havea, perché ha monstro non lo volere'; and on 6 January 1480, Lorenzo himself, writing from Naples, pointed out to the *Dieci* (ASF, Dieci, Responsive, 25, fol. 439) that he had not 'tenuto qua grado o termine di ambasciadore, ché m'è paruto meglo a proposito stare chome privato'.

[4] The mandate (a copy is in ASF, Notarile antecosimiano, B 2320, fols. 126^v–127^r) gave him full powers to conclude peace and alliances with the

The successful conclusion of the negotiations, completed after he had left Naples, forms a landmark in his diplomacy, as well as in his position as head of the regime. His official participation in the conduct of foreign policy as member of a public office, interrupted after he had ceased to be a member of the *Dieci* in December 1478, was resumed, on a different level, and on a practically permanent basis, after the creation of the Seventy in April 1480. A new magistracy, the *Otto di Pratica*, which was elected every six months from its personnel, replaced the *Dieci*, in peace as well as in war; but the Seventy took the final decisions, and Lorenzo was a member of that council. The new structure of government brought with it a further decline in the authority of the Signoria, as well as of the old statutory councils. Supreme authority in the republic was now concentrated in a council which, while meeting in the Palace of the Signoria, represented the inner circle of the regime. The contrast between Palazzo Vecchio and Palazzo Medici had been settled, though not in the way which the opponents of the Medici had envisaged. It was the beginning of a new period in the development of Lorenzo's statecraft.

King of Naples and other powers, 'prout eidem Laurentio libere videbitur et placebit'. In fact, Lorenzo kept in close contact with the *Dieci* throughout the negotiations. The Milanese ambassadors in Naples report on 13 January (ASM, SPE, Napoli, 229) that Lorenzo had decided to tell the King 'che la voglia et parer suo saria de ritornare a Fiorenza, perché con la presentia sua poteria più facilmente indure quella Excelsa Signoria a questi effecti, alli quali lui non ardiria aconsentire da si stesso'.

[*Bibliographical Note*: Lorenzo de' Medici, *Lettere*, vol. i (18 November 1460 to 12 July 1474), vol. ii (3 August 1474 to 14 March 1478), vol. iii (26 April 1478 to 5 February 1479), vol. iv (17 February 1479 to 23 March 1480), Giunti–Barbèra, Florence. Vol. iv will be published in 1979.]

T. S. ELIOT: LANGUAGE, SINCERITY AND THE SELF[1]

By JOHN CASEY

Read 19 May 1977

I

IT is perhaps not enlightening to elicit a set of propositions from a poet's work and present them as his 'beliefs'. And if it is not enlightening this will not be because it is always difficult to make such inferences, but because beliefs do not enter into poetry in the same way that they enter into philosophy and religion. To say that is not exactly to utter a commonplace, since we are no longer agreed upon an aesthetic theory that will distinguish between beliefs and assertions as they exist in art and as they exist elsewhere. Yet it was T. S. Eliot's own view that poetry offered not thought but its emotional equivalent, and that it was Shakespeare's business 'to express the greatest emotional intensity of his time, based on whatever his time happened to think'.[2] In this lecture I shall be talking about the self as it is explored in Eliot's poetry; but to find the echo, or trace of philosophical ideas in the verse cannot be an end in itself. An idea of the self does enter centrally into Eliot's poetry, and it carries with it the weight of a whole philosophical tradition; but it depends upon a strictly poetic exploration of experience. By 'a strictly poetic exploration of experience' I mean an exploration of experience that is at the same time the exploration of the possibilities of language, so that the possibilities of what can be believed, even in a philosophical or religious sense, will finally be connected to what the poet can find to say.

In *The Love Song of J. Alfred Prufrock* we certainly find the traces of a philosophical theory of the self. The opening lines are as memorable as those of any poem in the language:

Let us go then, you and I,
When the evening is spread out against the sky,
Like a patient etherised upon a table;

[1] I am grateful to Roger Scruton for helpful criticism and suggestions.

[2] 'Shakespeare and the Stoicism of Seneca'.

But who is the 'you' and who the 'I'? One critic has quite confidently asserted that the 'you' is the woman whom Prufrock loves. This assumes that the poem is more or less like a Browning dramatic monologue, with a speaker whose character is revealed as the poem progresses. (In *My Last Duchess*, for instance, we learn that the Duke who is speaking—a man of consummate vanity, a sort of Renaissance Gilbert Osmund—has somehow procured the death of his wife, and is now relating the story to the very person through whom he is negotiating a new marriage.) But *Prufrock* is not at all like a Browning dramatic monologue, and there is no other person to whom Prufrock addresses himself. We do indeed have a sense of a fragmentation of personality, and of a consciousness with uncertain boundaries. There is the self of Prufrock that is merely self-conscious:

> (They will say: 'How his hair is growing thin!)
> My morning coat, my collar mounting firmly to the chin,
> My necktie rich and modest, but asserted by a simple pin—
> (They will say: 'But how his arms and legs are thin!)

This self is merely self-conscious in the sense that it is unable to present an identity which validates experience. Self-consciousness in Prufrock goes with no self-knowledge, since there is no self-will ('Should I, after tea and cakes and ices, / Have the strength to force the moment to its crisis?'). He sees himself from the outside, as it were, as the subject of speculation on the part of others, having no identity that is achieved from within. The self of Prufrock is constantly overwhelmed by its impressions and images, since it can give them no meaning that is its own. His experiences come to him as though they were the experiences of another man, lacking the imprint of an active self; so the self constantly dissolves into its impressions—and indeed bears the closest possible resemblance to the picture of the self, as a bundle of impressions, that we find in the empiricist philosophy of Hume. One might say that Prufrock does not possess his experience but is possessed by it—the yellow fog, the lonely men in shirtsleeves leaning out of windows—and is incapable either of action or of organizing his impressions into significance:

> To have squeezed the universe into a ball
> To roll it towards some overwhelming question
> To say: 'I am Lazarus, come from the dead,
> Come back to tell you all, I shall tell you all' . . .

It is a central Idealist doctrine that the self is not a substance, in which experiences and thoughts somehow 'inhere'. In that respect the Idealist tradition is in agreement with Hume. But Idealism, unlike Hume, does not dissolve the self into a bundle of impressions. Rather it reconstitutes it as an activity, an activity of 'self-realization' in which to be a self is seen as an achievement rather than as a given fact. The self (to use the language of Hegel and Sartre) is a way of being *in* the world, not a way of being *for* the world. According to some thinkers (for instance, F. H. Bradley) the self is achieved when an active unity is created amongst sensations, thoughts, and feelings. The Prufrock who is self-conscious, and who cannot compel his kaleidoscopic impressions into a unity, is defeated in his attempt to be a self. He thus does not exist *in* the world but *for* the world. His self-consciousness is no more than a sense of what he is in the eyes of others.

But in *Prufrock* we are not presented with the predicament of an individual. Prufrock tries several different styles of language in order to try and construct a sense of himself. The most diffident seem closest to reality, but furthest from giving a secure sense of the self. The most confident are the least sincere and collapse the most completely. It is interesting that when Eliot wanted to define the quality of Dryden's use of language, he did so by contrasting him with Swinburne. Whereas Swinburne's poetry is all suggestion and no denotation, Dryden's verse 'states immensely, but its suggestive power is almost nothing'. And talking again of Swinburne, he wrote: 'Language in a healthy state presents the object, is so close to the object that the two are identified. They are identified in the verse of Swinburne solely because the object has ceased to exist, because the meaning is merely the hallucination of meaning, because language, uprooted, has adapted itself to an independent life of atmospheric nourishment.'[1] Yet it is clear the Prufrock's language has more in common with Swinburne than it has with Dryden. Prufrock regularly resorts to what one critic[2] calls 'the authorised sonorities of the best English verse *circa* 1870'; and he does this in order to evoke a poignancy that is in excess of anything that can actually be grasped in his situation:

> For I have known them all already, known them all—
> Have known the evenings, mornings, afternoons,
> I have measured out my life with coffee spoons;

[1] 'Swinburne as Poet'.

[2] Hugh Kenner, *The Invisible Poet*, p. 6.

Here the plangencies produced by control of sound and rhythm give an illusion of meaningfulness in excess of meaning. The best example of course is a couplet the grandiloquence of which is almost entirely a matter of its control of sound.

> In the room the women come and go
> Talking of Michelangelo.[1]

The speaker cannot say just what he means, but he invests his own situation, which he cannot define, with all the grandeur of Victorian eloquence. Even the most blank observations are invested by a control of sound and rhythm with a suggestion of significance: 'And sawdust restaurants with oyster shells'.

But Prufrock is not entirely immersed in a world of words, or in reminiscence of a worn-out poetical fashion. Irony enters in the contrast between his general sense of the poignancy of his situation and his plans—slightly deranged in their increasing precision—to do something about it:

> I grow old . . . I grow old . . .
> I shall wear the bottoms of my trousers rolled.
>
> Shall I part my hair behind? Do I dare to each a peach?
> I shall wear white flannel trousers, and walk upon the beach.

The world Prufrock inhabits is one of on the one hand sharp, particular sensations—'Arms that are braceleted and white and bare / (But in the lamplight, downed with light brown hair!)', and on the other muffled echoes of poetic rhetoric.

Twice the rhetoric becomes eloquence; first, in the Hamlet section (the only lines that Pound thought would be immediately popular) where Prufrock, nagging at the fact that he is not the Prince, manages to suggest that that is a cause of sorrow in lines of rhythmic expansiveness that modulate wonderfully into the closing 'Almost, at times, the fool'. The second time is where the closing lines of the poem evoke another self, the buried, sexual self that might be able to tell her all:

> We have lingered in the chambers of the sea
> By sea-girls wreathed with seaweed red and brown
> Till human voices wake us and we drown.

The question of Prufrock's self is the question of what language he can use. And he does not seek a language that will adequately

[1] See Kenner, ibid.: 'The closed and open o's, the assonances of *room*, *women*, and *come*, the pointed caesura before the polysyllabic burst of "Michelangelo", weave a context of grandeur within which our feeling about these trivial women determines itself.'

express his predicament. It is only in a language and in a certain tradition of eloquence that Prufrock's situation can be identified. But because the poetic language that he inherits belongs to another world, and to another, grander realm of experience, it does not allow his predicament to be sincerely stated. The 'meanings' that hover on the periphery of Prufrock's experience fail to attach themselves to it, just as he is unable to make his experience genuinely a part of himself. What *Prufrock* is doing is playing with a range of devices for eloquence which in Victorian poetry can create significance, and can sometimes do so independently of what meaning they create. So *Prufrock* is bringing a tradition of poetic expression to bear upon a situation that cannot even be stated—except for some precise and unpoignant particularities ('Is it perfume from a dress / That makes me so digress?'). We might compare this with the way in which Joyce brings the whole history of the language to bear upon the unmomentous events of Bloom's day.

In being a poem about the self *Prufrock* is also a poem about language. The nineteenth century was well aware of the capacity for Tennysonian eloquence to develop into a sheer mimicry of meaning: ''Twas brillig, and the slithy toves / Did gyre and gimble in the wabe. / All mimsy were the borrogroves / And the mome rathes outgrabe.' And *Prufrock* employs and dissolves a tradition of eloquence by setting the grandiloquently suggestive against the precisely seen but atomic. The irony is Laforguian rather than Augustan. It does not presuppose an accepted frame of values and of moral rhetoric, the ideal with which the actual may be contrasted. The irony is in the experience itself, as a sense of an objective order that it is impossible (with this shabby equipment) to achieve. Hence the 'ideal' is itself ironized. We can further define the irony as Eliot did metaphysical wit: 'a recognition implicit in the expression of every experience, of other kinds of experience which are possible'.[1] But for Prufrock there is a disproportion between one sensibility, one way of using language, and another. The poem enacts an uncertainty about language, and hence about selfhood. Only an insincere rhetoric can offer to unite Prufrock's impressions, into which his self threatens to dissolve. His uncertainty about what he sees is also an uncertainty about what he is. And each moment of eloquence is self-contained: it suggests a mode of sensibility unconnected with any other.

Prufrock involves the summing up and criticizing of a tradition

[1] 'Andrew Marvell'.

of expression. Its protagonist is divided within himself because he is no longer sincerely within the tradition. We find Eliot saying of Swinburne: 'His language is not, like the language of bad poetry, dead, it is very much alive with [a] singular life of its own. But the language which is more important to us is that which is struggling to digest and express new objects . . . new feelings . . .'[1] The 'new feeling' expressed by *Prufrock* is really a feeling of being able to sum up, manipulate, and indeed abuse a certain poetic language. It is like using the technique of Rembrandt for the purposes of advertising.

An ability to choose a mode of expression, to be both within and outside a poetic tradition may not seem to point to a difficulty of sincerity or of the self. Yet it is precisely *that* moment of dislocation between experience and language that can be seen as crucial: 'Sensibility alters from generation to generation in everybody, whether we will or no; but expression is only altered by a man of genius.'[2] It is possible for a form of expression to outgrow the thoughts and feelings of an age, to cease struggling 'to digest and express new objects . . . new feelings'. How does one know when this has happened? We may take the analogy of a custom or ceremony: we perhaps become aware that it has lost its meaning when it becomes impossible for people to realize themselves *in* the ceremony, or to see a custom or institution as an expression of themselves, as rendering objective and intelligible their inner states. This may become apparent when, for instance, a ceremony is a self-conscious revival. It is in similar circumstances that we may become aware that language has become detached from what needs to be expressed. It is not that one has independent access to what needs to be expressed; rather the very availability of a tradition of expression, the ease with which it can be used unseriously or incongruously, may suggest that it is exhausted, that it has become a self-enclosed system of words. That is the case with Swinburne.

II. *Sincerity*

Perhaps this can be illuminated if we touch on a theme mentioned in the title: sincerity. Sincerity is an interesting word and a necessary concept. It begins as a moral concept, and refers to what is in a man's power, what he can be held responsible for, that for which he can be praised and blamed.

1 'Swinburne as Poet'.

2 *Introduction* to Johnson's *London: A Poem* and *The Vanity of Human Wishes.*

A man is insincere if he claims to feel what he does not in fact feel, if he pretends to believe what he does not in fact believe, if he promises what he does not intend to perform. And this normally involves a man's being responsible for his sincerity and insincerity. The picture this suggests is of our always knowing what we think, feel, and intend, and choosing whether or not to communicate our thoughts, feelings, and intentions to others. Let us call a certain model of the mind 'Cartesian' (even if in so doing we risk producing a slogan). According to this model, that understanding of sincerity will be central. We know what we feel, and we may choose to communicate it to others. Knowing what we feel, we sometimes search for the right words to correspond to what we already know.

But 'sincerity' is also a term that has been widely used by critics. Matthew Arnold, for instance, talks of 'the accent of high seriousness born of absolute sincerity' that gives Dante's 'criticism of life' its power.[1] And he talks of 'the profound sincereness with which Wordsworth feels his subject' and 'the profoundly sincere and natural character of the subject itself'. And sincerity is an important concept for Ruskin. It is a central notion in I. A. Richards and F. R. Leavis. But as these critics use the term it is remote from what we might call its primary, moral use. One critic insists that the poet's interest in his experience is inseparable from his interest in words, and that a poet is 'unusually sensitive, unusually aware, more sincere and more himself than the ordinary man can be'.[2] A poet's sincerity is a matter of his knowing what he feels; but the condition of his knowing what he feels is that he find a language capable of expressing what he feels. Here 'sincerity' has become something other than a moral matter; it has come to denote a power of imagination, and a mastery of technique, of language. Croce in fact suggests that when 'sincerity' is applied to works of art it has lost all its ethical content and acquired a quite different meaning; it has come to mean simply 'fullness of truth and expression'.[3]

In fact, these two uses of 'sincerity' point not only to a difference between the moral and the aesthetic, but also to two different pictures of the mind. Broadly speaking the second, 'aesthetic' use is, on what I have been calling the 'Cartesian' model, impossible. I know what I think and feel. I may choose

[1] 'A Study of Poetry'.

[2] F. R. Leavis, *New Bearings in English Poetry*, p. 13.

[3] *Aesthetic*, p. 53.

to express it, and I may or may not have the right words to express what I know. But my *finding* the right words will not at the same time be my acquiring new insight into what I think and feel. My discoveries in language will not also be extensions of self-knowledge; the possibilities of language will not at the same time be the possibilities of experience.

The other view goes as follows: an experience is essentially constituted by its expression both in action and in symbols; that is how we identify the experience both for others who may observe us and for ourselves. The possibilities of thought and action may determine the possibilities of experience. The sharp distinction between active and passive, between experience and will, becomes untenable. The forms of language, and the institutions through which self-knowledge is achieved are not unessential adjuncts to our private feelings: they determine what these feelings are to be. My ability to know my experience, in the sense of my ability to give it a meaning that derives from myself and which asserts its connection with my own self-identity—in short, my ability to be in possession of my experience and not merely possessed by it—this ability will be inseparable from my mastery of a form of expression. In particular, it will not bear an accidental relation to my mastery of language, and to my ability to use words to express what I feel. My interest in my experience will be inseparable from my interest in words. This corresponds, broadly speaking, with central tenets in philosophical Idealism.

These are philosophical doctrines, but they have their bearing upon how we might envisage a poet's task. The 'Cartesian' picture makes the task mysterious, even impossible. It becomes unclear why a poet might want to re-establish lines of communication with a literary past, indeed, why he might see his task as essentially one of finding a language for the present, or of purifying 'the dialect of the tribe'. The self is a substance, simple and unitary; my finding a language is not at the same time a finding of my *self*. The anti-Cartesian view can be expressed purely through philosophical argument—as Wittgenstein expresses it. Yet it can also be understood more informally. We might say that language is the most fundamental form of membership of a human community. One's use of language defines the self not only as something individual but also as something universal, and as part of an historic continuity. 'Cartesianism' not only isolates the individual, but also makes his use of language extrinsic to his real being. Therefore the poet, in searching for the right words, is never doing anything more than just that—looking for words. In 'Tradition and the Individual Talent' Eliot suggested that the historical sense was indispensable to 'anyone who would continue to be a poet beyond his twenty-fifth year'. The historical sense involves a perception 'not only of the pastness of the past but of its presence', a sense that 'the whole of the literature of Europe from Homer and within it the whole of the literature of his own country has a simultaneous existence and composes a simultaneous order'.

This points to something central to Eliot's understanding of the poet and his relation to language. The historical sense is what enables a poet to re-create a tradition: and the important thing is that it has to be *re-created.* It is not there as an inert, objective fact. Only the poet, and not the literary historian can discover what space there is waiting to be filled by *Prufrock*, and what connections with the literary past can be established in order to fill it. 'Tradition cannot be inherited, and if you want it you must obtain it with great labour.' The great labour does not consist in acquiring a great body of knowledge: 'Some can absorb knowledge, the more tardy must sweat for it. Shakespeare acquired more essential history from Plutarch than most men could from the whole British Museum.' Essential history involves a labour of selection, and that auditory imagination that can send 'tentacular roots' down into what is 'primitive'. Eliot talks of the 'mind of Europe' and says that it is a 'mind which changes . . . (and) this change is a development that abandons nothing *en route* . . .'. It would accord with Idealist thinking that as the self is achieved only in outward expression, and cannot exist as a mere Humean bundle of impressions or ideas, so the consciousness of an age cannot exist as a mere collection of individual thoughts and experiences, but only as an outward manifestation, a realization of the self-identity of the age in art and institutions. The consciousness of an age, the mind of Europe are not exactly metaphors—they are not more 'constructions' than is the self. But how do we *know* what can be thought and felt? The central criterion is what can be expressed, what is the language of the time. The man of genius is the man who can see through the superficial features of an age to something essential. If he is a poet he will find language for the mind of his own time: 'Sensibility alters from generation to generation in everybody, whether we will or no; but expression is only altered by a man of genius.'

As the expressive possibilities of an age create the consciousness of the age, so it may be possible for the expressive potential of different ages to come together (as it were) to create an impersonal consciousness that transcends the superficial differences. As the 'man of genius' penetrates to the heart of his age, is at the centre of its consciousness, and is able to find the language to body forth its consciousness, so the poet seeks to review the artistic past, bringing the essential present into relation with the essential past. The past becomes 'simultaneous with the present'. To see Jonson as a contemporary 'does not so much require the power of putting ourselves into seventeenth century London as it requires the power of seeing Jonson in our London'.[1]

III. *The Wasteland*

The Wasteland sets fragmentariness of experience against a postulated ideal unity. The opening lines, with their allusion to Chaucer's *Prologue* and (probably) to the late Latin poem *Pervigilium Veneris*, enact an awareness of 'the mind of Europe and of our own country':

> April is the cruellest month, breeding
> Lilacs out of the dead land, mixing
> Memory and desire, stirring
> Dull roots with spring rain.

But the mind of Europe soon disintegrates into a series of highly specific recollections—it becomes the mind of *Mittel Europa* with some very personal memories:

> Summer surprised us, coming over the Starnbergersee
> With a shower of rain; we stopped in the colonnade,
> And went on in sunlight into the Hofgarten,
> And drank coffee and talked for an hour.
> Bin gar keine Russin, stamm' aus Litauen, echt deutsch.
> And when we were children, staying at the arch-duke's,
> My cousin's, he took me out on a sled,
> And I was frightened. He said, Marie,
> Marie, hold on tight. And down we went.

The theme of spring, handled by the common European literary tradition has become the private recollections of minds that recollect experiences. From then on the 'heap of images' reflects, indifferently, the mind of Europe, the painful and sentimental memories of various women, helpless in the face

[1] 'Ben Jonson'.

of their recollected experiences, and a need to fit fragments of the European artistic and religious tradition into some sort of order.

We *could* say that in *The Wasteland* the mind of Europe, a mind more important than one's own private mind, is 'now very nearly exhausted by the effort to stay interested in its own contents'.[1] Yet in the poem that mind is in fact very interested in its own contents. The intense *interest* in the present is what prevents *The Wasteland*'s being a poem of exhaustion or disillusion. Sappho's evening hour that brings what bright dawn had scattered, the sheep, the goat, the child to its mother[2] really does bring also the typist home at teatime 'clears her breakfast, lights / Her stove, and lays out food in tins'. The allusion to Sappho both vivifies the scene and presents an ironic contrast. The intensity of the scene of the typist's seduction arises from the fact that this moment of evening is full of resonance, a fundamental human experience that needs to be captured. Sappho captured it and therefore the allusion to Sappho does not merely produce an ironic contrast, but also captures the deep meaning of the episode which escaped the participants, and is acknowledged only in the voice of Tiresias. Similarly the description of the modern Cleopatra in 'A Game of Chess' is not simply contrasted with the Shakespearean original. The transformation of a magnificence that was meant to be viewed by the multitudes on the adjacent wharves into a claustrophobic richness—infinite riches in a little room—which can only be stared at ('Staring forms / Leaned out, leaning, hushing the room enclosed') is a conversion of public magnificence into something rich and strange. Something else that is rich and strange is the modern, neurasthenic personality of the lady—a transmutation of Cleopatra's 'infinite variety'.[3]

The contrast between a 'realistic' present, and a past constructed from past literature *dramatizes* the present, and gives it all the meaning it could have. Eliot is doing what he had learned from the French symbolists—investing the imagery of modern life with the greatest possible intensity. In *The Wasteland*

[1] Kenner, op. cit., p. 137.

[2] And probably, since the poem was an epithalamion, 'Even so tonight bring thou home the bride to the bridegroom' would be the continuation.

[3] The phrase 'rich and strange' had a continuing resonance for Eliot. Cf. the poem omitted from *The Wasteland* 'Full Fathom Five Your Bleistein Lies', which contains the lines: 'Lower than the wharf rats dive / Though he suffers a sea change / Still expensive, rich and strange.'

we are certainly presented with a gap between experience and an ideal version of it, or between the sharply observed vignettes of modern life, and an eloquent version of them that fits them into a tradition, making them intelligible as well as vivid. In fact, this eloquent version of them makes them intelligible only because we see how far short of the ideal they fall. The language that seeks to capture the *essence* of these experiences, so giving them an identity which would make it possible for the person who suffers them to 'possess' them—that language persistently moves away from the experiences, and shows them as inadequate to their postulated meaning, just as the meaning is inadequate to them. So the neurasthenic woman is set against Cleopatra; the blankness of the typist after her seduction is set against St. Augustine's sense of sin; and Madame Sosostris with her Tarot pack is a withered version of the already withered Sybil with the leaves on which she wrote her revelations. These contrasts do not issue in a moralistic judgement: they express a characteristically modern consciousness. It is characteristically modern to think of the self as free to enter into any one of a large variety of forms of life. The past can be treated as a mythology which gives form to the present. In the non-Cartesian tradition, in which I am locating Eliot's poetry, the self is *both* something here and now, a centre of impressions, and something that stretches out through time, has a history. That we need to have such a sense of the self as stretching out through time has been expressed philosophically by the self's being described as a 'concrete universal'. A self cannot exist merely as an abstract idea. A man does not realize a self simply by accompanying his experience with the *idea* of a self, however elaborate that idea may be. The idea, as abstract, is a mere 'he', where what is needed is an 'I'. (This is what Kant refers to as the 'transcendental unity of apperception'.) Conversely, a self which is merely 'concrete'—a mere Humean bundle of atomic impressions—is not a self. ('And when we were children, staying at the arch-duke's, / My cousin's, he took me out on a sled, / And I was frightened. He said, Marie, / Marie, hold on tight. And down we went.') The self is truly such only if it is conscious of itself as persisting through time, forming intentions for the future, feeling regret about the past. My being thus in possession of myself is not a matter of my having theoretical knowledge, but more like practical knowledge, a consciousness of the persistence of the soul through time. And here again we may invoke the 'discovery' of tradition: Tradition must always be rediscovered, for it involves the constant translation of abstract or historical knowledge into felt experience, or of sensibility into expression.

The Wasteland enacts and dramatizes this construction of the self. In its movements from the simply experienced but unpossessed present to versions of the same experience from the literary, religious, and political past it dramatizes the very process of imposing a credible order upon ordinary reality, and thereby eliciting some perception of an order *in* reality.[1] Eliot presents this possibility as the only thing it can be for the modern mind—the mythologizing of experience. Subjective experience is rendered objective only by being held momentarily against a tradition of expression that can be experimented with or recapitulated, but not confidently possessed. And the situation of *The Wasteland* is one in which the necessary completion of experience has a mythological remoteness from it. The unity, or wholeness of experience which Eliot's notion of tradition (of writing with the whole of European literature in one's bones, from Homer to the present day) implies, and the unity or wholeness of experience, defined as a unity between language and object, which is a goal in Idealist thought, is in *The Wasteland* a series of gestures towards a pattern underlying the culture itself. The underlying pattern of the poem is given in the vegetation myths; and the Frazerian theory is that these vegetation ceremonies, differing as they do from each other, all have an underlying unity. One could say that Frazer helps create the characteristic myth of the present, and tries to redeem the fragmented experience of modern man by proposing a mythical unity for it. Frazer believed that there is a single form to all redemption myths, and tried to express what it was in anthropological terms. And the past has only a mythological relation to the present in the poem; the death of the past is its transmutation into myth.

A way of further exploring the same point comes if we reflect upon the following: the most influential modern view of art, deriving from Hegel, sees it as essentially the objectifying of the subjective. Hence art redeems the individual from the private, by finding an expression for something that is already universal. In art the universal is expressed in concrete form. With this idea will go the notion that any gap between actual, lived experience and its ideal, expressed form will involve

[1] Cf. the concluding sentence of *Poetry and Drama*.

anguish. (Collingwood sees the act of expression as lightening the burden of the emotions of ordinary life.) And it is a characteristic of modern writing to produce irony through a contrast between experience as it is in fact expressed, and a significance in the experience that is 'there' but cannot be seized by the characters. In other words, the *universal* is there in the work of art, the *concrete* in the individual experience represented, so that the artistic task becomes that of bringing universal and concrete together, to present this experience as bodying forth this meaning. It is often only through a certain kind of irony that this can be done—the irony of Joyce in *Dubliners* and *Ulysses* for instance, where what you might call the ideal form of the experience is revealed through an ironic contrast. The feeling, not fully grasped by the characters, must be described and identified in the light of this ideal form, which it vividly suggests precisely in the moment of falling short. Thus irony here becomes a mode not of criticism but of acceptance. Similarly the artist's task in dealing with the past, may be to evoke from it some such universal or prototype, so that it can convey a meaning, even when it is brought to bear upon experiences that are peculiarly modern. We always find that the truly creative artist of the nineteenth and twentieth centuries is able in this way to transform the material he receives from the past, whereas the academic poet typically leaves it in archaic form. Wagner, for instance, who is the characteristic 'modern', is always guided by a sense of how a form, an image can be found for modern experience. When he takes a legend or myth from the past he does so *entirely* in order to express and sum up modern experience. *Parsifal* is concerned with how to express the idea of renunciation as an experience for modern man; and a legend which is naïve and outward-looking is transformed into an evocation of neurasthenic eroticism.

This is precisely what we find in *The Wasteland*: the objective experiments in 'points of view' are constantly set against intensely personal, subjective feeling. So the mythological potency of hyacinths and sacred groves is broken in upon by the almost unbearably painful reminiscences of the (obscurely betrayed) girl in the hyacinth garden: the mystical mingles with the sexual. Sappo's evening hour brings a particular typist home for a particular seduction. This contrast between the sharp poignancies of particular experience and any received form that might console it *is The Wasteland*'s version of modern consciousness.

The *Vita Nuova* of Dante was always an important work for Eliot, and Dante's description of the love he felt for Beatrice when he saw her at the age of nine seems to have had a special significance for him. Eliot insists upon the actuality of the experience: '. . . the type of sexual experience which Dante describes as occurring to him at the age of nine is by no means impossible or unique. My only doubt (in which I found myself confirmed by a distinguished psychologist) is whether it could have taken place so *late* in life as the age of nine years.' The significance for Eliot of the episode is that Dante in recalling the experience gives it a meaning that it could not have had for him at the time:

> The attitude of Dante to the fundamental experience of the *Vita Nuova* can only be understood by accustoming ourselves to find meaning in final causes rather than in origins. It is not, I believe, meant as a description of what he *consciously* felt on his meeting with Beatrice, but rather as a description of what that meant on mature reflection upon it. The final cause is the attraction towards God. A great deal of sentiment has been spilt, especially in the eighteenth and nineteenth centuries, upon idealizing the reciprocal feelings of man and woman towards each other, which vigorous realists have been concerned to denounce: this sentiment ignoring the fact that the love of man and woman (or for that matter of man and man) is only explained and made reasonable by the higher love, or else is simply the coupling of animals.[1]

'Or else is simply the coupling of animals.' We see in that remark much that alarms some readers of Eliot: it seems to dismiss so much. What in eighteenth- and nineteenth-century literature is meant to be swept into that dismissive reference to 'sentiment' that has been 'spilt'? These words must be a stumbling block to some. Yet I suggest that they are seriously intended, relate to his central concerns, and point to what is central to *Four Quartets*. We might secularize Eliot's words, and say that a reference to 'final causes' might be taken to include that illumination by a tradition of expression that can save the moments of sensation, sheer emotion from being the painful things they are in *The Wasteland*. It is, indeed, the sheer fact of there being no 'reflection' in this sense that makes them painful. And a revealing example of modern man's not seeing in terms of final causes, and so producing a recollection that is a parodic re-enactment of Dante and Beatrice comes in *Dans Le Restaurant*

[1] 'Dante'.

where a waiter confidentially describes his earliest sexual experience, when they were seven, but were interrupted by a dog and stopped half way through: "It is a pity." "But then", replies the diner in whom he has been confiding, "you have your lust."

IV. *Four Quartets*

It is what we have been calling a 'Cartesian' notion that the inner life can be complete in itself independently of its outward expression. But if we take the opposing view, that the self is created in our commerce with the world both practically and through expression, then one's sense of oneself will be intimately related to a sense of one's place in the world. Pure experience, purely personal feeling will be intrinsically incomplete, defective, even painful or debased. It ceases to be defective only when it is completed by reflection, or by being taken into something that imposes order upon it—for instance, a cultural tradition, a religious tradition, or a continuing community (e.g. Little Gidding). One's sense of oneself may involve one's finding order in the world. In that case man's culture is not an accidental feature of the human world, something external in which he finds himself imprisoned—unless it has ceased to be a 'live tradition'.[1] In *The Wasteland* Eliot uses a mythographer, Frazer, who postulated an objective, inclusive pattern that underlies the fragmentary, over-personal experience of modern man. The opening lines of *The Wasteland* point to something that is anterior even to the common European literary tradition that celebrates spring. If we start from the Cartesian soul we are led further and further back through a series of literary and cultural reminiscences, in which the self becomes fragmented, and finally to a primitive, pre-literary myth that is entirely and reductively impersonal. And a similar effect can be traced to Freud, the other great myth-maker of the age, and one of the influences that makes the poem possible. The effect of the Freudian model of the mind is to dissolve the sense of a stable, unitary self. With different parts of the mind playing different (and conflicting) roles, with different desires and different intentions, the personality comes to seem like a series of archaeological layers. Frazer thinks that we gain a deeper, more complete knowledge of self by seeing modern man in relation to a primitive model. Freud believes

[1] Pound, *Canto* LXXXXI.

that self-knowledge, and hence integration, comes through a reconciliation of the present self with a past self. We re-live the past and hence cease to be prisoners of it.

The symbol of modern man's search for an identity must be his search for a language. Man is above all a language-user, and his linguistic capacities are the condition for all his expressive activities. For language to be liberating it must be language that expresses him in the present and is not a mere reminiscence of the past (for tradition must be acquired by great labour), and it must at the same time restore vital links with the past (the mind of Europe and our own country). The search for a language that shows continuities and yet is living will be at the centre of the search for a whole range of correlates that will allow for wholeness of human expression, and hence for sincerity. This wholeness will be a sense of self-identity, of being in possession of experience. That is why it is of a piece with sincerity, since without this sense of self-identity a self is not full achieved. If the self is to be regarded as in some sense an achievement, then sincerity must also be an achievement. That is why each of the *Quartets* contains a section of meditation on Language. Language here is the type of all forms of expression, forms through which an historical continuity can be realized, or in which fragmentation is most dramatically revealed. It is in such historical continuity that the self is a true universal, not as an abstract idea, but as a form of practical knowledge.

The question of the self arises in *Four Quartets* in another way: we feel that this is very much personal poetry. One recent critic says that the self presented in the poems is 'very much a "case"'. D. W. Harding speaks of the 'pressure of urgent misery and self-disgust' that is controlled in the *terza rima* passage in *Little Gidding* ('In the uncertain hour before morning / Near the ending of interminable night'). We do indeed feel that such emotions are faced and 'controlled' in the poem; no one can doubt their presence, and no one can doubt that the acceptance that comes at the close of *Little Gidding* is at least partly the acceptance of exhaustion. So perhaps the 'pressure of urgent misery and self-disgust' is the personal element in the poem. The future promised by the 'familiar compound ghost' in *Little Gidding* evokes the most inward agonies of an individual:

> First, the cold friction of expiring sense
> Without enchantment, offering no promise
> But bitter tastelessness of shadow fruit
> As body and soul begin to fall asunder.

Second, the conscious impotence of rage
At human folly, and the laceration
Of laughter at what ceases to amuse.
And last, the rending pain of re-enactment
Of all that you have done, and been; the shame
Of motives late revealed, and the awareness
Of things ill done and done to others' harm
Which once you took for exercise of virtue.

The 'rending pain' of the past is an experience of an individual, having that nightmare-like intensity, that suggestion of a guilty secret, that is suggested by the lines in *The Wasteland* about 'That corpse you planted last year in your garden, / 'Has it begun to sprout . . . O keep the dog far hence'. And the voice in the poems is sometimes a ruminating, uncertain one, not entirely unrelated to Prufrock's. The *starting* points of the poems are the strongly personal feelings of regret and remorse; and from these arises the desire to redeem time, the striving for the impersonal, and the attempt to master language. The universal self comes from history, involves an awareness of oneself as persisting through time, of regretting and hoping. But to find the self in history must also mean finding a community with the language of the past. Not every way of discovering the past is adequate or amounts to a sense of community. There is the merely nostalgic, uncreative reminiscence, either in the form of romantic reaction (following an 'antique drum') or of artistic pastiche ('A periphrastic study in a worn-out poetical fashion'). That is why tradition must be discovery: the past must be created out of the present, just as the present is knowable only through being brought into relation with the past. The self which tries merely to re-live the past in its own idioms and with its own sense of itself does not cease to be merely here and now.

In moving from a purely 'personal' experience to explore an ideal version of the experience, *Four Quartets* does not evolve a set of doctrines, or assert belief. Rather it gives the sensory equivalent of certain ideas; any pattern in experience that is suggested is shown by how it is *felt*. The 'sincerity' of the exploration of the poems is a matter of a felt order. In these poems the personal basis is twice the poet's own history, or family history (in *East Coker* and *The Dry Salvages*). In all the poems something impersonal—perhaps a religious tradition, or the recollection of a society that existed in a particular place, but partook of a universal set of beliefs—is set against the personal.

And we can say that this reflects the fundamental concern of the poem: What, finally, gives meaning to the personal, to personal history? And what is the relation between the simply immediate and that which is reflected upon and taken into a larger whole? The poem does not contain an abstract—and in that sense, philosophical—*exploration* of this question, but rather presents the emotional basis upon which it might come to be asked. The 'timeless moment' in *Burnt Norton* for instance is not presented as an intellectual speculation (although it is preceded by lines of rumination—'Time present and time past / Are both perhaps present in time future, / And time future contained in time past'—that *look* like intellectual speculation.) It has an emotional origin, which is the recall of childhood from an adult point of view. The pain of recall is all the more intense in that it is recognized as both impossible and still longed for. It is given in the dream-like image (reminiscent of *Alice in Wonderland*):

> Down the passage which we did not take
> Towards the door we never opened
> Into the rose-garden.

But the longing for what presents itself almost illusionistically as a *present* possibility is immediately turned into something spoken of, recalled and certainly dead:

> My words echo
> Thus in your mind.
> But to what purpose
> Disturbing the dust on a bowl of rose-leaves
> I do not know.

The moment in the rose-garden is thus both present in that it is longed for, and beyond recapture. The past is presented not as an object of speculation, but of regret, and later remorse and guilt.[1]

And the present in the poems is the mechanical, the hurried; it is composed of 'intense' 'rending' 'burning' moments. The present is sometimes expressed as fire (an image taken from Heraclitus, suggesting that the present is constant flux), a fire that burns as well as purifies. Indeed the burning present is, in the Dantean passage in *Little Gidding*, almost a burning embarrassment:

> Then fool's approval stings, and honour stains.
> From wrong to wrong the exasperated spirit

[1] Cf. *The Family Reunion*.

Proceeds, unless restored by that refining fire
Where you must move in measure like a dancer.

The time that might be 'eternally present' is also a time of burning shame, and of the 'agony' which 'abides'.

In his distinguished critique of *Four Quartets* F. R. Leavis suggests that in registering his recoil from mechanistic determinism Eliot denies life's essential creativity. He says also that there is in Eliot a 'lack of courage in the face of life' and that 'the profoundest and completest sincerity, that which characterises the work of the greatest writers, is . . . impossible for him'.[1] Indeed, confidence in the self and the courage and sincerity that might simply be based upon it are precisely the values that are explored and questioned in *Four Quartets*. We see how Dr. Leavis's view has, despite all of Eliot's qualified presentations of the sincere and the courageous, an intuitive plausibility. The concept of eternity that the poems generate often does seem to be something that stands over against life, and that reduces life to 'appetency' and 'metalled ways'. So one might be moved to agree that there is a reduction of 'that which is only living' to something less than human, and that the spiritual and eternal deny the living.

Dr. Leavis is also right to connect 'courage in the face of life' with the completest sincerity. I have already tried to suggest that sincerity and the activity of expression must ultimately be regarded as a kind of achievement, an achievement best described (as the Idealists described it) in terms of a notion of Self. Yet we must also see that the conditions for such achievement, its possibility—and in particular its possibility for modern man—is very much Eliot's preoccupation in the *Quartets*. The poems regularly start with a particular experience or memory—the moment in the garden, childhood memories of the Mississippi–Missouri and the Massachusetts coast—which is then treated as the starting-point for reflection. The reflection does not issue in argument or assertion, but in the finding of abstract analogies—philosophical or religious—for the primary experience. These reflections regularly return to the experiences from which they start, suggesting that meaning may be revealed ('And approach to the meaning restores the experience / In a different form, beyond any meaning / We can assign to happiness.') They give an indication of what an experience might be like were it not *just* an impression, but

[1] *The Living Principle*, p. 189.

rather the experience of an achieved and continuous person. So the childhood moments are both preserved—since they are not different experiences—and at the same time transformed —since they are recognized in reflection as an initial experience of what is intrinsically enduring. Dante's procedure in the *Vita Nuova*—of describing the experience of childhood in terms that are not available to a child—is reaffirmed. That is why we might wish to reject the view that the poems make statements or doctrinal assertions, or express philosophical theories. The meaning of the general statements derives from the original experiences which they transform. 'Sincerity' here means that responsible search for a language that will bring the experience into the experience of a community. It involves the search for an objective self which can possess and give meaning to experience. As Eliot presents the theme, the search for meaning is inseparable from a kind of responsibility—responsibility not in the sense in which Dr. Leavis understands it, but in the sense of a re-creation of private experience in objective form. In particular it involves the re-creation of links with institutions and with a community, and the consequent transformation of experience through the 'sense' of history. This outward movement, from private to public, which is essential if the private is to become fully intelligible, is not only a kind of responsibility, but also, in the *Quartets*, a preparation for love.

If the idea to which the *Quartets* move is Love, it is elicited with the most elaborate indirection. Images of stillness are set against movement (e.g. the centre of the wheel and the rim), suggesting Love as undesiring, and the Unmoved Mover. The notion of Love is dependent upon the rejection and depreciation of desire; and desire is itself reduced to 'movement', and therefore to something mechanical, the appetency of metalled ways, that which is 'only living' and can only die. In this way is developed the set of oppositions, between movement and stillness, desire and Love, the fleeting moment and art (or the 'pattern'), experience and knowledge, time and eternity. There is no doubt that the way the poet builds up the oppositions between desire (and all that that suggests of 'that which is only living') and Love, time and eternity devalues one term as against another. It is clear also that this is his way of reformulating a traditional religious position—the Way of Negation. (And it also enables him, incidentally, to bring together Eastern and Western asceticism to much the same effect as he did in *The Wasteland*. In the notes to that poem he says that 'the collocation of these two representatives of eastern and western asceticism . . . is not an accident'.) To explore Love (as that term is used in the *Quartets*) is to explore fundamental conditions of the self. And the starting-points for this exploration in personal experience—the timeless moments—are of ambiguous significance. They are deceptive, a childlike desire for 'our first world', opposed to reality:

> And the pool was filled with water out of sunlight,
> And the lotus rose quietly, quietly,
> The surface glittered out of the heart of light,
> And they were behind us, reflected in the pool.
> Then a cloud passed and the pool was empty.
> Go, said the bird, for the leaves were full of children,
> Hidden excitedly, containing laughter.
> Go, go, go, said the bird: human kind
> Cannot bear very much reality.

In contrasting Love (which is stillness) with the 'movement' of desire, the poet is approaching an idea that has usually been given a religious significance. Love is always an approach to God, even when what is loved is here and now ('Quick, now, here, now . . .'). Of course, since Eliot does not make any such statement, despite the frequent allusions to Christian tradition (e.g. St. John of the Cross) through which it has been expressed, it is impossible to say that the poems present that or any other Christian thought as *doctrine*. Yet the movement and imagery of the poem is inseparable from religious concepts; and without an understanding of religious concepts, and without an understanding of religion, we may doubt that *Little Gidding* would even be intelligible. The poet is therefore faced with the problem of what religious poetry can be. *Four Quartets* is not devotional verse. Its not being devotional verse means that it does not cultivate interests and attitudes separate from those of the rest of life. To call *Four Quartets* 'religious poetry' is certainly to refer to their radical exploration of experience and of personal value, combined with their taking for granted certain religious doctrines. However, the beliefs themselves are not what is expressed or even explored in the poetry: rather is it the consequences for our sense of human value of holding these beliefs. We are brought back, in fact, to Eliot's stated view that poetry expresses the emotional equivalent of thought, and that belief in poetry is a different thing from belief in philosophy or religion.[1]

[1] 'In truth neither Shakespeare nor Dante did any real thinking—that

The problem of writing a poetry of religious belief is really no different from that of finding the language of one's time. This is, indeed, warranted by Eliot's remark that the poet must express the greatest possible intensity of his time based on whatever his time happens to believe. It is not the beliefs themselves that present the difficulty, but the finding of language that will carry the accent, resonance—what Frege called 'tone' —that surrounds and gives confidence to what may be affirmed. (It is ignorance of that basic truth that has led the Anglican and Roman Churches to the absurd conclusion that particular beliefs themselves are stumbling-blocks for modern man, and to initiate the dissolution of the whole attitude of belief by their philistine debasements of language and liturgy.) This corresponds to what Eliot called 'feeling', and which he distinguishes from 'emotion', regarding it as attached to words, images, and phrases.[1] It is new *feelings* in this sense that the poet discovers when he discovers new language; and a language which can relate the feelings of the present to those of the past is one which enables the modern mind to be also 'the mind of Europe and of our own country'.

In his invocation of the concept of eternity in the *Quartets* Eliot uses the analogy of art:

> Words move, music moves
> Only in time; but that which is only living
> Can only die. Words, after speech, reach
> Into the silence. Only by the form, the pattern,
> Can words or music reach
> The stillness, as a Chinese jar still
> Moves perpetually in its stillness.[2]

But this does not suggest that the 'pattern' art can give to experience, or the pattern language can give is of unambiguous value. 'Words, after speech, reach / Into the silence'. Perhaps this means that although language is the essential means of ordering our feeling, it is accompanied with, reaches out to all those other forms of symbolic human behaviour—including the creation of institutions—that also discipline and render accessible human emotion. Indeed, most human emotion is disciplined by a lived tradition more than by words. The act of speech permanently alters one's vision, one's experience.

was not their job . . . What every poet starts from is his own emotions' ('Shakespeare and the Stoicism of Seneca').

[1] Cf. 'Tradition and the Individual Talent'.

[2] *Burnt Norton* V.

Perhaps also the pattern of words that *have* been spoken ('where prayer has been valid') is something that is *moving*. We are moved by the recollection of the language of others:

And what the dead had no speech for, when living,
They can tell you, being dead: the communication
Of the dead is tongued with fire beyond the language of the living.[1]

Speech can express only the present moment ('Quick, now, here, now, always'); but in choosing words one is choosing to align oneself with, or to reject the words or traditions of others. To choose words is also to choose a relation to something communal, and to the past. It is also to reveal and to create one's own consciousness. So to recapture the language of others is to 'sympathize' with their world. The 'pattern' which enables words or music to reach the stillness is necessarily a pattern 'beyond the end you figured', for it may exhibit relations to the past and the future that are hidden.

The language and images that relate us to a community may, in true symbolist fashion, be unpredictable in their ability to reach into the depths of our feeling.[2] The visit to the country house in Gloucestershire gives an image of time and eternity, adulthood and childhood, regret, love of people whose lives were lived in the past, and who are thought of as invisible parents, or first parents, or simply dignified, benevolent, observing presences:

Quick, said the bird, find them, find them,
Round the corner. Through the first gate,
Into our first world, shall we follow
The deception of the thrush? Into our first world.
There they were, dignified, invisible,
Moving without pressure, over the dead leaves,
In the autumn heat, through the vibrant air,
And the bird called, in response to
The unheard music hidden in the shrubbery,
And the unseen eyebeam crossed, for the roses
Had the look of flowers that are looked at.

[1] *Little Gidding* I.

[2] 'Why, for all of us, out of all that we have seen, heard, felt in a lifetime, do certain images recur charged with emotion, rather than others? . . . an old woman on a German mountain path, six ruffians seen through an open window playing cards at night in a small French railway junction where there was a water mill: such memories may have symbolic value, but of what we cannot tell, for they come to represent the depths into which we cannot peer.'—*The Use of Poetry and the Use of Criticism*, p. 148.

In his criticism of the *Quartets* Dr. Leavis says: 'There is no acceptable religious position that is not a reinforcement of human responsibility.'[1] He takes these lines from *The Dry Salvages*:

But to apprehend
The point of intersection of the timeless
With time, is an occupation for the saint—
No occupation either, but something given
And taken, in a lifetime's death in love,
Ardour and selflessness and self-surrender.

He comments: 'What—"given"—to be passively "taken" he attains to apprehending at "the point of intersection" is the pure otherness postulated in Eliot's conception of the supreme Real.' And he goes on: 'In fact, a conception of pure non-human otherness can hardly be a conception; it can be no more than the ghost of one—a mere postulate. The space cleared for the Other by the elimination of all that "human kind" can recognize as life, value and significance is a vacuum: nothing is left to qualify it.'[2] One understands what Dr. Leavis means by 'human responsibility' and why it makes it impossible for him, in the end, to endorse the 'negative way' of the *Four Quartets*, and therefore its spirituality. One can see the way in which the poems are not a 'reinforcement of human responsibility' if we make a comparison with the Yeats of *Sailing to Byzantium*:

That is no country for old men, The young
In one another's arms, birds in the trees
—Those dying generations—at their song,
The salmon-falls, the mackrel-crowded seas,
Fish, flesh, or fowl, commend all summer long
Whatever is begotten, born and dies.
Caught in that sensual music all neglect
Monuments of unageing intellect.

Yeats expresses a duality between the fleshly and the spiritual, and, later, a sense of fleshly decay that makes an acceptance of the spiritual necessarily the acceptance of something deathly, mechanical: 'such a form as Grecian goldsmiths make / Of hammered gold and gold enamelling / To keep a drowsy Emperor awake'. But although Yeats establishes a complex relationship between the fleshly and the spiritual, he is confident about the basis of each. The contrast is confident and does not involve

[1] Op. cit., p. 236. [2] Op. cit., p. 245.

any exploration that carries him beyond the traditional framework. He accepts the framework in which there is a contrast between the Platonic and anti-Platonic. His disgusted rejection of nature is qualified by the negative way in which he presents the 'artifice of eternity'. The picture of the heart 'sick with desire / And fastened to a dying animal' powerfully suggests what it ought to know, and what it desires—the fish, flesh, and fowl that 'commend all summer long / Whatever is begotten, born and dies'. There is no unqualified rejection of the temporal and living in *Sailing to Byzantium*; and the invocation of eternity manifests an attachment to what is not eternal.

The sexual longing in *Sailing to Byzantium* is unassuaged, an unconsolable longing in age for the youth that would allow such desire to be enjoyed. In the framework of the *Quartets* this sensual music (unlike the music and the dance in these poems) is not a meaning but an hallucination of meaning. Looking back on such a desire one can see no pattern, but can only feel despair because it is *past*. Such a past is present in time future, but only as something external, as the pleasure of another being—a self whom one cannot recapture—and not as a satisfaction of the present self.

The spiritual is in *Four Quartets* set much more starkly and blankly against the living than it is in the Yeats. The intersection of the timeless with time involves a response that is purely passive. The notion of humility, so important in the poems ('humility is endless') itself suggests a stark opposition to something equally blank. We might remember Eliot's use of Coriolanus as a figure of pride in *The Wasteland* and in *Coriolan*—the figure who has

> No interrogation in his eyes
> Or in the hands, quiet over the horse's neck,
> And the eyes watchful, waiting, perceiving, indifferent.

The full extent of the poet's questioning of what might be consoling in human experience is shown in the beautiful passage in *East Coker* where he imagines an actual communal life in the past which is in some sense his own past—East Coker being the village of his English ancestors, one of whom was a figure in the beginning of English prose, a Renaissance pioneer. Here Eliot uses his texts with the utmost subtlety. 'In my beginning is my end' involves the main philosophical and religious texts from Heraclitus and St. John of the Cross; it implies the connection of living with dying; and it suggests the possibility that significance comes from reflection upon 'that which was the beginning'—the past and one's own past. (And it is difficult for the reader not to make the connection also with Eliot's decision to be buried in East Coker, where the monument consists of the first and last lines of the poem meeting in an ellipse.) The whole passage suggests both an attachment to the personal, living world, and an alienation from it:

In that open field
If you do not come too close, if you do not come too close,
On a summer midnight, you can hear the music
Of the weak pipe and the little drum
And see them dancing around the bonfire
The association of man and woman
In daunsinge, signifying matrimonie—
A dignified and commodious sacrament
Two and two, necessarye coniunction,
Holding eache other by the hand or the arm
Which betokeneth concorde.

But the magical invocation of not just a personal but a communal past—'In that open field, if you do not come too close, if you do not come too close, / On a summer midnight . . .' is not to be taken at its face value. The sense of an actual communal past, so movingly evoked, is also a picture of a civilized, articulate sense of *community* as it was understood by a Renaissance man, to whom the 'pattern' was literally in 'the dance', for whom the image of the dance can really stand for a spiritual and religious order which unites the individual with the communal, and the physical with the spiritual—'The association of man and woman / In daunsinge, signifying matrimonie- / A dignified and commodious sacrament.' On one level it is certainly true that the poet betrays the expectations of the reader by dissolving the social and spiritual vision expressed in the words of Sir Thomas Elyot, resolving a social, cultured vision into mere animal activity, thought of as 'only living' and therefore as having only died:

Round and round the fire
Leaping through the flames, or joined in circles,
Rustically solemn or in rustic laughter
Lifting heavy feet in clumsy shoes,
Earth feet, loam feet, lifted in country mirth
Mirth of those long since under earth
Nourishing the corn. Keeping time,
Keeping the rhythm in their dancing

As in their living in the living seasons
The time of seasons and the constellations
The time of milking and the time of harvest
The time of coupling of man and woman
And that of beasts. Feet rising and falling,
Eating and drinking. Dung and death.

The High Renaissance picture of the 'dance' of human society has been resolved into its primitive elements, into movement, then into animality, and finally into dung and death. But on another level this dissolution of the meaning into its ephemeral moment may be said not to reduce the meaning, but rather to elevate the moment. Where people 'move in measure, like a dancer' the refining fire restores. The refining fire is present among them not because the 'only living' is made 'eternal', but because there is an eternal significance in what these 'only living' creatures do. The significance is revealed in the possibility of describing their movements in the dignified words of Sir Thomas Elyot, words which in their associated thought and institutions embody a meaning beyond the moment to which it seems to be reduced. His words are *achieved* because they stand for an order that has been achieved, and one that is there only because men can see the world in terms of it, can impose a significance through its terms, and so find a pattern where there is otherwise only dung and death.

There is something similar in *The Dry Salvages*: the poem begins with the recall of boyhood memories of the Mississippi–Missouri and of Cape Ann, Massachusetts. These remain very much sea and river, but become also symbols for the growth of the poet's consciousness:

His rhythm was present in the nursery bedroom,
In the rank ailanthus of the April dooryard,
In the smell of grapes on the Autumn table,
And the evening circle in the winter gaslight.

As much as Proust Eliot is finding images for 'the pastness of the past and of its presence'. Again there is the subtlety with which he suggests both a consoling memory, a memory that sees one as by nature part of a human community—'Home is where one starts from'[1]—and at the same time suggests something that disturbs and alienates. The presence of the river's rhythm 'in the nursery bedroom' is not at all consoling. And from this sense of the menace of what is pre-human the symbol

[1] *East Coker* V.

of the river is developed. It is what is non-personal in our experience:

> The river is within us, the sea is all about us;
> The sea is the land's edge also, the granite
> Into which it reaches, the beaches where it tosses
> Its hints of an earlier and other creation . . .

The presence of the river in these childhood memories loosens our grip upon them, our sense of personally possessing them. Again something personal dissolves into something inhuman. Childhood is not a point of return, not the 'end'. The poem powerfully challenges any sense we might have that somewhere or some state is 'home' or the 'end'.[1]

Conclusion

I began by saying that to elicit a set of abstract propositions from a poet's work and present them as his beliefs might not yield us insight into his poetry. Yet it may seem that with this exploration of the idea of the self in Eliot's verse, that is exactly what I have done.

However, the philosophical ideas about the self that we have been exploring were themselves the product of something more than purely philosophical speculation. Idealism itself, in all its profound influence over art, literature, and politics, cannot adequately be understood if it is thought of simply as the outcome of certain arguments against the empiricists. The picture of the self that I have (with some looseness) been calling 'Cartesian' can itself be regarded as a denial of 'human responsibility'. The simple, abstract substance in which experiences inhere has no intelligible connection with the self that acts and suffers. 'Cartesianism' elicits no intimate connection between the self as consciousness and the self as Will. It can be seen as expressing and giving a warrant to all those individualist philosophies that separate man from history, from culture, from responsibility for what spiritually and intellectually he is.

The Idealists tried to restore to men a responsibility for their own essence. (Marx also in his early writings, influenced by Hegel, did the same.) Their doctrines can certainly be expressed purely philosophically. Hegel, for instance, posits an ideal of a wholeness of experience that has its roots in Kant's doctrine of the 'transcendental unity of apperception'—a sense of the

[1] Cf. Leavis, op. cit., p. 218.

unity of the self that is also a sense of its unity through time. Time is 'the form of the inner sense'. (In the *Parologisms* of the *Critique of Pure Reason* Kant argues that the unity of the self is the very fact of its *sense* of self-identity. The unity of the self arises from our ability to ascribe states to ourselves, to express in speech our ownership of our experiences.) The unity of the self is not simply a state of affairs that can exist independently of one's awareness of it.

Eliot did not, as a poet, set out to express philosophical doctrines. To explore and make explicit these doctrines is simply one way of coming to understand the enormous effort of intelligence with which he explored modern consciousness. (And indeed Idealism was the first philosophy to uphold the notion of being 'modern' as an ideal, as vital to one's ability to make sense of experience.) Eliot's awareness of the difficulty and at the same time necessity of finding a language that would relate us to the past while giving us a precise sense of our distance from it, is an essential part of his poetic genius. To discover a self is not just to receive impressions, but also to find a language that will relate to past and future, and that will express one's necessary community with and necessary separation from the lives of others. It is to 'urge the mind to aftersight and foresight'.

Eliot wrote finely of Blake's poetry: 'It is merely a peculiar honesty, which, in a world too frightened to be honest, is peculiarly terrifying . . . Nothing that can be called morbid or abnormal or perverse, none of the things which exemplify the sickness of an epoch or a fashion, has this quality; only those things which, by some extraordinary labour of simplification, exhibit the essential sickness or strength of the human soul.'

We cannot confidently say that Eliot himself, or Yeats or any poet of the century has achieved that Blakean impersonality of vision. Yet his positing an ideal which no contemporary poet could achieve is (paradoxically) a further sign of his miraculous sense of the possible and impossible. This great poet showed throughout his career a 'peculiar honesty' in his poetry that is indeed disturbing, and is the outcome of a supreme integrity.

MORTIMER WHEELER ARCHAEOLOGICAL LECTURE

BRITAIN AND JULIUS CAESAR

By CHRISTOPHER HAWKES

Fellow of the Academy

Read 10 December 1975

I AM happy to be speaking in the presence of these lectures' eponymous hero, Sir Mortimer, in the twentieth week of the fifty-first year of our friendship. Here tonight too is Mr. C. E. Stevens, my friend from early schooldays, when he and I delved together in that fat red volume by T. Rice Holmes, *Ancient Britain and the Invasions of Julius Caesar* (1907). Holmes had excessive trust in Caesar's good faith. But he was ample, and averse to textual surgery—more favoured then by others than today. Robust, he was also acute; and for dates, prior to the Julian Calendar, I follow his system—not Le Verrier's, in spite of M. Michel Rambaud, the French Caesarian of today. (The lecture as printed here includes much that in speaking I omitted for brevity, besides rewordings required to accord with my reading during 1976. Of my helpers here to be acknowledged in notes as I go,[1] death has overtaken Derek Allen and C. E. Stevens; and Sir Mortimer's presence to hear me was the last occasion of our seeing one another.)

I. *Prologue: The Ocean, Alps, and Rhine, to 58 B.C.*

Caesar marched to supremacy over the Roman world from the West. From Britain came a little—less indeed than he had

The reference key throughout is the Bibliography, pp. 185–92; I have tried to serve archaeologists equally with classicists.

[1] This Mortimer Wheeler Lecture was the fifth. My debts to acknowledge, in preparing and revising it, are many: to Sir Mortimer himself, to C. E. Stevens, and to D. F. Allen, all running far back; to my wife Sonia Hawkes; and more lately incurred, to Professors Kenneth Jackson, Leo Rivet, and Charles Thomas, and to Michael Avery, James Dyer, John Kent, Michael Mackensen, Daphne Nash, Stuart Rigold, and Warwick Rodwell. Dr. Nash has given me help from the Heberden Coin Room (Ashmolean Museum, Oxford); for photography I thank Robert Wilkins (Institute of Archaeology, Oxford); and for drawing so skilfully the figures and maps from my originals, Marion Cox.

hoped—of the Western wealth that equipped him. Ancient trust in that wealth was old: Carthaginian, Greek, Phoenician, prehistoric. It started from Spain, when men discovered

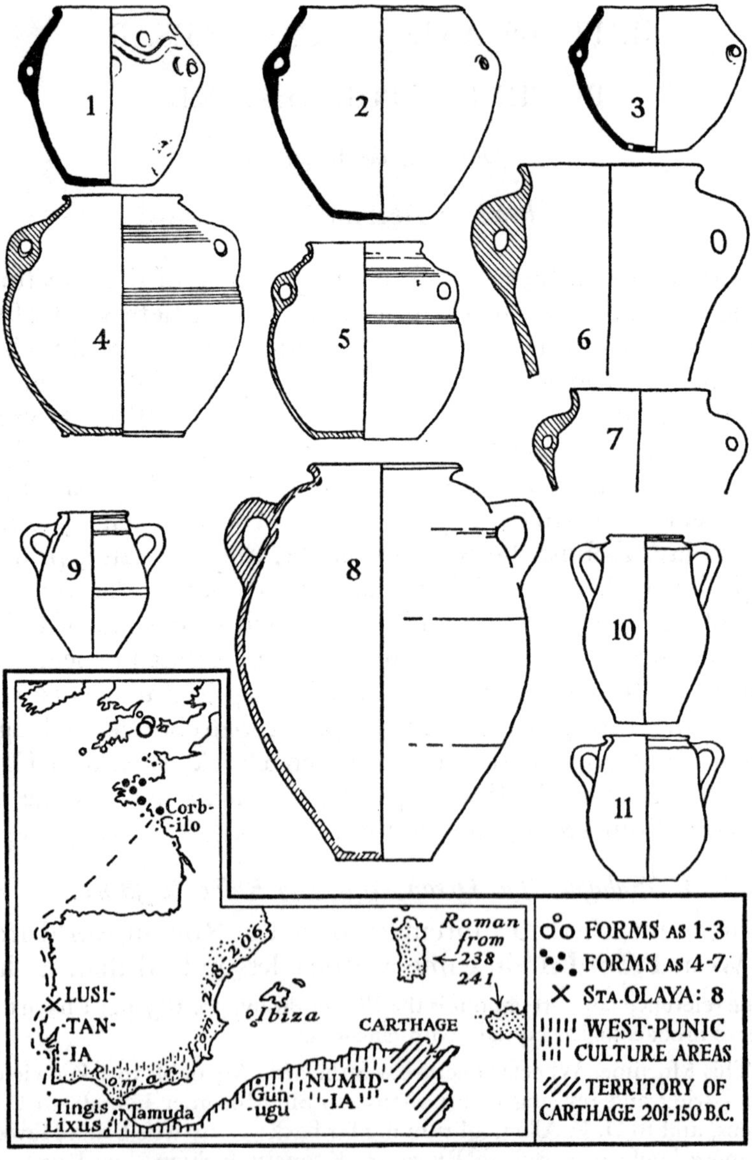

FIG. 1. Countersunk-handled pottery: 1–3, Britain; 4–7, Brittany; 9–11, Carthage

MAP. 1. Rome, Carthage, and coasts to Corbilo and Britain

wealth in metals there; most of them are southern yet recur as north-western too. And tin (for making copper into bronze) is rare, unlike Spain's copper, in the south, but grows in abundance up the Ocean coast to Galicia, drawing traders north, and thence into farther explorations, to Gaul's north-western or Armorican wealth: tin in Brittany, and more then in Britain.[1] So Carthage was drawn; and from the final years of her trading, till the middle second century B.C., there may even be Punic derivation for the pottery with countersunk paired loop handles, adopted in Brittany and thence into south-west

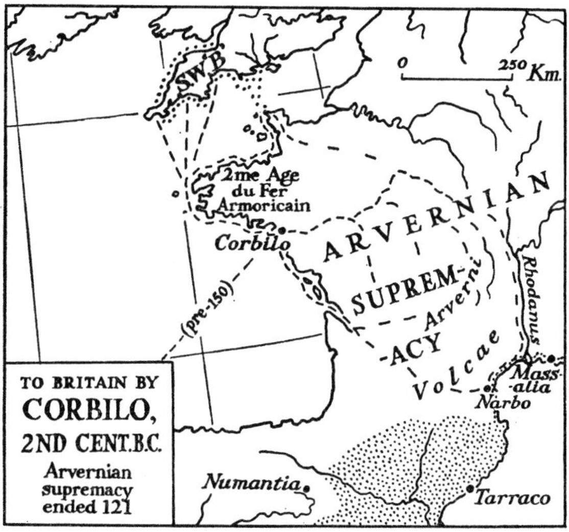

MAP 2. Routes from Greek Massalia to Corbilo and Britain

Britain (fig. 1 and map 1).[2] Transmission would have been by Corbilo, known (on the Loire) since the voyage of Pytheas, the Greek fourth-century explorer who came from Marseilles.[3] That Greek city-state, foe of Carthage and ally of Rome, had routes

[1] Hawkes 1977, map 7, distribution of Western tin-ores.

[2] Two-handled jars, so typically Punic, persisted till the third–second centuries, in simple forms such as spread to Hispanic coastlands: Harden 1962, 150–1, using Cintas, *Céramique punique* (1950). In my fig. 1 with map 1, nos. 9–11 are from Carthage, 8 (painted) from the mouth of the Mondego (Portugal: site of Sta. Olaya, excav. A. dos Santos Rocha, Mus. Figueira da Foz). Sailings to the Loire may be guessed till the tin trade languished after Carthage's fall (middle second century along with death of Massinissa, old king of Numidia, rich (Walsh 1965) and I think placed better for a hand on such traffic). Brittany, so getting the idea of two handles, could apply it in the countersunk form (4–7, grey), whence Britain derived its own, as on sites from Cornwall to Dorset (Maiden Castle, 1–3): Wheeler 1939; 1943, 56, 206–9, 383; Wheeler and Richardson 1953, 100–1, fig. 31; Thomas 1966, 77 with n. 21; start here within second century, Frere 1961, 86–90; this Punic suggestion of mine was not in print till now.

[3] Hawkes 1977, 40–2, 44–5.

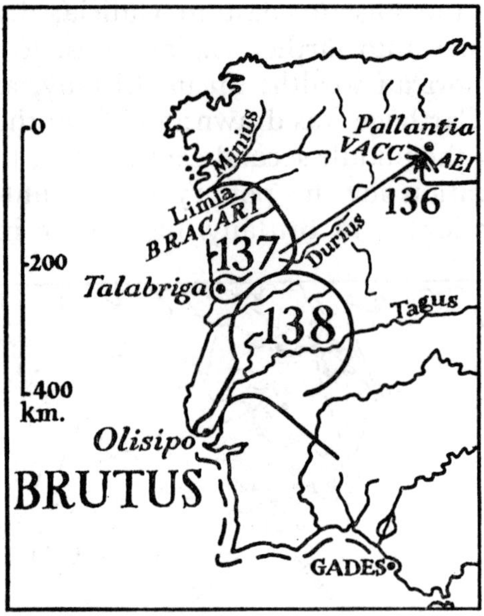

Map 3A. Campaigns of D. Junius Brutus

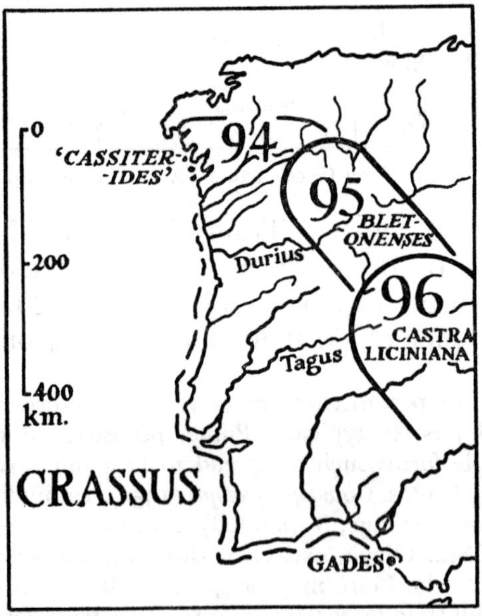

Map 3B. Campaigns of P. Licinius Crassus

by land, avoiding Spain through Gaul, towards Britain and especially for British tin (map 2). But the central-Gaulish Arverni could exert control; and only their defeat, later in the second century when Marseilles brought Rome into Gaul, let the south then prosper as a new Roman province with the old Greek city set within it. Provinces in Spain, at first taken from

Carthage, were two: Hither (with Tarraco) and Farther—opened to the Ocean in 139, when the native resister Viriatus fell[1] and left Rome with the whole south-west. The incoming governor was Decimus Junius Brutus.[2] He advanced to the Douro and beyond: into Galicia (map 3A), whose name Callaecia supplied an additional name for himself, Callaicus. But although he crossed the river Lima and reached the Minho he had to fall back; from the Bracari and coastal Talabriga he was summoned away. No record connects him with the 'Tin Isles' (Cassiterides), fabulous mart for the tin of a far north-west. The frontier down on the Tagus stayed; and only forty years on, crossing higher up, did the consular Publius Licinius Crassus advance, by Salamanca and doubtless Zamora (map 3B), on Galicia from the east.[3] So the 'Tin Isles' coast, of which sailings from the south had at last reported a discovery, had its shallow mines and peaceful men observed by Crassus, who 'sailed across' to them.[4]

[1] Texts in *FHA* iv. 96–135.

[2] Texts in *FHA* iv. 135–40, essentially Appian, *Iberica*, 73–5 (composed about A.D. 145 on these wars, from good ultimate sources). Map 3A for him in 138 and 137, and 136, called off to siege of Pallantia, town of the Vaccaei. Names here in Latin: Minho Minius, Lima Limia, Douro Durius.

[3] Texts in *FHA* iv. 152–3: his base-camp (*castra*) *Liciniana*, Ptol. *Geogr.* ii. 5, 6 (mis-spelt in *Itin. Ant.* 438, 5), was on the middle Guadiana between Toledo and Mérida for 96; 95, he was around Salamanca, for there he forbade the Bletonenses (of Bletisa) to continue appeasing their gods by human sacrifice (Plutarch, *Q.R.* 83; it had just been abolished at Rome with himself as consul, 97: Pliny xxx. 12); 94, from there to a Galicia too far north for Brutus, his route would have to be that from the east by Zamora.

[4] To the men, not islands which in Greek would have the pronoun feminine. Most have read masc. *autous* as though fem. *autas*—including Schulten: *FHA* vi. 89, 301. The account is Strabo (iii) 176, end of chapter that has begun on 175. Crassus can have crossed one of this coast's deep 'rías' or firths, both its sides then of course being equally mainland. The islands along it seem not to have tin, except perhaps a little on Ons. Strabo here will have drawn on Posidonius, who was travelling around in Spain not very much later; but he starts the chapter with the isles of old false conjecture, 'out at sea', ill-suited to what follows and contradicting the chapter's concluding words, 'Iberia and the islands lying off it': writing far away, he failed to perceive the discrepancy. Strabo here finishes on Spain: book iii. As Britain comes in iv, with Gaul, that alone shows his Crassus not Caesar's officer (pp. 133–4, 147–9), who thus cannot visit British tinners in Cornwall (as fancied by too many), or a Scilly archipelago, really mostly formed from a large single island through local submergence later: unknown to Dion 1952, 310, when expounding the contemporary changes on the lowermost Loire; here he should be set beside Hawkes 1977, 1, 23, 26. I owe thanks to Charles Thomas for advising me on Scilly; much of his work on it is in Ashbee 1974.

And he pronounced the sea-voyage free for traders from the south, although it was longer than the crossing to the tin in Britain.

Map 4, with all Spain, shows Gaul and the Channel so crossed. With Marseilles (Massilia in Latin) the traffic now was

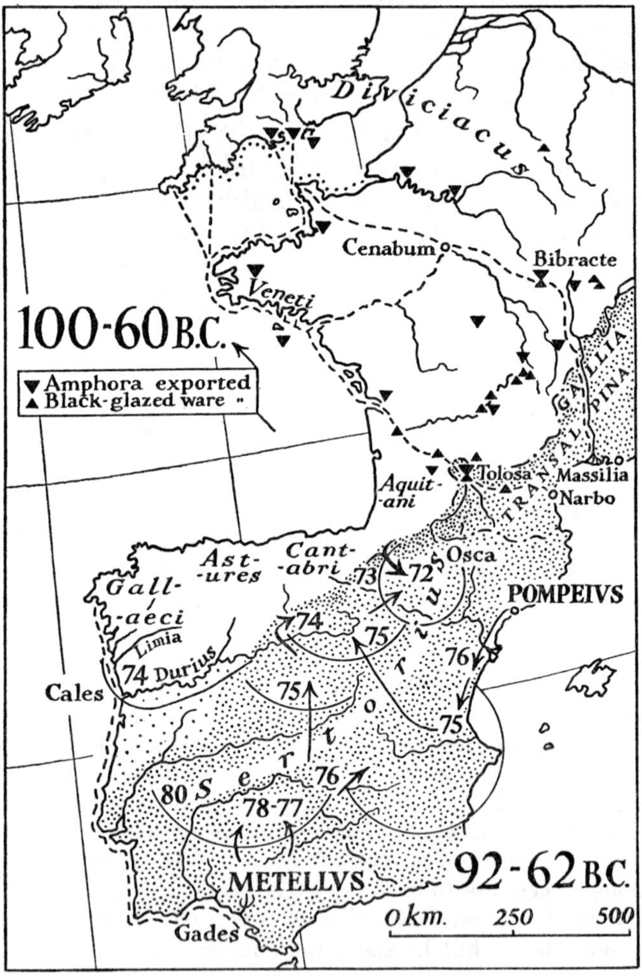

Map 4. Gaul 100–60 B.C. and Spain between Crassus and Caesar

shared by Roman Narbonne (the colony Narbo), and two descriptions were preserved by Diodorus (*c.* 60–40). He took one if not both from Posidonius, it seems (whom Strabo, rather after, used for Crassus); this leader in Greek ethnography himself had been in Spain and Gaul early in the century. Keeping the details here to a note,[1] I shall return to this tin-trade later. Its

[1] Diodorus's accounts are v. 22, 2 and (briefer) 38, 5. In the latter, the

augmenting by the Spanish had as yet no more than begun; and in Spain, after Crassus, there again was war. Rome's new government, from 80, had to wage it with the natives drawn to revolt (map 4) by the dissident Roman leader Sertorius. Galicia's miners could still prefer to be peaceful: Sertorius's man Perperna

tin comes 'out of the Brittanic island', is conveyed to 'Gaul lying directly opposite', and 'through the inland middle of Celtica is carried on horses by the merchants, both to the people of Massalia and the city named Narbo'. Usually the source has been presumed to be Posidonius, who was in Gaul some forty years earlier than D was writing. Corbilo at mouth of the Loire (map 2) is not mentioned: primarily only by Polybius (preceding century); in my opinion (p. 134) it was destroyed, in 104 or 103, by the Teutoni. So the route will indeed have run inland from the coast 'directly opposite', the 'island' being Britain as a whole—or alternatively Wight (p. 145).

The account in 22 was seen formerly as coming from the early third-century Timaeus (thus Holmes 1907, 499–514), because its tin, from Belerion (tip of Cornwall) is shipped at a tidal island there (St. Michael's Mount), Iktis, and Timaeus in a passage known only from Pliny (iv. 104) has tin obtained in an island, frequented by Britons, which his text spells 'Mictis'. Pliny did not think of the Isle of Wight; yet its spelling, in authentic Latin Vectis, means a Celtic name beginning with a W-sound, which Greek spells Ou-. Professor Kenneth Jackson's assuring me that therefore its name cannot ever have been Iktis, so that 'Mictis' ought to be a manuscript error for *Victis or else Greek *Ouiktis (or actually for Vectis or Ouektis), is here acknowledged with my gratitude, as equally in Hawkes 1977, 28–30. It demolishes the false equation Iktis = Vectis (as though English 'ill' could = 'well'), and thus the sole ground for supposing that Timaeus can have here been Diodorus's source.

Timaeus's own source must have been Pytheas (Hawkes 1977, 7, cf. 9), at whose fourth-century date (and after) tin ingots would be those known to Cornish archaeology, not of astragalus form as in D but essentially plano-convex: Tylecote 1966 (some are Roman; post-Roman ones are different again). To call the unique one from Falmouth Harbour off St. Mawes an astragalus, with Aileen Fox (1964, 116, 240), was shown to be impossible by Hencken (1932, 166); its weight of 158 lb. (71·67 kg. approx.) and its narrow yet wide-barred H shape, nearly 0·864 m. long, recall the Mediterranean 'ox-hide' ingots of copper, which are second-millennium. Pytheas's date would be surprising too (though the early first century is not) for the tin's reaching Iktis as D describes, on waggons, and for the merchants' thirty-day pack-horse trail through Gaul 'to the mouth of the Rhone', in which his first account is consistent with his second, quoted above. Both were left aside by Mette when he edited the texts that have a bearing on Pytheas (Mette 1952: in England barely noticed), though including of course the Pliny from Timaeus. If Posidonius were not the source for both D's accounts, despite their measure of agreement, the other would be one of the explorers mentioned by Strabo, (i) 63, as having seen, besides Ireland, Britain and small isles round it. He speaks of them as modern, and again so on Ireland, (ii) 115; none should be prior to 100, so the time of Posidonius should in any case stand.

had to march in arms there, plainly for their metals;[1] so the sea-trade doubtless was serving Metellus, the government commander in the south. He and Pompey, commander in the east, were forcing Sertorius gradually north, to encirclement at Osca by Pompey and then to be murdered there. Four years afterwards, in 68, there arrived in Spain from Rome, as a quaestor in the south, young Gaius Julius Caesar. Seven years more, and he was back (map 5) in Farther Spain, as its governor.

In Rome he had just been praetor, and speaking at the funeral of Julia his aunt, widow of the great and redoubtable Gaius Marius. Marius had served in both Spains; in 114 he had governed the Farther. Caesar, now almost forty, had known him in boyhood; he had learnt, from his glory as a soldier, memorable lessons. Farther Spain still had glory to offer, and wealth. Big debts that he owed in Rome being settled for him there by Marcus Crassus, son of old Publius and also rich from Spain, he squeezed new riches for himself from there—though protecting provincial debtors.[2] His province's Atlantic side, still unruly, he tackled in arms.[3] Over the Tagus, he could quell the Herminian hillmen if he captured their hillforts. But success this way (as Marius had known) took time: his dash on past the Douro was checked by Herminians revolting in his rear. Back then, and driving them down to the coast, he had trouble at an island: tidal—it is now the peninsula Peniche—and for assailants a death-trap. He took it only by combined operations, with ships from Gades (Cadiz): another lesson. Lastly, embarking with his fleet, he sailed up north, to the coast with the 'Tin Isles'; surpassing both Brutus and Crassus, he rounded the cape, to the north-facing bay of La Coruña and took by storm its citadel Brigantium, where such a navy, never seen by any before, struck terror. This late-summer visit to a harbour that could serve for adventuring farther, like Pytheas, who had sailed to

[1] Texts in *FHA* iv. 182 ff., 224–5 ff.: Perperna arrived in winter 77/6; he wintered with Sertorius 75/4 in Lusitania, south of Galicia; by the end of 74 they were forced north to the Ebro, and never gained any initiative again. So 74 is the year for Perperna to lunge into Galicia, taking Cales (at mouth of the Douro) and in action north of it on the Lima (named superstitiously 'river of oblivion'): *FHA* iv, 233, from fragments 43–4 of the *Histories* of Sallust (contemporary of Caesar). His motive, obscure to Schulten, would be gaining more metals, with tin to make bronze, for the sinking Sertorian army.

[2] Texts in *FHA* v. 10–12, 14–15 (Appian, Suetonius, Plutarch, Cicero, etc.).

[3] His whole campaign (ib. 12–13), Dio xxxvii. 52–3.

Armorica and all round Britain, is revealing. North-western Spain itself, he had learnt, would be a conquest lengthy and hard; eastward, it led to the lands in which Sertorius had fallen to Pompey; Pompey was jealous for his own renown in Spain,

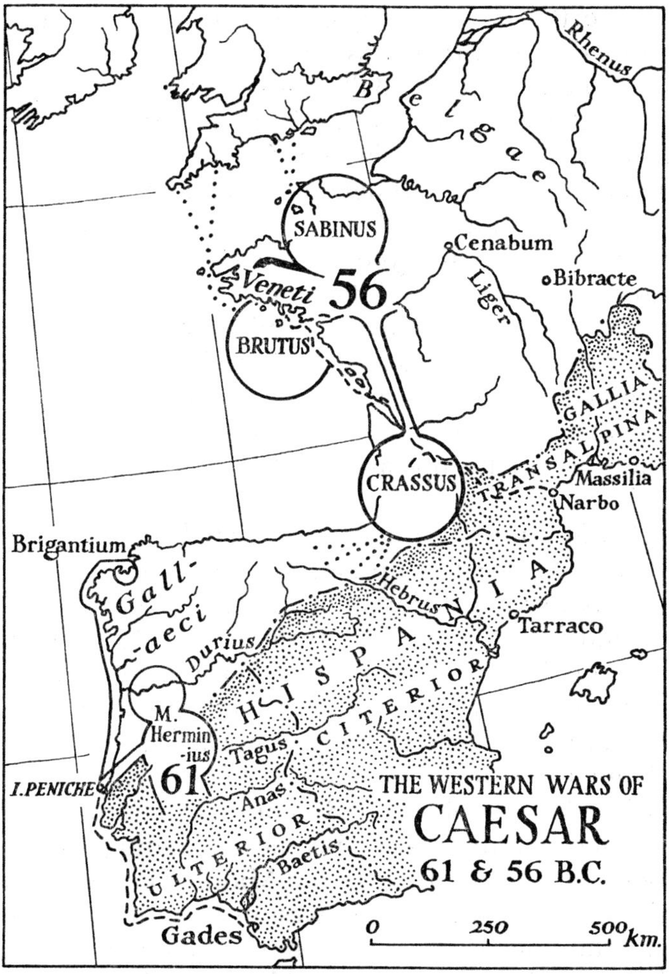

MAP 5. Caesar's theatres of war, 61 and 56 B.C.

and Pompey was important, along with Marcus Crassus, in Caesar's politics. Might he then instead reach Armorica and Britain through Gaul? So he turned back south. Next June he was in Rome once more, soon balked of a triumph but set for his consulship, to be gained through his private supporting by Pompey and Crassus. Three years on from that, through Gaul in arms, he was facing Armorica, and the Veneti who there controlled the crossing to Britain. And his best young officers were Decimus Brutus, of the family of old Callaicus, and a Publius Crassus who was son of his wealthy supporter, and grandson of old Publius Crassus of the 'Tin Isles'.

Yet the Gallic side of the West had its inland part. It was open to Central Europe, where currents from the East met others from the North. The Cimbri, in the late second century, had come from the North: against Bohemia first, which repulsed them, and on toward the Balkans—to return soon after, fight Romans in the Eastern Alps, and proceed to Gaul. With the Teutoni now, they arrived in 109. Celts from the Alpine fore-lands had joined them, Tulingi and others; next year the consul Silanus, rashly opting to advance, was beaten; so was Cassius in 107, by the Tigurini (though they then went home); the bigger force of 104 met total disaster; Spain was assailed, much of Gaul overrun—and, I fancy, Corbilo destroyed. Only Marius —reformer of the army—saved Italy and Rome. The invaders' destruction in 102 and 101 was never forgotten. So Caesar knew that Italy and the West must be guarded from dangers on their inland sides. Inner Europe and the North lay there behind; and also the East.

The Pontic king Mithradates, known best for his reign in Asia Minor, his Aegean irruption, Armenian alliance, and defeat in 66 by Pompey, had dominions north of the Black Sea too (map 6); and from these in his last three years, to 63, he planned a thrust through Europe into Italy.[1] With his death, the threat very soon took a further form. Within the Carpathian Ring, between the Pontus and Danube, was Dacia; Mithradates will have planned his thrust in political accord with it. Its king, young when he was old, was Burebista. Archaeology shows—besides much commerce—its people expanding to west, and Celts there having to retreat to the Middle Danube.[2] Burebista had only to cross, and push on west overrunning Pannonia, to endanger Italy next by the Alps and Adriatic. The Pannonian lands between, however, were held by the Celtic Boii. From their Hercynian home (Bohemia), they had formed now a big

[1] No one aware of the ambience shown by East-European archaeology, on its Pontic side from long before Mithradates, can think his design as far-fetched as have many historians.

[2] The trade, Glodariu 1976 (in English): conclusions 97–102. The advance (though with Daicoviciu H. 1965, 1972): Zirra 1973, esp. 806–19, using his 1971a and b and for this century especially c; Benadik 1971; behind all are Filip 1956, and Daicoviciu C. 1945 (though position since then much altered). Burebista's reign, at conclusion of Berciu 1967, is equated there with an archaeological horizon very well marked.

Middle-Danube realm, conjoined with Taurisci, and ruled by a king Critasirus. Burebista, more probably in 60 than any time later, smashed it in a battle.[1] Till then, they were masters in Central Europe and a danger to Italy themselves. If invading it now, they could thus forestall any Dacian invasion from the east; and to tempt them were former Boian lands now Roman, the

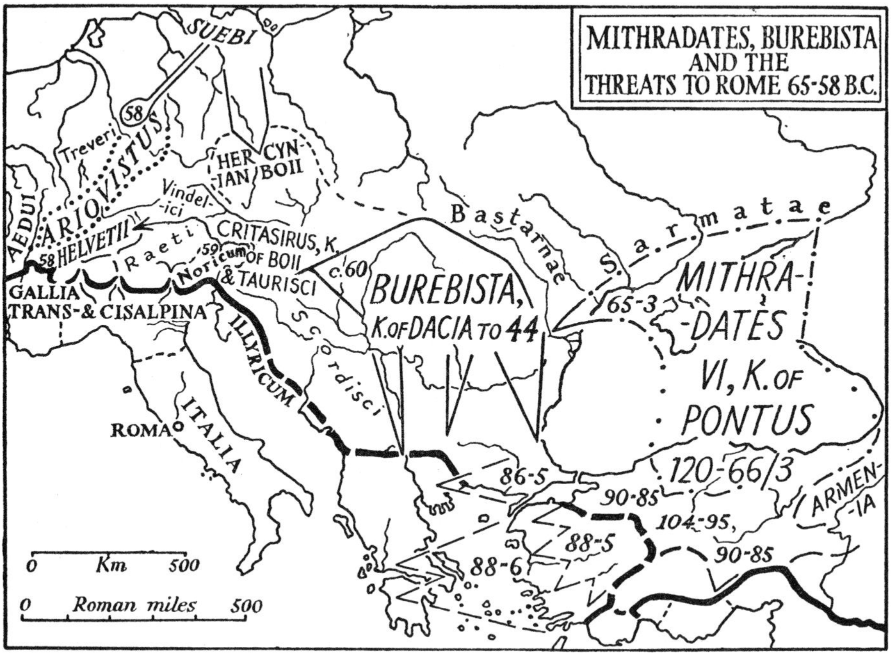

Map 6. Threats to the West, 65–58 B.C.

lands round Bologna. If Burebista hit them later, as is still believed by some[2] (after his harrying the Black Sea coast and Macedonia),[3] this would be a Boian threat; if he hit them in 60, the threat was himself. A threat in 59, through the Eastern Alps, was being felt then in any case at Rome.

[1] Strabo (vii) 298, 303–4, 313, 315, with (v) 213; (vii) 292, the resulting 'desert of the Boii' adjoins a lake, which (though there confused with L. Constance) is clearly Pannonian, and the same (Neusiedler See) as the 'lacus Peiso' that is placed by Pliny, iii. 146, beside this 'desert', with Norici as (westerly) neighbours.

[2] Strabo as n. 1 and (xvi) 762; Suetonius 44. 3; Gelzer 1969, 322 with n. 6; see n. 3.

[3] Gelzer as n. 2; and 87 with his n. 1 on the date, citing *PWRE* (1959) and E. Swoboda's *Carnuntum* (ed. now for citing is 1964). Two views on it stand in contrast (for that of Mócsy see p. 138, n. 5); Hungarians and Germans have mostly preferred the 'late'—upheld Sept. 1976 by Professor

Caesar was consul; and was given by the People, in the Law of Vatinius the tribune, two provinces for nearly five years: Cisalpine Gaul—North Italy—and Illyricum, adjoining it beside the Adriatic and the Eastern Alps. Adjoining both, within those Alps, was the kingdom of Noricum: equally at risk from beyond, it was friendly to Romans. A pact with Noricum also now was made, with a royal marriage, by the formidable Ariovistus, over on the Rhine.[1] His tribes, with the name Germani, had territories formerly all on its east; his crossing it to Gaul, to side with a grouping of powerful peoples there, led in 60 (at Magetobriga)[2] to his beating opponent peoples, whose leaders—the Aedui—had long been friends of Rome. Yet now, in 59 with Caesar as consul, she bestowed her coveted friendship on Ariovistus.[3] He prized its prestige, Rome wanted him appeased; but his Norican commitment and the Illyrican for Caesar, effecting a triple deterrent, could avert the threat from farther east, whose-ever this was. Of unknown leanings are only the Vindelici, in modern Bavaria. And at this point, Boii—whether recouping or forestalling Burebista's onset from the east—invaded Noricum in force: it was a mass migration.[4] But they failed. And he did nothing. So the threat dissolved.[5] Ariovistus now could be treated

A. Nagy (Debrecen) at the Nice international congress, against my doubting. Czechoslovaks and Romanians, however, and some Germans, favour the 'early', dating the battle towards or no later than 60; see also p. 138 n. 5 for Alföldy 1974. For date 'about 60', Filip 1962, 74 (with behind him his 1956) claims support from recent research in Hungary itself, besides Romania; '60' is the date in Neustupný 1961, 161; from Romanian discussions (Macrea 1956; Pippidi 1965, 266–87; Vulpe 1968, 27–31) '60' comes as the latest possible in Daicoviciu C. 1969, 21–2. The disjunction explains my attitude here, but the 'early' is still what I prefer: see p. 136 n. 5 and n. 3 on the Boii who in 58 joined the Helvetii (p. 138).

[1] *BG* i. 53–4: the king in Noricum, Voccio, sends him his sister, to marry (in bigamy) after his going into Gaul. For his going there not before 61 or 60, see text below with n. 5 and pp. 137 n. 1, 138 n. 1. Voccio's inscribed coinage will cover that time.

[2] *BG* i. 31, 12; 44, 3. Name-form and date, Holmes 1911, 554–5; location somewhere in eastern Gaul, but unknown.

[3] *BG* i. 40, 2; 43, 4, 8; 44, 5.

[4] *BG* i. 5, 4.

[5] Gelzer 1969, 87, threat from Burebista 'sooner or later'; but see here above, p. 135 with nn. 1–3, and below p. 138 with n. 5 on the Boii: their invasion of Noricum has to be 59, and their fighting force was leading a mass migration. The Helvetii to whom they recoiled are in Caesar set apart from Ariovistus; *BG* i shows vividly his art of disjunctive concealment (Stevens 1952b; Rambaud 1953, 1966). Ariovistus, now his foe but only the year before his friend, was an embarrassment needing this art to carry him over; it was from non-Caesarian sources, never coming through to us

as the western danger that he always had been. South Gaul, the Transalpine Province, went to Caesar (from 1 January) for 58, with a legion which (then) his Cisalpine three, and any more he might raise, would reinforce. Thus in arms, as in

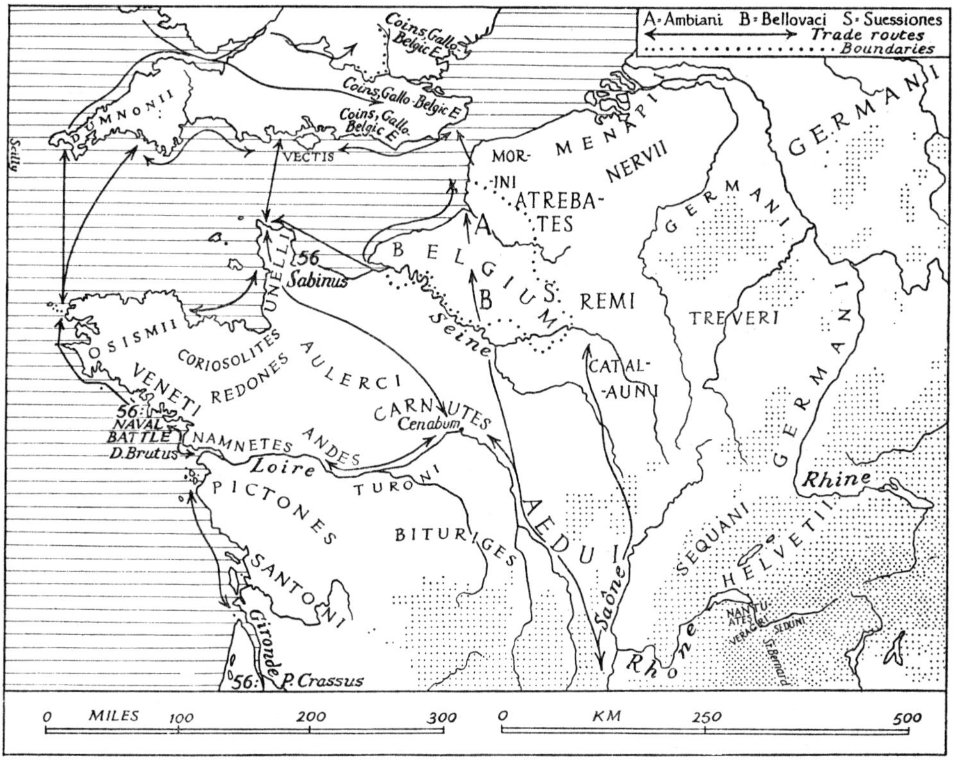

MAP 7. Gaul and the Channel shores, 58–57–56 B.C. A = Ambiani, B = Bellovaci, S = Suessiones. The Jura divides Helvetii from Sequani

diplomacy till now, he could uphold his determined protection of the West.

Ariovistus was beyond the mountain chain of the Jura (map 7). Within it, holding the forelands of the Alps in Switzerland, were the Helvetii, with a High Rhine frontier on the north where they faced Germani. I believe that Ariovistus himself had previously forced them back to it, from the older one farther north, on the Main, from which Tacitus mentions their retreat.[1] To Caesar in 58 he boasted of fourteen years in the field, and

directly, that the Boii and Burebista were known to Strabo, sixty years on; little as it is, what he tells us has clues we can follow. See next Part II.

[1] Tacitus, *Germania*, 28, 2; cf. Ptolemy, *Geogr.* ii. 11, 6.

most of those years should be prior to his entering Gaul.[1] There was warfare on the High Rhine still,[2] and within it they were cramped; here were their tribes who had fought against Rome with the Teutoni.[3] Their famous plan of migration,[4] not now on to Roman soil but to the west, was moved by their noble Orgetorix in 61 to serve his ambitions, yet after their exposure and his consequent death it was persisted in. By early 58 they had been joined by neighbours and by Boii: those who had invaded Noricum and failed, last year, and were not going home.[5] Caesar broke them all, and sent most of the survivors

[1] *BG* i. 36, 7. Thus the position of Ariovistus's people the Nemetes, at vi. 25, 2 (in the 'German excursus'), is beside the Helvetii and the Raurici round Basel, where the Black Forest (head of the 'Hercynian') flanks the Rhine. Their stretching out over it to upper Alsace was thus part of his movement into Gaul. The Rhine peoples' list at iv. 10, 3 has Nemetes in the two chief second-class manuscripts (where the better have Nantuates in error: see p. 146 with n. 5) placed next to the Helvetii, therefore on the High Rhine; it turns then north down the Rhine till it reaches the Triboci, who again were one of the peoples of Ariovistus. The river's flowing 'through' them should suggest their being stretched out over it: about Mainz and Worms (so it seems) where next they were followed by his Vangiones, they themselves moving south to the region of Speier. On all these three see p. 140 with n. 3. For iv. 10 see Rambaud 1967, 66–9, against the doubting of the chapter by Klotz and Fuchs, from von Göler and Meusel (who persuaded even Holmes: 1911, 455–6, 481–2, 692–3 nn. 2–3). The idea that A crossed the Rhine at the *start* of his fourteen years is an error.

[2] Warfare *BG* i. 1, 4; 40, 7; frontier location 1, 5 and 2, 3.

[3] Notably the Tigurini (p. 134), whose victory over Cassius is recalled *BG* i. 7, 4; 12, 4–5; 13, 2.

[4] *BG* i. 2 ff.

[5] Why not? and where had been home? 'Beyond the Rhine', *BG* i. 5, 4, is unhelpfully obvious. Filip has them fleeing (1962, 74) out of Pannonia after the smashing by Burebista: for this as in 60 at latest, see notes 1 and 3 to p. 135. Filip reinforces his belief in it from *BG* i. 29, 1–2: when Caesar has broken the Helvetic migration that they joined after failing in Noricum—having fruitlessly assailed Noreia there, i. 5, 4—the peoples numbered in the Greek-written list that he finds (one-quarter being warriors) are 368,000 in total, 32,000 being Boii. Stevens 1952b, 168, takes 157,000 as the total recorded by Livy (from his excerptor the early fourth-century Orosius, *Hist. adv. Paganos* vi. 7, 5); this is greatly the likelier truth, so the Boii can be not quite 14,000. But any such very large host with non-combatant majority (females, old men, and boys were listed apart) means a mass migration: p. 136 n. 5. Thus an exit from Pannonia is to that extent more probable, and therefore the 'early' date for the Dacian assault on it. So Alföldy 1974, 39–41, 45, 50 and 295 (notes): at the Magdalensburg in Carinthia, to be accepted as Noreia, excavation shows damage to the *murus gallicus* defence-wall, close before the middle of the century, so assignable to Boian assault in 59. Mócsy 1974, 18, propounding a date between 56 and 50, inferred

back. But their intended destination on the Atlantic coast of Gaul, in the land of the Santoni around the Charente, was not so perilously near the Roman Province as he pretends.[1] What he skilfully hides is that out of the Province that way, along the Garonne, where a native ruler quite lately had been named Rome's friend,[2] ran the trade-route linking Roman Narbonne with the Ocean, at the Gironde estuary's mouth, of which the Santoni held one side (map 7): no place for a greedy Helvetic intrusion. They had sea-going ships; so also had the Pictones[3] who stretched to the Loire; the Veneti beyond (as I have said) held the sea-way to Britain. So the Helvetic migration's story has a British connection; and Caesar will have known.

As for Ariovistus, the group that had brought him in arms into Gaul had as its strongest power the Arverni (p. 128 with map 2): they could threaten all routes between south and north, the chief of which passed through the Aedui. These in 61 had appealed to the Senate in Rome. As its reply, Transalpine governors were told to defend them and Rome's other friends, where there might be advantage to Rome; yet it added no teeth.[4] But Caesar had the teeth, and after the Helvetii he had them for Ariovistus; he bit and on the next day crushed him

from Burebista's not having conquered the Dardani in Serbia till after 57 (he wants both offensives near together: see his map, fig. 5), has no reason, 17, for the Boian assault on Noreia. Nor has Swoboda 1964, 230–2 (cited also by Gelzer: my n. 3 p. 135), unless by supposing a confusion with the Cimbri, at latest in 113. Even the 'late' date, surely, would be better than that. If preferring it still, and guessing these Boii as migrating from a home in Bohemia, one could see them as in Noricum to clear the way into Italy; but this is a further guess, and I would rather follow Filip. Clearest, in any case, is Roman awareness of an Eastern-Alps threat in 59; it dissolved, whose-ever it was, but it still is what I think should explain (despite n. 1 below) the award of friendship to Ariovistus, not any slackening of Caesar's care for the West.

[1] *BG* i. 10, 1–2. For Stevens, 1952b, 168, 172, the plan of migrating here was a fabrication; if so, the false destination was adroitly chosen. This whole account by Stevens of book i, with Helvetii, Aedui, Sequani and Ariovistus, should be read beside mine; in 1974 he told me that he held to it. It makes the matter Gaulish entirely, and omits any elements from Central Europe. It perhaps could be adapted to include them, but I need not attempt this.

[2] Mentioned by Caesar in a different context, not till 52. He was Ollovico, father of Teutomatus of the Nitiobriges (region of Agen) and implied to have been his predecessor as their king, *BG* vii. 31, 5.

[3] These ships come also in a different context only, iii. 11, 5: p. 147 n. 1 (147–8).

[4] *BG* i. 31, 9 with vi. 12, 5, their envoy disappointed. Terms of the decree and its date, i. 35, 4.

in battle (September 58), somewhere in upper Alsace not far from the Rhine. The king fled over, in a boat, and very few others; those left on the bank were slaughtered by Caesar's cavalry.[1] As this was only the mounted part of his auxiliaries, and the men in his legions—six—were fewer than the enemy's, other fugitives, left unslaughtered, will have formed a fair proportion of the total.[2] So Caesar has barely concealed what is anyhow obvious, that defeated Germani were left on the Rhine's left bank. Vangiones, Nemetes, and Triboci henceforward remained there.[3] The line of the Helvetii and these, then, held it from the Alps to the Middle Rhineland; and it suited a political decision that he made a year after. This was to extend the name 'Germani' to denote all east-bank peoples, whether Celts though differing from Gaul's, as were these, or folk between Celts and the North, or distinct and genuine Northerners, notably the Suebi. Ariovistus indeed had made a marriage alliance with those, before he left home;[4] and a hundred septs of them marched to his aid against Caesar. Not many can have sped (though Sedusii might) to the battle, as the main mass heard of

[1] *BG* i. 53, 1–3.

[2] Holmes 1911, 653 from *BG* i. 51, i; 654–5 with 240–1, on the list of migrants, Helvetic and the rest, cited here, p. 138 n. 5.

[3] Gelzer 1969, 112, declaring this, has behind him Mommsen, *Röm. Geschichte* iii (1889) 257–8, transl. *History of Rome*, v (1894), 48–9; with his citations (n. 4: Pliny, Tacitus, Ptolemy) for their all being there hereafter, archaeology agrees. Basic, for the Mains-Worms region, is Behrens 1923. See n. 1 on p. 138 on Triboci in the list *BG* iv. 10, 3; if in Caesar this comes from Posidonius and so does Strabo (iv) 193, where they had moved into west-bank lands of the Mediomatrici, their taking that region should be prior to Ariovistus; but their replacing by Vangiones there, and moving to upper Alsace, should anyhow belong to his movement, like the Nemetes' arrival round Speier (same note). What he twice was told by Caesar was intolerable, i. 35, 3 and 43, 9, was that the masses he brought across the Rhine should be increased still further. That he might not be able to send home any crossed already, is expressly acknowledged by Caesar at 43, 9; these two passages were those that Mommsen relied on (Holmes 1911, 455–6, quite wrongly disapproving). Upper Alsace had belonged (iv. 10, 3 shows it) to the peoples who had brought him into Gaul, the Sequani (map 7: i. 31, 10); his demand for more of their lands was to admit the Harudes—people from the North, to be noticed here directly below. Till his defeat, he could expect to go on like that, as the Aeduan noble says in i. 31, 11; after it, there was only the room that was held by the three Rhine peoples, who themselves would be threatened if any more multitudes came. So Mommsen rightly saw them as entrusted by Caesar with the frontier's guardianship. Only from the Middle Rhine northward had he trouble any further: they guarded the rest.

[4] *BG* i. 53, 4; cf. p. 136 with n. 1.

it when still far away, and went home;[1] but other true Northerners already were at hand, the Harudes. News of these Northern accessions struck Caesar with dismay.[2] His swift advance and victory saved the situation. He was right to see thenceforward that from over the Rhine, Northerners would make the worst potential danger. But his giving them the name 'Germani' cannot make Ariovistus a Northerner, nor any of his three tribes left along the Rhine's west bank.[3] Their king had led them to defeat, and then saved his own skin; Caesar, after the blood-letting, left them to keep 'Germani' out—on a long stretch of his frontier guarding the West. How his first *Gallic War* book simplifies and dissembles the competing threats to it, by deceits that some still fail to apprehend, is a prime illustration of his cunning. On the Channel and again in Britain, we must watch for more of it.[4]

II. *Britain over the Channel, 57–56 B.C.*

Caesar's frontier had now to be stretched still farther, to reach the Ocean (map 7). He had secure communications with his Province through the lands of the Aedui; he wintered his army in those of the Sequani, farther outside it still.[5] Between him

[1] *BG* i. 37, 3, they have reached the Middle Rhine (opposite the Treveri), whence they retreat soon for home, i. 54, 1. Yet Ariovistus's order of battle, i. 51, 2, has a unit of Suebi; and of Sedusii (Northerners, named nowhere else in *BG*). Unit-size not being stated, neither need be large; Triboci, Vangiones, and Nemetes must be main units. Its Harudes call for no doubt (text and note 2). Its 'Marcomanni' after these, which cannot be genuine, as this was a group not formed till the time of Augustus, can be a later gloss on Harudes by someone who thought it was their up-to-date name. The historical Marcomanni, an emigrant group coming down from the North, were essentially Suebic but might have included some Harudes.

[2] *BG* i. 31, 10 (see p. 140 n. 3); 37, 2–5 ('vehementer commotus').

[3] This abridges, of necessity curtly, what I first read in Stümpel 1932: still the best presentation of the case that I know, although the boldest. For Caesar's soon calling peoples 'Germani' who were neither German Northerners nor Celts, but anyhow were east of the Rhine, see Hachmann, 1962; though close to my position, going further was hardly his concern there. It is not contradicted by Caesar when at i. 40, 5, in his speech to his officers, he calls Ariovistus's host 'that enemy' whom Marius had met when he beat the Cimbri and Teutoni (and whose prisoners joined the slave-revolt in Italy, 73): those forces were mixed; so was this one; and he goes on next to call it (40, 7) 'the same' as had fought the Helvetii, which really was of SW. Germany's Germani (p. 137 with n. 1). A pep-talk speech by Caesar can afford such liberties. Space fails me for more about Germani.

[4] Stevens on this: 1952a and b.

[5] *BG* i. 54, 2.

and the Ocean were the peoples called Belgae. His advance among them, spring 57, brought him first to the Remi,[1] whose ambassadors, senior nobles, brought him their friendship. In the past, they explained, Germani had crossed the Rhine to settle hereabouts; mostly descended from these, they were now reckoned Belgae. They enumerated all the peoples so called, extending on the west to the Channel; it becomes clear later that the country this way was distinctively and separably Belgic, so that Caesar on three occasions calls it 'Belgium'.[2] Where the name of Belgae now prevailed farther east, the Germanic settlers of old had been merged in its unity. For distinction from Ariovistus's, 'A-Germani', and the Northerners, *Deutschgermanen* or 'D-Germani', we may call those settlers 'B-Germani', as merged by now in the Belgae. The ambassadors also named others 'who are called Germani *uno nomine*' (besides their particular tribe-names),[3] north of the Ardennes. These joined the Belgae now against Caesar politically;[4] being on the Belgic side of the Rhine, so Germani *Cisrhenani*,[5] we may call them 'C-Germani' to set them apart from 'B' and from 'A'; all were differentiated Celts (unlike the 'D').

Caesar, through getting his Remic friends attacked by the patriot Belgae, took excuse for subduing these tribes, and the C-Germani, each in turn. Their league against him, formed in the winter before for their common defence,[6] under Galba the king of the powerful Suessiones (round Soissons, map 7), can initially explain the gold uniface coins (blank obverse), plentiful in Britain, as dispatched there in hopes of a purchase of British support[7]. The sovereignty of Galba's precursor Diviciacus had

[1] *BG* ii. 4, 1 ff.

[2] *BG* v. 12, 2; 24, 3 (despite some manuscripts' 'Belgis'); 25, 4; less clear location only by Hirtius in viii. 46, 4, 7; 49, 1; 54, 4 (with 5). See Hawkes 1968, 6–9 with maps, correcting Hawkes (and Dunning) 1931, 240–3, after Hachmann 1962, 46–8 with n. 69. So thought Holmes already 1911, 395–7.

[3] *BG* ii. 4, 10.

[4] *BG* ii. 3, 4.

[5] *BG* vi. 2, 3. They will have included the peoples who later emerge as Tungri, whence Tacitus on the name: *Germania*, 2, 5. Archaeology, latest: De Laet 1974, ch. 11, esp. 515–18, 519–30.

[6] *BG* ii. 1, 1 ff. (in 1 citing i. 1, 1–2); ii. 5, 4–11, 6, Caesar contrives the attack on the Remi and reverses it; deals then with tribes in turn, ii. 12 ff.

[7] Allen (1961, 113–16 and 1962) ascribed these, his Gallo-Belgic E group of coins, to an invasion, in approximately 60, spread from Essex inland, from Kent into Surrey, and westwards in coastal Sussex, where they would oust Armorican coins and also his prior Gallo-Belgic D group, letting this and a retreat from Surrey explain the ensuing new coinage in Dorset; summary, Hawkes 1968, 11–12 with fig. 3 map E (some also on eastern

reached to Britain—though today less probably reflected in coins than I thought some years ago.[1] But Caesar defeated Galba, storming his fortress of Noviodunum—an action

coast). Yet Allen's phrase 'major surge of invaders or refugees' (1961, para. 59) hardly suits his admission that the coins (para. 58) 'had remarkably little lasting effect here'. Scheers 1972, 6 says only 'émigrations', and does so in concluding her article's new demonstration (1–6) that these E coins—uniface, as also the Sussex Xc (Allen para. 53) came here from the Ambiani (region of Amiens): later than C, which were also theirs (n. 1 below), as were A in the century before (p. 144 n. 5; the succession, her 1969b), and dated, by quality, weight, and certain hoards, to the attempted Belgic stand against Caesar. They are the Ambianic portion of a simultaneous chain of issues, by Belgic tribes and Treveri, belonging accordingly to winter 58–57: cf. *BG* ii. 1–4 and my p. 142. Britain, next summer, was the refuge of vanquished chiefs (14, 2: Bellovaci, the Ambiani surrendering next, 15, 2); but as Caesar noted quiet British aid to the Gauls that year (as in 56: on just these years as implied in iv. 20, 1, see Rambaud 1967, 100–1, beside Collingwood 1936, 32, n. 1), these coins in Britain mean missions to obtain that aid, and only secondly emigrating refugees. Combined, the two will explain their distribution much better than would forcible invasion, which I took too readily from Allen: he admitted refugees but with invaders first. Hence Mackensen 1974, 26 (with 45 n. 120 on Dorset), referring further to Scheers 1973; next has come her 1975; and all have prompted my repentance in the text, encouraged by Dr. John Kent's having presented, to the Society of Antiquaries November 1976, his own reassessment of the coinages in general, embodying this point with numerous others. See further: next note; p. 144 n. 5; p. 164 n. 2; p. 165 n. 1; p. 177 n. 2; p. 184 n. 1.

[1] Hawkes 1968, 12–13, on Allen's coin-group Gallo-Belgic C, and his series of insular groups, to British K from British A which most closely resembles it (11, fig. 3, map C), must now be held excessively rash, and for two good reasons. Gallo-Belgic C cannot be made Suessionic, any more than Atrebatic as was once supposed. It is a coinage of the Ambiani (Scheers 1969b; 1970, 142; 1973 i, 6 ff. and ii. 388 ff., with iv, figs. 100–5), and not commencing till the years just after 70, which must anyhow be thought too late for Diviciacus. His hegemony stretching to Britain (*BG* ii. 4, 7) need not—as Suessionic coins themselves are later than 70—have involved any community of coinages at all: Scheers 1970b (on their coins altogether), 153; and on the looseness of such 'hegemonies' (high-kingships) Nash 1975. Secondly (Mackensen 1974, 45 n. 110, using Scheers 1970b, 155; 1973, ii. 388–9, 441–2), the main southern-insular versions, British A1–A2, B1–B2, form a series which not only stretches off into the west (where B2 awaits location beside B1), but becomes so much later as it goes that it extends into the 50s. None the less, Gallo-Belgic C must still be the primary prototype of all, and its proving to be Ambianic cannot impair this sign of its prestige; its distribution here (Mackensen 11, Abb. 1) is densest in Kent around the Medway, and the prestige could accordingly stem from a seizure of power there, soon after 70, by forces with impulsion from the Ambiani of Amiens. See p. 165, with n. 1 (these coins) and p. 164 n. 2 (those of potin here; dates overlapping).

illumined by Mortimer Wheeler's explaining the nature of its earthworks[1]—and advanced against the Bellovaci (region of Beauvais). These, well inside the distinctively Belgic 'Belgium' (again map 7), had long had a friendship with Rome's old allies the Aedui;[2] their opposing Caesar now had brought him to provoke them with an Aeduan force.[3] Yet on his own approach they surrendered, leaving the Aedui expecting gain from them, but the irreconcileables in angry retreat to Britain.[4] Thus Britain's south-eastern quarter, linked with these Belgic peoples opposite, was left in Caesar's mind as potentially troublesome.[5]

[1] In Wheeler and Richardson 1957, 12, accepting it as l'Oppidum de Pommiers (Aisne), an example of their 'Fécamp' type of wide-ditched massive defence, 8–12 with fig. 2; description of Pommiers and refs. by Mrs. M. A. Cotton, 129–30 in course of gazetteer 126–32; Fécamp (le Camp du Canada) excavations 1939, 62–75; le Châtellier, Duclair, 75–83 (both now dépt. Seine-Maritime).

[2] *BG* ii. 14, 2.

[3] *BG* ii. 5, 2–3; 10, 5; 14, 1.

[4] *BG* ii. 14, 2–3, 4–5; surrender on Caesar's approach, ii. 13.

[5] *BG* iv. 20, 1. On the evidently earlier invaders of Britain's 'maritime part' out of 'Belgium', see pp. 168–70, with nn. Mentioned not in Caesar's narrative but only in his 'British excursus', v. 12–14, and there without dates, they need them from archaeology, supported perhaps, in part, by appropriate coin-groups. Forms of weapon, other metalwork and ornament, adopted or adapted in Britain out of Gaul, start afresh in La Tène II times, second century B.C.: Hawkes 1968, 13–14. In distribution, indeed, these are far from being 'maritime' strictly, and are scattered both west and north from the south-east corner; yet 'maritime' in the excursus need not signify the same as in the narrative, being contrasted with *interiores* mostly non-agricultural and skin-clad (14, 2), claiming to be native (12, 1), and only credible if mainly in the Highland Zone. Thus 'maritime part' will perhaps just be loosely the Lowland, extending farther than the narrative's 'maritime states' (11, 8).

As the signs of La Tène II influence do so extend, they may perhaps be a clue for tracing the invaders. And if some, not all, used coins (as ought to be expected in the second century), such coins (beginning within it) are to hand: in the first place, Gallo-Belgic A. Scheers has now shown that these are of the Ambiani (inside 'Belgium'): her 1968; more fully 1969a, confirming her date (like Allen's) for their start at about 150, and explaining their arrival by invasion (in successive instalments). For Gallo-Belgic B, brought from elsewhere on the coast into a Lower Thames enclave, see her 1970a: dating these from rather nearer towards 100 (again like Allen), she explains them by what she here calls 'émigration'. With Rodwell 1976 independently concurring, and Allen 1961–2 on both groups now expanded yet essentially confirmed, my linking them with some of our La Tène II features is upheld. Brought from Gaul and in A's case circulating long, they mean ascendancy, and never any mass displacements. The La Tène II features are likewise drawn into older British metalwork traditions, and are evinced indeed partly in the furnished inhumations introducing this custom from abroad, but

His next year's aim, however, was not that end of the Channel, but the other. Here was the Armorican Gaul to which I already have drawn attention; it was the western and a northern part of the country of the peoples 'beside the sea' (*Aremoricae*):[1] Brittany round to the Loire, and the Cotentin where dwelt the Unelli (map 7). The Veneti, controlling traffic with Britain as I said, were now its chief power; like the Osismii of Finistère, they had a land with metals—and of Britain's, plainly, they drew upon the trade in tin.[2] Of this I have spoken already in regard to the record supplied by Diodorus: p. 130, to which my note (prolonged p. 131) gives the background now for the subject. If the two Diodorus accounts mean two chief routes for the crossing of the Channel, the longer which names Belerion, in Cornwall, should be over to the harbours of the Veneti; the shorter, which names 'the Brettanic island' only, but the Gaulish end as 'lying directly opposite', should be over to north Armorica straight from a British south-coastal *entrepôt*, such as would serve for trade with the British south-east, not only for the traffic with Gaul, and doubtless at different times could be locally varied. We can believe that Pytheas was told of such a mart on Vectis, the Isle of Wight (same note). One at Lulworth Cove, to be guarded by the Bindon Hill dyke, protective though unfinished, might have been tried from the Cotentin, by those who had the coves along its north-west tip, together, all guarded by the Hague-Dick, of Late Bronze date.[3] And on our coast

often still in river-depositions, our traditional rite. Just as those features stretch in space beyond the coins, so in time they need not strictly be held confined to the coins' own dates. But in the Ambiani who along with them did bring coins, our Gallo-Belgic A, we now have forerunners of those who brought C (p. 143 with n. 1). So a quite long background lay behind Caesar's disquiets over Belgic Britons. And its mention in his British excursus was to suit him further, as we soon shall see.

[1] Thus Armorica (Western) above, pp. 127, 133. *Aremoricae civitates*: *BG* v. 53, 6; vii. 75, 4 (enumerated by name); viii. 31, 4, 'in the farthest confines of Gaul adjoining the Ocean'. In iii. 34 their appellation is translated, as *maritimae*.

[2] Above, p. 127 with nn. 1–2 and maps 1–2; from Corbilo, mentioned no longer now and I think destroyed by the Teutoni (p. 134), the trade will have passed to Venetic control already by the time of P. Crassus the elder (pp. 129–30 with map 4).

[3] Bindon Hill linear earthwork, Wheeler 1953; pottery not later than an early moment in the Iron Age. For La Hague-Dick (crossing the neck at the tip that runs to Cape de la Hague), the dating was got by radiocarbon from Swedish excavations in its rampart; I hope to write on it further on another occasion.

between those two, strong evidence attests one at Hengistbury Head, in precisely the time of the trade that we know from Diodorus. Just west of Vectis (map 7), shielding Christchurch Harbour, and protected by great double dykes across its landward neck, it has yielded from harbour-side sites many pieces of Italian amphoras for wine; Dr. Peacock has dated them, from near to 100 till the years around 50 B.C.[1]

His Gaulish distribution for such, from the Province in the south, furthermore shows trade routes: one leads northward through the Aedui up among the Belgae, one from round Narbo to near the Gironde and the Atlantic; there are wreck-finds off the Morbihan coast, and fragments from the excavations, Wheeler's and Leslie Murray Threipland's, in Brittany forts.[2] This is just the route, meeting sea beside the Santoni (p. 139), that Caesar had determined to keep well away from the Helvetii. And while Narbo appears in Diodorus as one of the terminals for British tin, the other was of course Massilia, the trade's old mistress. The *Gallic War* twice shows care for Narbo;[3] Massilia it never even names. Small wonder then that in autumn 57, while preparing 56 for Armorica, Caesar tried to by-pass Massilia[4] with a shorter route to Italy than any by the Western Alps: over the Great St. Bernard pass (map 7). Beyond the Nantuates (on the south of Lake Geneva and the lowermost Alpine Rhône)[5] the pass was blocked by Veragri, allied with Seduni from higher on the river; they fought his task force hard, but the Seduni at least were repulsed, and the Veragri left with

[1] Hengistbury excavations (1911–12), Bushe-Fox 1915, with all the pottery-associations; amphoras, Peacock 1971, 171–4, fig. 37 Hengistbury specimens, fig. 36 distribution-map with Gaul; chronology (Dressel types 1A and start of 1B) 162–6; bibliography 185 ff.; British sites from Cornwall to I. of Wight, 180–2, now most notably augmented by finds from Winchester.

[2] Morbihan wreck-finds, Peacock 185, citing André; in forts, Wheeler and Richardson 1957, 33–6, figs. 5–6, nos. 43, 77, 79, from le Camp d'Arthus, Huelgoat (Finistère), and 80–1, fig. 21, nos. 24–5, 30, from le Châtellier, Duclair (now Seine-Maritime).

[3] *BG* iii. 20, 2; vii. 7, 2.

[4] As pointed out by Rambaud 1965, 3, 9.

[5] Nantuates here, Holmes 1911, 453–5, quite rightly (though initial N restored by editors). At iv. 10, three good manuscripts put them on the Rhine, where a less good pair have correctly Nemetes: p. 138 n. 1. That short chapter 10, thought spurious by Germans, has some other geographical errors, but Rambaud 1967, 66–8, follows Constans in judging it suited to its context, though taken by Caesar from a note that his dossiers had got from some Greek geographer. An addition (10, 1) about the Maas has been interpolated later. Nantuates instead of Nemetes, however, will rather be the

the pass are not heard of again.[1] His other preparations were effected in the west itself.

Armorica' wealth, in the metals long exploited—gold, copper, iron, lead, and the tin of the trade with the south—had behind it in Britain so much for augmenting the trade's available resources, that Venetic and Massilian profits were alike best served from the British supply.[2] Caesar had recoiled from the Spanish; and now, in the fresh deal he aimed at with Pompey and Crassus, Spain would go as one of the prizes for requiting Pompey's support for himself, in getting his existing proconsular command prolonged. Protection of the West seemed assured along the Rhine's whole length; thus a deep impression had been made by his Belgic campaign. He wintered some of his legions close to the scenes of it, which must mean south and south-west of them down the Seine, and some between it and the middle and lower Loire; both the locations were to serve for Armorica next.[3] As a western prelude to this, he had sent one legion on a march among its peoples, through Normandy, past the Unelli and touching the Veneti and Osismii, under young Publius Crassus (p. 134), to assure him of their total submission.[4] Gaul as a whole, he declared, was therewith pacified; its still unvisited centre would be soon surrounded.[5] Next spring, while sending an officer Sabinus to grasp the Armorican north, Caesar would take the Venetic navy, and add to it further ships: a fleet for Decimus Brutus (p. 134). The year would give him all the coast of the Ocean from Seine to Gironde: not simply for

note's mistake, amended later in some but not in all good copies, after Caesar himself had carelessly overlooked it. His way with his notes, very seldom so careless, will be illustrated soon from Britain.

1 *BG* iii. 1–7, 1.

2 Armorican metal resources, Briard 1965, 15–25 (three maps). South-West British, Fox A. 1964, 21–4 (map of copper and tin lodes). And her 116, 131, 240: tetradrachm of silver, issued 93–2 by the quaestor Aesillas (Macedonia) found near another, of Alexander the Great (after 326, so could be time of Pytheas), both near native fort in S. Devon, *Antiq. Journal*, xxx (1950), 152–4 (Holne Chase, metalliferous area); also 116 (and Allen 1961, 121, 281), from Paul, near Penzance and close to coast of Belerion area, hoard of forty-three Cisalpine silver drachms imitating Massilian, minted (approx.) late second century B.C. The natives, unlike the Armoricans, refrained from issuing coinage themselves; these finds should mean cross-Channel sailings to Devon and Cornwall from long before Caesar.

3 *BG* ii. 35, with Rambaud 1965, 125–8; historical setting, 1–5 with map 1.

4 *BG* ii. 34 with Rambaud 123–5 and 1–5.

5 *BG* ii. 35, 1 with Rambaud 8–10 and map 2, for the campaigns of 56 (143 ff.).

surrounding interior Gaul but as base for getting quickly to Britain. Meanwhile, back in Italy and witnessing Illyricum as quiet,[1] he could proceed with the politics of gaining his prolonged command. Wooing first Crassus, then Pompey, he brought them to Lucca to confer with him in private. A share-out of power was agreed upon, for years to come. He would ensure for the two, by sending in troops out of Gaul to sway the election, fresh consulships in 55 which would let them fix his tenure of his provinces, and tenures elsewhere for themselves: not even discussable till 1 March 50 so allowing no successors till he passed, from 49, into his own fresh consulship, promised for 48.[2] For clinching his assurances at Lucca to his partners, everything now depended on Gaul, and on Britain in hand at latest in 55.[3] But already when there—early spring 56 (their calendar's middle April was today's late March)—he knew, through his Crassus in Gaul, that the tribes of Armorica were out in revolt. For months they had been seeing just what his ambitions would lose them. They revolted against his design upon their ships for Britain—though his book never says so. Non-Caesarian accounts, here most succinctly summarized by

[1] *BG* ii. 35, 2; iii. 1, 1 and 7, 1; here no more about either, as Caesar has concealed the entire chronology, from now until the following May, for reasons of his own. See Stevens 1952a, 9–11; Rambaud 1965, 143–51; the naval preparations, iii. 9, 1–2, must have been ordained so 'swiftly' in autumn 57 already, for they could not be swiftly finished for Brutus to take command next spring. They gave him (11, 5) not only warships built on the Loire (9, 1) but Gallic ships commandeered from 'pacified regions': two farther south but the remainder not specified, and guessed by Stevens (11–12) as on the Channel facing Britain—commandeered, originally, then, for the right-wing army in a double invasion, with the left in the ships of the Veneti and southerly neighbours. I agree that 56 would be the year for it if Caesar had his mainland bases secure enough, but (with Rambaud) have taken this proviso as allowing 55 to be a likelier alternative.

[2] With my text, offering essence of Gelzer 1969, 119–25, I would rather (G at 122 is too chilly) set Cuff 1958. Share-out of provinces: Stevens 1953, 18–19.

[3] For there even were sceptics who declared that no Britain existed: Plutarch 23. 2, well cited by Stevens (1953, 21 n. 1, with also Dio xxxix. 50, 3), scenting Livy behind, and behind the fourth-century Eutropius, *Breviarium* vi. 17, Britons ignorant even of the name of Romans till Caesar arrived. Writers prior to Caesar on Britain were Greek; they will not have filled Roman readers all with trust in what Pytheas had claimed, but Greek Polybius had scorned, large isles in the Ocean (cf. Hawkes 1977, 40). Caesar, whose reading of Greeks (*BG* vi. 24, 2) included Eratosthenes, a chief upholder of Pytheas, of course knew better; but to validate Britain he had got to invade it himself.

Strabo,[1] must be seen to have declined his own story and recorded the truth. As outstanding interpreter here, our debt is to Stevens.[2] While the natives' forts inland could be reduced, by Sabinus in the north and in the west by Caesar, their coast's cliff-castles made a problem that could only be resolved by operations on the water.[3] His warships now built, and Gallic ships from farther south—the Pictones and Santoni I noticed before (p. 139)—made him a fleet, under Decimus Brutus, for a naval battle (maps 5 and 7). The enemy fleet, in that battle, was totally destroyed.[4] But this was the Armorican fleet he had relied on for transporting his army to Britain.

All his long-nursed project was therefore in ruins. Fierce vengeance on prisoners could not help—and of course there were survivors. Young Crassus he had sent to Aquitania, past the Garonne; he did extremely well,[5] and his were the troops that went to Rome to get his father and Pompey made consuls.[6] When the father went on to his chosen tenure of Syria, the son went too—both going to their deaths, in 53.[7] Pompey took the

1 iv. 4, 1 = (iv) 194.

2 Stevens 1947, 4; 1952a, 8–16. He was praised rather faintly by Wheeler (Wheeler and Richardson 1957, 17–18, where for Crassus see my p. 129 n. 4 and for 'Diodorus Siculus' read Strabo), and rather under-used by Rambaud (1965, 13, 144–74; 1966, 421–2), probably less because too clever than too ambitious: in projecting for Caesar a full-length conquest of Britain, and of Ireland as well, to be approved as essential for a Gaul meanwhile being steadied for provincial status (by the 'ten legati' of Stevens 13–14, n. 7: citations from Cicero). But is ambitiousness ever out of place when the subject is Caesar? And where else, if he had pacified Gaul in 57, would he go?

3 Armorican hillforts, Wheeler and Richardson 1957, 1–4, 19; gazetteer 102 ff.; reduction 56 B.C. declared from excavations 1938: le Camp d'Arthus, Huelgoat (Finistère), 23–38; le Camp du Chatellier at Le Petit Celland (Manche), 38–54, presumably by Sabinus; in Finistère see also 54–61, Kercaradec at Penhars. Cliff-castles, 4–8; Morbihan, trial excavations 1939, (Murray) Threipland 1944, 128–49, on Ile de Groix and Belle-Isle and at Vieux-Passage, Plouhinec. These I name for Wheeler's and his colleagues' sake; French activity has long had its own renewal: see the *NAA* (*Notices d'Archéologie Armoricaine*) in every year's *Annales de Bretagne*, and most recently P.-R. Giot in Duval (ed.) 1973, 595–607.

4 *BG* iii. 12–16. On 16 with Caesar's claim to have blotted out the Veneti, by slaughter and enslavement, see Rambaud 1965, 172–3, citing Merlat in *NAA* 1954, 167–9: the claim is hyperbolic, but his crediting fugitives to Britain can no longer have archaeological support in the form adduced by Wheeler (Frere 1961, 86–90: phase dated from '56' must have begun no later than second century).

5 *BG* iii. 11, 3; 20–7.

6 Dio xxxix. 31, 2; Gelzer 1969, 127 with notes.

7 In battle with the Parthians at Carrhae (Haran), 53.

Spains; though he governed them by legates, from Rome, his controlling Spanish wealth must have sharpened the pangs in the breast of Caesar. He had staked so much upon Gaul and Britain that he now was in extremely sore straits. He never could appear to be failing. He must make a fresh plan, holding Gaul, to get to Britain besides: as soon as he could manage it when once the new year had assured him, by the law that his partners would carry, his prolonged command.[1] He would have to go back to Belgic Gaul, and to Britain's more troublesome corner. The south-west, although the Armoricans had called on it for aid,[2] was inaccessible now. He would have to invade the south-east. And opposite this were two Belgic peoples, Morini and Menapii, never subdued in 57. Autumn was coming, but he marched right across to them and straight into action, braving the weather.[3] He did everything he could in the time. All yet would be well.

III. *Britain invaded by Caesar, 55 and 54 B.C.*

55 B.C.

Britain, for all to be well, must give him safe access, swift advance, and somehow a prospect of profitable wealth. Access risks in the Straits should be minimal; advance could be speeded through action by cavalry; as for the wealth (other than in slaves), though its chief known source was the tin that now seemed so remote, yet clearly Britain must have widespread markets and routes of its own, like Gaul's, some stretching far enough east for him to lay his hands on. What Armorica had been taking could only have been part of the output; and although he had ruined its western traffic, the northern may still have been in business, as coins of the Coriosolites and some

[1] The Law of Pompeius and Licinius (Crassus); passed between January and April 55, say many, as Gelzer 1969, 128; also Rambaud 1967, 1–10, at 2–4 countering Stevens 1953, who yet might be right in his retarding its date till Caesar had been into Britain. And the troops that had swayed the elections at the start of January (p. 149) were with Publius Crassus, so only need march from Aquitania: 1965, 8, map 2. Rambaud's belief ibid. 9, n. 1, in a Crassus cruise to Britain just before (my p. 129 n. 4) seems implicitly retracted in his 1967, 4–5.

[2] *BG* iii. 9, 9; response not vouched for, but implied in iv. 20, 1, Rambaud 1967, 100–1. For the Cornish cliff-castles just like the Armorican, and cordoned pottery Armorican in style or derivation of around this time, showing more than just trade relations, see Fox A. 1964, 122 with pls. 67–8; 127–8 with pl. 74; Thomas 1966, 75–92.

[3] *BG* iii. 28.

of the Hengistbury amphoras allow.[1] Victories in south-east Britain should assure him much; and trouble through its fugitives from Gaul should be amenable to remedy. What was not so safe was his base, too near (map 7) to the Lower Rhine frontier. The Middle Rhine's Treveri indeed seemed quiet. But the 'C-Germani' on their north-west side were being reached by an intrusion over the Lower: Usipetes and Tencteri had crossed, being driven from their homes by aggressions of the Suebi. Britain then had to be postponed. Caesar's first fight with the intruders led to their massacre; to his bridging the Rhine, at news of which the Suebi retired; then to dealings with others; he could only return to north Gaul when already it was August.[2]

He writes as if only then did he settle, though so late, on even venturing to Britain: a look at the coasts and country would be helpful; also Gauls had been receiving British help. No one seeks to go there, he says, but merchants; and personal inquiry, from a round-up he made of them, showed they knew nothing of the country unless just opposite, nor of harbours to shelter a fleet on the coasts they did know. He therefore sent an officer he trusted, Volusenus, in a fast-rowing warship, to explore. The ship was back, after more than four days, about a week before the start. By that time Caesar, with his Tenth and Seventh legions, had arrived at the place where the crossing would be shortest; this was the beach of Wissant, rather east of Cape Gris Nez. Assembling Belgic ships there, and last year's fleet that had defeated the Armoricans, he was ready—when a number of British states sent envoys, promising submission. He sent these amicably home, and with an influential envoy of his own:

[1] Amphoras: Peacock 1971, 162–4, Dressel type 1, forms A and B (fig. 35, 1 and 2); 165–6, 1A until middle first century B.C., 1B from slightly before that; 173 (with 174, fig. 37), Hengistbury mostly 1A, but the few 1B could run past 56. (Perhaps hardly past 52: see below, p. 178.) Coriosolites coins in Britain, Allen 1961, list (to date) 272–3, mainly south-coastal Devon-Sussex so with Hengistbury central; Allen 1962, map 7, adding Jersey. Michael Avery, with cross-Channel routes as Avery 1973, 536–42, 551, map fig. 11, allows me to refer to his unpublished Oxford thesis of 1971, in which this slight prolongation of the traffic implied by the coins was first proposed.

[2] *BG* iv. 1–19; Holmes 1911, 95–100, 689–724; Rambaud 1967, 10, 39–99. The August date, with all dating for Caesar's invasion of Britain in 55, is independent of the Roman calendar, and taken from his note of full moon, on a night soon after he had landed, which modern astronomy has fixed—at 3.33 a.m. on 31 August: Holmes 1907, 600–3; 706–7. See further n. 1 on p. 153. Standard accounts since Holmes of both expeditions, 55 and 54: Collingwood 1936, 32–53; Frere (1967) 1974, 42–54; Bayly 1962 should be set beside both, with Colvin 1959, 1963: my p. 154 n. 1.

Commius, a Belgic noble of the Atrebates (region of Arras), whom after their subjection in 57 he had made their king. Through dispatching him thus to Kent, he hoped for a bridge-head of friendly power: any move against this would give him grounds for hitting back (as at the Belgic onset on the Remi), in the terms of the Senate's decree (p. 139) for the defence of Rome's friends in Gaul. His preparations, as all these doings make plain, had been started well before his camping at Wissant. Commius would get picked up by Caesar already when returning from the Rhine, and passing his capital, the Oppidum d'Étrun near Arras; Volusenus's start, not specified by Caesar, was on 10 August, and probably from Boulogne.[1] Lastly, the eighteen cargo-ships for the cavalry, at Ambleteuse (fig. 2), an *ulterior portus* ('lower down' the coast), became wind-bound there, so the cavalry was sent to them, while Caesar, unwilling to wait, was able to set sail. The first wind they presently got soon changed to a second which drove them up the Straits, till blown by a third into Sangatte (*superior portus*). Trying again, a new first wind let them nearly reach Caesar, but a second blew a gale. It swept them past; some made Ambleteuse, but others were borne towards Sussex, and thence were lucky in regaining the Continent anywhere. Fig. 2 shows both of the attempts, from Rambaud who explains the rotation, due to shifting depressions, of winds that could be stormier then than now.[2] First by this, then, Caesar's plans were spoilt. He would now (apart from a troop of thirty taken across by Commius) have to do without cavalry altogether.

[1] Between the Canche (too marshy) and Ambleteuse on which see text with n. 2. Rambaud 1967, 103, suggests the Somme, altogether farther south, but only perhaps through his taking him to Beachy Head, 106; for my own account of his voyage, see text and map 9. On Caesar's preparations in sum, as presented *BG* iv. 20–2, I follow Rambaud gladly in general, 1967, 10–12, 15–16, 100–12, and in particular firmly on Wissant as the main fleet's starting-point (11 and 104), against Holmes who (with Jullian) chose Boulogne: 1907, 306, 552–95, and has been followed by all who have not seen that this 'shortest crossing' (iv. 21, 3) is contrasted by Caesar with the 'most convenient', from Boulogne which he adopted next year: namely Portus Itius, v. 2, 3 (with my n. 1 on p. 157). To Dover from Boulogne is 49 km., from Wissant 35. And on the ports that the cavalry transports used see next note.

[2] Rambaud 1967, 11–12, 108–11 with map 2, 126–8; tides and meteorology 1966, 423; *BG* iv. 22, 4; 23, 1; 26, 5; 28, 1–3. Holmes (n. 1), insufficiently briefed on the meteorology, got 'inferior' and 'superior portus' interchanged: on the Latin, see Rambaud (but his 1966, 422 besides, on the view of R. Dion).

He and the infantry, expecting no such thing and putting out from Wissant by night, next morning (27 August)[1] had arrived off Dover. The painter of pl. XXI, *c.* 1690, would be anchored at the self-same spot,[2] where he waited for his legions and regarded the Dover scene, as Volusenus had already. Of what he

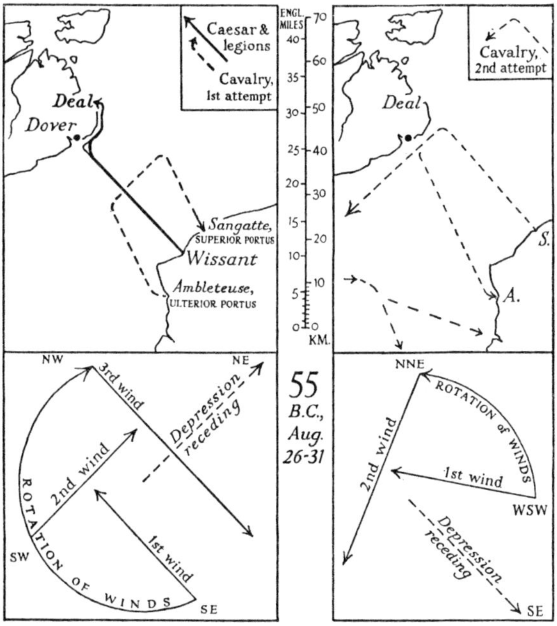

FIG. 2. 55 B.C.: crossing of the Straits and landing; cavalry's misfortunes. Diagrams and sketch-maps after Rambaud 1967.

did then expect, he says nothing: it was surely a boat, coming forward to meet him, with friendly Britons from Commius to welcome him ashore.[3] None came. Up there on the cliff, where the painting has Dover Castle, looking much as today, was the big British hillfort that has left its chalk rampart—though eroded

[1] *BG* iv. 23, 1: the third watch of the night, when he started to put out, began at midnight, the small hours of the day that Holmes thought probably 26 August but perhaps 27th (1907, 603), which I follow Rambaud in preferring (1965, 126, 128, 16); the full moon of night 30–1 (n. 2, p. 151) followed his 4th day in the island, iv. 28, 1 with 29, 1.

[2] Wheeler 1930, 41 for this painting, his pl. IX (in the Mowll collection, Dover); the claim for the spot for Caesar here is my own: *BG* iv. 23, 2–5; 6, he takes the fleet to Deal (as text here ensuing).

[3] The natural harbour usable by Britons began to be Romanized some 150 years later: Rigold 1970, with plan fig. 1 opp. p. 89; on his evidence, Rivet 1974, 63, suggests it as the 'New Haven' of Ptolemy ii. 3, 3.

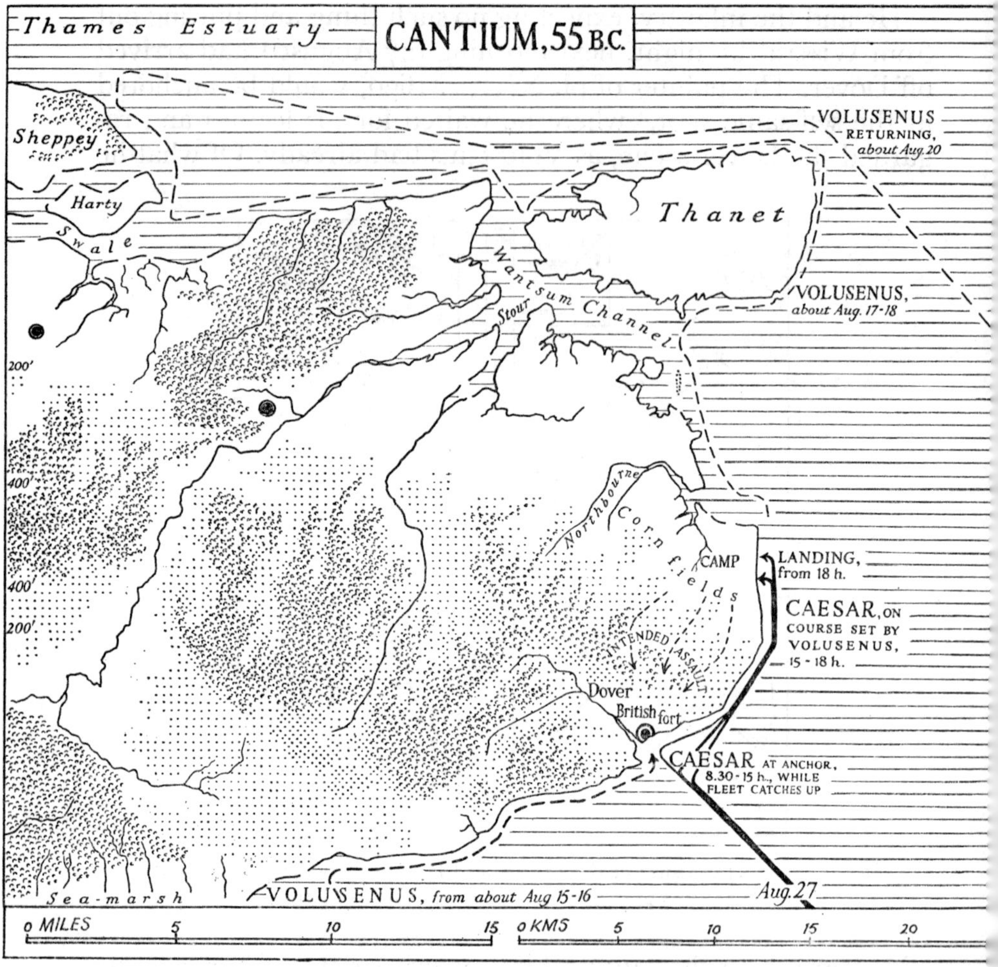

MAP 8. East Kent, 55 B.C.: Volusenus's cruise, and Caesar's landing and soon-frustrated intentio[n]
⊙ = British hillfort; stipples, land above 200 and (closer) 400 ft.; woodland inferred from geolog[y]
coastlines adapted from Sonia Hawkes 1968.

in front—as the Castle's outer work. Re-discovered by Colvin,[1] this major fortress is the key to the expedition's understanding. Caesar would be given its harbour and all its district, if Commius prevailed there; if not—as was seeming now likely—Volusenus will have shown him how to take it: from behind (map 8). Towards Deal, he will have found that the cliffs fall away; beyond, from off-shore, he saw all the south-eastern Kentish downs rising up—their high reverse side he will have seen while

[1] Colvin 1959, noting the overlapping-earthwork entrance; 1963, 630 with plan 1, fig. 53; pottery (his n. 1) Bayly 1962, xlviii. Mr. Colvin has cordially encouraged my adducing him here.

west of Dover—and sloping north-eastward to low ground close to the sea. The shore then receded into a bay, where the fleet, if a British one appeared, could be bottled up; once landed on the beach at its corner, however, the legions could ascend that slope, and pin the defenders of the hillfort against their cliffs. So Caesar, who had waited since morning while the fleet closed up, got the tide about 3 p.m., with a south-west wind—the same that deflected his cavalry's ships, had he known it, at sea (fig. 2)—and sailed round to Deal. By 6 he was off the beach (near Walmer Castle), and could land. The eagle-bearer's plunge, the fight, the surrender, yielding Commius back stultified, are familiar to us all; then the gale that bore away the cavalry and rose, that night (30–31 August), with the new-moon tide, to the smashing of the fleet—warships on the beach and transports at anchor—and its sequels, the reaping of the cornfields for food and the chariots' attack down the slope from the woods, the fight against a larger force, surrender renewed, and final withdrawal (26 September) make Caesar a well-told tale.[1] Yet it has hidden his original objective: a foothold for starting on Britain from Dover.

His goddess Fortuna served Caesar more amply when he made his report to the Senate. The thanksgiving voted was the longest in Roman history, twenty days.[2] Thus reassured that his doings were officially approved, to the pleasure of the public, he was soon ordaining a better and a much bigger fleet.[3] For what he next year was to do with it, however, his designs owed most to Volusenus (map 8). The bay beyond the 55 landing-place was wide, not choked as now by alluvium and banked with shingle.[4] Volusenus saw it first fed by the Northbourne, ending the slope north-east from the downs, and bordered next by a beach—which he duly noted. Past that, it ran back into an open channel, the Wantsum; the mainland there faced an island, Thanet, which ended in a steep north cape. Doubling this, he met the channel's other end, where the coast led him west, as far as Sheppey; it was the estuary coast of the Thames.

[1] *BG* iv. 24–36; Rambaud 1965, 116–44, and 18–23 on composition (24) from basic notes on file and his own campaign-report.

[2] *BG* iv. 38, 5; Stevens 1947, 5–6 (with Plutarch on Cato's lone vote against it) is vivid on the public acclaim for even such a short expedition into Ocean.

[3] *BG* v. 1, 1–41; 2, 1–3; 5, 1–2: all bearing on his special concern for the shipbuilding.

[4] See pp. 161–2 with n. 3 on my wife's documentation; with the late Mrs. Mary James, she was indispensable equally in our field-work.

And he must have expected it. For Caesar had found that the merchants had known what was opposite to Gaul, and the coasts of Kent (though nowhere with a harbour for a fleet); his negative manner of saying so (p. 151) has concealed their awareness of

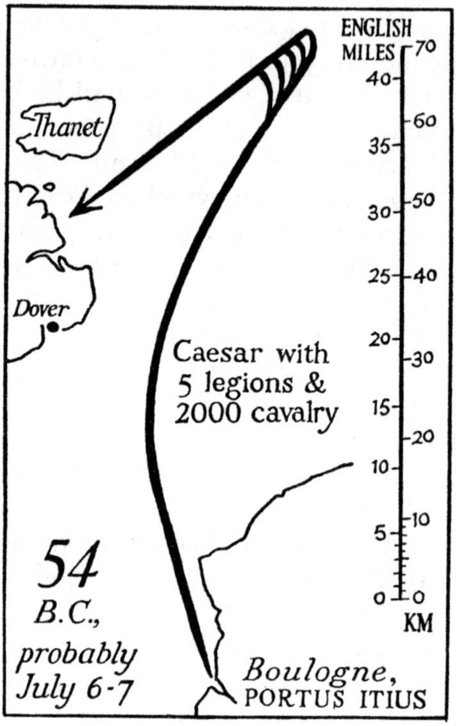

FIG. 3. 54 B.C.: crossing of the Straits, turn of the tide, and landing.

the estuary, yet some must have known it, past Sheppey at least to the Medway. That large-mouthed river is the centre of one of our scatters of Gallo-Belgic coins (p. 143, n. 1), and we shall further see evidence soon that the Medway was reached in fact by merchants, evidently round from the bay between the Wantsum and Deal. The beach in this bay, just mentioned, was chosen by Caesar for his landing next year. He will have been told of it first by Volusenus, but reveals from him nothing that would bear on 54—though the fast ship he had given him (lateen-rigged and oared) in more than four days at sea would do at least 1,200 km., quite enough to justify the course that I show on map 8.[1] And the coasts lying north from Deal, round

[1] Beach, *BG* v. 8, 3; 9, 2. Volusenus's ship, iv. 21, 1 and 9; Rambaud 1965, 103 and 106, but in error where guessing that he passed to Kent from the Somme by Beachy Head: that Sussex coast, the westward *inferior pars*

to the Thames estuary and up it, were to be crucial in 54 to Caesar's designs.

54 B.C.: Kent, and the prospect of Essex

The start again was late: an affair in Illyricum, trouble with the Treveri, the dissident Aeduan Dumnorix, and prolonged contrary wind, made it July, about the 6th (by the calendar then, 31st),[1] when Caesar sailed with his fleet, at dusk, from Boulogne. No more Dover. His course was north (fig. 3); the tide bore him on till at dawn on the 7th, seeing coast away behind, he waited for the ebb and set his soldiers to row, hard across it. Their effort got the fleet to the beach about mid-day.[2] Not closely located in his book, it is agreed to have been north of the beach of 55,[3] and modern research can let the bay, between that and what then was the Wantsum channel, have nowhere a beach like Caesar's, 'soft and open' for his anchoring his fleet—of more than 800 ships—save one, long buried by the choking-up of the bay, and close to Worth. At Worth, in 1925, excavation of a small Roman temple (map 9) found under it pottery, running from early in the Iron Age; and from late in it—broadly of Caesar's time—three little bronze shields, which are votive.[4] Here then prior to the temple was a beach-side

of 28, 2, had nothing to do with Dover and Deal. Excluding it secures to V his time for the estuary coast of the Thames.

[1] *BG* v. 1–8, 2. On the date, and contemporary calendar-date, Holmes 1907, 706–30, refuting (with others) Le Verrier as followed by Stoffel (for Napoleon III) and still by Rambaud. Boulogne as Portus Itius, Holmes 552–95; Rambaud 1967, 59–60, with my p. 152 n. 1. But see his 1966, 422–3, for French views other than his own.

[2] *BG* v. 8, 1–5: tellingly evoked by Collingwood, a mariner himself (1936, 33), but seemingly with South Foreland for North.

[3] Holmes 1907, 595–674, though with a physical topography largely obsolete today (518–52), established the 55 beach as at Deal, near Walmer Castle, and stretching (we can add) to a point about the railway-station, where it turned for the corner of the bay. On the 54 beach, which he established at least as north of it, he was hampered through non-recognition of the bay's existence, but rightly put the camp on a gentle rise of ground near Worth, though of the temple there (see text) he could not know; the off-shore water, which at Deal is part of the Downs, opposite Worth is called the Small Downs, and there he put the anchored fleet. But why, after the gale of 55, Caesar exposed it there, neither he nor anyone I know has seen hitherto.

[4] Temple, Lewis 1966, 3, 40, 51 (later Roman), 170 plan fig. 31 from Klein 1928, excavations; pottery (and brooch) *Antiq. Journal*, xx, 115–21 (Hawkes), votive shields, Reginald Smith ibid. viii, 79–81, fig. 11, whence

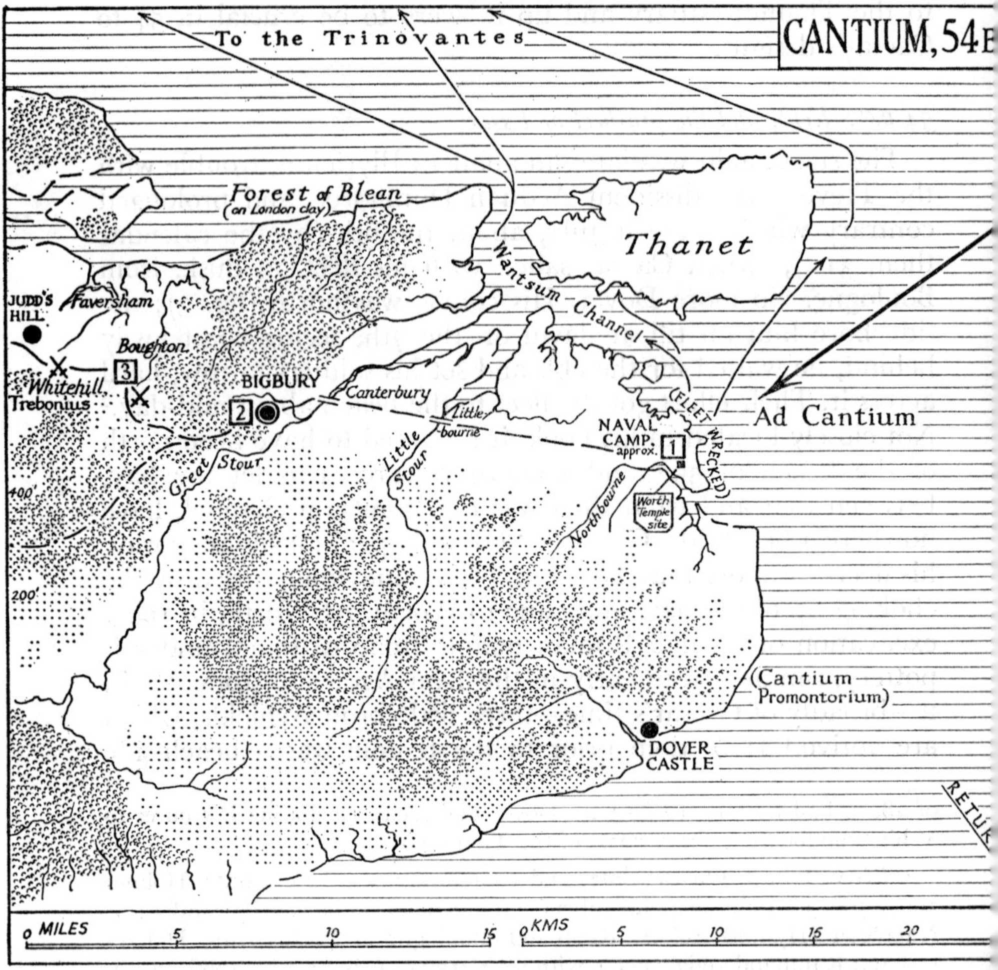

Map 9. East Kent, 54 B.C.: Caesar's landing, intentions (thin arrows) frustrated by wrecking fleet, and march with main army (broken line). ● = British hillfort, ⊙ (ringed) = stormed Caesar; ⨯ battlefield; 1, 2, 3, his successive camps; ═ ford; —·— British ridgeway; stipples, land ab 200 and (closer) 400 ft.; woodland inferred from geology; coastlines adapted from Sonia Hawkes 19

sanctuary; not surprising, for this whole bay was where ships from Gaul nearly all put in, as Caesar records only later—the harbour *ad Cantium*. Protecting it, the South Foreland (now stunted by the sea) was the Cantium promontory. The Isle of Thanet's cape, the North Foreland, Caesar will have seen, receding when the tide had borne him past it (fig. 3); yet never does he mention the island, nor its Wantsum channel. We know

Cunliffe 1974, 296–7, fig. 15: 5 (all three shapes); Harding 1974, 103–5, fig. 25 (two only, C–D), comparing others of the period from elsewhere (A–B).

its name Tanatos from later geographers only.[1] Yet how can either have escaped Volusenus's report? Why Caesar has hidden the geography, we soon shall see.

From Worth, where his camp (map 9, camp 1) will have been somewhere close to the sanctuary, the plain stretches west to the Little Stour, with a ford at Littlebourne, then gently rises to the ridge looking down upon the Great Stour ford at Canterbury. The way from Worth, quite straight, must have been the trackway to Cantium harbour. The Roman road from Canterbury later had the same alignment on Worth, till its swerve toward the Romans' Richborough port (my map's small island in the Wantsum). Caesar now, ashore unopposed, and at Worth taking prisoners (people doubtless in the sanctuary), learnt from them where the native forces, scared at his fleet, had gone. At midnight, up the trackway, leaving behind his anchored fleet (as its guard, ten cohorts only, with some horse), he marched. Twelve miles forward at dawn, he saw them in retreat across the Great Stour ford; when cavalry drove them up higher ground past it, they climbed through woods to a fort, and this can only have been Bigberry, up above Harbledown. Sadly ill treated today, it was planned some forty-five years ago by Ronald Jessup, who illumined then Boyd Dawkins's earlier find of a wrought-iron firedog, recently discussed by Piggott, and of continental type that can befit this period.[2] The occupants had blocked all its entrances with logs—Caesar guessed, for a prior tribal war; most of its habitation appears (from its excavated pottery) as earlier, and he calls it 'excellently fortified both by

[1] Rivet 1974, 66, after Bradley (1881 as cit. 1885) and Müller 1883 as noted 57 and 80; 66 also, Cantium promontory not North Foreland but South.

[2] Piggott 1971, 249, 253–4 (type B, this firedog), 259, 265; illustration, Fox C. 1958 pl. 26C, text 75, 132; old excavations (1864 and all before 1887) found pottery and much more ironwork: Boyd Dawkins 1902; Jessup 1930, 144–6, 257; 1933, full description with his own fine plan (and the firedog, 110); excavations 1933–4, Jessup and Cook 1936 (whence Cunliffe 1974, 66, simpler plan fig. 5: 4); dating of their pottery reconsidered 1976 by Dr. T. C. Champion, whom I gratefully thank for his judgement given me in writing, from examining all in the light of modern comparisons: hardly any should be reckoned so late as the time of Caesar. 'Bigbury' was Dawkins's spelling, 'Bigberry' more usual now, as Jessup, and already Belloc 1904 (1948, 273–6); both described and reflected on the site before most of its modern disfigurement, by house and garden enclosures in addition to older tree-planting and gravel-digging. For an earlier-occupied fort thus later less used but resorted to in war, compare (p. 174) Ravensburgh as *oppidum Cassivellauni*.

nature and by works', omitting his usual hillfort word, which is *oppidum*. Anyhow his Seventh Legion stormed it; and Caesar put his camp, most probably, near it to the west (map 9, camp 2).[1]

Why had he made this dash? Keeping back ten cohorts only from his force of five legions? Some twenty thousand infantry, plus cavalry,[2] in motion, means deployment on his flanks, protecting his centre's advance and fanning out; Bigberry thus would be the apex of a broad enough front to guarantee him security. The centre legions and horse he led in person to success, but it assured him much more. With his left flank watching the downs and their woods, and his right the mouths of the Stours, both wide open to the Wantsum, watched at its opposite end by his ships, he had its channel, and Thanet's island beyond, cut off. Yet all this he hides, with all that undoubtedly he knew about the coasts and the Thames. In the regions beyond its mouth dwelt nearly their strongest tribe, the Trinovantes. Their Essex coast faced Kent. But in recent warfare, along with the rest, they had been fought by an inland neighbour who proved to be stronger, Cassivellaunus. Their king had been killed, and his son Mandubracius had barely escaped with his life. This prince, to seek Caesar's protection, had come to him in Gaul. We are not told when; and the record of the warfare and his flight is split apart, between separated points in Caesar's narrative. Both are farther on, disjoined from the present position in Kent; but a third shows Mandubracius in Caesar's train.[3] Caesar, as his deal with the Remi showed, and his attempt at one in Kent through Commius, required a friendly power that he could claim to be defending, under the Senate's decree (p. 139), against the rest. Commius, thrown into chains at Dover and returned looking foolish, had failed him; Mandubracius would not—and now had told him much more

[1] *BG* v. 9: the whole narrative, from the landing. Bigberry is not wide-ditched nor massively banked, like Fécamp (p. 144 n. 1), so the soldiers could lock their shields, fill the ditch with an *agger*, and climb more easily. Briefer, Rivet in Jesson and Hill (eds.) 1971, 191, 194.

[2] Any legion might be fielding fewer than its full 6,000 men, yet Caesar's five now (*BG* v. 8, 2), less the ten cohorts left at base (9, 1), can imply a good 20,000 infantry advancing; his cavalry totalled 2,000 (v. 8, 2 with 5, 3). The 5,000 legionary average thus suggested is admittedly a guess, but within the limits of Holmes 1911, 559–63. Rambaud 1965, 7 can make it appear too low. See further his 1958 on all the war's individual legions.

[3] In his train, *BG* v. 20, 3; with him in Gaul, v. 20, 1; warfare with Cassivellaunus, 20, 1 with 11, 9.

View of Dover from the sea, about 1690, from a contemporary painting in oils (51 × 30 inches) in the Mowll Collection, Dover, reproduced by Wheeler 1930. The painter must have been anchored in just the same position as Caesar, on the morning of 27 August 55 B.C.

PLATE XXII

Portrait of Julius Caesar, 44 B.C., on silver denarius of the moneyer Marcus Mettius: Crawford 480/17.

Ashmolean Museum, Oxford

than any merchant, Volusenus, or Kentish hostage.[1] His tribesmen would welcome his return, if Caesar brought him and avenged his father. The fleet was ready. It had Thanet to take, but Peniche (p. 132) had been an ample lesson. Squadrons then would sail, round the Foreland and through the Wantsum, leaving guard enough at his base-camp, over to Essex. Caesar would be saved any forcing of the Thames higher up, against Cassivellaunus. Like his Gallic province's old proconsul Domitius, whose grandson was his enemy in Rome, he could impress the natives mounted on an elephant: it seems he had an elephant actually brought with him.[2] Fortuna was turning. But in the night of those dreams beside Bigberry she turned to double-cross him. Before the morning's triple pursuit of its fugitives was all out of sight from his camp, gallopers came from the fleet: it had been ruined by a gale. He had left it at anchor to be ready for the Wantsum, for Thanet, and next for the Trinovantes. Its ruin was the ruin of his plans. He must again make new ones.

54 B.C.: from Kent to the Thames

Accounts of Caesar in Kent have allowed too little for its changes of coastline; my own estimations may themselves be too conservative. Though exactness is by nature unattainable, the essentials are as valid as research can make them. My guide has been Sonia Hawkes, my Kent-born wife; her knowledge, from periods earlier to later,[3] has helped me on the map and in

[1] *BG* iv. 38, 4: at the end of 55, two Kentish tribes had sent hostages as promised; the rest had not.

[2] Stevens 1959, dismissed too sweepingly by Scullard: 1974, 194 with n. 136. Our informant is Polyaenus (about A.D. 160–180), who has the elephant clearing Caesar's passage of a river, panicking the British warriors and chariot-teams of 'Kasolaunos'. Romans all knew that horses could be terrified by elephants, but Stevens gave Caesar a political motive for bringing one: Domitius, proud of his elephant-riding grandsire in southern Gaul, should be made to stomach an elephant-riding Caesar. In *BG*, writing when conscious that in Britain he had formed no province like Domitius's in Gaul, Caesar would retract and say nothing of his elephant; yet its clearing the river will at least have been told to the Senate, including Domitius, in his report for 54—which Livy can afterwards have used, Polyaenus then Livy. Stevens was possibly rash (as also Dayet 1960) in adducing the event to account for Caesar's issuing the well-known coin, his 'elephant' silver denarius (Crawford 443/1), which for Scullard is irrelevant (and equally for Crawford: his ii. 735). But detach this, and Stevens's case from Polyaenus remains; see therefore p. 164, n. 1, p. 170, n. 3.

[3] Hawkes S. 1968, with all relevant coastal documentation (for the

the field, both coastwise and on through inland country—which had now to be traversed by Caesar. Ten days, in continuous day and night shifts, got the ships and wrecks ashore, their repairing put in hand, and the camp defences extended around them as a single great naval camp. Recording this, Caesar omits what steps he must have taken to ensure himself local security, minimizing risks both from Thanet and from Dover, where most of the downs must now have escaped his grip. Back at last beside Bigberry again (map 9, camp 2), he found resistance ready in force and with a new commander. The Cassivellaunus he had meant to assail from Essex was a fighter so famed from his wars, that his former foes, now Caesar's, had joined in awarding him supreme command.[1] His tactics for Kent were to muster with chariots and horsemen in the up-hill woods, and fall upon the Romans in the open low ground, whether marching, camping, or foraging. The topography puts the battle at Caesar's third camp near Boughton, below the tail of Blean Forest, and the biggest battle close to Whitehill; a factor in it must have been the Judd's Hill fort, in Syndale Park beside Ospringe. It was won under Gaius Trebonius, and cleared the way for advancing further (map 10). In front of three legions, the cavalry routed the assaulting Britons at last; when their chariots were rushed into flight by the charge, their forces dispersed.[2] But destroyed they were not;

Wantsum's N. end, add C. L. So, *Arch. Cantiana*, lxxxvi (1971), 93–7), has full discussion and conclusions for NE. Kent, and map (her fig. 24), starting-point for mine: 9 with 8, 11 with 10, and the SE. portion of 12. Her map is for the Roman period, and may even for that be too conservative on coastlines; for Caesar's, a century before that started, my own may in places err more that way. They are nowhere at all too radical.

[1] *BG* v. 11, 9, Trinovantes unmentioned, but *Britanni toti* had done so; *bello imperioque* (*praefecerant*) may appear as if hendiadys: (had put him in) 'command of the war'. Yet *imperium* is Caesar's usual word for a Celtic or Belgic high-kingship, whether as war-lord (here; vii. 4, 6, Vercingetorix; ii. 4, 7, Galba) or long-term (ibid., his father Diviciacus, p. 143 with n. 1); and for Caesar, this war-*imperium* will condition the terms of peace (p. 177).

[2] *BG* v. 15–17: Caesar on the British chariot-fighting here (from notes used also in iv. 33: p. 167 with n. 1) describes its effect on both infantry and cavalry, 16, 1–2, and its final overcoming by cavalry charge, 17, 3–4. Battle here close to Whitehill, and previous at camp (3) near Boughton, are my estimations from the moves in Caesar with maps, Geological (Drift) and Ordnance Survey. Judd's Hill, former hillfort round Syndale Park: *Arch. Cantiana*, i (1868), 167; xiii (1880), 2, C. Roach Smith; 13, Flinders Petrie; *VCH Kent*, i, 460; Jessup 1930, 159. All, among the earthworks in G. Payne's survey of 1888 (*Archaeologia*, li) and in *VCH* i, have other Kent forts, some

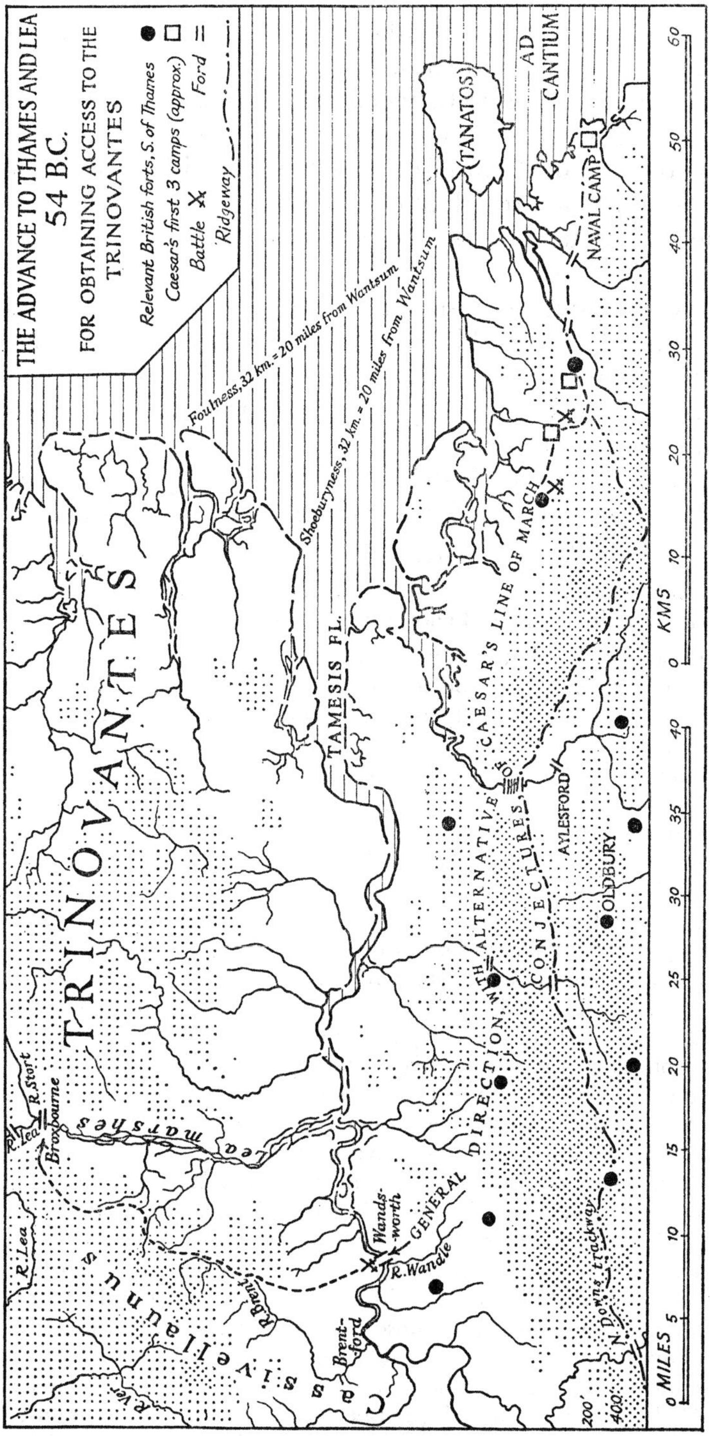

Map 10. Caesar's advance to the Thames, and through Cassivellaunas's lands to the Lea. ═ford; stipples, land above 200 and (closer) 400 ft.

among their downs and woods to the south, they would wait until the Romans were away inland. Cassivellaunus then would throw them at the naval camp.

The advance was thus between the downs and the estuary coast, on which Caesar is silent, as also on his having the Medway to cross: upstream from where it was tidal, so doubtless at Halling and Holborough and Snodland, where are fords that have the downs behind them.[1] These silences also muffle the Medway's affording an entry from the sea. Yet here are centred not only those gold Gallo-Belgic coins that I have mentioned (p. 143), but also, and this way reaching inland Kent, class I of our cast coins of potin, which imitate Gaulish imitations of the bronze of Marseilles. They were cast in rows; and one type, from some twenty until eight or ten years before Caesar, had had its moulds impressed with strips of Egyptian papyrus[2]—in this, Marseilles must have dealt. As middlemen, the Aedui would pass it into 'Belgium' (map 7), down the Seine or to their friends

equally now neglected. Map 11 has those here relevant; for Oldbury and Loose (Quarry Hill) see p. 168 end of n. 4 from p. 167.

[1] On these fords exhaustively, Thornhill 1974. From prehistoric to medieval times, through marine transgression at the estuary, the point of high tide was pushed gradually up-river. But in Caesar's time the fords (between Cuxton and Aylesford) will all have been usable, though the water-volume, slowed by the level at the mouth, would be greater. Hilaire Belloc, when the tide's prehistory here was unknown, was the first (I think) to view them in regard to trackway-borne communications; his topography was seldom at fault: Belloc 1904 (1948, 234–55 with his neat small map). For the Medway as the 'great river' (unnamed) in Polyaenus, forced for Caesar by his elephant (p. 161, n. 2) against 'Kasolaunos', see p. 170, n. 3 on his passage of the Thames soon after.

[2] Allen 1971, 128–30, developing with E. G. Turner's help the discovery by J. P. Wild: *Antiquity*, xl (1966, June), 139–42. This type G's date (his Class I, G A–B–C), Allen 133, 136, 143; illustr. pls. I–III, V (52–5): with the liberty of using approximate years to represent the indications of his wording, one can run it from a start a little after 75 to a conclusion before 60, so for ten or a dozen years. The earlier types, without papyrus, are rarer; when the later, again without it, have reached type L, there are eight known hoards; two on Thanet, four on the lower Thames, and one in inland Kent, with one (Snettisham in Norfolk) farther off. As the home of the whole Class I is north Kentish (Thanet–Surrey) with the Medway in the middle, Allen ascribed these hoards, round its edges, to escapers from the onset of Caesar. See his 136–7 with map fig. 33, 142–3 and lists 144–6, 147–8. As for dating prior to the onset, the need for 'small change' which the potin supplied, felt first in Kent through its trade with Gaul where potin was current already, will have started them here before the arrival of the gold Gallo-Belgic C. For this (p. 143, n. 1.) starts later now than Allen believed. Thus the only gold locally existing would still be the old Gallo-

the Bellovaci, neighbours of the Ambiani on the Somme;[1] it could be shipped from either—with bulkier commodities—to Britain. That at its south-east corner, *ad Cantium*, nearly all ships from Gaul put in (p. 158), is told us in the 'British excursus' in Caesar's text, before Trebonius's battle. Any bound for the Medway—or the Thames itself—would do so on their way into the estuary. Having veiled the existence of this to hide his failure at crossing it to Essex, he has the Thames named only in his narrative, up where he now had to cross it as a river. But the coins, and perhaps already Gaulish-like pots as at Aylesford, higher on the Medway,[2] show acquaintance from the water with the whole of north Kent; moreover Thanet might itself have held another island market, like the Isle of Wight's touched upon already (p. 145), drawing barterable metals—including tin—from the west. Not tidal like Belerion's St. Michael's Mount, it has for this no ancient authority, but the modern writings on all the three have a review from Mr. I. S. Maxwell;[3] in spite of his still thinking Pytheas the source of the Diodorus accounts (pp. 130–1), it should serve to remind us of our loss through silences of Caesar's.

The 'British excursus', all or part, has been by some judged spurious. Yet one can see how Caesar used his dossiers now for narrative, now for gathering matter up into excursuses like this; it should nowhere be later than his finishing the whole, in the winter 52–51. Its matter where not from his campaign-reports, or staff notes, will be excerpts from earlier writers: Posidonius doubtless among them but others besides. What does, however,

Belgic A, none new being wanted (same note) for Diviciacus. There would anyhow be potin in his time (Scheers 1970b, 'towards 80–75'); and the type made with papyrus, showing trade from the south through Gaul, will be current at Gallo-Belgic C's new date of arrival, from the Ambiani. Among the aims of the take-over (p. 143 n. 1 once more) would be profits from the trade. And this is Gaul's trade with Kent in Caesar's excursus (text above).

[1] Ambiani being responsible (p.143) for our Gallo-Belgic C, and in 57 surrendering to Caesar next to the Bellovaci (*BG* ii. 15, 2), their neighbours on the south, who were influential (15, 1) and friends of the Aedui (14, 2), one can clearly see the route of the trading connection with the south and Marseilles (map 7). The alternative harbour on the Seine was in a region that had shared in our Gallo-Belgic B, though this had gone out before Caesar's time (Scheers 1970a). The scene of course is much more clear through eliminating E as a coinage of invasion: p. 142 with n. 7 (142–3).

[2] Birchall 1965, 243–9, 256–8, 288–91, 296–8, 301–4, 329–34, figs. 6–11; Rodwell 1976, 215–34, fig. 15, 13; fig. 14 map; add Stead 1976, my p. 192.

[3] Maxwell 1972; many points of interest.

seem to have happened to it later is misplacement of a codex leaf, so that the three excursus chapters, now our 12, 13, 14, had a previous order 14, 12, 13. And either for meeting unconformity so caused, or through mistranscription already, an occasional sentence may be out of its intended place. (So 14, 1 could follow 12, 1–2, leaving only the rest of 14 after end of 12.)[1] Of the excursus's contents—dimensions of Britain (these better than the extant older ones),[2] climate and trees, people and dwellings, habits and currency—one notices the tin, 'in inland regions', while the iron (small in amount) comes in the 'maritime'. Only in Cornwall is that so; is the note from the dossier of 56?[3] But if Kent's using iron from the Weald is meant,[4] the tin could seem 'inland' to a note-writer hearing of

[1] Rambaud 1974, with text and commentary 81–7, has introduction 29–33 on treatment of dossiers in annalistic structure, 34–8 on this treatment's disordering through leaf misplaced, as hère and perhaps at v. 18–19 (my p. 167 n. 4 (167–8)), and occasional dislocation of a sentence; cf. Holmes 1914 ad loc. on similar principle, against recourse to excessive rejections of text; hence Collingwood 1936, 34 ff., 476, excursus 'substantially genuine'.

[2] *BG* v. 13, Britain as triangle (obtuse-angled at Cantium), Ireland on W. and Man between, ultimately from Pytheas through recension of data by Eratosthenes: Rivet 1974, 59–60, using Tierney in *Journ. Hellenic Studies*, lxxix (1959), 132–48. Pytheas estimated Britain's circumference from his days of coastwise sailing; Strabo (ii) 104, from Polybius, gave his total as 'more than 40,000 stades' (or 6,280 km.). Pliny iv. 102 has it as 4,825 Roman miles which = 39,000 stades, and quotes him for this together with Isidore of Charax who is extant for 39,000: *Geogr. Graec. minores*, ed. Müller, ii. 509, 32. Diodorus v. 21, 4 still has 42,500: longest side 20,000, east side 15,000, short side (next to Continent) 7,500. All three are exaggerations, natural in view of their ultimate source; the total = nearly 6,700 km., against an actual nearly 2,600, and short side = 1,180 km. against an actual about 540. Caesar's sources, however, allowed him circumference of some 2,960 km. namely 2,000 Roman miles, and this is only some 400 km. more than actuality. Yet his short side is still some 200 km. too long, at 740 km. = his 500 Roman miles. He says nothing of an earlier source for this, and it might have been (I fancy) transferred, from some recent measurement of Gaul's N. coast, taking Finistère as opposite Land's End, which the tin trade would have prompted (p. 130 n. 1 (131), p. 147 with n. 2): by navigator's points between there and the capes at the Straits, it could make the length of the Channel 4,000 stades, = 740 km. and Caesar's 500 miles. His figures show anyhow his turning to data far more realistic than the older Greek figures, which were ultimately Pytheas's sailing-days artificially turned into stades: Hawkes 1977, 11.

[3] *BG* v. 12, 5; this was Stevens's explanation, repeated to me vigorously 3 October 1974.

[4] Jessup 1930, 141–2, affirming this, saw it probably explaining the ironore smelted in the furnace discovered at Swarling: Bushe-Fox 1925, 49–53, Appendix by its excavator C. L. (later Sir Leonard) Woolley. Bushe-Fox's

an inland route for it eastward (map 7), unaware of it as landed at the mouth of the Severn from Cornwall. Either way, care was here neglected; and Caesar could himself neglect it on occasion, as in Gaul (p. 146 with n. 5) on the Nantuates. In the excursus there is anyhow some matter from what must have been his autumn report for 55; but conversely, his 55 account of British chariots has them dashing amongst his cavalry—not at hand till 54.[1] The excursus then, altogether, is a patchwork quilt.

Its dividing Britain up, into 'interior', with wild aborigines, and 'maritime part', invaded and settled 'out of Belgium', gives an ethnography, handy for Caesar's decrying an interior he never had reached, that is foreign—and in matter thus prior—to his first-hand narrative. Schematic in the manner of a Greek ethnographer, the bipartition is false to fact. The 'maritime shore and those regions that are opposite Gaul', known to the merchants whom he questioned in 55, are in the excursus just the 500-mile line of the coast. Its corner and the harbour for ships from Gaul are in Kent, 'which is maritime entirely'; but the excursus never limits to Kent the invader *civitates*, with their names still as in 'Belgium', nor mentions the names. Essex being maritime really, was one the Trinovantes? Though I once thought not, archaeology now has made it indisputably probable;[2] and for Caesar's concealing their maritime location, we have seen, he had reasons of his own. He gives 'maritime *civitates*' a frontier at only one point of his narrative. They are divided by the Thames, 'about 80 miles from the sea', from the borders of his leading enemy Cassivellaunus.[3] The excursus follows immediately, then comes Trebonius's battle; then at once Caesar marches to the Thames—no Medway, no details, no hillforts (though there were plenty: map 9).[4] One can only

well-known cremation-cemetery close by, studied afresh by Birchall 1965, 242–3, 245–9, 256–8, 288, 295–301, 324–8, figs. 1–5, is claimed as beginning no later than Caesar by Rodwell 1976, 215–29, 232–4; the furnace was anyhow in broadly contemporary use.

[1] Rambaud 1967, 21, 137–8 on *BG* iv. 33; 1974, 6, 87–9 on v. 15–17.

[2] Rodwell 1976, 214 (but on coins see my p. 142 n. 7), 216–19 with map fig. 11, 225 ff. with map fig. 14, 238–40 with map fig. 18 (after Peacock 1971).

[3] *BG* v. 11, 8–9; cf. 18, 1.

[4] On the placing of the excursus here between v. 11 and 15, and resumption at 18, 1 (*cognito consilio eorum*) from 11, 8 where Cassivellaunus has command *communi consilio*, see Rambaud 1974, 81, 87, 92, and 34–7 with my n. 1 to p. 166. The placing here is not to mask any slowness of advance

give a general line for his march to the river-bank: probably at Wandsworth.[1]

54 B.C.: in the country of Cassivellaunus

Cassivellaunus, on the other bank, fought with his country at his back. He and his dominant people there have long seemed Belgic invaders themselves; their name in later record, Catuvellauni, seemed suggestive of the Catalauni, dwelling on the Marne in Gaul round Châlons. But those, by Caesar unnamed, no doubt because a client tribe, probably of the Remi, were well outside his 'Belgium' whence the excursus brings the invaders. My pointing this out (from Hachmann)[2] led to a new view of Cassivellaunus, not as recent Belgic arrival but as native Briton. Archaeology and studies of coins, moving on past subsequent essays that I wrote,[3] have enabled their comparison with Caesar

by Caesar, but to draw away notice from the fact that Cassivellaunus had now the initiative, Caesar having lost it when the gale wrecked his fleet and his design of assailing him from Essex. Rambaud 36–7 entertains (from Meusel) a further misplacing of a leaf, whereby chapters 18 and 19 have interchanged places; the existing 19 begins with Cassivellaunus dejected through Caesar's successful crossing of the Thames, but if placed before 18 the cause would be his beating in Trebonius's battle (17). As the text now stands, his dejection's noting at 19, 1 as *ut supra demonstravimus*, can only have referred to his feelings at losing that battle which are not, in fact, brought into the account of his defeat at end of 17; if the change is made, that defeat will then become the whole prime cause of his dejection, and the note *ut supra demonstravimus* has to be interpolated later, not by Caesar. In any case the course of events has been obscured by what was evidently Caesar's purpose, of high-lighting only the Trebonius battle and the forcing of the Thames: nothing else. Yet he may have found the Medway contested (p. 164 n. 1; p. 170 n. 3, suggesting why suppressed), and have had to deal with such hillforts as map 11 shows (p. 162 n. 2); for Oldbury, Ward Perkins 1944, with added defence of Fécamp type (p. 144 n. 1), the dating now is high enough for this: Hawkes 1968, 10 from Mrs. Cotton; Rodwell 1976, 191–3, noting also the Quarry Wood fort at Loose, SE. from Aylesford on my map: Kelly 1971, not necessarily post-Caesar.

[1] Holmes 1907, 692–9, 742, really got nowhere. Stevens 1947, 6, n. 21, gave Wandsworth because the crossing is at the only ford (*BG* v. 18, 1), therefore the Britons' own, and the clue to it thus distribution of British (La Tène) finds in the river; 'the vicinity of Wandsworth' was declared to him as the place by the man with the greatest knowledge of all such finds, G. F. Lawrence: *Archaeo. Journal*, lxxxvi (for 1929), 69–98; Wandsworth, 90–1. See too G. M. Willcox in *Trans. London & Middlesex Arch. Soc.* 26 (1975).

[2] *BG* v. 12, 22; p. 142 with note 2; Hawkes 1965 from Hachmann 1962, 46–8. Catalauni in Gaul, Holmes 1911, 445, 468.

[3] Hawkes 1968, 6–10, 15–16; 1972, 109–11; 1973, 607–18. In Frere (ed.) 1961, 12 (chart fig. 4), 15–16, I had Belgic invasion no longer '75' but near

to present that view in corroborated forms:[1] upholding the Catuvellauni as British, as against the invaders who were 'maritime', it has even made their territory belong to the excursus's 'interior part' of Britain. But Caesar's Thames about 80 miles from the sea (that is, from his landing-place, Worth)[2] divides them from 'maritime states' without assigning them to any 'interior'; and if the recent wars were of Cassivellaunus as a Briton against those states, the Trinovantes he beat will be a 'maritime state', though beyond the Thames—at its estuary: the estuary that Caesar was having to hide. So between his excursus and narrative he juggled with 'maritime'. Cassivellaunus is never that, and though never 'interior' either, there is nothing in Caesar against the archaeology and coins that

100; ibid. 84–5, Frere put it just before, to fit Allen's dates for coins and let it have chariotry from Gaul (abandoned there shortly after 90), not borrowed in Britain from the north, as Piggott had once suggested. But none had as yet reckoned Cassivellaunus and his chariots in the south both native.

[1] Michael Avery, original article of 1969, unpublished, has summary in Harding (ed.) 1976, 142 n. 103; Harding 1974, 223–6 with map fig. 81, developed same or essentially similar views; for the train of thought that led to both, see opposite, with nn. 2–3.

[2] *BG* v. 11, 8: *mare* as in 9, 1; 80 Roman (118 km.) = 73 English miles, three more than the crow-flight Worth to Wandsworth Bridge. The clause *cuius fines . . . LXXX* is in all the manuscripts and perfectly clear: Cassivellaunus's bounds are divided from 'maritime states' by the Thames where its distance from the sea (at Worth) is about 80 miles. Caesar reached it (18, 1–4) having learnt, from deserters and prisoners, that it only could be forded (with difficulty too) at one place, where the farther bank, with sharp stakes lining it, and more under water, was held by the enemy; he saw them there when he came to the place, having led his army to the Thames *in fines Cassivellauni*, *in* being purposive ('for entering' them: so Rambaud, *pour entrer dans le territoire*). The 80-mile point, the ford and the frontier upon it, are all one place: the description here in 18 fully fits the clause in 11, 8, *cuius fines a maritimis civitatibus flumen dividit quod appellatur Tamesis, a mari circiter milia passuum LXXX.* Against over-critical editors, whether rejecting the whole clause (Knoke), suspecting words lost before *cuius* (Fuchs), or rejecting them from *cuius* to *Tamesis* (Meusel), the text has been upheld by Du Pontet, whose model was old Nipperdey (see his preface) not Meusel, Holmes (against Meusel), Klotz, Constans, Seel, and Rambaud. Stevens (*viva voce* 3 October 1974) assured me that he too was for Holmes against Meusel: Caesar, whether or not correcting a figure got already (if from Britons or Gauls, perhaps '50 leagues', = 75 miles), will have had the approx. 80 measured as his marching total to the Thames, entered it then in the notes for his report, and thence used it when composing *BG*. He put it here, not in 18, so that Cassivellaunus should be seen as remote, and recently (11, 9) at war with neighbours who in 20 will include the Trinovantes; we can see why he hid these till then, and left them still seeming equally remote, but he made Cassivellaunus seem here to be remote because his choosing by

present him as native.[1] His people can well have begun to adopt some 'maritime' elements of culture, but at that time still much less than they afterwards adopted, when Caesar had gone.[2]

From the forcing of the Thames that he had hoped to avoid, against fierce resistance and the famous sharp stakes (some possibly from older wars?),[3] Caesar had to pass through Cassi-

the Britons as war-lord (9 again) enhances thereby the aggrandisement implied for himself. Altogether the text of 11, 8 must stand.

1 'Native' thus does not mean 'interior' as in the excursus; what it means is 'not maritime' as either in that or in the narrative. Rodwell 1976, 208–11 (acknowledging Frere), comes nearer to this than those whom I cite here in p. 168, nn. 2–3 and 169 n. 1.

2 Interpreting of coins, as my notes on them show (pp. 142–4, 164–5, 177, 178, 184), is at the time of writing still in a movement of transit: Allen's of 1961–2 was not so much too 'invasive'—apart from Gallo-Belgic E (and probably D)—as too exposed in his datings of gold, after A and B, to correction from the Continent. So too Rodwell 1976, who on A and B thus is at his best, with important maps. And Allen 1976, posthumous, is altogether basic. Interpreting of pottery and other material culture, as evidence has grown through the fifty years from Bushe-Fox, seems also in transit: to a reconciliation of 'invasionist' and 'pacifist' standpoints, on the basis of one between chronologies lower and higher, and of more excavation. (My 1972 and 73 were meant as pointers along the way.)

3 *BG* v. 18: on the tactics for crossing, described with extreme compression, still see Holmes 1907, 698–9; stakes in bank perhaps previous, Harding 1974, 225. Too often ignored, however, as there, is the story I have mentioned already (p. 161 n. 2, p. 164 n. 1 with map 10) of a 'great river' held against Caesar by 'Kasolaunos', and crossed in safety when his Britons and their chariot-horses all fled in terror from the elephant, armoured and with turret on its back full of archers and slingers, which Caesar sent ahead into the water: Polyaenus, *Strategica* viii. 23, 5. See Stevens 1959; Scullard 1974, 194, with 279 n. 136; both have assumed that the river was the Thames, so that it seems to Scullard 'hazardous to accept Polyaenus against Caesar'. For the Thames, Caesar's account of course must stand: sending in cavalry first, next legions, he prevailed through the speediness and shock of their attack. So if the elephant was there, though suppressed in *BG*, it could only have been leading the cavalry—which, with the legions, Polyaenus suppressed to make his tale more remarkable without them. Yet the Britons' sharp stakes were not only in the bank: as Caesar had been told, they were also under water; did the Britons know this elephant already? Would he risk it against their stakes? So the river, unnamed in Polyaenus, though 'great', should be not the Thames but the Medway. If held by the Britons in advance of the Thames, as 'great' enough to baffle the Romans—it was plainly the river so judged in A.D. 43, Dio lx. 20, 2–4—Polyaenus will be telling us why Cassivellaunus lost it. Suppressed in *BG* by Caesar along with all mention of the elephant (Stevens), and along with the whole of his advance to the Thames (which its clearing him the Medway will have sped), the story (transmission as Stevens) will be all the better credible. And

vellaunus's country now, to reach the Trinovantes' landward corner, where friends and food would be ready. Only so could their natural frontier, the Lea, be reached and crossed (map 10) at fords higher up than its length of great marshes, impenetrable down to the Thames. Cassivellaunus evacuated homes and fields into forests overlooking the advance, where his chariots could muster and burst on any cavalry that scattered for ravaging and plunder; thus infantry forays alone could be allowed, never far from the columns on the march,[1] and this just suits the physiography in Hertfordshire, with forest on the drift-clad upland, while the valleys' thin cover over chalk makes them arable and viable.[2] Thus Caesar marched up the Brent, and on till he descended on the Lea about Broxbourne. But he must have been still on the march, with the Lea far ahead and the Thames across his rear, when Cassivellaunus played the stroke for which he now had his best opportunity. He sent orders for the kings in Kent, who were four, to collect the whole of their forces, for capturing Caesar's naval camp by surprise. While he waited for the outcome of that, the Trinovantes learnt that Caesar was nearing the Lea—of course their frontier: nowhere else hereabouts can its line have been (map 10)—so dispatched to him envoys who promised their submission, and asked to be given Mandubracius back.[3] And this is where Caesar in his book first states that Mandubracius existed at all. His escape, from his father's fate, to Caesar in Gaul can be at last here told, as distantly as possible from the gale that had wrecked the fleet, left at anchor for reaching his country across the estuary (pp. 158–61). Caesar on reaching it instead by land, though never saying just where it was, explains Mandubracius now when assured of the friendship of his people, and their readiness with hostages and corn for the hungry army, on his giving them the prince as king and fending Cassivellaunus off. This defending of friends of Rome from a foe, as in Gaul the

Claudius, with elephants brought in the supports for his invaders, together with himself (Dio lx. 21, 2), will have thought both of panicking horses and of emulating Caesar. Scullard, 198–9, has neither.

[1] *BG* v. 19.

[2] So (over chalk) on all sides of London, as mapped for Royal Commission on Historical Monuments, *London iii, Roman* (1928), 12, plans C and D (text by Wheeler); area of Verulamium (St. Albans), Wheeler and Wheeler 1936, 13, map fig. 2: valley woodland clearable, upland forest; 24, map pl. X, from this to Welwyn area, by Wheathampstead (other sites excluded): lands wooded thickly, lightly, open (chalk) and alluvial.

[3] *BG* v. 20.

Aedui and Remi, legitimized his war, as will now be understood.

It moreover so impressed five other British tribes, that they all sent missions of surrender: Cenimagni, Segontiaci, Ancalites, Bibroci, Cassi.[1] Among them are those (unnamed) from whom Caesar hears (note his vivid present tenses) that 'not far from that place' (where they have met) 'is the *oppidum*, Cassivellaunus's, protected by woods and swamps, to which a sizeable number of men and of cattle has' (just now) 'gathered together'. No permanent capital *oppidum* this, or Trinovantes would have told him of it first; he at once explains 'Britons call an *oppidum*' (a place) 'to which, when with rampart and ditch they have fortified difficult woods, for avoiding enemies' incursion, they gather by custom.' Setting out for this place, with legions, he finds it 'excellently fortified by nature and by works'. (He has used that phrase already (p. 159) of Bigberry—though not called *oppidum*.) Never mind: his rapidly assailing it, on two sides, soon had the enemy in flight from a third. Captures in the flight, and slayings, were many; inside was found very much cattle. Modern search for a capital *oppidum*, viewed in terms of 'urbanization', onwards from the days recorded by Holmes,[2] has had a number of sites to choose from (map 11). On the brow above Roman Verulamium, facing St. Albans, the fortification that starts in Prae Wood was by Wheeler proved to have a date too late; he preferred the more massively fortified site above Wheathampstead, with its 'Devil's Dyke' western side and semblance of opposite ditch at 'The Slad'. His pottery within, from a transverse gully, he dated from around this time, lasting till Prae Wood's date around 10 B.C.; he had also then a brooch. But when was its beginning? Ann Birchall said as early as Caesar if Wheeler be believed; Rodwell prefers not later but depends on duration of the critical pot-forms. Certainty can only be attained from renewed excavation. The glory that Wheeler won here was a pioneer's.[3] Of my map's strongest other sites (bivallate earthwork), Gatesbury at Braughing is unduly far east; The Aubreys at Redbourn, unexplored, has the weakest site; Bulstrode has no effective finds, while Cholesbury, like Wheathampstead most in pottery and vallation (smaller, but a

[1] *BG* v. 21, 1–3. [2] Holmes 1907, 699–702.

[3] Wheeler and Wheeler 1936, 6–16, 22–4, 40–9, Prae Wood; 16–22, Wheathampstead, with the Beech Bottom Dyke that I omit because not directly related to Caesar (derivative plans, Cunliffe 1974, 66, 83); Birchall 1965, 287–8, cautious; Rodwell 1976, 221–7, 230–1, 234.

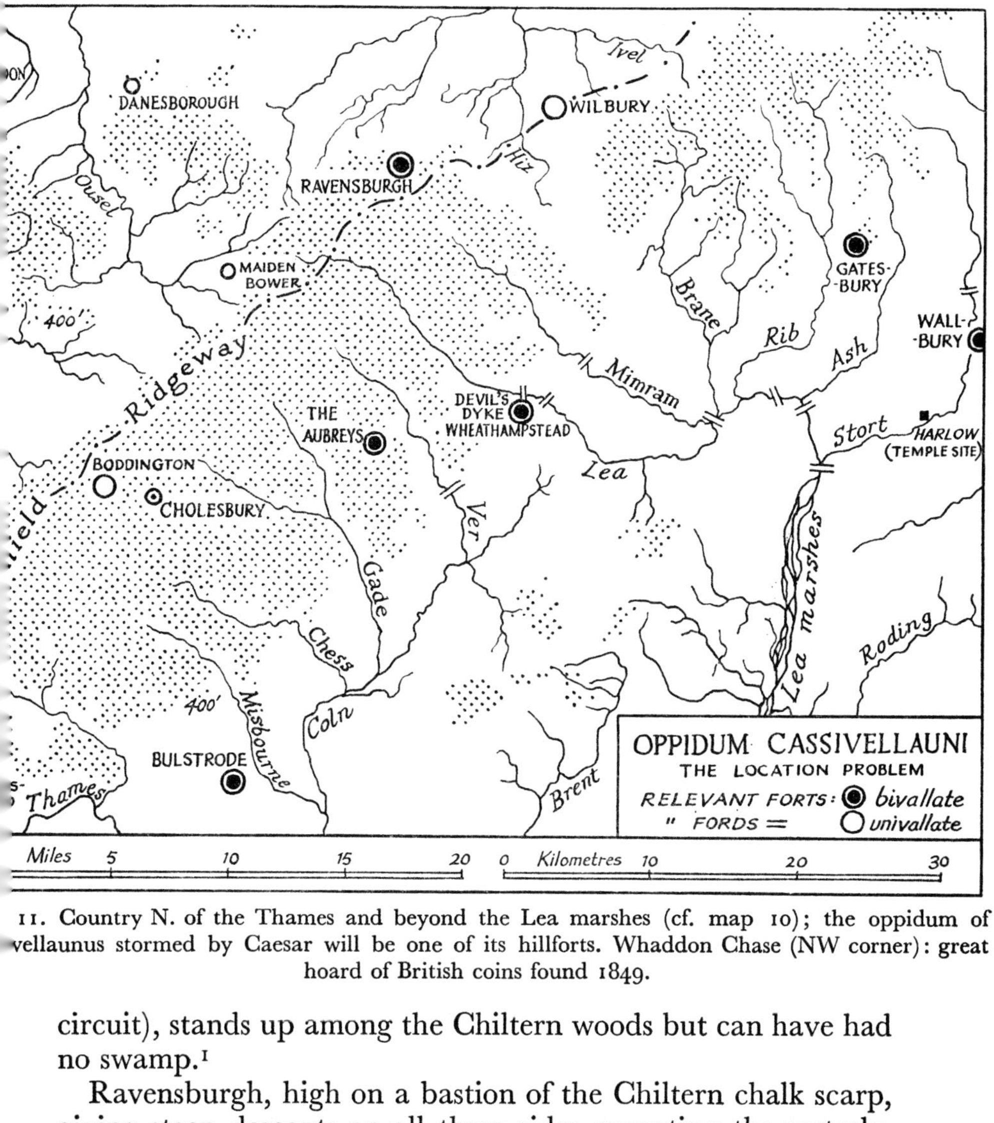

11. Country N. of the Thames and beyond the Lea marshes (cf. map 10); the oppidum of vellaunus stormed by Caesar will be one of its hillforts. Whaddon Chase (NW corner): great hoard of British coins found 1849.

circuit), stands up among the Chiltern woods but can have had no swamp.[1]

Ravensburgh, high on a bastion of the Chiltern chalk scarp, giving steep descents on all three sides excepting the easterly, remains. It is adequately far from Trinovantes (25 miles) yet near enough for Caesar. As the scarp should not be very far from Cassivellaunus's northern border, any fort on it might be known among northern neighbours. At Ravensburgh, Mr.

[1] Gatesbury (smallest), Rodwell 1976, 328–9, 364–5, citing C. R. Partridge; Aubreys, Bulstrode, briefly in *VCH*, *Herts*, iv, *Bucks*, ii; Bulstrode (8·5 ha. enclosed) suggested *oppidum Cassivellauni* by Revd. B. Burgess, 1883, *Records of Bucks*, v. 326–7; Cholesbury, survey, excavation and finds (pottery, Hawkes), Kimball 1934; Chiltern area, Dyer 1961 (with *Antiquity*, xxxvii, 46–9); Saunders 1972; Matthews (i–xiii Hawkes) 1976.

James Dyer's excavations[1] show an early primary rampart, a lengthy interval, then a reconstruction, and a fourth period next, to which the interior stripping published assigns large post-holes set in rows (44 holes in 0·1 hectare). Cattle-pen posts can have stood in them; besides, there was purposeful slighting

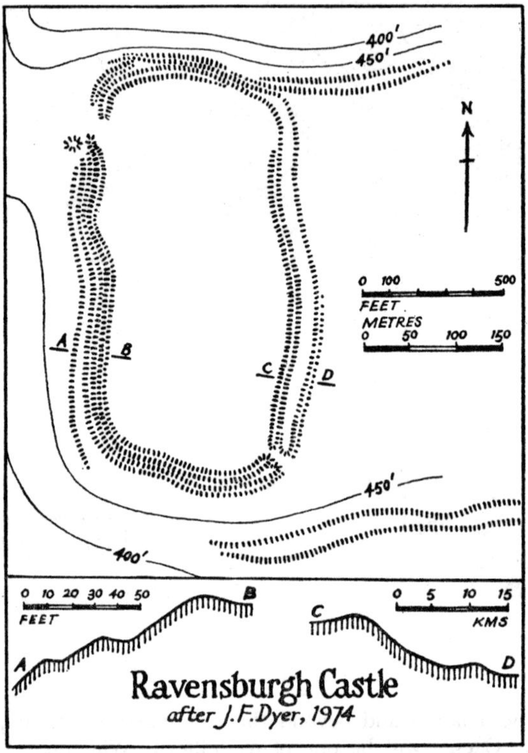

FIG. 4. Ravensburgh Castle hillfort (Bedfordshire: location, map 11): plan and profiles in actual state, after J. F. Dyer 1974.

of the rampart—on the east, where a ditch-fill rapidly followed, with a 'Belgic pedestal' pot-base. This base can be after Caesar (later additions to the works are undated), but the slighting could be his, upon a capture with cattle in the pens. Having forest to south and swamp to south-east, neither open to doubt, excellent natural and earthwork strength, and a size that is eastern England's biggest—almost 6·5 hectares internally—Ravensburgh stands (fig. 4) quite likely to be shown, with

[1] Dyer 1976; excavations 1964, 1970, 1972. With cordial approval from the owner of the site, Mr. James Ashley Cooper, James Dyer has briefed me on all, with copy of plan for my fig. 4; marsh just SE. at Burwell spring, his 158–9, fig. 1. Caesar's description of *oppidum* and capture, *BG* v. 21, 4–6.

further excavation, as the *oppidum Cassivellauni* taken by Caesar. Legions would easily march by the ridge north-west from the Lea to arrive here; and Wheathampstead will need, for competing, a proof that its 'Slad' is true ditch—Mr. Dyer believes it natural. Of Cassivellaunus, Caesar says not that he was present in the fort thus stormed, but that now he got the news that the surprise attack that he had ordered on the naval camp, to cut Caesar off from Gaul at a stroke, had failed. After suffering so much, lands ravaged, worst of all the defection of tribes he had relied on, he let it be known that he was ready for his own surrender.[1]

Caesar had been in Britain for some four weeks.[2] Within them, pulling disappointment into gain, he had certainly accomplished wonders. But he had had to drop the notion of his wintering his army there; in Gaul, he says, it might be needed for sudden troubles. So he would now, and this he does not say, quickly ride to the naval camp, praise the defenders, inspect the ships, start planning the return, and dictate correspondence. His letters to Rome included the one for Cicero, whose recording it, as written from the coast on '1st September', modern 5 August, has alone disclosed the fact and timing of the visit.[3] There was also personal tragedy at hand for Caesar. His daughter Julia, in her early twenties but married five years to Pompey, and loved by them both, had just now died in childbirth. That his bond with Pompey would be loosened, he might foresee.[4] Yet all the more, he must make the best of Britain; a return kept clear of the autumn equinox would leave him, at the most, six weeks. Enough for what he needed to do, if only he ensured success at the start of it. That was, to draw terms of surrender out of Britain which would let him guarantee himself a profit, from its wealth—that wealth which he had hoped for through Armorica, and now must get at here, both to justify his venture and to yield the profit for his use. Treating Cassivellaunus as still a commander-in-chief, although

[1] *BG* v. 22, 1–3.

[2] As declared at the start, I follow the chronology not of Le Verrier but of Holmes (1907, 707–35), whose case appears to me (with 669–71) to be as firm as ever.

[3] In a letter to his younger brother Quintus Cicero, in Britain with the army but not with Caesar then at the coast: Cicero, letters *ad Quintum fratrem* iii. 1, 25.

[4] Julia: Gelzer 1969, 21, 80, 147–8; a sequel, 170. Dies, Caesar still in Britain (Cicero, Seneca), news on his reaching Gaul (Plutarch): Rambaud 1974, 21.

a beaten one, he must get him to open the surrender talks by sending a mission to himself, and persuade him to this through means that were sure to succeed. The most urgent, therefore, of his business will be sending for Commius, perhaps forewarned already at his capital by Arras, and pressing him on Cassivellaunus to facilitate the mission. And Caesar records, not explaining his presence at all, that 'through Commius the Atrebate' the mission in fact was sent, and that hostages, lest the war should be prolonged, were demanded and duly supplied. He then says he fixed 'what Britain, each several year (*in annos singulos*), was to pay to the Roman People as *vectigal*'. His orders to Cassivellaunus (he continues) were to do no harm to Mandubracius, nor his people the Trinovantes—he now being king. All this happened inland, for Caesar states that after getting the hostages, he marched his army back to the sea and found the ships reconditioned.[1] He was there by 29 August (his calendar's sixth day prior to October), when as Cicero records he wrote him a letter once again.[2] Caesar's time on the parleys will therefore have been not less than a fortnight; and the hostages had only all arrived (so it seems) when the army was ready for the march. What profit had the terms guaranteed him? The question leads on to my concluding theme.

IV. *From Britain through Gaul to Civil War, 54–49 B.C.*

'Britain is finished off', was what his last mail told to Cicero; no booty, but hostages got, and *pecunia* ordained. The number of Caesar's prisoners, however, was great; he says so when telling how his army was brought, in two successive convoys, safely to Gaul in spite of the approaching equinox—our 26 September.[3] He limits his account to 'ships for military transport', but private merchantmen, numerous in July when the fleet had set out, must have been carrying prisoners for sale as slaves, and material booty besides; Strabo in fact records both slaves and booty.[4]

[1] All this is v. 22, 3–5 and 23, 1: most masterly compression.

[2] Cicero, letters *ad Atticum*, iv. 18, 5: he has had one from his brother (p. 175 n. 3) besides Caesar, both being back at 'the nearest coasts of Britain' by that day; (*litoribus*) *proximis*, emending the manuscripts' *proximo*, is generally accepted.

[3] *BG* v. 23: Holmes 1907, 706 with nn. 3–4; Rambaud 1974, 101; with this the Le Verrier chronology naturally accords.

[4] Strabo (iv) 200. Private ships in fleet at outset, *BG* v. 8, 6; its ships altogether had been more than 800. Not booty, but from Kent coast oysters, would be Caesar's pearls: Suetonius 25, 2; Pliny iv. 16.

More profitable even than immediate loot, moreover, would be that *pecunia*, that annual tribute to the Roman People: a tax, defined as *vectigal*. Best interpreter here has again been Stevens.[1] Every tribe's recorded surrender, and Cassivellaunus's own as leader, had been a *deditio*: term in public law for unconditional surrender, whereby the surrendered are liable to *vectigal*. The terms for Cassivellaunus warning him off the Trinovantes are only a special addition for him to the terms for 'Britain' as a whole; they imply a corollary for Mandubracius, as Trinovantian king, that he, having come to Caesar seeking protection (*in fidem*), may expect the surrender to bring him the status of a 'client king' by treaty. *Britannia* was envisaged meanwhile as a 'provisional province', for entering the Empire; the tax lay on all of it. What was this *Britannia*? Cassivellaunus's supreme command, given him by all the resisting tribes, is treated now as an *imperium* over every tribe, so wide that Caesar can use *Britannia* inclusively. The 'interior part' in the excursus (p. 167) is of course here out of the reckoning, but the tribes will include non-maritime besides the 'maritime'.

They are Cassivellaunus's own (in subsequent record the Catuvellauni), four under kings in Kent, the Trinovantes, and the five that had surrendered next; one of these at least lay north of his own, as having given information of his *oppidum*, and another can have been the Iceni beyond the Trinovantes on an inland side, if the name, in Caesar *Cenimagni*, as many have thought, means 'the greater Iceni' (the surrender not extending to any 'lesser'). All five should be anyhow north of the Thames; but south of it is Surrey, part of which Caesar had traversed marching west out of Kent, so had somehow subdued (map 10). The tribes are then eleven or twelve. And in Surrey there begins, stretching west into inland Hampshire, the preponderant distribution of the 'British A' coins, derived from Gallo-Belgic, and now being seen as late enough for this same time. From some in West Sussex and a neighbour group ('British D'), with another such ('British C') in the Isle of Wight, there begins the 'British B' distribution, over western Hampshire and Dorset, clearly now later than Allen believed, so again to be put at this time.[2] None of the states with such coins

[1] Stevens 1947, 7–8, advancing from Holmes 1907, 355–6, and augmenting his authorities. Cf. Rambaud 1974, 16, 99–100: two traditions, one commending or magnifying Caesar's achievement, one disparaging. Further, with Stevens 1951, see p. 179, n. 2.

[2] Mackensen 1974 (after 1973), slightly (but firmly) lowering the dates

as these were 'maritime' in Caesar's own sense; nor, as we have been deciding, was Cassivellaunus. As for those extending out west, they need not have joined in his parleys with Caesar, but they were linked in geography to those of the *Britannia* that did—and the links will have been often economic.

Caesar, through the trade that will have always been supplying it with shares in the metals of the west (pp. 150, 166–7), the north-west probably, and any Midland iron, could include without closer inquiry shares for himself in assessing it to tax, and thus, with the rest of the assessment, profit from quarters that he never was to visit. Reckoning the value in *pecunia*, he thus could get tin out of Britain after all, along with whatever other wealth the *vectigal* was laid upon. We have seen that there may also still have been cross-Channel trade in it, from southern Britain over to northerly Armorica (pp. 150–1 with n. 1); from there by land, the route would reach Cenabum on the Loire (at Orléans: map 7), where now were many merchants up from the south. So Caesar could anyhow partly retrieve his disappointment of the year 56.

Just as well. That October, in north-east Gaul, revolt burst out. He had planned next year for Germany again, reasserting the Rhine as his frontier;[1] he managed to, bridging it again, but the year 53 was grim for Caesar, and for his second-in-command, the tough Labienus. Still within winter, Cenabum was assailed, and the merchants and his corn-supply officer all of them massacred. Events moved swiftly into the great revolt of 52—and in that, despite the rewards he had had from Caesar, Commius joined.[2] Then again, after finishing in winter his *Gallic War*, in seven books, Caesar had resistance still to stamp out in 51. Commius rose, with his peoples and the Bellovaci, and was furiously active; moreover he knew too much, about those dealings in Britain especially. But when Caesar sent Volusenus to kill him at a parley, he escaped with a wound. When back from dealing with south-west Gaul's last stand, and with Aquitania, Caesar wintered with the northernmost four of

implicit in the Jersey Le Câtillon hoard, on which Allen relied: his 1961 and 62; distributions, 1962 map 1, whence Hawkes 1968, 11, map C; E's (from Allen, map 2) no longer explained by invasion, n. 1 on p. 143, from Scheers as there cited (with Mackensen).

[1] Rambaud 1974, 16–22, 102 ff. on v. 24–58, explaining the winter dispositions as prepared for this, and amending, with legions nine not eight, my account 1968, 7–9 with map fig. 1. Campaigns of 53: vi. 1–12, 29–44.

[2] *BG* vii; Commius, 75, 76, 79.

his legions at Arras, by Étrun the old capital of Commius—who himself had still been in arms and busily harassing Roman supply-trains. Worsted (though he nearly killed Volusenus) at last in a cavalry fight, he offered hostages: for his life, if nevermore within sight of any Roman, he would go and do whatever he was told.[1]

All this has led to disbelief, among some, that the tax due from Britain was paid at all. We have no statement that it was, even in the eighth of the *Gallic War* books, which Hirtius afterwards wrote to complete the set. Yet does this hide a tribute unpaid, by a Britain thus cheating Caesar? Or hide its being paid, because it swelled the supplies for his preparing, never avowed, of civil war? That it was paid, most English opinion has agreed with Stevens.[2] Yet his belief that it continued for long seems not so binding; and all-important for Caesar were the first few years. If civil war came, against the party of his enemies in Rome, the right-wing senators, drawing in Pompey as they might, he could win enough against them in the West for invading Spain, and could hope to subdue it. Whatever happened next, there would be wealth for him from there. But in the meantime, Gaul was being bled; in gold alone, what Caesar took away sent the market price plummeting;[3] to estimate the loss to the country in wealth of all kinds is beyond possibility. Yet the widespread ruin he had brought it needed a sequel now in appeasement: from directly after the fighting of 51 and for all of 50, bland generosity was plainly essential for peace.[4] So a steady British tribute would make him an offset. And the great camp by Arras where he passed that winter had Boulogne very near, and a straight road down through the Remi to the Alps, for Italy, if business required it. To the Britons, his previous years' punishments inflicted in Gaul were a terrible warning:

[1] *BG* viii; Commius, 6–7, 10, 21–3, 47–8. The final deal was previous to Caesar's reaching Arras, and was made with Marcus Antonius, now his quaestor. But when Commius fled none the less, we are told it was from Caesar, who will thus have come just in time—unless the flight was next summer. See text below with p. 183 n. 3.

[2] Stevens 1947, 7–8 (where Livy); fuller, 1951, 332 ff., whence Frere 1967 (1974, 55–6). Trinovantes prosper under treaty, drinking-vessels imported and wine in amphoras (Dressel IB Italian, and other), Peacock 1971, 171–7; Rodwell 1976, 237–43.

[3] Suetonius 54.

[4] Declared viii. 49, a very forthright statement—though of course with nothing of his need of unopposed recruitment of auxiliary troops, horses, and materials of war for the expected struggle.

they had to expect that he was presently going to return. So for four years or five, I believe that the tribute was paid. But what happened next?

I have tried to show it on a map (map 12). The escape of Commius to Britain, on this, seems dwarfed by the events on the Continent; but from there, very soon, I shall turn to look back on it, and deal with its date and implications. Caesar's base was still at Arras when he called, in the middle summer of 50, the whole of his army to a place 'on the bounds of the Treveri' for high ceremonial: its solemn lustration from stain by the horrors of the war—to be clean for the next one. (The required big stretch of open land would be between the Ardennes and the Woèvre and Argonne, out on the borders of Lorraine round Bouzonville and Basse-Yutz.)[1] After that, striking camp at Arras and moving south to his other great camp, by the Aeduan capital Bibracte on the Mont-Beuvray, he placed Labienus in Cisalpine Gaul—whence he soon would be defecting to Rome. How Caesar, joining his Thirteenth Legion at Ravenna on the Adriatic coast, faced there the dictates of the right-wing party, with Pompey drawn in—that celebrated story yet has lost the locations of the two further legions he was counting on. While three legions more were now with Fabius about Narbo, confronting the Pyrenees and Pompey's Spain,[2] Caesar will assuredly have moved the Twelfth and Eighth into south-east Gaul: whatever the season, they had to cross the Alps to him without any danger from snow. His December, when the Rome situation reached climax, began in our calendar's mid-October. But could he be sure so soon that the normal western pass—the Mont-Genèvre—would be open when he summoned them? Safe then would only be the snow-free pass behind Genoa, reached along the coast-road. And Massilia, though included in his policy of appeasement, might still resent his

[1] Lustration of 'army' (so en masse): viii. 52, 1. Rolling country everywhere, between those forests, no doubt long cleared through native occupation under lordships such as that which in early fourth century, from a lordly tomb undoubtedly (others are renowned both to east and to west), is evinced in the British Museum by the sumptuous four bronze vessels of Basse-Yutz.

[2] *BCiv* i. 37, 1: not disclosed till he is set for the Pyrenees. Legions set to follow these (37, 2) were 'more distant'; but where? My map's route for the Thirteenth into Cisalpine quarters already (whence called to Ravenna, *BCiv* i. 7, 8 with 6, 5) is by the Genèvre, reaching the upper Durance from the Drôme and Col de Cabre, rather than by Grenoble: cf. Holmes 1911, 615–16 (Caesar 58 B.C.) with the tribal geography.

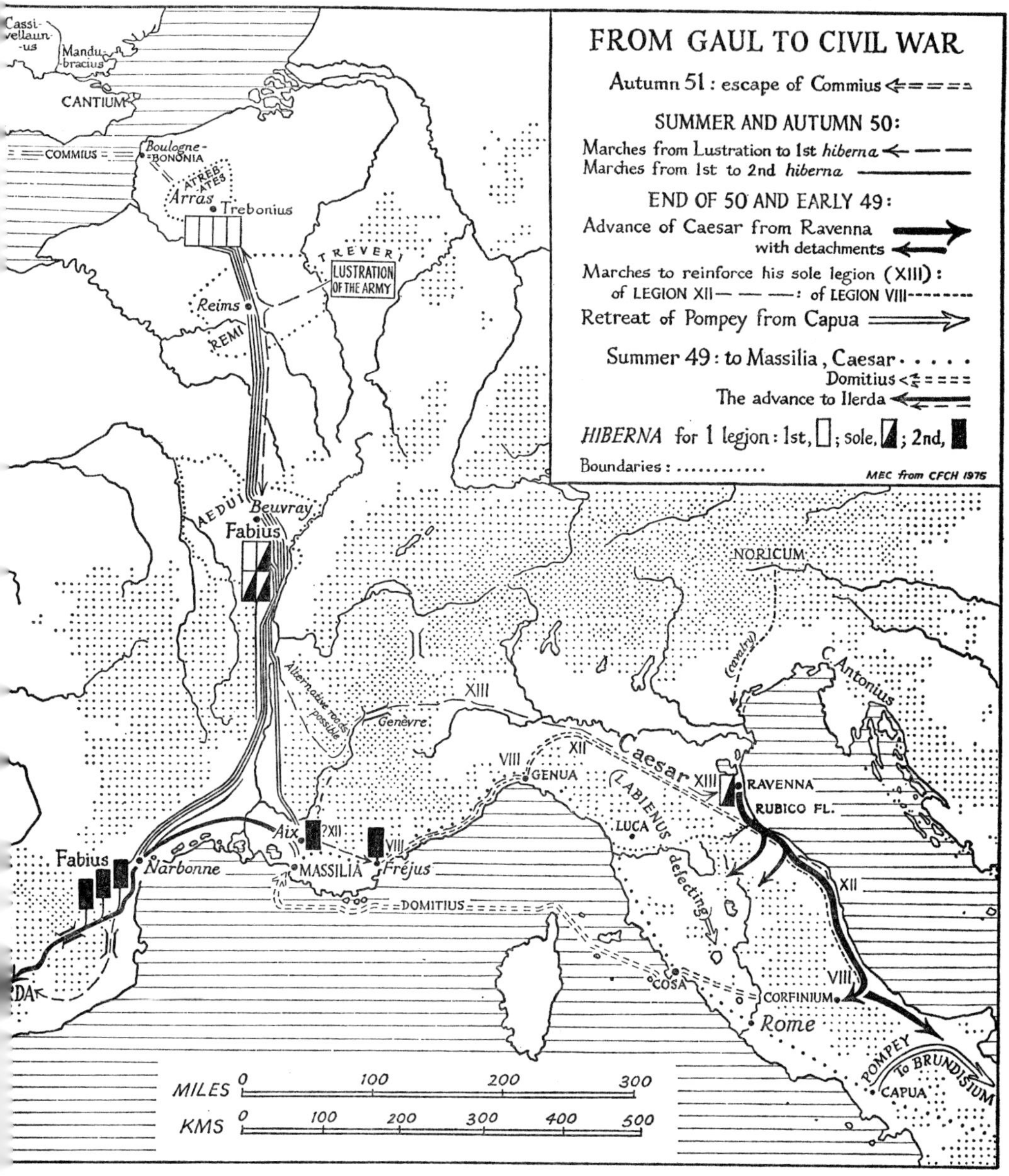

AP 12. Caesar's transition from the Gallic to the Civil War, 51–49 B.C. Topography as text and notes pp. 182–5. *Hiberna* are legionary winter-quarters (normally ordained at the end of summer).

robbing it of trade; at first, one legion could watch it, so I fancy the Twelfth camped somewhere near Aix, for advance, if not by the Genèvre, then along past Fréjus. By Fréjus, not yet Roman nor ever with its harbour taken up by Massilia, the road towards Genoa passed (at that time, climbing the Estérel); when Caesar got power he founded its town *Forum Julii*, and made it a veterans' colony soon—for the Eighth. So the Eighth is here now; the Twelfth will be joining it, and both are called to Italy by Caesar, in time for setting out within Rome's mid-December, last week of the modern October. In Rome's early February, the modern mid-December, he gets the Twelfth to him in eastern Italy; the Eighth had to shepherd twenty-two raw cohorts, just raised, and be joined by some horse from the king of Noricum, so reached him with these some ten days later, at Corfinium.[1]

For his opening the Civil War, from Ravenna by the Rubicon and on, securing Apennine passes, Pompey soon now heading for retreat, this was how Caesar reset the scene: by hidden intermediate steps from the Beuvray and his northern base-camp at Arras, which was kept secluded just as long as he required it, for the Belgae and the tax from Britain. Now at Corfinium, with various notables and troops in force, stood Domitius—grandson of Domitius of the elephant (p. 161), and Caesar's most deadly enemy. Yet the troops, ringed round, came

[1] Thus the coast-road's blocking by Ligurian revolt for Pompey, in February (during our December) at Ventimiglia, put down with small forces by Caelius (as he wrote to Cicero: letters *ad Familiares* viii. 15, 2), was after the legions had passed, to prevent its re-use; so Caesar's hiding those events will accord with his hiding its ever being used, and with his feigning that he summoned these legions with others in January (our late November): from Rimini, *BCiv* 1. 8, 1, after leaving Ravenna. To get them moving in time, he must have summoned them well before he left it: before mid-December (our late October). The deceit has been notorious, but most have thought he called them straight from Beuvray and Arras, not from secondary camps; the diagrammatic lineation of my map can show how he switched the dispositions.

Fréjus, *Forum Julii Octavanorum Colonia*, as among colonies founded by Caesar, through Tiberius Nero in 46: Rambaud 1966, 432 (older view: Caesar founds *Forum*, in Cicero already 43, *Colonia* for Eighth being later, *c.* 30 when entitled *Pacensis Classica*); latest account will be P. A. Février, *Forum Julii* (*Fréjus*) ed. 2; ed. 1 was 1963; his summary now, with new excavations, is in Goudineau (ed.) 1976, 41–62; I thank him for further demonstration on the spot, September 1976, notably of road over Estérel. On Alpine passes' onsets of snow (ref. esp. Mt.-Genèvre) I thank for advice professors Marc Sauter and colleagues (Geneva) and Nino Lamboglia, Inst. Ligurian Studies (Bordighera), who has shown me the Colle di Tenda as

over. And the notables were spared, including Domitius.[1] He went, from Cosa on the western coast with a squadron of ships, to Massilia, and there brought about a resolve of the city, in Caesar's despite, to withstand him.[2] And this is where I think of the escape—late autumn 51 (or up to middle summer 50)—of Commius, over to Britain out of northern Gaul. The trouble to expect in his case, of course, was in Gaul if he had not made the escape. But his making it affected Britain very much, so I turn to it.

The story of his flight is told not in the *Gallic War*, but in the *Stratagems* of Julius Frontinus, who, a century and a quarter later, was governor of Roman Britain, and might have collected the tale from there.[3] It has him pursued by Caesar, who thus will still have been based on Arras, but has him bluffing the pursuit by setting full sail while his ships were aground at low tide. Was Caesar so simply deceived? or was the pursuit a shrewd bluff of his own, intended to fail so that Commius was thus got rid of? But whereas at Corfinium Caesar's clemency was public, to gain him political advantage (which it did), this would have been secret indeed: how few could have guessed it? It looks as if Britain, whatever might be done there by Commius, was now dispensable. If its tribute-tax continued, all

impossible and moved me to adopt the coast-road. See in general Gabert and Guichonnet 1965, 38, 74–7, 82–3 map fig. 7, 95–6, 99.

[1] *BCiv* i. 8–23, Caesar's narrative from Ravenna to Corfinium, masterly in vividness yet also in omissions and slants (cf. Pollio in Suetonius 56, 4); on others' views of his veracity (Mommsen, Meyer, Holmes, Adcock, Syme) Rambaud 1966, 133–4 with n. 88, compares O. E. Schmidt, von Fritz and himself; on the march and summoning of legions, 106–7, and Fabre 1972, xxvii, both starting from Stoffel (*Guerre civ.*, 1887); but only from secondary camps can the summoning be just when the crisis demanded it—just after Caesar's 7–10 December (third week of our October), when he had the latest news from Rome (brought first by Hirtius, then by Curio). Domitius spared at Corfinium, and even financed, i. 23, 2–4; proceeds by sea to Massilia, 34, 2.

[2] *BCiv* i. 34–6, Caesar somewhat juggling the sequence of events.

[3] Julius Frontinus, governor 74–77/8: *Stratagemata*, ii. 13, 11. For escape-date as autumn 51, see p. 179 (from *BG* viii. 48) with n. 1. Otherwise it has to be in 50 at a time when Caesar was at hand for a pursuit. Commius could have planned the escape (flotilla of ships) when the army was away for the lustration, but on starting found Caesar was back from it sooner than he reckoned. Yet after it (viii. 52, 1–2), though Caesar was in movement, we are not told where he went. An escape in middle summer at latest, before he left for Italy (54, 4–5), is the only alternative to one in late autumn 51, which I rather prefer.

the better for Caesar; if not, he had at least had the profit while he needed it most. What Commius did there, we can judge from coins. From the type of Allen's Gallo-Belgic F (now seen as Suessionic) is derived his 'British Q', displaying a horse with triple tail. It is distributed in coastal Sussex and inland on the middle and upper Thames and all around; furthermore, after twenty or twenty-five years the type gets an inscription—Commius's name. His dynasty's later story is not here relevant; but what must be, is the quantity of Q coins appearing in the great gold hoard of Whaddon Chase (map 11), which has otherwise a quite new class, 'British L'. This has divisions, related obscurely; but the whole brings change, in distribution, to the former pattern seen north of the middle Thames. In the centre there, Cassivellaunus had not struck coins; now, his country is brought into the L coin area, which stretches outside it. These Whaddon Chase coins have been by some believed his; but Allen's and the lower modern datings tell against it;[1] what the change means, surely, is Cassivellaunus's death. So perhaps what Commius did was to foment, or join, a revulsion against him, by tribes that surrender to Caesar had forced to pay the tax. It would henceforth cease. It should cease in the very early 40s, when Caesar had the Civil War fully on his hands.

Pompey had withdrawn to Brundisium, eluded Caesar, and sailed to the Balkans. Caesar, speeding now from Rome to Massilia, set Trebonius and Decimus Brutus to besiege it. On into Spain, adding three to Fabius's legions, he defeated the legates of Pompey at Ilerda. So in Farther Spain soon, he could assure himself the wealth he had withdrawn from in 61, beside the Ocean. Through many worse frustrations, often hidden by his deceits, his successes had put the West, which he had guarded

[1] These lower datings however leave Gallo-Belgic F itself, and so the start of British Q, not so late as believed by Allen but actually earlier. This follows from F's recognition by Scheers as Suessionic, as prior to her last classes (4, 5, and *Criciru*), and as passing elements to Q that are all from her previous classes (1–3). So Q will have started here a little before 60, not from the flight of Commius: Scheers 1970b, 154–6. Commius will then have been received among people who already had Q, and were using it before the termination of the sequence British A1–A2–B1–B2: Mackensen 1974 and my p. 143 n. 1. None the less he can have quickly been in action; and the coin-map contrast north of the Thames, marked by the Whaddon Chase hoard's combination of Q and British L, remains sharp. Rodwell 1976, with L Trinovantian, makes it sharper; though his E needs correcting (my n. 7 pp. 142–3), his L could start just after 54 (Mandubracius), and spread wider on Cassivellaunus's death, which I think should account for the contrast. See text to his maps fig. 3, 4, 10, 19, 20.

by the Rhine, all into his hands—with the trade that he had robbed from Massilia. He arrived in time for its surrender, achieved through the efforts of Trebonius and Brutus. In spite of setbacks (in Illyricum with C. Antonius, in Africa, and briefly through a mutiny)[1] this freed him for the next year's ultimate reckoning with Pompey. Caesar when supreme (pl. XXII) had a price to pay. In only the fifth year after, on the Ides of March, Trebonius and Brutus joined in extracting it in blood. Yet he was history's force: driving to power from the West, where his spoils, essential to his triumph, will have included—in the critical years—that tax from the Britain he had had to let drop.

BIBLIOGRAPHY AND ABBREVIATIONS

Alföldy 1974	G. Alföldy, *Noricum*, London and Boston (Routledge).
Allen 1944	D. F. Allen, 'The Belgic Dynasties of Britain and their Coins', *Archaeologia*, xc, 1–46.
Allen 1961	—— 'The Origins of Coinage in Britain: A Re-appraisal', in Frere (ed.) 1961, 97–308.
Allen 1962	—— 'Celtic Coins', in *OS. Map S. Br.*, 20–32.
Allen 1971	—— 'British Potin Coins: a Review', in Jesson and Hill (eds.) 1971, 127–48.
†Allen 1976	—— 'Wealth, Money and Coinage in a Celtic Society', in *To Illustrate the Monuments*, ed. Megaw: Essays to Piggott, London (Thames and Hudson), 199–208.
Ashbee 1974	P. Ashbee, *Ancient Scilly*, London (David and Charles).
Bayly 1962	E. H. Bayly, 'Activities round Dover, 1962', *Arch. Cantiana*, lxxvii, (p.) xlviii.
Behrens 1923	G. Behrens, *Denkmäler des Wangionengebietes*: Germanische Denkmäler der Frühzeit I, Mainz (Röm.-Germ. Zentralmuseum).
Belloc 1904 (1948)	H. Belloc, *The Old Road*, London (Constable), reprint 1948 from ed. 1910.
Benadik 1971	B. Benadik in Filip (ed.) 1971, 907–12.
Berciu 1967	D. Berciu, *Romania before Burebista*, London (Thames and Hudson).
Birchall 1965	Ann Birchall, 'The Aylesford-Swarling culture . . .', *Proc. Prehist. Soc.* xxxi, 241–367.

[1] Siege of Massilia, *BCiv* i. 36, 56–8, ii. 1–16; Spanish campaign and attainment of victory at Ilerda, i. 37–55, 59–87; Caesar in Farther Spain, ii. 17–22; C. Antonius, iii. 10 (implied prior mention seems lost); Africa, ii. 23–44; mutiny of Ninth Legion at Placentia (Cisalpine) told by Suetonius, Appian, and Dio, concealed by Caesar.

Bishop 1971 — M. W. Bishop, 'The non-Belgic Iron Age in Surrey', *Surrey Arch. Collections*, lxviii, 1–30.

Boyd Dawkins 1902 — (Sir) W. Boyd Dawkins, 'On Bigbury Camp and the Pilgrims' Way', *Archaeo. Journal*, lix, 211–18.

Brady 1952 — S. G. Brady, 'Caesar and Britain', *Classical Journal* xlvii, 305–16, with 348.

Briard 1965 — J. Briard, *Les Dépôts bretons et l'âge du bronze atlantique*, Rennes (Lab. d'Anthrop. préhist. de la Faculté des Sciences).

Bushe-Fox 1915 — J. P. Bushe-Fox, *Excavations at Hengistbury Head in 1911–12*, Rep. Research C'ttee Soc. Antiq. London iii, Oxford (OUP).

Bushe-Fox 1925 — —— *Excavation of the Late Celtic Urnfield at Swarling, Kent, in 1921*, Rep. (as 1915) v, Oxford (OUP).

Caesar *BCiv* — Gaius Iulius Caesar, *Commentarii de Bello Civili*: ed. and transl. P. Fabre, *César, la Guerre Civile* i–ii, Coll. des Univs. de France Assoc. G. Budé, Paris (Belles-Lettres), tome i, 1936, 8th printing 1972; Rambaud 1962 ed. bk. i.

Caesar *BG* — —— *Commentarii de Bello Gallico* i–vii, with viii by A. Hirtius: Oxford ed., R. Du Pontet 1901 (1924); Teubner ed., O. Seel 1961 (1968). Eds. with comm.: Holmes 1914, Rambaud 1965 bks. ii–iii, 1967 bk. iv, 1974 bk. v. My citations by book-chapter-section may omit, where superfluous, the *BG* prefix.

Collingwood 1936 — R. G. Collingwood in Collingwood and Myres, Oxford History of England, i (*Roman Britain and the English Settlements*, chapter iii), Oxford (Clarendon Press).

Collis 1971 — J. R. Collis, 'Markets and Money', in Jesson and Hill (eds.), 97–104.

Colvin 1959 — H. M. Colvin, on Dover Castle in *Antiquity*, xxxiii, 125–7, with official plan fig. 1.

Colvin 1963 — —— on the same, in Colvin (ed.), *The History of the King's Works*, ii, London (HMSO), 629–41 with period plans fig. 53.

Crawford — M. H. Crawford, *Roman Republican Coinage*, 2 vols., Cambridge (CUP) 1974.

Cuff 1958 — P. J. Cuff, 'The terminal date of Caesar's Gallic Command', *Historia*, vii, 445–71.

Cunliffe (ed.) 1968 — B. W. Cunliffe (ed.), *Fifth Report on the Excavations at Richborough, Kent*, Rep. Research C'ttee Soc. Antiq. London xxiii, Oxford (OUP).

Cunliffe 1974 — —— *Iron Age Communities in Britain*, London and Boston (Routledge).

Cunliffe and Rowley (eds.) 1976 — —— and T. Rowley (eds.), *Oppida: the Beginnings of Urbanisation in Barbarian Europe* (conference, Oxford Oct. 1975), BAR Supplementary Series 11, Oxford (British Archaeological Reports).

Daicoviciu C. 1945 — C. Daicoviciu, *La Transylvanie dans l'antiquité*, Bucarest.

Daicoviciu C. 1969 — —— in *Römer in Rumänien*, Köln (Röm.-Germ. Mus. exhib. catalogue-vol.).

Daicoviciu H. 1965 — H. Daicoviciu, *Dacii*, Bucarest.

Daicoviciu H. 1972 — —— *Dacia de la Burebista la cucerirea romana*, Cluj.

Dayet 1960 — M. Dayet, 'Le Denier de César au type de l'éléphant', *Revue arch. de l'Est et du Centre-Est*, xi. 1, 42–7.

De Laet 1974 — S. J. De Laet, *Prehistorische Kulturen in het Zuiden der Lage Landen*, Wetteren (Universa).

Dio — Cassius Dio Cocceianus, *Roman History*: comp. over years to *c.* A.D. 230 (vulg. 'Dion Cassius').

Diodorus — Diodorus Siculus, *Bibliotheca* (of history to 54 B.C.): comp. *c.* 60–30.

Dion 1952 — R. Dion, 'Le Problème des Cassitérides', *Latomus*, xi, 306–14.

Du Pontet (ed.) 1901 (1924) — R. (L. A.) Du Pontet (ed.), *Caesaris opera I* (*Comm. de BG*), Oxford (reprint 1924).

Duval (ed.) 1973 — P.-M. Duval (ed.), *Études celtiques*, xiii, tome 2, *Actes du IVe. Congr. Internat. d'Études celtiques, Rennes 1971*, *Archéologie celtique*, Paris (Belles-Lettres).

Dyer 1961 — J. F. Dyer, on Chiltern Iron Age territorial boundaries, *Antiquaries Journal*, xli, 32–43.

Dyer 1976 — —— 'Ravensburgh Castle, Hertfordshire', in Harding (ed.), 153–9.

Fabre 1972 — See Caesar *BCiv.*

FHA — *Fontes Hispaniae Antiquae*, ed. A. Schulten, Barcelona (Bosch). 1937: fasc. iv, *Las Guerras de 154–72*; 1940: fasc. v, *Las Guerras de 72–19*; 1952: fasc. vi, *Estrabón, Geografía de Iberia* (= Strabo iii, etc.).

Filip 1956 — J. Filip, *Keltové ve Střední Europý: Die Kelten in Mitteleuropa*, Prague.

Filip 1962 — —— *Celtic Civilisation and its Heritage*, in New Horizons ser., Czech Acad. Sci. (Engl. transl. from orig. 1960), Prague.

Filip (ed.) 1971 — —— (ed.), *Actes du VIIe. Congr. Internat. des Sciences Pré- et Protohistoriques, Prague 1966*, tome 2, Prague.

Fox A. 1964 — (Lady) Aileen Fox, *South West England*, London (Thames and Hudson).

Frere (ed.) 1961 — S. S. Frere (ed.), *Problems of the Iron Age in Southern Britain*, from conference (Council for British Archaeology) Dec. 1958, London (Univ. Inst. of Archaeology, Occasional Paper II).

Frere 1961 — —— 'Some Problems of the later Iron Age', in Frere (ed.), 84–92.

Frere 1967 (1974) — —— *Britannia: a History of Roman Britain*, London: 1967 (Routledge); my refs. are all to 1974 (Sphere Books' Cardinal ed.) paperback.

Gabert and Guichonnet 1965 — P. Gabert and P. Guichonnet, *Les Alpes*, Coll. 'Magellan' (La Géographie et ses problèmes) no. 14, Paris (Presses Universitaires de France).

Gelzer 1969 — M. Gelzer, *Caesar: politician and statesman*, reprint (slightly rev.) of 1968 Engl. transl. of German 6th ed. (1960), Oxford (Blackwell).

Glodariu 1976 — I. Glodariu, *Dacian Trade with the Hellenistic and Roman World*, BAR Supplementary Series 8, Oxford (British Archaeological Reports).

Goudineau(ed.) 1976 — Ch. Goudineau (ed.), *Sites de l'Age du Fer et Gallo-Romains de la région de Nice*, Livret-Guide de l'excursion B3 du IXe. Congrès UISPP (Nice).

Hachmann 1962 — R. Hachmann, 'Germanen und Kelten am Rhein in der Zeit um Christi Geburt', in R. Hachmann-G. Kossack-H. Kuhn, *Völker zwischen Germanen und Kelten*, Neumünster (Wachholz).

Harden 1962 — D. B. Harden, *The Phoenicians*, London (Thames and Hudson).

Harding 1974 — D. W. Harding, *The Iron Age in Lowland Britain*, London (Routledge).

Harding (ed.) 1976 — —— (ed.), *Hillforts: Later Prehistoric Earthworks in Britain and Ireland*, London (Academic Press).

Hawkes 1965 — (C. F.) C. Hawkes, 'Celtes, Gaulois, Germains, Belges', *Celticum*, xii (Ogam Suppl. 98, Congrès Sarrebruck, 1964), 1–7, with corrigenda and map pl. I.

Hawkes 1968 — —— 'New Thoughts on the Belgae', *Antiquity*, xlii (no. 165, March), 6–16.

Hawkes 1972 — —— 'Europe and England: Fact and Fog', *Helinium*, xii, 105–16.

Hawkes 1973 — —— 'Cumulative Celticity in Pre-Roman Britain', in Duval (ed.), 607–28.

Hawkes 1977 — —— *Pytheas: Europe and the Greek Explorers*, Sir John Myres Memorial Lecture 1975, Oxford (Blackwell).

Hawkes and Dunning 1931 — —— and G. C. Dunning, 'The Belgae of Gaul and Britain', *Archaeo. Journal*, lxxxvii (for 1930), 150–335, 531–41.

Hawkes S. 1968 — Sonia (Chadwick) Hawkes, 'Richborough—The Physical Geography', in Cunliffe (ed.), 224–31.

Hencken 1932 — H. O'N. Hencken, *The Archaeology of Cornwall and Scilly*, London (Methuen, County Archaeologies series).

Hirtius — A. Hirtius, *de Bello Gallico* viii, see Caesar *BG*.

Holmes 1907 — T. Rice Holmes, *Ancient Britain and the Invasions of Julius Caesar*, Oxford (Clarendon Press).

Holmes 1911 — —— *Caesar's Conquest of Gaul* ed. 2, Oxford (Clarendon Press).

Holmes 1914 — —— ed. Caesar *BG* (i–vii with viii), Oxford (Clarendon Press).

Itin. Ant. — *Itinerarium Antonini Augusti*, so called (vulg. 'Antonine Itinerary', road-book of Roman Empire), essentially of third cent. A.D. (ed. O. Cuntz, *Itineraria Romana* i, 1929).

Jesson and Hill (eds.) — M. Jesson and D. Hill (eds.), *The Iron Age and its Hillforts: papers presented to Sir Mortimer Wheeler*, Southampton (University Monographs I), 1971.

Jessup 1930 — R. F. Jessup, *The Archaeology of Kent*, London (Methuen, County Archaeologies series).

Jessup 1933 — —— 'Bigbury Camp, Harbledown, Kent', *Archaeo. Journal*, lxxxix (for 1932), 87–115.

Jessup and Cook 1936 — —— and N. C. Cook, 'Excavations at Bigbury Camp, Harbledown', *Arch. Cantiana*, xlviii, 151–68.

Kelly 1971 — D. B. Kelly, 'Quarry Wood Camp, Loose: a Belgic oppidum', *Arch. Cantiana*, lxxxvi, 55–84.

Kimball 1934 — D. Kimball, 'Cholesbury Camp', *Journal Brit. Archaeo. Assoc.*, new ser. xxix part 1, 187–212.

Klein 1928 — W. G. Klein, reports his excavations on temple site at Worth, Kent, *Antiquaries Journal*, viii; votive shields, 79–81 by Reginald Smith, with fig. 11.

Lewis 1966 — M. J. T. Lewis, *Temples in Roman Britain*, London.

Livy — T. Livius the Roman historian was covering this period, in books now lost, about A.D. 5.

Mackensen 1973 — M. Mackensen, in *Jahrbuch f. Numismatik und Geldgeschichte* (Munich), xxiii, 45–51.

Mackensen 1974 — —— 'Die älteste Gold- und Silberprägung in England', same *Jahrbuch*, xxiv, 7–63 and 6 pls., 6 maps.

Macrea 1956 — M. Macrea, 'Burebista şi Celţii la Dunaréa de mijloc', *Studii şi Cercetări de Istorie Veche* (Bucarest), v, 119 ff.

Matthews 1976 — C. L. Matthews, *Occupation-sites on a Chiltern Ridge*, BAR 29, Oxford (British Archaeological Reports).

Maxwell 1972 — I. S. Maxwell, 'The Location of Ictis', *Journal of the Royal Institution of Cornwall* new ser. vi, part 4, 293–319.

Mette 1952 — H. J. Mette, *Pytheas von Massalia*, Berlin (De Gruyter).

Mócsy 1974 — A. Mócsy, *Pannonia and Upper Moesia*, London and Boston (Routledge).

Nash 1975 — Daphne Nash, 'The Chronology of Celtic Coinage in Gaul: the Arvernian "Hegemony" reconsidered', *Numismatic Chronicle*, 7th ser. xv, 204–18.

Neustupný E. and J. 1961 — E. and J. Neustupný, *Czechoslovakia before the Slavs*, London (Thames and Hudson).

OSMap S. Br. — *Ordnance Survey Map of Southern Britain in the Iron Age*, Chessington (Ordnance Survey).

Peacock 1971 — D. P. S. Peacock, 'Roman Amphorae in Pre-Roman Britain', in Jesson and Hill (eds.), 161–88.

Piggott 1971 — S. Piggott, 'Firedogs in Iron Age Britain and Beyond', in *The European Community in Later Prehistory* (J. Boardman, Margaret Brown, T. G. E. Powell, eds.), London (Routledge), 243–70.

Pippidi 1965 — D. M. Pippidi, Part 2 of Berciu and Pippidi, *Din Istoria Dobrogei*, i, Bucarest.

Pliny — C. Plinius Secundus (the elder), *Historia Naturalis*; its final revision was in hand at his death A.D. 79.

Plutarch — Plutarch(us), *Caesar* (Life of), written probably about A.D. 105.

Plutarch *QR* — —— *Quaestiones Romanae*, the 'Roman Questions' (ed. H. J. Rose 1924).

Ptol(emy) *Geogr.* — Claudius Ptolemaeus of Alexandria, *Geographia*, on which see Thomson 1948, 229–30, and Rivet 1974; comp. around A.D. 150.

PWRE — *Pauly-Wissowa . . . Real-Encyclopädie der klassischen Altertumswissenschaft* and Supplements, Stuttgart.

Rambaud 1953 — M. Rambaud, *L'Art de la Déformation historique dans les Commentaires de César*, Annales Univ. Lyon 3e. sér., Lettres fasc. 23, Paris (Belles-Lettres).

Rambaud 1958 — —— 'L'Ordre de bataille de l'armée des Gaules', *Rev. Études anciennes*, lx, 87–130.

Rambaud 1962 — —— ed. *César, BCiv.* i, Coll. Érasme, Paris (Presses Universitaires de France).

Rambaud 1965 — —— ed. *César, BG* ii–iii, Coll. Érasme, Paris (Presses Universitaires de France).

Rambaud 1966 — —— *La Déformation historique chez César* (ed. rev. from 1953), Coll. d'Études anciennes Assoc. G. Budé, Paris (Belles-Lettres).

Rambaud 1967 — —— ed. *César, BG* iv, Paris as 1965.

Rambaud 1974 — —— ed. *César, BG* v, Paris as 1965.

Rigold 1970 — S. E. Rigold, 'The Roman Haven of Dover', *Archaeo. Journal*, cxxvi (for 1969), 78–100.

Rivet 1974 — A. L. F. Rivet, 'Ptolemy's Geography of Britain', *Caesarodunum*, ix *bis* (Mélanges R. Dion), 55–81.

Rodwell 1976 — W. Rodwell, 'Coinage, Oppida and the rise of Belgic Power in South-eastern Britain', in Cunliffe and Rowley (eds.), 181–367.

Saunders 1972 — C. Saunders, 'The Pre-Belgic Iron Age in the central and western Chilterns', *Archaeo. Journal*, cxxviii (for 1971), 1–30.

Scheers 1968 — Simone Scheers, 'Le Premier Monnayage des Ambiani', *Revue belge de numismatique*, cxiv, 45–73.

Scheers 1969a — —— 'Un Monnayage ambien attribué aux Bellovaci', same *Revue*, cxv, 1–55.

Scheers 1969b — —— 'Les Monnaies d'or attribuées aux Atrébates et aux Morini ne sont-elles pas ambiennes?', *Bulletin de la Société française de numismatique*, xxiv (juin), 412–14.

Scheers 1970a — 'Un monnayage gaulois non attribué de la côte maritime belge', *Revue* as 1969a, cxvi, 65–89.

Scheers 1970b — 'L'Histoire monétaire des Suessiones avant l'arrivée de César', *Ancient Society*, i (Louvain, Catholic University), 135–60.

Scheers 1972 — 'Coinage and Currency of the Belgic tribes during the Gallic War', *British Numismatic Journal*, xli, 1–6.

Scheers 1973 — *L'Histoire monétaire de la Gaul Belgique du IIIe. au Ier. siècle avant J-C.*, doctoral thesis (same university), vols. i–iv. Unpublished, but photocopies have been granted to certain libraries.

Scheers 1975 — *Les Monnaies gauloises de la collection A. Dannicourt à Péronne* (Travaux du Cercle d'Études Numismatiques, no. 7), Brussels; reviewed *Britannia*, vii, 399–400 (R. Reece).

Schulten 1937, 1940, 1952 — See *FHA*.

Scullard 1974 — H. H. Scullard, *The Elephant in the Greek and Roman World*, London (Thames and Hudson).

Seel (1961) 1968 — O. Seel, ed. *C. Iulius Caesar*, Band I, *Bellum Gallicum*, Leipzig (Teubner: 1968 = stereo of 1961).

Stevens 1947 — C. E. Stevens, '55 B.C. and 54 B.C.', *Antiquity*, xxi (no. 81, March), 3–9.

Stevens 1951 — 'Britain between the invasions (54 B.C.–A.D. 43): a study of ancient diplomacy', in *Aspects of Archaeology in Britain and Beyond* (Essays for O. G. S. Crawford, ed. W. F. Grimes), London, 332–44.

Stevens 1952a, b — 'The Bellum Gallicum as a work of propaganda', *Latomus: revue d'études latines* (Brussels), xi. 1, 3–18; 2, 165–79.

Stevens 1953 — 'Britain and the Lex Pompeia Licinia', again *Latomus*, xii. 1, 14–21.

Stevens 1959 — 'Julius Caesar's Elephant', *History To-day*, ix, 626–7.

Strabo — Strabo, *Geographia*; comp. over anyhow 30 or perhaps approx. 50 years, to about A.D. 21.

Stümpel 1932 — G. Stümpel, *Name und Nationalität der Germanen*, Klio Beiheft xxv (new ser. Heft xii), Leipzig.

Suetonius — C. Suetonius Tranquillus, *Divus Iulius* (in his 'Lives of the Twelve Caesars'); comp. about A.D. 121.

Swoboda 1964 — E. Swoboda, *Carnuntum*, ed. 4 (Vienna).

Tacitus — The Roman historian Cornelius Tacitus; his *Germania* is of A.D. 98.

Thomas 1966 — Charles Thomas, 'The character and origins of Roman Dumnonia', 75–92 in CBA Research Rep. 7, *Rural Settlement in R. Britain*. ed. Thomas, London (Council for British Archaeology).

Thomson 1948 — J. Oliver Thomson, *History of Ancient Geography*, Cambridge (CUP).

Threipland 1944 — (Mrs.) Leslie Murray Threipland, 'Excavations in Brittany, spring 1939', *Archaeo. Journal*, c (for 1943), 128–49.

Tylecote 1966 — R. F. Tylecote, on ancient ingots of tin found in Cornwall, *Cornish Archaeology*, v, 30–3; cf. S. M. Warner, ib. vi (1967), 29–31, on Romano-British.

UISPP — Union Internationale des Sciences Pré- et Protohistoriques.

VCH — *Victoria History of the Counties of England.*

Vulpe 1968 — R. Vulpe, Part I of Vulpe and Barnea, *Din Istoria Dobrogei*, II, Bucarest.

Walsh 1965 — P. G. Walsh, 'Massinissa', *Journal of Roman Studies*, lv, 149–60.

Ward Perkins 1941 — J. B. Ward Perkins, 'The Pottery of Gergovia . . .', *Archaeo. Journal*, xcvii (for 1940), 37–87.

Ward Perkins 1944 — —— 'Excavations on the Iron Age Hillfort of Oldbury, near Ightham, Kent', *Archaeologia*, xc, 127–76.

Wheeler 1930 — R. E. M. Wheeler (Sir Mortimer), 'The Roman Lighthouses at Dover', *Archaeo. Journal*, lxxxvi (for 1929), 29–46.

Wheeler 1943 — —— *Maiden Castle, Dorset*, Rep. Research C'ttee Soc. Antiq. London xii, Oxford (OUP).

Wheeler 1953 — —— 'An Early Iron Age "Beach-Head" at Lulworth, Dorset, *Antiquaries Journal*, xxxiii, 1–13.

Wheeler and Richardson 1957 — —— and K. M. Richardson, *Hill Forts of Northern France*, Rep. Research C'ttee Soc. Antiq. London, xix, Oxford (OUP).

Wheeler and Wheeler 1936 — —— and T. V. Wheeler, *Verulamium: A Belgic and Two Roman Cities*, xi. in same Reports series, Oxford (OUP).

Zirra 1971a — V. Zirra, 'Les Celtes dans le nord-ouest de la Transylvanie', in Filip (ed.), 890–4, with map and lit. to 1966.

Zirra 1971b — —— in *Dacia* (Bucarest), xv, 171–238.

Zirra 1971c — —— in *Archeologické Rozhledy* (Prague) xxiii, 529–47.

Zirra 1973 — —— 'Les Celtes en Roumanie', in Duval (ed.), 795–820.

Zirra 1976 — —— on the same, in *Journal of Indo-European Studies* iv. 1 (Washington D.C.), 1–40.

Addendum

Stead 1976 — I. M. Stead, in *Problems of Economic & Social Archaeology*, ed. G. Sieveking et al., London (Duckworth), 401–16: Aylesford pots (my 145) post-Caesar as sepulchral; Rodwell 1976 begins some sooner as domestic (his 219–37).

RALEIGH LECTURE ON HISTORY

GLADSTONE AND IRELAND

By JOHN VINCENT

Read 5 October 1977

THE Irish nationalists, so Mr. Gladstone reflected as his mind moved towards Home Rule, were like vermin about a man's person, troublesome and disagreeable, able to give annoyance, but not to interfere with his action.[1] Bearing this warning against making simple assumptions about the relation between Irish cause and British response very much in mind, this paper seeks to ascertain what underlay Gladstone's calculations about, and attitudes towards Irish matters.

The questions involved are many. They refuse to converge readily on a single focus. There is the question of the kind of Ireland Gladstone wished to see, and its converse, whether Gladstone wished to see the kind of Ireland that actually emerged. There is the question of how far Gladstone recognized Irish nationality. There is the question of the degree of deliberateness with which Gladstone approached Irish affairs, and its converse, how far apparently deliberate results derived from improvisation and opportunism. There is the question whether his views differed substantially from those of other politicians. If there is a common element behind these questions, it is to be found in relation to the perplexing matter of Gladstone's greatness. With Gladstone's greatness as an individual now more clearly understood than ever,[2] it has become needless to rest his fame on an Irish Church Act that was at best a plausible distraction, an 1870 Land Act that was largely unnecessary or inoperative, an 1881 Land Act whose central ingredient Gladstone denounced as robbery, an 1884 Reform Act ostensibly aimed at splitting nationalist opinion, and an 1886 Home Rule

[1] '. . . He did not think the Parnellites strong enough ever to cause real danger or to do serious mischief; they would be, he said, like vermin about a man's person, troublesome and disagreeable, able to give annoyance, but not to interfere with his action' (Lord Derby's diary, 8 October 1883, reporting a private conversation with Gladstone).

[2] Except, it may be hinted, in matters of finance.

Bill which gave no prospect of Home Rule. As to peasant ownership of the soil, Gladstone's own legislation on the subject failed to work, and he condemned the first effective scheme of land purchase, Ashbourne's Act, as 'mischievous and dangerous'. Of all his Irish policies, the one which worked best was the repression of 1881–5, yet even here he can claim only a small part of the credit for one of the most distinct British successes of the later nineteenth century.

Gladstone's Irish policy is normally explained in terms of continuity, intention, and natural development, rather than as sharply discontinuous, somewhat haphazard, and as much a matter of response as of initiative. Certain notorious quotations[1] have been allowed to speak too strongly in favour of continuity. The 1880s are seen as a development, not as a contradiction, of what went before; and throughout, what Gladstone did is represented as significantly in advance of what others did or thought.

Ireland was a possible political direction for Gladstone but not, up till 1867, an actual or even probable one. In a career so multifarious, there are of course traces of interest, but the simple conclusion can hardly be avoided that Gladstone steered clear of Ireland until he was 57. In this there is one feature that does not become less extraordinary as one dwells upon it: the fact that he only stayed in Ireland once,[2] in 1877. He was an inveterate traveller to uncomfortable places, and the Irish Mail practically went past his door each night. Moreover, he had time to spare. From 1845 to 1859, fourteen of the best years of his life, he was in office for only two and a half years, and was

[1] On 12 October 1845 Gladstone's Catholic sister Helen, then in Germany with her brother, was held down by force to have leeches put on (*Diaries*, vol. iii, p. 488). Gladstone began a letter to his wife before the leeches incident, but completed it the following morning. It is the latter part of this letter which contains the famous apostrophe, bearing no intelligible relation to the main thread of the letter: 'Ireland, Ireland! that cloud in the west, that coming storm, the minister of God's retribution upon cruel and inveterate and but half-atoned injustice!' (A. Tilney Bassett ed., *Gladstone To His Wife*, p. 64).

Every biographer knows that Gladstone said in December 1868, 'My mission is to pacify Ireland' (Sir P. Magnus, *Gladstone: A Biography*, 1963 ed., p. 193). Few have related this aspiration to the statistics of agrarian crime and eviction, which show an Ireland already as pacified as it was ever to be during Gladstone's career. Agrarian crime only once subsequently fell below the 1868 figure. Evictions reached their lowest point between 1846 and 1886 in 1869.

[2] He also put ashore for a few hours in 1880 on a cruise.

not leading an opposition. Yet on only one occasion, prior to his eventual visit, did he so much as consider a tour that was increasingly obligatory for a rising politician.

In the late 1830s and first half of the 1840s, Gladstone gave much thought to Ireland, but with what objects in mind it is not easy to say. In 1841 he hoped to be made chief secretary for Ireland:[1] 'the idea of Ireland had nestled imperceptibly in my mind'.[2] What curious project lay behind this has not been brought to light. Gladstone had spoken on Ireland in 1835, 1836, and 1838, but between 1838 and his resignation on Maynooth in 1845 he left the subject alone.[3] It would be unwise to read into his frame of mind at this time any element of precocious liberalism on Irish matters. His deep emotion about Rome continued unabated. O'Connell was 'a man regardless of all laws human and divine',[4] and Gladstone made inquiries about the extent to which he broke the Sabbath. It was in 1842, moreover, that Gladstone wrote urging his father that his Catholic sister Helen should be required to leave the family home. Finally, there is the question of Maynooth. Gladstone emerged from the Maynooth controversy in 1845 wearing the mantle of a soul won for liberalism. What is less remarked, but was probably more important at the time, was that Gladstone entered the Maynooth controversy when it commenced in 1844 as the leader of the hard-line Protestants in the cabinet. The Maynooth episode is normally treated as the vagary of a stainless spirit. There was more to it than that. It gave Gladstone a future if anything happened to Peel. It gave Gladstone a 'Protestant' power base without giving him a reactionary image.

[1] Morley, *Gladstone*, vol. i, p. 244; *Diaries*, vol. iii, p. 136; John Brooke and Mary Sorensen ed., *The Prime Ministers' Papers: W. E. Gladstone. I: Autobiographica.* (1971), vol. ii, p. x.

[2] *Diaries*, 1 September 1841.

[3] Cf. Arthur Tilney Bassett, *Gladstone's Speeches: Descriptive Index and Bibliography, with a Preface by Viscount Bryce O.M. and Introductions to the Selected Speeches by Herbert Paul* (London, 1916), pp. 7–11; Gladstone's own list of 'important speeches' printed in the *Diaries*.

[4] By 1881, however, Gladstone was drawing a highly flattering contrast between 'the leadership and doctrines of O'Connell and the leadership and doctrines that are now in vogue', and discovered no less than five principles from which O'Connell never swerved: loyalty to the Crown, a desire for friendly relations with Great Britain, he 'respected law and human life', 'he used the remarkable expression that political change, political improvement, was not worth having at the expense of a drop of blood', and he respected property (speech at Knowsley, *The Times*, 28 October 1881, p. 8).

It even raised thoughts of a Wellington–Gladstone or a Stanley–Gladstone ministry.[1]

By 1852 Gladstone was ready to say, in respect of the New Zealand constitution of that year, that 'every question in which you cannot show the Imperial interest shall be left to be dealt with and managed by the Colonies themselves'. A lesson had been learned, a liberal imperial rhetoric had been created, but it no more had an Irish dimension than it (or his ecclesiastical or economic or Italian liberalism) determined his party allegiance. He had arrived at a view of imperial statesmanship common to his generation, and in common with them did not apply it to Ireland. Indeed, he explicitly denied in a somewhat embarrassed way that the new doctrine could apply to Ireland, in his correspondence with Manning. In his only two important ventures into Irish affairs in the twenty years between 1845 and 1865, the introduction of income tax into Ireland in 1853, for which he was directly responsible, and his part in the Peelite capture of the Irish Brigade in the period following the Papal Aggression of 1851, the tendency of his actions was to unite Ireland more closely with Great Britain than before. In the case of income tax, Gladstone overcame a cabinet majority who still thought Ireland should be treated as a special case. Gladstone pressed his argument that there was no difference between well-off Irishmen and well-off Englishmen, and pressed it without any show of sympathy.[2]

[1] When Louis Philippe suggested a Wellington–Gladstone ministry to replace Peel, Disraeli replied 'I told the king that he was quite equal to Peel, with the advantage of youth' (Disraeli to Manners, n.d. but Dec. 1845, in C. Whibley, *Lord John Manners and his Friends* (1925), vol. i, p. 196).

[2] The financial changes of 1853 were complicated. Gladstone remitted £240,000 in Irish annuities, chargeable locally mainly on poor districts in the south and west of Ireland. In return, he imposed an income tax bringing in an estimated £460,000 (actually £480,000), an Irish spirits duty producing £198,000 (actually £213,000), and, thirdly, succession duties producing a variable amount. His measures in one way produced a redistribution of burdens from the poorer areas and people in Ireland to the richer ones, but also left a considerable gain for the Exchequer, even on his own reckoning. Three points should be remembered. The income tax of 1853 was meant to be a temporary tax for seven years only. Secondly, the spirits duty in Ireland was set at 8*d*., against 1*s*. in Scotland, and a previous level of 8*s*. in England. Thirdly, Irish income tax was assessed in a way which made it much less burdensome than in Great Britain. In England, the landlord paid tax on the full nominal rental, whereas in Ireland he paid on the Poor Law valuation, which was perhaps a third less than he really received. Irish tenant farmers also paid income tax on much more favourable principles of assess-

Gladstone, indeed, saw Ireland with the eyes of a Chancellor of the Exchequer, not of a Peelite social engineer. In certain obvious ways he did not take up the legacy of the Devon Commission. He did not speak on the Irish land acts of 1849 and 1860.[1] Up to 1863, indeed, Gladstone spoke very rarely on Ireland. Between 1853 and 1859 he made no speech of any length on Ireland. The intricate financial questions raised by the Famine found him silent, suited though they were to his special abilities. He had no obvious commitment for or against coercion. On the other hand, he was every inch committed against the mixture of regional policy, graft, and special pleading for infant industries, which was the form in which Irish policy most impinged on the Exchequer. On one occasion he noted 'all the Irish were there, most of them vying with one another in eagerness to plunder the public purse'. His opposition to making Galway a second Liverpool at public expense is one example.[2] While local log-rolling remained paramount, and Irish national issues lay in the background, Gladstone could not emerge as a friend to Ireland.

Besides, the Liberals were the enemies of the Pope in Italian

ment, so that it cost them probably half what it would have done an English tenant farmer (cf. *Parl. Deb.*, *3*, vol. clxxi, col. 833, 12 June 1863.) Cf. Morley, *Gladstone* (1903), vol. i, pp. 646–7, for Gladstone's memorandum on the question, and his Aberdeen speech of 26 September 1871 for Gladstone's remarks on the burdens avoided by the Irish taxpayer. See below, pp. 232–6.

[1] He was unable to speak on Stanley's Compensation for Improvements Bill of 1845, as the measure was introduced into the Upper House and never reached the Commons.

[2] The collapse of Lever's Galway packet station project had a curious sequel. The project in some way involved the Whig magnate Lord Clanricarde; both he and his son Lord Dunkellin spoke on the subject in parliament. In 1866 it was Dunkellin whose amendment led to the fall of the ministry. A letter from Clanricarde illuminates the kind of Irish politics with which Gladstone had no wish to associate: 'I am afraid that as you narrate, Lever is making a sad fool of himself and injuring the prosperity of our company, by his attempts at meddling in Party Politicks. I have tried to stop him and I hope not wholly without effect, we have put before him that his colleagues and shareholders are mostly Liberal (at least)—that the present ministry will most likely be out of office before the Co. is ready to sign a contract, and that if he gets himself in antagonism with their successors, he cannot expect favours, or more than scant justice from them' (Clanricarde to W. H. Gregory, 11 March 1859, Clanricarde MSS., Leeds, Bundle 42. I owe this reference to Dr. K. T. Hoppen). Lady Clanricarde 'detests' Gladstone (Lord Stanley's diary, 16 May 1865) and her husband was hostile to any reform bill (ibid., 23 June 1866).

politics. Gladstone was an enthusiast in the Italian cause. His last major speech on Italy was in 1862.[1] His first hint of Irish interests came in 1863.[2] In 1864 Garibaldi's visit again placed Gladstone at the head of a Protestant frenzy. It was not until the election year of 1865 that Gladstone was free enough of Italian connotations, and of a Protestant constituency,[3] to take up the threads of friendship with Catholic Ireland.

It is worth reflecting on Gladstone's view of what Ireland was, and where it was going. He did not deliver himself very fully on the matter, except on his visit in 1877, but all the hints tell the same story, whether we look at the 1860s or 1870s or 1880s. He believed in Irish landlords 'whose social and moral influence we must look upon as absolutely essential to the welfare of the country'.[4] If he wished for a change, it was not that Irish landlords should exert less power, but that they should become more like English landlords, that is, a strong and active force in the life of the community. Even in 1870, he defined his object in terms of the landlord's mission as a guarantor of a free but orderly, hierarchical society. 'We ought to look forward', he said, 'with hope and expectation to bringing about a state of things in which the landlords of Ireland may assume . . . the position which is happily held, as a class, by the landlords of

[1] *Parl. Deb.*, *3*, vol. clxvi, cols. 933–50, 11 April 1862. In this speech Gladstone dismissed as 'victims of credulity' leading Irish Catholic members of both parties who had raised the issue of alleged Piedmontese atrocities in Naples. (Gladstone's attitude resembled that of Disraeli to the Bulgarian atrocities.) Later that year the Liberal chief whip wrote, 'You are losing the support of the Irish R. Catholics, the natural enemies of a Liberal Govt. . . . In the south [of Ireland] our prospects are very bad: and all that we can hope to do is to save a few seats from the general wreck' (Brand to Palmerston, 24 August 1862, Hampden MSS., House of Lords Record Office).

[2] *Parl. Deb.*, *3*, vol. clxxi, cols. 825–36, refusing a request from an Irish Conservative for a select committee on Irish distress. This was Gladstone's first substantial discussion of Irish policy since 1853, and it was a response (to Irish distress, and to a backbench request), not an initiative.

[3] The University Elections Act of 1861 (24 and 25 Vict. c. LIII) provided for university electors to vote by means of voting papers. This gave greater weight than before in Gladstone's Oxford University seat to the non-resident electors, many of them strongly Conservative clergy. Whether such constituency matters affected Gladstone's behaviour between 1861 and 1865 is hard to compute, because it has not been established that he expected to lose Oxford. It may, however, be noted that his speeches to popular audiences began in the session following the University Elections Act, and not in 1860 or 1861. It should also be remembered that the Catholic vote in S. Lancashire was considerable.

[4] *Parl. Deb.*, *3*, vol. clxxi, col. 827, 12 June 1863.

this country, a position marked by residence, by personal familiarity, and by sympathy with the people among whom they live.' Though he in later days spoke harshly of Peel's 'great failure in regard to Ireland',[1] there is no sign that he wished, before 1865, to go as far as Peel had wished to go in 1845.

Gladstone, for a large part of his middle life, thought Ireland was not a problem. All the recent statistical and social research, he argued in 1863, showed that until the bad season of that year, Ireland was making great and clear progress in everything connected with agricultural and manufacturing wealth.[2] These views were not quickly abandoned. They were still firmly held in 1877. He might concede the case for greater liberality in lending public money to enterprise in Ireland than in Scotland, but this was only because Ireland was climbing the same ladder of progress as the other countries, if a rung or two lower down. Even in 1866, when moving the suspension of Habeas Corpus, he offered a perspective which linked progressive Unionism and evolutionary optimism, saying 'it is our duty . . . to record the signs of progress made . . . Some progress, at least, has been made towards unity of sentiment . . .'[3] Up to the end of 1866, there was nothing about Gladstone's Irish statements that gave any hint of what was to come, or that set him apart from other leading men. If Gladstone had qualms concerning the Irish Church, about which he pledged himself to take no action in his speech of 1865 and his letter of that year to Dr. Hannah, so had most of his contemporaries. That most average of official Liberals, Sir Charles Wood, said 'that for himself he thought the Irish Establishment an abomination, and believed most public men did so, but to attempt to meddle with it would be madness'.[4] That most moderate of Conservatives, Lord Stanley, thought: 'The truth is that to settle the Irish Church question satisfactorily is impossible, except by total disendowment; . . .'[5] If there was a bee buzzing in Gladstone's bonnet in

[1] 'His great failure was in regard to Ireland. He thought he could cobble up the Irish difficulty by endowing Maynooth, and establishing what the strong Protestants called "Godless Colleges".'—L. A. Tollemache, *Talks with Mr. Gladstone* (London 1898), p. 127.

[2] *Parl. Deb.*, *3*, vol. clxxi, col. 836, 12 June 1863.

[3] Ibid., *3*, vol. clxxi, col. 723, 17 February 1866.

[4] Stanley diaries, 16 March 1865, recording Wood's private conversation with Stanley.

[5] Ibid., 10 April 1866. Stanley had prepared a speech against the Irish Church in 1866, but did not deliver it because of its possible bad effect on Conservative unity over parliamentary reform.

1864–7, it was that he was 'decidedly in favour of the plan of buying up the interest of the [railway] companies on behalf of govt'.[1] The question to be asked is why Gladstone, having steered clear of Irish issues until the end of the session of 1866, then took them up in the session of 1867. There is no single answer. The suggestion that it was a response to serious unrest in Ireland fails to fit chronologically. The nearest one can get at present is to say that Gladstone took the question up in early 1867 because Russell was taking it up; that he pursued Irish questions later in 1867 because they reunited the party and enabled him to avoid more divisive issues; and that in 1868 he pressed forward to attack to avoid the danger of Disraeli dealing with the question. In other words, he did what the changing position made him do, and would have made any leader in comparable circumstances do.

As Gladstone twice said,[2] Ireland had little to do with his first steps in Irish policy. There is no difficulty in showing that he, like his colleagues, was turning over Irish issues, particularly the Irish Church issue, throughout 1867, and that his and their intentions to do something antedated both the fragmentation of the Liberal party in the spring of 1867, and the sensational Fenian incidents of the autumn.[3] Gladstone's first major speech

[1] Stanley diaries, 18 March 1865. In the winter of 1865–6 Derby and Disraeli were more nervous about a rumoured financial 'sensation measure' from Gladstone than about reform of parliament. Their anxiety was that the certain profits of railway nationalization would allow Gladstone to make dazzling tax cuts. Had not Russell's radicalism and proletarian distemper retarded progress, Gladstone might have initiated the mixed economy in 1866. For Gladstone's evident enthusiasm for railway nationalization in 1864, see the correspondence about this 'very great and fruitful measure' in Philip Guedalla ed., *The Palmerston Papers. Gladstone and Palmerston, being the Correspondence of Lord Palmerston with Mr. Gladstone 1851–65* (London, 1928), pp. 291–2, 308–9, 315–20.

[2] Gladstone said that Fenianism 'had not been an influence in determining, or in affecting in the slightest degree, the convictions which we have entertained with respect to the course proper to be pursued in Ireland' (Morley, *Gladstone*, 1903, vol. ii, pp. 241–2, citing *Parl. Deb.*, *3*, 31 May 1869). Subsequently, in his twelfth Midlothian speech, he broadened the terms of the proposition. 'In the case of Ireland, it was not the decision of the people of Ireland that led to the destruction of the Established Church. The people of Ireland had borne it so long, had been so accustomed to the work of submission, that they hardly stirred upon the subject.'

[3] Gladstone took a strong line about the Manchester Martyrs. He firmly refused to support a miscellaneous Irish and radical request for allowing them to appeal, leave having been refused by the courts. He argued 'the judgment of those judges shall be final' (*Parl. Deb.*, *3*, vol. cxc, col. 126, 21

to a popular audience on the Irish issue followed within a few days of the Clerkenwell bombing,[1] but what he said had been foreshadowed during the session.[2] The first stirrings on the question perhaps came from Russell,[3] and it was probably because of Russell rather than Gladstone that by February 1867 it was generally known that the Irish Church was marked for the axe. Gladstone's involvement in the Irish Church question was less than entirely voluntary, for had he not taken up the question he ran the risk of being badly outflanked by Russell.

Gladstone's Southport speech[4] revealed another dimension of his Irish intentions. In it he not only used the Irish question to reunite a demoralized party, but also made it serve to rule out popular education and the ballot as party commitments. Gladstone's choice of the Irish Church issue was therefore as much a rejection of two issues he regarded as unsuitable, as an espousal of a cause he preferred for its own sake. As to the kind

November 1867. The execution took place on the 23rd). At Southport Gladstone argued that the Fenian assailants of the police van did not fire their revolver in order to break open the lock, thus only accidentally killing the policeman inside, but that they fired through the ventilator grill and that the death was therefore no accident.

[1] His speech at Southport on 19 December 1867 followed directly upon the Clerkenwell bomb explosion of 13 December. However, on 30 November Gladstone had told Bright that he was willing wholly to suppress the state church in Ireland (*The Diaries of John Bright*, ed. Walling, p. 313), a statement which went beyond his remarks at Southport.

[2] On 7 May 1867 Gladstone strongly attacked the Irish Church in parliament, saying, 'I refuse to give my countenance to that strange, anomalous, and most injurious state of things which prevails in Ireland', and denied that there were any grounds on which the Irish Church could be maintained. On 29 May 1867 the House decided to defer the subject until the next session. On 18 July 1867 Gladstone reminded the House, 'It was time that in some at least of these Irish questions progress should be made'; on 24 July Bright found Gladstone 'earnest, especially on Ireland' and thinking 'the Irish question the most urgent'; on 1 August Gladstone pressed in bold terms for nationalization of Irish railways. Before the Fenian incidents of autumn 1867, Gladstone had put forward a whole programme of Irish reform.

[3] In the winter of 1866, when Russell was at Florence and Gladstone at Rome, Russell took the initiative in asking Gladstone to have a talk about the Irish Church. Gladstone made an excuse, but Russell later claimed to have ascertained that Gladstone was 'as little disposed as I was to maintain Protestant ascendancy in Ireland' (Lord John Russell, 1st Earl Russell, *Recollections and Suggestions, 1813–1873* (1875), p. 345, where no documentation is given).

[4] 19 December 1867.

of Ireland he wished to see, Gladstone's tone was grating. 'What we want is to have Ireland like Scotland', he asserted; 'that union of heart and spirit which is absolutely necessary for the welfare of the country has not yet been brought about.' His ultimate object was 'that end of which I never despair—viz. of redeeming the reproach of total political incapacity to assimilate to ourselves an island within three hours of our shores . . .' Governing by Irish ideas was a programme, however well meaning, for integrating Ireland more firmly within the British political structure, just as the working class had been so integrated.

Gladstone's involvement in Irish reform, then, was not a response to particular phases of external agitation. It was not an intelligent anticipation of agitation, unless it is intelligent to have prior knowledge of one's own decision to agitate. Nor was it a response to the ailments of the Liberal party, since it both preceded those ailments and it was uncertain until late in the day whether it would cure them. Reform was not an attempt to satisfy the new democracy, except in the special sense that it served to head them off from more radical or more divisive areas of policy, such as the ballot and education.[1]

Gladstone not only had to pull his party together. He had to prevent Disraeli from keeping his options open. The danger was that the Conservatives might confine themselves to platitudes on the Irish Church until after the election. If Disraeli had retained office uncommitted until after the election, he could have offered a 'reform' of the Irish Church which would have

[1] *A Chapter of Autobiography* is, as apologetic for Gladstone's course in 1867–9, sadly defective. His main assertion, that since his resignation over Maynooth in 1845, he had never said one word 'which could pledge me on principle to the maintenance of the Irish Church' perhaps explains his benevolent neutrality between 1845 and 1867. 'True I did not say that I was thenceforward prepared at any moment to vote for removal of the Established Church in Ireland . . . on the contrary, I was willing and desirous that it should be permitted to continue . . .' What the pamphlet does not even try to explain is why Gladstone ceased to be benevolently neutral in between 1866 and 1867, and became actively hostile. After much circuitous statement of positions of the most ordinary kind, he concludes by saying that his reason for dealing decisively with the Irish Church now must be treated elsewhere. As the reasons lay in 'the dialectic of party', they could not form part of his apologetic. Irish land legislation was not part of the election programme of 1868; rather, it was part of the pre-election consensus of 1866–7 which emerged again as cabinet business in autumn 1869, but did not require either Gladstone or political upheaval or 'democracy' to obtain a place on the agenda of the reformed parliament.

had attractions for some Irish and more Whigs. It was true that the Catholic prelates were almost all for complete disendowment—nothing for nobody. Their austerity did not, however, derive from any particularly profound aversion to money, but from a belief that they needed Liberationist votes to topple the Church. If Disraeli were to offer them the same result based on Whig votes, then their voluntaryism was an uncertain quantity. Disraeli's most vigorous and idiosyncratic election campaign, that of 1868, was forced on him against his better judgement by the inability of his cabinet to agree on an opposite policy. It was good luck[1] which gave Gladstone a reactionary response from the ministry, rather than a situation in which the Conservatives made sensible reformist proposals to which Gladstone offered doctrinaire opposition.

The parliamentary situation was primary. The Irish prelates supported the voluntaryist section of the Liberals because of their power, not because of their views; but it is likely that concurrent endowment had a more numerous and influential following in the party. But its Whig supporters could not defect to Disraeli's radical opportunism with ease, even if Disraeli had been able to offer a policy tailored to their needs. The voluntaryists were powerful, not because they were any stronger than they had been while in the wilderness since 1847, but because the events of 1867 had destroyed the Conservative alternative for moderate Liberal opinion.

The Land Act of 1870, unlike the Church Act, was not part of Gladstone's election programme. A compensation for improvements bill was expected, having been proposed by both parties; the much larger bill that emerged from the cabinet was not. Yet the Act of 1870, with its general attempt to protect tenants against unreasonable eviction, was as close to average opinion in 1870 as the compensation bills had been in 1866 and 1867, perhaps closer, because average opinion itself had moved on. Both landlords and Conservative politicians took the view 'it might be worse', thinking Gladstone's measure 'not practically injurious' and 'a tolerably fair bill'.[2] The bill passed the

[1] The luck took the form of having Cairns, a Belfast Protestant, and Hardy, the member for Oxford University and a militant churchman, as the two best debaters, party men, and strong personalities in a rather weak Conservative cabinet.

[2] Cf. Derby's notes on two meetings of Conservative leaders: '[The landlords] . . . expected a more stringent and revolutionary proposal, and on the whole seem disposed to say "It might be worse". In fact the power of eviction which the bill limits is one which few landowners are able to exercise,

House of Commons by 442–11, the House of Lords without a division. With the Conservatives *hors de combat*, cabinet opponents of the bill like Clarendon and Lowe were in a weak position. Lowe, as a doctrinaire, detested the bill in principle; as a politician, he was not anxious to lose the chance of passing his popular budget of 1870. Clarendon, a dying man and a poor man with family interests to think of, was not well placed to make a stir. The current assumption was that radical democracy was master, and no one, least of all its opponents, wished to bring that force into play by necessitating an election.

The Act, if not a failure, was a modest success as an old-fashioned compensation for improvements bill, its least revolutionary and controversial feature. As far as land purchase went, the Bright clauses were virtually inoperative. This too helped the tenant, by saving him from buying at the top of the market. Tenant-right was given only to those who already had it, namely the Ulstermen. Otherwise, the bill did not protect against evictions, which were never so low again.[1] This is only to say that evictions followed the economy, not the statute-book, in the 1870s and 1880s. Even if state intervention in the relations of landlord and tenant be taken as a great change of principle, it was a change that was meant to lead nowhere, that did in fact lead nowhere, and whose effect on the legislation of the 1870s was to make it more supine by reaction.

If the Act failed to prevent evictions, make the hens lay more eggs, or effect land purchase, it achieved something politically more significant. If it satisfied no one else, it satisfied Gladstone, and his satisfaction, indeed his complacency, about his handiwork dominated his approach to Irish affairs in 1870–81, and but for unforeseen calamities of weather, price collapse, and disaffection, would probably have continued to determine

in the actual state of popular feeling, and considering the prevalence of assassination on the most trivial pretexts' (Derby diary, 19 February 1870).

'. . . All the members of the H. of C. agreed that our friends there are inclined to accept the bill—some being in fear for their seats, others really thinking it a tolerably fair bill, and all agreeing that they expected something worse. . . . I do not think the bill practically injurious, though doubtful as to its justice in principle' (ibid., 5 March 1870; Derby was still a large Tipperary landowner at this time).

In 1871 Derby described the Act as 'more revolutionary in principle than any Act which Parliament has yet sanctioned, though in practice it works fairly enough' (6 May 1871).

[1] The number of evictions rose from a low of 374 families evicted in 1869, to within the range 463 to 726 in 1870–7.

his views for the rest of his life. With Irish fickleness he was, however, disgusted.

At the 1874 election Disraeli accused Gladstone of being too hard on the Irish. Gladstone accused Disraeli of having links with the Irish Catholic prelates. After the election, Gladstone, distinctly avowing that he would never need the Irish Catholics again, launched his offensive attacks on Vaticanism. Disraeli planned a visit to Ireland. Gladstone was as ready to play an anti-Catholic hand as Disraeli was to play a pro-Catholic one. Once he believed himself no longer in need of their votes, Gladstone lost no time in erecting an apparently insuperable barrier of theological insult between himself and his former Irish clients.

Gladstone resumed interest in Ireland in order to re-establish himself as a Liberal leader.[1] By 1877 he was back in business, and this meant among other things rebuilding his standing as a friend of Ireland, in a series of speeches between 1877 and 1880. His optimism about Ireland was boundless:

> Now, gentlemen, I had something to do in introducing into Ireland that state of things in which we can say that justice is the principle which regulates the relation of government and governed. . . . I have an undoubting and cheerful confidence—it is as certain, I believe, as the revolution of heavenly bodies—that what has been done for Ireland will have its fruits, and that the little inconveniences and secondary evils of which we may now, perhaps, complain . . . will pass away and be forgotten, but that the Union of these countries may be said now to rest upon something like a firm foundation; . . .[2]

[1] In August 1876, just before his return to politics, he told an effusive Irish correspondent, 'The feelings you describe are not the less valued by me because all probability has ceased of their finding in the future any scope for action' (*The Times*, 18 August 1876, p. 9, col. f). Gladstone was replying to an 'Irish Catholic Layman', who expressed gratitude for what Gladstone had done for Ireland and expected to see him premier again. 'When the time for taking that position arrives, your old and grateful friends in Ireland will prove to the world that Irish Catholics are never ungrateful, and that honesty of purpose, even when directed against what they hold most dear, cannot blot from their memory past favours.'

[2] *The Times*, 2 June 1877, p. 12, col. a, reporting speech of previous day to the Birmingham Liberal Association. Gladstone's dominant idea was that Ireland could and should be regained for the Liberal party. Gladstone set out to solve the question why Ireland was still dissident after 'changes which have removed by far the greatest and most crying, and the most searching and the most pervading evils.' (He did not consider the possibility of nationalism.) His reply to the Home Rulers' wish to obtain prosperity through particularism was 'I need not say . . . they make a great mistake.' He believed

In autumn 1877 Gladstone at last visited Ireland.[1] His report to Granville was that of an innocent abroad. He radiated optimism about economic prospects and gloom only about parliamentary ones. 'The upshot is that with the social condition of Ireland and the prospects of its future solid happiness

'that we have laid in Ireland the foundations of national content', and that the Irishman 'will learn—to a great extent has learnt—to cease to view in the law of the government of his country his natural enemy'. Now that 'a more genial temper possesses the national mind', he expected 'all our questions with Ireland will now be symptomatic and superficial'. If there was an Irish problem, it was a problem of parliamentary faction. The existence of the Home Rulers was 'an evil—it is a public evil, it is a serious evil', but only at a parliamentary level.

[1] Gladstone, accompanied by his wife and daughter and his nephew Spencer Lyttelton, arrived at Kingstown on Wednesday, 17 October, leaving for home on Monday, 12 November, when he addressed a deputation on his arrival at Holyhead. His visit was an active and successful one. On arriving, he was recognized by a newsvendor, who cried, 'Welcome to Ireland!' to which Gladstone raised his hat, saying, 'I thank you!' His hosts were Lord Meath (17–25 October), Lord Fitzwilliam (25–9 October), Lord Powerscourt (29 October–1 November), Lord Monck (1 November), the Duke of Leinster (1–6 November), Lord De Vesci (7–10 November), and Lord Annaly (10–12 November). On 20 October he lunched with the Lord-Lieutenant, the Duke of Marlborough; on the 22nd he lunched with the Provost and Fellows of Trinity College, and spoke impromptu to a crowd of students; on the 23rd he visited the Lesser Sugarloaf mountain, and on the 24th Kilkenny Hill near Bray, in the latter case with Judge Lawson and Judge Keogh, infamous in nationalist eyes; on the 30th he spoke to boys at Powerscourt Reformatory, exhorting them, at the behest of a priest, to humility; on 5 November he visited Maynooth, then dined with the Protestant Archbishop; on the 6th visited Cardinal Cullen, received a deputation from the County Down Farmers Association, and dined at Trinity College. On the 7th he received the Freedom of the City of Dublin, making two speeches in reply, one at the presentation, one at a *déjeuner* at the Mansion House. His miscellaneous sightseeing included Christ Church Cathedral, the Synod House, the Bank of Ireland, the Royal Irish Academy, St. Patrick's Cathedral, the National Gallery, the College of Physicians, and the Industrial Schools. He was also presented with a 'sprig of shillelagh' cut from the famous oak at Aughrim. He appears to have extended his visit, his reported original intention having been to depart before the first week in November.

Gladstone declined an invitation from Major Crawford, brother of Mr. Sharman Crawford, M.P., the Ulster Liberal leader, to visit the north of Ireland on the grounds that 'in the present state of Irish opinion he should do best to keep silent on public affairs'.

In his Knowsley speech (*The Times*, 28 October 1881, p. 8), Gladstone emphasized that he had received the Freedom of the City of Dublin by a unanimous vote, and that the honour was so rarely awarded that his name then stood alone on the list with that of Butt.

I am thus far quite contented, and this is the thing really important: but in its politics, the politics of the day and on the surface, I do not at present see any daylight. I think there is a sense of shame about them but they do not know how to mend their ways.' On the eve of the Land War, Gladstone foresaw 'future solid happiness' for Ireland, and his main anxiety was that its politicians had cut loose from the Liberal party.

On returning, he regarded his visit with some complacency. Cardinal Cullen may have said 'You know, Mr. Gladstone, we could have given you a warmer reception if it had not been for certain pamphlets which we in Ireland did not like very well',[1] but for Gladstone nothing was so striking 'as the apparent eagerness of the Parish Priests to meet me, and their warmth'.[2] He saw no real difficulty in coming to a sensible arrangement with the Home Rulers. 'Had the Home Rulers a real leader whom they were disposed to follow I cannot think it would be difficult to arrange a *modus vivendi* with them.'[3]

His Dublin speech[4] showed what Gladstone hoped and expected to see in Ireland during the rest of his political career. He waxed lyrical on the modernization of the Irish economy. He deplored emigration, but thought it at an end; noted a halving in crime; dwelt on the rise in the value of agricultural produce; and claimed 'we have arrived . . . at the real stage of improvement'. He showed no false modesty in his assessment of his 1870 Land Act. 'The landlord is better, the farmer is better, the cottager is better . . .' he asserted with gusto. The only weakness in the 1870 Act, it appeared, was in the purchase clauses inserted by Bright; and here Gladstone was not attacking purchase, but deploring its rarity.[5]

Since all was for the best in the best of all possible Irelands,

[1] Morley, *Gladstone* (1903), vol. ii, p. 571.

[2] Gladstone to Granville, 20 November 1877, in A. Ramm ed., *The Political Correspondence of Mr Gladstone and Lord Granville 1876–1886* (1962), vol. i, p. 58.

[3] Ibid. Gladstone was silent while in Ireland on 'the one subject on which I am now in thorough accord with the popular party in Ireland'. This was the question of amnesty for the two Fenians still confined for the Manchester murder of 1867. Gladstone had, however, recently urged amnesty in parliament, on 20 July 1877, which must have done something to smooth his Irish visit. See Ramm, loc. cit., n. 1 and 2.

[4] 7 November 1877.

[5] Five thousand purchasers, amounting to three-quarters of Church tenants, had bought under the 1869 Church Act. The Bright clauses of the 1870 Act created only 870 owners in 1870–81.

it followed that there was no need for a split between English Liberals and Irish Home Rulers, and that the latter should be gently admonished. The sinner, not the sin, was to be rebuked; home rule might be accommodated by calling it local government, but to create a separate body of men called Home Rulers, distinct from the British Liberals, was an unnecessary blunder.[1] For Gladstone, whether in 1877 in Birmingham and Dublin, in 1879 and 1880 in Midlothian, or in 1880 in office, the expectations were clear. Gladstone saw no reason why his later years should be much involved with a country whose problems were so largely solved, and solved by him.[2] His visits in 1877 and 1880 had been agreeable.[3] For the Irish in parliament, some accom-

[1] Gladstone's line on this point hardened in a textually curious way. In his Ninth Midlothian speech, he misquoted his Dublin speech as follows: 'I ventured to expostulate with them upon the policy they had adopted . . . I said, "I will take the liberty of saying that the present state of the representation with this formation of a Home Rule party is deplorable".' This 1879 version was much sterner than what he had actually said in 1877. It leaves no doubt that the common assertion that Gladstone only once and lightly attacked Home Rule suppresses a truth about Gladstone's public expressions towards Home Rulers. Gladstone repeatedly made it clear that Irishmen might support home rule, but they should not set up as Home Rulers.

[2] Gladstone's optimism about Ireland was, even in November 1877, not quite up to date. After a spring and summer of quite appalling rainfall, the potato yield had fallen to less than half the 1876 level. Gladstone eulogized Irish economic growth a few months after continuous decline had actually begun. But his opinions, if a year or so out of date, represented a general consensus about Irish serenity. Beach, Disraeli's chief secretary for Ireland, wrote of the Home Rule Party, 'Their humbug helps to keep the country quiet'; Trollope, the only English pundit who had lived in rural Ireland for a long period, wrote at this time a peculiarly radiant passage on Irish tranquillity: 'Rents are paid with more than English punctuality. And the religious enmity between the classes, though it is not yet dead, is dying out Home-rule no doubt is a nuisance—and especially a nuisance because the professors of the doctrine do not at all believe in it themselves' (Anthony Trollope, *An Autobiography* (World's Classics ed. 1947), pp. 65–6.)

[3] In August 1880 Gladstone put ashore in Dublin Bay while on a cruise in the *Grantully Castle*. 'On the quay a considerable crowd had collected, by whom the Premier was cheered. Rough working men, grey-haired priests, and railway porters came forward and shook him by the hand, some of them crying out, "You are a friend to Ireland". The Prime Minister was evidently very much pleased with the visit which he had determined to pay to Irish soil . . . Mr. Gladstone proceeded to Dublin by the first train and drove in an outside car to Christ Church Cathedral . . . Mr Gladstone walked back to the station, being greeted with great enthusiasm on the way. The station was crowded and so was that at Kingstown, where the ticket collectors were too much engaged in cheering, and waving their caps to attend to their

modation could be made using such elastic quantities as local self-government and land purchase. What none of these things amounted to, especially against the backcloth of 'Beaconsfieldism', was an idea of a mission to Ireland of which a first stage had been completed but a second had yet to be fulfilled. When Gladstone returned to office in April 1880, and for about six months afterwards, he thought his Irish work had been completed, not that it was just about to begin.

The Midlothian speeches, taken as a whole, offered no Irish programme or policy.[1] They showed openness towards some mild form of devolution, interest in peasant proprietorship, and disapproval of Home Rulers. On no topic was there anything amounting to a commitment.[2] Irish disturbances, Irish distress,[3] Irish nationality were not mentioned. Gladstone supported the

business of taking the tickets' (*The Times*, 30 August 1880, p. 8, col. 4). This 'truly warm Irish reception' must take its place along with dogmatic claims about the tense state of Irish opinion in 1880. According to the *Illustrated London News*, the premier 'was received with loud cheers by an immense crowd' on arrival at Kingstown (*I.L.N.*, 4 September 1880, vol. lxxvii, p. 230), although his landing had been delayed by fog.

[1] The second Midlothian speech tried to detach the question of Home Rule from political nationalism by making it a matter of parliamentary reform, local government, and 'the constitution of secondary and subordinate authorities', and by refusing to treat Ireland as a special case: 'I will consent to give to Ireland no principle, nothing that is not on equal terms offered to Scotland and to the different portions of the United Kingdom.' In the sixth Midlothian speech, Gladstone said, 'In Ireland, I have not the least hesitation in saying it is most desirable to encourage the formation of a small proprietary.' The ninth Midlothian speech attacked the Home Rule party as deplorable and a Tory front. (In personal vein, Gladstone made capital out of Beaconsfield having appointed a Conservative Home Ruler, King-Harman, as Lord-Lieutenant of Roscommon.)

[2] In January 1879 when Granville raised the question of an accommodation with the 'reasonable' Irish, Gladstone responded with much the same ideas as in 1877. Denominational education and *local* government (Gladstone's underlining) were seen as suitable areas for meeting Irish wishes. As Gladstone was a whole-hearted denominationalist, it was easy for him to overlook what was clear to Granville, that a Liberal party dependent on English Nonconformists could never gratify the priests. The areas which Gladstone marked out in the late 1870s as ripe for action—education, local government, land purchase—were precisely those not tackled in the 1880s.

[3] The story of the Conservative reaction to Irish distress in 1879 has not been fully told, but see C. H. D. Howard and P. Gordon, 'The First Balmoral Journal of Dudley Ryder, Viscount Sandon (later third Earl of Harrowby), 6–14 November 1879', *Bulletin of the Institute of Historical Research*, vol. xlx, May 1977, p. 90: 'I told her [the Queen] that the condition of Ireland and probable famine in certain districts, had occupied us [the cabinet] largely.'

creation of a peasant proprietary; so did Hartington.[1] Nothing came of this when the Liberals were in power. It was a minority Conservative government which, within weeks of taking office, and at the end of the session, passed the first effective legislation on the subject in 1885.

Not having an Irish policy appeared to the incoming government of 1880 entirely adequate. Gladstone himself later acknowledged his initial complacency.[2] He hardly knew there was a land war on, financial and foreign policy claiming all his attention. What was true of Gladstone was true of his colleagues. The uniform despondency of winter 1880 was preceded by an equally uniform complacency.

Ministers readily abandoned coercion.[3] They produced a Disturbance Bill,[4] but barely reacted to its defeat in the Lords.

[1] When Derby pressed Hartington for an exposition of his Irish views, 'the only definite decision' which Derby could extract was 'that he would support a plan for buying by help of the State the lands of willing sellers, to be resold to the tenants. He seemed to think obstruction would die out of itself, in a new parliament: Parnell nearly mad, and not unlikely to go quite so' (Derby diary, 26 October 1879).

[2] Gladstone's election address of 10 March 1880 made no reference to Ireland, except to say that the Conservatives were the party whose past actions had endangered the Union (W. Saunders, *The New Parliament 1880*, n.d., p. 31). Gladstone wrote to Granville, 18 December 1880, commenting on the rather weak appointment of Cowper as Lord-Lieutenant: 'There can be no doubt that if in April [1880] we had anticipated what we now have to encounter we should have sought for a man of more experience' (A. Ramm ed., op. cit., vol. i, p. 231). Speaking at Edinburgh, 1 September 1884, Gladstone explained, 'I freely admit that I had much upon my hands connected with the doings of the Beaconsfield government in almost every quarter of the world, and I did not know, no one knew, the severity of the crisis that was already swelling upon the horizon that shortly after rushed upon us like a flood' (Morley, *Gladstone*, vol. iii, pp. 47–8). One source refers to a speech made at Edinburgh in 1880 when Gladstone spoke of 'an absence of crime and outrage, with a general feeling of comfort and satisfaction, such as was unknown in the previous history of the country': see Bernard Holland, C.B., *The Life of Spencer Compton, Eighth Duke of Devonshire* (London, 1911), vol. i, p. 264, but not traced in press.

[3] 'When the new parliament assembled for business, there were only twelve days,—from the 20th of May to the 1st of June,—before the time at which the Peace Preservation Act of 1875, and all the older laws kept in force by it, would expire' (Roundell Palmer, Earl of Selborne, *Memorials. Part II. Personal and Political, 1865–1895*, vol. ii, p. 8). Cf. Selborne, ibid., pp. 6–10, for the arguments against renewal of coercion in 1880. Ireland had been continuously under coercive legislation in the quiet decade from 1870 to 1880.

[4] In the Queen's Speech, ministers offered Ireland no land legislation,

Forster[1] and Gladstone[2] thought a good harvest would dispose of the difficulty. Such complacency[3] in hindsight seems strange. The reaction to the Land War of 1879–80 was a decision to drop coercion and to let events take their course.

If Gladstone was slow to recognize the Land War as a problem, he was slower still to recognize the Parnellites as speaking for Ireland. So long as the Parnellites were the truly anti-English, socially radical group that men like Dillon seemed to be achieving in 1881, Gladstone rejected any suggestion that they were more than 'a few individuals'.[4] Gladstone accepted the Parnellites only when they came to heel, and only when it had become apparent that the Conservatives were not above joint parliamentary action with them. In 1881, however, Gladstone saw his task as crushing radical nationalism, and peremptorily denied 'there were more than 10 or 12 really disaffected Irishmen in the House. He believed the Irish people as a body to be loyal'.[5] Gladstone's heart was never more thoroughly

but only an irrelevant trifle in the form of an adjustment of the Irish borough franchise. The Disturbance Bill was an afterthought.

1 *Parl. Deb.*, *3*, vol. cclv, col. 315.

2 Gladstone considered that an imminent good harvest 'may dispose of a great portion of the difficulty' and 'may help to bring about that improvement between classes which in some districts of the country is so much to be desired'. If this failed, the government would provide for law and order especially by pressing landlords to stop evictions (Gladstone to Granville, 3 August 1880, in A. Ramm, ed., op. cit., vol. i, p. 155).

3 Childers was sent to Ireland to report. Hamilton, Gladstone's private secretary, wrote on 26 September 1880: 'Ireland seems quieting down. Childers writes cheerfully of the country and says the good harvest has worked wonders.'

4 As late as six months before Kilmainham, Gladstone made great play with the fact that Parnell and Dillon had been refused the Freedom of the City of Dublin, which he, Gladstone, had been awarded unanimously.

5 Derby's diary, 28 October 1881, reporting Gladstone's private conversation. See also Gladstone's speech at Knowsley, *The Times*, 28 October 1881, p. 8. Gladstone denounced 'not the Irish party in general' but 'the knot of men associated with Mr. Parnell' for making 'every effort to damage and discredit, and if possible to overturn the Land Bill in its passing, to make its enactments hopeless . . .' 'It is idle', he said, 'to talk of either law or order or liberty or religion or civilization, if these gentlemen are to carry through the reckless and chaotic schemes that they have devised. Rapine is the first object; but rapine is not the only object. It is perfectly true to say that these gentlemen wish to march through rapine to disintegration and dismemberment of the Empire, and, I am sorry to say, even to the placing of different parts of the Empire in direct hostility one with the other. . . . Our opponents are not the people of Ireland. We are endeavouring to relieve the people

in his Irish work than when he undertook in autumn 1881 to show that 'the resources of civilization were not exhausted' in the face of Irish lawlessness.

By November 1880, complacency had given place to dismay in English ruling circles.[1] Gladstone, however, went on denying that there was an Irish question until well beyond the last moment. Early in November, Gladstone opposed Forster's request for coercion. Later in the month, he argued against immediate legislation to repress crime as being justified only 'in the face of a great outburst of crime, which neither has occurred, nor is likely at an early (I doubt it at a later) date, the case we have to deal with being a paralysis of certain most important civil rights'.[2] This view that boycotting, not crime, was the root problem was hardly borne out by the dramatic rise in Irish agrarian crime.[3] Gladstone's instinct was to respond by letting well alone.

One of his reasons was that a coercion bill would entail remedial land legislation to which he was opposed. Another was that concentration on Irish measures would deprive him of any chance to bring forward a great financial scheme.[4] Gladstone in fact had to be dragooned into action. His second phase of Irish legislation was no more voluntary than his first. He was at heart a principled opponent of his greatest legislative achievement, the 1881 Land Act, and his real views slipped out when he told parliament that no country in the world would eventually derive more benefit from perfect freedom of contract

of Ireland from the weight of a tyrannical yoke.' Gladstone at this time was guarded by ten policemen day and night, and was under formal sentence of death from an Irish-American 'court'.

[1] On 8 November 1880 Gladstone's secretary Hamilton wrote, 'Never had a Government a more difficult problem to solve than that of Ireland at the present moment.'

[2] Gladstone to Granville, 18 November 1880, in A. Ramm ed., op. cit., vol. i, p. 220. As late as 19 December 1880, Lord Cork found Gladstone saying there was very little crime. When introducing the Land Bill on 15 April 1881, a measure prompted in no small part by homicide or fear of it, Gladstone thought it proper to stress that 'The homicides of Ireland have shrunk to a mere fraction of what, within my recollection, they habitually were.'

[3] Agrarian crime rose from 136 cases in 1875 to 2,590 in 1880. Families evicted rose from 667 in 1876 to 2,119 in 1880.

[4] What Gladstone hoped to achieve in 1881 was a large plan for rearranging the succession duties so that property paid more. Cabinet opposition led to the plan being dropped (Lewis Harcourt's diary, 2 April 1881).

in land than Ireland.[1] Whether one looks at land or coercion, the idea of a progressive Gladstone restraining a repressive Forster is untrue[2] for all but the last few weeks of the Forster regime of 1880–2. As late as April 1882, Gladstone could tell Forster, 'If you go, and go on Irish grounds, surely I must go too'. Gladstone's resistance to the introduction of coercion, based partly on lack of information, partly on unwillingness to admit that Irish problems could recur in serious form, partly from a desire not to be lumbered with consequential changes in land legislation, must be coupled with his steady support for Forster's policy once it had been introduced. If Gladstone differed from Forster over coercion prior to their final quarrel, it was because Gladstone was looking for more effective ways of attaining the same ends. Where Gladstone fell behind Forster was over the Land Act; and over Irish local government he barely kept abreast of him.[3]

Some facets of Gladstone's policy on coercion have been misunderstood. Gladstone was against coercion not because it punished Irishmen unfairly, but because it did not punish them enough. Thus he was anxious to change Forster's method of repression by means of administrative detention into repression by use of the criminal law. This looks, on the face of it, like a Liberal scruple about Habeas Corpus. But administrative

[1] On introducing the Land Bill, 7 April 1881. In the process of passing the measure, Gladstone as usual developed an enthusiasm that was distinctly lacking at first. The Bill was undoubtedly a difficult one to steer through parliament, but it would have been much simpler but for complications introduced to meet Gladstone's qualms. In 1870 he had committed himself in the strongest terms against fixity of tenure, not once, but many times, e.g. '. . . I am irreconcilably opposed to fixity of tenure'.

[2] See A. B. Cooke and J. R. Vincent, 'Select documents: XXVIII. Herbert Gladstone, Forster, and Ireland, 1881–2', in *Irish Historical Studies*, vol. xvii, no. 68, September 1971, pp. 521–48, and ibid., vol. xviii, no. 69, March 1972, pp. 74–89. See especially Gladstone's letter to Forster, 5 April 1882 (cited above, p. 527, from Sir T. W. Reid, *Life of the Rt. Hon. W. E. Forster*, vol. ii, p. 413): 'I do not admit your failure, and I think you have admitted it rather too much—at any rate, by omission: by not putting forward enough the fact that in the main point, namely, the deadly fight against the social revolution, you have not failed . . . If you go, and go on Irish grounds, surely I must go too.'

[3] Gladstone said Forster 'also is broad in his ideas as to what will have to be granted to Ireland in the way of local government' (Gladstone to Granville, 16 September 1881, in Ramm, op. cit., vol. i, p. 293). One other area of Irish policy, that of tenant purchase of their holdings, strongly urged by Gladstone in 1877, 1879, and 1880, had fallen by the wayside, an early victim of the Land War.

detention was notoriously a gentlemanly affair: a change towards using the criminal law for the same clients would mean inflicting on them ordinary imprisonment, a much severer deterrent, though not one which breached Habeas Corpus.[1] The other point, perfectly clear in the printed sources, but muddied since in popular tradition, is that Gladstone would have dropped coercion at the time of the Kilmainham Treaty had it not been for the Phoenix Park murders; that getting rid of Forster meant getting rid of repression; and that Parnell's terms, indeed Parnell's victory, included an agreement to drop coercion. One hesitates to refute a tradition so edifying, so comprehensive, and so perfectly groundless. However, Parnell's terms did not include coercion;[2] the differences with Forster turned on personality rather than policy; and Lord Frederick Cavendish was working on 'a bill to replace the coercion bill' as the euphemism went, immediately prior to his death. If there was a golden chance of reconciliation in 1882, it arose from the fact that Parnell, not Gladstone, was willing to make very large, perhaps very generous concessions.

This is not the place to discuss the collusive drama of Parnell's arrest and the destruction of the Land League in 1881–2, nor the tragic dénouement of Kilmainham, the breaking of Forster, and the murder of Lord Frederick Cavendish. This is the best-known aspect of the Irish policy of Gladstone's second ministry. What preceded it, Forster's regime of 1880–2, is not so much little-known as unfairly judged in the light of contemporary nationalist propaganda and Gladstonian hindsight.

Gladstone began his second inquiry into the Irish land question with the advantage of knowing the answer. Before taking office, he had publicly stated his belief in supply and demand.

[1] Gladstone claimed in retrospect that what he had wished, instead of the 1881 Coercion Act, was to suppress the Land League. The abortive plan to establish Provincial Councils in spring 1882 should probably be understood as a pre-emptive strike designed to prevent the situation which arose at the 1885 election. The object was to get Provincial Councils working while radical nationalism was, in Ireland and in parliament, safely under control. The first signs of Tory–Irish tactical co-operation in 1882 must have hastened Gladstone's wish to avoid the opportunist settlement that he already foresaw.

[2] For Gladstone's announcement, prior to the Phoenix Park murders, of further coercive legislation, see *Parl. Deb.*, *3*, vol. cclxviii, cols. 1965–70, 2 May 1882. The new legislation was 'to strengthen the ordinary law', unlike Forster's act of 1881 which overrode the ordinary law; but, this apart, there was no change of policy. See Cooke and Vincent, *Irish Historical Studies*, loc. cit., p. 81, n. 27.

With mid-Victorian certainty, he declared in his Sixth Midlothian speech 'that the relation of landlord and tenant will unquestionably be decided by the true state of the market'. This did not presage an easy abandonment of market economics. When he heard the news that the Bessborough Commission were coming out in favour of 'the Three F's', Gladstone exclaimed, 'I have not heard', adding, 'it is incredible!'[1] He did not accept the incredible with a good grace. Early in January he spoke strongly against both fixity of tenure, and fair rents, saying that both were a robbery of the landlord.[2] For Gladstone, robbery of the landlord was the central issue against which he fought in 1881, and fought with considerable success. The famous Three F's were so contrived that they became a snare and a delusion. 'Fair Rents' meant a compulsory 15-year lease on terms which soon became unfair to the tenant. 'Free Sale' meant that one peasant could charge a rack-rent in capital form to another peasant. 'Fixity of tenure' had little effect in preventing evictions caused by inability to pay unfair 'Fair Rents'.[3] Evictions remained high, far higher than in the 1870s. Even in 1886, with Gladstone in power for half the year, and 'fixity of tenure' in operation, they were at three times the highest annual rate reached under Disraeli (in 1879).

Putting aside those complexities which have baffled lawyers and farmers down to the present day,[4] one should ask three

[1] Morley, *Gladstone* (1903), iii. 56. There were other sharp reminders of Gladstone's attitude. '. . . I, at least, shall never be a party to the introduction of the Irish Land Act into England', closed one door (*The Times*, 8 October 1881, p. 6, col. c), while Gladstone's speech at his own tenants' dinner warned them in no uncertain terms that there were to be no 'Fair Rents' on the Hawarden estate, only supply and demand (*The Times*, 13 January 1882, p. 6, col. a). Gladstone showed that market forces could respond adequately to agricultural depression, by lowering his farmers' rents by 25 per cent in 1880–1 (*The Times*, 12 January 1881, p. 9, col. f).

[2] 'The Premier called on Ly D[erby] this afternoon, and talked with her freely on current events. . . . I gather that he expressed himself strongly against the Irish schemes of fixity of tenure, and settlement of rents generally by a court, saying that both one and the other were a robbery of the landlord: which confirms what we heard last month, that he is more moderate in his proposals than even the moderate section of the Cabinet' (Derby's diary, 8 January 1881).

[3] Purchases under the 1869 Church Act tenants' clauses created 5,000 owners by 1877. The Bright clauses of the 1870 Act created only 870 owners in 1870–81. The 1881 Act created only 733 owners in 1881–5.

[4] Farmers and lawyers in Northern Ireland, where these Acts still apply, were in 1971 still so apprehensive of these complexities, that they avoided at

questions: what was Gladstone trying to do, what was the Act as eventually passed designed to do, and what did it in fact do?[1] In practice the bill produced a general reduction in rent of nearly 20 per cent. This reflected the views of the land courts rather than of the creators of the bill. The balance of opinion among ministers principally involved was in favour of true fair rents fixed from time to time in court, with freedom of contract thrown overboard. The object of the cabinet was rather to avoid exorbitant raising of rents, than to effect a general reduction; for Irish rents were known to be low. Gladstone's purpose was to preserve freedom of contract wherever was possible. He was successful only to the extent that he prevented true fair rents and created an extremely complex bill. His colleagues, especially his Whig colleagues and Forster, were amongst his severest critics. Forster, indeed, said that Gladstone's first ideas of the bill were so inadequate, that he had told Gladstone he could not be a party to such a measure and must resign. Har-

all costs the creation of agricultural tenancies. Instead they used conacre and agistment (licences to enter on land to cultivate and graze on a seasonal basis). Such licensees took everything they could out of the soil and put nothing back. The present state of affairs is thus, because of Gladstonian legislation, exactly what that legislation was intended to remedy: the non-owning cultivator has no incentive to improvement. Cf. *Survey of the Land Law of Northern Ireland.* By a working party of the Faculty of Law, The Queen's University, Belfast. Chairman Professor L. A. Sheridan. (H.M.S.O., Belfast, 1971), pp. 111–12. For another outburst against the complexities of the 1881 Act, see Michael McCarthy, *Five Years in Ireland 1895–1900* (London and Dublin, 6th ed., 1901), pp. 234–6. J. C. W. Wylie, *Irish Land Law* (London, 1975) points out that Gladstonian legislation on agricultural tenancies still bedevils both parts of Ireland in the 1970s, and will gradually become more important as such tenancies increase, their creation having until recently been severely restricted.

[1] Because the bill changed its character in its passage through the cabinet, even experienced observers thought when it was announced that it was a bill, not for, but against, the Three F's. 'The [Queen's] speech was read after dinner . . . [On Irish land] the language is studiously and skilfully moderate. The object is declared to be to amend and supplement the Act of 1870, not to supersede it—which at once excludes the "three F's" and absolute fixity of tenure. I said to Cork after the reading, "This means that you break with the Ultras": he answered, "It certainly does, and I am very glad of it". On the other hand Ld O'Hagan looked grave and gloomy, and feared that what was proposed would never go down in Ireland' (Derby's diary, 5 January 1881). Even in the debate on the second reading, Derby noted, the common remark was that Gladstone dwelt little on the justice of the bill, but treated it exclusively as a matter of political expediency (ibid., 20 May 1881).

court, a vehement supporter of a strong bill, said Gladstone's first project would have been laughed out of the House as utterly inadequate. Gladstone's initial cabinet paper of 17 December 1880 on Irish land was described by Carlingford, then serving on the Richmond Commission, as 'very insufficient and confused'. Another high authority, the official draftsman Thring, thought a broad and simple bill giving judicial rents and qualified fixity of tenure would have been enough, but Gladstone had introduced the distinction between present and future tenants, and all the complications. When the bill was published in April 1881, Carlingford, the minister responsible for it in the House of Lords, noted, '. . . after a first reading I find it hard to see clearly its bearing and effect'. Gladstone's (private) outline of its provisions showed him 'very averse to interference with freedom of contract'.

The simplest explanation, and one often resorted to, is that Gladstone alone really understood Irish land, and any divergence between him and colleagues represents a failure on the part of the latter fully to apprehend the issues. But in 1880–1, unlike in 1870, Irish land was not an unexplored issue. Two Royal Commissions had examined it. Again, in 1880–1, unlike in 1870, Gladstone was under pressure from the moderates in the cabinet to make large changes. In this the moderates reflected average opinion in both parties and both Royal Commissions, which took judicial Fair Rents as a basis and was willing to accept qualified fixity of tenure. What has to be explained is why a simple bill establishing a permanent settlement on the basis of dual ownership was not pushed through on the grounds of practical necessity. Instead, Gladstone's conception of an emergency to be dealt with in a way which would not block the return to traditional landlordism and freedom of contract, struggled within the cabinet and within the bill against far more collectivist ideas. The result was a legislative hybrid.

Had the Act been designed to lower rents below market levels, then the 1881 Act would have been a revolutionary measure, at odds with the whole tradition of Victorian legislation. As the Act was designed to make the free market work, in the rather special circumstances where the price mechanism worked more freely in the courtroom than the world of boycotts and hedgerows, it simply carried out by special means the general aims of Victorian legislation. Gladstone's object, indeed, was only to use judicial arbitration to pave the way to a return to free individual bargaining[1] in more stable circumstances. 'My great desire', he said, 'is to avoid arbitration upon rents generally and prospectively',[2] that is, he wished to make a once-for-all judicial reduction of exorbitant rents, with landlords thereafter to get what they could when vacant possession occurred. It was the Land Courts, not Gladstone, who made the 1881 Act what in the event it was, an Act for the general reduction of rents.

Gladstone himself must have thought that, after Phoenix Park,[3] the course was set. He entered a period of partial retirement. His career as an Irish statesman seemed likely to conclude without further upheaval. He said in May 1882, 'It is enough for me to have conquered the most formidable social revolution of modern times.' In 1882, also, Gladstone reassured Granville: 'There is not the least chance of any question as to any sort of

[1] The legal history of the Act's working is curious and reflects the divided intentions of its creators. Fixity of tenure, supposedly created by the 1881 Act, was found in practice to terminate with the fifteen-year statutory period of tenancy, after which ejectment became possible. It was the Land Law Act of 1896 that gave real fixity of tenure, or apparently did so until a judgement of the Court of Appeal in Northern Ireland removed fixity of tenure from non-statutory tenancies (by then the great majority). For a few years in the late 1920s Northern Ireland got on well enough without the supposed necessities of Fair Rent or Fixity of Tenure. The extreme rarity of agricultural tenancies in Northern Ireland today makes it impossible to say what the position now is. Expert opinion favours a return to a pre-Gladstonian freedom of contract. Cf. Wm. A. Leitch, 'Present Day Agricultural Tenancies in Ireland', *Northern Ireland Legal Quarterly*, vol. 16 (1967), pp. 491–507. Mr. Leitch makes the incidental suggestion that the majority of tenants, having had their Fair Rents fixed by Gladstonian methods twice, say over the thirty years 1881–1911, then relapsed into negotiating their own tenancies with their landlord.

[2] Gladstone to Granville, 1 December 1880, in Ramm, op. cit., vol. i p. 226. In this letter Gladstone said, 'I certainly wish that on the vacancy of a farm the landlord should be free to take what rent he can get.'

[3] Before Phoenix Park, Gladstone was the driving force behind Irish policy both in its repressive aspects (as in autumn 1881) and in conciliation through victory (as at Kilmainham). From 1882 to 1885 Gladstone ceased to be the driving force in Irish affairs, which passed into the hands of the executive, namely Spencer and Harcourt. The lack of a biography of Spencer, the relative remoteness of his large and well-ordered archives, and the lack of stature and archives on the part of Spencer's two Chief Secretaries, Trevelyan and Campbell-Bannerman, have tended to lead to an underestimate of the Gladstonian repression of 1881–5. Agrarian crimes in Ireland fell from 4,439 cases in 1881 to 762 cases in 1884. While Gladstone toyed with paper exercises for Irish constitutional reform, Spencer executed the decisions of 1881–2.

assembly in Dublin.' Perhaps, therefore, this is the place to classify Gladstone's various initiatives and responses according to their degree of deliberateness.

There were the schemes long approved by Gladstone which ran into the sand. These included peasant proprietorship, his only Irish policy to achieve the status of a pet idea in the late 1870s, and possibly also the state acquisition of Irish railways, which had fascinated him as far back as the mid-1860s. Virtually nothing was heard of these schemes after 1880.

Then there were the schemes which grew out of Gladstone's 1879 doctrine of home rule as a mixture of parliamentary reform, local government, and administrative devolution. These were Erskine May's Grand Committee proposal of 1880; the elective county government promised in the Queen's Speech of 1881; the Provincial Councils scheme of 1882; the local government bill of 1883; and the Central Board scheme of 1885. All these vanished readily enough into the dustbin of history, though they represented the consistent centre of Gladstone's thought and intentions.[1] All these schemes can be taken, as Hammond takes them, to show that Gladstone already approved of Home Rule. They can equally well be read as showing that he wished to forestall Home Rule.

Finally, there were the projects which were not a product of deliberate intention, but arose from an immediate crisis, from parliamentary forces, or from chance. Among these we may include the 1881 Land Act, the 1881 and 1882 Coercion Acts, the inclusion of Ireland in the 1884 Reform Act,[2] and more ambiguously the Home Rule Bill itself. These were responses to situations.

Looking at these questions as a whole, one can but note the darkening tone of distrust which the Irish agitation produced in

[1] His comments on these projects were not flattering to their supposed beneficiaries. In one case he wrote of allowing Irish M.P.s 'to knock their heads against one another upon questionable theories'; in another, that it would show, 'the antics of a Central Board essentially municipal, not parliamentary'. Every year from 1880 to 1886 some constitutional change for Ireland was mooted. Of these, only the reform bills of 1884–5 passed, and these only because the government took the line of least resistance.

[2] Gladstone argued in cabinet that a mass electorate in Ireland would split nationalist opinion on class lines. Tactical reasons almost certainly weighed more heavily with him. To get the bill through, he needed Irish support and could not afford Irish antagonism. Tory-Parnellite collusion was to be expected in 1884, unless the Irish could be bought. The Tories therefore secured the Irish labourer his vote.

Gladstone's mind. This distrust was not confined to the 'handful of men' who 'follow Mr. Parnell',[1] or to contempt for Irish M.P.s generally, whom he found, in 1886, 'gloomy, monotonous, and vulgar'.[2] The pessimism extended to the Irish people. The buoyancy about Irish prospects to be found in the 1860s and 1870s had disappeared.

The fears that moved Gladstone towards Home Rule were all anti-Irish in tone and mostly wrong. He feared a violent rising: 'There is a Parnell party and a Civil War party, and the question which is to have the upper hand will be decided in a limited time.' He feared that the nationalist M.P.s would set up a Dáil in Dublin. He feared the Irish tenant would not pay his debts while Britain ruled: 'The Irish tenant cannot, in my deliberate opinion, be safely accepted as a debtor on a large scale to the Imperial Treasury.'[3] These views were shared by others, including competent officials; but taken as a whole, they amounted to a picture of Ireland which was unduly alarmist and which showed Gladstone as really not a competent judge of the position there. How far Gladstone was in 1886 from thinking that the Irish were fit to be trusted, is shown by his assumption that Irish land was an imperial matter which could not be left to Ireland to decide.[4]

Land purchase, as Ashbourne said when introducing the first effective measure in 1885, was '. . . a non-party question'. It contained many cross-currents. The first measures enabling tenants to purchase, those of 1869, 1870, and 1881, affected only small numbers. In so far as they prevented Irish tenants from buying at the peak, the ineffectiveness of Gladstone's legislation did them a notable service. Gladstone had created,

[1] *Leeds Speeches*, p. 13.

[2] Cooke and Vincent, *The Governing Passion* (1974), p. 328: Cooke and Vincent, *Lord Carlingford's Journal: Reflections of a Cabinet Minister, 1885* (1971), 141–2. The only exception made by Gladstone to this condemnation was a certain Callan, a nationalist at daggers drawn with Parnell. Callan was distinguished by his drunkenness and by being a tool of Chamberlain and Churchill; Gladstone singled him out for praise.

[3] Gladstone to Granville, 13 April 1882, Ramm, op. cit., vol. i, p. 360. The House of Lords committee of inquiry into the working of the 1881 Land Act impelled Gladstone to produce an outline of a provincial councils bill (printed, Hammond, 259–62).

[4] Besides the three excessive fears about Ireland (civil war, secession, non-payment) there was the quite separate issue of Scottish devolution, which had shown signs of becoming intermittently troublesome in the early 1880s. No statesman, especially one with a Scottish seat, could take up questions of Irish government without recognizing their possible Scottish implications.

by 1885, only about 6,500 peasant proprietors, against the 250,000 created by Wyndham's Act in 1903. It was not that kind words and fond hopes were wanting. Gladstone spoke in 1877, 1879, and 1880 in favour of a peasant proprietary. In May 1882 Granville announced that revision of the 1881 Purchase Clauses was being considered. In 1883 Lord George Hamilton, son of a great Ulster landowner, carried a unanimous motion calling for the purchase clauses to be made effective. In May 1884 Trevelyan, the chief secretary, introduced a bill offering easier terms to the purchaser, including abolition of any deposit. This idea of 100 per cent advances turned opinion against the bill and killed it. The Liberals tried, but not very hard, to turn consensus into fact, but land does not sell readily in a falling market, and when they went out of office nothing had been done.

The real question is not why the Liberals' actions were ineffective, but whether their sympathies were at least in spirit with the enterprise. This question really arose over Ashbourne's Act of 1885, the legislative foundation of modern Ireland. The Act passed without controversy, despite its avowed motive of removing 'the block in the land market', i.e. buying up land which landlords could not sell. Spencer, for the Liberals, opposed the 100 per cent advances for fear of a rent strike,[1] and his coldness suggested deeper doubts.[2] Gladstone was unable to speak on the measure because of a throat strain,[3] but a year later he condemned Ashbourne's Act as 'dangerous and mischievous'.[4] The question that arises is whether a peasant proprietary did not mean one thing to the Liberals and another to the Conservatives: in the first case the creation of a class of kulaks, in the second the elevation into owners of the mass of existing occupiers. Apart from his own land scheme of 1886, which he took a leading part in extinguishing, Gladstone notoriously opposed further land bills, partly for tactical reasons. Romantic though Gladstone could be in his occasional

[1] *Hansard*, vol. 299, col. 1344, 21 July 1885.

[2] Spencer's papers at Althorp are unenlightening on the Liberal response to Ashbourne's Act. A hint of his views may be gained from Thring's letters to Spencer of 18 and 22 July 1885, which suggest that Spencer was troubled by the bribes offered to both buyer and seller, by the possibility that the Act might unduly raise the price of land, and by the fear that it was open to improper manipulation. I owe this information to Dr. P. Gordon.

[3] On 14 July 1885 Gladstone's doctors ordered him to be silent 'almost like a Trappist'. Morley, *Gladstone* (1903), vol. iii, p. 216.

[4] Gladstone to Bright, 2 July 1886, *The Times*, 3 July 1886, p. 11, col. e.

references to *petite culture*, no one could claim that Gladstone was an enthusiast for an Ireland of peasant proprietors, or that he would have followed Arthur Balfour in describing the Irish land system after the Gladstonian reforms as 'essentially and radically rotten' and requiring 'heroic measures'.[1] If there is a residue of continuous intention to be extracted, after deductions made for tactical constraints, in Gladstone's view of the Irish land system, it would be this: that he could not see much beyond a reformed landlordism because he had no wish to; that he distrusted projects which depended on Irish honesty; and that he naturally overrated the efficacy of his own reforms.

When the 1885 election precipitated a crisis that was far more parliamentary than Irish, it found Gladstone in no particularly good shape to mould a policy. He was prey, as we have seen, to alarmist assumptions about what might happen in Ireland. He thought, or wished others to think, that there was an Irish crisis as well as a parliamentary one. He had nobody particularly sensible telling him what to think about Ireland, and his personal contact with Irish politicians could hardly have been less. (It was in January 1886 that he and Parnell, finding themselves on the same platform at Chester station while waiting for different trains, ostentatiously avoided each other.) He had no burning ambition, such as was to fill Arthur Balfour, to set to work upon Irish society as a social engineer or 'professional humanitarian'. His emotions on the subject of Ireland were nevertheless running at a higher pitch than anything he had mooted in the last five years would justify. His expressions were not those of the strictly rational supporter of devolution, of the Peelite imperial statesman. They were the emotions of a deeply moved man. It will be necessary for purposes of analysis to draw a sharp line between the sober garb of Home Rule before Easter 1886, and its wild and extravagantly radical tendency in the summer of that year. In doing so, we must not forget that the passion so embarrassingly to the fore in the election campaign, was also to be found in the preceding Christmas vacation.

[1] Ashbourne's Act of 1885 made £5m. available for purchase. Ashbourne's Act of 1888 provided another £5m.; Arthur Balfour's Act of 1891 (introduced in 1890, but delayed by Gladstonian and Irish obstruction) provided £33m. (Dugdale, *Life of Balfour*, vol. i, p. 181). 24,900 tenants purchased their farms under the Acts of 1885 and 1888. Out of this number, only twenty-two were considered in 1896 as bad debtors. The Liberals opposed land purchase in 1888 and 1891, and did nothing to forward it while in office in 1892–5.

How was this emotion to find a focus, given that he did not greatly want to change Ireland, and that he could hardly become passionate against his own stewardship? One answer lay in the instant creation of a tradition of historical interpretation centring on the wickedness of the Act of Union. Unable openly to preach Irish nationalism, or to condemn his own years in office, Gladstone centred his argument on immemorial oppression. This endorsement of native Irish traditions of hatred was the real concession to Ireland made in 1886.

He talked of the Union—called it a frightful and absurd mistake, thought Pitt had been persuaded into it by the King, who believed it would act as a check upon the Catholics, said that every Irishman 'who was worth a farthing' had opposed it, and if he had been an Irishman he would have done so to the utmost. He believed in nationality as a principle—whether Italian, Greek, Slav, or Irish—quoted as I had heard him do before, a saying of Grattan about 'the Channel forbidding Union, the ocean forbidding separation'—which he considered as one of the wisest sayings ever uttered by man—then dwelt on the length of time during which Ireland had possessed an independent, or at least a separate legislature.[1]

This belief in the wickedness of the Act of Union, suddenly discovered in 1886, provided a ready target for Gladstone's opponents, but there is no doubt that what might be called the historical case for Home Rule was there within him and that it provided a focus for the irrational passions that stirred him. Nationalism he could not openly preach, and perhaps did not, in the Irish case, quite believe. The historical doctrine of the oppression of 1800 served as an indirect relief for the emotions of nationalism. Added to other weaknesses, this reliance on what even then was weak polemical history limits even further his title to be regarded as acting from motives of insight and wisdom.

Nor can he be given much credit for his ideas as to how Home Rule was to pass. One is left with the rather unpleasant choice between assuming he was acting in bad faith, or assuming he was acting wildly. When pressed upon the point, his answer suggested an excitable unreality about strategy, not in keeping with his shrewd daily tactics:

He had his answer at once. Why should the peers reject it? who could tell that they would? and if once, would they do it a second time? What need was there for a dissolution? He then went into an argument as to the right of the peers to force a dissolution, as if he had contemplated the case occurring.[2]

[1] Derby's diary. [2] Ibid.

Going rather beyond the normal duties of his office, Gladstone had apparently offered the Queen odds of 40 to 1 against Home Rule passing; and if he did so, he was surely correct. There was no conceivable situation in the 1880s or 1890s in which the House of Lords would have passed a Gladstonian Home Rule Bill. The resistance would have had an absolute quality such as no Liberal premier had had to encounter since 1832. A dissolution would not help. A creation of peers was most improbable. Resignation aimed at leaving the country without a government required a degree of Liberal unity and popular enthusiasm which did not exist.

The mystery about how Gladstone would achieve Home Rule implies a greater mystery as to why and even whether he set out to achieve Home Rule. There are some strange clues, among them an account from one of those interviewed for office on the formation of the 1886 government:

> Gladstone drew a distinction between Home Rule—a phrase which he said he disliked—and the local autonomy which he thought it possible to create. . . . I should note that in the early part of the conversation he drew a distinction which I could not well follow, but to which he seemed to attach some importance—he said he disliked the name of Home Rule and preferred to call it 'local autonomy'. He did not explain the difference.[1]

The course of events requiring construction is as follows: Gladstone, by the Hawarden Kite, was able to draw the Irish back into his orbit, without making any public or private commitment, and without coming to an arrangement with Parnell. Gladstone, in fact, secured the Irish for a song, or rather a press leak. His *faux naïf* overtures to the Conservatives did much to ensure that they played the Orange card. When he was asked to form a government, what did he do? To some extent he was simply trying to form whatever could be formed; but to a surprisingly large degree he offered places on a basis which would have created a Unionist cabinet. Some of his offers were no doubt not intended to be accepted.[2] Even so, there was no real guard against what in retrospect looked like unwanted Unionists taking a large number of cabinet places. When we come to Sir Henry James, all ambiguity ceases. Gladstone undoubtedly wanted to build his House of Commons team round James, a doormat, but a Unionist doormat. Home

[1] Derby's diary, 30 January 1886.

[2] Hartington and Selborne may have carried away from Gladstone a false impression that Irish M.P.s were to remain at Westminster.

Rule was not a condition of entry into the 1886 cabinet; indeed, explicit disclaimer was possible. Gladstone could not have foreseen in advance that he would be able to form a cabinet; he could not have foreseen in advance that the cabinet would be so much less Unionist than he apparently was willing for it to be; and having once formed it, he could not then foresee what line the cabinet, or indeed those who were not yet its declared opponents, would take.

It was not a Home Rule cabinet. Harcourt and Chamberlain, the chief lieutenants in the Commons, hated Home Rule and had only to lift their little finger jointly to stop it ever getting past the cabinet. Harcourt 'thought Home Rule would inevitably lead to Civil War'.[1] Herschell, the Lord Chancellor, was privately opposed or at best very doubtful. Trevelyan was obsessively opposed, without Chamberlain's qualifications. Rosebery kept to himself in the Foreign Office and was probably Hartington's man in the cabinet, grooming himself to be Hartington's Foreign Secretary. Kimberley and Ripon were Whig pessimists and did not count outside their departments and imperial policy. Mundella and Campbell-Bannerman had done their best to undergo instant conversion but were barely of ministerial calibre. Of the 'true' Home Rulers, John Morley had hesitated to join Gladstone, and put land ahead of Home Rule; Childers tried to sabotage the bill by press leaks at a crucial stage; Granville had nearly refused to serve on grounds of *amour propre* because of his relegation; and Spencer's support on Home Rule was conditional on a land settlement which quickly proved a phantom. On normal expectations of how cabinets behave, then, the balance of power in the cabinet did not permit of a Home Rule Bill being even introduced.

There was, moreover, no distinct need to introduce a bill.

[1] At a dinner in autumn 1886 Harcourt's son had to stuff his father's mouth with a napkin to restrain his denunciations of Home Rule and the Irish. Chamberlain's position, commonly said to have always stopped short of Home Rule, may possibly have been more open:

'I had also some interesting talk with Chamberlain as to the future of Ireland: he admits to almost universal hatred of England: thinks it may die out, as a similar feeling has done in Scotland: he seemed to me to admit that a federal union is practically impossible, and that federalism is only a step to separation. He did not say in so many words that he was ready to accept separation as a possible solution, but implied it by arguing that after all the danger that could arise from Ireland being free was rather imaginary than real: that the Irish could do us no harm "a miserable little island at 4 hours distance": but he seemed to ignore the possibilities of French or American alliance' (Derby's diary, 4 January 1884).

The Parnellites and the Tories had, for the present, cut themselves off from reunion. Gladstone's majority was safe, and large.[1] Ireland was in a manageable state. The need to do anything was not apparent. The cabinet were not actually pressing for legislation, indeed were quite in the dark as to their Irish programme. The Liberal party was united and Hartington in a state of almost lukewarm friendliness.[2] On 4 March 1886, indeed, Gladstone obtained what was presumably his largest majority[3] on a major Irish vote, when he defeated Holmes's motion to withhold supply on the grounds of the disturbed state of Ireland by 364 to 204. Gladstone was in a position where it was easier, far easier, to do very little. Why then did he go decisively for Home Rule? The obvious answer is that that was what he wanted to do. Certainly the mystique that he was able to engender around Home Rule in the next few months cannot have come from nowhere, and the answer as to his personal commitment cannot be fully known until Oxford makes his diaries as accessible as they were to Hammond. But we must not make too much of his intense response to so ambiguous a writer on Anglo-Irish relations as Burke; this has normally been taken as a clue, but it is a clue open to many interpretations. Nor can we neglect the fact that from 1879 to 1885, Gladstone's views, in private as well as in public, seemed to settle on average at the level of a central board 'essentially municipal'. It may be, then, that Gladstone's private views on this as on so many other occasions were not the most powerful forces shaping his course. Instead, one would use the ample tools of common sense and dwell on three inescapable causes of Home Rule: the question of the parliamentary timetable, the question of the choice between two evils, and the question of the Chamberlain *démarche*.

Gladstone, in the spring of 1886, was understood to be going to introduce an Irish Land Bill and a Home Rule Bill. One did

[1] It is a common fallacy that the Parnellites held the balance of power in the 1886 parliament. Numerically this is so. Politically it meant nothing. After the Conservatives came out for coercion on 26 January 1886, the Irish vote became a cipher. The Parnellites were less powerful than before.

[2] Hartington's political factotum, Sir Henry James, speaking at Bury on 1 March 1886, said, 'I am going to take up my abode in no cave' (*The Times*, 2 March 1886). On 5 March Hartington spoke to the Eighty Club, stressing that 'up to the present time we, the Liberal party, are still one, and all of us are free and uncommitted' (*The Times*, 6 March 1886).

[3] Hartington, James, and most of the leading Liberal Unionists of the future voted with Gladstone on this occasion.

not have to be an old parliamentary hand to see that both bills could not possibly pass within one session, merely on grounds of time. One of the two bills, therefore, was a dummy—a well-intentioned dummy, perhaps, betokening concord and the promise of things to come, but nevertheless so far as that session went, a dummy. In hindsight, we take it for granted that the Land Bill was the dummy, and that Spencer, in particular, was Gladstone's dupe. This was not necessarily so at the time. Both Spencer and Morley expected the land legislation to precede that on Home Rule, and moreover the Land Bill was actually the first of the two to reach the cabinet. What we have, up to mid-March, is a premier with two bills on his hands, one of which looks as though it will have to be dropped or postponed, and the Home Rule Bill running in second place. Nor can one neglect the weighty and generally accepted reasons for giving priority to a settlement by Westminster of Irish land: the landlords had to be protected from a predatory parliament in Dublin. In parliamentary terms, too, the Land Bill was easier to try first. The outgoing Conservative ministry had in their last days of office committed themselves to prompt legislation to extend land purchase, which in any case they liked; and potential Whig dissidents, too, were friendly to the idea of protecting the landlords by purchase. Even from a Home Rule point of view, priority for land meant that one of the strongest arguments against devolution, namely that it would imperil the landlords, would be removed. If Gladstone wished to represent the consensus of British opinion, while isolating the Conservatives as harbingers of conflict, and retaining Irish goodwill, his proper course was to carry a Land Purchase Bill, building on the acknowledged success of the Conservative Bill of 1885. As Gladstone up to Easter 1886 appeared to wish to proceed by consensus, it is especially hard to see why this did not happen.

One reason why it did not happen was the strong feeling among nearly all Liberal and many Conservative politicians that Irish policy was a choice of evils: there was repression, which nobody believed would really work; and there was Home Rule, which few people believed would work well. Gladstone, with his long-standing instinct that Parnell was the man to back if one wanted an orderly Ireland, went further than most, but even with him it is unlikely he had positive enthusiasm for Home Rule at the time he first endorsed it, that he supposed it would bring better government, or that he had much regard for those to whom it would hand power. His reasons were negative, and therefore may be called 'Peelite': Home Rule was an expedient to adopt lest worse befell, rather than a Liberal reform based on 'gorgeous reckless optimism'. Since the Conservatives had chosen repression, and it had done them little good in parliamentary terms, the Liberals were driven willy-nilly towards Home Rule. It was 'the devil or the deep blue sea' as Gladstone said; and 'the devil' having been pre-empted, the only real question was why some compromise was not possible leaning towards, but falling short of, Home Rule. One reason, but not the decisive one, was that Parnell was less willing than ever to compromise; another, probably more weighty, was that Liberal politicians genuinely expected a compromise of the 'Central Board' type to produce the worst of both worlds. The Liberals took up Home Rule because there was no other available position. Choice or conversion, in the early stages, appeared to play less part than necessity. There was sugar on the pill, for Home Rule appeared to mean the expulsion[1] of the Irish from Westminster, and, for many, to have an attractively punitive aspect. In this matter of choice between almost balanced evils, Gladstone faced what he and other Liberals saw as an unpleasant dilemma rather than an exciting opportunity. In this he was characteristic. Where he was uncharacteristic was in his power of developing and transmuting his initial position into positive belief.

Then there was Chamberlain's *démarche*. On 13 March 1886 the cabinet discussed Irish legislation for the first time. The matter before them was the Irish Land Bill, and perhaps only that. Chamberlain, so far as one can collect from the imperfect accounts remaining, switched the business of the meeting by raising the question of Home Rule. It is not now possible to reconstruct what Gladstone had intended to happen at the meeting, and what should develop from it. What is clear is that as late as 12 March, Gladstone was finding opportunities to put the stress on Irish land legislation. His letter[2] to the leader of the southern Irish landlords, seeking a solution to the Irish land question by agreement, implied developments in that

[1] 'Converting Ireland into a colony *pur et simple*', as Harcourt said (Cooke and Vincent, *The Governing Passion*, p. 395).

[2] Gladstone wrote to Lord De Vesci, 12 February 1886, inviting 'free communication of views' from responsible individuals in Ireland on the subjects of Gladstone's re-election address, namely social order, land, and government in Ireland. The letter was printed in *The Times*, 16 February 1886, p. 6, col. c.

direction, while the bait of Home Rule tomorrow kept the Parnellites in tow. Up to 12 March Gladstone had avoided using Irish questions as an issue which might radicalize the Liberal party. It is also clear that, whether he wanted it or not, Gladstone could not have foreseen so early and so direct a confrontation with Chamberlain on the Home Rule issue which, though entwined in the land legislation, the premier may have wished to keep below the surface. Much of this is speculation. What we can say is that the cabinet entered Downing Street on 13 March 1886 with no distinct Irish policy known to most of its members, and emerged from it committed to Home Rule in principle rather than as a practical and immediate legislative commitment. The next cabinet, before Chamberlain's resignation was written, was called to work over details of Irish land, the Land Bill retaining its priority. It was Chamberlain's resignation which made Home Rule the central issue and which created a situation to which Gladstone had to respond. The unfavourable parliamentary reaction to the Land Bill in April was its *coup de grâce*, but the Land Bill had already fallen from first to second place by the time of the cabinet of 29 March. Gladstone began March 1886 as a discreet, possibly procrastinating, Home Ruler who was anxious to legislate on Irish land while avoiding radical overtones; he ended the month as an unenthusiastic land reformer whose chief immediate commitment was to Home Rule. The details are uncertain, but it is likely that 13 March 1886 was the point at which history jumped from one set of tracks to another. The result was to make Gladstone's burning intensity of the Christmas vacation, his Home Rule legislation of April 1886, and his somewhat manic election campaign in June, appear as three closely linked expressions of a single inner moral experience and an outer political radicalism, which was not necessarily the case.

The decision to put Home Rule in the foreground of immediate politics was of far greater significance than the earlier decision to form a ministry to which Home Rule leanings could be imputed. The earlier decision, it may be argued, created the Irish-Liberal alliance, for it enabled the Parnellites to support Gladstone. This ignores the fact that the Parnellites became Gladstonian fellow travellers not because of what Gladstone did, or because Parnell secured certain terms from the Liberals, but because the Conservatives made it impossible for the Irish to support them in any circumstances. It was only with the decision to make Home Rule legislation the central issue in the 1886 session that the stage was set for a conflict in which moral Gladstonian 'masses' encountered the upper 'classes' in a crusade—exactly the situation which Gladstone had been trying to avoid, with some skill and success, in the first three months of 1886. Gladstone's manifesto of 1 May 1886 announced that Chamberlain's and Hartington's bid for the centre before Easter had left Gladstone free to establish his position on the left, and to carry out that 'democratic' polarization of parties which Chamberlain had unsuccessfully attempted at the 1885 election. What Gladstone was doing was not passing Home Rule, but carrying out the reorganization of party structure on lines which Gladstone had ably resisted when it had been pressed by Chamberlain.

If Gladstone had been primarily concerned with Home Rule, he should have given more serious thought to passing on the torch to Hartington than he did. What mattered about Hartington was not what he had said against Home Rule, but what he had not said in favour of coercion. Hartington, having made an appropriate show of resistance, was in a strong position to make, and to carry, some form of accommodation with the Irish, under a different form of words. He would have faced the usual dilemma whether to govern with or without bayonets, and as the Liberal party would certainly not have supported bayonets, the rest followed. Gladstone could not have put Hartington in office as his successor, leading a united and pro-Irish Liberal party, because the Queen's actions were so unpredictable; but he could have done something to make the matter possible. Instead, he used the device of a crusade to make a Hartington succession impossible.

Gladstone did not idealize the Irish. It would be too simple to say he did not like Irishmen, though the outward and social forms which commonly express liking were absent.[1] What is lacking is something more impersonal and significant, that process of idealization which attended a Gladstonian enthusiasm. Gladstone idealized the Waldenses in youth,[2] the Italians in

[1] e.g. his refusal to visit Ireland in autumn 1886 when invited by the Irish ladies' deputation which visited Hawarden (*The Times*, 5 October 1886, p. 10, col. a). Davitt had already in an interview spoken of Gladstone being 'tendered a grand banquet in Dublin in October . . .' (*The Times*, 20 August 1886, p. 9, col. f).

[2] Cf. his 'To Violets in a Vaudois Valley', March 1832, in *The Prime Ministers' Papers: W. E. Gladstone. I: Autobiographica*, ed. John Brooke and Mary Sorensen (1971), pp. 232–3.

middle age, the Montenegrins in age,[1] and the Scotch always. From about 1870 he began to idealize that 'strong, stern, masculine race', as he called them, the Welsh. In his great speech at Swansea, Gladstone made startling assertions, going far beyond what politics demanded. He took issue with those who thought Wales a mere geographical expression. He asked his audience to consider whether Wales was a nationality or not—a question 'on which I for one have a strong opinion'. He affirmed 'that Welsh nationality is as great a reality as English nationality' and referred to the Welsh saints 'to show how absurd it is to deny this nationality of Wales'. Then, going still higher in the scale of compliment, he added:

> With the traditions and history of Wales, with the language of Wales, with the feelings of Wales, with the intention and determination of Wales, I maintain that the Welsh nationality is as true as the nationality of Scotland.[2]

It would be hard to find any parallel affirmation of Irish national identity, or even any extolling of Irish virtues. In his least political speeches, those given to the villagers of Hawarden, Gladstone never wearied of holding up the virtues of the Scotch, and of Aberdonians in particular, for their emulation. In these rustic homilies addressed to a Welsh audience, he dwelt repeatedly on Scottish superiority.[3] It might be difficult to find a single gratuitous and non-political compliment falling from his lips about the Irish.[4] He leaves us in doubt whether he recognized in Ireland the qualities that made up national identity in Scotland and Wales. He even pointed a finger at the Irish for letting their language decay, while the language of Wales flourished.

When all is weighed, it comes to no great sum. Gladstone did not want to see the kind of Ireland the Conservatives and the Free State created, the kind of Ireland that actually emerged, and preferred to reform landlordism rather than destroy it. He did not give cordial recognition to Ireland as a nation, as he

[1] Cf. his 'Montenegro: A Sketch', in *The Nineteenth Century*, May 1877.

[2] Speech at Swansea, *The Times*, 6 June 1887.

[3] In 1875, 1877, 1879, 1882, 1888, and 1890.

[4] When discoursing on Shakespeare, he let fall this pearl (to a Welsh audience) '. . . If you take his ideas of the Irish, they are very soon disposed of. He mentions them very seldom, and when he does mention them it is in a manner far from agreeable to the Irishman' (*The Times*, 5 September 1888, p. 6, reporting a speech at Wrexham).

[5] See below, p. 236.

did to Scotland and Wales. His main achievements in Irish affairs were unpremeditated, the Irish Church Act being the chief exception. What he promised or hoped for of his own accord, as with Irish railway nationalization in the 1860s, land purchase in the late 1870s, and moderate devolution in the early 1880s, came to nothing. His two Irish phases overlaid and erased deeper layers of intention concerning his schemes as a financier. Ireland sidetracked him, hiding from view important parts of his genius. Where he set his great parliamentary gifts to do what other men could not, it was in the cause of legislation like that of 1870 and 1881, which in both cases only partially represented his intentions and only partially worked. Doubts arise also as to whether the Irish tenant benefited economically from Gladstonian legislation, which either gave him formally what he already had informally, or else introduced rack-renting under the name of tenant-right. What was tenant-right to a selling tenant, was tenant's wrong to an incoming occupier; and for every seller there was a buyer.

It is only if one puts oneself in the shoes of Parnell (or still more of Dillon) that a pattern of achievement can be seen: the suppression of radicalism and the peasant movement by the twin Acts of 1881, the imposition of responsibility by the Kilmainham Treaty of 1882, the clerical reconstruction of Irish electoral politics by the Seats Act of 1885, the demolition of the Tory-Irish alliance and thus of Parnell's independent parliamentary power, the absorption of the Home Rulers into Liberalism by the events of 1886—this, seen as a pattern, shows Gladstone as the most masterly upholder of Unionism since Pitt, one who with a minimum of real concession put the United Kingdom on a satisfactory working basis which could, so far as Ireland went, have lasted well beyond 1922.

APPENDIX A: GLADSTONE ON HOME RULE, 1871

Gladstone's speech[1] on receiving the Freedom of the City of Aberdeen deserves special attention, as the most developed and least guarded exposition of his views on Home Rule before 1886. Much in the speech is representative of Gladstone's views on Ireland at least up till 1880; the customary dismissal of it as a merely humorous and momentary aberration will not stand examination. After the usual courtesies, Gladstone took as his theme the sterling efforts made by the people of

[1] *The Times*, 27 September 1871, p. 6, cols. a–f.

Aberdeenshire in setting up their own scheme for controlling cattle plague without waiting for governmental guidance:

'. . . I wish to say here that which I have said elsewhere in public and in private—that it was an admirable spectacle when all over the country we were wandering and groping about, some proposing the most absurd measures by way of remedy and precaution, and others feeling themselves to be totally in the dark—it was an admirable spectacle when gentlemen and farmers of the county of Aberdeen associated themselves together with nothing to rely upon except their own energy, except their own prudence and intelligence, to devise for the ready, rapid, and complete extinction of that plague a remedy which, at a later period, after much ineffectual discussion, the Legislature found themselves counselled by prudence to adopt. I cannot recollect . . . so remarkable an example of local activity, self-reliance, practicability, and wisdom, holding up for the nation a standard which that nation was ultimately glad to follow. . . . That transaction brings to mind the extraordinary value of the principles and practice and habits of local government and local management of affairs in this country. Our great and illustrious neighbour, the French nation, probably never would have undergone the frightful calamities which it has been destined to experience during the last fifteen months had its people had that kind of training, and acquired that kind of personal and individual self-reliance by which the people of this country are so largely distinguished, and which for my own part I look upon as one of the greatest public blessings that they enjoy. That is the kind of Home Rule, such as you practised on the occasion of the cattle plague, which every man must witness with satisfaction, and I trust feel that it is, after all, in the energy of individual character and the sense of individual responsibility for public matters, and the facility of combination in our local community that we see laid the broad and solid basis upon which is erected the fabric of the national greatness . . . the very remarkable exhibition of Home Rule which I have spoken of in the county of Aberdeen reminds me of another cry for Home Rule which is now raised across the Channel in Ireland, and with which I own I find it not so easy to deal in a satisfactory manner. I am not quite certain what is meant in Ireland by the cry of Home Rule. I am glad to know from the mouths of those who raised that cry what it does not mean; they have told us emphatically by their principal organs that it does not mean the breaking up into fragments this United Kingdom. [Applause.] Well, that after all, is a most important matter. This United Kingdom, which we have endeavoured to make a united kingdom in heart as well as in law [applause], we trust will remain a united kingdom [loud applause]; and although as human beings the issues of great events are not in our hands, but are directed by a higher Power, yet we intend and mean every one of us, both high and low, not those merely who meet within this hall, but those who crowd the streets of your city, and every city from the north to the south of this island—we intend it shall remain a united kingdom. [Loud applause.] And, my Lord Provost, as the subject has been brought into discussion and has attracted considerable attention in the sister island, I for one, have not the slightest hesitation in saying that I am extremely glad that the distinguished lawyer who has just been returned for Limerick [Mr. Butt][1] has again found his way into Parliament; it will be an immense advantage in dealing with this question that its chief advocates should be there. It is in this way that in this country we deal with all political difficulties. If there are wild ideas abroad, depend upon it the place where they can most safely be promulgated is within the walls of the House of Commons. I may regret, perhaps, that a particular constituency seems to show a momentary sympathy with ideas which are very unintelligible and superfluous; but, presuming that that disposition exists, I say it is of great public benefit that the champions of any impracticable scheme should come before the representatives of the people in the House of Commons, and should there have the opportunity of stating all that they can state on behalf of their views, and should there be subject to have those views brought to the test of discussion and of searching examination, and when that learned gentleman makes his appearance in Parliament we shall be very glad and we shall be very anxious to do our best to discuss all about this matter of Home Rule. [Laughter and cheers.] We are told that it is necessary for Ireland to close her relations with the Parliament of this country and to have a Parliament of her own. Let me do the promoters of this movement the fullest justice. Always speaking under the conviction, as they most emphatically declare, and as I fully believe them, that the union of the kingdoms under Her Majesty is to be maintained, but that Parliament is to be broken up—"Well now", we shall say to this learned gentleman, "Why is Parliament to be broken up? Has Ireland great grievances? What is it that Ireland has demanded from the Imperial Parliament and that the Imperial Parliament has refused?" [Cheers.] It will not do to deal with this matter in vague and shadowy assertions. I have looked in vain for the setting forth of any practical scheme of policy which the Imperial Parliament is not equal to deal with, or which it refuses to deal with, and which is to be brought about by Home Rule. So far as my research has gone, and I confess it is not extensive, we have not had the advantage of hearing all that is to be said. I have seen nothing except that it is stated there is a vast quantity of fish in the seas that surround Ireland, and that if they had Home Rule they would catch a great deal of these fish. [Much laughter and cheers.] But there are fish in the sea which surrounds England and Scotland. England has no Home Rule, and Scotland has no Home Rule, but we manage to catch the fish. [Cheers and laughter.] Unhappily, my Lord Provost, it has been one consequence of the policy towards

[1] Isaac Butt, the leader of the Home Rule movement, had been elected for Limerick City earlier in the month.

Ireland in former times that those principles of self-reliance, those powers of local action, that energy and public spirit which are the inherited possessions of this country have been steadily enfeebled and crippled in the Sister Island; and therefore it is that these things, which in this country every day and every month that we live the various classes and the various communities are doing for themselves the Irish people have not yet learnt in the same way to do; but I am bound to say they have not had the same opportunity of learning in the same degree to do for themselves, and hence they are liable to become more or less the victims from time to time of this or that political delusion. [Applause.] You would expect when it is said that the Imperial Parliament is to be broken up, that at the very least a case should be made out showing there were great subjects of policy, and great demands necessary for the welfare of Ireland, which representatives of Ireland had united to ask, and which the representatives of England, Scotland, and Wales had united to refuse. [Cheers.] There is no such grievance. There is nothing that Ireland has asked and which this country and this Parliament have refused. This Parliament has done for Ireland what it would have scrupled to do for England and for Scotland [cheers]. There remains now a single grievance—a grievance with regard to University education, which is not so entirely free in Ireland as it has now been made in England; but that is an exceptional subject, and it is a subject on which I am bound to say Ireland has made no united demand upon England; still, I regard it as a subject that calls for legislation, but there is no demand which Ireland has made and which England has refused, and I shall be very glad to see such a demand put into a practical shape in which we may make it subject of candid and rational discussion. What are the inequalities of England and Ireland? I declare that I know none, except that there are certain taxes[1] still remaining which are levied over Englishmen and Scotchmen and which are not levied over Irishmen, and likewise that there are certain purposes for which public money is freely and largely given in Ireland and for which it is not given in England or Scotland. [Cheers.] That seems to me to be a very feeble case indeed for the argument which has been

[1] Cf. Gladstone, *Parl. Deb.*, *3*, vol. clxxi, col. 827, 12 June 1863: 'Men who can keep horses and carriages, or who have considerable estates in Ireland, are as rich as the same class in England. They are richer, indeed, because an income of £1,000 a year is worth more in Ireland than in England, and gives a higher social position there than here. We have in England duties on hackney coaches, horses, railways, and stage carriages, amounting to £700,000 or £800,000 per annum. All these duties are levied in England and Scotland, but not one shilling of them is paid in Ireland. We have also the assessed taxes, the land tax, and the inhabited house duty, which produce about £3,250,000 to the Exchequer in this country. Not a single shilling is paid in respect of any one of these duties in Ireland.' Gladstone pointed out that these exemptions benefited only the Irish rich; the Irish poor enjoyed, by 1863, full equality of taxation.

made by means of which, as we are told, the fabric of the United Parliament of this country is to be broken up. But while I have thus freely criticized the promoters of this movement, and endeavoured to give expression to what I believe to be your feeling and the feeling of this country about it, let me say I admit that large allowance is to be made for our friends and fellow countrymen in Ireland. Political virtues such as we have been just referring to—I mean the virtues of self-reliance and practical energy—are not the creation of a day. The circumstances under which Ireland was too long governed were hostile—nay, almost fatal to their growth, and, on the whole, we ought rather to be pleased that Ireland is what she is, for, after all, we believe this to be but a partial and superficial manifestation. We ought rather to be pleased with regard to her growing industry and her general freedom from crime than to complain that she is not something better than she has ever had an opportunity of becoming. But if the doctrines of Home Rule are to be established in Ireland I protest on your behalf that you will be just as well entitled to it in Scotland [hear hear]; and, moreover, I protest on behalf of Wales, in which I have lived a good deal, and where there are 800,000 people, who to this day, such is their sentiment of nationality, speak hardly anything but their own Celtic tongue—a larger number than speak the Celtic tongue, I apprehend, in Scotland, and a larger number than speak it, I apprehend, in Ireland—I protest on behalf of Wales that they are entitled to Home Rule there. [Applause.] Can any sensible man, can any rational man suppose that at this time of day, in this condition of the world, we are going to disintegrate the great capital institutions of this country for the purpose of making ourselves ridiculous in the sight of all mankind, and crippling any power we possess for bestowing benefits through legislation on the country to which we belong? [Applause.] One word more only, my Lord Provost, on this subject, and it is this:—People say that we have tried to conciliate Ireland, and that we have failed. I do not admit that Ireland is not going to be conciliated [applause], but I say this—that we must always keep in mind that there is a higher law to govern the actions of Parliament and of politicians than the law of conciliation, good as that law may be. [Cheers.] We desire to conciliate Ireland, we desire to soothe her people—the wounded feelings and the painful recollections of her people. We desire to attach her to this island in the silken cords of love [cheers], but there was a higher and a paramount aim in the measures that Parliament has passed, and that was that it should do its duty. It was to set itself right with the national conscience, with the opinion of the world, and with the principles of justice [loud cheers]; and when that is done, I say fearlessly that, whether conciliation be at once realized or not, the position of this country is firm and invulnerable'.[1]

[1] Gladstone then proceeded to discuss non-Irish subjects. In 1886, when his speech of 1871 was used in Unionist polemics, Gladstone wrote to Bright,

APPENDIX B: LORD HARTINGTON ON HOME RULE 1886[1]

Sunday, 24 January 1886. . . . My conversation with Hartington yesterday was too long and turned too much on details to be noted in full. He dwelt on the impossibility of any business being done in parliament while the Irishmen sat there: this evil he seemed to think incurable by any regulations or systems of procedure. He thought it absolutely necessary that they should be turned out. 'Then', I said, 'you must give them full control over their own affairs in a local parliament.' He did not see that, thought it did not follow, was not for making concessions to them, would get rid of them for our own sake, not for theirs, assumed that in any case there must be a power in the English parliament to override a local legislature set up in Dublin—in short, he would restore the Irish parliament as it was before Grattan and 1780. 'Did he suppose that would satisfy the Irish? Would they not be worse off than before?' He could not tell, and did not much care. 'But will Gladstone agree to a plan quite different from his own?' That he did not know either. 'Would he, Hartington, agree to Gladstone's plan, by which the Irish are to be retained in the House?' 'No, certainly not'. 'Then what is to happen if the government[2] go out?' Much discussion followed. He seemed to think that Gladstone would try to make a government and fail, and that possibly matters might end in the present Cabinet coming back with Whig support. He distinctly assured me that he would not take office on the mere chance of being able to agree on Irish policy afterwards, but would insist on knowing what was proposed.[3]

'Never since Home Rule was started fifteen years ago have I once condemned it in principle' (*The Times*, 28 June 1886, p. 6, col. c).

[1] From Lord Derby's journal.

[2] Lord Salisbury's administration of 1885–6.

[3] The assumption that Hartington's position on Home Rule was the simple contrary of Gladstone's is a good example of how conscientious archival history can mislead. The archives at Chatsworth present a picture of a splendidly conventional Hartington who never budged an inch on the principle of Home Rule. This is not because of weeding of his papers, but because his correspondents imposed this stereotype on him, and expected him to write back in the same terms, which he did. Only in certain places which have no obvious association with Hartington will the truth be found that his and Gladstone's views, if not their interests and situations, at one moment almost converged. The 'Home Rule' Hartington of *c.* 23–6 January 1886 may be found in the Grey MSS., Durham; Mrs. Courtney's diary, L.S.E.; Kay-Shuttleworth MSS. in an estate office in Upper Ribblesdale; Hartington's letter to Lansdowne speaking well of Home Rule; a short paragraph in *The Times* reporting a pro-Irish kite flown in a speech of Hartington's brother; and the phenomenally long meetings with Gladstone reported in

the press in January 1886, which showed the two men were meeting to consider joint party strategy. Hartington's little acts of friendliness to Gladstone in succeeding months deserve thoughtful interpretation, as does his benevolent line in early March. Until Chamberlain's *démarche* forced Hartington into the open for fear of losing the centre–right to Chamberlain, it is not clear that Hartington meant to break openly with Gladstone. The Hartington who had the leadership of a united Liberal party almost within his grasp, not the Liberal Unionist secessionist, is the figure we should see in spring 1886.

DAWES HICKS LECTURE

PRE-ESTABLISHED HARMONY *VERSUS* CONSTANT CONJUNCTION: A RECONSIDERATION OF THE DISTINCTION BETWEEN RATIONALISM AND EMPIRICISM[1]

By Hidé Ishiguro

Read 19 October 1977

THE grouping of European philosophers of the seventeenth and eighteenth centuries into rationalists and empiricists seems to me to be unfortunate and unhelpful. It suggests that there are two self-contained mutually incompatible sets of views, which are clearly demarcated and based on opposing principles: one claiming that the source of all substantial truths about reality is reason; the other claiming that all knowledge derives from experience. To divide these thinkers into Continental rationalists and British empiricists is even more misleading. It suggests that the grouping of people with opposing sets of beliefs and theories coincided with their nationalities.

Not only did thinkers like Descartes, Spinoza, and Leibniz take great interest in the experimental sciences of their day, they also thought that the data we obtain from our senses played an important role in the formation of our knowledge of the world.[2] On the other hand, as J. MacIntosh has pointed out, Berkeley went so far as to write that intellect and reason are alone the sure guides to truth,[3] and even Locke, who proclaimed that all our knowledge comes ultimately from the senses, defended a theory of knowledge in which an indispensable role is played by elements which, as many have pointed out, cannot be derived

[1] In writing this paper I profited from comments on an earlier version made by David Wiggins and by my colleagues, Myles Burnyeat, John Watling, and Richard Wollheim.

[2] This has been argued in a convincing way by others. See, e.g., R. M. Blake, 'The role of experience in Descartes' Theory of Method', *Philosophical Review*, 38 (1929), and E. M. Curley, 'Experience in Spinoza's Theory of Knowledge', in *Spinoza*, ed. M. Grene, p. 25. For Berkeley's views on the importance of reason see J. J. MacIntosh, 'Leibniz and Berkeley', *Proceedings of the Aristotelian Society*, 1971. It can be seen, however, that I do not agree with much of what he says on Leibniz on causation.

[3] Berkeley, *Siris*, p. 264.

from sense–experience. We will see that the same can be said of Hume's theories.

What I would like to draw your attention to today is the view of causation developed by Leibniz, who is often thought to be the rationalist philosopher *par excellence*. His views on causation are widely misunderstood. A proper understanding of them will go against the received view of the contrast between rationalism and empiricism. Three points in particular will be important.

The first is the considerable similarity between Leibniz's theory of causation, namely the doctrine of pre-established harmony, and the opinion of Hume on this subject so familiar to the British philosophical public—in contrast, for example, to the views of Descartes or Locke. We shall see that the experiential evidence for pre-established harmony is not different from the experiential evidence for constant conjunction.

Second, by examining how Leibniz linked his views on causation with the concept of the nature of things and of force, we shall see, despite all their similarities, the ultimate difference between Leibniz's views and those of Hume. It is impossible, however, to do justice to this difference in terms of the ordinary stereotypes of rationalism and empiricism. It involves Leibniz's belief in the possibility of *a posteriori* knowledge of real essence, which Locke thought unknowable.

Third, it should become apparent how Leibniz's views compare with recent theories of causal explanation: especially theories related to counterfactual conditionals and nomological deductive theories. I hope that the comparison will suggest how misguided are the standard criticisms of Leibniz's account of causation.

1. *Hume and Leibniz*

It is well known that Leibniz denied the philosophical doctrine of causal interaction. It is seldom understood what it was that he was denying. Russell, for example, wrote, that, according to Leibniz, 'nothing really acts on anything else'.[1] But what is the difference between really acting on something and seeming to act on it? Many people seem to have thought that Leibniz's denial of causal interaction amounted to the claim that there was no connection between what happens to one thing and what happens to other things. If this were a correct interpretation, it would be a mystery that Leibniz was always interested in the investigation of the laws of dynamics and the correct mathematical

[1] *The Philosophy of Leibniz*, p. 93.

formulation of them. He wrote several treatises on dynamics. His disagreement with Descartes and with Newton about the laws of dynamics never concerned the question whether there exist laws stating the interconnection of material things. They related only to how the laws should be formulated. Noticing law-like regularities was what made nature comprehensible to men. As Leibniz writes, the central concept of dynamics was that 'there is always a perfect equivalence [by which he means equality of energy] between the full cause and the whole effect'.[1] Leibniz is far from denying the existence of conditions or events that are causes and conditions or events that are effects. Nor does he deny the importance of the causal explanation for macroscopic physical things. As far as macroscopic physical things were concerned his views were very much in the spirit of the mechanism of his time. As he says, 'But in phenomena everything is explained mechanically and so masses are understood to impel each other'.[2]

Some philosophers have said that Leibniz's denial of causal interaction concerns only monads, which were, strictly speaking, the only individual substances for Leibniz, and therefore has nothing to do with the causal explanation of physical events, which are according to Leibniz phenomena. It must be recalled, however, that Leibniz first expressed his denial of causal interaction in an article concerning the mind-body problem; and in his discussion on causation he repeatedly refers to the relationship between mind and body, as well as to that between the mind and phenomenal changes in the outer world. The body is an aggregate according to Leibniz—an infinite complex machine—and also something we identify as a spatial, extended thing, i.e. a phenomenon. Leibniz even wrote that his system of pre-established harmony has the advantage of conserving what he calls the 'great principle of physics', the inertial laws of bodies, in its full rigour and generality.[3] The scope of the doctrine is not as limited as these critics have supposed.

[1] Reply to Abbé Catelan in *Nouvelles de la République des Lettres*, Feb. 1687.

[2] Letter to de Volder, 1703. *G* II, p. 250; *L*, p. 529. (*G* is Gerhardt, *Philosophische Schriften*, vols. I–VII. *L* is *Leibniz's Philosophical Papers*, ed. Loemker, published by Reidel.)

[3] 'Consideration on Vital Principles and Plastic Natures', 1705. *G* VI, p. 541; *L*, p. 587. In a letter to Arnauld he reflects that his denial of causal interaction between corporeal substances may be even more surprising than his denial of causal interaction between monads, since action of the body on another may appear so undeniable. Letter to Arnauld, 14 July 1686. *G* II, p. 58; *L*, p. 338.

Many popular commentators have claimed to be puzzled by an analogy, which Leibniz made in the *Monadology* for a popular audience. He says that monads have no windows; they are like mirrors which reflect the rest of the universe. But there is no puzzle here. Leibniz does not use the contrast between the mirror without windows and a thing with windows to point to an esoteric fact hidden behind appearances. His concern is with a familiar recognizable truth. The analogy reminds the reader of something he should already know about if he is to think about the problems without preconceived ideas: viz. what is involved in causal explanation. When we think that a moving billiard ball causes another ball to move by impact, we do not need to suppose that something goes out of one ball and into another. The motion of one ball does affect the motion of the other ball. But it is the velocity, motion, and direction of *each* ball that changes. The denial that there is something literally transmitted in these causal transactions is the point of Leibniz's analogy of windowless monads. Whereas we do think of a reflection in a mirror as a typical case of a state caused by external events. Corresponding to the changes in the vicinity of the mirror, there will be changes in the image on the mirror—but not because a bit of the external world enters the mirror. The (intact) mirror by its (very) own nature, changes its state in a manner corresponding to the change outside. Of course, light waves of certain kinds travel to the surface of the mirror. But they do not go into it. If anything, Leibniz's analogy of the mirror shows not only that he believed in the existence of what we would now call causal relation; it shows that he thought it much more far-reaching than is normally assumed. Every entity has a causal relationship with everything else in the universe.

I therefore think it is misleading to write as many have done[1] that according to Leibniz there is no such thing as causal interaction since each substance is separately 'programmed' for the whole of its history. Each substance has its nature. Given that the substance finds itself in a universe with other things, this nature programmes its history. The nature of the substance is such that the substance will be affected by other things, in a specific way, and is such that the substance will affect other things in a particular manner. The nature of the monad also determines the nature of aggregates of which it is a constituent, and determines how the aggregate is affected by other aggregates. Leibniz writes, 'Who would deny that a substance is modified

[1] e.g. N. Rescher, *The Philosophy of Leibniz*, p. 83.

through the effect of another substance, for example, when a body is thrown back by an opposing obstacle?'[1] Leibniz goes on to say that we shall, therefore, have to use the concepts of *both* bodies in order to know distinctly the recoil of one of the bodies. He, nevertheless, is careful to add that the recoil is only a mode of that body—it is not as if something alien to the body has come into the body, like a disembodied force, as if from a window, to make it recoil. It was the very nature of that body, with its particular mass and elasticity, to recoil the way it did, given the impact of the other in those particular circumstances.

Now, although the physical objects which we perceive were, according to Leibniz, phenomena of aggregates, interacting with one another by collision and impact, Leibniz did say of monads, which make up these aggregates, that he did not 'admit any action of substances upon each other in the proper sense since no reason can be found for one monad influencing another'.[2] We must, however, give an interpretation of the denial of action 'in the proper sense' between substances, which is compatible with his theories of nomic regularities between phenomena of aggregates. A helpful way is to see what Leibniz was opposing.

The doctrine of causal interaction which Leibniz rejected is not a doctrine of what we today mean by cause and effect. It was a doctrine which was in traditional scholastic textbooks of his time and one which had slipped without much resistance into the vocabulary of the Cartesians and the new physicists: the doctrine of influx.[3] According to this view, when A interacts with B, a form or a quality or a mode which A has, passes from A to B. Thus, if a hot metal bar, A, heats a cold metal bar, B, the heat which was in A is said by the view Leibniz was attacking to move from A to B. If a moving object A collides with another object B, which is at rest and moves it, then the motion of A is said to be transferred from A to B. But Leibniz thought that this theory entailed an absurd idea—the idea that qualities can be detached from substances. Thus, in the passage of the *Monadology*,[4] where Leibniz asserts that monads have no windows

[1] Letters to de Volder, July 1701. *G* II. p. 226; *L*, p. 524; *Leibniz: Selections*, ed. Wiener, p. 169.

[2] Letter to de Volder, June 1703. *G* II, p. 251; *L*, p. 530.

[3] Suarez's definition of cause was 'what flows being into something else'. Suarez (1548–1617), *Disputationes Metaphysicae*. For Leibniz's fierce criticism of this view see Preface to an edition of Nizolius, 1670. *G* IV, p. 148; *L*, p. 126.

[4] *Monadology* § 7 *G* VI, p. 607; *L*, p. 643.

through which anything could enter or depart, he explains that this is so because 'accidents cannot be detached from substances and march about outside of substances as the sensible species of the Scholastics once did'. Leibniz is not saying that the Scholastics, nor his physicist contemporaries, put forward a doctrine of detached accidents. He is saying rather that the Scholastics' talk about the transfer of forms or the Cartesians' talk about the exchange of motion, if taken literally, commits them to such a doctrine. For example, Suarez has defined 'cause' as 'what flows being into something else'. But what is it to flow being? Leibniz remarks that even the [syntactical] construction of this phrase is inept since 'flow' (*influere*) is used by Suarez as a transitive verb, whereas we only understand its use as an intransitive verb. (What is it that does the flowing? And what is the 'being'? Is it another substance or an accident?) Leibniz concludes that this is a barbarous and obscure definition. For 'flow' is only to be understood metaphorically, and the definition is more obscure than the concept of cause which it defines.

But is Leibniz right? We do say, for example, when a physical body A collides with another body B, that there is a transfer of momentum. We must realize, however, that this is a metaphorical expression. What we mean by this is that there is a correlation between the decrease of momentum of body A and the increase of momentum of body B, and that a certain conservation principle is observed. We do not mean that any transfer really takes place.

What could transfer themselves? Are they substances or qualities? Let us follow Leibniz's query. If the mind and body are substances then 'it is impossible', Leibniz says, 'to conceive of material particles or of species or immaterial qualities which can pass from one of these substances into the other'.[1] How can a material particle get detached from the body and then pass into a mind which is not extended, or how could an immaterial quality—say intelligence—get detached from the mind and pass on to a material body? It is evident in the case of mind and body, which are supposed to be different categories, that nothing that belongs to one category, whether it be bits of the substance itself or the attributes peculiar to the substance, can transfer itself to the substance of another category. The difficulty remains, however, even between causes and effects, which are events belonging to the same category.

[1] 'Second Explanation of the New System', *G* IV, pp. 498–9; Wiener, p. 118.

There are then two quite distinct points Leibniz was making in his denial of the traditional doctrine. Leibniz's first point is that to think of free-floating attributes or forms moving from one thing to another is nonsense whether this be between things of different categories or of the same category. Secondly, he holds that to explain causation as *requiring* particles to move from one thing to another leads one to an infinite regress. Transfer of particles does often happen between aggregates. As we will see, Leibniz believed that parts of all bodies are changing continuously. Understanding the pattern of motion often makes us see why certain corresponding changes happen in bodies. But we cannot go on explaining *why* these constituent particles move, by further exchange of particles. (It may be pointed out that Quine, together with many contemporary physicists, has said that causality is the flow of energy. But again we must be careful what is meant by 'flow'. That the propagation of energy can be expressed by wave equations does not mean that we can say of the energy, which is said to flow, that it is the same energy which moves from one place to another, in the way in which we can talk of the same water flowing from one place to another. We are merely talking about the quantity of energy at each contiguous place.) And transfer must be excluded between the simplest entities. By definition, the simplest units, be they Leibniz's monads or the fundamental particles (if contemporary physics admits such ultimate fundamental elementary particles), are not made up of further particles. So not all nomic regularities —nor all of what we call cause and effect—can be explained in terms of exchange of constituent particles, if one accepts as Leibniz did that there are ultimate simple entities.

So much for what he was denying. What was he affirming? We believe we can understand many phenomena. We do give causal explanations of what happens and we predict what will happen, often successfully. Now, we may believe, as, for example, Professor Anscombe has done, that our concept of causation comes from that of derivation, which can be immediately grasped; i.e. that we often perceive that one thing causes another, by simply grasping that the latter derives from the former, prior to any idea of regularity or necessitation. Or we may believe that our causal notions are dependent on something else. Leibniz was of this view, despite the fact that he was quite clear that this something else was not 'influx'. It was, therefore, necessary for him to give an account of what we call cause and effect in a way which does not require exchange of particles or qualities. In this way Leibniz arrives at a view which is very close in certain respects to that which David Hume was to express just over half a century later. Leibniz asserts that 'what we call causes are in metaphysical rigour only concomitant requisites'[1] (*quae causas dicimus esse tantum requisita comitantia in metaphysico rigore*). Compare Hume's claim in the *Treatise* that 'the relation of cause and effect totally depends on the constant conjunction of objects'.[2] Hume even goes so far as to define a cause in the *Enquiry* 'to be an object, followed by another, and where all the objects similar to the first are followed by objects similar to the second', or in other words where, if the first object had not been, the second never existed.[3] In this definition, which is *one* of at least two quite different definitions of causation which Hume gives in both the *Treatise* and the *Enquiry*, Hume is saying that a cause and effect are concomitances, and that the cause is a requisite for the effect: but that is exactly what Leibniz says. Notice that Hume's definition here (unlike his other definition) is not an epistemological one. He is not saying that constant conjunction of impressions constitutes causation, or that regular observation of conjunction of objects makes causation; he is not even saying that all the objects similar to the first have in the past been followed by objects similar to the second. Since causes and effects are said to be objects, they can exist even without being observed. What Hume is saying is that even when cause and effect *are* observed, no further necessary link between them can be observed.

Similarly, half a century before Hume, Leibniz had asserted that for causality the only thing one need require, and the only thing one can directly observe, is concomitance or the harmony itself. In other words, what one observes in observing a harmony is nothing other than the constant conjunction of which Hume was to speak. In a letter to the Dutch physicist de Volder, Leibniz recounts the reply he made to a French Jesuit, Tournemine, who approved of his doctrine of the pre-established harmony—as it explained well the agreement we perceive, for example, between the mind and the body—but said that he still wanted to know the reason for the union between the two. Tournemine claimed the union was different from the agreement. Leibniz replied that this metaphysical union '. . .which the

[1] 'First Truths', *c.* 1680–4. Couturat, *Opuscules et fragments inédits*, p. 521; *L*, p. 269.

[2] *Treatise of Human Nature* (Selby-Bigge edition), p. 173.

[3] *An Enquiry concerning Human Understanding*, Section VII, Part 2, p. 76.

scholastics assume in addition to their agreement, is not a phenomenon . . . there is no concept and therefore no knowledge of it'. It follows that no reason can be given for it.[1]

Leibniz criticized Locke's definitions of cause as well as the traditional view. According to Locke, cause is that which produces any simple or complex idea and the effect is that which is produced. Not only did Leibniz find in Locke's talk confusion between an idea and what it is an idea of; even if we allow cause to be what produces an event or a change in the object, the explanation is empty. As Leibniz writes, 'in saying that efficient cause is that which produces . . . you make use only of synonyms'.[2] This was a point that Hume was to raise, in almost the same words in his *Treatise*.[3] Leibniz then was not denying causation when he rejected the metaphysical doctrine of causal interaction. He tried to clarify what his denial amounts to and writes, 'Just as Copernican can talk truthfully of the rising of the sun . . . I believe it is very true to say that substances act upon one another, so long as one understands that one is the cause of the change in the other as a consequence of the laws of harmony'.[4]

Nothing which Leibniz says leads to the view that the cause has temporally to occur before the effect. It is even easier to establish regular concomitance between two kinds of contemporaneous events. Indeed, many of the examples of concomitances that Leibniz uses are contemporaneous ones. Thus, in so far as Hume was to insist on the temporal precedence of cause in his elaboration on causation, there is a difference between what Leibniz says on concomitance and what Hume was to say on constant conjunction.

We will see, however, that when events are not contemporaneous, Leibniz claimed that whatever is the cause must precede the effect. This is related to an important difference between Leibniz's view and that which Hume explicitly stated at least in the *Treatise*. And here I come to the second point of my lecture: by linking the concept of causation to the nature of objects and to the concept of energy Leibniz succeeds in giving an objective realist basis to the causal concept, despite the fact that he thinks that causality consists only of a certain kind of concomitance.

[1] Letter to de Volder, 19 Jan. 1706. *G* II, p. 281; *L*, pp. 538–9.

[2] *New Essays Concerning Human Understanding*, II, 26, § 1.

[3] *Treatise*, Part III, Section 4, p. 157.

[4] 'Explanation of the New System of the Communication of Substances', 1695. *G* IV, p. 495.

2. *Concomitance and the nature of things*

Regularity or regular concomitance is what makes nature comprehensible. The necessity of this concomitance is not produced by any propensity of the mind such as that which comes from habit. The mind may well acquire such propensities and certain expectations, some of which may be right and some wrong. But the fact that certain perceptions follow each other is itself based on concomitance between changes in the external world and changes in one's perceptions. If the regularity of the changes in the external world have grounds at all, be they causes and effects or two different effects of the same cause, it comes from the nature of things in the external world. Change from night to day is due to the rotation of the earth. The fact that *we observe* night followed by day repeatedly is no ground for claiming that we will continue to have similar experiences. If we understand that the regular change in our perception comes from a regular change in the outside world, in this case the earth, and, if we understand that this rotation of the earth comes from its stable nature, then that is the basis for expecting our experiences to continue. Leibniz speculates on what he calls the great analogy between the earth and the magnet. And, just as magnetism depends on the nature of the matter of the magnet and the matter of the things attracted to it, so regularities in nature come from the nature of things.[1] Leibniz does not think that necessity is a quality of an object, or even a perceivable quality of a relation, any more than Hume did. But it is not something conjured up by the mind. It is a feature of certain regularities in nature, which is based in turn on the nature of things.

Think of the example mentioned above of two bars, one hot and one cold, standing adjacent to one another. Eventually, the bars would be of the same temperature. Even if the size of the bars and the initial temperature of the two bars were fixed, the time it would take for the two bars to become the same temperature would differ enormously if the bars were made of copper, or if they were made of porcelain. This entirely depends on the nature of copper or porcelain itself. If it were just a question of disembodied heat travelling from one bar to another, there would be no difference in the time required.

In one of his early works, Leibniz had defined the nature of a

[1] Letter to Huygens, Sept. 1692. *GM* II, pp. 141–6; *L.* p. 415.

thing as the cause in the thing itself, of its appearance.[1] When in 1682 Robert Boyle caused a controversy by writing an attack on what he called 'vulgarly received notions of nature', and suggested that the vague term 'nature' be replaced by the more precise term 'mechanism', Leibniz wrote a paper called 'On Nature itself, or on the inherent Force and Actions of created Things'.[2] According to Leibniz, any particular mechanism can be understood by something further—the inherent force which endures in the things that enter into mechanical laws. Thus, it is not correct to say that nature is the mechanism of bodies. The force of energy is in the bodies permanently, even when they are at rest. Force is not identical with the mass spoken of by his physicist contemporaries, which was something passive. Force is active in that it corresponds, Leibniz says, to the law which gives the series of states of the body in motion—given what is happening in the rest of the universe. There is no inconsistency in asserting that everything happens mechanically in nature: that is, according to certain mathematical laws that express a relation, which holds between a plurality of things, and saying at the same time that everything acts according to its own nature.

Let us remind ourselves of Leibniz's own formulation of the doctrine of pre-established harmony. He gave this name to his system of explanation comparatively late in life, and talks of this doctrine by this name only in connection with the mind–body problem where efficient causes and final causes seem to meet. Pre-established harmony is a system of explanation, which is applicable to all substances, however, and is based on his view, which he espoused very early, about what is involved in all causation, even that involving only efficient causes. (One may compare here the Cartesians, who expressed their doctrine of causal interaction only in connection with the mind-body problem, but never thought that causal interaction operated only between mind and body.) Leibniz says that the harmony or correspondence between the mind and body is not a perpetual miracle, but the effect of the nature of each of them, and is no more nor less miraculous than any regularity between the states of change of any natural thing. It is 'a perpetual wonder', he writes, but 'a perpetual wonder as many natural things are'.[3]

Thus, Leibniz claims that it is true not only of the soul, but of

[1] 'An Example of Demonstrations about the Nature of corporeal Things drawn from Phenomena', 1671. *L*, p. 142.

[2] 1698. *G* IV, pp. 504–16; *L*, pp. 498–508.

[3] Leibniz–Clarke Correspondence, Letter V. *G* VII, p. 412; *L*, p. 711.

every other real unity that '*everything in it must arise from its own nature by a perfect spontaneity with regard to itself, yet, by a perfect conformity to things without*'.[1] This he calls the doctrine of pre-established harmony. What does Leibniz mean? What would it be for a thing to lack spontaneity with regard to itself? What is added by 'spontaneity'? This is added in order to rid people of the notion that change could happen to things in ways quite unrelated to the nature of the things themselves. Every change, every event that occurs to a thing, expresses the nature of the thing. As Leibniz explained to Pierre Bayle, a thing continues to change when it changes 'always following a certain law . . . And this law of order which constitutes the individuality of each particular substance, is in exact agreement with what occurs to every other substance and throughout the universe.'[2] The acknowledgement of the pre-established harmony then is nothing other than the recognition that things are created with natures such that they behave in law-like regularity in the universe. Although the nature of each substance is different, many substantiating a different set of laws and each substance substantiating even the same laws in different ways, the laws themselves apply to all substances, and thus the concept of 'law' here does not become empty and trivial, as Russell feared.

Leibniz claims that to believe in the existence of the laws of nature is not to believe in the existence of laws disembodied. God cannot create disembodied laws. Substances and laws are fixed simultaneously. In creating a universe governed by law-like regularity, God does *not* carry out two distinct acts of creation. By establishing the laws, God does not merely give us a way of describing things by the extrinsic or contingent relational properties.[3] To say of God that he established laws is, Leibniz insists, to say that he conferred on things some imprint that endures within them. We should not, however, think of this in too pictorial a manner. The physical world with its mass has its laws of nature within it. And this is to say that each thing down to the simplest substance in it acts in accordance with the internal force and laws of its own nature. This is the only fact

[1] 'New System of the Nature and Communication of Substances', § 14, 1695. *G* IV, p. 484; *L*, p. 457.

[2] Clarification of the difficulties which M. Bayle has found in the new system. *G* IV, p. 518; *L*, p. 493.

[3] It is not that 'the law had bestowed upon things only an extrinsic denomination'. 'On Nature itself, or on the inherent Force and Actions of created Things', 1698. *G* IV, p. 507; *L*, p. 500.

which is common to things on the macroscopic level, i.e. aggregates, and to simple substances. As he writes, 'For me nothing is permanent in things except the law itself, which involves a continuous succession and which corresponds in individual things to that law which determines the whole world.'[1] In the case of a simple substance, *ex hypothesi* it has no structure. The only way we can specify its nature is to give the law which generates the events it partakes in, in aggregation with other simple substances.

In fact, Leibniz says the foundation of laws of nature is the principle of the conservation of active force or energy and he defended his view against Newton's spokesman, Clark. (Clark had claimed that when soft inelastic bodies collide there is no conservation of energy.) But how can the law of conservation of energy be embodied in individual things? Does this not lead to the view that the momentum of each body remains constant, which is obviously false? No. Leibniz is not committed to such a blatant mistake. What he says is that each thing embodies a law such that the thing acts in correspondence with other things so that *the totality of energy in the world is preserved*. This is not a correspondence by 'fluke', since for Leibniz each substance by its own nature also registers at each moment what is happening to the other things in the world. We can see that the concept of laws of nature is inseparable from the concept of energy. All that we perceive is magnitude, figure, and motion. But we can understand that the nature of matter is not merely extension, for instance, by perceiving that it is not the quantity of motion, which is constant. What we observe is a particular over-all relationship which holds for the plurality of things between direction and quantity of mass. At any instant we can measure the momentum of a thing. This is what Leibniz calls derivative force. By thinking about what we observe we obtain the concept of active force which resides in things. This is what Leibniz calls primitive force, or the nature of the thing, which is the law of the series of the changing momentum of the thing, given the states of the other things.

There are two trains of thought which lead Leibniz to his belief in the inherent active force of simple substance. First is his conviction that action must ultimately arise from something active. Anything that is merely passive, such as Descartes's matter whose essence is extension or a mere plenum, cannot bring about action. On the other hand, Leibniz believed that

[1] Letter to de Volder, Jan. 1704. *G* II, p. 263; *L*, p. 534.

inertia and impenetrability of matter was neither a primary property, nor a property derivable from the extension of matter, but needed to be explained by an active force in the thing itself.[1]

Second, Leibniz thought that the concept of extension was 'incomplete'.[2] In this context he understands by this what we mean by second order concept. Strictly speaking, this paper is not extended and white. It is extended paper that is white. Leibniz had said, as Frege was to say almost two centuries later, that number was a concept which depended on other concepts—sortal concepts. There must necessarily be something numbered. Nothing can be three and apples, though there may be three apples. Leibniz held that extension shares this feature with number and multitude. All extension is an extended something. Leibniz concludes, therefore, that what is extended is something prior to extension, something prior to plurality or repetition. This must be active force. Active force is ascribable even to a simple monad, which, on its own, has no extension.

Now, as is well known, Hume gave two quite different accounts for the necessity involved in causation. On one hand, he wanted to say that the necessary connection between objects, which is part of the idea of cause and effect is *nothing* but our propensity to pass from an object to the idea of its usual attendant.[3] On the other hand, he did say that causation depended entirely on the constant conjunction of objects, and not on the constant conjunction of our perceptions; and necessity seems to be ascribed to the relation of the objects themselves. This is most clear in the *Enquiry*, when in defining cause, he writes that 'if the first object had not been, the second never had existed'.[4] This is clearly a necessary relationship that exists between two objects, quite independent of whether anyone observes it or not. And *that* necessity cannot be explained just by the mind's propensity or custom or any psychological fact as Hume thought, even if it is also a psychological fact that we have an ability to recognize certain patterns and form certain expectations when we have repeatedly encountered causes and effects which hold between objects of certain types. Hume must have been influenced by his reading of Leibniz, when in one passage in the *Enquiry* he acknowledges that we can learn from the succession of our ideas only if there is agreement between our

[1] e.g. Letter to de Volder, Mar.–Apr. 1699. *G* II, pp. 169–70; *L*, p. 516.

[2] Ibid.

[3] *Treatise*, Part III, Section 14, p. 165.

[4] *An Enquiry concerning Human Understanding*, Section VII, Part 2, p. 76.

ideas and objects in nature, and says, 'here then, is a kind of pre-established harmony between the course of nature and the succession of our ideas'.[1]

It is Leibniz's strength to have explained causation in terms of concomitance or conjunction, and yet to have accounted for the necessity of the concomitance in the nature of the objects themselves. This also enabled him to link the concept of cause with the direction of time. He claimed quite clearly in at least one paper that, if one of two states which are not simultaneous involves a reason for the other, the former is held to be prior, the latter posterior.[2] Past states, unlike future states, can leave traces, or generate a process and thus affect future states. These traces or impressions remain in objects; processes go on in the external world, and not only in the mind of the observer. Thus, the temporal precedence of a cause is based on objective grounds pertaining to the external world, not merely on habits of the mind of observers.[3]

It might be thought that this difference between Leibniz and Hume is a simple reflection of the difference between rationalism and empiricism. One can perceive the repeated conjunctions, it may be said, but one cannot observe internal forces or past histories. The problem is not so simple, however. For one thing, Leibniz thought that there were observable differences between physical things, which acted out of the internal force which was enduring in them, and things which could be explained in terms of motion of passive matter. Our view about force is an assumption or a hypothesis, but it is based on our observation.

Leibniz thought that one could assess the probability of such hypotheses empirically. 'Some hypotheses can satisfy so many phenomena, and so easily, that they can be taken for certain . . . a hypothesis of this kind is like a cryptograph, and the simpler it is and the greater number of events that can be explained by it the more probable it is.'[4] There can be no empirical *proof* of a hypothesis for, as Leibniz goes on to say, the same phenomenon can always in principle be explained in several different ways, and, thus, no firm demonstration of the truth of a hypothesis can

[1] Ibid., Section V, Part 2, p. 54. This was pointed out to me by Dr. J. Watling.

[2] 'Metaphysical Foundations of Mathematics', *GM* VII, p. 17; *L*, p. 666.

[3] This claim of Leibniz does not by itself give us any adequate topological features of time. It is compatible with time being discontinuous. For him time is continuous because it is the order of all possible as well as actual states.

[4] 'An Introduction on the Value and Method of natural Science', *L*, p. 283.

be made from the success of a hypothesis. Nevertheless, according to him, empirical data do and must affect the way we accept or reject the hypothesis.

We must also notice that the ways we come to know the nature of macroscopic objects and the nature of simple monads are somewhat different.

(*a*) *Complex objects*

Everything that is extended and has parts, be it a clock or an atom of contemporary physics, is a complex aggregate. Leibniz writes that material bodies are almost like a river which always changes water or like the ship of Theseus which the Athenians were always repairing.[1]

In the case of complex objects, Leibniz did think that we can come to an understanding of how force operates by coming to know the structure (or 'contexture') of the object itself and of the changes that are occurring in it. For example, he writes that by coming to know a particular structure of a clock, whether it moves by spring or by wheels, we can understand why a hammer of a clock strikes when a given time elapses.[2] For even if we do not observe any force transferring itself out of the wheels and into the cog, because there is none, we can see how the equal quantity of motion in one is made to correspond to the equal quantity of motion in the other. (We can similarly see how certain electric phenomena correspond to the flow of electrons within a bigger conglomerate of atoms.) Leibniz was not persuaded by Locke that the real essence or real constitution of physical things is unknowable to us.[3] We are, as a matter of fact, ignorant about the constitution of many physical things, just as we have vague confused ideas about the qualities of many objects. But just as we may come to have empirical knowledge of the constitution of the clocks, we may come to have empirical knowledge of the constitution of more minute things. For example, he says, 'it is possible that bodies which are exceedingly subtle and cannot be caught or perceived by sense in one substance can be caught in another'.[4]

Locke had said not only that the real essences of things 'are unknown to us. We cannot discover so much as that size, figure

[1] *New Essays*, Bk. II, Ch. 27, § 4.

[2] Ibid., Bk. III, Ch. 6, § 39; Bk. IV, Ch. 6, § 7.

[3] Locke, *Essays Concerning Human Understanding*, III, p. 17.

[4] 'On a Method of arriving at a true Analysis of Bodies and the Causes of natural Things.' *G* VII, p. 267; *L*, p. 174.

and texture of their minute and active parts, which is really in them, much less the different motions and impulses made in and upon them by bodies from without.'[1] He went on to claim that such consideration should put an end to all our hopes of ever having the ideas of real essences. In so far as Locke admits the existence of these real essences—for which he, unlike Leibniz, thinks there is no possibility of empirical knowledge—he is the one who breaks the so-called canons of empiricism.

As will have been clear from what has gone before, Leibniz did not believe that we always *know that we know* the real constitution when we do. But having arguments of his own against the idea that *to know is to know that one knows*, he does not rule out knowledge of the structure of things by which we can comprehend the workings of their inner force.

In aggregates, which are complex processes of simple substances for Leibniz, there are exchanges of entities at all sorts of levels. We will understand the processes better by tracing the exchanges. However, it is not always the case that nomic regularities between complex objects at one level have to be explained by the movement and exchange of entities of a less complex level. What happens when a billiard ball hits another is not like what happens when the nucleus of an atom is split in a synchrotron and an isotope is made. It is not necessary, according to Leibniz, to account for the impact of the billiard ball by the transfer of particles. As I mentioned before, what is standardly called transfer of momentum is not literally a transfer of anything. A billiard ball A's motion does affect the motion of a billiard ball B, but it is the velocity and direction of each ball that changes.

(*b*) *Simple substances*

If there were ultimate elementary particles with no parts then we cannot have structural knowledge of them, and causes and effects between events concerning these particles could not be explained by further constituent particles going out of one elementary particle and going into another. We only observe the structure of the aggregate—an atom or molecule or aggregates of atoms—and we observe the corresponding motions of elementary particles within the structures. The same can be said of Leibniz's simple substance. By definition it has no parts and no further constituents. Leibniz concludes, 'Thus the action of one substance on another is not the emission or transplantation of an

[1] *Essays*, IV, Ch. 12.

entity as is commonly conceived'.[1] The possibility of fission of atoms only shows that atoms are not the elementary, or simple, substances in Leibniz's sense. Leibniz's arguments against explaining causation by emission of particles, unlike his arguments against detached properties, depend on his belief in the existence of simple, indivisible substances or ultimate particles (i.e. belief in a kind of axiom of regularity).

3. *Pre-established harmony and counterfactual truths*

I come now to the third and last point I would like to make to-day. It is to examine Leibniz's doctrine in the light of recent views on nomological explanation and on counterfactual analysis of causation, and try to defend Leibniz's view on the pre-established harmony from some traditional attacks. We will then try to see if in any sense we can say that Leibniz's doctrine is a rationalist view of causation as opposed to an empiricist one.

As we have seen, many philosophers have taken Leibniz's denial of the metaphysical doctrine of causal interaction and his doctrine of the pre-established harmony as saying that even if things *seem* to interact according to dynamic laws, they do so, as it were, by fluke, each substance acting out a pre-fixed programme, quite independently of whatever happens to other things. Leibniz is partly responsible for this, since he gives bad analogies to illustrate his doctrine (like that of the two clocks which always give the same time because they were set and wound up in the right way in the beginning. The difficulty about this analogy lies in the fact that one of the clocks can very well break down, or begin to lose time, without the other doing so); he also talks misleadingly about good and bad reasons for God's actions. Nevertheless, such an interpretation is odd because our talk of laws of dynamics is normally taken to entail the truth of certain counterfactuals. To say that the motion of object A after collision with object B can be explained by the laws of dynamics is to say, amongst other things, that had the mass of B or the direction or the velocity of the motion of B at the time of its collision with A been different then A's motion after the collision might not have been what it was. Leibniz thought in the same way. Far from believing that one object would behave in a fixed way, no matter what happened to other things, Leibniz thought that any difference in the state of other things would bring about a change to the object. (It seems to me that, if he errs, he errs in the opposite direction.) He was quite

[1] 'New System of Nature', § 17, 1695. *G* IV, p. 486; *L*, p. 459.

clear about the truths of many counterfactual conditionals, which followed from his commitment to the laws of nature or the pre-established harmony. He writes, '. . . in reality, because of the interconnection of things, the entire universe with all of its parts would be wholly different, and would have been another world altogether from its very commencement, if the least thing in it happened otherwise than it has'.[1]

What then is fixed in an individual when a harmony is pre-established? What is pre-fixed is the nature in each substance to act in accordance with other things, or to act and react to other things not at random but with mutual lawlikeness, whether individually, or in aggregates. In his words, it is 'this mutual agreement, regulated in advance in every substance of the universe'.[2] The pre-fixed nature of magnets and of iron is such that when iron is in the vicinity of a magnet it is drawn to it out of its very own nature in response to the nature of the magnet. Leibniz's own favourite example is perception. The nature of mind (which is a simple substance) is such that spontaneously, by its own nature, it perceives things external to it corresponding to the change in the person's body, which in turn corresponds to change in external phenomena (which are aggregates). This entails the truth of the counterfactual: 'Had the states and changes in the external world been different the perceptual states of the mind would also have been different'.

The introduction of the talk of the pre-established harmony, or pre-fixed nature, allows us, therefore, to give truth-values to certain counterfactuals. This is something which the observation, however repeated, of concomitance does not allow us to do. It does *not*, therefore, make each aggregate and each substance behave independently of other things. On the contrary, it is an attempt to explain each thing as causally dependent on other things *by the very nature it has*. It commits us to accepting the necessity of certain universally quantified conditional propositions in this world, *given the laws of nature that we do have*. A Leibnizian view thus leads to the acceptance of a nomological deductive theory explanation for all cases which do not involve human action (which is said to be inclined by prior states involving reasons and desires but not necessitated). Given a set of antecedent conditions, which is the state of the world at a given

[1] 'Remarques sur la lettre de M. Arnauld touchant ma proposition: que la notion individuelle de chaque personne enferme une fois pour toutes ce que luy arrivera.' *G* II, p. 42.

[2] 'New System of Nature', § 14. *G* IV, pp. 484–5; *L*, p. 458.

time, plus all its history up to that time, one can, in principle, deduce the consequent state, by reference to the laws of nature. As in all such theories, Leibniz's doctrine does not enable one to distinguish causes from antecedent conditions or from other effects of the same cause in any clear-cut way. Leibniz would probably not have minded this. What was important for him was not so much to pick out a cause for every condition or state, but to show how comprehensibility was linked with the stable natures of things and the way they change in correspondence with changes in others. This expressed itself as a functional relationship between the state of one thing and the contemporaneous and ulterior states of other things.

An important point about Leibniz's scheme of explanation is, however, that the identification of antecedent conditions cannot be made independently of the identification of the laws of nature. Laws of nature cannot, as we have seen, exist disembodied. For example, the specification of what kind of things exist, carries with it the laws of nature in virtue of which we can distinguish one kind of thing from another. Thus, in creating a world, God does not carry out two distinct acts of creating substances and their aggregates, and creating the laws of nature. To create substances and their aggregates with natures of certain kinds is to create the laws of nature. We must also notice that there is nothing in what Leibniz says that makes it impossible for the laws to be probabilistic or statistical ones. Nor is there anything that prohibits antecedent conditions from including specifications of whether the subject finds itself within a certain vicinity of certain objects, thereby determining their position in what physicists would now call fields.

As I have said, Hume himself unwittingly committed himself also to objective necessity when he realized that his definition of cause as 'an object followed by another, and where *all* the objects similar to the first are followed by objects similar to the second' leads to the acceptance of a counterfactual, which he formulates as 'if the first object had not been, the second never had existed'. But it is Hume who was to fail to give an empirical justification of his *own* concept of cause, at least in the case of open classes of events or objects. For, as many have pointed out since Kant, our propensity to infer in a certain way after repeated observation of conjunction of events in no way justifies the universality of the conjunction.

Leibniz tried to give an intelligible account of the uniformity of the constant conjunction by linking it to the structure of things (which are phenomena of aggregates), this structure being in principle empirically accessible; and to the active force in things.[1] The existence of this force is postulated because it makes sense of observable phenomena. He was very clear that one cannot ask for further links to explain every conjunction. It was not in his opinion an accidental defect on our part as observers that we fail to perceive such links. It was a conceptual or metaphysical impossibility to explain all regularities between objects by further exchange of particles; and it was conceptual confusion ever to explain anything in terms of transference of detached qualities or modes. But this does not lead to the claim that further investigation of the structure of complex objects, or a hypothesis about the nature of simple objects, can never give the grounds for the regularities.

Now, as has often been pointed out, Leibniz writes in many places of the importance of intelligible realms as distinct from sensible realms. But these two realms are not composed of distinct entities which exist side by side. The two realms correspond to what is given to the senses and what, in perceiving the same reality, is understood by using concepts and theories. We cannot have the concept of justice, which belongs to the intelligible realm, without perceiving the needs and desires of men. We cannot have the concept of active force, which pertains to the intelligible realm, without perceiving motion, rest, and direction. As a matter of fact it is not Locke, but the Cartesians, whom Leibniz attacks for being 'content to stop where the sense perceptions stopped'.[2] He believed that they mistakenly thought that extension was the essential attribute of matter and that the quantity of motion is conserved, because they had not tried to understand clearly enough what they perceived.

The realm of the intelligible in reality is not something one can have access to independently of our senses. It corresponds to the way we draw conclusions from and correctly understand

[1] Bas Van Fraassen has raised the following interesting question. Consider two worlds α and β. Exactly the same thing happens in them; but in α they happen in accordance with laws of nature, while in β there are no laws of nature nor any physical necessity, but as a matter of fact things behave exactly as in α. Are they really distinct worlds? Now, for Leibniz, these would only be distinct worlds if in β things behave the way they do because God or some external power is constantly making the things behave the way they do. If not, then β is the same world as α since to assert that the laws of nature exist is nothing more than to say that things behave in a regular way of themselves and β is a world in which *ex hypothesi* things do so behave.

[2] Letter to de Volder, 30 June 1704. *G* II, p. 269; *L*, pp. 536–7.

what we observe. We do not depend on any one sense to obtain information about the external world. Against Locke, Leibniz does insist that it is possible for a blind man to understand what colour is, even if he has no visual data, and hence does not know what it is to experience perceiving colours. But, in so far as we are bodily people and not angels, what we understand about the external world is not independent of what we perceive. For one thing, Leibniz believed, as did Spinoza, that the mind always represents all changes in the body. Thus, if there is any change in the retina or the ear-drums due to the changes in the light waves or sound waves that reach them, these corresponding in turn to changes in objects further away, then the states of the mind change accordingly.[1] We cannot ignore what we perceive. We can merely make better and better theories to fit in to greater and greater numbers of our perceptions.

Is there any point at all in the traditional labels of rationalist and empiricist? (In the account of mathematical knowledge or of ethics there may be important relevant differences which I will not discuss.) So far as our knowledge and theories relating to the external world are concerned, all philosophers traditionally put under either of these labels seem to have thought that experience was necessary but not sufficient. Thus, if empiricism is supposed to be the doctrine that all knowledge of the world comes entirely from sense perception and rationalism to mean the doctrine that knowledge of reality comes from our understanding independently of the data of our senses, both are positions held by no one and better forgotten. Nor do the traditional labels of nominalism and realism help us. Leibniz considered himself a nominalist, and he was undoubtedly a nominalist in the sense of the medieval dispute—i.e. one who does not believe that universals exist in reality independently of things that instantiate them.

There is, however, a different kind of contrast which we can perhaps make to characterize the kind of difference we have found obtaining between Leibniz's and Hume's account of causation. This is the contrast between the attitude of thinkers who believe that, even if ultimately one can only *describe* the concomitant changes which occur within the structure, the understanding of the global structure of things adds to our understanding of the processes or movements of things in it, and thinkers who want to stick to the case-by-case description of the

[1] See, e.g., Letter to de Volder, Mar.–Apr. 1699. *G* II, pp. 171–2; *L*, p. 517.

concomitances. In this sense Descartes, Spinoza, and Leibniz as well as Locke all belonged to the former group whereas Hume and Berkeley seem to belong to the latter.

It is interesting to notice that in eighteenth-century Japan when there was a great debate between medical doctors who followed the tradition developed in China and Japan on one hand and those who wanted to develop the European medicine introduced by the Dutch in the seventeenth century, the traditionalists described themselves as empirical, and as upholding medicine based on experience against the medical doctrine of the Europeans. The traditionalists claimed that medicine must proceed, and can only proceed, by establishing by repeated observation that certain sets of symptoms and certain sufferings can be cured and men made healthy by the taking of certain herbs or the application of certain ointments.

One of the Japanese physicians who defended European medicine in the eighteenth century, Sugita Genpaku, argued that the strength of the European practice of that time lay in the fact that, by a search for the understanding of the anatomical structures and workings of the body as well as of the material components of the medicines, one comes to understand why a particular medicine has a particular effect on a patient and how the cure comes about.[1] I am not saying that he is necessarily right about what European medical science actually does even at the present day. It may also, to a great extent, be based on case-by-case observations of cures and alleviations rather than on any further understanding of the reasons. What is interesting though is that, in so far as Sugita believed that a holistic structural knowledge leads to understanding of the reason why, and holds the view that however descriptive it may be only global knowledge can give real understanding, he reflects the ideas held by Leibniz and others hitherto labelled rationalist.[2] The traditional oriental doctors were much closer in spirit to Hume.

[1] Genpaku, Sugita, *Words of a Mad Physician*, 1775. Sugita did not deny that the traditional Chinese physicians had views about the structure of the body. He nevertheless thought that their views on the matter were very inexact, and that this came about from their failure to link the understanding of particular ailments with the understanding of the exact structure of the body.

[2] The affinity between Sugita's view and that of Leibniz is remarkable. Leibniz even found himself defending the importance of anatomy against the noted physician and chemist of his time, Stahl. The latter failed to attach proper importance to the study of anatomy.

Let us then reconsider the widely accepted distinction between rationalism and empiricism. In recent decades we have seen much discussion about the status of observation terms and theoretical terms. It is now a commonplace to point out that there are no theory-free descriptions of observation, nor any statements of theory that are free of words with meanings impinging on observable phenomena. If we accept this (and I do), the contrast drawn in the traditional manner between rationalism and empiricism becomes even emptier. In its place there is a real contrast to be drawn among philosophers as well as scientists between two types of thinkers: those who believe that the concepts which they use to explain one type of regularity can be understood only by placing the regularity in the context of a general picture of the structure of the universe, and those who merely express and predict particular types of regularity in what is observed and who avoid or reject linking it to any general concept of reality. The latter are interested in the question whether the particular equations work. To characterize this contrast, as is so often done, in terms of a distinction between realism and operationalism is as misleading as are the labels rationalism and empiricism when applied to the seventeenth and eighteenth century. For even the so-called operationalist presumably believes that the equations express a certain correlation between the commonly observable phenomena or measurements of an external world, which *exists* independently of us even if the measurements are relative to our methods of obtaining them.

The important problem here is whether, without a theory or hypothesis about the whole, one refuses to be satisfied by equations or descriptions of particular types of regularities of observable data, or holds that one should be content with piecemeal descriptions and the mathematical expression of different kinds of regularities. This is not a difference of attitude about quantities of information but about the nature of concepts: about how globally concepts need be or need not be interconnected.

Global theories, like conspiracy theories, perhaps need to be resisted. Precisely because of the temptation we have to build models to explain away whatever we observe, there is a purist satisfaction we feel in refraining from going beyond codifying regularities of particular kinds. (From the original Buddhists who stuck to the description of the suchness of concrete things and their law-like changes, to Paul Valéry who wrote that 'the problem of the totality of things . . . comes from the most naïve of intentions',[1] we see the mind of people anxious to avoid the self-deceiving solace which the appeal to hidden meanings and global theories often bring.) We have seen that Leibniz likened a theorist to a cryptographer. But when people claim to see everywhere signs, clues, and confirmation of their own facilely built models and weary us with their self-indulgence and banality we cannot help but be drawn to the dry elegance of self-imposed particularism.

Perhaps only those who are interested by temperament in a wide variety of particular areas of observation, and are rigorous in developing theories to explain the data in each particular area, can allow themselves the luxury of the attempt to make a global theory. Leibniz not only denied that his philosophy constituted a unitary system, he developed and interested himself in many theories for their own sake, not *because* they linked up with his philosophical doctrines or other areas of investigation.[2] The doctrine of pre-established harmony (like Leibniz's other theories on probability, or on infinitesimals) is the creation of a mind insatiably interested also in *a posteriori* knowledge of various phenomena. It is a theory in which the concepts of laws of nature, of the nature of individual substances, of force, and of the direction of time are all intricately linked; it is a global theory but one which tries to account in a unified way for the nature of particular explanatory theories, carefully worked out, which are based on observation.

[1] Paul Valéry, 'Au Sujet d'Eureka' in *Variété*, p. 137.

[2] Think of his invention of differential calculus, his interest in probability theory, palaeography, the building of computer machines, hydraulics, law, deontic logic, educational reform, etymology, etc.

FOURTEENTH BIENNIAL ALBERT RECKITT
ARCHAEOLOGICAL TRUST LECTURE

CASTLE-BUILDING IN THIRTEENTH-CENTURY WALES AND SAVOY

By A. J. TAYLOR

Fellow of the Academy

Read 23 November 1977

ON this Wednesday thirty-three years ago our much lamented Fellow the late Sir Goronwy Edwards delivered to the Academy his Sir John Rhŷs Memorial Lecture on the subject of 'Edward I's Castle-building in Wales'.[1] In a characteristically penetrating and lucid paper he examined and set before us, in a way unlikely to be superseded, the documentary evidence preserved in the Public Record Office for the creation of eight new royal castles: Builth, only its Norman earthworks now rising beside the Wye; Aberystwyth, war- and weather-worn since the time of Glyndŵr; Flint and Rhuddlan; Conway and Harlech; Caernarvon and Beaumaris. These were all castles which King Edward began, and in all but two cases completed, in mid and North Wales between 1277 and 1295. The study broke new ground in that it was the first time the building of these great works had been considered as a single state enterprise, costing so much money, requiring the recruitment and movement of so much labour, calling for special expedients of finance, and taking this or that number of years to carry through. It will not be unknown to some of you here this evening that I have myself been moved to devote a good deal of time to pursuing one aspect which Sir Goronwy specifically excluded, namely the architecture of the castles, and in particular its authorship and affinities. Though many of my findings have already been published over the years,[2] I think the time has perhaps come for me to give some account of the investigations that led to them.

[1] *Proceedings of the British Academy*, xxxii (1953), 15–81.

[2] 'Master James of St. George', *English Historical Review*, lxv (1950), 433–57; 'The Date of Caernarvon Castle', *Antiquity*, xxvi (1952), 25–34; 'A letter from Lewis of Savoy to Edward I', *English Historical Review*, lxviii (1953), 55–62; 'The Castle of St. Georges-d'Epéranche', *Antiquaries Journal*, xxxiii (1953), 33–47; 'Castle-building in Wales in the Later Thirteenth Century:

I make no apology for doing so within the ambit of an archaeological lecture, for to observe and study the architectural minutiae of medieval constructions is often to elucidate their archaeology. One of the purposes of the Trust under whose auspices this lecture is given is defined as the encouragement of 'the exploration of ancient sites in any part of the world . . . and the publication of the results thereof', and provided ancient sites may be construed as including medieval castles I think I may claim my subject falls within the terms of reference. Indeed, what I am now going to place before you is the account of how one such exploration was carried on and correlated not in one part of the world only, but in two parts simultaneously, over a period of more than twenty years. In both the regions concerned it has been an exploration not only of buildings but also of records, so that a sub-title of the paper might have added the words 'in the light of field-work and archives'. At all events I take my cue from Sir Mortimer Wheeler's light-hearted description of the Reckitt Fund as one whose mild restrictions 'have enabled it to be used profitably over a wide range of projects in which "research" and "discovery" are not too narrowly defined and discriminated'.[1]

It has been said that what historians seek is affected by what they see.[2] I do not claim any special perceptiveness but I certainly enjoyed unusual opportunities. As Inspector of Ancient Monuments for Wales from 1946 to 1955 I had the chance to become totally familiar with the North Wales castles, to notice things that were like and things that were unlike, to compare resemblances of detail, checking the treatment of this or that feature in one building against its corresponding treatment in another, looking if need be at three or four castles in the course of a single summer day for the repetition or absence of

the Prelude to Construction', in *Studies in Building History: essays in recognition of the work of B. H. St. J. O'Neil*, ed. E. M. Jope (London, 1961), 104–33; 'Some Notes on the Savoyards in North Wales, 1277–1300, with special reference to the Savoyard element in the construction of Harlech Castle', *Genava*, N.S. tome XI (Genève, 1963) (Mélanges d'histoire et d'archéologie offerts en hommage à M. Louis Blondel), 289–315; 'The King's Works in Wales, 1277–1330', in *The History of the King's Works*, ed. H. M. Colvin (London, 1963), i. 293–408, ii. 1027–40; 'The Walls of Conway', *Archaeologia Cambrensis*, cxix (1970), 1–9; 'Who was "John Pennardd, leader of the men of Gwynedd"?', *English Historical Review*, xc (1976), 79–97.

[1] Mortimer Wheeler, *The British Academy 1949–1968* (London, 1970), 52–3.

[2] Margaret Aston, 'English Ruins and English History: The Dissolution and the Sense of the Past', *Journal of the Warburg and Courtauld Institutes*, xxxvi (1973), 254.

some particular constructional quirk, and storing in memory or on film impressions for comparison elsewhere when occasion might arise. The familiarity thus gradually gained led me to identify five constructional or architectural features that were not to my knowledge paralleled in other English or Welsh castles and were therefore likely to be directly derived from a continental source. They were as follows:

1. First there is the use, in the construction of towers and curtain walls alike, of helicoidal or inclined scaffold paths up which materials could be hauled or winched as buildings advanced in height. Evidence of this is to be seen in the sloping lines of putlog holes which are prominent throughout the castles of Conway, Harlech, and Beaumaris and on the town walls of Conway and Caernarvon (Plates XXIII–XXIV). For an example reflecting the use of orthodox horizontal scaffolding one may contrast the long rows of putlog holes to be seen in the walls of the Bishop of Chichester's fourteenth-century castle at Amberley, Sussex.
2. Next there is the sporadic use of the full-centred semicircular arch, over doors, gateways, embrasures, and windows. Examples are to be seen in embrasures at Flint, Conway, and Harlech; in the gatehouse at Harlech and in the great end window of the hall at Conway; in the barbican gate at Beaumaris; and high up over the Queen's Gate at Caernarvon (Plates XXVI–XXIX).
3. At Harlech there occur two distinctive types of garderobe construction. In the first the shaft is contained in a shallow projection occupying the angle of inner curtain and corner tower and extending almost the full height of the curtain wall; in the second we have a large half-round projection corbelled out from the outer curtain at courtyard level to overhang the rock-cut ditch below (Plate XXX).
4. A fourth feature is the embellishment of the crenellation of Conway castle with groups of three stone pinnacles or finials originally surmounting the cresting of every merlon. The same treatment was applied to the town walls, where today only one finial is left out of the hundreds there must have been originally (Plate XXXI).[1]

[1] Stumps of finials surviving on pieces of original cresting at Caernarvon castle, particularly on the Watch Tower and the curtain wall to the east of it, may indicate original decoration similar to Conway's, and not necessarily the repetition of the sculptured figures seen on the Eagle Tower.

5. Fifth and last, Harlech has a series of notably distinctive windows, lighting the four principal rooms of the castle gatehouse; nothing closely comparable to them appears to have survived elsewhere in this country. There are eight windows altogether, three facing west into the courtyard on each of the two main floor levels, and, on the topmost floor only, one in each of the short north and south end walls. The six westward-facing windows have at some time been severely modified, their tracery lights having been suppressed, their segmental heads lowered and reset at the level of the transoms, and the resulting space under the relieving arches filled up with blocks of ashlar. Only in the two end windows does the stone framing survive to its full original height, but between them these two retain enough fragments of their destroyed mullions, transoms, tracery, shutter fittings, and glazing grooves to allow accurate reconstruction of the original form of the whole group (Plate XXXII).

These, then, the helicoidal scaffold holes, the full-centred arches, the distinctive forms of certain garderobes, the triple finials at Conway, and the gatehouse windows at Harlech, stood out as five well-defined features whose area of origin seemed to be unknown and to deserve location and exploration. Moreover, if that area could be discovered, and its relationship established on a basis not merely of architectural resemblances, which can be deceptive, but of resemblances backed by documentation, which may be decisive, then the way might also be opened to the explanation of an unknown of even greater interest than the resemblances themselves: namely the problem, for such it then was, of the identity and previous whereabouts of the Master James of St. George who from at least 1285 onwards is referred to in our English records as the *magister operacionum Regis in Wallia*. As long ago as 1937 I had noted the earliest references to him as *Magister Jacobus Ingeniator*, or *Magister Jacobus Le Mazun* in the 1277–8 wardrobe book,[1] and as time went on I was led increasingly to believe that Master James probably had not, as such men as Robert of Beverley or Walter of Hereford presumably had, an English professional background.

It was with these two purposes in view, therefore, to search on the one hand for architectural parallels and on the other for authentic sources for dating them, which might also perhaps

[1] PRO, C47/4/1, fos. 11d, 16d, 22d, 34.

throw light on the overriding problem of authorship, that I set out from England in the autumn of 1950.[1] If one went with little hesitation to Savoy, this was only because there were many pointers in the direction of that historic princedom lying astride the Alpine passes, its thirteenth-century bounds embracing territories that are today partly in western Switzerland, partly in north-west Italy, partly in eastern France. First, was there not the close family relationship between King Edward I and Savoy's ruling Count Philip, whose sister Beatrice was the mother of Eleanor of Provence and grandmother of the king? Philip's more famous predecessor Peter of Savoy, to whom Henry III had given the honour of Richmond and lordship of Pevensey, and Archbishop Boniface of Canterbury were his brothers; his nephew Amadeus, later (1285–1323) Count Amadeus the Great, was with King Edward's army at Montgomery in the first Welsh war of 1277 and captain of the army of Chester at the beginning of the war of 1282.[2] It was from this family tie that there arose the remarkable arrangement under which succesive counts of Savoy actually held of, and did homage to the kings of England as their feudal overlords for, the castle of Avigliana within distant sight of Turin, the town of Susa, the palace and castle of Bard, beyond Aosta, today covered by a derelict Napoleonic fort, and the town of St. Maurice in Chablais with its watch-tower commanding a vital Rhône crossing, each of them a key point on one of the transalpine routes over the Mont Cenis or the Great St. Bernard.[3]

Furthermore one could hardly forget that Edward had chosen a Savoyard, his lifetime friend and confidant Sir Otto de Grandison, to be the first justiciar of North Wales under the settlement of 1284. Amongst many Savoyards brought by the

[1] The journey owed something of its inspiration to T. E. Lawrence, *Crusader Castles* (Golden Cockerel Press, 2 vols., 1936), a copy of which had been given me in 1949 by E. T. Leeds, sometime Keeper of the Ashmolean and a good friend to both Lawrence and the writer.

[2] For references to Amadeus in Wales, see *Eng. Hist. Rev.* lxviii. 56, n. 2. It is not unlikely that he was the writer of a letter addressed 'Au Roy de Engleterre' and sent on 3 April 1277 from the besieged Welsh castle of Dolforwyn near Montgomery (*Cal. Anc. Correspondence Wales*, ed. J. G. Edwards, 30–1). Its writer's expressed unwillingness to entrust the surrendered castle's repair to Master Bertram, who had by then already been thirty years in the king's service (cf. *Hist. King's Wks.* ii. 1036–7), may foreshadow the procurement of Master James of St. George from Savoy for Wales early in the following year.

[3] F. M. Powicke, *King Henry III and the lord Edward* (Oxford, 1947), i. 365, ii. 612–13 and n.

dynastic connection into the circle of the English royal household Otto was pre-eminent, and to Otto had been given, according to his biographer C. L. Kingsford, a special charge for the building and care of Edward's new castles.[1] Otto's own castle of Grandson (Plate XXXIV*c*)[2] beside the lake of Neuchâtel might indeed still be visited, as likewise could his tomb (Plate XXXIV*b*)[3] in the cathedral of Lausanne above Lac Léman. And again, the chief residence of the counts of Savoy used to be the island castle of Chillon, still standing intact on the margin of the Léman (Plate XXXIV*a*), and it was here that Amadeus, whose presence in Wales with King Edward we have already noticed, had been married in 1272.[4] I also retained a vivid picture of having twice seen from the train somewhere in this same region a ruined castle, afterwards identified as Saillon in the Valais, whose very stance and build had seemed to me even from a mile away to have an affinity of form and line with Conway, different in scale as they might be. Finally, I had not forgotten reading how in 1854, when the House of Lords' Committee of Privileges was hearing the claim of Sir Henry Paston Bedingfield to be co-heir to the abeyant barony of Grandison, counsel for the petitioner, in order to substantiate the Grandison pedigree, gave evidence (and I quote) 'of certain Charters which had been made to and by members of the Grandison family, and which had been preserved among the Muniments of the Counts of Savoy at Turin, the Lordship of Grandison having been formerly held under the Counts of Savoy; and . . . put in duly attested copies of those Documents'; numbering five in all, and dating from 1257 to 1303, they were sworn to by a barrister from Genoa who appeared before the Committee to testify in person that such deeds would be admitted in evidence in a nineteenth-century Sardinian court.[5] The Savoy archives at Turin certainly seemed to demand urgent investigation. Indeed, had not Galbreath's *Inventaire des sceaux vaudois* shown that one of the items they preserved was an instrument dated in 1279 at Evian, across the lake from Chillon, and still bearing the seal of John de

[1] C. L. Kingsford, 'Sir Otho de Grandison', *Trans. Royal Hist. Soc.* 3rd ser. iii (1909), 133.

[2] Description in Victor H. Bourgeois, *Les Châteaux historiques du canton de Vaud* (Bâle, 1935), 8–15.

[3] For Otto's tomb, see Marcel Grandjean, *Les Monuments d'art et d'histoire du canton de Vaud*, ii (Bâle, 1966); *La Cathédrale de Lausanne* (Berne, 1975), 50–1.

[4] To Sybil de Baugé (Ilio Jori, *Genealogia Sabauda* (Bologna, 1942), 34).

[5] Grandison Claim of Peerage, *Evidence and Documents, 1854–1858* (London, 1858), 166–74, cited in Kingsford, op. cit., p. 178, n. 2.

Bonvillars?[1] I could see no reason to doubt that this was the same John de Bonvillars as was already known to me as being engaged only four years later, in 1283, in supervising Edward's new castle works (*ad supervidendum castra*) in Wales, and to have been given the constableship of Harlech, then still being built, in 1285.[2]

Fig. 1. Seal of Sir John de Bonvillars, deputy justiciar of North Wales and constable of Harlech Castle 1285–7, enlarged from the original attached to a deed dated at Evian, 22 March 1279 (Turin, Archivio di Stato, Baronnie de Vaud 27, Mézières 1).

Accordingly it was to Turin that I went first, and I found the Bonvillars deed[3] and copied it. At that time I knew nothing, and alas in two days' work discovered nothing, of the existence of several Savoy household rolls, not unlike our contemporary English wardrobe and household accounts, nor of the survival of many thirteenth-century castellans' accounts, similar to our own Ministers' Accounts, for castellanies in many parts of Savoy. Thus it was with a feeling of having rather drawn a blank on the archives that I soon set off again to cross the Alps from Italy into

[1] Donald L. Galbreath, *Inventaire des sceaux vaudois*, Mémoires et Documents publiés par la Société de l'histoire de la Suisse romande (Lausanne, 1937), 49.

[2] For Sir John de Bonvillars, see *Eng. Hist. Rev.* xci. 79–97.

[3] Turin, Archivio di Stato (henceforth cited as AST), Baronnie de Vaud 27, Mezières 1; printed in *Eng. Hist. Rev.* xci. 95–6.

Switzerland to see if I might fare better with the castles. Within the next few days (20–4th September 1950) I visited for the first time the castles of Grandson and Chillon, Yverdon and Champvent, and stayed a night in the house that incorporates what is left of the Carthusian priory of La Lance, which Otto and Peter de Grandison founded in 1318–20 and where Otto's heart is reputedly buried. The 'breakthrough' came on 22 September, when a day spent in the University Library at Lausanne introduced me to Albert Naef's great study, *Chillon, La Camera Domini* (1908),[1] and Victor van Bercham's pioneer paper *La 'ville-neuve' d'Yverdon, Fondation de Pierre de Savoie* (1913),[2] both of them well-documented works by good scholars. 'This day's work has made it clear to me', I wrote in my diary, 'that I must go back to Turin, tedious journey as it will be, and look at the "comptes savoyardes" for myself and see how much early stuff there really is there.' My first week was gone and I had only one week left.

The following morning was spent at the castle of Yverdon (Plate XXXV*a*), one-time home of the first school of Pestalozzi, and today occupied as part school, part museum, and with extensive wine storage in the cellars below. Points of particular interest were the overall plan which, with its four-square ward, three corner towers attached and the fourth much larger and originally offset and detached, seemed to anticipate Flint (Plate XXXV*b* and *c*); indications that there had been tall angle garderobe shafts which seemed to anticipate one of the types we noted at Harlech (Plate XXX*a*); and remains of original segmental-headed and mullioned windows which in a simplified form might have anticipated Harlech also. I spent the afternoon at Champvent (Plate XXXVI*a*),[3] whose interest for us derives initially from the fact that it was the castle of Peter de Champvent, cousin of Otto de Grandison and another lifelong friend and servant of Edward I in England, Wales, Gascony, Scotland, and Flanders, a witness to the foundation borough charters of Flint, Conway, Caernarvon, and Beaumaris, and king's chamberlain from 1284 or earlier to 1298 or later.[4] The basic ground

[1] Albert Naef, *Chillon. Tome I, La Camera Domini: La Chambre des comtes et des ducs de Savoie à Chillon*, Genève, 1908.

[2] Victor van Berchem, 'La "ville-neuve" d'Yverdon, Fondation de Pierre de Savoie', in *Festgabe für Gerold Meyer von Knonau* (Zürich, 1913), 205–26.

[3] For Champvent, see Arthur Piaget, 'Le Château de Champvent et le comte Louis de Neuchâtel', *Musée Neuchâtelois*, 1937, 217–33.

[4] For Peter de Champvent, see Kingsford, op. cit., p. 180; T. F. Tout,

a

b

Inclined scaffold lines on curtain walls

a. Conway *b*. Beaumaris

PLATE XXIV

a

b

c

d

Helicoidal scaffold lines

a. Conway, Watch Tower *b*. Conway, Upper Gate
c. Harlech, Gatehouse *d*. Beaumaris, North Gatehouse

a

b

c

d

e

Helicoidal scaffold lines

a. and *b.* Saxon (Valais)

c. Harlech, SW tower *d.* Conway, Prison tower *e.* Saillon (Valais)

PLATE XXVI

a

b

Full-centred semi-circular arches

a. Conway Castle, E window of hall

b. Harlech Castle, window embrasures in SE tower

a

b

Full-centred semi-circular arches

a. Beaumaris Castle, barbican

b. Harlech Castle, arch in S tower of gatehouse

PLATE XXVIII

a

b

c

d

Full-centred semi-circular arches

a. and *b.* Saillon (Valais), Porte du Sex   *c.* and *d.* Harlech, outer gateway

a

b

c

d

Full-centred semi-circular arches

a. Harlech Castle, embrasure in NE tower

b. St. Georges-d'Espéranche, embrasure in SE tower

c. Conway Castle, embrasure in King's tower

d. Harlech Castle, door-head in gatehouse

PLATE XXX

a

b

c

d

Garderobe construction

a. Harlech Castle, NW tower *b*. St. Georges-d'Espéranche (Isère), SE tower

c. Harlech, above S ditch *d*. La Bâtiaz (Valais), NW curtain

a

b

c

d

Triple finials on battlements

a. and *b.* Conway Castle, western towers

c. and *d.* S. Giorio in Val di Susa, crenellation of (?)*c.* 1300

a

b

c

d

Harlech gatehouse windows

a. Gatehouse from W *b*. Gatehouse, restoration drawing by David Neal

c. S window, restoration drawing by the late Leonard Monroe *d*. S window

a

b

c

d

Harlech and Chillon windows

a. Chillon, view from lake *b*. Chillon, window to courtyard (ext.)

c. Harlech, window to courtyard (int.) *d*. Chillon, window to courtyard (int.)

PLATE XXXIV

a

b

c

a. Chillon from SE

b. Lausanne Cathedral, tomb of Sir Otto de Grandison

c. Château de Grandson

a

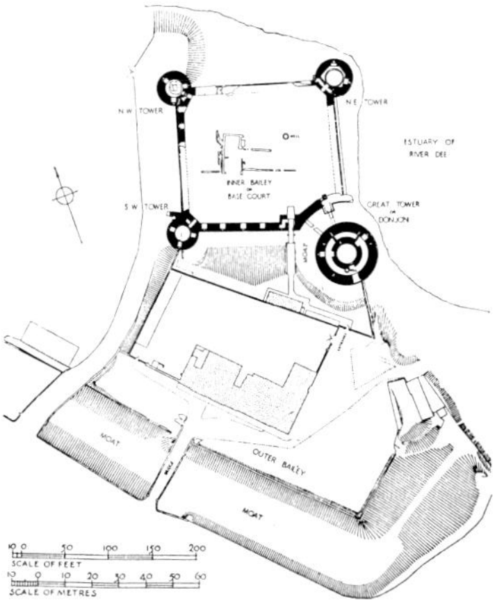

b

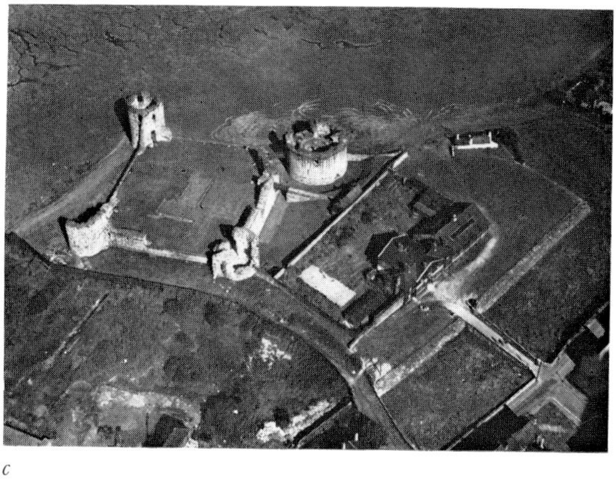

c

a. Château d'Yverdon (begun 1261), air view

b. Flint Castle (begun 1277), plan

c. Flint Castle, air view

a

b

a. Château de Champvent (Vaud), general view

b. Conway Castle, N façade

a

b

c

a. Château de Saillon (Valais), general view

b. Conway Town Walls and Castle from Bangor Road, by Moses Griffith, 1806

c. Conway Town Walls, view from W

a

b

c

a. Château de Saillon (Valais), curtain wall and flanking tower

b. Conway, Town Walls with flanking tower

c. Saxon (Valais), original putlog and remains of surface rendering

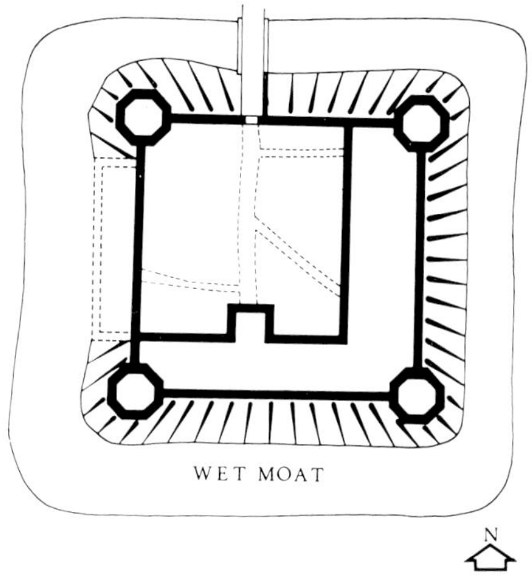

a

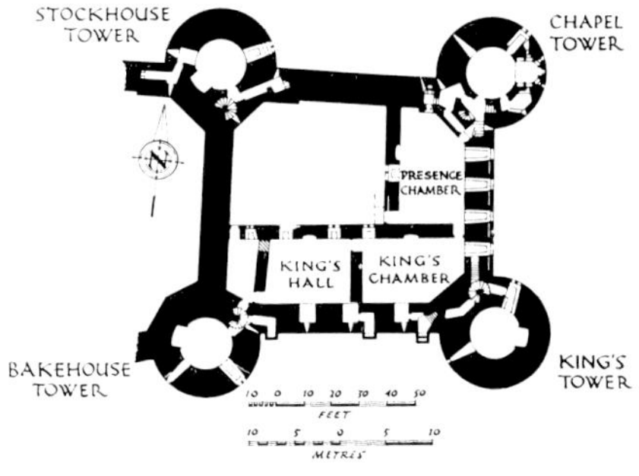

b

c

a. St. Georges-d'Espéranche, plan based on drawing of 1794

b. Conway Castle, 1st-floor plan of inner ward

c. St. Georges, air view from E, with castle in left foreground

PLATE XL

a

b

c

d

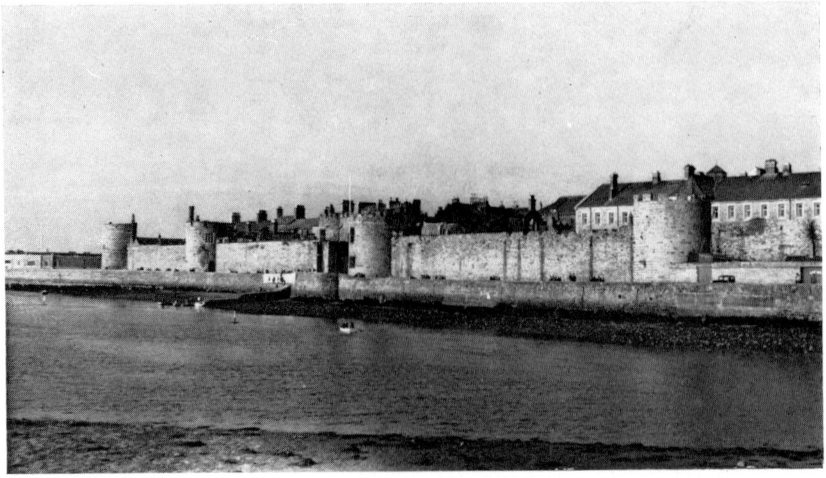

e

Caernarvon and Constantinople

a. Caernarvon Castle from SW *b*. Caernarvon Castle, Queen's tower

c. and *d*. Constantinople, Theodosian Walls

e. Caernarvon, W wall of town, showing Porth-yr-aur or Golden Gate (named as 'Gildyn yeate' in 1524)

a

b

c

d

a. Lausanne Cathedral, W window before restoration (drawing of 1902, from Marcel Grandjean, 'Chronologie et Maîtres d'Oeuvre de la Cathédrale', *Geneva* NS XI (1963), 261–87)

b. Conway Castle, E window of hall, reconstruction drawing by Sidney Toy, *Archaeologia* LXXXVI (1937), 186

c. Valle Crucis Abbey, Denbs., showing W gable as rebuilt after 1284

d. St. Etienne, Moudon (Fribourg), E end (first quarter of fourteenth century).

a

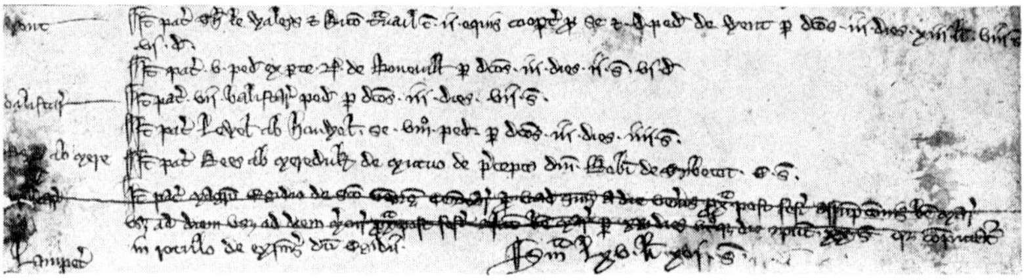

b

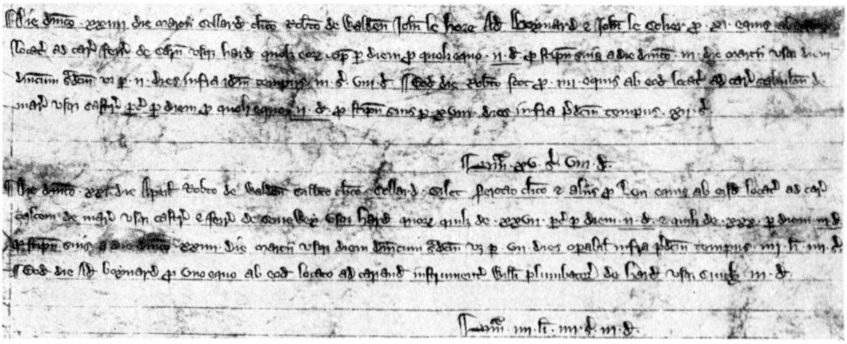

c

a. Contract between Count of Savoy's chaplain and Tassin of St. George, mason, for building works at Falavier (Isère), St. Georges, Wed. after Easter 1278 (Archs. de la Savoie, Chambéry, Inv. 135, fo.17. pqt.14, no.7)

b. Cancelled payment to Master Giles of St. George at Aberystwyth, Aug.–Sept. 1282 (PRO, C47/2/4)

c. Payments to transport contractors, including 'Gilet' and Adam Boynard, Harlech, March 1286 (PRO, E101/485/27) plan of Champvent is again that of Yverdon or Flint; the accommodation on the principal floor appears to have been almost exactly that of Edward and Eleanor's apartments at Conway—a south range joining at right angles with an east range which terminates in a chapel occupying the north-east corner tower.[1] As we shall see later, exactly the same arrangement, even to the orientation, appears to have obtained at Count Philip's palace-castle of St. Georges-d'Espéranche.[2] Champvent is, and probably always has been, an inhabited house; it is rendered with plaster, so that it still wears the same outward aspect of whiteness as did its North Wales analogues and of which Conway in particular still shows substantial traces (Plate XXXVI*b*). Having been the castle of a feudatory, however, it lacks, as does Grandson, the early documentation that illumines so many of the castles of the counts.

The next day, Sunday the 24th, was Chillon day. It is easier to remember, than to communicate, one's impressions on visiting this marvellous building for the first time, impressions no doubt coloured by those superimposed in a score of later visits, each adding some new piece to previous knowledge.[3] Here, surely beyond doubt, were the ancestors I was seeking of the Harlech fenestration, dating as I learned later from the middle 1260s (Plate XXXIII). In these matters one does not look for replicas and duplicates, but for parallels in essentials, and at Chillon and Harlech we surely have them. We have already noted how, where the dressings of the Harlech windows have perished, sufficient evidence has none the less survived to allow a faithful reconstruction; the Chillon dressings have, in fact, already been largely renewed by Naef, whose records show that he did the work with great sympathy and scrupulous accuracy.[4]

Chapters in Medieval Administrative History, vi (Manchester, 1933), 45, where the reference to him as chamberlain from 1292 can be advanced to 25 Sept. 1284, on which date he is named as 'camerarius noster' in the Liberate Roll of 12 Edward I (PRO, C62/60).

[1] Plan in Sidney Toy, 'The Town and Castle of Conway', *Archaeologia*, lxxxvi (1937), 189. The archetype of this whole Anglo-Savoyard group may have been the castle of Grandson, where the fourth tower of the thirteenth-century quadrangle was the pre-existing twelfth-century square donjon, now demolished.

[2] See below, pp. 279–80.

[3] The best short account of the castle is that by J.-P. Chapuisat: *Chillon, son histoire illustrée de documents iconographiques* (Lausanne, 1965).

[4] See his measured drawings of the original stonework in *La Camera Domini*, 20, 36, 37.

In English terms we might almost call the Chillon windows 'Harlech-type' windows, even though they are the earlier by twenty years; they occur throughout the Peter of Savoy work in the castle, and it was especially rewarding to row out in a little boat and discover them ranged on the side towards the lake, basking like their Merioneth counterparts in the strong light of the western sun (Plates XXXII*a* and XXXIII*a*). Later scrutiny at both castles was to show that the word 'counterpart' is used advisedly; for there is an inner similarity to match the outer, and it can also be shown to be as real as it is apparent. The diagram and table given below (fig 2) illustrate measurements taken

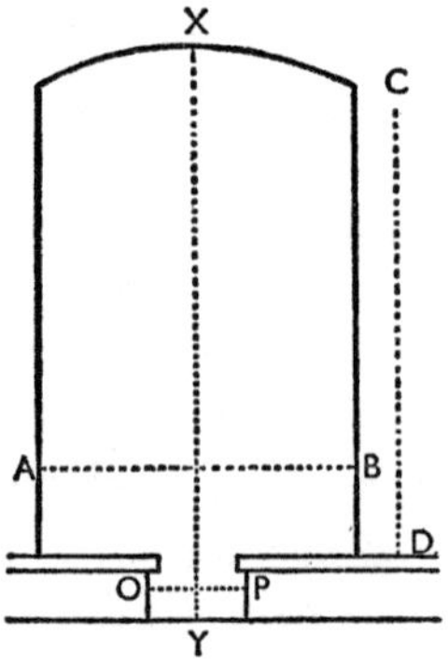

Measurements in metres

	Harlech	Chillon				
	*	i	ii	iii	iv	v
A-B	1.52	1.53	1.53	1.53	1.53	1.45
X-Y	3.88	3.86	3.86	3.74	3.62	3.58
C-D	3.09	2.93	2.93	2.93	2.78	2.77
O-P	0.88	0.82	0.82	0.81	0.84	0.76

* S. window, 2nd floor of gatehouse.
i-iv Windows on Lake side, "Bâtiment Q", south to north.
v S.E. window of *Pelium*, "Bâtiment G".

Fig. 2. Diagram to illustrate comparative measurements of windows at Harlech and Chillon.

independently by my friend M. Jean-Pierre Chapuisat in Switzerland and by myself in Wales. The difference between the dimensions of the selected Harlech window and the average of the corresponding dimensions of five selected windows at Chillon proved to be of the order of only 6 mm for dimension A–B, 15 cm for X–Y, 22 cm for C–D, and 7 cm for O–P. In each case the Harlech measurement is very slightly the greater, a discrepancy perhaps partly to be accounted for by the continued existence of surface rendering in the roofed and habitable rooms at Chillon in contrast to the open and weathered condition of ruined Harlech (Plate XXXIII*c* and *d*). It is hard to avoid the conclusion that these two sets of windows, although they are 950 miles apart, derive at least their dimensions, their frame design, and their relieving arches from a common pattern book, or a sketch-book such as Wilars de Honecourt's. It was only much later that I discerned the evidence, not easily seen, of helicoidal scaffolding having been used in building the flanking towers added by Peter of Savoy along Chillon's landward front.

It sounds like a forgotten era to recall that at 3.37 a.m. the next morning I was leaving Lausanne on the Orient Express for Arona, bound once more for Turin. The next 3½ days, Tuesday to Friday the 26–9 September, were as productive of crucial sources as any I have ever spent. Suffice to say that through the great helpfulness of Signorina Dott. Augusta Lange, to whom my indebtedness at Turin both then and through the succeeding years merits more than mere footnote acknowledgement, I procured the three volumes of Chiaudano's *La Finanza Sabauda nel secolo XIII* (1935–8), which print *inter alia* the earliest surviving castellans' accounts for Chillon, Yverdon, and Saillon as well as a selection of Count Philip's household rolls.[1] This left me free to devote the little time I had left (the Archivio closed at 2 p.m.) to unprinted material covering roughly the decade 1268–78, especially the fragile and invaluable household rolls for the years 1273–9.

These few days produced six discoveries:

First, that the building of Yverdon, castle and new town together, was begun in May 1261 under a Master John the Mason and his son Master James; Master John was paid 12*s.* 0*d.* a week, i.e. at the same level as a Master Peter Mainier, the *custos operum domini* or 'keeper' of the count's works, while Master James received 10*s.* 6*d.*[2] By 1266–7 Master John had disappeared from the scene, a payment of £15 for 1½ years' wages being then made to Master James alone.[3]

Second, that included in works payments recorded at Chillon in 1266–7 there is an unspecified item of £15 paid to a recipient whose name, 'Jacqueto de sancto Jorio', sounds uncommonly like 'James of St. George'.[4]

Third, that during the years 1271–5 the count's household

[1] The principal contents of the Turin archives are listed in Max Bruchet, 'Répertoire des sources de l'histoire de Savoie', extrait de la *Revue des Bibliothèques* (tirage à part, Paris, 1935, pp. 1–142).

[2] Mario Chiaudano, *La finanza sabauda nel sec. XIII* (3 vols., Torino, 1933–8, being vols. cxxxi–cxxxiii of Biblioteca della Società Storica Subalpina), i, 63 (henceforth cited as Chiaudano, *FS*); the passage is quoted in full in *Eng. Hist. Rev.* lxv. 453.

[3] AST, Inv. Sav. 70, fo. 205, mazzo 1, no. 1, '*In acquietancia Magistri Jacobi Cementarii hoc anno et de anno preterito, qui Jacobus percipit Yverdun' de domino in feud' decem lib. vien. singulis annis, xv. li.*'

[4] AST, Inv. Sav. 69, fo. 5, mazzo 1, no. 4, *Idem liberavit Jaquetto de sancto Jorio per litteras domini xv. li.* If, as seems likely, this and the entry quoted in the preceding note refer to an identical payment, then we have here the only reference so far discovered in Savoy records to Master James the mason as being 'of St. George'.

rolls show many payments of expenses to *Magister Jacobus lathomus* in respect of travel all over Savoy, often to places where works are evidently in progress.

Fourth, that one such place, namely St. Georges-d'Espéranche, in the Viennois, south-east of Lyon, is coming to the fore in the early 1270s with the building there of a new 'palace castle' by Count Philip, giving rise to the possibility that it might be from *this* St. Georges that the Master James who makes his début in English records in 1278 took or was given his local surname.[1]

Fifth, the Christian name 'Ambrosia', which English records show was the name of the North Wales Master James's wife, is sometimes encountered in Savoy records.[2]

Sixth, that the earliest castellan's account for Saillon shows that the building of the new tower there (Plate XXV*e*) in 1261 was entrusted as a task (*ad taschiam*) to a certain Francis the mason (not a master, simply *Franciscus Cementarius*) by a Sir John Masot, who later, in the 1270s, appears frequently as a travelling companion of Master James and is sometimes associated with him (as, for example, at St. Laurent-du-Pont in 1274) in the assignment of works 'tasks' and the awarding of contracts;[3] Sir John's function at Saillon is to settle the form of the tower (*ad turrim de Sallon devisandam*) and see to its positioning (*ad supervidendum situm turris*)[4] and, presumably, to draw up appropriate agreements with Franciscus. Saillon was the very castle whose affinity to Conway had by now more than once struck me from the railway. I reflected that, besides this evidence, printed by Chiaudano, for its tower having been built by this mason named Francis, an unprinted Chillon account of 1266 listing payments to masons, carpenters, and others included one of 75*s.* to a John Francis (*Johanni Francisco*);[5] and I recalled also that in our own Conway accounts of 1286 a John Francis (*Johanni Franceys*), also not styled 'master', twice appears as the first name

[1] *Ant. Journ.* xxxiii. 33–40. In a letter of 3 Feb. 1952 apropos James of St. George the late Louis Blondel writes, 'Comme j'ai pu le remarquer très souvent les maîtres d'œuvres sont désignés d'après le *dernier* grand chantier où ils ont travaillé. Or il n'est pas douteux que le château de St. Georges construit entre 1270–1272 était le plus important à ce moment-là.'

[2] e.g. 'Ambrosia, uxor Petri Bonivardi', burgess of Chambéry (Archs. Depts. de la Savoie, Chambéry, Inv. 65, fo. 1).

[3] Archives de la Savoie, Chambéry, Inv. 32, fo. 14, no. 66; just as we find Sir John de Bonvillars and Master James of St. George associated in assigning tasks ten years later at Conway (*Eng. Hist. Rev.* xci. 86).

[4] Chiaudano, *FS*, i. 58, 59, 68.

[5] AST, Inv. Sav. 69, fo. 5, mazzo 1, no. 3(c).

in lists of contractors undertaking particular 'tasks' on Conway town walls under Master James of St. George.[1] We last hear of this 'Conway' John Francis at Beaumaris under Master James in 1296;[2] if he were then, say, 70, he would have been 60 at Conway in 1286, 40 at Chillon in 1266, 35 at Saillon in 1261, and 31 at Conthey and Brignon (where he was probably the builder of Peter of Savoy's now vanished *turres*) in 1257.[3] Was it, is it, too much to think that perhaps we are dealing with one and the same life all through?

It was thus towards Saillon that I headed when I left Turin and crossed the Alps northwards again on 28 September, briefly visiting *en route* the site of Conthey and the castle and the Valère, the former cathedral of the bishops of Sion, famous for its fourteenth-century organ. It was the bishops of Sion who in the mid thirteenth century were the principal opponents in the Valais of the expansionist counts, and the towers of Conthey and Brignon, Saillon and La Bâtiaz built by Count Peter in the years preceding his succession in 1263, and the tower of Saxon built by Count Philip in 1279–80, bear witness to a long-drawn conflict.[4] Saillon, La Bâtiaz, and Saxon all proved to have much to contribute to the final story.

Saillon, like Chillon, at once revealed examples of the architectural parallels I was seeking. The simple round-headed gate arches of the town walls, for which the castellan's accounts give a firm date of 1257–8 (Plate XXVIII*a* and *b*), bear striking resemblance to the form of the entrance arch through the outer curtain at Harlech, as also to the great internal arch in the southern tower of the Harlech gatehouse (Plates XXVII*b* and XXVIII*c* and *d*). The donjon, securely dated to 1261, is of helicoidal construction, has a round-headed entrance door, and, like the towers of Conway castle, rises compass-perfect despite the irregularity of the rocky crag on which it sits (Plate XXV*e*). As with the towers of the North Wales castles generally, it was floored on close-set joists integrated into the original building and not stone vaulted at any level. Though the curtain and its

[1] PRO, E101/485/28; one of the passages referred to is reproduced in facsimile in *Archaeologia Cambrensis* cxix (1970), Plate II (a).

[2] PRO, E372/158, rot. 48.

[3] Chiaudano, *FS*, i, 26, where payment is recorded to him of £20 for a new building beside the keep at Conthey, '. . . pro tascheria nove camere iuxta turrim de Conteis . . .'.

[4] For the political background, see Victor van Berchem, 'Les dernières campagnes de Pierre II, comte de Savoie, en Valais et en Suisse', *Revue hist. vaudoise*, 1907, tome XV.

flanking towers are slighter and on a smaller scale than Conway's in the proportion of voids to solids and in details like the vaulting of embrasure heads there is a remarkable sameness between them (Plate XXXVIII*a* and *b*). Granted the difference in scale and terrain, the siting and conception of the Conway walls could well reflect the application of the same principles as those followed at Saillon twenty-five years earlier (Plate XXXVII). Even today, with its narrow alleys and passages within and its big rough-timbered barns and storehouses without its weathered and partly hidden walls, Saillon has extraordinary charm and tranquillity, and in its tiny way seems still to retain a feeling of continuity uninterrupted from medieval times.[1]

La Bâtiaz, the castle of Martigny, crowns a similar spur of rock about 7 miles down the Rhône from Saillon, not far from where the main river is joined by the Durance; its position high above the great Rhône bend affords extensive views northwards towards St. Maurice, eastwards towards Sion, and southwards up the entrance to the valley of the Great St. Bernard, the ancient road to which crosses the Durance immediately below the castle rock. The castle of La Bâtiaz was surrendered to Peter of Savoy by the Bishop of Sion after a siege in 1260, and there is documentary evidence which suggests the keep may have been building in 1265; in any event it is a product of the same *chantier* as Saillon, and here the evidence of helicoidal construction is even more plain to see. La Bâtiaz was afterwards recovered by the bishops, who undertook extensive repairs to its other buildings in 1280–1; we shall have occasion to look at these later.[2]

In September 1951, almost exactly a year after that first trial run, the help of a Leverhulme travel grant enabled me to return and devote a whole month to exploring other parts of Savoy and other archives. Indeed, the frequent mentions of St. Georges-d'Espéranche in the household rolls of the 1270s, and the fact that works which had once had their own building accounts had been in progress there in 1270–2,[3] were already turning my mind in that direction even before I left Turin for the second time in 1950. When I reached home the potential significance of St. Georges at once became apparent to me from Sir Maurice

[1] For a short account, with plan and illustrations, see André Donnet, *Saillon, bourg médiéval* (*Trésors de mon Pays*, Neuchâtel, 1950).

[2] For the castle of La Bâtiaz, see A. Donnet et Louis Blondel, *Châteaux de Valais* (Olten, 1963), 121–4.

[3] *Eng. Hist. Rev.* lxv. 457, n. 2.

Powicke's references to it in *Henry III and the lord Edward*, a book then only six years old.[1] For it was actually at this St. Georges, on Sunday, 25 June 1273, that the 66-year-old Count Philip did homage to his great-nephew Edward, the 34-year-old uncrowned king of England, for the nominal overlordship of those Alpine towns and castles enumerated earlier, through two of which, Avigliana and Susa, Edward and his knights would have ridden not many days before on their homeward journey from the Crusade.[2] A little before Susa the old road passed close beside the church and castle of S. Giorio in Val di Susa. This is relevant to our subject, as the castle provides a parallel for battlementing decked with triple finials, as at Conway (Plate XXXI); it is also remarkable for the extent ot which the medieval rendering has survived on the surface of its rubble walls, as well as for a gate arch bright with coloured voussoirs, and with traces of surmounting coloured shields of arms.[3]

When I eventually arrived in St. Georges-d'Espéranche myself the first thing to catch my eye was an obelisk flanked by two Union Jacks, erected by the French Resistance to the memory of seven English airmen who had fallen to their deaths over St. Georges in 1943. As I soon learned, it had been placed, doubtless quite unknowingly, almost on the site of the castle entrance through which Edward I must have passed seven centuries ago, a poignant reminder of Trevelyan's poetry of history.[4] Let me explain, as shortly as I may, in the light of this and eight further visits in subsequent years, what St. Georges once was and what it is now. A sketch-plan of 1794 preserved in the Archives de l'Isère at Grenoble shows that the castle was quadrangular with attached octagonal towers at the corners; the main buildings were ranged along the south and

[1] Above, p. 269, n. 3.

[2] There are several references in the castellans' accounts to King Edward's progress, as, for example, in that of Albert de Bagnol, bailiff of Savoy and keeper of the castle of Montmélian, for the year beginning Thursday, 12 January 1273: *In expensis domini Alberti ballivi euntis obviam domino Regi Anglie in Maurienna, xx. sol. Navigantibus qui transierunt dominum Regem per Yseram, ultra illud quod solutum eis fuerat per dominum Bosonem, de mandato domini comitis, v. sol.* (Archs. Depts. de la Savoie, Inv. 51, fo. 257, mazzo 1).

[3] For history and description, see Eugenio Olivero, *Il Castello e la Casa Forte di S. Giorio in Val di Susa* (Torino, 1925), for a copy of which I have to thank the late Dott. Ing. Guglielmo Lange of Turin. A single centre finial of this type remains on one of the towers added to the precinct wall of St. Mary's Abbey, York after 1318 (RCHM, *City of York*, vol. 2 (1972), 160–1, and Plate 58).

[4] G. M. Trevelyan, *An Autobiography and other Essays* (London, 1949), 13.

east sides and faced on to a square courtyard, the north wall of which contained the entrance gateway. Thus the residential blocks were planned, and orientated, exactly as at Champvent and Conway, leading one to wonder whether here too the north-east tower may have contained a chapel (Plate XXXIX). The plan was concentric, in that the built quadrangle was surrounded by a sloping berm, perhaps 30–40 feet in width, with this in turn enclosed by a water-filled moat said to have been 30–50 feet wide and 10–18 feet deep, but there does not appear to have been an outer curtain between berm and ditch. This, and the fact that all the walls, those of the towers included, were only 5–6 feet thick, emphasizes that St. Georges was much more a *palacium* (as the records sometimes name it), much more a *château de plaisance* than a true *château fort*. Two of the towers remained standing to full height until about the middle of the nineteenth century, but today only the south-east tower is left, standing to two-thirds of its original height, together with a fragment of the south and most of the adjacent east range, both much altered. Indeed, the east range has long been divided up into a warren of separate dwellings, mutilating but not wholly obliterating the medieval structure; their gardens usefully keep open the site of the berm or outer ward on this side. In particular there remain valuable traces of original door-heads and fenestration, the former including a characteristic semicircular arch, the latter proving to be almost identical with that of Yverdon. It is also not impossible that a window recess in the south-east tower may preserve the form and dimension of the thirteenth-century embrasure that preceded it; if so, comparison with Harlech is apposite (Plate XXIX*a* and *b*). Most significant of all is the garderobe shaft that occupies the tower's adjacent eastern re-entrant angle, and whose measurements proved on comparison to correspond to within a few centimetres with those of the similar adjunct to the north-west tower at Harlech (Plate XXX*a* and *b*).[1]

When I was first at St. Georges in 1951 I was told[2] of the survival in the Archives de la Savoie at Chambéry of a contract made at St. Georges in the year 1278 for masonry work at the neighbouring castle of Falavier (Plate XLII*a*). Falavier's stand-

[1] 'The Castle of St. Georges-d'Espéranche', *Ant. Journ.* xxxiii. 33–47; Plate XI (*c*) reproduces the original 1794 plan on which our own plan (Plate XXXIX*a*) is based.

[2] By the late Dr. Joseph Saunier of Heyrieux, physician and antiquary, who gave me the greatest possible help and kindness at St. Georges.

ing remains are heavily overgrown and it was not possible to recognize the works in question, if indeed they still remain. The contract is none the less of much interest in itself, for its date, for the form of the agreement with Boso the count's chaplain, for the name and style of the contractor 'Taxinus de sancto Georgio lathomus', and the survival of fragments of Boso's and Tassin's seals, the latter bearing a mason's toothed hammer-axe and remains of the legend 'S. TASS . . .'.[1] Little or nothing now remains of the other three castles in the Viennois, La Côte St. André (*Costa*), Voiron, and St. Laurent du Pont (Sanctus Laurentius in Deserto), where works are mentioned in the household rolls of the early 1270s.

Let us now return to the Valais, as I myself did in 1951, and look again at La Bâtiaz, this time not at Peter of Savoy's *donjon circulaire* but at a detail of the buildings adjacent to it built or rebuilt by Bishop Pierre d'Oron of Sion in 1281. We have no accounts for this work, but in March 1281 the Sion chapter agreed to grant the bishop the first-fruits of vacant benefices, '*cum episcopus sumptuosum opus inceperit in castro Martigniaci*'.[2] Earlier we remarked that at Harlech there are two specially distinctive garderobe types and we have just noted one of them paralleled at St. Georges. Here at La Bâtiaz we find a parallel to the other in the shape of a corresponding pair of projecting constructions which probably belong to this work of 1281. Though less well preserved and built of a different stone, the shoots at La Bâtiaz are essentially of similar pattern and similar corbelled form, and are similarly positioned, to the shoot at Harlech. The Harlech and La Bâtiaz shoots are the only known examples of their kind (Plate XXX*c* and *d*).

Five miles from La Bâtiaz stands the rock of Saxon,[3] which I visited for the first of many times, in a quick dash up the hill and down again, between trains, on 27 September 1951. It is only

[1] Archs. Depts. de la Savoie, Chambéry, Inv. 135, fo. 17, pacquet 14, pièce 7. 'Ce nom de *Tassin* est du nord d'Italie ou de la Lombardie en partie dans les états de Savoie . . . Tasse est avec St. Victor un des saints de Milan' (Louis Blondel, 3 Feb. 1952). The name 'Ambrosia' is also derived from the Milanese St. Ambrose.

[2] Abbé J. Gremaud, *Méms. de la Soc. d'histoire de la Suisse romande*, tome XXX, 298–9.

[3] The authoritative account of Saxon is by Louis Blondel, 'Le château de Saxon', *Vallesia*, ix (Sion, 1954), 165–74 and X. 87–8. It was the late M. Blondel, at that time the doyen of antiquarian studies in western Switzerland, who first drew my attention to Saxon, as well as giving much other help and advice. Amongst many papers on the castles of the region, his

gradually that I have since come to realize that a relationship between the building and the builders of this tower in 1279–80, and the buildings begun in North Wales in 1282–3, is perhaps more convincingly demonstrable, both visually and in terms of records, than is the case with any of the other instances we have considered up till now. For the tower of Saxon, the *turris Sayssonis*, we not only still have the tower itself in a good state of preservation, but we also have in the Archivio at Turin two detailed and well-preserved castellan's accounts relating to its construction.[1] Next day, therefore, I crossed the Great St. Bernard by bus, a journey unforgettable for the drove upon drove of bedecked and tinkling cattle winding their slow way down to the valley for the winter, spent a day looking at the castles of Aosta and Châtel Argent, both with round towers built by the helicoidal method,[2] and then went on to spend five days in the Via S. Chiara at Turin, copying amongst others the two Saxon accounts in question.

It is Saxon and its documentation that must now claim our attention. First the structure. Being dated precisely by the accounts to the years 1279–80, it comes closer in time than do any others we have considered hitherto to the castles begun in North Wales in the ensuing decade, and the resemblances are close; for example, the round-arched doorway (Plate XXV*b*), the perfectly graded batter (Plate XXV*a*), support for the floor joists provided at each level by two parallel cross beams,[3] and a classic exemplification of helicoidal construction, with some of the putlogs still sound and in place (Plate XXV*a* and *b*). It is fortunate indeed that we should still have contemporary records of such a building's erection in considerable detail. Here we can only note what they have to tell us of some of the principal contractors, in whose identity perhaps lies the most conclusive endorsement of the relationship between the building of these additions to the little Savoy castles and the building of the much bigger and more elaborate North Wales castles which it was the purpose of my exploration to attempt to establish. We need

'L'Architecture militaire au temps de Pierre II de Savoie, Les Donjons circulaires' (*Genava*, xiii (1935), 271–321) is of first importance, surpassed only in scale by his great study of the *Châteaux de l'ancien diocèse de Genève* (Genève, 1956).

[1] AST, Inv. 69, fo. 69, mazzo 1, no. 1; ibid., fo. 5, mazzo 1, no. 7.

[2] AST, Inv. 68, fo. 2, mazzo 1, no. 2 is a detailed works account for Châtel Argent.

[3] For plans and sections see L. Blondel, 'Château de Saxon', *Vallesia*, ix. 173.

concern ourselves with three names only, viz. first Tassin of St. George whom we have already come across at Falavier; second, Giles or Gilet, whose full style is given as '*Giletus de sancto Georgio lathomus*' and who is Tassin's brother; and third, someone whose name is given as '*Beynardus rex ribaldorum*', who shares with another a payment of £18. 5*s.* for digging the tower's foundation, and whose picturesque title means, in a building context, the man in charge of the barrows and hand-carts, 'celui qui dirige les brouettes'.[1]

These last two names Giletus and Beynardus, provide, I believe, a link which takes us back to Wales, where our journey began, bringing us first to Llanbadarn, i.e. Aberystwyth. By the merest accident, indeed thanks solely to a clerical blunder which though erased was fortunately not obliterated, our own records have preserved a reference,[2] given in facsimile below (Plate XLII*b*), to the presence at Aberystwyth castle in September 1282 of an individual who it is hard to believe is not identical with 'Giletus de sancto Georgio lathomus'. If 'Egidius' is synonymous with 'Giletus', and 'cementarius' for all practical purposes with 'lathomus'—and who will deny that they are?—then here at Aberystwyth, not so very long after we left him at Saxon, we are surely with our friend Giles of St. George again, and he is now 'Master' or 'Mr.' Giles. And what has been happening in the meantime? What has happened is this. Last Palm Sunday, 22 March 1282, the Welsh princes Llywelyn and Dafydd launched a well-concerted revolt, laid siege to the castles of Flint and Rhuddlan, and a day or two later sacked the unfinished castle of Aberystwyth.[3] Count Philip's nephew Amadeus of Savoy, captain of King Edward's army at Chester, raised the siege of Rhuddlan but then had to return to his own country on account of the death of his brother Thomas.[4] Not only are unfinished or damaged castles standing in need of completion or repair, but bigger and stronger castles are going to have to be built, castles that will bring Snowdonia into the king's peace once and for all, and additional professional help is going to be needed in the

[1] Ibid., x. 87; cf. *Hist. King's Wks.* ii. 1038–9.

[2] PRO, C47/2/4, m. 3. Entry of payment in September 1282, '*Magistro Egidio de Sancto Georgio Cementario pro vadiis suis . . . per xx. dies . . . xx.s.*' cancelled, because entered more appropriately on his own expenses roll, now lost.

[3] For the political background, see J. Goronwy Edwards (ed.), *Littere Wallie* (Cardiff, 1940), lxi–lxix.

[4] 'A letter from Lewis of Savoy to Edward I', *Eng. Hist. Rev.* lxviii. 55–62.

planning and the building of them. There is much to suggest that in the emergency of 1282 Edward did indeed invoke the help of Count Philip, at once his 'man' in feudal, his great-uncle in family terms. In a letter dated 26 August 1282 his mother, Queen Eleanor of Provence, reminded Edward how in some unspecified time of crisis Philip had come to his aid, and how friendly he had been to him in 1273 when the king was returning from Crusade: 'Et pensez comme il vous fut ami en votre grant besoigne d'Angleterre et au moment ou vous veniez d'Outremer.'[1] That the master of the works, Master James, should go to Aberystwyth in May, as he did, to see to the resumption of the building of the castle[2] is natural enough; but it can only be against something like the background outlined above that we can explain the arrival of Master Giles from Savoy in June. The two men must already have been at least known to one another. How well known can only be a matter of speculation, and it is one upon which we shall touch again before we conclude.

Meanwhile, what of 'Beynardus rex', the 'officer i/c carts and carters' (if we may so describe him) at Saxon? One can only repeat a suggestion already made elsewhere, namely that he is to be identified with a so-named 'rex dictus Adam' who receives a Christmas box of £5 from Count Amadeus in 1296, and that he turns up under a combination of the two names as 'Adam Boynard' at Harlech in the 1286 particulars account, having probably come with Giles of St. George to Aberystwyth in 1282.[3] That there was an ex-Aberystwyth element in the Harlech work force is indicated by the presence of a William de Lanpader, and when we encounter the names Adam Boynard and Gilet together at Harlech in 1286, in lists of contractors whose horses have been employed in carting building materials to the site (Plate XLII*c*),[4] it is hard not to suppose that 'Gilet' may be none other than the 'Giletus de sancto Georgio' of the Saxon accounts *alias* the 'Magister Egidius de sancto Georgio' of the Aberystwyth account. Harlech's full-centred arches, its many indications of inclined scaffolds, its 'Chillon' windows,

[1] Quoted in Francois Mugnier, 'Les Savoyards en Angleterre au XIIIe siècle', *Mémoires de la Société Savoisienne*, tome XXIX (Chambéry, 1890), 333–4.

[2] *Hist. King's Works*, i. 304.

[3] *Genava*, N.S. xi. 307–8. At the same time as the payment of 100*s*. 'Regi dicto Adam', another of 50*s*. was made to a William of Pontefract the coachman ('quadrigario'), and Richard his companion 'redeuntibus in Angliam' (AST, Inv. 38, fo. 46, mazzo 2, no. 5).

[4] PRO, E101/485/26, printed in full in *Hist. King's Wks.*, ii. 1030–5.

its St. Georges- and Bâtiaz-type garderobe shoots, its little rectangular staircase lights which are replicas of those at Saxon—all these seem to postulate a strong Savoy element in the castle's conception and execution, and may be indicative of the presence of others from that background besides the controlling figures of Master James of St. George and Sir John de Bonvillars, of whose close association at Harlech I have written in another place.[1]

I think that by now I have explained the stages by which my exploration of buildings and documents came to convince me of the reality of the connection between North Wales and Savoy. I should now like to examine the question of possible family relationships between some of the principal personalities. Early in our inquiry, at Yverdon in 1261, we found two masters, John and James, working side by side and named as father and son. Twenty-one years later, at Aberystwyth in 1282, we have again found ourselves in the presence of two masters, James and Giles, having 'St. George' as their common surname. During the interval, in what are at best but intermittent and imperfectly examined records, we only once (in 1266 at Chillon) found this local surname applied to a Savoy James, but in our English records, from 1278 onwards, it is applied to the North Wales James increasingly and eventually almost always. Assuming that it is with only one James that we are dealing, what is likely to have been his age when he first appears, already a 'master', in the company of a father probably by then well on in years, in 1261? Allowing for an apprenticeship of seven years from age 15, he would not have been less than 22, which would make the year of his birth 1239, the same as that of Edward I, and his age at death in 1309[2] 70. Yet the Savoyards tended towards long life: Otto de Grandison was at least 90 at his death in 1328 and his brother William must have achieved much the same tally at his death in 1339.[3] Master James of St. George may easily have lived to be well over 70. Let us therefore assume instead that he was at least 80 in 1309 and 32 or more in 1261. If he married at the age of 25 this would then have been not later than 1254, so that a further step into the realm of controlled conjecture would give 1255 as a likely date for the birth of his eldest child. Supposing that child to have been Tassin, and Giles to have been two years younger, they would have been 25 and 23 respectively at Saxon in 1280, and Giles would have been 25 at

[1] *Eng. Hist. Rev.* xc. 91–5. [2] Ibid. lxv. 452.
[3] C. L. Kingsford, op. cit., 170, 174.

Aberystwyth in 1282, not too young an age to have been a 'master' if he served his apprenticeship from age 15 or thereabouts, particularly with so distinguished a father. Thus it is not impossible—at present we can put it no higher—that the Master James of St. George and the Master Giles of St. George who appear briefly together at Aberystwyth in the records of 1282 were father and son, like Master John and Master James at Yverdon in 1261; if so, Giles would in all likelihood have been apprenticed under his father during the busy castle-building period at St. Georges-d'Espéranche and elsewhere in the Viennois during the early 1270s. This allows us to suppose that the other son, Tassin, remained behind to represent the family and carry on the family profession in Savoy, where indeed we can in fact still trace him, as 'Tassinus lathomus', at Chillon in 1286–7 and Geneva in 1288,[1] and as 'Magister' Tassinus at Treffort in 1291–2.[2] As to the subsequent career of Master Giles, a possibility—it can be no more—is that he is the 'Master Giles the mason' named at Edinburgh in 1304 (with Walter of Hereford and others previously in North Wales) in the context of preparations for the coming siege of Stirling castle.[3]

We may thus here be in the presence not of two but of three generations of master masons, Master John (d. after 1261 and before 1268), Master James (d. 1309), and Master James's sons Master Tassin and Master Giles. What, then, can be said of the grandfather, Master John? A great deal can be said of *a* Master John, and it has lately been brilliantly said in the writings of M. Marcel Grandjean, the Professor of Regional Art History at the University of Lausanne. Professor Grandjean has shown, on the evidence of Lausanne chapter records, that the *magister operis Lausannensis* of the second quarter of the thirteenth century, the master responsible for the latest, more westerly parts of Lausanne Cathedral, was a Master John, to whom there are no fewer than nineteen references, mostly in the cathedral cartulary, between 1210 and 1318, the first five belonging to a time before 1225 when not *he*, but *his* father was *magister operis*, while the last four indicate that by 1268 he was no longer alive; the remainder, dating from 1227 to 1236, show Master John in office as 'master of the Lausanne work', which office he may well have continued to hold, in the absence of his having been superseded or of his being deceased before the mid 1260s, for some, perhaps

[1] AST, Inv. 69, fo. 5, mazzo 1, no. 9.

[2] Archives de la Côte d'Or, Dijon, B.7083.

[3] Bain, *Cal. Docts. relating to Scotand,* ii. p. 399.

many years longer. What is of particular interest is that in July 1234 the chapter assigned to Master John land and ground for a house in their own newly founded *ville-neuve* of St. Prex, on the lakeside eight miles to the west of Lausanne, on condition that he and his eldest son after him should continue to occupy it at an annual rent to the chapter of 10*s*. Only a few months afterwards, in 1236, we find John named both as *magister operacionis Lausannensis* and *castellanus sancti Prothasii*, i.e. in effect the chapter's resident commandant and administrator of their new-built defended town, of whose layout and defences he may well himself, as M. Grandjean suggests, have been the planner and constructor.[1]

When we turn from the Lausanne chapter's St. Prex of 1234 to Peter of Savoy's Yverdon of 1261,[2] we find the records provide us with a valuable statement of the terms of employment of three men who will be principally responsible for the new works.[3] Presumably the most important of the three is the one mentioned first, namely Master John the mason; we may note that the account does not by implication downgrade John by saying that he gets the same pay as Master Peter Mainier the *custos operum domini*, but rather the reverse—Peter Mainier is to

[1] Marcel Grandjean, 'A propos de la construction de la cathédrale de Lausanne (XII–XIIIe siècle); notes sur la chronologie et les maîtres d'œuvre', *Genava*, N.S. tome XI (Genève, 1963), 261–87; *La Cathédrale de Lausanne* (Berne, 1975), 47–8. One of the posthumous references (1270) gives Master John's surname as 'Cotereel' ('. . . *tenementum quod fuit magistri Johannis dicti Cotereel* . . .'); according to M. Grandjean (p. 278) the name is foreign to the Pays de Vaud and its vicinity, but is found as a place-name in north-east and north-west France, in Flanders, Brabant, and as far away as England. Nevertheless we may note (i) that in 1271–2 the castellan of Rue, in the Pays de Vaud, accounts for a render of oats paid 'apud Cotterel' (Chiaudano, *FS*, i. 214), and (ii) the existence in Veytaux of a lane named 'Chemin de Cotterd' leading off the old road from Lausanne to Chillon. It is also not without interest to note the name Jacobus de Coterel' in one of the lists of recipients of livery gowns distributed by King Henry III to a variety of royal servants at Christmas 1261 (*Close Rolls, Henry III*, xi (1261–4), 15). For the probability that Master John's father was also 'magister operis Lausannensis' before him and the possibility that the father (who would thus have been Master James's grandfather) had served under William of Sens or William the Englishman at Canterbury, see Grandjean, *Genava*, N.S. xi. 275 and note; for the Canterbury/Lausanne relationship, see Jean Bony, 'The resistance to Chartres in early thirteenth-century architecture', *Journ. of Brit. Arch. Assn.*, 3rd ser., xx–xxi (1957–8), 35–52, esp. 47–8.

[2] For the early history, see Roger Déglon, *Yverdon au Moyen Âge* (Lausanne, 1949), 17–31.

[3] Chiaudano, *FS*, i. 63; cf. above, p. 8, and n. 27

get the same pay as Master John. And yet it is this Peter Mainier whom the Swiss archaeologists and art historians from Albert Naef onwards have again and again insisted, as I believe quite wrongly, on calling 'le véritable architecte et ingénieur militaire de Pierre II',[1] the chief architect and designer and builder of his castles. The 'keeper' or 'warden' of the works is not rightly to be confused with their 'master', who is the skilled professional practitioner. Peter Mainier's position in regard to the works of Yverdon, Chillon, and Romont, all three of which seem to be implicitly covered by the 1261 statement, is no different to that of, say, William de Perton or Nicholas Bonel in regard to the Flint and Rhuddlan works between 1277 and 1286, or of John of Candover at Conway in 1283–4.[2] Essentially they were all of them clerks of works and accounting and supply officers, not craftsmen or professionals. When we give to the position of Master John, which is implicit in the 1261 statement, the evaluation it evidently deserves, the possibility—to put it no higher—that he is the same John as the *magister operis Lausannensis* can hardly be excluded; clearly it would be no novelty for one with the experience of having planned and started St. Prex to be entrusted near the end of his life by Count Peter with the planning and founding of Yverdon. Moreover, while the ground-plans of the two towns are far from being duplicates,—they occupy very different sites and are twenty-five years apart in date—nevertheless they have certain basic characteristics in common; each has a layout based on three streets radiating from a point near the south-eastern extremity of the site; both are fully provided with water defences, St. Prex's (fig. 3) mainly natural and partly man-made, Yverdon's (fig. 4) mainly man-made and partly natural; the parallelism of their orientation is striking. And, if we are right in our thinking, there is a parallelism too between a versatile father who builds great churches, lays out new towns, and is put in command at St. Prex by the chapter of Lausanne, and a versatile son who builds great castles, lays out towns, and is put in command of Harlech or at Linlithgow by the king of England.[3] Occasionally, as in the resemblance of the end hall window of the castle of Conway to

[1] Albert Naef, op. cit., 33. Naef's work is well documented, but as an architect he would not have been equipped to distinguish between the roles of the 'custos' and the 'magister' of the count's works.

[2] A. J. Taylor, 'Castle-building in Wales . . . the prelude to construction', 105, 108 and notes.

[3] *Eng. Hist. Rev.* lxv. 451.

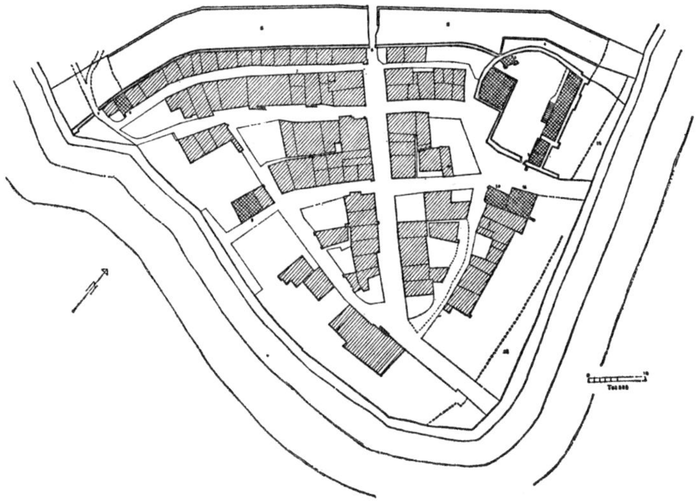

Fig. 3. Plan of town of St. Prex (Vaud) in about 1741 (from Marcel Grandjean, '. . . la construction de la Cathédrale de Lausanne . . . la chronologie et les maîtres d'œuvre,' *Genava* N.S. xi (Genève, 1963), 283.

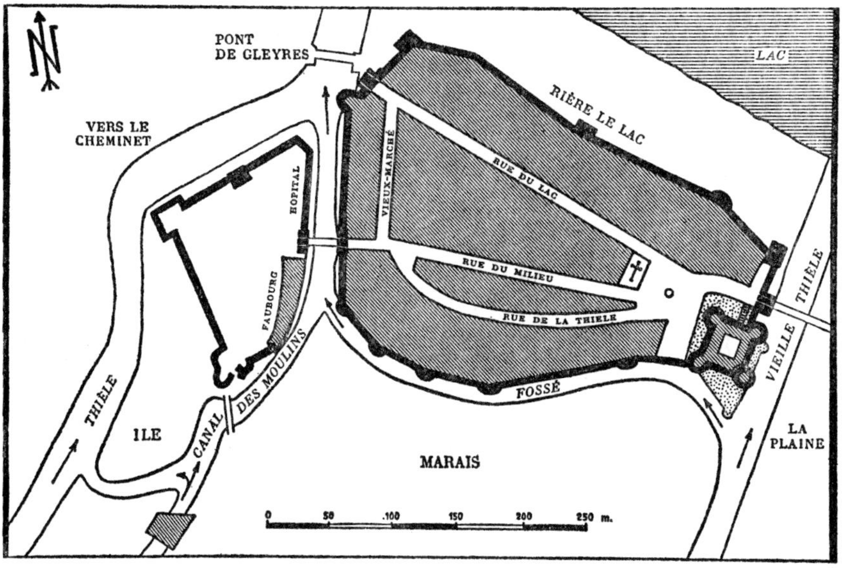

Fig. 4. Plan of town of Yverdon (Vaud) in about 1686 (from Roger Déglon, *Yverdon au Moyen Âge* (Lausanne, 1949), xxiii.

the western window of the cathedral of Lausanne, the military architect may reflect the source of his inspiration (Plate XLI*a* and *b*).[1]

Master James of St. George's versatility would scarcely be in

[1] One wonders whether Master Bernard de Sancto Georgio, master

question even were there only Flint and Rhuddlan, Conway, Harlech, and Beaumaris to make up the sum of his surviving achievement in Wales. It was Thomas Rickman who first remarked on the contrast between Caernarvon's polygonal towers and angular planning and the rounded towers of the others,[1] and the view has often been expressed that the explanation is to be sought in a different architectural authorship. I have stated elsewhere the grounds for believing that, on the contrary, the real explanation is the much more fundamental one of the king's intention that Caernarvon, as the capital of a new dynasty of English princes, should be a palace-castle, reflecting in its symbolism its own Roman origins and using the likeness of the Theodosian walls of Constantinople to invoke the imperial theme (Plate XL).[2] Moreover, all the documentation that we have points to the conclusion that Master James's over-all responsibility as *magister operacionum Wallie* was undivided, and, no matter how able and experienced may have been such colleagues as Richard of Chester or Walter of Hereford, Caernarvon as the prestige commission is the one least likely of all to have been delegated.[3] Though the style is different and the degree of embellishment greater, the resemblances both in detail and in general plan to Conway are unmistakable. It is not to be forgotten that versatility is one of the marks of the great architect: few looking for the first time at Barry's Houses of Parliament, the Reform Club House in Pall Mall, and the Quadrangle at Devonport dockyard would guess, or perhaps even readily believe, that they were all products of the same drawing-board. It would be a poor tribute to hold that Master James, given the great site differences and widely different commissioning requirements, could not have conceived the palatial majesty of Caernarvon as well as the military strength of Conway, Harlech, Beaumaris, and the rest.

mason at Bordeaux Cathedral in the 1360s (Archives de Gironde, sér. G, fo. 240v° and sér. H, no. 6, fo. 11v°), may perhaps have been a descendant. In 1314 Pope Clement V, Edward I's former clerk Bertrand del Goth, Archbishop of Bordeaux 1300–5?, left a bequest of 100 florins to a Bertrand de Sancto Georgio. A Perreninus de Sancto Georgio, *macon*, was working at the castle of Poligny (Jura) in 1429 (P. Brune, *Dict. des artistes et ouvriers d'art de la Franche-Comté*, Paris, 1912, p. 259).

[1] Thomas Rickman, *An Attempt to discriminate the styles of Architecture in England*, 3rd edn. (London, 1825), 362. The castle of Henry de Lacy earl of Lincoln at Denbigh also has polygonal towers but is without the coloured stone banding that distinguishes Caernarvon.

[2] *Hist. King's Wks.* i. 369–71.

[3] Ibid. 391–3.

In availing himself of specialists from abroad to carry through the great building programme in Wales Edward I was following accustomed practice. We have only to recall the origins of his doctors and surgeons, Simon and Philip of Beauvais; of his lawyers, the Accursii of Bologna; of his bankers, the Riccardi of Lucca or the Bardi and Frescobaldi of Florence; of his saddler, Felyseus of Paris;[1] of the German miners employed to search for copper near Dyserth in Flintshire;[2] of the canal expert Master Walter of Flanders, employed to make the moat at the Tower of London,[3] or of Master Manasser of Vaucouleurs to order the ditch-digging at Caernarvon;[4] and that even Edward's musician, Guilottus *vidulator*, sounds like an Italian, whilst the thousand Welsh minstrels who came to play to the king and queen at Overton, when Nevin was over, in 1284, doubtless also gave of their native best.[5] When it came to the castle-building it is true that the workmen, as Sir Goronwy reminded us,[6] were brought mainly from England, masons, carpenters, and diggers coming in their tens and fifties and hundreds from every corner of the land; but it need cause no surprise, that with Amadeus, and Otto, and Peter de Champvent to advise and recommend, and with the memory of his own sojourn at St. Georges-d'Espéranche in mind, the king should have turned to Savoy for the expert direction and deployment of so widely drawn a labour force. That Savoy may not have been entirely the loser, that some who came returned, is suggested not only by the plan of Champvent, which is likely to reflect that of Conway rather than vice-versa, but also by the extraordinarily close resemblance of the early fourteenth-century east end of the church of St. Etienne at Moudon to the west front of Valle Crucis abbey (repaired after war damage in 1282–3) (Plate XLI*c* and *d*).[7] No easy explanation can be offered, but the suggestion of a direct connection seems inescapable. There are

1 PRO, E101/351/9, m. 11; 351/12; *Archaeologia*, xvii. 306–7.

2 Arthur Jones (ed.), 'Flintshire Ministers' Accounts, 1301–28', *Pubs. Flints. Hist. Soc.* 3 (Prestatyn, 1913), 95–6.

3 *Hist. King's Wks.* ii. 716

4 Ibid. i. 372 n. 2.

5 *Bull. Bd. of Celtic Studies*, xxvii (1977), 254, quoting PRO, C47/3/21(11).

6 *Proc. Brit. Acad.* xxxii. 17; diagrams showing their numbers and catchment areas are in Taylor, 'The Prelude to Construction' pp. 107, 111.

7 For the history of Moudon see Charles Gilliard, *Moudon sous le Régime savoyard* (Méms. et Docts. publ. par la Soc. d'histoire de la Suisse romande, sér. 2, tome XIV); for St. Étienne, see Gaëtan Cassina, 'Saint-Étienne de Moudon' in series *Guides des Monuments Suisses*.

many unknowns in the story traced in the foregoing pages, and their solution may safely be left to the future.

Acknowledgements. I am indebted for permission to reproduce illustrations as follows: Crown Copyright reserved, Department of the Environment: Plates XXIII*a* and *b*, XXIV*a* and *d*, XXVI*a* and *b*, XXVII*a* and *b*, XXIX*a* and *c*, XXXII *a* and *c*, XXXIII*c*, XXXV*b* and *c*, XXXVIII*b*, XL*a*; Crown Copyright reserved, Public Record Office, Plate XLII*b* and *c*; Royal Commission on Ancient and Historical Monuments in Wales, Plate XL*b*; Max F. Chiffelle, Lausanne, Plate XXXIII*b*; J. Cellard, Lyon, Plate XXXIX*c*; Musée d'Art et d'Histoire, Genève, Plate XLI*a*, figs. 2 and 3; F. Rouge and Cie S. A. Lausanne, fig. 4; Society of Antiquaries of London, Plate XLI*b*; Archivio di Stato, Torino, fig. 1; Archs. Dept. de la Savoie, Chambéry, Plate XLII*a*.

[1] Besides debts of thanks acknowledged in the text or in previous footnotes, I gratefully recall help given me by MM. R. Avezou and Jean Sablou, and M. Sablou's successor M. Perret, Archivistes en chef of the Archives de l'Isère and de la Savoie at Grenoble and Chambéry respectively in the 1950s; by the late Baronne Elisabeth de Blonay at Grandson; by the late M. Hugues and Mme Jéquier at La Lance; and by M. Péclard at Champvent. I also have to thank Professor Marcel Grandjean for help in regard to the cathedral of Lausanne, and M. Gaëtan Cassina for help in regard to St. Etienne de Moudon. I am also infinitely indebted to M. Jean-Pierre Chapuisat for constant help and advice and companionship over a period of twenty years on visits to castles and churches in all parts of medieval Savoy, and to Jeanne and Lionel Stones for help during the preparation of this paper. The reconstruction drawing of Harlech (Plate XXXII) was kindly made by Mr. David Neal, and the redrawing of the 1794 plan of St. Georges by Mr. Frank Gardner, both of the Ancient Monuments Illustrators Branch of the Department of the Environment.

PROVENANCE AND PROBLEMATICS OF 'SUBLIME AND ALARMING IMAGES' IN POETRY

By EDWIN MORGAN

Read 14 December 1977

I STARTED off the speculations in this essay—and I should add that they are speculations rather than things I shall necessarily hope to prove—from a remark of Thomas Warton in the Postscript of his *Observations on the Fairy Queen of Spenser*, where he speaks of 'those sublime and alarming images, which true poetry best delights to display'. Warton writes this in his general advocacy of an earlier literature of romance and chivalry to which his own 'age of reason and refinement', as he calls it, might give short shrift, but one senses, behind what he says, something that opens out the whole matter towards a wider conception of the importance of the imagination. Those images of the marvellous, the sublime, and the terrible have, he suggests, a function: to 'rouse and invigorate all the powers of imagination'. If this is so, why has the idea of the sublime been such an intermittent one? Has it, in fact, any permanent usefulness? What should we make of it today? We know Longinus *On the Sublime*; we know Burke's *A Philosophical Enquiry into the Origin of our Ideas of the Sublime and Beautiful*; we could list some works which most people would agree in finding 'sublime' or at least containing unmistakable touches of sublimity—*The Divine Comedy*, *King Lear*, *Paradise Lost*. But Warton's 'sublime and alarming images' have not always been thought to be useful or desirable, and it seems that the imagination may be invigorated in other ways. This is the area into which I wish to insert some questions and tentative answers.

Since the sublime is a concept that is notoriously difficult to define, it may be best to begin from the period of its maximum discussion in English literature, the middle and later eighteenth century. The title of Edmund Burke's treatise at least served to indicate that what was beautiful was not necessarily sublime, and vice versa; and from a reading of the treatise it would become clear that the sublime was a higher category than the beautiful, something to be strained for by the utmost use of the faculties of the artist and something to be received with awed recognition by anyone to whom representations of it were exposed. Indefinable though the sublime might seem, it was a quality he was sure did exist, and it existed in nature for all who had eyes to see; indeed during times of crisis it was an inescapable and monstrous *donnée*—an earthquake, an eruption, a hurricane, a great fire which must make any observer realize how hard it is to disentangle thrill from pity. A true recognition of the sublime involved an intense and uncommon emotional response, a response characterized by the presence of opposites: 'not pleasure, but a sort of delightful horror, a sort of tranquillity tinged with terror; which, as it belongs to self-preservation, is one of the strongest of all the passions. Its object is the sublime. Its highest degree I call *astonishment*' (IV. vii). To the general requirements of astonishment and terror, Burke added such other factors as obscurity (the vague and shifting portrait of Milton's Satan being more sublime than clearly delineated monsters in paintings of the temptation of St. Anthony), power (because power is associated with violence and danger, or, in religion, with a salutary dread), privation (emptiness, darkness, silence, solitude all being natural associates of fear), vastness (whether of the very large or of the very little, but suggesting the pull of infinity in either direction), and what he called magnificence (instancing the apparently confused but grand richness of a sky of stars). Of these, it might seem that 'privation' and 'magnificence' are in prospect of contradiction; but presumably Burke was acknowledging that there are different manifestations of the sublime, and that not all the named qualities would always be found in an experience of sublimity.

The eighteenth century found these qualities in James Macpherson's Ossianic poems of the 1760s; we, looking back, would be more likely to see them in Wordsworth's *The Prelude*, or in some of the poetry of Blake, Coleridge, or Shelley. Yet Macpherson influenced Wordsworth, and influenced Blake even more, and in his introduction to a recent reprint of the Ossianic poems[1] John MacQueen invited a reconsideration of Macpherson's achievement in terms of a Tolkien-like creation of an imaginary but self-consistent world—a world which never really existed in either Scottish or Irish history or legend but which

[1] *Poems of Ossian*, Mercat Press, Edinburgh, 1971.

was devised to fit the shadowy, portentous workings of the pre-Romantic imagination. Macpherson's contemporaries were hungry for grandeur, for liberation, for the primitive, for the sublime, and they absorbed what he had to offer—an inchoate sublime rather than sublimity in truth—unaware that better was to come. Macpherson is a good example of how, if the time is ripe for it, powerful impulses and large general emotions can be conveyed through imperfect or even windy and pretentious verbal expression.

As a hundred winds on Morven; as the streams of a hundred hills; as clouds fly successive over heaven; as the dark ocean assails the shore of the desart: so roaring, so vast, so terrible the armies mixed on Lena's echoing heath. The groan of the people spread over the hills: it was like the thunder of night, when the cloud bursts on Cona, and a thousand ghosts shriek at once on the hollow wind.[1]

It might seem hard to deny sublimity to a passage that strives so manfully to reach it! Yet the effect, not at all bad to begin with, is weakened, not strengthened, by the final strained and melodramatic touch of the thousand shrieking ghosts; later poets would manage such a scene without recourse to Macpherson's blatant Gothic buttonholing. At the same time, it is by no means impossible to see why Macpherson's readers were impressed by the sense of vast interlocking clashes in human and natural life, and were also attracted by it, as something quite new in that century's literary experience. The images, if not sublime, were at least alarming, and had something of that pleasing terror that Burke demanded.

Yet the image in that quoted passage which will perhaps stick in the mind of a modern reader is that of the 'dark ocean' which 'assails the shore of the desart'. It is hard not to connect this with Wordsworth's story, in Book V of *The Prelude*, of his friend's dream of the Arab

riding o'er the desert sands,
With the fleet waters of the drowning world
In chase of him; whereat I waked in terror . . .
(V. 135–7)

Wordsworth, more than any other poet, seems to have been created to make something of the eighteenth-century ideas of the sublime, and all these ideas can be persuasively illustrated from his work. The association of the sublime with the alarming, the importance of elements of awe and terror, is particularly

[1] 'Fingal', Book III, *Poems of Ossian*, p. 105.

his, as the episode of the stolen boat in Book I of *The Prelude* makes very clear. The fright the boy receives when he imagines the peak striding after him is no doubt some kind of moral lesson for his nocturnal escapade, but the whole power of the passage lies in how far it goes beyond such moral questions, in the boy's being haunted later by 'huge and mighty forms', sublime masses half-way between inorganic and organic which trouble his waking hours as well as his dreams. Mountains, traditionally sublime, are here given virtually another dimension.

A rocky steep uprose
Above the cavern of the willow tree,
And now, as suited one who proudly rowed
With his best skill, I fixed a steady view
Upon the top of that same craggy ridge,
The bound of the horizon, for behind
Was nothing but the stars and the grey sky.
She was an elfin pinnace; lustily
I dipped my oars into the silent lake,
And, as I rose upon the stroke, my boat
Went heaving through the water like a swan;
When, from behind that craggy steep till then
The bound of the horizon, a huge cliff,
As if with voluntary power instinct,
Upreared its head. I struck and struck again,
And growing still in stature the huge cliff
Rose up between me and the stars, and still,
With measured motion, like a living thing,
Strode after me. With trembling hands I turned,
And through the silent water stole my way
Back to the cavern of the willow tree;
There in her mooring-place I left my bark,—
And through the meadows homeward went, with grave
And serious thoughts; and after I had seen
That spectacle, for many days, my brain
Worked with a dim and undetermined sense
Of unknown modes of being; in my thoughts
There was a darkness, call it solitude
Or blank desertion. No familiar shapes
Of hourly objects, images of trees,
Of sea or sky, no colours of green fields;
But huge and mighty forms, that do not live
Like living men, moved slowly through my mind
By day, and were the trouble of my dreams.

When Keats spoke of Wordsworth's 'egotistical sublime' he was perhaps paying him a greater tribute than he intended, since an unembarrassed feeling for sublimity was an innate part of Wordsworth's character, and would have found some outlet whether stimulated by Lakeland landscape or not. The argument as to whether sublimity resides in manifestations of the natural world or in some quality of soul in the experiencer of these manifestations comes to a head in Wordsworth's awareness of it. When he tells how, in his youth, 'the midnight storm / Grew darker in the presence of my eye' (*The Prelude*, II. 392–3) we must believe him, yet no poet has done more to recommend to us a belief that the natural world has in it sublime powers, or powers pointing towards sublimity, and that this sublimity is important to us, much in the way Thomas Warton described, in its capacity to 'rouse and invigorate all the powers of imagination'. The soul, in Wordsworth's experience, keeps

> an obscure sense
> Of possible sublimity, to which
> With growing faculties she doth aspire.
> (II. 336–8)

This assertion of the 'beyondness' of the sublime, like Burke's mention of the idea of infinity, suggests that on a lower level of finding communicative images for poetry, the poet might be hard put to it to avoid abstraction, high-flown generalizing, or wrong assumption of common ground with the reader. Wordsworth, however, had a remarkable gift for taking the reader with him to the brink, and hopefully leaving him there. Not all readers will quite know what is happening to them, or what is being asked of them, but to any who are sympathetic, the experience is both vertiginous and exhilarating—sublime, in short. As his own imagination is baulked, but productively and illuminatingly baulked, by the thought of his having crossed the Alps without realizing it (*The Prelude*, Book VI) and been unwilling to admit that there was no further summit to scale, so the reader's understanding is jolted beyond any simple-minded idea that a mountain is climbed 'because it is there' into the far more audacious conception of climbing into a beckoning infinitude, into 'something evermore about to be'.

> Our destiny, our nature, and our home
> Is with infinitude, and only there;
> With hope it is, hope that can never die,
> Effort, and expectation, and desire,
> And something evermore about to be.
> (VI. 538–42)

Wordsworth, although he is pre-eminently a poet of nature, extends the sublime firmly into human life and action. Landscape sublimities abound in 'Tintern Abbey' and *The Prelude*, but it would equally be difficult to deny a human sublimity to solitary figures like the discharged soldier in *The Prelude* (Book IV). The image here is admonitory and awesome, yet at the same time perfectly realistic: a tall, gaunt, muttering figure leaning against a milestone on a lonely road in the moonlight: a soldier on his way home after service in the tropics. Wordsworth at first observes him in secret, and is rather frightened, but then he speaks to him and they walk on together. It is interesting that the word 'sublime', though qualified, is used here by the poet himself, aware of the potential of the incident.

> Towards the cottage without more delay
> We shaped our course; as it appeared to me,
> He travelled without pain, and I beheld
> With ill-suppressed astonishment his tall
> And ghastly figure moving at my side;
> Nor, while we journeyed thus, could I forbear
> To question him of what he had endured
> From hardship, battle, or the pestilence.
> He all the while was in demeanour calm,
> Concise in answer; solemn and sublime
> He might have seemed, but that in all he said
> There was a strange half-absence, and a tone
> Of weakness and indifference, as of one
> Remembering the importance of his theme
> But feeling it no longer.
>
> (IV. 464–78)

In real life he only 'seemed' sublime, but in the poem he has become sublime in Wordsworth's presentation of him. His strangeness, his desolation, his loneliness, his history affect the poet more deeply than the man could possibly imagine, and change a happy self-congratulatory mood into one of troubled thoughtfulness. So one does not need the expected grandeurs of Alpine peaks; a simple human encounter on a country road will suffice. It is perhaps in the same way that Shakespeare's *King Lear* shows its sublimity not only in the violent elements of nature and extremes of human feeling in the storm scenes, but also and even more supremely in the reconciliation-scene between Lear and Cordelia, when in answer to his comment that she, unlike her sisters, has some cause to hate him, she replies 'No cause, no cause' (IV, vii. 75). This, from Lear's tormented point of view, might be regarded as a sublime lie; on the part of Cordelia, it is the simple truth. The sense of awe which is the core of the sublime is here very clear, coming from a revelation of the extraordinary forgivingness and self-abnegation of Cordelia's nature, and it contrasts with the much less definable awe that lurks in Wordsworth's encounter with the soldier; Shakespeare's is more moving, Wordsworth's is more interesting. Awe at what happens to human beings, whether or not they are placed in awesome circumstances, is surely one of the directions the sublime can take, and once the excitement of the pre-Romantic and Romantic rediscovery of nature and its grandeur had passed its main first phase, while at the same time the novel was rapidly developing as a rival to poetry, it was possible for such a novelist as Dickens to obtain effects at times which have something of this 'human sublime'. The death of Jo the crossing-sweeper in *Bleak House* might be taken as an example. Jo has quite an important part in the plot of the book, but it is on his death that Dickens pulls out all the stops. It is an emotional scene, perhaps too emotional for our anti-sentimental age, but Dickens concludes it with a splendid distancing device which raises it at least somewhere near the sublime.

After a short relapse into sleep or stupor, he makes, of a sudden, a strong effort to get out of bed.

'Stay, Jo! What now?'

'It's time for me to go to that there berryin-ground, sir,' he returns, with a wild look.

'Lie down, and tell me. What burying-ground, Jo?'

'Where they lead him as wos wery good to me, wery good to me indeed, he wos. It's time fur me to go down to that there berryin-ground, sir, and ask to be put along with him. I wants to go there and be berried. He used fur to say to me, "I am as poor as you to-day, Jo," he ses. I wants to tell him that I am as poor as him now, and have come there to be laid along with him.'

'By-and-bye, Jo. By-and-bye.'

'Ah! P'raps they wouldn't do it if I wos to go myself. But will you promise to have me took there, sir, and laid along with him?'

'I will, indeed.'

'Thank'ee, sir. Thank'ee, sir. They'll have to get the key of the gate afore they can take me in, for it's allus locked. And there's a step there, as I used fur to clean with my broom.—It's turned wery dark, sir. Is there any light a-comin?'

'It is coming fast, Jo.'

Fast. The cart is shaken all to pieces, and the rugged road is very near its end.

'Jo, my poor fellow!'

'I hear you, sir, in the dark, but I'm a-gropin—a-gropin—let me catch hold of your hand.'

'Jo, can you say what I say?'

'I'll say anythink as you say, sir, fur I knows it's good.'

'OUR FATHER.'

'Our Father!—yes, that's wery good, sir.'

'WHICH ART IN HEAVEN.'

'Art in Heaven—is the light a-comin, sir?'

'It is close at hand. HALLOWED BE THY NAME!'

'Hallowed be—thy—'

The light is come upon the dark benighted way. Dead!

Dead, you Majesty. Dead, my lords and gentlemen. Dead, Right Reverends and Wrong Reverends of every order. Dead, men and women, born with Heavenly compassion in your hearts. And dying thus around us every day.

(Chap. XLVII)

The sudden switch from the exclamatory 'Dead!' to the level straight admonitory 'Dead, your Majesty', the dislocation from the fictional crossing-sweeper to the real Queen Victoria, is a touch of genius producing something of that Burkean astonishment we are warned to expect from the sublime.

The position of the novel, in respect of the sublime, is ambiguous. On the one hand, it would not be difficult to obtain general agreement that some novels, *Wuthering Heights*, *Moby Dick*, and *The Return of the Native* among them, are as sublime as anything in poetry. In these three books, grandeur of nature—wild moorland, wind and storm, wild seas—combines with extremes of human feeling to deliver the genuine elated *frisson* and the requisite enlargement and amazement of mind; certainly the imagination of both writer and reader is stimulated and shaken to an unusual degree. As Emily Brontë, Herman Melville, and Thomas Hardy were all in fact poets as well as novelists, it may be thought that they are special cases. The novel has origins in both romance and documentary, but if realism was the mainstream nineteeth century development in fiction, then that development was on the whole a powerful force working against the sublime. If George Eliot's *Middlemarch* is taken as an outstanding and central book of the period, it is clear that its heroine, Dorothea, is not to be allowed, in her life and environment, any of the sublimity George Eliot might have found in the St. Teresa she is compared with in the novel's Prelude: indeed, Dorothea at the end, having made one ardent but disastrous marriage and settled for a less than brilliant but contented second one, is left in our minds almost as a figure symbolic of the values of the anti-sublime—of the ordinary, the everyday, the domestic, the 'hidden life' and the 'unvisited tomb'. It is true that the associations of the word 'sublime' are so complex that it can be used even in a domestic context, as we are reminded by Robert Burns in his 'Epistle to Dr. Blacklock':

To make a happy fireside clime
    To weans and wife,
That's the true pathos and sublime
    Of human life.

Perhaps in this case it was Burns's own wife, Jean, who showed the sublime by looking after his illegitimate children as well as her own! I think, however, it can be taken as generally true that in so far as the novel became a popular and dominating form during the course of the nineteenth century, its concerns were not those of the sublime, and so sublimity was driven back into the arms of poetry, but a poetry less and less interested in that particular quality. It is only by straining the word 'sublime' considerably, and softening its contours, that one could find it in either Tennyson or Browning. There is some kind of desperate sublimity in Hopkins, but peripheral to the category as being so specialized, so idiosyncratic, so compressed. In Arnold's 'Sohrab and Rustum' there are some slightly suspect but still very fine touches of the sublime. But the most convincing approach to the sublime in Victorian poetry is surely James Thomson's long poem *The City of Dreadful Night* (1874), where vastness and obscurity, darkness and terror, power and astonishment, all discover a new lease of life. The sublime has now migrated from the heathery battlefields and tossing seas and blustery mountain-tops and settled in a large city. This, one feels, is as it should be, with the huge growth of cities, especially industrial cities, during the nineteenth century, and with the sense that a heightening, often an alienated heightening, of human experience was associated with them. The solitary wanderer through a remote and empty landscape, traditionally open to sublime encounters and visionary experiences, could readily give place to the wanderer in city streets who might know as much loneliness in the midst of hurrying crowds. Wordsworth was aware of this, as was Baudelaire, and later T. S. Eliot; but it was James Thomson's lot, for a variety of reasons, to express most powerfully the sublime potential of the new urban environment.

Thomson's city in the poem is not any actual city, though it is certainly based on London, and probably also uses his early memories of Glasgow. It is very large and very old, it has huge buildings, great bridges, squares, cathedrals, mansions, slums, endless streetlamps. Since the time is night, the streets are relatively empty, but because it is a metropolis there are plenty of shadowy nocturnal prowlers who are the denizens of the night city and the actors of the poem—the outcasts of daytime society, the tramps, the drunks, the drug addicts, the half-crazed, the lonely, the homeless, the sleepless (insomnia, after drink, was Thomson's own particular torment). The poem has a certain grandeur which comes from its relentlessness, from its over-all drive towards a pessimistic philosophy, but I would like to single out two particular images which seem to me useful examples of Thomas Warton's 'sublime and alarming' classification. The first of these is descriptive of sudden violent movement in the otherwise largely dead city, a little incident which is 'alarming' because unexplained, a part of the nightmare.

It is full strange to him who hears and feels,
  When wandering there in some deserted street,
The booming and the jar of ponderous wheels,
  The trampling clash of heavy ironshod feet:
Who in this Venice of the Black Sea rideth?
Who in this city of the stars abideth
  To buy or sell as those in daylight sweet?

The rolling thunder seems to fill the sky
  As it comes on; the horses snort and strain,
The harness jingles, as it passes by;
  The hugeness of an overburthened wain:
A man sits nodding on the shaft or trudges
Three parts asleep beside his fellow-drudges:
  And so it rolls into the night again.

What merchandise? whence, whither, and for whom?
Perchance it is a Fate-appointed hearse,
Bearing away to some mysterious tomb
  Or Limbo of the scornful universe
The joy, the peace, the life-hope, the abortions
Of all things good which should have been our portions,
  But have been strangled by that City's curse.

(IX)

The other image appears near the end of the poem, and is by contrast static. On a bleak northern ridge of the city there is a colossal bronze statue of a winged woman who is based on the figure of Melencolia in Dürer's well-known engraving. She is seated, and her wings are folded. Thomson makes her the presiding deity or patron saint of his night city—she is the embodiment of whatever it is that makes the night city dreadful. She possesses a strange mixture of lethargy and enormous latent power, and in her we can recognize, more strongly than in the first image of the thundering wagon, something that is both sublime and alarming.

Anear the centre of that northern crest
  Stands out a level upland bleak and bare,
From which the city east and south and west
  Sinks gently in long waves; and thronèd there
An Image sits, stupendous, superhuman,
The bronze colossus of a wingèd Woman,
  Upon a graded granite base foursquare.

Low-seated she leans forward massively,
  With cheek on clenched left hand, the forearm's might
Erect, its elbow on her rounded knee;
  Across a clasped book in her lap the right
Upholds a pair of compasses; she gazes
With full set eyes, but wandering in thick mazes
  Of sombre thought beholds no outward sight.

* * *

Titanic from her high throne in the north,
  That City's sombre Patroness and Queen,
In bronze sublimity she gazes forth
  Over her Capital of teen and threne,
Over the river with its isles and bridges,
The marsh and moorland, to the stern rock-ridges,
  Confronting them with a coëval mien.

The moving moon and stars from east to west
  Circle before her in the sea of air;
Shadows and gleams ride round her solemn rest.
  Her subjects often gaze up to her there:
The strong to drink new strength of iron endurance,
The weak new terrors; all, renewed assurance
  And confirmation of the old despair.

(XXI)

That was Thomson's city of the imagination, and its images linger in the imagination of readers. But it is worth quoting a fragment of prose the poet wrote about the real London he lived in; this was written in 1872, when he was in the midst of writing *The City of Dreadful Night.* 'The isolation of thought is sometimes almost appalling. Walking in the streets at night and sunk in musing, I come up to the surface and regard the moving people; and they seem to me distant and apparently unrelated as ships on the horizon traversing the ocean between unknown foreign ports; and there are moments when they seem incalculably and inconceivably remote, as stars and star systems in infinite space.'[1] This, although prose, is almost like the sketch of a poem. It is as if Thomson was searching for the images that would extend his observation of people's self-abstractedness in a crowd out into a world of the imagination, comparing them to ships on major oceans, then to stars, and finally to galaxies. The effect, perhaps because it is being pushed in the direction of the infinite and the sublime, is ambiguous: the mind is at the same time aware of the awful trap of human isolation and exhilarated by the spendour of the company in which the isolated move and have their being.

Thomson's 'stars and star systems' reminds us that by the later nineteenth century science was delivering a new sort of sublime, for any who wanted to take it up. The enormous stretches of time being revealed by geology and palaeontology, the concept of biological evolution, the new discoveries in astronomy, were all potential sources of sublimity, especially if one believed it was necessary to counteract grubby Zola and dreary Gissing with something more uplifting. And since the sublime may involve the alarming in any case, it would not matter too much whether one was optimistic or pessimistic about descents or ascents of man. Yet not much came of all this; poets remained, by and large, aloof from science. At least Edward FitzGerald had perceptively laid his finger on the problem, in a letter to Edward Cowell in 1847:

> Yet, as I often think, it is not the poetical imagination, but bare Science that every day more and more unrolls a greater Epic than the Iliad . . . I never take up a book of Geology or Astronomy but this strikes me . . . So that, as Lyell says, the Geologist looking at Niagara forgets even the roar of its waters in the contemplation of the awful processes of time that it suggests . . . [This vision of Time] is in itself more wonderful than all the conceptions of Dante and Milton.

The 'wonder of science' is in some ways a very Victorian idea, even if saying that it is more wonderful than Dante and Milton is highly idiosyncratic, considering the reverence paid then to these

[1] *Poems, Essays and Fragments*, 1892, p. 261.

two poets. One would agree with FitzGerald that a contemplation of Niagara might result in a fine poem if any means could be found of dealing with it. However, despite Tennyson's reference to evolutionary ideas in *In Memoriam*, which are impressive enough as far as they go, it is perhaps in prose rather than in poetry that we find really productive use being made of the 'new sublime' of the enlarged time-scale shown by science. In one novel already mentioned, Hardy's *The Return of the Native* (1878), the generally agreed sublimity of the background landscape of Egdon Heath (and it is actor more than background) is attained not only from traditional associations of bigness, darkness, deprivation, solitude, and wind and storm, but also from a careful imaginative rolling back of the heath layer by layer through medieval history to Roman roads to prehistoric Celtic burial-mound to the last Ice Age. The heath would be a formidable, alien presence even if we knew nothing of its history, but Hardy likes to use the new knowledge of prehistory to remind his readers (if they were unaware of such things) that 'even the trifling irregularities were not caused by pickaxe, plough, or spade, but remained as the very finger-touches of the last geological change' (Chap. 1).

So far, I have been discussing writers who were working within a literary tradition that included ideas about the sublime, and even if they did not avail themselves of these ideas they had not thrown them out, nor, if asked, would they have brushed them aside as completely irrelevant. James Thomson, for instance, uses the words 'sublime' and 'sublimity' in *The City of Dreadful Night* and clearly is not unaware of the high area he is attempting to work in. Thomas Hardy in *The Return of the Native* refers to the 'chastened sublimity of a moor, a sea, or a mountain' as being for his age more congenial than the 'orthodox beauty' (and we notice the Burkean opposition of sublime and beautiful) of spas and vineyards and southern gardens. But when we ask what has happened now to the idea of the sublime, how it has fared in the twentieth century, we find it much harder to receive any very intelligible reply. If any eager student was to look up the elegant and learned *Princeton Encyclopedia of Poetry and Poetics* in its most recent edition, all he would be told is that the sublime is 'not greatly in fashion today'. At this point my lecture might, no doubt, come to a stop. But I am nothing if not curious, and one of the things that attracted me to this subject was precisely the apparent reaction against the sublime in twentieth-century poetry. How thoroughgoing was this? Are there exceptions, and if so how did they arise? Does the idea survive in other, possibly disguised forms or formulations? Or is it, in any case, perennially available, as the *Princeton Encyclopedia* to its credit does suggest, with a last nod back towards Longinus and the concept of a 'great soul'?

Modern poetry set itself against the idea of a hierarchy of subjects or of feelings, and this being so, it would not be surprising if the sublime, like other very grand but sometimes rather hollow or pretentious things, had to take its chance with the rest, and might not survive if less-exalted material proved more resilient and more suited to the needs of the time. T. S. Eliot and William Carlos Williams have other qualities than sublimity—great qualities; sublimity they were not trying to obtain. But with others the situation is less clear-cut, and I would mention specifically Ezra Pound, Hugh MacDiarmid, and Wallace Stevens.

Ezra Pound's poem, or suite of poems, *Hugh Selwyn Mauberley* (1920), opens with the much-quoted and at least partly autobiographical 'Ode pour l'Election de son Sepulchre', which begins:

> For three years, out of key with his time,
> He strove to resuscitate the dead art
> Of poetry; to maintain 'the sublime'
> In the old sense. Wrong from the start—
>
> No, hardly, but seeing he had been born
> In a half savage country, out of date . . .

Mauberley is full of ironies, far from straightforward, but it is not in doubt that the speaker still sees 'the sublime' as a category, and one to which he bears an ambivalent relation. The self-correction between lines 4 and 5 leaves a door open, but a door to what? As a leader of the modern revolution in poetry, Pound might hardly be expected to want to maintain anything that belonged to a dead tradition, and the sublime, as we have seen, had become weakened and sporadic in English poetry since the time of the great Romantics. Nor would he, in any case, admire the visionary and obscure grandeurs of a concept of the sublime that went against all his passion for clarity of delineation. His 'sublime' seems to hark back rather to Greece, to Homer and Sappho, and to the sense that pervades *Mauberley* of the gulf between the exalted, exemplary arts and culture of ancient Greece and the 'tawdry cheapness' which he says 'shall outlast our days'. The sublime then reverts to its simplest (etymological) meaning of 'high, elevated', and Pound is not saying that he wants it given up, but as an American from 'a half savage country' he admits a certain bafflement as to how, if at all, the sublime in his simplified sense can be embodied.

Well, he did not embody it in *Mauberley*, or in his early poems in general, but *The Cantos*, unfinished though they are, do offer hints of sublimity as well as having satire, lyricism, historical documentary, and virulent propaganda. The sublimity comes through some of the vistas of time as they recede through history into legend and myth in a remarkable way that forces even the unsympathetic reader to raise his sights and, for a moment or two, to wonder. It also emerges when some of the central ideas are fused into a telling image, as in the startling first lines of Canto 95:

> Love, gone as lightning,
> enduring 5000 years.
> Shall the comet cease moving
> or the great stars be tied in one place!

In may be that since *The Cantos* is a modern re-tooling of the idea of an epic poem, some of the sublimity traditionally thought to adhere to epic writing has brushed off on Pound's poem, despite its many structural differences from previous epic. Its distinctive feature, of course, is that it willingly, and very much in a modern spirit, juxtaposes the sublime and the anti-sublime, as in the transition from the Confucian tranquillity of Canto 13 to the foul 'Hell' Cantos 14 and 15. Cinematic, anti-decorum effects like that are very much a part of their period, and Pound protests too much in *Mauberley* when he taunts the age for its 'kinema' and its pianola, and even more for its having allowed its Caliban to oust its Ariel—who more Caliban than Pound (yet Ariel too; he is himself pure 'kinema', a restless montage of opposites)?

One of Pound's admirers is the Scottish poet Hugh MacDiarmid. His poetry, and his interests, differ in many ways from those of Pound, but he shares with the poet of *The Cantos* a belief that the sense of awe is important. Many of MacDiarmid's poems are meditations on some object or theme or situation which he has chosen to allow himself a very free-ranging imaginative journey into high matters of human fate, whether biological, political, or social. He is an uneven but certainly a great poet who is not afraid to take the risk of being thoroughly serious, in a period which finds it easier to disguise serious concerns in irony or black comedy. But undoubtedly he has within himself many of those leanings towards vastness and power and solitude, and above all a sense of the importance of the non-human part of the universe (if human beings would only see it), which characteristically move towards the sublime. Even in a short four-line poem like 'The Skeleton of the Future', an evocation of Lenin's mausoleum in Moscow, there is an unmistakable flash of the sublime, particularly under the Burkean aspect of mingled delight and terror:

> Red granite and black diorite, with the blue
> Of the labradorite crystals gleaming like precious stones
> In the light reflected from the snow; and behind them
> The eternal lightning of Lenin's bones.

But almong his longer poems, I would instance 'On a Raised Beach', 'The Glass of Pure Water', and 'Stony Limits', to say nothing of the book-length *A Drunk Man Looks at the Thistle*, as examples of a modern sublime. *A Drunk Man* has a comic sublimity, where the fantasy world of the imagination is richly peopled with images and characters and ideas thrown together audaciously, yet bringing out, through the shock of contrast as well as through reiterated images, a steady pulse of serious ideas on Scotland, on evolution, on man in the universe. In this poem it is the presence of the infinite, of the undefined and indefinable ends of life, rather than such specific images as that of light or wave or crystal which we find Ezra Pound reaching for, that suggests sublimity. In other poems, too, this stretching out towards the infinite is a marked feature, a token of an almost religious spirituality sometimes thought very strange in one who claims to be a scientific materialist and Marxist. But in 'Stony Limits', which is an elegy on Charles Doughty (1843–1926), he praises Doughty for being somewhat similar—a great explorer of Arabia, a trained geologist, but also a man open to the mysterious admonitions of the loneliest landscapes of endless desert and infinite stars:

> I have seen Silence lift his head
> And Song, like his double, lift yours,
> And know while nearly all that seems living is dead,
> You were always consubstantial with all that endures.
> Would it were on Earth! Not since Ezekiel has that faw sun ringed
> A worthier head; red as Adam you stood
> In the desert, the horizon with vultures black-winged,

And sang and died in this still greater solitude
Where I sit by your skull whose emptiness is worth
The sum of almost all the full heads now on Earth
—By your roomy skull where most men might well spend
Longer than you did in Arabia, friend!

'On a Raised Beach' removes the prop of any figure or character and presents the speaker face to face with nature at its most formidable and uncommunicative: stones. Tantalized and almost maddened by the knowledge that if stones could speak, or if they retained in code and not merely in contour the story of what they have been through in millions of years, they could take us back long before man and all organic life, the poet nevertheless persists in his belief that (like birds) stones have gates which are always open; no more than birds can they shut them, and therefore the stone should also have its song, if it was possible to hear it.

Nothing has stirred
Since I lay down this morning an eternity ago
But one bird. The widest open door is the least liable to intrusion,
Ubiquitous as the sunlight, unfrequented as the sun.
The inward gates of a bird are always open.
It does not know how to shut them.
That is the secret of its song,
But whether any man's are ajar is doubtful.
I look at these stones and know little about them,
But I know their gates are open too,
Always open, far longer open, than any bird's can be,
That every one of them has had its gates wide open far longer
Than all birds put together, let alone humanity,
Though through them no man can see,
No man nor anything more recently born than themselves
And that is everything else on the Earth.
I too lying here have dismissed all else.
Bread from stones is my sole and desperate dearth,
From stones, which are to the Earth as to the sunlight
Is the naked sun which is for no man's sight.
I would scorn to cry to any easier audience
Or, having cried, to lack patience to await the response.
I am no more indifferent or ill-disposed to life than death is;
I would fain accept it all completely as the soil does;
Already I feel all that can perish perishing in me
As so much has perished and all will yet perish in these stones.
I must begin with these stones as the world began . . .

That poem was published when MacDiarmid was living on a remote Shetland island, very poor and very ill, in the 1930s.

It shows the sublime through a hard and awesome environment, like Hardy's Egdon Heath, or Emily Brontë's Yorkshire moors, or Wordsworth's Lake District, or the nocturnal deserts of James Thomson's London. Granted that particular kind of recurring context for the sublime, where can we fit in Wallace Stevens, who seems at first sight too gorgeous and too happy and too playful to join any such company?

Perhaps two adjoining poems from his volume *Idea of Order* (1935) will offer some pointers. 'The Idea of Order at Key West' presents a woman walking by the sea at dusk, and singing. The noise of the sea—its own song—is there in the background but is not what the listeners listen to. The poem suggests how the two very different voices may indeed interrelate:

> It may be that in all her phrases stirred
> The grinding water and the gasping wind;
> But it was she and not the sea we heard.

But out of her singing comes something else, something to put the theatrical sublimity of the scene—the 'meaningless plungings of water and the wind', the high horizons, the vast stagy distances—in its place. The human voice creates and imparts an order that in the process of solidifying, paradoxically abstracts, refines, redefines, shimmers in outlines of a new sublime, far removed from, yet no doubt making use of, the melodramatic 'mountainous atmospheres / Of sky and sea', sublime enough things in their own limited world. The poem concludes by stealing off into the sublime it has set up:

> Ramon Fernandez, tell me, if you know,
> Why, when the singing ended and we turned
> Toward the town, tell why the glassy lights,
> The lights in the fishing boats at anchor there,
> As the night descended, tilting in the air,
> Mastered the night and portioned out the sea,
> Fixing emblazoned zones and fiery poles,
> Arranging, deepening, enchanting night.
>
> Oh! Blessed rage for order, pale Ramon,
> The maker's rage to order words of the sea,
> Words of the fragrant portals, dimly-starred,
> And of ourselves and of our origins,
> In ghostlier demarcations, keener sounds.

Much of Stevens's poetry is concerned with the search for a supreme or perfect quality, a good, a reality of the highest kind, and it would not be surprising if ideas of the sublime were suggested by this search. But is it a different, a special kind of sublime? The poem which follows 'The Idea of Order at Key West' is called 'The American Sublime', and its title forces us to ask that question. Here is the poem:

How does one stand
To behold the sublime,
To confront the mockers,
The mickey mockers
And plated pairs?

When General Jackson
Posed for his statue
He knew how one feels.
Shall a man go barefoot
Blinking and blank?

But how does one feel?
One grows used to the weather,
The landscape and that;
And the sublime comes down
To the spirit itself,

The spirit and space,
The empty spirit
In vacant space.
What wine does one drink?
What bread does one eat?

Although this remarkable little poem does make one or two statements, it is mainly putting questions, and the questions could only come from one who believed in the importance of the sublime but who was puzzled, even baffled, as to how one could approach it, as an American living in the twentieth century. How does one stand, how does one feel? Money-conscious pragmatists and materialists are not in touch with it. But then even the great American landscapes, sublime in the old sense, Grand Canyons but not of the spirit, frontiers of a too naïve myth, are not helpful: one grows used to them. And as for 'wine and bread': ritual sacrifice, sacramental faith seem irrelevant to him, he finds no entry into the sublime through exalted traditions. All that is left is 'the spirit and space', both of them empty and blank, the one inhabiting the other and the sublime becoming the result or accompaniment of this. Perhaps the old 'terror' of the sublime lurks here, not in wind and wave, or in precipice and torrent, but in sheer blankness and vacancy. Looking from this poem back to 'The Idea of Order at Key West', we can believe that the 'ghostlier demarcations' of its last line, the quasi-invisible reclamations of the work of art, are beginning to form themselves towards vacancy, like melting crystals, and at their finest will draw us into the sublimity of the apparently uninhabited space, where there is nothing but art and the artist's figuring of the artist, which is not to say the artist himself.

The 'American sublime' is a protean concept, and it would apply to Norman Mailer as well as to Wallace Stevens. It might encompass Whitman and Ginsberg, Hart Crane and Thomas Wolfe. But its existence would not be denied: it is part of the nature and history of the place. The European sublime, on the other hand, has fallen on evil days. Who was more sublime than Rilke it might be asked? Yet Rilke, great poet though he was, may be said to have given the sublime a bad name. Certainly, to many poets writing from the Second World War onwards, the sublime would seem an insulting category; survival rather than heroics, irony rather than high meditation, the everyday rather than the beckoning gleam, have been in order. If one wants poetry diametrically opposed to the sublime, it is there—and very good poetry it is too—in the books of Zbigniew Herbert in Poland or Miroslav Holub in Czechoslovakia. The sense of living through a violent and cruel era, when it is best to preserve a wary stance and check ideals ceaselessly against reality, counteracts all the old attractions of the sublime. Here is a short poem by Holub which says much in meagre space. It might be described as a concrete poem, since it has five lines with five letters in each line—a perfect square. A perfect State would have a like sublime simplicity and symmetry; all people would fall into their place, and contribute to the regularity of the structure, and to its unshakability. The poem is called, however, 'Very Brief Thoughts on the Letter M':

A, b, c, d, e,
f, g, h, i, j,
k, l, n, o, p,
q, r, s, t, u,
v, w, x, y, z.

This does not mean that the sublime is not a permanently accessible idea. The images of the sublime, drawn from whatever is most powerful or startling in nature or from the greatest human artefacts, and even in the absence of such images, the delineation of great energy and astonishment in emotional or imaginative human situations, go, as Longinus said, with certain great qualities in the mind itself, and are therefore always liable to return. Perhaps the sublime is being reborn in science fiction, and the last refuge of the sublime is in the stars. The popularity of this genre, in fact, probably indicates that it is fulfilling a need not otherwise supplied. No doubt poets have to do what they have to do, but it would be surprising if sooner or later some of them did not find ways of reintroducing a note of acceptable grandeur.

THE LOST BEGINNING OF MENANDER, *MISOUMENOS*

By E. G. TURNER

Fellow of the Academy

IN October 1977 a particularly dirty scrap of papyrus from the Oxyrhynchus collection (inv. 7 1B.5/C(c)) was found to contain parts of verses which occur in the, as yet, unpublished fragments of another Oxyrhynchus papyrus (inv. 47 5B.46/D1 (a)+(2)) already identified as holding the opening verses of one of Menander's best comedies, the *Misoumenos*. The new text, though itself deplorably damaged, acted as skeleton on which could be mounted the *disiecta membra* of the one already identified. In the upshot about one hundred consecutive verses from the opening of this play have proved amenable to reconstruction. It has seemed desirable to make this interesting discovery public with the least possible delay, and without waiting for a solution to all the textual problems involved.

What is published here is the bare minimum for a scholarly understanding: diplomatic transcripts and critical apparatus, reconstructed edition together with a selection of possible supplements, and an English translation. I offer no literary appreciation of the play, no exegesis of the text, no reasoned explanation for the supplements adopted, and, alas, no photographs. These essential companions to interpretation have already been put together by me. Text, commentary, and plates will appear in a forthcoming volume of the *Oxyrhynchus Papyri*, a general appreciation elsewhere. For permission to publish this advance text thanks are due to the Egypt Exploration Society.

It will be convenient to continue the system of papyrus notation devised by Professor F. H. Sandbach for his Oxford Classical Text of Menander. He had reached the figure of O18, so I shall assign O19 to papyrus 5B.46 D(2) and O20 to 7 1B.5/C(c). I have also followed Professor Sandbach's excellent practice of prefixing an A to the line numbers to avoid disturbing existing numeration. O19 was identified by Dr. John Rea in 1971, and its opening eighteen consecutive verses were published by me as an appendix to my *The Papyrologist at Work* (*G.R.B.S.*, supplement 6, 1972). Attached to this first column of writing were six consecutive more or less complete lines from the head of a second column. Completely detached from it were six other fragments (one largish) and a number of scraps; they could not be positioned in relation to the first fragment by any objective criterion. O20, which takes up at the end of v. 12 of O19, includes at the foot of its first column (which is not complete at that point) parts of the first three verses which begin column ii in O19. The mutilated second column of O20 has beginnings of verses, some of which are more or less complete in O19. All except one of the fragments of O19 (the one here labelled fr. C) have now fallen into place inside a framework of two columns. O19 turns out to have been a manuscript having 50 lines to the column. Since the foot of col. ii survives (though much damaged), the text can be arranged with some confidence as far as v. 100. As already stated, of O19 only fr. C is unplaced. If it is not to be located fairly high up in the second column of O19, it must be assigned to a location in a subsequent column of which it will then be the only representative.

O19 is written on the back of a roll, the front of which had already been used for a documentary register recording payments in the month of Thoth in an unnamed year made at a place in the Oxyrhynchite nome for a local tax (amounts are constant, either 1 drachma 2 obols or 2 dr. 4 ob.). Both this register and the Menander on the back of it should be assigned to the third century after Christ. The scribe of the Menander text wrote a medium-sized fast hand of no calligraphic pretensions in a black to brown ink. Letters are formed in several different ways, are of differing sizes, and relative stance. Normally *scriptio plena* is used (the occasional exception being marked by an apostrophe). The scribe rarely inserts punctuation (only two high stops). He does not employ the dicolon to show change of speaker, contenting himself with initial paragraphus and sometimes also a space in the line. There is an occasional marginal *nota personae*, and at least one interlinear example. The copying is inaccurate, sometimes grossly so, as is proved by O20. Where the edition rests only on the evidence of O19, conjecture may be allowed a freer hand than is normally permissible.

O20, on the contrary, also in roll form, is a careful piece of copying, though not impeccable (there is a certain metrical error at A46, an almost certain error at A23; a necessary dicolon is absent from A36, paragraphi at 83–4, 91, 93 are aberrant). The Menander is written on the front of the roll and the writing goes with the fibres. It is in a single piece and, somewhat unusually, consists of two papyrus sheets pasted to each other. The explanation for this is probably that this section, being at the beginning of the roll and being subject to much use, was strengthened in antiquity. The sheet pasted on the back is not part of the normal *protokollon*, since its fibres also ran horizontally, and carried writing. This writing, along the fibres, about 20 lines in two hands from an official property register, was probably already there when the sheet was pasted on as a strengthener. Both this hand and the Menander hand should be assigned to the third century after Christ. The copyist of the Menander wrote a small, somewhat flattened, quick, slovenly hand of no more beauty than O19: similarly varying letter forms, spacings, letter stances. For punctuation he occasionally uses a high stop; and normally he elides vowels in hiatus (occasionally marking the elision by an apostrophe; *scriptio plena* once at A85). Change of speaker is shown by dicolon and paragraphus; and when the left margin survives, it occasionally carries a *nota personae*. He corrected his text *currente calamo*. An editor will not depart from his version lightly. Each column of text contained about 55 lines. In col. i about 8–10 letters are lost from the beginnings of verses.

After these texts had been worked on it was realized that another fragmentary third-century papyrus manuscript (O21; inv. 1B5 layer 5), put together from three scraps by Dr. W. E. H. Cockle, also contained portions of verses A30–43. At one point (A32) it inverts the order of the first metra in the verse and supplies a certain restoration, at another (A41) it offers welcome confirmation of change of speaker. No transcript or discussion of it is offered here. It will be discussed in full in the *Oxyrhynchus Papyri*. Mention may be made in passing of a fourth papyrus fragment, this time to be dated to the late first or early second century after Christ, of which nothing survives except the title *Misoumenos of Menander*.

These fragments have gained greatly from study at a seminar held in the Institute of Classical Studies of the University of London in autumn 1977. I have tried to record the authors of suggestions, whether adopted here in the text or recorded for further discussion, attributing them by initials. I am particularly grateful to Dr. Colin Austin (C.A.) and to Dr. W. E. H. Cockle (W.E.H.C.)—who performed the difficult and delicate task of cleaning the papyri—Mr. Alan Griffiths (A.H.G.), Professors E. W. Handley (E.W.H.), F. H. Sandbach (F.H.S.), and M. L. West (M.L.W.). Professor Handley has been constantly available for questioning and advice, and has reread the originals. Dr. Austin and Professor West have also both read the originals. All unattributed supplements are my own. So are all the errors.

I have used the ordinary papyrological conventions. But I should add that where square brackets are used together without intervening dot, thus [], the intention is to show a tear, hole, or stripped surface where no writing need have been lost.

ΜΕΝΑΝΔΡΟΥ

ΜΙϹΟΥΜΕΝΟϹ

O19 col. i

ωνυξ ϲυγαρδηπλειϲτ̣οναφ[. . .]ειτηϲμεροϲ
μετεχειϲθεων·ενϲο̣ιτ̣επ̣[ερ]ι̣το̣υ̣τωνλογοι
πλειϲτοιλεγονταιφρο̣ντιδε̣[. . . .]ρωτ[.]κ̣αι
αρααλλονανθρωπω̣ν̣[. . . . .]θ̣λιωτερον
A5 εορακαϲ αραερωντ̣α̣[. . .]π̣οτμω[.]ε̣ρον
προϲταιϲεμαυτουν[.]νθυραιϲεϲτηκ̣α̣ε̣γω
εντωϲτενωπωπεριπατωντεα[.]ω̣κ̣ατω̣
αμφοτεραϲμεχ̣ρ̣. . . . . .ϲ̣ουϲηϲϲουχε̣δ̣ο̣ν̣
εξωκαθευδειντηντεερωμενηνεχει
A10 παρεμοιγα[.]εϲτινενδονεξεϲτιντεμοι
καιβουλομ[.]ι̣τουτοωϲανεμ̣μανεϲτατα
ερω[. . .].· ουτωωδευπαιθριωδεμοι
χειμ[. . . . . .]εϲτιναιρετ̣.τερον
εϲτη[. . . . . .]ρ̣εμο̣ντ̣ι̣καικ̣αλουντιϲοι

A15 Γεταϲ τ̣οδ[. . . . . .]ενονο̣υ̣δε̣[. . . . .].τ̣ω̣θεω̣[
νυ.[. . .].ητεονεϲτ̣[. . . . .]δε̣ϲ̣π̣οτηϲ
ω̣.[ ]π̣ερθε.ο̣υϲμεϲο[ ]. . .
τοϲ. .τ̣.[.]πολ̣.[

. . . . .

O20 col. i

A12 Traces
]ν̣τ̣οϲε[. . . .]αιρετωτερον[
]τ̣ρεμοντι̣[.]αιλαλουντιϲο̣[ι
A15]ενονουδεκυνιματο[
]ο̣νεϲτιν. δεμοϲ̣δεϲπο̣[
]υϲμεϲ̣ο̣υ̣π̣ε̣ριπατειφιλο. .[
]ε̣ι̣[ ].ουδρυϊνοϲ[.]. . . . .ε̣π[
]ι̣α̣τ̣ρ̣ι̣βων.᾿ εγ̣κ̣α̣. . .πεϲ[

P.I.F.A.O. (from the photograph)

A15]ενονουδ̣ε̣κ̣υ̣[ ]ατουϲθ[
]νεϲτιν·.[
]υ̣[.]μ̣[

. . . . .

A15 O20 end stripped   A17 O19 papyrus is warped   part of cross bar of π visible before the break   after θε, tip of descender of ρ   O20 end, ϲο[acceptable   A18 O19 πο followed by λ, δ, even μ   O20 ι of ει represented by low ink of ligatured descender, space and trace rather wide for one letter, μ less unsatisfactory than δ, no apostrophe   after ινοϲ rubbed, 1 vertical, 2 low curve on line, high tip of ascender curving to right, 3 cap with horizontal below, ε or ϲ, 4 clear loop of α, 5 low vertical, then indeterminate, 6 ε or υ ligatured to π ([ο]υχ εαν επ[compatible)   A19 γ̣᾿   after κα, 2 letters, then ε, α, ϲ (not εγκατεπ[εϲ- or εγ καλω)

(Thrasonides) ὦ Νύξ – cὺ γὰρ δὴ πλεῖcτον Ἀφροδίτηc μέροc
μετέχειc θεῶν, ἐν cοί τε περὶ τούτων λόγοι
πλεῖcτοι λέγονται φροντίδεc τ' ἐρωτικαί –
ἆρ' ἄλλον ἀνθρώπων τιν' ἀθλιώτερον
ἑόρακαc; ἆρ' ἐρῶντα δυcποτμώτερον;
πρὸc ταῖc ἐμαυτοῦ νῦν θύραιc ἕcτηκ' ἐγώ,
ἐν τῷ cτενωπῷ περιπατῶ τ' ἄνω κάτω
†αμφοτεραc μέχρι νῦν μεcούcηc cου cχεδόν,
ἐξὸν καθεύδειν, τὴν ἐρωμένην ἔχων.
παρ' ἐμοὶ γάρ ἐcτιν ἔνδον ἔξεcτίν τέ μοι
καὶ βούλομαι τοῦθ' ὡc ἂν ἐμμανέcτατα
ἐρῶν τιc, οὐ ποῶ δ'· ὑπαιθρίωι δέ μοι
χειμ[ῶνοc ὄ]ṿτοc ἐcτὶν αἱρετώτερον
ἑcτη[κέναι] ṭρέμοντι και λαλοῦντί cοι.

Γέτας τὸ δ[ὴ λεγόμ]ενον οὐδὲ κυνί, μὰ τοὺc θεούc,
νῦṿ [ἐξι]ṭητόν ἐcτιν. ὁ δ' ἐμὸc δεcπότηc
ὥc̣π̣ερ θέρουc μέcου περιπατεῖ φιλοcọ[φῶν
τοcọῦτ'· [ἀ]πολ̣ε̣ῖ̣ μ̣'· οὐ δρύϊνοc; [.]..ε̣α̣..π[
δ]ịαṭρ̣ịβων γ̣'εγκα...πεc[

Sandbach's apparatus is not repeated here. A3 πλεῖcτοι already conjectured by Kraus A4 E.W.H. A8 ἀφ' ἑcπέραc cj. C.A., ἀμφότερ' ἀεὶ cj. M.L.W. A9 ἔχων (omisso τε) E.W.H., cf. Eustath. 236.31, Schol. Ar. *Ach.* 1164b (p. 144 Wilson) *et al.* =com. adesp. 282 K A14 ἑcτη[κέναι J. R. Rea A15–16 τὸ δ[ὴ λεγόμ]ενον C.A., E.G.T. ἐξιτητόν, M.L.W. comparing Alciphron 3.30.1 οὐδὲ ⟨κυ⟩νὶ (cj. M.L.W.) ἐξιτητόν A17 θέρουc cf. χειμ[ῶνοc A13 φιλοcο[φῶν E.W.H., cf. Theognetus fr. 1 K A18 ἀπολεῖ μ' cf. Ar. *Thesmoph.* 2, 1073, Men. fr. 144 Kö δρύινοc, cf. Philo, *de fuga et inventione* 39, 42 alibi (F.H.S.) and cf. πρίνινοc, πρινώδηc etc.

(Thrasonides) O Night—I address you since among the gods you have the largest portion of Aphrodite's joys, and in your timespan fall most words of love and lovers' cares—have you ever seen any man more wretched than me? Any more star-crossed lover? I am standing now at my very own front door, and in the alley walking backwards and forwards . . . now when you are at midnight almost, when I could be fast asleep and holding my beloved in my arms. She is indoors in my house and I could do it and I want it like the maddest of lovers, but I don't do it. I'd rather choose to stand out of doors, for all the winter storm and my chattering teeth, talking to you.

(Getas) As the saying goes, by the gods it's not fit even for a dog to go out at the moment. But, as though it were midsummer, my master is walking about philosophizing (?) and going on so. It will be the death of me. Not heart of oak? . . . discourses (?), . . . the door.

O20

A20]. . ε̣ι̣τ̣η̣ν . [ ]. . ανωδυστυ̣χ̣η̣ς
`.'
[τιουκαθευ]δ̣ειc·cυμ'α [π]οκναιειcπερι̣πατων
]υ̣δ̣ειc·περ [.]μενε̣ι̣μ̣'εγ̣ρ̣η [.]ορωc //
]υδι̣αυτοc̣ . [.]εληλυθαc *vac.*
]με̣ν [.]cποτ̣ [ ]ρακελευcθ̣ε̣ [ ]c̣υποτ̣ε
A25]ητοτοιουτο [ ]αποcαυτουπ̣ [. .]ων
]κ̣ελευονοι̣ [ ]αθευ̣δ̣ [.]ντεc: [ ]ετα [
]ε̣οικεκηδ [.]μωνεμοc *vac.*
[ειcελθεκ]α̣ινυνωμ [α]καρι [ ]εν̣π̣α̣ [. .]ι̣γ̣αρ̣
]α̣ρχο̣c̣τ̣ιc: [ ]υτωδεινωc . [
A30]. ταμ̣εγιcτ̣ [ ]λ̣ουδεπω *vac.*
]ρ̣ανc'εχ̣θε̣c̣ [.]α̣ρειcτηνοικ [.]αν
]τηνημετε [. .]νcυδιαχρο [. .]υ:
]πε̣δου̣γαρ [. .]. πη̣ρ̣α̣καταλ [ ]π̣ων
].ωcε̣ . ψυ [.]. [.]. δ̣ . . αττομ . .
A35]α̣ραπομπη̣ [. . .]ν̣λαφυρωνε̣ [. .]ατοc
`ρ'
]υ̣πουνc'ε . [ ]. υβιζομαι:
A37]υποτηcαιχ̣ [. .]λ̣ω̣τουπριαμ̣ε̣νοc

O19 fr. B

A33]. [
]ωcε̣υ̣ψυχ̣ο̣c̣ [ ]. [
A35]αραπομπηcτ̣ [
`θρ'
]. υπουνc . ε̣ . . . . [
A37 [υποτηcαιχμαλωτουπ [

A20 . [high downward facing curve,] . . high dot, tiny high loop, θυραν (E.W.H.) acceptable A20–1 Men. frr. 137+341 K = 124 Kö+*Misoum.* fr. 3 S recognized by W.E.H.C. A21 interlinear ink above cυμ' A23 δια, ι ligatured by high horizontal to α τοc . [, compatible with ε A28 *Misoum.* fr. 4 S recognized by W.E.H.C. a gap between καρι and ε A29 . [, high horizontal, e.g. τ A30–43 partly covered by P. Oxy. ined. Tin box 1B5 layer 5 = O21 (not published here) A33 O19 recommences O20]. πηρα̣ first letter of group π, not ν, and preceding trace suits only α Traces of ink after πων belong to col. ii At verse end O21 app. diverges from O19, O20 A34 O20]c̣, π less likely Before δ̣, vertical (ν, η?), then διαταττομαι acceptable A36 O20 interlinear ρ added by 1st hand no dicolon, but O19 has interlinear θρ

Hallo there! Poor man, why aren't you sleeping? You will wear me down walking up and down. [Or are you walking in your] sleep? Wait for me—if you are awake [and can see me].

[(Thras.) Getas,] have you come out of the house in person [to see what is going on?]—I never [instructed you]—or are you acting so strangely of your own accord?

]. . ε̣ι̣ τὴν θ̣[ύ]ρ̣αν. ὦ δυςτυχής,
τί οὐ καθεύ]δειϲ; cὺ μ' ἀποκναίειϲ περιπατῶν.
καθε]ύδειϲ· περ[ί]μεν' εἶ μ' ἐγρη[γ]ορὼϲ
(Thras.)]υ δ' αὐτὸϲ ἐ̣[ξ]ελήλυθαϲ
]μ̣ε̣ν̣[.]ϲ· πότ̣[ε]ρα κελευϲθε[ὶ]ϲ—⟨ο⟩ὔποτε
] ἢ τὸ τοιοῦτο[ν] ἀπὸ ϲαυτοῦ π[οι]ῶν;
(Get.) ἐ]κ̣έλευον οἱ [κ]αθεύδ[ο]ντεϲ. (Thras.) [Γ]έτα,
παρῆϲθαϲ, ὡϲ] ἔοικε, κηδ[ε]μὼν ἐμόϲ.
(Get.) εἴϲελθε κἂν νῦν, ὦ μακάρι'· (Thras.) ἐν πα̣[ντ]ὶ γὰρ
]α̣ρχόϲ τιϲ· (Get.) [ϲ]ύ τ' ὦ δεινῶϲ τ̣[
]. τὰ μέγιϲτ['—· (Get.) ἀλ]λ' οὐδέ πω
]ραν ϲ'· ἐχθὲϲ [γ]ὰρ εἰϲ τὴν οἰκ[ί]αν
ἐλήλυθαϲ τὴν ἡμετέ[ρα]ν ϲὺ διὰ χρό[νο]υ.
(Thras.) τοῦ ϲτρατο]πέδου γὰρ [ὡϲ] ἀ̣πῆρα καταλιπὼν
]ϲ̣ωϲ εὔψυχο̣ϲ̣ [.]., δ̣ι̣α̣τ̣άττομαι
ἐπὶ τῆϲ π]αραπομπῆϲ τ[ῶ]ν λαφύρων ἔ̣[ϲχ]ατοϲ
Μυϲῶν· (Get.) τί τὸ λ]υποῦν ϲ' ⟨ἐϲτ'⟩; (Thras.) ἐλεῖν' ὑβρίζομαι.
(Get.) ὑπὸ τίνοϲ; (Thras.)] ὑπὸ τῆϲ αἰχμαλώτου· πριάμενοϲ

A22 [ἢ καὶ καθε]ύδειϲ F.H.S. A23 [ὁρᾷϲ: Γέτα] F.H.S. ϲὺ δ' E.W.H. ἐ̣[ξ]ελήλυθαϲ C.A. A24 e.g. [ἐποψό]μεν[ο]ϲ E.W.H., alii alia πότ[ε]ρα F.H.S. κελευϲθε[ὶ]ϲ-⟨ο⟩ὔποτε C.A. A25 [ὑπ' ἐμοῦ γάρ–] F.H.S. A26 [μὰ Δί' ἀλλ'] E.W.H. A27 [παρῆϲθαϲ, F.H.S. ὡϲ] ἔοικε, κηδεμὼν read by W.E.H.C. A28 Σ Dem. κἂν νῦν ἐ̣ν̣ π̣α̣[ντ]ὶ γὰρ E.W.H. A29 e.g. [ϲὺ δὴ πολέμ]αρχόϲ τιϲ;, ὕπ]αρχόϲ, E.W.H., [ἔγωγ' ἂν]αρχόϲ C.A. End τ̣[ρέμων—? A30 e.g. [(Thras.) ἔα με ϲημῆνα]ι̣— A31 e.g. [ϲχολὴ παρο]ρᾶν ϲ' A32, ἐλήλυθαϲ O21 A33 ϲτρατο]πέδου recognized by W.E.H.C. [ὡϲ] ἀ̣πῆρα E.W.H. A34 e.g. [Κύπρον μέ]ϲωϲ εὔψυχοϲ [ἦ]ν̣· or [ἐφάνην ἴ]ϲωϲ . . . [ὤ]ν̣ A35 ἔ[ϲχ]ατοϲ [Μυϲῶν, cf. frs. 50, 175 Kö; A.H.G. 'cf. Paroemiogr. Gr. II 47 ἐπὶ τῶν ⟨ἐπὶ⟩ δυϲχερῆ ἐπιταττομένων' A36 τί τὸ λ]υποῦν ϲ' C.A., M.L.W.

[(Getas) I don't imagine] I had my orders from those who are asleep.
(Thras.) Getas, it looks as though you had come here to look after me.
(Getas) Come in now, if ever, dear man.
(Thras.) In everything [you are a] true [colonel].
(Getas) Your teeth are chattering—
[(Thras.) Allow me to take] supreme [command].
(Getas) I haven't had [time to be insubordinate] yet. It was only yesterday that you came back to our home after a long absence.
(Thras.) When I sailed from headquarters and left [Cyprus? I was more or less] stout-hearted. My posting is to take charge as escort of the spoils, I'm a mere dog's body.
(Getas) What is upsetting you?
Thras. I'm being insulted in a way that calls for sympathy.
(Getas) By whom?

O19 fr. B

A38]. . . ε̣ι̣ϲ̣. ελ[ ]ευθερ. . [. . . . .]. [
]. ναπο. . . [ ]ξαϲ. θε. . π̣αιναϲχρυ[
A40]. . . . [ ]. . ϲ·ειτατι[
]α̣ι̣ϲχυνομ̣[
]. . . . ωϲ. . α̣ϲ̣ο̣ν̣[
]ν̣. . . . [
]α̣νθρωπινον
A45]τιν̣[ ]ουδ̣[ ]. . [

. . . . . .

O19 fr. A col. ii

A51 ϋονταπολλωνυκτοϲαϲτ. . π̣αϲβρονταϲ[
εχωνδεαυτηνκατακειμαι ειτατι

———

κεκραγαπαιδιϲκηβιδιϲαιγαρφημϊδει[
ηδημεπροϲτονδεινα ειπαϲονομα̣τ̣ι̣

O20

A38]ρ̣ι̣θειϲελευ[. . .]. α. τηϲοικιαϲ
]. ναποδειξα[.]θεραπ̣α̣ιναϲχρυϲ̣ια
A40]υϲ γυναικανομ[.]ϲαϲ: ειτατι̣
]. ι̣ζει: καιλεγειναιϲχυνομαι
]α̣ιναν: αλλ’εμοιϲ’ομωϲφρα[ϲο]ν:·
]μεμειϲοϲ: ωμ̣[.]γ̣νητιϲ. . [
]α̣γαρυπονο̣ειϲ[ ]ηνθρωπιν. [
A45]ντ’εινα. . οδεϲ̣τιν:ουδε[ ]κ̣[.]. ια
]. . . [.]. αν. [.]. [ ]. αιϲφοδρ[
]. . [ ]ϲ̣τειναιγα̣[
]πειρ. . . [
]. [.]. . . . [
A50]. [.]. . . [
]ηϲαϲτρα[
]ατακειμ[
]διϲαι. . [
A54]. [

. . . . . .

A41 O20]., trace of loop A43 O20 νητιϲ, then vertical, compatible with η, not υ A44 O20 before νθρ, vertical, part of cross-bar and 2nd hasta of η A45 O20 trace of horizontal cross-bar before οδε A46 O20 below τ of A45 high ink as of cap of ε after αν, left facing curve A47]ϲτ: ϲ, high and low trace, hardly κ A48 πειρω̣μ̣ A49 tops]. [.]. π̣α̣ϲ. [? A50 O20 nothing recognizable. See commentary. A54 O19 δεινα, α has long tail, indicating a stop

πε]ριθεὶϲ ἐλευθερίαν, τῆϲ οἰκίαϲ
δέϲποιν]ạν ἀποδείξαϲ, θεραπαίναϲ, χρυϲία,
ἱμάτια δο]ύϲ, γυναῖκα νομίϲαϲ. Get. εἶτα τί;
πῶϲ οὖν ὑβ]ρ̣ίζει; Thras. καὶ λέγειν αἰϲχύνομαι
]αιναν· Get. ἀλλ' ἐμοὶ ϲ'· ὅμωϲ φράϲον.
(Thras.) μιϲεῖ . . . .] με μῖϲοϲ. Get. ὦ Μ[α]γνῆτιϲ. .
]α γὰρ ὑπονοεῖϲ· ἢ 'νθρώπινο̣ν̣
]ν τ' εἶνα̣ι τ̣όδ': οὐδὲ κ̣[υ]ρία
(Thras.) ⌊τηρῶ τὸν Δία⌋
ὕοντα πολλῷ νυκτόϲ [οὔϲ]ηϲ, ἀϲτρα̣πάϲ,
βροντάϲ, ἔχων αὐτὴν δὲ κατάκειμ'. (Getas) εἶτα τί;

(Thras.) κέκραγα "παιδίϲκη, βαδίϲαι γάρ", φημί, "δεῖ[
ἤδη με πρὸϲ τὸν δεῖνά ⟨μ'⟩". "εἶπαϲ ὄνομα τί;" —

A38 πε]ριθείϲ E.W.H. A39–40 χρυϲία|[ἱμάτια] cf. Men. *Sam.* 382S, fr. 951 Kö i 2; [ἱμάτια] C.A., F.H.S. (parallels F.H.S. *Sam.* l.c.) A40–1 or τί|[παθοῦϲ' ὑβ]ρίζει, E.W.H. A42 ? θεράπ]αιναν or (E.W.H.) λέ]αιναν ἀλλ' ἔμοιγ' ὅμωϲ cj. M.L.W. (ἀλλ' . . . ὅμωϲ Men. *Aspis* 317) A43 cf. Men. *Epitrep.* 433 S θεῖον δὲ μιϲεῖ μῖϲοϲ [νέον] C.A., i.e. as at Eur. *Hec.* 217, where Schol. ἤτοι καινὸν ἢ δεινόν, cf. Men. fr. 774 Kö? end ἦν̣? Μαγνῆτιϲ (λίθοϲ), cf. Eur. fr. 567 N², Eubulus fr. 77K, ('Ηρακλεία), Plato *Ion* 533D, etc. A44 ?[ληρεῖϲ M.L.W., attributed to Thrasonides then (E.G.T.) ἄτοπ]α A45 e.g. [δοκεῖ καλό]ν τ' εἶναι τόδ': οὐδὲ κ̣[υ]ρ̣ία, cf. Men. *Pk.* 497S ἑαυτῆϲ ἐϲτ' ἐκείνη κυρία A46 ?[αὕτη γ' ἑαυτῆϲ] A50–1 τηρῶ τὸν Δία ὕοντα πολλῷ, Porson apud Dobree's *Adversaria* IV 291 = fr. 721 Kö, identified and placed here by W.E.H.C. οὔϲηϲ, E.W.H., who also placed βροντάϲ in A52, and cites [Dem.] lix (Neaera) 103 interpretation of this passage adopted in the translation owes much to E.W.H. and A. Bulloch κατάκειμ' 'at bed or board' E.W.H. A53 κέκραγα Thrasonides calls for his cloak, etc. βαδίϲαι cf. Men. *Epitr.* 752–3S A54 δεῖνά ⟨μ'⟩, εἶπαϲ . . . τί E.W.H. δεῖν' ⟨ἐπ⟩είπαϲ . . . τι, M.L.W., C.A.

(Thras.) By the girl prisoner. I purchased her, I gave her her freedom, I treated her as mistress of the house, I presented her with maids, gold ornaments, frocks, I treated her as my wife.

(Getas) Then what? How are you being insulted?

(Thras.) I am ashamed even to talk about it . . . [I've caught a Tartar?].

(Getas) So are you to me! But out with it.

(Thras.) She has conceived an extraordinary hatred of me.

(Getas) Oh, she's the magnetic stone!

(Thras.) [Nonsense! an absurd] notion. This conduct is truly human and . . .

(Getas?) Even if she were [legally her own mistress] she wouldn't . . .

(Thras.) [My idea was that] I wait for the moment when the heavens open at night, and for lightning and thunderclaps, and there I am at her side, in possession.

(Getas) Then what?

(Thras.) I call out 'maid' and 'I've got to go out at once' I say 'to see a man'. 'What did you say his name was?'—that's what

O19 fr. A col. ii

A55 πασαν . . νηδητ̣ [.] . [ ] . ιποιτουδ̣ι . . [
ϋοντοσωταλαν [ ] . πovτινα [
σκ . π̣ . [ ]α̣στα . [
] . ηδ̣ [.
. [
A60 [
[
[
[
. . . [
A65 του [
ε . . [
ο . . [
A68 εκ̣ . [
. . . . . .

O19 fr. B col. ii

A85 . . . . [. .]ος̣ε̣χ̣ω̣φι . [
πα̣ρ̣ρ̣ωμενωδ . . . [
φι̣ . . νικιαν . ονο [.]μ̣α̣ν̣ι̣ [
τι̣ω̣κακοδα̣ι̣μον[]αλλεγ̣ω̣γ̣ε̣α̣ν̣φι̣ [
A89 κ . η̣ [.]ε̣ι̣σμο̣νονθυσαιμιπασιτοισθε̣ [.] . [

O20 col. ii

A78 φησωνμο̣ [
οτοιχοσου . [
A80 ερεισεαυτ [
ουκεικοτ [
Γετ ωταντατπ̣ [
τ̣ρ̣ . π . ν̣τ̣ε̣ . [
υπ̣ερ . ντρ . [
A85 α . τ̣η̣εστ [
παρορωμ [
φιλ [. .]ικιαν̣ [
τι [.]κ̣ακ [
A89 κλ [

A55 after πασαν, γ̣ likely; stroke following reaches vertically above the line A57 after σκ, ε̣? Not ω, η . [, ? τ A58 marginal *nota personae*, [Γε]τ ? A59 δ[? A79 . [, τ̣ A83 τρο̣πο̣ ? A83, 84 No paragraphus A84 π after υ anomalous, high horizontal of π continues to right to form cap of ε after ρ, curved foot, ε? A85 O20 after α, top of right hand upper fork of υ, possible bar of τ O19 α̣υ̣τ̣η̣ε̣στι̣ [acceptable A86 O19 end δε̣πε̣ [or δε̣το̣ [A88 O19 indication of change of speaker in the hole? end, feet only of letters

A55 πᾶϲ᾽ ἂν γυ̣νὴ δὴ τ̣[ο]ῦ̣[τό γ᾽] ε̣ἴποι — "τοῦ Διὸϲ
ὕοντοϲ, ὦ τάλαν; [μέθεϲ τρ]ό̣πον τινά,
A57 ϲκ.π̣.[ ]α̣ϲτα.[

A78 (Thras.) (?) φηϲωνμο̣[
ὁ τοῖχοϲ ουτ̣[
A80 ερειϲεαυτ[
οὐκ εἰκότ[

Getas ὦ τᾶν, ταπ̣[
τρ̣ό̣πο̣ν̣ τ̣ε̣.[
(Thras.?) ὑπ̣ερε̣ντρ[υφ — (?)
A85 αὕτη ᾽ϲτι· [πρ]όϲεχ᾽ ὦ φιλ[τάτη τὸν νοῦν ἐμοί,
παρορωμένῳ δε..[
φιλ[ο]νικίαν π̣όνον μανί[αν

(Get.) τί ὦ κακόδαιμο[ν;] (Thras.) ἀλλ᾽ ἔγ̣ωγ̣᾽ ἂν̣ φί̣[λτατοϲ
A89 κλη[θ]εὶϲ μόνον θύϲαιμι πᾶϲι τοῖϲ θε̣[ο]ῖ̣[ϲ.

A55 supplements and punctuation E.W.H. A56 [μέθεϲ], E.W.H. [πρὸϲ ἄνθρω]πόν τινα C.A., M.L.W. A57 e.g. ϲκε̣π̣τ̣[έον A79 οὗτ[οϲ or οὐ τ[οϲοῦτο a talking wall? A85 αὕτη ᾽ϲτι cf. Men. *Pk.* 513S προϲέχειν τὸν ν. cf. Lys. i 6, Plato *Laws* 783E A86 παρορωμένῳ cf. Men. fr. 183 Kö, *Sam.* 634 e.g. δὲ π̣ε̣[ριβαλεῖϲ παραχρῆμά μοι

any woman would say—'What, poor man, in pouring rain? [Relax a little] . . .'

(Thras.) . . . she is the one. Give your heart to me, dearest; if you pass me over, you will fill me . . . with envy, distress, madness . . .
(Getas) You were born under an unlucky star.
(Thras.) If she would only call me 'dearest' I should sacrifice to all the gods.

O19 fr. B col. ii

π̣[..]ονανειητοκακονουδεγαρϲφοδραει
...ωϲαηδηϲωϲτεγεειπειν· αλλαϲο[
.[.]μεικροναμε̣λε[.]τουϲτρατι⟦ ⟧τικου[
ˋηνˊ
.[..].ψινυπερα̣ϲ̣τε̣ι̣οϲ̣αλλαμ⟦μ⟧ηνα.[
...η̣.ι̣κ̣ι̣...[]ναα̣..ε̣...π.θε̣ν.[
———
κακωϲα[.]ο̣λ̣ο̣ι̣οδειτοπραγμαευρει̣ν̣[
.ϲ̣τ̣ινπ.[.].αιτιαναναγκ[.]ιαντ̣ι̣να[
].αι̣[]μια.[.].το̣φυ̣λον̣[..]τιδεϲ[.]..[
3/4].παρη̣[.]ϲ̣υ̣.εγ᾽αδιηγειδεϲπ[
4/5].μο.[]...επρο̣ϲ̣[..]ϲῡκαζειτε[
4/5].ομο[..].καε̣..[...]υ̣λογοϲτε.[
foot

O20 col. ii

τι[
⟦...⟧ ακ̣.[
———
το.[
αλ̣[
———
A94 τ̣[
. . . . .

A91 O20 after α, slightly sloping vertical, trace diverging to right at top, possible lower trace diverging obliquely downwards, if so κ rather than η O19 indeterminate, slight preference for α̣κ̣ over α̣ρ̣ A92–3 large ink blot at end of line A93 O19 end, α links to top of a vertical (γ? ρ, κ possible) A94 O19 between η̣ and ι̣κ̣ι̣ descending oblique after ι̣κ̣ι̣ 1 high wedge 2 top of curve 3 χ, λ, α̣ after ναα̣ two strokes join short vertical, then τ or π A97]., high ink, like tip of ξ in A39 αι̣ read by M.L.W. μια.[, ρ or ι το̣: ο high on broken fibres but acceptable A98 η read by M.L.W. after ϲ̣υ̣ flat base on line (? δ), tip of ε̣ A99]., high down-facing curve, ϲ, θ, ο after ο, low curve, descending oblique after tear, then top of vertical and high horizontal ϲῡκ longum added by 2nd hand A100]., high trace high dot before κ, ? υ after κα, ε or ϲ, then ? ι before λ, high oblique curve end τ, π

(Get.) τί ⟨τοῦτ'⟩ ἂν εἴη τὸ κακόν; οὐδὲ γὰρ cφόδρ' εἶ
ἄκ̣ρ̣ωc ἀηδὴc ὥcτε γ' εἰπεῖν· ἀλλὰ co[ὶ
τὸ μικρὸν ἀμέλει τοῦ cτρατιωτικοῦ [βλάβη·
ἀλ̣[λ'] ὄψιν ὑπερά̣c̣τειοc· ἀλλὰ μὴν ἄγ[ειc(?)
τ[ῆc] ἡλ̣ικία̣c̣ ... πο̣θεν.[

(Thras.) κακῶc ἀ[π]όλοιο· δεῖ το πρᾶγμ' εὑρεῖ̣ν̣ [ὅ τι
ἐ̣c̣τ̣ί̣ν πο̣[τ'], αἰτίαν ἀναγκ[α]ίαν τινὰ
[δεῖ]ξαι. (Get.) μιαρ̣[ὸ]ν̣ τὸ φῦλόν [ἐc]τι, δέc[π]ο̣τ̣[α.
(Thras.)].πάρῃ[c]· (Get.) c̣ὺ̣ δ̣ἐ̣ γ' ἃ διηγεῖ, δέcπ[ο̣τ̣α
] ὀ̣μό̣c̣α̣ι̣ τ̣ε̣ πρόc [τι] cυκάζει τέ [cε,
].ομο[.·ο]ὐ̣κ ἀ̣εὶ γ̣[ὰρ ε]ὔλογοc τε.[

A90 O19 suggests π[οῖ]όν ⟨γ'⟩, O20 τί ⟨τοῦτ'⟩ A91 ἄκρωc with adjective, cf. Hero *Def.* 76; for cφόδρα and second adverb cf. fr. 198 Kö, *Kolax* 9 ἀηδήc, cf. fr. 451 Kö; (of facial appearance α. ἰδεῖν, Men. *Pk.* 302S, 309) Ἄρεωc ἀήθηc cj. C.A. A92 τὸ cτρατιωτικόν, S. West, cf. Dem. xiii 4 A93 ὑπεράcτειοc, Hegesander fr. 9 A97 [:] E.W.H. μιαρόν, τὸ φῦλον, M.L.W. cf. fr. 718 Kö ἔθνοc μιαρόν A98 e.g. [ἂν μ]ὴ πάρῃ[c]– A99 e.g. [τάδ' ἂν] cυκάζει, cf. Strattis *Atalanta* fr. 1 M, (Hesych. κνίζειν ἐν ἐρωτικαῖc ὁμιλίαιc), Arist. *Birds* 1699 A100 e.g. [αὐτό]ν̣ομο[c· ο]ὐκ ἀε̣ὶ γ̣[ὰρ ε]ὔλογόc τέ τ[ιc | πιθανή τε πρόφαcιc;]

(Getas) What on earth could this trouble be? It isn't as if you were utterly downright rude, well not enough to speak of. Of course the meagreness of your service pay is a drawback. But your face, an aesthete's. However, you bring . . .

(Thras.) Damn your eyes. We must discover what the trouble can possibly be, demonstrate some compelling reason.

(Getas) Actually females are a wanton lot, master.

(Thras.) [Unless you drop it—]

(Getas) But your report, master, [that's what she] would swear for some purpose or other, and she caresses you into it, [taking an independent line (?)]. Isn't there always a specious [and plausible excuse(?)]

O19 fr. C

This scrap containing the middles of 8 verses cannot be positioned on objective grounds. On the principle of Occam's razor one would like to place it in col. ii. The only position available is below A57 and before A85 (?A78). The principal speaker is clearly Thrasonides. I do not know to what extent he may be quoting conversations held with others (as in A53–7). It is also possible that he may be steeling himself to sterner measures, such as keeping Krateia a prisoner. If the speaker of v. 5 is Getas, as is prima facie likely (he is addressed v. 2, and presumably speaks v. 4), the fragment cannot be placed in col. ii. If in fact Getas does suit action to the word and go into the house at vv. 5–7, v. 8 could be the beginning of a monologue by Thrasonides once more left alone. No restoration is so clearly cogent as to establish the extent of the loss at the beginnings of verses.

. . . . .

].π̣[..]...[.]δ̣.[].ωκαταβη.[
]..νη.ουκ...ουςηςγε̣τα[
]νηϲ·.....[...]·απιουϲαδ̣[
` ´
..
]ο̣λλονκα̣ι̣μ̣α̣λ̣α̣ϲτρατιωτ[
]α̣ϲαινυνοραϲειϲερχομα[
].λωποδυτ̣αϲμοιπεριπ̣[
]ουτουϲτεφ[.].γωνε..υ̣τ̣[
αι
]τεροϲω̣ταλ[[αν]].[

. . . . .

1]., ι, ϲ for π̣[, τ.[is also possible]..., ϲε̣ι̣? after δ, low trace]., ι, τ, ν end, lower part of down-stroke 2].., ε̣ι̣ possible after κ, anomalous α, ε or θ, uncertain whether 2 or 3 letters between it and ου 3 after νηϲ·, two verticals, one on each side of a tear (? π, η), then rounded letter (ο, α, δ) and tops 4 interlinear *nota*: part of a vertical, then low horizontal 6]. low trace 7]., oblique above line after ε 1 vertical curving to right at top (not ρ), 2 high trace; not εἰκότ[ωϲ τ̣[or ϲ[8 αν blotted and αι added above line .[a vertical

(Thras.)].π̣[..]...[.]δ̣.[].ω καταβη.[
ἐκ]ε̣ί̣νης ουκ...ούϲης, Γέτα [
]νηϲ· ....[...]· ἀπιοῦϲα δ̣[
(Get.)? Ἄπ]ολλον· καὶ μάλα ϲτρατιωτ[ικόν
]α̣ϲαι· νῦν, ὁρᾷς, εἰϲέρχομα[ι.
].λωποδύταϲ μοι περιπ̣[ατῶν
τ]ούτουϲ τε φ[ε]ύ̣γων ἐκ̣λ̣ύτ̣[ωϲ.
(Thras.)]τεροϲ ω̣ ταλαιπ̣[ωρ

1 e.g. π[εύ]ϲει, ϲπ[εύ]ϲει καταβήϲ[ομαι, καταβῆν[αι 2 οὐ κελευούϲηϲ, E.W.H., M.L.W. οὐκ ἀλυούϲηϲ, C.A. The passage has resisted verification 3 end e.g. δ' [ἄν (M.L.W.) κνίζοι μ'], or (quoted words of Krateia) δ[ὲ λείψω ϲ' 5 e.g. π]ᾶϲαι, preceded by verb (μιϲοῦϲι?) 6 e.g. [μή ποτ' ἐπάγῃϲ τοὺ]ϲ 8 e.g. ἕ]τεροϲ (πῶϲ οὖν ἄν ε., οὐκ ἔϲτιν ε., *vel sim.*) ᾧ ταλαιπ̣[ωρητέον (so F.H.S.) (or ὦ ταλαίπ̣[ωρ' . . .)

(Thras.) . . . come downstairs . . . since she [does not request it], Getas. If [she] goes away, [she would hurt me].

(Getas) What an extraordinary thing! And a good soldierly [action you've watched][1]. Now, as you see, I am going indoors, for fear you bring down muggers on me by walking up and down, [leaving you (?)] and escaping them in relaxed fashion.

(Thras.)(?) [. . . another who must suffer distress . . .]

[1] See *Addenda*

ADDENDA

A 20/1 Following up a suggestion by M. D. Reeve, ὦ δυϲτυχήϲ, [τί οὐ καθεύ]δειϲ might be assigned as 'self-address' to Thrasonides, ϲὺ μ' κτλ. to Getas. The interlinear ink above ϲυ might be Γε.

A 24 e.g. [τί βουλό]μεν[ο]ϲ; F. H. S., W. S. Barrett.

A 28/9 ἐν παντὶ γάρ [καιρῷ *vel. sim.* H. Lloyd-Jones

A 29 δεινῶϲ π̣[αθών, H. Lloyd-Jones.

A 36 The translation 'dog's body' was suggested by Dr. Holford-Strevens, the O.U.P. reader.

A 41/2 or αἰϲχύνομαι / [κακῶϲ τάλ]αιναν, S. West.

A 44 e.g. [λίαν ἄτοπ]α, J. G. Griffith.

A 85 ? [αὐτή rather than αὕτη, O.U.P. reader.

A 88 e.g. φι̣[λοφρόνωϲ], H. Lloyd-Jones.

o 19 Fr. C

4/5 Perhaps better ϲτρατιωτικὸν / [ἔργον τεθέ]αϲαι· E. G. T.

Publication numbers have now been assigned to the four new texts, viz. P. Oxy. XLVIII, 3368–71.

MAURICE HERBERT DOBB

MAURICE HERBERT DOBB

1900–1976

THE death of Maurice Dobb, on 17 August 1976, has robbed the world of economics of an outstanding and well-loved scholar, who over a period of fifty years established and maintained his position as one of the most eminent Marxist economists in the world. These fifty years were spent almost entirely at Cambridge, where his scholarship, integrity, and great international reputation were eventually recognized by his appointment to a Readership in 1959. To the very many students and colleagues whom he so unstintingly helped and inspired over the years, Cambridge will never seem quite the same again.

Maurice Herbert Dobb was born on 24 July 1900, the son of Walter Herbert Dobb and Elsie Annie Moir, of London. He was educated at Charterhouse—an establishment not particularly noted for its output of Marxist intellectuals—and remained a loyal Carthusian to the end of his life. Having become a socialist in the last stages of the war (partly no doubt under the inspiration of the October Revolution in Russia), and saved from the call-up by the armistice of November 1918, he entered Pembroke College, Cambridge, as an Exhibitioner in 1919 in order to read economics. In those days economics was still a rather unfashionable subject, and socialism was a rather unusual creed for a young man of impeccable upbringing and appearance to profess. Dobb himself (as reported by Professor Hobsbawm) used to recall with amusement 'his first attempt to join the small band of Cambridge University socialists, and being intensively interrogated by H. D. Dickinson (later Professor of Economics at Bristol), who was clearly under the impression that so spruce and conventional-looking a young man must be a provocateur'. A socialist economist—and particularly one who had the temerity to call himself a Marxist—was indeed a *rara avis* in the immediate post-war Cambridge scene.

Having taken a First in both parts of the Economics Tripos, Dobb went on to spend two postgraduate years at the London School of Economics, reading for his Ph.D. under Edwin Cannan. He then accepted an invitation to come back to a University lectureship at Cambridge, where he was to teach for the remainder of his career. Thanks to the efforts of the late

Professor D. H. Robertson he eventually became attached to Trinity, but for reasons which may not have been unconnected with his political views, it was not until 1948 that he was actually elected to a Fellowship at this (or any) college.

Dobb had joined the Communist Party in 1921, and was to remain a loyal, though conspicuously undogmatic, member of that organization to the end of his life. To a man of his political convictions, and great integrity, the atmosphere at Cambridge in the 1920s must have seemed incredibly uncongenial. He wrote in a letter about that time that he was finding it rather distasteful 'teaching embryo exploiters how to exploit the workers in the most up-to-date and humane way'. And one can imagine how this distastefulness must in Dobb's eyes have been exacerbated by the absence of any really significant group of radical students in the University, by the lack of any industrial working class to speak of in the town, and, after the General Strike, by the virtual collapse of even that miniscule left-wing movement which had previously existed. It was not until the stormy period of the 1930s that the Cambridge left was resuscitated, and Dobb's political isolation somewhat diminished.

It was during the 1920s, however, that the foundations of Dobb's future work as a scholar were laid by the publication of two important books—*Capitalist Enterprise and Social Progress* in 1925, and *Russian Economic Development Since the Revolution* in 1928. These two books did not constitute the whole of his output in this period, of course: there were also several journal articles; there was the first edition of what was to become a very popular textbook on *Wages* (commissioned by Keynes for the Cambridge Economic Handbooks series); and last, but in Dobb's eyes certainly not least, there were several outline courses on economic topics written for left-wing educational organizations like the Labour Research Department. But it was the two books —and particularly *Capitalist Enterprise and Social Progress*—which most clearly manifested Dobb's scholastic ability and foreshadowed the remarkable work which was soon to come.

Re-reading *Capitalist Enterprise and Social Progress* today, more than half a century after its first appearance, one is struck above all by the way in which the three parts into which the book is divided ('Analytical', 'Historical', and 'Applied') faithfully reflect the three major fields which Dobb was later to make his own—first, economic analysis (with particular reference to its history and methodology); second, economic history (particularly the history of capitalism); and third, the practical problems of economic planning under socialism. One is also struck by the appearance, in this very early work, of certain concepts and distinctions which were destined to become the motifs of much of his later work: the concept of profit as the fruit of an 'institutional' monopoly limiting the supply of entrepreneurs, for example, and the distinction between 'uncertainty' in the normally accepted economic sense and 'uncertainty' in the sense of the ignorance of each individual entrepreneur (under competitive capitalism) as to the actions and intentions of his rivals. Finally, one is struck by the extent to which this book provides evidence of the fact—sometimes forgotten or misinterpreted by Dobb's critics—that he was in fact brought up not only in the Marxist but also in the Marshallian and Pigouvian traditions. His ability to translate Marxian ideas into non-Marxian language, and his belief that one *ought* so to translate them if one wanted to make Marxism accessible to academic audiences in the West, are both very clearly indicated in his first book. And the particular field in which his interest in the problems of economic planning under socialism was mainly to be displayed was indicated with equal clarity in his second book, *Russian Economic Development Since the Revolution*—a pioneer study which was to be only the first of a long series of writings by Dobb dealing specifically with the Soviet economy.

In the 1930s Dobb's political isolation was lessened greatly as a result of the explosion of left-wing ideas among intellectuals, and he soon became one of the best-known members of a group of Cambridge Marxists whose influence both inside and outside the University was out of all proportion to its size. His strong sense of duty and hatred of all kinds of privilege, which always overcame his appreciation of the social benefits of the division of labour, led him to share in the more mundane activities of this group on the same basis as everyone else: contemporaries recall how he served on anti-fascist committees, licked stamps and sealed envelopes, knocked on doors, and took part in demonstrations. He was one of the handful of Cambridge dons who in 1932 marched out to Girton to meet the north-eastern contingent of hunger marchers. But his main political work was, as always, in the educational field: he became widely known and respected in left-wing circles as a lecturer, and he published a large number of popular pamphlets on Marxism, the U.S.S.R., and the economics of socialism.

In the official academic world, however, he still remained a somewhat lonely and isolated figure—almost, one might say, on the periphery of academic life. This was not due to any failure on his part to contribute to academic publications, or to produce scholarly books: on the contrary, he published in the 1930s a very large number of articles and reviews in academic journals, and also produced what may well come to be recognized as his most original and impressive book, *Political Economy and Capitalism* (1937).

This book deserves much more than passing mention. Marked by the same careful scholarship and close argument which characterized all his work, *Political Economy and Capitalism* was the first really *creative* contribution to Marxist economics ever to appear, at any rate in the English-speaking world. Although some of its leading ideas had been anticipated in a much shorter work which Dobb had published a few years earlier (*An Introduction to Economics*, 1932), it is from the appearance of *Political Economy and Capitalism* that future historians of economic thought will probably date the emergence of Marxist economics as a really serious academic discipline in this country. In this book, Dobb discussed in turn the requirements of a theory of value in economics; the nature of classical political economy (with particular reference to its relation to Marxist economics); the theory of economic crises; the basic trends and tendencies of modern (non-Marxist) economics; imperialism; and the question of the operation of economic laws in a socialist economy. This wide range of subjects was discussed from a point of view which was unmistakably Marxist: the book is at the same time a powerful defence of Marx as the logical successor and developer of the tradition of classical political economy, and a penetrating Marxian critique of the then predominant subjectivist or 'marginal utility' school in economic theory. But this defence and critique are conducted with such depth, perception, originality, and sheer charm that one would have imagined that nobody—not even one whose political views were opposed to Dobb's—could possibly have overlooked or underestimated the book.

Nevertheless, it is probably true to say that at that time its impact was still felt predominantly in left-wing circles. In how many libraries of ageing left-wing scholars, I wonder, are there to be found treasured and heavily underlined copies of Dobb's *Introduction to Economics* and *Political Economy and Capitalism*, from which so many of us in so many different countries learned for the first time not only what intellectual Marxism was, not only what economics was (or could be), but also what real scholarship was? In more orthodox circles, however, its impact was very much less, and the amount of intellectual excitement which it generated was minimal. The whole tradition of orthodox economic thought was then permeated with the notion that the introduction of 'social' or 'institutional' data into economic theory, as an integral factor in the explanation of prices and incomes, was essentially political rather than scientific. And when this introduction was performed by an immensely civilized person like Dobb, who possessed to the full the uncomfortable ability to translate Marxian ideas into Marshallian language, the instinctive tendency of orthodoxy to resist this invasion from an alien world was naturally heightened. In addition, as Professor Hobsbawm has perceptively noted, Dobb's critique of economic orthodoxy at this time

> ran parallel to the more influential Keynesian one, but hardly touched it except in the common rejection by both of theories whose refinement was bought at the cost of gross unrealism. Nor did either side make much effort to approach the other. The Keynesian preoccupation with controlling economic fluctuations within the capitalist economy was one which Marxists in the 1930s were not likely to share, and conversely, Dobb's argument, intellectually able as it unquestionably was, seemed quite remote from the practical policy questions which British economists, always potential Treasury advisers at heart, sought to, influence.

The years of the Second World War brought for Dobb various new strains: a doubled teaching load, intensified political activity (particularly after the U.S.S.R. became an ally), A.R.P. and Home Guard duties, and so on. But there was no interruption in the flow of journal articles, reviews, and popular books and pamphlets from his pen. Many of these, as one would expect, were concerned with aspects of life in the U.S.S.R.; but there were others on different subjects, notably a splendid and very influential essay on *Marx as an Economist* which first appeared in 1943. Nor did Dobb, always an indefatigable worker, allow all this to interfere too seriously with his long-term research—a fact which was abundantly evidenced by the appearance, in the years immediately after the end of the war, of two new and important books.

One of these, *Soviet Economic Development Since 1917* (published in 1948), was in effect a revised and enlarged edition of his *Russian Economic Development Since the Revolution*, which as we have seen had appeared in 1928. The other book, however—*Studies in the Development of Capitalism* (1946)—although it certainly had its germ in what Dobb with characteristic modesty now called 'some jejune chapters of twenty years ago about the origins of capitalist enterprise' (i.e. his *Capitalist Enterprise and Social Progress*), was essentially the product of new thinking and research. It is possibly upon this book—as well as, perhaps, upon his *Political Economy and Capitalism*—that Dobb's reputation as a scholar will finally rest. In it he employed his great theoretical ability and historical flair in order to throw light on certain crucial problems relating to the economic development of Western capitalism. The book was motivated, as Dobb put it in his preface, 'by the obstinate belief that economic analysis only makes sense and can only bear fruit if it is joined to a study of historical development, and that the economist concerned with present-day problems has certain questions of his own to put to historical data'. In these *Studies*—which were based on an exhaustive analysis of the then extant secondary sources—Dobb showed a degree of insight and originality which commanded the respect even of those who disagreed fundamentally with the Marxian view of history which he deployed as a tool throughout the book. In particular, his account of the transition from feudalism to capitalism raised very sharply certain controversial issues which have ever since been the subject of intense debate. Among Marxists, the stimulation afforded by Dobb's book was reflected almost immediatəly in a well-known international discussion of these issues early in the 1950s—a discussion which is still proceeding today, as witness the appearance in 1976 of a reprint of the original contributions to this discussion together with a number of more recent essays relating to it. Among non-Marxists the effect was less immediately and directly felt, but felt it eventually was: there must today be few economic historians who are prepared to deny at any rate the *relevance* of the problems in this field which Dobb was one of the very first scholars to raise.

In the 1950s, however, the changes which took place in the political climate were hardly conducive to a more widespread acceptance of Dobb's ideas. They also rendered his political life at Cambridge much less comfortable: in the middle and late 1950s support for the Communist Party at the University dwindled considerably; and Dobb once remarked at this time that it was quite disconcerting walking in the streets of central Cambridge because so many ex-Communists crossed to the other side when they saw him coming. Although he rarely showed any outward sign of discomfiture, and continued to give his usual constant and quiet encouragement to the young graduates in his Party branch, he must have felt this temporary return to the semi-isolation of the 1920s very keenly indeed. So far as his writing was concerned, however, the only visible sign of this was a decline in his output of *popular* books and pamphlets; and this was much more than compensated for by an appreciable increase in the flow of journal articles, many of which were of very high quality. A collection of some of these articles of the 1950s, together with a number of earlier ones, appeared in 1955 under the title *On Economic Theory and Socialism*. In the 1950s, too, there was published the monumental edition of the works and correspondence of David Ricardo, edited by Piero Sraffa with the active assistance and collaboration (since 1948) of Dobb.

But so far as the development of Dobb's thought was concerned, the 1950s were above all marked by his increasing concern with the problems of the economic development of pre-industrial economies—a field in which he was able fruitfully to combine (and extend) the results of his analyses both of the development of Western capitalism and of the Soviet economy. The first major products of this concern were the three lectures on *Some Aspects of Economic Development* which he gave at the Delhi School of Economics when he went there as Visiting Professor for a short period in 1950–1. Quite a few of his journal articles in the 1950s were also devoted to this subject, and in 1960 he published what was probably his most important contribution in the field—the short but classic volume which he modestly entitled *An Essay on Economic Growth and Planning*. In this book he discussed with great technical skill and profound analytical understanding the central problems of investment choice in a planned, developing economy. The argument is very tight indeed, and owes little (except by way of general 'philosophical' inspiration) to the work of Marx. One of the main points which Dobb makes, to put it in his own words, is that correct decisions by a central planning authority about the choice of techniques in the consumer goods and investment sectors 'may contribute much more to human welfare than could the most perfect micro-economic adjustment, of which the market (if it worked like the textbooks, at least, and there were no income-inequalities) is admittedly more fitted in most cases to take care'. Strategy, in other words, is more important than tactics in this sphere; and it is therefore to the delineation of the principles which ought to govern the correct strategy that Dobb turns his main attention in this seminal book.

It is of course the Maurice Dobb of the 1960s and early 1970s that most of us will best remember. His economics students will remember him as an immensely careful, painstaking, and sympathetic supervisor and lecturer. His friends will remember him most typically—if I may quote from Professor Hobsbawm again—

> sitting in an armchair, rosy-faced, still elegant in an informal but carefully colour-checked shirt and disclaiming, against all probability, any special competence on any subject under discussion, diffidently intervening in conversation, with a natural and deep-seated courtesy which once led a visiting foreigner to say that he had always heard about English gentlemen, but he had never met one until he met Maurice Dobb. Or else we think of him on those long discussion-laden walks through Backs, Fellows' Gardens, or the woods near Fulbourn, which are so inseparable from the intellectual life of the older universities.

Few who knew him at any stage in his life, even if they came to disagree with him politically, could ever have lost their great respect and affection for him.

The last fifteen years of Dobb's life were marked by an increasing recognition of his achievements which must have done much to compensate for the long years which he had been obliged to spend on the borders of the academic wilderness. His retirement from his Cambridge Readership was marked by a *Festschrift* (*Socialism, Capitalism and Economic Growth*, 1967) to which an extremely distinguished array of economists contributed. He was awarded an honorary doctorate at the University of Prague in 1964; and another at the University of Leicester in 1972. (The latter occasion he shortly afterwards described in a letter to me as a 'bright day' which was 'not only very pleasant but also rather overwhelming—a little like one's first party as a child'.) And the award of his British Academy Fellowship in 1971 also meant a great deal to him.

But the last fifteen years of his life were also—and perhaps even more importantly—marked by an intensification of his intellectual activity which, viewed in retrospect, is really quite extraordinary. I am thinking here not so much of his second collection of essays (*Capitalism, Development and Planning*, 1967), although that is impressive enough, but more particularly of his *Welfare Economics and the Economics of Socialism* (1969) and *Theories of Value and Distribution Since Adam Smith* (1973). In the first of these two books he attempted, as he put it, to sort out the wheat from the chaff in the modern theory of welfare economics, rejecting at the same time both the uncritical admiration displayed towards this branch of theory by its more ardent supporters and the nihilistic opposition to it displayed by its more sectarian critics, and applying those of its propositions which came out unscathed from his own searching criticism to the problems of economic choice in a socialist economy.

It is in his *Theories of Value and Distribution Since Adam Smith*, however, that the remarkable freshness and continuing vitality of his intellectual vision revealed themselves most prominently. In a certain sense, this last book of his represented a return by Dobb to the territory he had explored thirty-five years before in his *Political Economy and Capitalism*. It would be quite wrong, however, to regard the *Theories* merely as a kind of updated new edition of the earlier book, since the general orientations of the two works are quite different. In *Political Economy and Capitalism*, Dobb's main aim was to show that Marxian economics was the logical successor of classical economics, and to develop Marxian economics in such a way as to provide better answers than orthodox economics was then capable of providing to certain key problems relating (for example) to imperialism and socialism. In his *Theories*, by way of contrast, his main aim was to rewrite the history of economic thought (with special reference to value and distribution theory) in the light of the present-day controversy over capital theory, and, more particularly, in the light of the so-called 'Sraffa revolution' ushered in by the appearance in 1960 of Piero Sraffa's *Production of Commodities by Means of Commodities*. In carrying out this aim, Dobb took the opportunity of correcting what he had now come to believe were certain errors of emphasis in *Political Economy and Capitalism* (a book, he told me a few years ago, that he sometimes now regretted that he had ever written), and reinterpreted nineteenth-century economic thought in terms of the emergence and development of what he called 'two quite distinct and rival trends' in value and distribution theory. The *Theories* is an extremely perceptive and stimulating book, which—if economics is in fact now at an important turning-point in its development, as Dobb believed—is bound to have a profound effect on the writing of the history of economic thought.

Sraffa's *Production of Commodities*, which embodied in effect both a kind of rehabilitation and development of Ricardian and Marxian theory and at the same time a critique of modern 'neo-classical' theory (particularly capital theory), not only directly inspired Dobb's *Theories* but also had the additional—and equally happy—effect of bringing him closer to a number of economists, at Cambridge and elsewhere, with whom his relations in earlier years had at times been rather more uneasy. In the last years of his life, Dobb began to feel that if this new alliance could be preserved and strengthened there was a real possibility that what he called 'the century-old dominance of orthodox doctrine over economics teaching' might fairly soon be overcome. But he was also very much aware that the battle was by no means won; that the defenders were mounting a powerful counter-attack against the Sraffian critique; and that under these conditions 'leftist' criticism of what had come to be called (pejoratively) Sraffa's 'neo-Ricardianism' could only be harmful and divisive. In a moving passage at the end of what must have been almost his last journal article, Dobb wrote:

> When such an ideological contest is being joined I would suggest that Marxists have more to gain by stressing what they have *in common* with their allies, in the shape of fellow-critics of prevailing bourgeois orthodoxy who would not perhaps go all the way with them in positive statements of what they believe; and that it is weakening and divisive (and in this sense sectarian) to focus attention on *differences* between Marxists, near-Marxists and others (even if such differences are not to be ignored). Joined with this consideration is the question of the audience one is addressing . . . This audience should be largely, if not mainly, those still unconvinced by recent criticism. In the present context the sectarian critics have in my view much underestimated the extent to which rehabilitating Ricardo, for the great majority of people schooled in orthodox teaching . . . is *ipso facto* an introduction to the study of Marx.

Looking at Dobb's life and work as a whole, one is struck in particular by two things. The first is that although he was from the beginning a convinced Marxist, he always firmly resisted, in all its manifestations, the vulgar notion that Marx's ideas constituted a kind of self-contained, encapsulated system which had had no history and was incapable of further development. On the contrary, he always insisted that there was an important sense in which Marx as an economist had worked within a broad analytical tradition established much earlier by Smith and Ricardo (a fact which suggested a ready way of introducing Marx to British audiences); that Marxian economics could and should be developed, and even where necessary transcended; and that this should be done not only with the aid of tools fashioned by Marxists, but also with the aid of at least *some* of those fashioned by 'bourgeois' economists. Why, he asked in effect, should the devil have all the good tools? Dobb always refused to join in the wholesale denigration of Marshall and Pigou which became fashionable in certain quarters; and when it came to modern welfare economics, although he severely criticized a number of its leading propositions and attitudes, he was very careful (as we have seen) not to allow the wheat to escape with the chaff. Dobb once told me of an amusing 'economists' dream' which he had just had. One of the economics tutors at St. John's, it appeared, was giving a sherry party (in an attic room somewhere above the chapel) for the Economics Faculty in order to introduce Karl Marx to Alfred Marshall. The party was apparently a great success: the two old men were talking together with tremendous animation and in perfect amity. The tutor who had organized the party, however, was not satisfied. 'What a pity Sraffa isn't here,' he said to Dobb, 'Marx would have been so interested in his new edition of Ricardo.' Can one perhaps see in this dream, besides its obvious charm, an indication of Dobb's lifelong concern to have Marx placed in a historical—and British—setting?

The second thing which strikes one about Dobb's life and work—and it is something which I think he himself would have liked to see emphasized—is the way in which throughout his whole life his political and academic activities were so closely linked together, with no loss of integrity and very little sense of strain. He always considered it part of his everyday duty, as a politically conscious academic, to make the results of his research available not only to the *cognoscenti* but also to interested lay people. And his popular books and pamphlets, whatever their level of discourse, are marked by the same meticulous scholarship, precision of argument, and refusal to make concessions to dogmatism, as his major 'academic' works. The other dimension of this which should be noted is that the level of objectivity which Dobb managed to achieve in all his work was very high—quite remarkably high, in fact, if one remembers the political circumstances in which he found himself. It must have been extraordinarily difficult, for example, for a Communist academic like Dobb to write as objectively as he usually did about the U.S.S.R., while giving so few hostages to the dogmatists at either end of the political spectrum. If there are few economists of our time who can match Dobb in the range, quality, and originality of his contributions, and few who can match him in his great modesty and humanity, there are even fewer who can match him in his integrity and honesty.

Acknowledgements. I have made considerable use in this memoir of the tribute to Dobb written by Professor Hobsbawm for the *Festschrift* mentioned above, and also of some articles on Dobb which appeared in the August 1967 issue of *Marxism Today*. A number of Dobb's friends and associates have also assisted by providing me with reminiscences and further information.

RONALD L. MEEK

PLATE XLIV

SIR GODFREY ROLLES DRIVER, C.B.E., M.C.

GODFREY ROLLES DRIVER

1892–1975

THE first thing to be said about G. R. Driver is that he was the son of a great Hebrew and Old Testament scholar. Samuel Rolles Driver, Regius Professor of Hebrew and Canon of Christ Church, Oxford, formerly Scholar and then Fellow of New College, was the most distinguished British Hebraist of the late nineteenth and early twentieth centuries, and played an influential part in winning acceptance in this country for the use of critical methods in the study of the Old Testament.

Godfrey Rolles Driver was born on 20 August 1892 as his parents' eldest child in the house in Christ Church that his father occupied as a canon. His mother, born Mabel Burr, was a niece of the wife of T. K. Cheyne, the Oriel Professor of the Interpretation of Holy Scripture, another distinguished Old Testament scholar, although his work became intellectually unbalanced in his later years. Mrs. Driver was not only the wife of an eminent scholar: she was a character in her own right, who was able, among other things, to insist that a parrot should be placed in her husband's study contrary, it is said, to his own wishes. Their son began his formal education at an excellent school in Bradmore Road, North Oxford, run by a certain Miss Owen whose pupils included a number who were to rise to bishoprics and other prominent positions. The young Driver's knowledge of the Old Testament was already sufficient to stand him in good stead, for he was able effectively to challenge his teacher's assertion that there was no book of Obadiah in the Bible. From Miss Owen's school he moved to Summerfields, also in North Oxford, where one of his contemporaries was Harold Macmillan, the future Prime Minister and Chancellor of Oxford University. Driver did not much like Summerfields, he said, because he was kept too clean, but it was from there that he won a scholarship to Winchester College where his father had been. Now, for the first time, he lived away from Oxford, and Winchester became, like his native city, an object of his loyalty and devotion for the rest of his life. In later years, the only tie he wore, except when in evening dress, was a Wykehamist one.

Even in those days, the foundations of Driver's future work

as a Hebraist were being laid. His father taught him Hebrew and would ask him to read to him from an unpointed text. A. E. Cowley's preface (dated in September 1910) to the second edition of his translation of *Gesenius' Hebrew Grammar as edited and enlarged by the late E. Kautzsch* expresses thanks to 'my young friend, Mr. Godfrey R. Driver, of Winchester College, for some welcome help in correcting proofs of the Hebrew index and the index of passages'.

In 1911 Driver followed his father's example by going up to New College as a Scholar to read for Classical Moderations. Although he was placed in the second class (his failure to get into the first class may have been because he had been driven, and had driven himself, too hard), his distinction as a classic was shown by his winning the Gaisford Prize for Greek Prose in 1913 and for Verse in 1916. He also showed evidence of his promise as a student of Hebrew by winning in 1912 both the Junior Hall–Houghton Septuagint Prize and (like his father) the Pusey and Ellerton Hebrew Scholarship at the same time that he was studying classics.

S. R. Driver died in February 1914, and the war broke out a few months later. G. R. Driver joined the army in the following year. His military service was distinguished by the award of the Military Cross and by his being mentioned in dispatches, and he attained the rank of Major. He was wounded in the thigh by shrapnel in Serbia. The next part of the world to which he was sent was to have an influence on his future work, for he was moved to the Near East and began to gain the first-hand acquaintance with Palestine to which he was always to attach so much importance. He became acquainted with colloquial Arabic, and a report on Kurdistan and the Kurds was prepared in 1919 (and he later published several articles about the Kurds).

In 1919 Driver returned to Oxford, and was offered a Fellowship at Magdalen College while he was considering a similar invitation from another college. He accepted the offer at Magdalen, and he was a Fellow and, after his retirement, an Honorary Fellow for the rest of his life. He served the college in various ways—as Pro-Proctor in 1923, as Librarian from 1923 to 1940, and as Vice-President in 1931–2, and he was from the time of his election a Classical Tutor; he always stressed to his pupils in later years the value of a training in classics for anyone who wished to study the Old Testament. Although Driver taught classics for his college, Semitic languages were his own chief interest, and from 1920 onward he published numerous articles on Hebrew and related languages, and he was elected in 1921 to the Senior Kennicott Hebrew Scholarship (his father had been a Scholar in 1870). In 1924 he married Madeleine Mary Goulding and so began an extremely happy marriage. The following year he taught as a Visiting Professor at a summer course at Chicago University. His first books appeared in 1925. *A Grammar of the Colloquial Arabic of Syria and Palestine* made use of what he had learned while serving in the Near East. *The Bazaar of Heracleides* was edited jointly by Driver and Leonard Hodgson, who was then also a Fellow of Magdalen and was later to become the Regius Professor of Divinity. Driver was responsible for the translation from Syriac of this work attributed to the heresiarch Nestorius, and Hodgson contributed the patristic learning. A different branch of Semitic scholarship appeared in *Letters of the First Babylonian Dynasty*, which established Driver's reputation as a promising Accadian scholar. Thus, in one year three books showed Driver's ability in no fewer than three Semitic languages other than Hebrew. The University appointed him a Lecturer in Comparative Semitic Philology in 1927, and a Reader in the following year, and he then gave up his Classical Tutorship.

Driver was now able to concentrate his energies on Semitic languages, though he was, in addition, an editor of the *Journal of Theological Studies* from 1933 to 1940. His learning in both Greek and Hebrew made him a suitable holder of the Grinfield Lectureship on the Septuagint, which he occupied from 1934 until 1939. He served as Deputy Professor of Hebrew in 1934, during a vacancy in the Professorship. His scholarship would have made him an obvious person to be appointed to the Regius Chair of Hebrew, which his father had occupied, but it was annexed to a canonry at Christ Church and G. R. Driver was not in Holy Orders. He was a practising lay member of the Church of England, but it would have been completely contrary to his principles to seek ordination merely to qualify himself for the Chair. A few years later, S. A. Cook was about to retire from the Regius Professorship of Hebrew at Cambridge, and Driver was invited to become his successor. He refused, primarily because the Chair was not attached to a Fellowship at any Cambridge College and Driver valued his Fellowship at Magdalen—though it would, in any case, be difficult to imagine Driver at home in any university but his own. Instead, he had the satisfaction of seeing one of his first pupils, D. Winton Thomas, going to the Chair in Cambridge in 1938.

Throughout these years, articles and reviews by Driver

continued to appear. His edition of *The Assyrian Laws*, which was written jointly with Sir John Miles, was published in 1935, and *Problems of the Hebrew Verbal System* a year later. The University of Oxford recognized his attainments in 1938 by conferring on him the title of Professor of Semitic Philology. In the same year he was the President of the Society for Old Testament Study, whose meetings he attended regularly throughout his academic career until poor health made it impossible for him to be present, and he was elected a Fellow of the British Academy (of which his father had been a Fellow since its foundation) in 1939. He was also awarded in 1939 a Leverhulme Fellowship, which he hoped to use for travel abroad, but the outbreak of war compelled him to resign the award.

The Second World War again took Driver to Palestine, and he later served at the Ministry of Information in London. During the war, he had to go for a time to hospital on account of low blood pressure, but he later delighted to tell how he was envied by the other patients because he was told that he must take whisky. Despite his commitments, he was the Schweich Lecturer of the British Academy in 1944, and his lectures were published as *Semitic Writing from Pictograph to Alphabet* in 1948.

The years between the end of the war and Driver's retirement in 1962 were full of activity. Numerous articles continued to appear. Together with Sir John Miles he edited *The Babylonian Laws*, of which the two volumes were published in 1952 and 1955 respectively. Another book of the same period was an edition of texts in a different Semitic language—*Aramaic Documents of the Fifth Century* B.C. (1954). He was also working on an edition of texts in yet another Semitic language, Ugaritic, which was published as *Canaanite Myths and Legends* in 1956. Hebrew, however, was not neglected: he had been interested from the beginning in the Qumran scrolls. His brief work *The Hebrew Scrolls* (1951) gave his first impressions, and his later theories were worked out at length in *The Judaean Scrolls* (1965). He was the President of the International Organization for the Study of the Old Testament from 1953 to 1959, and their Congress was held in Oxford in the latter year. He was a member of the Advisory Committee of *Vetus Testamentum*, the Organization's quarterly journal, for the rest of his life. He also devoted much time to the preparation of the New English Bible (as his father had helped to prepare the Revised Version), and he became the Convener of the Old Testament Panel in 1957, and Joint Director (with Professor C. H. Dodd) in 1965. Nor did he neglect his university duties, for he played a leading part in planning the building of the Oriental Institute, and he was a conscientious and enthusiastic teacher: he lectured regularly and frequently to small but keenly interested audiences on various books of the Hebrew Bible, the Qumran scrolls, Ugaritic texts, and Semitic philology, and he supervised research students. When, in 1959, Dr. C. A. Simpson, the Regius Professor of Hebrew, was appointed Dean of Christ Church, Driver was again appointed Deputy Professor of Hebrew, and he carried a very heavy teaching load during the interregnum. He had long believed that it was wrong for the Chair to be restricted to men in priest's orders, and he led a campaign to detach the professorship from the canonry. The campaign was successful, and Dr. W. D. McHardy, one of Driver's pupils, became in 1960 the first non-Anglican to hold the Chair. Driver, who had been allowed to retain his own post beyond the normal retiring age because of the changes to the statutes of the Regius Chair, eventually retired in 1962 at the age of 70.

The academic year that began in 1962, when Driver became Emeritus Professor of Semitic Philology, was what he described as his *annus mirabilis*. Magdalen elected him to an Honorary Fellowship, and two collections of essays were published in his honour: volume vii, part 2, of the *Journal of Semitic Studies* (1962), edited by Edward Ullendorff, a former pupil; and *Hebrew and Semitic Studies presented to Godfrey Rolles Driver* (1963), edited by two other pupils, D. Winton Thomas and W. D. McHardy. Driver received various honours both before and after his retirement. The British Academy awarded him the Burkitt Medal for Biblical Studies in 1953. The School of Oriental and African Studies of London University made him an Honorary Fellow in 1963. He received several honorary doctorates: a D.D. from Aberdeen University (who had similarly honoured his father forty years before) in 1946, and from Manchester University in 1956; a D.Litt. from Durham University in 1948, and from his own University of Oxford in 1970; Cambridge University, which had given his father an honorary Litt.D. in 1905, conferred the same honour on him in 1964. He was made a C.B.E. in 1958, and received a knighthood in 1968. Shortly before his death, he was glad to learn that he had been elected to an Honorary Fellowship by New College, where he had been an undergraduate.

Driver's retirement was far from inactive. Most of his time was devoted to the New English Bible and to writing articles, but he was pleased to lecture again in Oxford for a few weeks when Professor McHardy was unwell. Early in 1967, he had a heart attack and, although he was soon able to return to work and would not have been happy if he had been unable to do so, the rest of his life was dogged by ill health. Happily, he was able to attend the service in Westminster Abbey that marked the publication of the complete New English Bible in 1970, to walk in the procession, and to read the first lesson in a way that earned much praise but had been made possible only by taking a double dose of pills. He continued to work afterwards, and the flow of articles did not cease, although his writings showed some signs of his poor health. In January 1971, when the Society for Old Testament Study met in Oxford under the Presidency of Professor Edward Ullendorff, his former pupil, he was able to read a paper. Despite his poor health, he seemed full of vigour and held the attention of his audience—much to the delight of all, particularly his pupils for whom the lecture brought back inspiring memories of the past. He died on 22 April 1975, and the funeral was held in Magdalen College Chapel, where he had so often worshipped.

In character, Driver was an honest and straightforward person, who spoke his mind plainly. Although some were opposed to him, he was not a man to take pleasure in nursing malice, and he would never descend to anything underhand or mean. His honesty was accompanied by a genuine humility: he did not pretend to be a lesser scholar than he was, but he put on no airs, and he was always willing to learn and to change his mind if there was a good reason for doing so. He did not claim to be infallible,[1] and he was the more respected for his good sense in being willing to learn as well as teach. His mind was always open to new ideas.

Driver's married life was stable and happy, and he was devoted to his wife and three daughters. Yet, for all his love of his family and home, he was never in the least domesticated. He had never lived in an ordinary house until he married at the age

[1] I once wrote an essay for him on the Semitic verbal system and ventured to criticize his theory on the ground that it did not account for the origin of *yaqṭul* in West Semitic. He replied that he could not at once remember what his own theory was but that he would look into the question. At the following week's tutorial, he admitted that there was a weakness in his theory. Such frankness, without any attempt to cover up the difficulty, left no doubt in a young man's mind that his teacher was a true scholar.

of 32, and his wife's efficient management of the home relieved him of many domestic cares which often fall to husbands and for which his upbringing in a Victorian canon's home at Christ Church had not prepared him. It was not that he was unwilling to help. When, for example, Lady Driver once asked him if he would open the door of a garden shed that had stuck, he said he would be glad to do so provided she told him where it was. To the end of his days he continued to refer to 'the servants', even when the words bore little relation to the realities of the second half of the twentieth century. Similarly, he would ask his wife what time dinner would be served, and the answer would be simply that his poached egg would be on the table at 7 o'clock. Only once, in the severe winter of 1962–3, did he ever eat a meal in the kitchen, and he said he found it a very uncomfortable place.

One of Driver's characteristics was the possession of a boisterous sense of humour. As a small boy he loved practical jokes and was known to put dates in the gloves of old ladies who were visiting his home. Even in later years he enjoyed hiding in wardrobes and jumping out at people, or lowering children's teddy bears on strings from windows. It is not surprising that he got on well with children—at least, once they were no longer babies. Adults too found him good company. When he was sitting next to ladies at dinner parties or attended by nurses in hospital, his conversation was always entertaining, and a male guest invited to dine with him in college was sure of a good evening. One was often reminded of the spontaneous enthusiasm of a schoolboy, and it was quite in keeping with his personality for him to point to the decanter of claret that was set before a guest in Hall at Magdalen and say, 'There's your booze'.

Driver drove himself hard, and he was not happy unless he could devote long hours to his work. Yet his interests were not restricted to Semitic languages. He was interested in flowers, and it was one of the lasting disappointments of his life that, when he found a new orchid while he was still at Winchester and sent it to Kew, he was told that someone else had reported the same discovery just a few days before. Another long-standing interest was birds, and this interest impinged on his scholarly work, and he published several articles in the *Palestine Exploration Quarterly* for 1955, and in the revised edition of Hastings's *Dictionary of the Bible* in 1963. He read a paper on 'Owls and Ostriches' in Cambridge in 1953 at a meeting of the Society for Old Testament Study, while his pupil D. Winton Thomas was the President, and he sought to show that the Hebrew names for some birds were attempts to represent the sounds they made. Much to the delight of the audience, a small bird flew to the window-sill behind him and perched there, apparently to listen to the bird-like sounds that were being made by the lecturer. Not only did Driver's interests sometimes influence his choice of subjects for papers: his attempts to determine the meaning of biblical passages would also arouse his interest in various subjects. He would, for example, inquire about astronomical matters in order to understand biblical references to constellations, and the help of a medical colleague would be enlisted to identify the disease from which the Philistines in 1 Samuel 5 suffered or the skin diseases in the Old Testament that were traditionally, but inaccurately, known as 'leprosy' (and he claimed that he himself had 'true leprosy'). Similarly, despite his professed ignorance and lack of interest in scientific matters, he learned how alcohol can rise up the side of a glass by capillary attraction—a phenomenon to which he believed there was a reference in Proverbs 23: 31.

His interests did not include sport or organized games. Happily, Winchester was reasonably enlightened, and he did not have to go to the gymnasium more than once. When he went for a cross-country run, he would regularly start with the other boys but leave them near a railway bridge and sit under a bush with a text of Xenophon or Homer, and then rejoin the party on the way back. The same attitude remained in later years. 'The one good thing the scientists have done', he once said in a lecture, 'is to teach us to work in the afternoon.' That was high praise from one who had been to the school chemistry laboratory only twice. Driver's regular exercise was walking from his home to college or, in later years, to the Oriental Institute. He gave up riding a bicycle when he was young, and it is inconceivable that he should ever have driven a car. Lord Wolfenden, who was a Fellow of Magdalen for some years, reports that Driver 'maintained that the only exercise he ever took was following to their graves the coffins of people he knew who played games'.[1]

Another subject in which Driver had no interest was music. Yet he regularly attended services in Magdalen College Chapel, which were renowned for the excellence of the organist and the choir. In that chapel, he used to try out draft passages of the Old Testament for the New English Bible by reading them at

[1] J. H. Wolfenden, *Turning Points. The Memoirs of Lord Wolfenden* (1976), p. 55.

the first lesson at Evensong. Driver was a faithful lay member of the Church of England, and he worshipped in his parish church, St. Andrew's, when there were no services at Magdalen. He also served on the Council of Wycliffe Hall, a theological college in Oxford. His opinions were decidedly low church, and he professed a suspicion of bishops, although a number of them were, in fact, among his friends, and he was pleased that he had once examined F. D. Coggan, the future Archbishop of York and then of Canterbury, for a Hebrew scholarship—and awarded it to him. His religious convictions were firmly held, but he was not a man to talk about them. The one religious principle of which he was prepared to speak was *laborare est orare*, and it is interesting that, when he read J. A. T. Robinson's controversial book *Honest to God*, he said that the only part of which he approved was the chapter on prayer.

When it came to assessing a man's academic ability and character, Driver was a shrewd judge. Though he sometimes made mistakes, he was usually right both in perceiving scholarly promise and in seeing through sham and pretension. If he believed a pupil was worthy of support, he would do all he could to help him, and his recommendations for vacant academic posts carried considerable weight. The late Sir James Duff, for example, the Warden of the Durham Colleges and Driver's former fag at Winchester, consulted him on several occasions about appointments in Hebrew or Old Testament studies. Nor did Driver's help for his pupils stop then. If they—or, indeed, other scholars—wrote to ask his opinion about the meaning of a Hebrew word or about the draft of an article, they would receive a letter or a postcard written in a hand that was regarded by some as pleasing to the eye, or even beautiful, but was found by all to be difficult to read.[1] The contents, which were invariably helpful, usually drew on the resources of his filing cabinet with its many thousands of slips containing lexicographical information.

Driver was primarily a philologist, and much of his work was concerned with the light shed by Semitic languages on one another. He became a general Semitic scholar at a time when it was still possible for one person to make a substantial contri-

[1] When Driver wrote to me to tell me my marks in the Final Honour School of Oriental Studies, he commented—with every justification—that what had counted most against me was my bad handwriting. It was some time before I could decipher his card.

bution to the study of several Semitic languages. During his life, scholarship grew more and more specialized, and it became increasingly difficult for one man to master the problems of several languages. There were limits even to Driver's work, for he wrote primarily about East and North-west Semitic languages. His first published article was, indeed, on 'The linguistic affinities of Syrian Arabic' in the *Journal of the Royal Asiatic Society* for 1920, but he made little contribution to the study of South Semitic languages after his *Grammar of the Colloquial Arabic of Syria and Palestine* in 1925, although he made extensive use of Arabic in his publications on other Semitic languages.

His work as an Assyriologist began early, and he showed his ability in 1925 in *Letters of the First Babylonian Dynasty*. The following year, he contributed an appendix on 'Problems in the book of Genesis in the light of recent Babylonian, Assyrian and Egyptian research' to the twelfth edition of his father's commentary, *The Book of Genesis*; and he was also the author of an article on 'The [Old Testament] Psalms in the Light of Babylonian Research' in *The Psalmists*, edited by D. C. Simpson, whose pupil he had been.[1] He continued to be interested in Accadian studies until the end of his life, and his books on the Assyrian and Babylonian laws were important works. Nevertheless, it was beyond the powers of a scholar with interests as wide as those of Driver to keep in touch with all the most recent developments in Assyriology in later years.

An interest in Aramaic was also shown early. A review in the *Oxford Magazine*, xli (1922) of C. F. Burney, *The Aramaic Origin of the Fourth Gospel*, was followed by two articles on the same subject in the *Jewish Guardian* for 1923. Of the three books of his that were published in 1925, one was, as we have seen, the translation of a Syriac work, *The Bazaar of Heracleides*. A number of articles on Aramaic appeared in later years, but his major work was *Aramaic Documents of the Fifth Century* B.C., which was published in 1954, and in a revised and abridged form in 1957. It is an edition of thirteen letters in the Bodleian Library concerned with the Persian administration of Egypt. The most substantial part of the book is the philological commentary, which displays Driver's usual erudition although he acknowledges the help received from other scholars.

[1] The continuing interest of Driver's article for Old Testament scholars half a century later is shown by the fact that a German translation was recently published in P. H. A. Neumann (ed.), *Zur neueren Psalmenforschung* (1976).

The year after Driver was appointed to his Readership in 1928, texts in a hitherto unknown script and language were discovered at Ras Shamra, the site of the ancient city of Ugarit, on the coast of Syria. Driver played no part in the decipherment of the tablets and early stages of the study of the Ugaritic language, but he followed with characteristic interest developments in this new branch of Semitic studies. His *Canaanite Myths and Legends* (1956) combines in a single volume of moderate size an introduction, bibliography, transliteration of poetic texts, translation, grammatical notes, and glossary. This inexpensive work of reference has helped large numbers of Hebraists to acquaint themselves with the religious poetry of Ugarit and its language, and to see something of their great importance for the study of the Hebrew Bible. Driver's lexicographical suggestions and translations are often tentative, as he would have been the first to admit, but unlike some translators he offers readers the evidence for his renderings so that they may be able to form their own judgements. The book is undoubtedly a major contribution to the understanding of Ugaritic. Driver's work on the subject continued, and he wrote several further articles. He hoped to publish a revised edition of his book, but he eventually committed the revision to Dr. J. C. L. Gibson, a former pupil, and it was published in 1978.

Driver's publications on texts and problems in particular Semitic languages make use of the comparative method, and two of his books are devoted to general Semitic subjects. *Problems of the Hebrew Verbal System* (1936) deals, not only with the problems of the language named in the title, but also with the evolution of the Semitic verbal system in general, and with other, related subjects such as the 'Basis of Semitic Roots' (chap. 2). The principal question discussed is one 'in which I confess a hereditary interest', as Driver says in the preface (p. v), for his father had published *A Treatise on the Use of the Tenses in Hebrew* in 1874 (3rd edn., 1892). S. R. Driver had understood the difference between the imperfect and perfect as a difference of aspect, and had sought to explain the so-called consecutive tenses, in which the usual meanings appear to be reversed, on the basis of that understanding. His son offers an entirely different explanation, partly because he is able to use Accadian evidence[1] not available to his father, and partly because of

[1] He was also aware of the Ugaritic evidence, and said in the preface (p. vi) that it was 'likely to support what is here said in several respects', but he did 'not think it prudent to use a language which is in course of being

publications since the appearance of his father's book. In particular, he is indebted to Hans Bauer, although he rejects a major part of Bauer's theory. Driver argues—if I may present his theory in an oversimplified form—that the original Semitic verb was **qátil*, a primarily stative and intransitive form which could be used of past, present, or future. The second form to be developed was **yaqátil*, an active and transitive verb which was used of the present and the future. The third was the preterite **yáqtul*. In Hebrew, **qátil* has developed into the perfect *qāṭál*, an active and transitive form which is normally used of the past; and **yáqtul* has become the imperfect *yiqṭṓl* with a meaning not unlike that of **yaqátil*. However, traces of earlier meanings survive in the consecutive tenses, in certain other idioms, and in poetry. Hebrew is a mixed language: its consecutive tenses exhibit an affinity with East Semitic and an earlier stage of development, and the ordinary tenses represent the later, West Semitic stage. There are difficulties and inconsistencies in Driver's theory, and it is scarcely surprising that it cannot be accepted in its entirety forty years later. Indeed, one of Driver's pupils, T. W. Thacker, has suggested in *The Relationship of the Semitic and Egyptian Verbal Systems* (1954) some ways in which it needs to be modified. Nevertheless, Driver's book has an important place in the history of the subject, and it cannot be neglected by any scholar interested in the problem. The other general Semitic work is *Semitic Writing from Pictograph to Alphabet* (1948, revised editions in 1954 and 1976), the Schweich Lectures for 1944. The three chapters discuss in turn cuneiform scripts, alphabetic writing, and the origin of the alphabet, and the work contains a mass of information and is well illustrated by diagrams, drawings, and plates. It is an essential book for anyone interested in the origin of the alphabet. Driver also planned a book on Semitic philology, on which he used to lecture, but he did not manage to complete it in a form suitable for publication.

While Driver published books and articles on several Semitic languages, classical Hebrew stood at the centre of his interests. Before we look at his work on the Hebrew Bible, it will be convenient to consider his writings on the Dead Sea Scrolls.

As soon as the discovery of the first scrolls at Qumran in 1947 was made public, Driver took an interest in these important new documents. After writing several letters to *The Times* and

deciphered largely with the help of Hebrew to throw light on unsolved problems in Hebrew itself'.

articles for journals, he delivered the fourth of the Dr. Williams Lectures in October 1950, and it was published (in a form that made use of more recent information) as *The Hebrew Scrolls from the Neighbourhood of Jericho and the Dead Sea* in the following year. He gave a summary of the information available at the time of writing, and then discussed the date. His independence of most scholars was shown by his arguing for a date between A.D. 200 and 500, much later than the pre-Christian date favoured by some. So late a dating was abandoned by him a few years afterwards, but it was not an unreasonable hypothesis at the time, and he advanced carefully reasoned arguments against a date before the Christian era. The palaeographical argument for an early date seemed to him unconvincing in view of the paucity of comparable material, and he rightly questioned the claim that the jars in which the scrolls were found came from the Hellenistic, not the Roman, period and the further argument that the scrolls must, therefore, have been written before the Roman conquest of Palestine—and R. de Vaux was soon to admit that his early dating of the jars had been mistaken. Driver's arguments were concerned chiefly with the paragraph division in the biblical manuscripts, the biblical text, and the orthography and the light it shed on the contemporary language. He believed that the scrolls had been written at a time when the text of the Hebrew Bible had begun to be standardized, and when Hebrew was no longer, in any sense, a living language, and that the evidence favoured a date in the Christian era, and not too near its beginning. In particular, he noted the spelling of the second person masculine singular pronominal suffix and the perfect with a final *-āh*, and the argument of E. Sievers and P. E. Kahle that it was a late phenomenon in Biblical Hebrew, though he did not date its origin as late as in Kahle's theory. It is now plain that the theories of Sievers and Kahle must be revised, and Driver later modified his own argument, but it, like the other arguments that he first advanced for the dating of the scrolls, seemed much more plausible in 1951 than it did in the light of further discussion. When the evidence showed that Driver's date for the scrolls was in need of revision, he was prepared to modify his first, provisional theory.

Within the next few years, Driver advanced a theory about the origin of the scrolls which was essentially the same as the one advocated by Dr. C. Roth, the Reader in Jewish Studies at Oxford. Driver read papers on the subject on various occasions, and worked out his theory at length in the Cadbury Lectures in Birmingham University in 1958, which were published in an expanded form in 1965 as *The Judaean Scrolls*. He argued that the Qumran sect was, not the Essenes as the majority of scholars held, but the Zealots, and that the Teacher of Righteousness (or rather, in his opinion, the Rightful Teacher) was a messianic pretender named Menahem who was killed in A.D. 66 by his enemy Eleazar, whom Driver identified with the Wicked Priest (cf. Josephus, *Jewish War*, II, xvii. 8, 9 [§§ 433–40, 448]). While he dated the Manual of Discipline *c.* A.D. 44–66, before the siege and destruction of Jerusalem, Driver believed that some documents at Qumran were written later: the Habakkuk Commentary about A.D. 70–3, the Thanksgiving Hymns soon after 73, the War Scroll between then and 115–17, and the Zadokite Document some time before 132–5. The caves at Qumran served, he maintained, as a *genizah*, in which heterodox writings and biblical texts that did not conform to the newly established standards were concealed by orthodox Jews in the first part of the second century A.D. Such opinions continued to be defended by Driver in a number of articles.

The Judaean Scrolls differs from most of Driver's publications in that it is concerned with historical questions, although it also shows his more usual linguistic interests. It contains much detailed information and discussion about Jewish sects, the historical background, contemporary beliefs and practices, different calendrical systems, ciphers and cryptograms, the bearing of the scrolls on the study of the New Testament, and a variety of other subjects. The main theses for which the book argues have not won wide acceptance among scholars, but there are two reasons why it is of great value even for those who do not share all the author's opinions. First, the detailed information relevant to the scrolls remains useful whether or not the inferences drawn from it by Driver are accepted. Secondly, it is healthy for a widely accepted theory, like the view that the Qumran sectarians were Essenes, to be challenged by a competent scholar, and for attention to be drawn to its difficulties and weaknesses. Driver argues his case forcibly with a wealth of relevant knowledge. The closing paragraph shows his modest awareness that his own conclusions might 'be disproved by subsequent discovery and research'. Many scholars believe that those conclusions are improbable, but they have no right to put forward different theories unless they have faced and answered Driver's arguments.

The grammar, the text, and above all the lexicography of the

Hebrew Bible were probably of greater interest to Driver than anything else. He published numerous articles on the subject of Hebrew lexicography, and he amassed many thousands of slips recording material of lexicographical interest for the Hebrew dictionary that he hoped to prepare in collaboration with Professor D. Winton Thomas. His influence is clearly to be seen in the translation of the Old Testament in the New English Bible, which has reached millions of readers outside the world of Semitic scholarship. In these parts of his work, he was conscious of the example set by his father, for S. R. Driver had shared in the preparation of the Revised Version of the Old Testament, and was, with F. Brown and C. A. Briggs, an editor of *A Hebrew and English Lexicon of the Old Testament* (1907).

There can be no doubt that the vocabulary of Hebrew was far more extensive when it was a living language than the entries in any standard lexicon of the Old Testament. Driver believed that many lost meanings could be recovered by comparison with other Semitic languages. In particular, he believed that a large number of problems that had led scholars to emend the text could be more satisfactorily solved by postulating that the text was sound (at least, the consonantal text, for the later vocalization was less reliable), and that the word, or words, in question had a meaning that had been forgotten in later times. Sometimes, too, it was necessary to distinguish between two different Hebrew roots, although they appear as a single root in the dictionaries. Brown, S. R. Driver, and Briggs, for example, regarded the Hebrew verb *ʿāḇar*, 'pass over, through, by, pass on', as cognate with Arabic *ʿabara* with a similar meaning, and derive from the same root *ʿeḇrāh*, 'overflow, arrogance, fury'. G. R. Driver, however, believed that the noun has nothing to do with 'overflow' and with the Hebrew verb, but that it is related to Arabic *ǵabira*, 'to bear rancour'; the roots are distinguished in Arabic, but the two Arabic consonants *ʿain* and *ghain* correspond to the one Hebrew consonant *ʿayin*, and most lexicographers have confused the roots in Hebrew. Such a use of Arabic, or some other cognate language, as an aid to the understanding of Hebrew was not, of course, invented by Driver. It has a long history behind it, and the example given above goes back to J. D. Michaelis in the eighteenth century. Driver developed the method in the light of the extensive modern knowledge of Semitic languages and the principles of comparative Semitic philology. Further, he argued, many meanings that were lost in later times are preserved in the ancient versions of the Old Testament, whose renderings are often confirmed by a comparison with words in languages cognate with Hebrew. The use of Driver's comparative method to discover a lost meaning of a Hebrew word involves: first, the existence of a difficult word in the Hebrew Bible that does not make sense if it is given its usual meaning; secondly, a suitable meaning in a cognate language or, preferably, languages; thirdly, if possible, a similar translation of the same word somewhere in one or more of the ancient versions. Thus use of this method has had the result that the New English Bible contains many translations not found in older English versions.

Driver's method needs to be used with caution. First, it is necessary to make sure that the difficulties of a passage cannot be solved by ascribing to the words meanings that are well attested elsewhere in the Hebrew Bible; and it cannot be assumed that the derivation of a meaning from a cognate language is always a superior solution of a problem to emendation of the text. Secondly, the meanings of apparent cognates need to be scrutinized very carefully. There are a vast number of words in the various Semitic languages, particularly in the massive vocabulary of Arabic, and it is necessary to check the exact meanings under consideration and to allow for the possibility that they are developments peculiar to a particular language. Thirdly, it is hazardous to use a particular word in an ancient version as evidence for a tradition about the meaning of a Hebrew word without considering the technique used by the translator elsewhere in the same book, and the textual history of the version. The handling of the ancient versions requires specialist skills of its own. There is a whole range of degrees of probability, and it is often difficult to be sure how probable a particular suggestion is. Moreover, while it is legitimate to register theories and suggestions in scholarly journals, it is arguable that greater caution should be exercised before a lexicographical theory is used in an official Church translation of the Old Testament. It is not surprising that there has been a reaction in recent years against the use of the comparative method. The criticisms made by James Barr in *Comparative Philology and the Text of the Old Testament* (1968) have been influential, although it must be stressed that Barr is not opposed to the use of the method provided proper safeguards are observed. It is generally recognized that Driver was sometimes carried away by his enthusiasm, and that a number of translations suggested by him and incorporated in the New English Bible need to be reconsidered. There are even places where resort is had to the questionable expedient of emending the text to produce a *hapax legomenon.*

Nevertheless, the fact that a number of Driver's suggestions are open to question should not lead scholars to lose a sense of proportion and to overlook his convincing contributions to the understanding of the Hebrew Bible. A comparison with cognate languages is undoubtedly helpful in determining the meaning of many Hebrew words, and the Ugaritic texts were translated largely with the help of other Semitic languages. If Driver went too far on occasions, it was usually because the excitement of discovery led him to overlook the principles that he himself advocated, not because comparison of Hebrew with cognate languages is of little value to a lexicographer. Further, he had the art of looking afresh at passages of the Hebrew Bible and seeing problems to which most scholars had been blinded by familiarity. Those who do not accept his solutions have not always offered satisfactory alternative explanations or even shown that they have recognized the problems.

Anyone who read Hebrew at Oxford while Driver was teaching and the late Canon H. Danby was the Regius Professor of Hebrew was fortunate in having the opportunity to learn two different approaches to the textual problems of the Hebrew Bible. Danby was not sympathetic to attempts to discover lost meanings of Hebrew words. Nor did he emend the text very often, not because he believed it to be sacrosanct and free from error, but because he was aware of the uncertain nature of emendations. His first aim was always to make sense, if possible, of the traditional Hebrew text by employing standard grammars and dictionaries, in which well-established meanings of words are recorded—and also, though not all undergraduates who heard him recognized this side of Danby's work, by studying medieval Jewish commentaries. His approach contrasted sharply with Driver's more ingenious method. Both methods are needed for Hebrew studies. Driver's method needs to be checked by Danby's caution. If, however, Danby's method were to be followed to the exclusion of more venturesome ideas, the door would be closed to the progress that can be made by new attempts to solve problems. Any Oxford undergraduate or graduate in the years when the two professors were teaching who was willing and able to learn from them both was well equipped to face the problems of the Hebrew Bible. Driver was undoubtedly the greater scholar of Biblical Hebrew, but it was good that Danby's voice was heard as well.

A most important part of Driver's contribution to the study of Hebrew was his teaching. He was a most stimulating lecturer. It was not that he had mastered the technique of lecturing. Indeed, he often broke the rules by, for example, writing words from various Semitic languages on the blackboard at high speed and then rubbing them out again before his pupils had had time to decipher and copy them. What made his lectures so exciting was his infectious enthusiasm. No lecture of his that I attended was ever dull: every one was a stimulating experience in which those present learned something new and shared something of Driver's excitement and interest. I was fortunate in hearing a number of good lecturers in the years I studied at Oxford, but none was as inspiring as Driver.

No attempt was made by Driver to fit his pupils into a mould. He valued independence of judgement and scorned any idea of founding a 'school' of pupils who would regularly follow the master; that would have seemed to him academical egotism unworthy of a scholar. He did his best to help his pupils, and he presented to them what he believed to be the truth, but he respected them if they made up their own minds and did not follow slavishly what he taught. He wanted them to think for themselves and to have a good knowledge of the relevant texts in the original language, and what mattered above all to him was, as he said, 'to do good work'.

A number of Driver's pupils and friends subscribed to the cost of a drawing of him by William Dring. It hangs on the wall of the top floor of the Oriental Institute,[1] which is itself a memorial to his enterprise and energy. Near it hangs a picture of his father.

J. A. Emerton

Note. A list of Driver's publications up to 1962 can be found in D. Winton Thomas and W. D. McHardy (eds.), *Hebrew and Semitic Studies presented to Godfrey Rolles Driver* (Oxford, 1963). It is hoped to publish a supplementary list in a future issue of *Vetus Testamentum*. I am indebted to Lady Driver, and to Professors W. G. Lambert and Edward Ullendorff for help in preparing this obituary.

[1] There is another drawing of him by the same artist in Magdalen College.

SIR RALPH HAWTREY, C.B.

RALPH GEORGE HAWTREY

1879–1975

I

THE increase in the number and importance of economists in government since the beginning of the Second World War is a fact which has been fully documented and widely discussed. Many of these have been academics who forsook their university posts temporarily or permanently to assist the work of various Civil Service departments through their expertise as economic advisers. This now familiar pattern was almost reversed in the career of R. G. Hawtrey—a career in the Home Civil Service lasting from 1903 to 1945 during which he used his spare time to write and publish more learned articles and books on economics than the majority of his academic contemporaries and established an international reputation for his contributions to the subject, mainly on the monetary side. As Claude Guillebaud wrote of him in 1944: 'An essentially academic economist, [Mr. Hawtrey] is attached to no teaching university, but looks out over the world from the Olympian heights of the Treasury.'

Like many distinguished servants of the Crown, Hawtrey came into the Civil Service by way of Eton and Cambridge. The family connection with Eton was an especially strong one; its members have been associated with the college, both as pupils and masters, for over four hundred years—the first Hawtrey was recorded as a King's Scholar at Eton in 1565.

Ralph Hawtrey's grandfather, John William Hawtrey, was Assistant Master of the Lower School at Eton from 1842 until 1869 and a second cousin of the famous Edward Craven Hawtrey, Headmaster of Eton from 1834 to 1853 and Provost from 1853 until his death in 1862. In 1869 John Hawtrey left Eton to establish a preparatory school, St. Michael's, at Aldin House, Slough, and later his son, George Procter Hawtrey, became assistant master there. Hence it was at Slough that Ralph was born on 22 November 1879, the third child of George Procter Hawtrey and his first wife, the former Miss Eda Strahan. The two other children of the marriage—Freda and Phyllis predeceased their brother, but Freda lived with him in his London house from the Second World War until her death in 1964.

It was not from Aldin House but from Mr. Brackenbury's school, Pinewoods, Farnborough, that Ralph Hawtrey came to Eton in 1893 as a King's Scholar, with Hugh Macnaghten, later Vice-Provost, as his classical tutor. Hawtrey's interests and abilities were not in classics but in mathematics; at that time, however, there were no mathematical specialists acting as modern tutors. A pupil of Dyer's in mathematics, Hawtrey won the Tomline Prize, Eton's highest mathematical award, in 1896. In the following year he gained a wider distinction, and even some notoriety, when his first article appeared in the *Fortnightly Review* for September 1897.[1] Entitled 'The Speed of Warships', it strongly criticized the then existing system of Admiralty steam trials as giving no accurate comparison of the capabilities of ships in the fleet, and concluded 'Certainly the present system seems anything but satisfactory and something ought to be done as soon as possible to make the trials more dependable'.

That the matter was 'one of great public interest and importance' was admitted by no less a person than Sir William Henry White, then Director of Naval Construction, in a rejoinder published in the next issue of the *Fortnightly* which amounted to an official examination and refutation of Hawtrey's charges. In the meantime it had become publicly known that the article was the work of an Eton boy and Hawtrey's father had been congratulated on his son's distinction by the aged Gladstone himself. In a somewhat ungracious postscript to his own article Sir William White declared 'Had I known the[se] facts I should have made no reply', but nevertheless conceded that 'in many ways the congratulation is deserved'.

From Eton Hawtrey went up to Cambridge in the autumn of 1898, gaining a Minor Scholarship to Trinity. There he read Mathematics and was twice a Prizeman—in his Freshman year and again in his third year. In 1901 he was nineteenth Wrangler —a result which, however creditable, disappointed his old Eton teacher, Dyer, and led another Eton mathematics master, Hurst, to hold Hawtrey up to another Eton pupil, Maynard Keynes, as 'a dreadful example of a person who has tried to do too many things'.[2]

Keynes, with whom Hawtrey's name and works were so often to be linked and contrasted in later years, could not bring himself to agree that Hawtrey had 'lost his soul in knowing something besides Mathematics'. With that judgement Hawtrey

[1] *Fortnightly Review*, 72 (New Series), 435–44.

[2] R. F. Harrod, *The Life of John Maynard Keynes* (1951), p. 41.

himself would surely have agreed; he might well have felt that he had not lost his soul but found it. As he himself wrote some seventy years later 'when I went up to Trinity, Cambridge, as an undergraduate I had the good fortune to come under the influence of G. E. Moore, who had just been elected a fellow'; and the influence of Moore's ethics upon him was profound and lasting.

Many of those who, like Keynes, came under the influence of that system of ethics at the beginning of this century later modified their views, but Hawtrey did not. The view which he learned from Moore, 'that the Good is a matter of direct judgment and is not to be explained away in terms of anything else' remained the core of his philosophy all through his long life.

With characteristic reticence, Hawtrey appears never to have written down any details of how he came to gain the interest and approval of Moore; but that he had it is unquestionable for as an undergraduate he was elected to the company of the Apostles, which then included E. M. Forster, Leonard Woolf, Desmond MacCarthy, Lytton Strachey, Roger Fry, and Saxon Sydney-Turner. Hawtrey was in fact one of the Apostles who elected Keynes to membership in 1903 and it was at this time that their long friendship began. Another friendship formed at Cambridge was with Bertrand Russell; here mathematical interests seem to have been the source and when Whitehead and Russell were writing *Principia Mathematica* in 1908, Russell was corresponding with Hawtrey concerning the proof of various theorems.

Many of Hawtrey's Cambridge friends and colleagues were later to form part of the Bloomsbury Group, and he continued his association with them when his career brought him back to London. Readers of the now extensive literature of and on Bloomsbury will thus encounter the name of Ralph Hawtrey frequently—staying in Cornwall with the young Stephens in the summer of 1905, spending Easter at Salisbury in 1908 with G. E. Moore, Lytton Strachey, Keynes, and Rupert Brooke, and from November 1914 joining the company at Lady Ottoline Morrell's Thursday evenings. That company often included the d'Aranyi sisters, all talented musicians, as befitted the great nieces of Joseph Joachim. The three sisters, of whom the youngest, Jelly d'Aranyi, was to become the best known, were then living with their mother at Beaufort Mansions, Chelsea, where Hawtrey also resided at this time. Hence it was that he met the girl who was to become his wife—Emilia d'Aranyi, second of the three. Like her sisters Emilia had exceptional musical ability but while Adila and Jelly were noted violinists, she enjoyed a considerable reputation as a pianist.

Emilia retired from the concert platform after she and Ralph Hawtrey were married in 1915. Their devotion to each other, remarked upon by Virginia Woolf when she encountered them as newly-weds, remained unaltered down the years, although shadowed by Emilia Hawtrey's long illness which lasted over fifteen years prior to her death in 1953.

Throughout the Bloomsbury years Hawtrey, like his fellow Apostle Sydney-Turner, was an established Civil Servant at the Treasury. He said in later years that his decision to work for the Civil Service examinations arose from the fact that while he was still at Eton he had been told that in the Civil Service one could be sure of an income of £1,000 a year by the age of forty, and of a pension too. At all events the prospects were sufficiently attractive in those days to produce intense competition and at least a year's preparation was considered essential for those who attempted the examinations. It seems to have been while engaged in this preparation at Cambridge that Hawtrey received such formal teaching in economics as he ever had—mainly from G. P. Moriarty, who was then acting as Director of Studies for those Cambridge men who intended to enter the open competition for the Home and Indian Civil Services. He also attended some of Clapham's lectures but was never a pupil of Marshall's—contrary to a widespread impression which seems to have developed from later attempts to categorize his theory of the demand for money as 'in the Marshallian tradition'.

A somewhat similar impression prevails that because Hawtrey spent so much of his career in the Treasury he also began it there. Yet in fact when he was successful in the open competition for the Civil Service in 1903 he went first to the Admiralty—perhaps because of his early interest in matters of naval policy. But in 1904 the Treasury's Upper Establishment of twenty-five was increased by the creation of one additional First Class Clerkship. As a result of the subsequent promotions, a new Junior Clerk was needed. One of the Joint Permanent Secretaries, Sir Edward Hamilton (who had begun his career as Gladstone's private secretary) proposed that the vacancy should be filled by 'the transfer from another office of one of the successful competitors at the last examination' and his choice fell on Hawtrey. Hence it was that the latter's long association with the Treasury began in January 1904, as a Second Class

Clerk in what was then the Third Division. In 1909 Hawtrey came into the First (Finance) Division as an acting First Class Clerk, but in 1910 Lloyd George, then Chancellor of the Exchequer, appointed Hawtrey to be his Principal Private Secretary and in that capacity he assisted in the work of preparing the Budget. He became an established First Class Clerk in the summer of 1911 and remained in that grade until appointed Director of Financial Enquiries in 1919.

The Financial Enquiries Branch had been established as a special branch of the Treasury in 1915 'to collect information upon all subjects of general financial interest and to prepare reports from time to time both on its own initiative and also upon any question which may be specially referred to it by the Chancellor of the Exchequer'. The post of Director of the branch was first held by Hartley Withers, but he relinquished it in July 1916, and the position was not filled until Hawtrey was promoted to it on 1 October 1919 with the rank of Assistant Secretary.

The rest of Hawtrey's career at the Treasury was spent in the Financial Enquiries Branch, apart from a period of nine months in 1928–9 when, unusually for a Civil Servant in those days, he was given leave of absence to take up a visiting Professorship at Harvard University. It had been intended that he should retire at the end of 1939, but with the outbreak of war he continued in post until his sixty-fifth birthday in November 1944. Even then his association with the Treasury was not at an end, for he was immediately re-employed to complete the chronicle of its wartime activities on which he had been working and only relinquished his appointment finally in October 1947.

It was in these years between 1919 and 1947 that Hawtrey made his most important published contributions to the development of economics, and between 1919 and 1939 he was the only established Civil Servant in the Treasury who could be considered a professional economist. An attempt to summarize and assess his achievement over these years in the twin spheres of monetary economics and economic policy cannot easily be combined with a narrative outline of his life, and is therefore attempted separately in sections II and III of this memoir.

Hawtrey's standing as a scholar in his chosen field, already recognized by his election to Fellowship of the British Academy in 1935, received further recognition in 1939 when London University conferred on him an honorary D.Sc. (Econ.). He was elected President of the Royal Economic Society for the years

1946–8 and in 1959 his old Cambridge college, Trinity, made him an Honorary Fellow. More significant perhaps was the fact that when the late Professor A. G. B. Fisher resigned the Price Chair of International Economics at the Royal Institute of International Affairs in 1946 the Advisory Committee set up to appoint a successor decided to offer the appointment to Ralph Hawtrey, and he took it up at the beginning of the academic year 1947–8, just after he finally left the Treasury.

Hawtrey served as Price Professor at Chatham House from 1947 until 1952. His position as the holder of a research chair gave him the opportunity to produce revised editions of some of his works—a fourth edition of his best-known book, *Currency and Credit*, and a second edition of his *Economic Aspects of Sovereignty.* He also began a new work, at that time provisionally entitled *Public Spirit, or the Ethics of Social and Political Motives*, an attempt to apply the ethical system of G. E. Moore to the problems of political judgements. His duties, however, required him to act as economic adviser on all aspects of the work of the R.I.I.A. and in consequence he became involved in work on Britain's balance of payments problem and early studies of the prospects and problem of Western European Union. Both of these studies resulted in publications—*The Balance of Payments and the Standard of Living* in 1950 and *Western European Union* in 1949; but the projected book on the ethics of politics did not appear.

After his retirement from the Price Professorship in 1952 Hawtrey seems to have considered that his first task was to use his knowledge of monetary economics to endeavour through public comment to change the course of what he considered to be the basically mistaken financial policies to which successive British governments committed themselves. This he continued to do in a series of books, pamphlets, articles, and newspaper comments right up to the time of his death in 1975. All these writings were dominated, some would have said and indeed did say, vitiated, by his unswerving belief that the devaluation of the pound in 1949 had been excessive and that its consequent under-valuation was the source of most if not all of Britain's international economic problems.

His work on philosophical problems was nevertheless continued; in the long tranquil evening of his life he went on thinking about that 'something else besides mathematics' which had first caught his interest at Cambridge some seventy years earlier, and he left behind at his death the completed typescripts of two books on ethics—*Right Policy: the Place of Value Judgments in Politics*, the final version of the study begun at Chatham House, and another more general work entitled *Thought and Things*.

Until the very end of his life Ralph Hawtrey remained active and interested in the world around him—a world which must have seemed to him almost incredibly different from the stable post-Gladstonian world of the Treasury of 1904, but which he yet looked on with more tolerance and understanding than many younger men could muster. At his Kensington home, 29 Argyll Road, W.8, where his domestic needs were well looked after by his faithful housekeeper Miss Ruse, he received hospitably many economists, making available to them his vast fund of recollections of the making of economic theory and economic policy in the first half of the twentieth century. Professor Richard Sayers who called on Sir Ralph (as he had become in 1956) to congratulate him on his ninety-fifth birthday in November 1974 noted afterwards 'I found him in most ways still the same charming and interesting man I first met some forty-two years ago'. It was Hawtrey's good fortune, perhaps not undeserved, to retain to the last that combination of great intellect and gentle character which impressed themselves on all who came into contact with him.

II

In the early 1960s a reviewer of one of the last in the long series of Hawtrey's books wrote that in it 'Sir Ralph Hawtrey does not disappoint the faithful who expect him to extol the importance first, of bank rate as an instrument of monetary policy and, secondly, of the alleged under-valuation of the pound sterling since it was devalued in 1949'. This neatly summarizes what may be said to be the current stereotype of Hawtrey's economics—dominated in the post-Second World War years by one King Charles's Head, the under-valuation of sterling, and in the inter-war years by another, the view that 'the trade cycle is a purely monetary phenomenon' which might be cured by appropriate adjustments of monetary policy in general and bank-rate policy in particular.

Like all stereotypes, this one contains an element of truth and an element of injustice. Certainly it draws attention to a central feature of Hawtrey's economics—that it was a monetary economics and monetary economics conceived in an international context. Yet that monetary economics was far more subtle and complex than the stereotype would suggest; and while it was certainly the major part of Hawtrey's economic thought it was not the whole; he also published ideas on the scope and method of economics and on the theory of production and distribution, the quality of which cannot fairly be judged by the neglect into which they have fallen.

A notable feature of Hawtrey's economics is its consistency. He was a contributor to the subject for a period of more than fifty-five years and many of the key ideas which he presented in his first book *Good and Bad Trade* (1913) are still to be found in his last, *Incomes and Money* (1967), as in many of the twenty other books which came between. As he himself wrote to Keynes in May 1937 'I have adhered consistently to my fundamental ideas since 1913 and in so far as they have developed and grown the process has been continuous since then. There has not been a departure followed by a relapse. I do not think this conservatism is a merit; indeed I should rather like to go in for something novel and extravagant if I could be convinced of it'.[1]

To some of his contemporaries Hawtrey's ideas appeared at times both novel and extravagant, but their development was undeniably continuous and based upon one fundamental and central idea—that of the wealth value of the monetary unit. Hawtrey, the Cambridge mathematician, came to this idea somewhat in the same way as Malthus, the first Cambridge economist, came to his central idea—through arguing with his father. In the political debates at the beginning of this century George Hawtrey was apparently convinced by the arguments of the tariff reformers while his son Ralph was equally firmly on the side of free trade. The latter was thus led to study with typical thoroughness the speeches of some of the leading politicians of the time and was particularly struck by a point made by Joseph Chamberlain in 1903, to the effect that British exports had not increased over the preceding thirty years. On looking into this he realized Chamberlain's figures related to the *value* of British exports in 1872 and 1902 and that the *volume* of those exports had actually increased substantially.[2] Hence the significance of changes in the general level of prices came home to Hawtrey and he began to study the forces affecting it—a study which was to become a life's work.

[1] Hawtrey to Keynes, May 1937; *Collected Writings of John Maynard Keynes*, xiv. 55.

[2] 'The Case for Tariff Reform', speech made in Glasgow by Joseph Chamberlain on 6 Oct. 1903, *Mr Chamberlain's Speeches*, edited by Charles Wood, 2 vols. (1914), ii. 145.

The basic ideas to which that study led him were outlined in *Good and Bad Trade* some ten years later and could be said to have emerged fully fledged in *Currency and Credit* (1919)—perhaps Hawtrey's most influential work and one which appeared just when he had first reached a senior level in the Treasury through his appointment as Director of Financial Enquiries.

Before examining the content of those ideas it may be useful to look briefly at their sources and the methods which Hawtrey employed in presenting them. It seems fair to say that Hawtrey arrived at the basic ideas of his system in almost complete independence from the work of other economists. In *Good and Bad Trade* there is a striking dearth of references to the contemporary literature of monetary economics—only Irving Fisher's work is actually mentioned by name. *Currency and Credit* has more references to current economic writings, but only from the rather obscure nineteenth-century work of H. D. Macleod on banking and credit does Hawtrey seem to have derived any of the ideas he put forward in the book. All of this is consistent with what Claude Guillebaud, writing with the authority of Sir Ralph himself, put on record in 1964—that 'he learnt his monetary economics as a Civil Servant in the Treasury, and cannot recollect having been influenced by Marshall; though he does acknowledge some indebtedness to Bagehot'.[1]

By what means exactly Hawtrey learnt his monetary economics in the Treasury can only be surmised; but it seems likely that he was considerably influenced by Sir John (afterwards Lord) Bradbury, who became Joint Permanent Secretary in 1913 and under whom Hawtrey had served in the Finance Division ('1D') from 1909. When, in his old age, Hawtrey reminisced about the Treasury he always described Bradbury as the ablest man he ever encountered in the Civil Service and stressed the intimate knowledge of City activities and the working of the monetary system which he possessed. Given the lack of close relations between the Treasury, the Bank of England, and the City before 1914, such knowledge was unusual and it seems likely that when the young Hawtrey began to look at the monetary system from the Treasury his view was largely formed with the aid of Bradbury's experience.

Although there seems no reason to question Hawtrey's disclaimer of any influence on him from Marshall, the method which he used in his economics was curiously similar to Marshall's. An able mathematician, as Marshall was, Hawtrey

[1] *Economic Journal*, 74 (June 1964), 475.

relegated any mathematics he used in his economic writings to footnotes and appendixes, and eschewed diagrams, as Marshall did. Clear, straightforward prose was the essential medium through which he conveyed his ideas. Many of those ideas were such as to admit of statistical testing and it must seem strange to modern economists that while Hawtrey sometimes discussed the possibilities of such testing he never attempted to carry it out; unlike Irving Fisher, that other leading theorist of the price level, he was not among the pioneers of econometrics. That cannot have been because of any lack of ability to command the necessary techniques; rather it may have been, as with Marshall, the result of a recognition of the qualitative complexity of reality. Certainly, like Marshall, Hawtrey had a great respect for the historical method; Keynes in 1920 remarked on the fact that 'so pure a theorist as Mr. Hawtrey should be so interested in economic history'. It was an interest which never waned and some of the historical studies which he made in search of evidence to support or disprove his theories are major works of scholarship in themselves; *A Century of Bank Rate* (1938) is the outstanding example.

Any attempt to outline the theories which Hawtrey developed with the aid of these methods must first set out the essentials of his monetary economics. Perhaps a summary can best begin from his own words in the Preface to the fourth (1950) edition of *Currency and Credit*:

> The theme of the book in its original form was the underlying unity of certain economic happenings: inflation; the cyclical alternations of activity and depression; financial crises; disturbances of the balance of payments and rates of exchange. All these were to be traced to changes in the wealth-value or purchasing power of the money unit, and changes in the wealth value of the unit, as indicated by the price level, are symptoms of changes in the consumers' income and outlay.
>
> The foundation of the whole theory is the function of the credit system as the source of money. The banks create the means of payment by lending, and thereby are in a position to regulate the flow of money.

Hawtrey conceived the economy which he sought to analyse as composed essentially of consumers and traders—a term which he used to include not only producers, but wholesalers, retailers, and dealers—to whom the interest cost of holding stocks is of special significance. 'Consumers' income' he defined simply as the total of incomes expressed in money, 'consumers' outlay' as the total spent *out of income*—whether on consumable goods and services or on the acquistion of capital assets. Any difference between the income and outlay of an individual consumer over an interval of time is reflected in his cash balance; the total of consumers' and traders' balances—the total of money and bank credit—Hawtrey referred to as the 'unspent margin'.

For each individual consumer the appropriate money balance will bear a determinate proportion to his income, and for each trader it will bear a determinate proportion to his turnover. Consumers and traders can release or absorb cash by altering these proportions—or as a result of increases or decreases in the supply of credit made available by the monetary authorities. Hence, to quote Hawtrey again, 'an expansion of credit is a device for causing a release of cash and a contraction of credit a device for causing an absorption of cash'. A contraction of credit, for example, will produce an absorption of cash, and a reduction of consumers' outlay. Retail sales will be reduced in consequence; retailers and wholesalers find themselves holding increased stocks and cut orders to producers who in turn reduce output and employment. Traders will seek to stimulate sales by reducing prices, and the fall of prices tends to relieve the situation but 'the process of readjustment will not be complete till wages are reduced in proportion to prices and pending that stage there is likely to be unemployment'.

Through the machinery of credit, bankers thus possess the power of regulating consumers' income and outlay, and hence the level of prices and of employment. But, Hawtrey argued, there is an inherent instability in the creation of bank credit. In the opening chapters of *Currency and Credit* Hawtrey showed with great clarity that a pure credit system would not be self-righting, but could generate cumulative falls or rises in money demand, employment, and prices because 'an increase in the supply of credit itself stimulates the demand for credit, just as a restriction in the supply of credit leads to a decline in the demand for credit'.

Pointing out that 'the expansive tendencies of credit are in perpetual conflict with the maintenance of a fixed standard of value, and a great part of our subject is taken up with the problem of how best to reconcile this conflict', Hawtrey moved to consider the case of an economy with a central bank which adheres to a gold standard and hence must be guided in its credit policy by the foreign exchanges. In these circumstances he argued that there would be a tendency for the instability of credit to take the form of a cycle. A period of expanding credit leads to rising incomes, prices, and employment, but ultimately also to a drain on the gold reserves of the banking system;

bankers are then forced to protect their reserves by contracting credit and raising rates of interest. The resultant effects on consumers' income and outlay and on traders' holding of stocks is to produce a period of falling prices and employment. Reserves are restored and ultimately bankers will seek to extend credit again at rates of interest which being below even the reduced profit rates experienced by traders serve to create a fresh expansion.

It was on this analysis that Hawtrey based his famous dictum that 'the trade cycle is a purely monetary phenomenon'. As such it could be controlled and even prevented by the use of monetary weapons, primarily Bank Rate. To the objection that rises in Bank Rate served only to over-correct an over-expansion when it had already gone too far Hawtrey always replied that this was because the Bank of England and other central banks under the gold standard were 'guided by a very tardy signal' in the state of the gold reserves. To prevent a slump it was necessary sooner to control the previous boom, through the use of a credit policy designed to stabilize consumers' income and hence general demand and the price level. Clearly no single national central bank could operate such a policy individually while adhering to the rules of the gold standard. Hence it followed that if the international gold standard system was to be preserved some form of international action to prevent variations in the wealth-value of gold was essential.

From this outline it can be seen that the theory of the trade cycle which gained so much attention from Hawtrey's contemporaries in the inter-wars years was in fact only a particular case of the general monetary model which he evolved—and a case of limited interest to him for he always insisted that the trade cycle as such had ceased to exist after 1914—the post-1918 world economy, whatever its instabilities, did not seem to him to exhibit the same regular periodicity.

The general monetary model itself might now be characterized as a fairly simple aggregate demand macro-model with near-perfect markets and a minimum of structural rigidities in it. Its originality and pioneering significance only becomes evident when it is remembered that Hawtrey developed it during the war of 1914–18 and that it was published in 1919, four years before Keynes produced his *Tract on Monetary Reform*. It is not surprising then that Keynes regarded Hawtrey as his 'grandparent in the paths of errancy'.[1]

[1] J. M. Keynes, 'Alternative Theories of the Rate of Interest', *Economic*

The question of the relations between the ideas of Keynes and the ideas of Hawtrey is a fascinating one which has already been the subject of one detailed paper and may well provide material for more.[1] The two men had ample opportunities for discussion, both at Cambridge and in the Treasury, prior to 1919 and the extent and effect of those discussions can only be a matter for conjecture. Yet there seems no reason to reject the view suggested by the quotation given above, that the first influence was of Hawtrey on Keynes, rather than Keynes on Hawtrey. Here Hawtrey's lack of contact with Marshall is significant, for while Keynes had to emancipate himself from the 'classical economics' which he had learned from Marshall, Hawtrey was always independent of it. So he was able to lead the way in the transition from the quantity-theory approach to the short-period analysis of changes in income prices and employment which characterized the monetary economics of the inter-war years.

The character of the relationship between the thinking of Keynes and Hawtrey as it stood before the appearance of *A Treatise on Money* was well stated by Keynes himself in a discussion at the Royal Statistical Society in December 1929: 'There are very few writers on monetary subjects from whom one receives more stimulus and useful suggestion than from Mr. Hawtrey, and I think there are few writers on these subjects with whom I personally feel in more fundamental sympathy and agreement. The paradox is that in spite of that, I nearly always disagree in detail with what he says!'[2]

In the case of both the *Treatise* and the *General Theory* Keynes sent copies of the proofs to Hawtrey before publication. Hawtrey took immense pains to produce detailed criticisms, which he afterwards published,[3] but in spite of the most sincere efforts to understand each others' doctrines, the differences between the approaches of the two men seemed to grow as Keynes's ideas developed from the *Treatise* to the *General Theory*. Yet it may well be, as Professor E. G. Davis has suggested, that Hawtrey was influential in setting Keynes on the path which led from one book to the other, by drawing his attention to the

Journal, 47 (June 1937), reprinted in *Collected Writings of John Maynard Keynes*, xiv. 202.

[1] E. G. Davis, 'The Role of R. G. Hawtrey in Keynesian Economics and the Economics of Keynes', *Carleton Economic Papers*, No. 77-12.

[2] *Collected Writings of John Maynard Keynes*, xiii. 127.

[3] His critique of the *Treatise* appears in the *Art of Central Banking*, pp. 332–411, that of the *General Theory* in *Capital and Employment*, pp. 164–232.

importance of changes in output at a time when, as Sir Austin Robinson put it 'Keynes was still thinking primarily of the factors which made prices go up and down'.[1]

After the *General Theory* there developed what Sir John Hicks in 1939 described as 'the great dispute about the working of monetary control—a dispute which has made most English economists either Keynesians or Hawtreyans'.[2] Hawtrey, following out the implications of his basic model, stressed the key influence of Bank Rate on short-term interest rates generally and thus on the cost to traders of holding stocks.

Keynes did not believe in the effectiveness of this mechanism and argued that only in so far as a change in Bank Rate affected the terms on which long-term capital could be raised by industry would it affect economic activity. Hawtrey devoted a great deal of effort to a detailed examination of the historical evidence on the effects of Bank Rate on short- and long-term borrowing and it is now accepted that the case he made against Keynes's view in *A Century of Bank Rate* (1938) was conclusive.[3]

If Hawtrey's reaction to the *General Theory* was mainly to reaffirm his belief in the correctness of his own basic monetary model he did nevertheless introduce some modifications and innovations in his own ideas as a result of his studies not only of the work of Keynes but also of other monetary theorists such as Hayek and Harrod. Some of these changes are to be found in *Capital and Employment*, others in the fourth edition of *Currency and Credit* published in 1949. Perhaps the most notable feature of *Capital and Employment* was an analysis of the time structure of production and the physical processes of long-term investment along the lines of Jevons and Böhm-Bawerk—something which had been absent from the earlier books. It was in this context that Hawtrey introduced the useful distinction between the processes of 'capital widening' and 'capital deepening'. On it he based the argument that 'if the widening of capital equipment is insufficient to absorb the available flow of new savings, it is this favourable state of the investment market that ought to induce the deepening process and restore equilibrium'.

This conviction of the ability of the market to produce

[1] E. A. G. Robinson, 'John Maynard Keynes 1883–1946', *Economic Journal*, 57 (Mar. 1947), 39.

[2] J. R. Hicks, 'Mr. Hawtrey on Bank Rate and the Long-term Rate of Interest', *The Manchester School*, 10 (1939), 21.

[3] For a fuller discussion of this see Sir John Hicks, 'Hawtrey', *Economic Perspectives* (1977), pp. 118–33.

equilibrium between savings and investment was probably one of the main sources of difference between Hawtrey and Keynes. But Hawtrey did modify his position on it to some extent, and in the 1949 edition of *Currency and Credit* conceded that in his earlier writings he 'took for granted too readily that money saved would be invested and that money invested would be spent'. Among his unpublished papers a piece which he had intended to use in this edition but did not suggests further concessions towards the Keynesian viewpoint—notably in these words: 'But over longer periods the fluctuations of working capital become less significant; the increments of working capital due to growth are small compared to the increments of instrumental capital. And the growth of instrumental capital is itself susceptible of wide fluctuations.'[1]

It was always a corollary of Hawtrey's analysis that the economy, although lacking any automatic stabilizer, could nevertheless be effectively stabilized by the proper use of credit policy; it followed that fiscal policy in general and public works in particular constituted an unnecessary and inappropriate control mechanism. Yet Hawtrey was always prepared to admit that there could be circumstances in which no conceivable easing of credit would induce traders to borrow more and in such a case government expenditure might be the only means of increasing employment.

This possibility of such a 'credit deadlock' was admitted in all Hawtrey's writings from *Good and Bad Trade* onwards, but treated as a most unlikely exceptional case. In *Capital and Employment*, however, he admitted that 'unfortunately since 1930 it has come to plague the world, and has confronted us with problems which have threatened the fabric of civilisation with destruction'.

So indeed it had, and in the years that followed opinion, both academic and political, became increasingly convinced that the solution lay in the methods of stabilization by fiscal policy which followed from Keynes's theories rather that in those of stabilization by credit policy which followed from Hawtrey's.

To quote Sir John Hicks, 'Hawtrey would not admit that that is the end of the story';[2] nor is it, but it is the end of a central chapter. For during his years at the Treasury, when his official position involved him in matters of policy, Hawtrey appeared to the world primarily as a theorist. When he had left

[1] Hawtrey Papers, Churchill College, Cambridge, 6/5/17.

[2] Hicks, loc. cit, p. 123.

the Treasury he used his monetary theory mainly to criticize policy. Hence a discussion of his post-1949 writings, especially on the alleged under-valuation of the pound, will follow more naturally after a consideration of his role in policy during his Treasury career.

III

It was not until he was appointed Director of Financial Enquiries in 1919 that Hawtrey was sufficiently highly placed in the Treasury to be party to the inner processes of policy-making. He was already in the Treasury at the time of the financial crisis of 1907 and could recall Bradbury watching the drain of gold from the Bank of England and considering the possibility of a suspension of the Bank Act. The resolution of the crisis must have given him an early lesson in the efficacy of Bank Rate, even if only as a spectator of events. When he became private secretary to Lloyd George in 1910–11 this seems to have remained his role; although Hawtrey had been sent to America with an Inland Revenue official to collect information on United States local taxes in connection with Lloyd George's land-tax proposals he did not write a report on this and in later years he recalled how he 'sat in a corner' while Lloyd George dictated his 1911 budget speech.

After his promotion to First Class Clerk and move to '1D' in the summer of 1911 Hawtrey began to be assigned to work of greater significance; thus he assisted Basil Blackett in the preparation of the Memorandum on Gold Reserves in May 1914, which the Chancellor had called for following the bankers' request for a Royal Commission to examine the whole question of the size and control of gold reserves in London.[1] In the more famous crisis of August 1914 Hawtrey worked with Bradbury and admired his swift appreciation of the need for a special issue of currency notes; in the formulation of the necessary policy and its implementation '1D' played a significant part and Hawtrey gained valuable experience as a member of that small team. No doubt that experience grew as the Treasury's functions in economic management expanded during 1914–18, but in the story of those years Hawtrey's name does not figure prominently —certainly not as prominently as that of Keynes, for whom the special 'A Division' was carved out of the Finance Division in 1917.

[1] See R. S. Sayers, *The Bank of England 1891–1944*, i. 65 and iii. 3–30.

Nevertheless it was the First World War which led to the creation of the Financial Enquiries Branch and it was his appointment as Director of this branch which gave Hawtrey the opportunity to comment on and sometimes to participate in policy-making in the inter-war years. Under the very broad remit which was given to the branch Hawtrey drew up many and varied reports and memoranda on economic and financial matters which are now to be found among the papers of senior Treasury officials of that period, but the impression prevails that they did not often receive much attention, and that the Financial Enquiries Branch under Hawtrey was something of a backwater. Churchill's jocular demand that 'the learned man should be released from the dungeon in which we were said to have immured him, have his chains struck off and the straw brushed from his hair and clothes, and be admitted to the light and warmth of an argument in the Treasury Boardroom' has been more than once quoted.[1] Sir Warren Fisher's explanation to the Public Accounts Committee in 1936 of the work of the Financial Enquiries Branch was rather in the same genre: he felt that the Committee probably knew of Hawtrey, 'who works away on metaphysics and writes learned books and concerns himself primarily with the theory of higher finance . . . he is really continually examining into the theoretical side (at least as it seems to me the theoretical side), and we pull a stop out when we want something from him'.[2]

In the Treasury of the twenties and thirties Hawtrey was no doubt a rather unusual figure, perhaps almost the first of the 'back-room boys'. It would be a mistake to think that as such he was unimportant. Sir Warren Fisher did go on to tell the Public Accounts Committee that 'supposing some rather delicate exchange issue comes along to the Under-Secretary . . . he would get hold of Hawtrey and say "you ought to know all about this" and he would advise'; and Churchill's sally can be read as a criticism of his officials for not making sufficient use of the special expertise which Hawtrey could provide.

In fact the advice which Hawtrey gave always followed logically from his conviction that the central objective of policy, national and international, must be to stabilize the wealth-value of the monetary unit. Consequently the extent to which it was acceptable to his administrative and political superiors inevitably

[1] P. J. Grigg, *Prejudice and Judgment* (1948), p. 82.

[2] Minutes of Evidence taken before the Committee of Public Accounts, 30 Apr. 1936; *House of Commons Papers 1935/36*, 131–48, p. 399.

varied. When Hawtrey took up his position as Director of Financial Enquiries in the autumn of 1919 the movement towards a dearer money policy was beginning and that winter the Cabinet accepted the recommendations of the Cunliffe Committee favouring financial retrenchment in preparation for a return to the gold standard at the pre-war parity. On the whole Hawtrey agreed with these recommendations at this time and in March 1920 he advised the Chancellor (Austen Chamberlain) in favour of an increase in the Treasury bill rate which would allow a rise in Bank Rate to 7 per cent. This was in line with his credit theory, according to which the prospect of dear money should serve to change expectations of a further rise in the price level. But, unlike Keynes, who was disposed to advocate a prolonged period of dear money, Hawtrey felt that high rates of interest should continue only for a short time and by the beginning of 1921 he was advocating a reduction. In April 1921 he was writing to Blackett that 'the drastic deflation effected, here and in America, since last spring [is a] most remarkable confirmation of the theory of control of credit through the discount rate' and later he advocated a return to pre-war practice of frequent changes in Bank Rate.

The problem, however, was that a return to the gold standard at the old parity seemed to require continued deflation. Hawtrey accepted that 'the justification for struggling back through all the admitted difficulties to our pre-war pound of 113 gr. of fine gold is that this parity would command confidence in a way that no other could. . . . The risk of a crisis arises chiefly from a too rapid reduction of prices. The best safeguard against it is to make the deflation slow.' In addition, Hawtrey did not consider that struggling back to the old parity necessarily meant restoring all the other features of the pre-1914 gold standard. His preference, stated in a paper to Section F of the British Association in 1919, was for a gold exchange standard with international agreements on uncovered paper issues and control of credit, with a view to keeping the gold value of commodities (measured by an index number) more or less constant.

An opportunity to have this plan, or at least something approaching it, carried into effect seemed to offer when an International Economic Conference was called by the Supreme Council of the Allies at Genoa in April 1922. Hawtrey was a member of the British Delegation and his participation in framing the resolutions on monetary policy and central banking adopted by the Conference was perhaps the highest point of his influence in economic policy-making; certainly the Genoa Resolutions always remained for him the most important guidelines in international economic co-operation. This was because they enshrined the principle of joint action by central banks to regulate credit 'not only with a view to maintaining the currencies at par with one another, but also with a view to preventing undue fluctuations in the purchasing power of gold'. To Hawtrey this was the key to stabilization not merely of prices, but of incomes and employment: the wealth-value of the money unit must be kept steady and there must be international action to achieve it.

In preparing his proposals for Genoa Hawtrey had discussions with Montagu Norman, with whom he had begun to build up contacts after his appointment as Director of Financial Enquiries gave him greater freedom to act in this way. The Board of Trade attempted to water down Hawtrey's proposals but with Blackett's support he contrived to have the full version brought forward at Genoa and adopted by the Conference.

Hawtrey himself recognized that 'in one respect the Genoa Resolutions are really unsatisfactory. It is impossible to point to any particular time at which effect can be given to them.' The twelfth Resolution did indeed request the Bank of England to call a meeting of central banks 'as soon as possible' and Norman sent out invitations with a view to a meeting in September 1922. Many felt that it should be postponed pending a political settlement of war debts with the result that 'there was never after 1922 any practical approach, and co-operation was left to develop in concerted attacks on particular problems rather than in general assembly round a single table'.[1]

At this time, however, Hawtrey still thought that a return to gold would afford a basis for developing international price stabilization along the lines of the Genoa Resolutions and that it might be achieved without rapid or serious deflation. To this end he pinned his hopes on a rise in the American price level and in 1923 he was writing memoranda in favour of an export of gold to the United States, ostensibly as part of debt repayment, but with the objective of provoking a rise in American prices. This proposal 'emanated from the Bank' but it is not surprising that Hawtrey gave it warm support at the Treasury for he had advocated something of the kind as early as 1920. For a time it was seriously discussed, but a fresh weakness of the pound in

[1] Sayers, *The Bank of England 1891–1944*, p. 162.

May 1923 put it out of court. Despite the opposition of Hawtrey and Niemeyer at the Treasury, who still favoured the gold shipment plan, Norman succeeded in having Bank Rate raised in July 1923 and the path to parity via orthodox deflation was resumed. Nevertheless even in March 1924 Hawtrey was arguing that 'it is still open to us to bring about an inflation of dollar prices and improve the exchange market without causing any set back to prices here'.

So in the debate which raged during 1924 concerning the priorities as between price stabilization and the return to gold there can be little doubt as to where Hawtrey's sympathies lay. Yet when the question of restoring the gold standard became practical politics in 1925 the answer which he gave to Churchill's well-known 'examination paper' was to the effect that it was 'both a British and world-wide interest that the pre-war system should be restored . . . exchange stability cannot be obtained at present by any other method than the gold standard'. However, he added that no active measures should be necessary before the end of the year; it was to be hoped that the exchange would come to par of itself and even if it did not credit contraction would still be undesirable.

Naturally Hawtrey was deeply disappointed and worried by the actual course of events which followed. Once he realized that the gambles on which the return to gold in 1925 had been based had not come off he moved into the position which he occupied at least until 1928, if not 1931, that of a persistent critic of British monetary policy and a persistent admirer of the American Federal Reserve. It was scarcely a popular stance for a Treasury official to take in those years; it placed Hawtrey in opposition to Norman and the Bank of England and sometimes to his own superiors as well, but he was fearless in his defence of it. When Bank Rate was raised to 5 per cent at the end of 1925 he characterized the move as 'nothing less than a national disaster' and he regarded its continuance as a major cause of falling prices not only in Britain but also in the United States. 'It is still true', he wrote in a Treasury memo at the end of 1927, 'that the Bank of England and the Federal Reserve Banks are pulling in opposite directions, the former contracting credit and the latter expanding. But whereas till last summer the Bank of England had prevailed and world prices had been falling now New York has the upper hand and world prices are either stationary or rising. From the point of view of this country that is a highly desirable state of affairs. . . .' Hawtrey had always a high admiration for the way in which Benjamin Strong had handled the credit policy of the Federal Reserve in the 1920s and considered that Strong's death in 1928 was a major misfortune for international monetary relations.

It could be said that Strong's task in these years was easy by comparison with Norman's; if the $4.86 parity was to be maintained how could it be done without the pressure of a high Bank Rate? One suggestion which Hawtrey put forward in 1927, when the amalgamation of the Bank of England and Treasury note issues was under consideration, was the abandonment of the principle of fixed fiduciary issue and indeed of any legal regulation of gold reserves—'there is no real need for the legislature to give any directions to the Bank of Issue except to maintain convertibility into gold'. It was a far-sighted proposal, but it drew from Niemeyer the comment, 'Far too theoretical, and dangerous for the Bank', and no more was heard of it.[1]

In fact Hawtrey was always prepared to be unorthodox within the terms of his own credit theory, but not beyond it. In 1929 the Liberal proposals for a major public works programme to reduce unemployment, supported by Keynes and Henderson, met with a bleak official response in the White Paper *Memoranda on Certain Proposals relating to Unemployment*. It was widely believed that Hawtrey had some responsibility for this 'Treasury view' of the inefficacy of public works to generate employment; certainly he saw no virtue in the public works proposals as such, but he was as eager as Keynes to see the level of unemployment reduced. The memoranda which he wrote on this subject in June 1929, only weeks after his return from Harvard, show him translating the Liberal proposals into his own terms:

> The virtue of Mr Keynes's plan, as advocated by the Liberal Party, is that the extensive schemes of capital outlay by the Government would affect the balance of payments by diverting part of the country's savings from external to internal investment. That would make possible an increase in the consumers' income, without which additional employment in one direction is bound to be offset by reduced employment in others . . . But there is another device which would likewise serve the purpose. Suppose the British government issues a loan on the London market and applies the proceeds to paying off Treasury Bills. . . . With fewer Treasury Bills the banks would seek other short-term commercial bills or advances. In so far as this occurs the government will have applied the resources diverted from external investment to provide additional working capital for industry and trade. . . . The fall of prices

[1] See ibid., p. 288.

and the unemployment are precisely the effects which ought theoretically to be expected from the policy of high discount rates which has prevailed since 1924. In so far as the funding of Treasury Bills stimulated short term lending . . . this disastrous tendency will be checked and, it is to be hoped, will be reversed.

Thus was Keynesian unorthodoxy translated into Hawtreyan unorthodoxy, but no hint of it appeared within the covers of the White Paper. As has been indicated above, Hawtrey's attitude towards the theoretical possibilities of increasing employment through public works underwent some modification in the thirties, but he nevertheless remained profoundly sceptical of their value in practice: in a 'Memorandum on Fiscal Policy during the Depression' prepared for the League of Nations in 1937 he compared British and American experience and concluded: 'The facts give no support to the theories of those experts who are inclined to assume that budget policy is the decisive factor in increasing or decreasing economic activity.'

These were not fashionable words even in 1937 and perhaps they give some indication of the reasons for the comparative decline of Hawtrey's influence in matters of policy which seems to have occurred in the thirties. For he held firmly to his basic monetary theories in a world where circumstances were changing rapidly and new advisers were growing up to interpret them in different ways.

In the evidence which he gave before the Macmillan Committee in 1930 Hawtrey was still arguing for international price stabilization along Genoa lines and urging that the Bank of England could and should give a lead in this respect by abandoning dear money. But by the spring of 1931 he had recognized that devaluation or depreciation of sterling was inevitable and was refusing to write memoranda in support of maintaining the $4.86 parity.[1]

After Britain had left the gold standard in September 1931 he was among those who produced memoranda on exchange-rate policy; his advice was to peg the pound at a new rate of £1 = $3.40, a 30 per cent devaluation, and subsequently to raise or lower the rate in line with movements of the world price level. Hawtrey's reasons for choosing a 30 per cent devaluation were typical—30 per cent was the extent of the fall in world prices since 1925, at which date he was prepared to assume that wages and prices had been in 'tolerable equilibrium'. At this time at

[1] Moggridge, *British Monetary Policy, 1924–1931*, p. 228.

least it seems that Hawtrey's views about the appropriate valuation of sterling and the concept of managing it in relation to world prices were in line with those of Keynes and of his Treasury superiors, although H. D. Henderson felt that the \$3.40 valuation was too low.[1]

Henderson at this time was Joint Secretary of the Economic Advisory Council, of which Keynes was a member, and in 1932 its Committee on Economic Information gave its backing to what has come to be known as the 'Keynes–Henderson plan' for an international note issue, as part of the proposals to raise world prices and revive trade to be submitted to the World Economic Conference in 1933. Initially Hawtrey, when asked to comment, was decidedly sceptical; despite his growing anxieties about the 'credit deadlock' he still felt that central banks could if they chose do all that was necessary for revival through open market operations. Nevertheless he went on to concede that 'if it *did* become a practical proposition, I should say by all means press it for all it is worth. . . . It would require very careful handling to avoid landing the world in a fresh series of monetary fluctuations, and that careful handling would certainly not be forthcoming, but this danger seems to me less serious than a continuance of existing conditions.'

On the whole, however, the Treasury reaction to the Keynes–Henderson plan was that it was not a practical proposition to put forward to an international conference. In the search for a simpler and less ambitious plan Hawtrey was involved with Sir Frederick Phillips, Sir Otto Niemeyer (now at the Bank of England), and Sir Cecil Kisch, Secretary to the Financial Department of the India Office. The result, the 'Kisch plan', called for a redistribution of existing gold stocks through an International Credit Institute, probably controlled by the Bank for International Settlements. Although it seemed unlikely that this plan would ever secure American official support, the Treasury still hoped to bring it forward at the conference. In the event, before this could be done the World Economic Conference was effectively broken up by Roosevelt's 'bombshell' declaration that stabilization was not a matter for governments and that he could not obligate the United States to approve the export of gold.

Earlier in 1933 Hawtrey had predicted that Roosevelt 'will make a great effort to avoid devaluing the dollar'. In spite of

[1] See Howson and Winch, *The Economic Advisory Council 1930–1939*, pp. 102–5.

this and of the blow to international co-operation which Roosevelt's later actions involved, Hawtrey was inclined to be sympathetic when Roosevelt adopted the so-called 'Warren Plan' and raised the domestic price of gold in September of the same year. Despairing of seeing effective international co-operation to raise and stabilize the world price level, Hawtrey now envisaged exchange depreciation as the only way in which a country like the United States could 'break the credit deadlock by making some branches of economic activity remunerative'. Not unnaturally there were those, like Per Jacobsson of the Bank for International Settlements, who found it hard to reconcile this apparent enthusiasm for exchange depreciation with Hawtrey's previous support for international stabilization schemes. To them his reply was 'the difference between what I now advocate and the programme of monetary stability is the difference between measures for treating a disease and measures for maintaining health when re-established. It is no use trying to stabilise a price level which leaves industry under-employed and working at a loss and makes half the debtors bankrupt.' Here, as always, Hawtrey was faithful to the logic of his system, which implied that if international central bank co-operation could not be achieved, each individual central bank must be free to pursue its own credit policy, without the constraint of fixed exchange rates.

The lessons of the breakdown of international economic co-operation during the thirties had much to do with what Sir David Waley described as 'A curiosity of history', the fact that 'during a Total War in which unexampled efforts and sacrifices had to be made to avert defeat . . . a large proportion of the time and energy of the Treasury was devoted to the elaboration of post-war Utopias'.[1] Again, as in the First World War, Hawtrey was not involved in the major policy decisions to the extent which Keynes was—much of his time in the later years of the war was devoted to compiling his detailed chronicle of the evolving activities of the Treasury since 1939—but he saw and wrote comments on most of the plans for the post-war economy which circulated within government. Some of the papers in his files from this period show him, as so often before and afterwards, swimming against the tide of received opinion—for at a time when most economists were concerned with the problems of

[1] Waley, 'The Treasury during World War II', *Oxford Economic Papers*, Supplement to vol. v (1953), p. 47; quoted in Henderson, *The Inter-War Years* (ed. H. Clay), Introduction, p. xxvii.

maintaining full employment after the war and expressing fears of renewed deflation, Hawtrey was warning of the dangers of inflation which the post-war world would face.

In these papers can be seen the first hints of ideas which Hawtrey published and kept on developing and presenting in later years. When plans for international monetary co-operation had finally taken shape in the International Monetary Fund he gave them a very qualified welcome in *Bretton Woods for Better or Worse* (1946). 'It is no part of my purpose to find fault with the plan itself', he wrote. 'Given effective safeguards against undue variations in the wealth-value of the principal money units, whether upwards or downwards, the Bretton Woods plan might be a useful instrument of international co-operation. But without such safeguards it is likely only to complicate and aggravate the resulting troubles. Especially is the much-vaunted "expansionist" policy likely to end in disaster. If depression is to be staved off by uninterrupted monetary expansion, the time is bound to come when the continuance of expansion is found intolerable.'

In the years immediately after the end of the Second World War it seemed to Hawtrey that the lessons of deflation, which he had so often had to explain in the twenties, had now been too well learned. Not surprisingly, he was critical of the continuance of cheap money and the neglect of bank rate. 'The demand is for a vehicle without a brake', he wrote in the Preface to the fourth edition of *Currency and Credit*, dated June 1949. 'Due regulation of the flow of money requires means not only of expansion but of contraction. For contraction Bank Rate remains the indispensable instrument.'

By 1949 it seemed to Hawtrey that in Britain 'redundant money and easy credit' had created a state of over-employment through demand inflation, but not an inflation of wage costs. In this situation as he saw it the devaluation of the pound was a policy mistake of the same order of magnitude as the return to the pre-1914 parity had been in 1925. 'Whatever the illusions in Government circles in 1949 as to the state of costs in the export industries, there was never any pretence that the devaluation from $4.03 to $2.80 was not far greater than any supposed disparity of costs could have justified', he wrote in 1955. 'The idea that wages and costs could be prevented from adjusting themselves to the rate of exchange thus reduced was quite chimerical. The rate of exchange set a standard for wages and prices, which in course of time they were bound to reach. If five years have passed without their attaining it, this is because the standard itself has been continually receding: it has risen higher and higher, as American wages and prices have been raised.'[1]

This was the essence of the message which Hawtrey continued to preach in books, articles, and letters to the press all through the fifties and sixties. In those years, when 2 or 3 per cent per annum inflation seemed a very small price to pay for full employment, it was not a message which many people cared to hear. There were some economists, like Harry Johnson, who recognized 'the suggestive value of an independent approach to the problem of sterling, which attempts to view it from a broader angle than that of the immediate state of the international reserves'. But to the great majority of the profession Hawtrey seemed to be a venerable figure incorrigibly attempting to apply the ideas of the past to the problems of the present; and as he went on reiterating his message they tended to become embarrassed and inattentive.

Yet Hawtrey's thesis was not without foundation; the authors of a recent carefully researched account of inflation in Britain argue that it is 'quite plausible to assume that in 1954 sterling was still undervalued following the excessive devaluation of 1949' and indeed find evidence for the persistence of undervaluation into the mid 1960s.[2] The authors of this particular study make no reference to Hawtrey's theories, but other aspects of his work have gained fresh recognition in recent years. Thus modern exponents of the monetary approach to the balance of payments, who stress that an excess supply of money will be reflected in all the other accounts of the balance of payments, recognize that this theory is to be found in *Currency and Credit* and was applied by Hawtrey in many of his factual studies.[3]

It is not hard to see the reasons for such a revival of interest in Hawtrey's work, nor to predict how far it may go. The more economists are convinced that 'money does matter' the more they are likely to be impressed by Hawtrey's analysis. For some thirty years after the publication of the *General Theory* they became and remained on the whole convinced that it did not matter, or at least not much, and Hawtrey's reputation declined. In the last ten or twelve years more and more of them have

[1] *Cross-Purposes in Wage Policy*, p. 71.

[2] R. J. Ball and J. Burns, 'The Inflationary Mechanism in the U.K. Economy', *American Economic Review*, 66 (1976), 475–6.

[3] Cf. J. A. Frenkel and H. G. Johnson, *The Monetary Approach to the Balance of Payments*, pp. 34 and 37.

become convinced afresh that money does matter and while this continues Hawtrey's reputation may well rise again. Economics is a very fashion-ridden subject and Hawtrey made few concessions to fashion. To him what he had thought to be true in 1913 still seemed true in 1973—in a money economy changes in the wealth-value of the monetary unit have consequences, which can be understood, but not escaped.

IV

The contributions to monetary theory and policy which have been discussed in the two preceding sections are numerous and distinguished. Whatever Hawtrey's reputation may now be or become it has never been disputed that in its day his monetary work was on a par with that of Keynes, Robertson, and other leading thinkers in that field. Consequently this tends to be seen as the whole of his achievement; but the fact is that if every one of his publications on monetary economics were deleted from it the list of his writings would still exceed in quantity and quality that of many of his contemporaries. For it would include books such as *The Economic Problem*, *Economic Aspects of Sovereignty*, *Economic Destiny*, *Economic Rebirth*, *and* articles such as his Presidential Address to the Royal Economic Society on 'The Need for Faith' and his 1960 paper on 'Production Functions and Land—a New Approach'.

In *Economic Destiny* (1944) Hawtrey identified two 'vital matters' besides the monetary in which he held that economics 'has failed to base guidance on conviction—it offers no accepted theory of profit . . . and . . . it has not taken sufficient account of power as a continuing and dominant object of economic policy'. Much of his own thinking and writing in the books and papers already mentioned was devoted to these problems. On them he formulated ideas of his own which, typically, were both unorthodox and durable. They have attracted little attention, but Hawtrey would himself have regarded them as ultimately of more significance than his better-known monetary work and an understanding of them is fundamental to any complete appreciation of his economic thought.

It seems to have been as a result of his emphasis on the place of traders in the economy that Hawtrey arrived at his concept of profit. He stressed that profit must be seen not merely as a margin between selling price and costs but also as a proportion of turnover, to which profit income is proportional. Profits depend on selling power—the skill, efforts, and opportunities of traders—and not on uncertainty, for without uncertainty there could still be great inequality in the amounts which different traders sell. 'Free competition', Hawtrey argued, 'tends to establish a common standard between incomes derived on the one hand from salaries and on the other from profit on a very modest turnover. Beyond that free competition has *no* tendency to keep down the incomes derived from profit.' Hence profit is 'quite definitely an exception to the general principle of the equalisation of rates of remuneration through the labour market. There is here a congenital malformation of the individualist economic system.'

Profits thus appeared to Hawtrey as the principal source of inequality under what he called 'competitivism', but he recognized that they were essential to it both as an incentive to enterprise and a source of accumulation. Within an economy this implied that a division of the product of industry between wage-earners and profit-makers which preserved the incentive to enterprise on the one hand without exploiting the workers on the other was of the greatest importance, but Hawtrey was extremely doubtful of the capacity of the collective bargaining process to achieve this because 'there is no independent and generally recognised standard of what is fair in wage agreements. What the defects of the profit-making and wage-fixing systems together could lead to in a market economy he saw clearly enough: 'If the existence of a level of profits no more than sufficient to provide the requisite stimulus to enterprise for maintaining full employment, is seized upon as a signal for demands for higher wages, the result can only be chronic unemployment combined with a progressive depreciation of the wealth value of the monetary unit, the worst of both worlds.'

On the other hand, Hawtrey attached much importance to the links between accumulation out of profits and the pursuit of power, both by the individual and the state. Wealth gave power to 'men of substance' who would seek to use it to influence public policy in their own interests. At the same time it afforded a source of power on which the state could draw through taxation and borrowing especially in time of war. Hawtrey also emphasized the relationships between accumulation, the export of capital, and imperialism. He was under no illusions as to the persistence of mercantilism in practice if not in theory, and while he expounded the benefits of international investment he also showed how it could be used as an instrument of power.

The pursuit of power by nation states could involve war or the threat of war and so contribute to what he often described, in a phrase borrowed from Lowes Dickinson, as 'the International Anarchy'.

This exposition of the defects of the competitive system might seem to be powerful enough to amount to an indictment of it—an indictment which would lead on naturally, as it did for many, to an acceptance of collectivism as a preferable alternative. Hawtrey did indeed devote much space in several of his books to a careful appraisal of collectivism, but he never accorded it unqualified approval. His condemnation of totalitarianism, whether fascist or communist, was unreserved; but he considered that democratic socialism was a possibility. The major problem it would present would be the establishment of an effective economic discipline to take the place of the profit motive, and Hawtrey predicted that 'in fact the reconciliation of liberty with economic discipline may turn out to be the greatest problem of our economic destiny'. Neither in competitivism nor in collectivism did he envisage an easy solution of it.

The reasons for this seemingly ambivalent attitude must be sought in Hawtrey's view of the relation between economics and ethics. 'Economics', he wrote in 1928, '*cannot* be dissociated from ethics' and there is no evidence that he ever departed from this position. It was a position almost diametrically opposed to that which was adopted, or was coming to be adopted, by most economists at that period: they were increasingly becoming uncomfortable with the propositions about utility which formed the basis of welfare economics as presented by Pigou and endeavouring to give their subject a strictly positive character. Hawtrey had no desire, however, to bring back the utilitarian ethics into economics. In fact he specifically attacked Pigou's conception of economic welfare as consisting of such satisfactions as are amenable to the measuring-rod of money. Hawtrey contested this identification of welfare with satisfaction, arguing that 'the consumer's preferences have a very slight relation to the real good of the things he chooses'. Hence it followed that 'the aggregate of satisfactions is not an aggregate of welfare at all. It represents good satisfactions which are welfare and bad satisfactions which are the reverse.'

Now this clearly implies an ability to define and distinguish good and bad satisfactions which most economists would have denied that, *as economists*, they possessed. They sought to narrow the scope of the subject by excluding all ethical considerations from it: Hawtrey sought to widen it by specifically importing into it a non-utilitarian system of ethics—the ethics of G. E. Moore. As has already been stressed in section I, Moore's view of an inherently valid Good was always the core of Hawtrey's philosophy. Hence while to most economists what is good would be subjective, to Hawtrey it was objective.

It was thus, as he explained to his colleagues of the Royal Economic Society in his Presidential Address in 1946, that he accounted for economists' lack of authority in public affairs: 'The answer, I believe, is to be found in a dissociation of their reasoning from any accepted ethical background.' Hence they did indeed fail to base guidance on conviction: yet 'if the economists' conclusions are to command faith, they must be directed to right ends. And surely a fundamental condition of any faith is that there *are* right ends.'

Hawtrey himself had no doubt that there are right ends, and also false ends. 'By a false end', he wrote in *The Economic Problem*, 'we mean something which is so generally and almost certainly valuable as a means, that people seek it without considering for what end it is to be used.' The cult of money-making and the cult of national-power he characterized as the pursuit of false ends. Both communism and individualism, he considered, shared the view that wealth was '*the* part that matters' in welfare, and he did not share it with them.

Hawtrey's union of ethics with economics enabled him to bring within it many topics which those who treat the subject as a strictly positive science would regard as excluded from it. Hence today when positive economics is somewhat out of fashion and economists permit, and admit to making, value judgements Hawtrey's ideas in this field are also beginning to be noticed again[1] and may be more attended to in future.

Whatever may be thought of Moore's system of ethics, there can be no doubt of its profound influence on Hawtrey's thinking over seventy years. That influence can be seen indirectly in many of his economic writings, but it was only in the unpublished works *Right Policy: the Place of Value Judgments in Politics* and *Thought and Things*, left behind at his death, that he endeavoured to set out his philosophy fully and directly. In the first of these works he sought to apply 'the ultimate criterion of the Good' not merely to economic problems but to political issues, both national and international. Part of his argument was that the study of value judgements was not dependent on philosophy,

[1] See, for example, Scitovsky, *The Joyless Economy* (1976).

but in his last book, *Thought and Things*, he turned to philosophical speculation itself, seeking in particular to develop his 'theory of Aspects', a theory of aesthetic perception which he had first presented at a meeting of Virginia Woolf's Friday Club in 1910, so that it could provide a means of reconciling the existence of differences about ends and means with the concept of an inherently valid Good.

V

Throughout this account of Hawtrey's life and work a certain element of paradox has been evident. A mathematician and a philosopher, he chose to spend his working life dealing with practical problems. An adviser on economic policy, he made a world reputation as an economic theorist. In debates on matters of economic theory in the twenties and thirties his name was most frequently linked with the name of Keynes and in a sense his career was almost the inverse of that of Keynes: for although it may be true, as Professor Patinkin has recently said, that 'the major revolution effected by the *General Theory* was in the field of theory, not of policy'[1] it is nevertheless the case that Keynes, who operated from an academic base, had an enormous influence on policy, and notably on Treasury policy in the Second World War. By comparison Hawtrey, who worked from an official base, had more influence on academic thought than ever he had on Treasury policy, although ultimately his influence was less than that of Keynes in both areas.

It may be suggested that Keynes's ideas were better adapted to the circumstances of his time than were Hawtrey's; the full reasons for Keynes's comparative success and Hawtrey's comparative failure remain to be investigated and assessed by historians of economic thought and policy. In that assessment, some part should be allowed to character and temperament. All those who knew him concur in the view that Ralph Hawtrey was truly a gentle man. He had the qualities of the pedagogue rather than the propagandist and consequently it was natural that he should have had more success in academic circles than in the corridors of power.

Writing about C. P. Sanger in 1930, Lowes Dickinson described him as belonging to 'a certain type' of Cambridge

[1] D. Patinkin, 'Keynes' Monetary Thought', *History of Political Economy*, 8 (1976), 19.

man: it seems fair to suggest that Hawtrey was another of that same type:

> It is a type unworldly without being saintly, unambitious without being inactive, warm-hearted without being sentimental. Through good report and ill such men work on, following the light of truth as they see it; able to be sceptical without being paralysed; content to know what is knowable and to reserve judgement on what is not. The world could never be driven by such men, for the springs of action lie deep in ignorance and madness. But it is they who are the beacon in the tempest, and they are more, not less, needed now than ever before. May their succession never fail![1]

R. D. Collison Black

For help in compiling this memoir I am indebted to Mr. J. H. P. Hawtrey; Mrs. E. Panton, Sir Ralph Hawtrey's executrix; Professor R. S. Sayers; Sir Alec Cairncross; and Lord Robbins. I am also grateful to Professor D. E. Moggridge and Mrs. Patricia Bradford who gave me much assistance in connection with Sir Ralph's manuscripts and papers now in the Archives Centre, Churchill College, Cambridge; to Mr. J. W. Ford for access to files remaining in H.M. Treasury; to Ms Susan Howson, who allowed me to see an advance copy of her paper on Hawtrey presented at the International Economic History Congress, Edinburgh, 1978; and to Mr Patrick Strong, Keeper of Eton College Library, for details of Sir Ralph's career at Eton. Mrs J. Wright, Research Officer in the Department of Economics, Queen's University, Belfast assisted in finding many references and preparing the bibliography of Sir Ralph's writings.

BIBLIOGRAPHY

1897 'The Speed of Warships', *Fortnightly Review*, 72 (New Series) (Sept.), 435–44.

1913 *Good and Bad Trade. An inquiry into the causes of trade fluctuations* (Constable, London).

1917 'Note on Mr. Middleton's Pamphlet on German Agriculture', *Economic Journal*, 27 (Mar.), 143–5.

1918 'The Bank Restriction of 1797', ibid. 28 (Mar.), 52–65.
'The Collapse of the French Assignats', ibid. (Sept.), 300–14.

1919 *Currency and Credit* (Longmans & Co., London).
'The Gold Standard', *Economic Journal*, 29 (Dec.), 428–42.*

[1] G. Lowes Dickinson, *Nation and Athenaeum*, 22 Feb. 1930. Quoted in J. M. Keynes, *Essays in Biography*, *Collected Writings*, x. 325.

* Reprinted in *Monetary Reconstruction*.

1921 *The Exchequer and the Control of Expenditure* (World of Today, London).
'The European Currency Situation', *Revue de metaphysique et de morale* (Armand Colin, Paris).*
1922 'The Federal Reserve System of the United States', *Journal of the Royal Statistical Society*, 85 (Mar.), 224–55.*
'The Genoa Resolutions on Currency', *Economic Journal*, 32 (Sept.), 290–304.*
1923 *Monetary Reconstruction* (Longmans & Co., London).
1924 'Discussion on Monetary Reform', *Economic Journal*, 34 (June), 155–76.
'The Tenth Annual Report of the Federal Reserve Board', ibid. 283–6.
1925 'Public Expenditure and the Demand for Labour', *Economica*, 5 (Mar.) 38–45.†
'Currency and Public Administration', *Journal of Public Administration*, 3 (July), 232–45.†
1926 *The Economic Problem* (Longmans & Co., London).
'The Trade Cycle', *De Economist*, 75 (Feb.), 169–85.†
'The Gold Standard and the Balance of Payments', *Economic Journal*, 36 (Mar.), 50–68.†
'Mr. Robertson on Banking Policy', ibid. (Sept.), 417–33.
1927 *The Gold Standard in Theory and Practice* (Longmans & Co., London).
'The Gold Standard', I–IV, *Journal of the Institute of Bankers*, 48 (Jan.–Apr.), 4–20, 53–67, 108–122, 176–90.
'The Monetary Theory of the Trade Cycle and its Statistical Test', *Quarterly Journal of Economics*, 41 (May), 471–86.
1928 'What is Finance?', *The Accountant*, 78 (Jan.), 13–19.†
Trade and Credit (Longmans & Co., London).
1929 'London and the Trade Cycle', *American Economic Association, Papers and Proceedings*, 19 (Mar.), 69–77.
'The Monetary Theory of the Trade Cycle', *Economic Journal*, 39 (Dec.), 636–42.
1930 *Economic Aspects of Sovereignty* (Longmans & Co., London).
'Money and Index Numbers', *Journal of the Royal Statistical Society*, 93 (Part I), 64–85.
'Charles Percy Sanger', ibid. (Part II), 316.
1931 *Trade Depression and the Way Out* (Longmans & Co., London).
'Consumers' Income and Outlay', *Manchester School*, 2, 45–64.
1932 *The Art of Central Banking* (Longmans & Co., London).
'The Portuguese Bank Notes Case', *Economic Journal*, 42 (Sept.), 391–8.
1933 'Mr. Robertson on "Saving and Hoarding" II', ibid. 43 (Dec.), 701–8.
'Public Expenditure and Trade Depression', *Journal of the Royal Statistical Society*, 96 (Part III), 438–58.
1934 '"The Theory of Unemployment" by Professor A. C. Pigou', *Economica*, 1 (New Series) (May), 147–66.
'Australian Policy in the Depression', *Economic Record*, 10 (June), 1–10.
'Monetary Analysis and the Investment Market', *Economic Journal*, 44 (Dec.), 631–49.
'Stabilisation of the Franc and French Foreign Trade: a Comment', ibid. 729–30.

* Reprinted in *Monetary Reconstruction*. † Reprinted in *Trade and Credit*.

1935 'Sir Basil Blackett', *Journal of the Royal Statistical Society*, 98 (Part IV), 775–7.
1936 'French Monetary Policy', *Economica*, 3 (New Series) (Feb.), 61–71.
1937 *Capital and Employment* (Longmans & Co., London).
'Alternative Theories of the Rate of Interest: Three Rejoinders, III', *Economic Journal*, 47 (Sept.), 436–43.
' "Essays in the theory of employment" ', *Economica*, 4 (New Series) (Nov.), 455–60.
'The Credit Deadlock' in *The Lessons of Monetary Experience, essays in honour of Irving Fisher* . . . , edited by A. D. Gayer (Farrar and Rinehart, New York), pp. 129–45.
1938 *A Century of Bank Rate* (Longmans & Co., London).
'Professor Haberler on the trade cycle', *Economica*, 5 (New Series) (Feb.), 93–7.
1939 'Mr. Harrod's Essay in Dynamic Theory', *Economic Journal*, 49 (Sept.), 468–75.
'Interest and Bank Rate', *Manchester School*, 10, 144–56.
1940 'Money and Money of Account', *The Accountant*, 102 (Jan.), 11–14.
'The Trade Cycle and Capital Intensity', *Economica*, 7 (New Series) (Feb.), 1–15.
'Mr. Kaldor on the Forward Market', *Review of Economic Studies*, 7 (June), 202–5.
1941 'Professor Hayek's Pure Theory of Capital', *Economic Journal*, 51 (June–Sept.), 281–90.
1943 'Competition from Newcomers', *Economica*, 10 (New Series) (Aug.), 219–22.
'W. A. Shaw', *Economic Journal*, 53 (June–Sept.), 290.
1944 *Economic Destiny* (Longmans & Co., London).
'Livelihood and Full Employment', *Economic Journal*, 54 (Dec.), 417–22.
1946 *Economic Rebirth* (Longmans & Co., London).
Bretton Woods for Better or Worse (Longmans & Co., London).
'The Need for Faith', *Economic Journal*, 56 (Sept.), 351–65.
'Sir Charles Addis (1861–1945)', ibid. 507–10.
'Lord Keynes', *Journal of the Royal Statistical Society*, 109 (Part II), 169.
1947 'Irving Fisher', ibid. 110 (Part I), 85.
1948 'Monetary Aspects of the Economic Situation', *American Economic Review*, 38 (Apr.), 42–55.
1949 *Western European Union. Implications for the United Kingdom* (Royal Institute of International Affairs, London).
'The Function of Exchange Rates', *Oxford Economic Papers*, 1 (New Series) (June), 145–56.
1950 *The Balance of Payments and the Standard of Living* (Royal Institute of International Affairs, London).
'Multiplier Analysis and the Balance of Payments', *Economic Journal*, 60 (Mar.), 1–8.
1951 'The Nature of Profit', *Economic Journal*, 61 (Sept.), 489–504.
1954 *Towards the Rescue of Sterling* (Longmans & Co., London).
'Relative Strength of the Pound and the Dollar', *Bankers' Magazine*, 178 (July), 1–8.
'Keynes and Supply Functions', *Economic Journal*, 64 (Dec.), 834–9.

1955 *Cross-Purposes in Wage Policy* (Longmans & Co., London).
'Bank Rate or Restriction of Credit?', *Bankers' Magazine*, 180 (Oct.), 265–72.
'Basic Principles and the Credit Squeeze', ibid. (Dec.), 447–51.
1956 'Employment and Bank Rate', *Bankers' Magazine*, 181 (Mar.), 219–25.
'Keynes and Supply Functions', *Economic Journal*, 66 (Sept.), 482–4.
'Mr. Harrod on the British Boom', ibid. (Dec.), 610–20.
'Approach to Convertibility', *Bankers' Magazine*, 182 (Dec.), 435–42.
1957 'Light on Montagu Norman's Policy', ibid. 183 (June), 505–9.
'Questions for the Radcliffe Committee', *Oxford University Institute of Statistics Bulletin*, 19 (Nov.), 307–13.
'Timing of Bank Rate', *Bankers' Magazine*, 184 (Dec.), 419–25.
1958 'Bank Rate: Progress and Prospects', ibid. 185 (Apr.), 285–91.
'New Credit Measures and the Balance of Payments', ibid. 186 (Aug.), 90–6.
1959 'Implications of Convertibility', ibid. 187 (Apr.), 281–7.
1960 'Production Functions and Land: a new approach', *Economic Journal*, 70 (Mar.), 114–24.
1961 *The Pound at Home and Abroad* (Longmans & Co., London).
1962 'The Chancellor's Letter', *Bankers' Magazine*, 193 (Feb.), 99–107.
'The Fourth Report of the Council on Prices, Productivity and Incomes', *Economic Journal*, 72 (Mar.), 251–4.
1964 'Diagnosis', *Bankers' Magazine*, 198 (Dec.), 341–5.
1966 'The Employment Tax and the Balance of Payments', ibid. 202 (July), 7–12.
1967 *Incomes and Money* (Longmans & Co., London).
International Liquidity (University of Surrey, London).
1969 'The Case for a Floating Pound', *Bankers' Magazine*, 207 (June), 343–8.
'The Return to Gold in 1925', ibid. 208 (Aug.), 61–7.
'A Stable Floating Pound', ibid. (Dec.), 275–80.
1970 'Stopping Inflation, Nine Per Cent', ibid. 210 (Nov.), 201–6.

PLATE XLVI

NORMAN McLEAN

NORMAN McLEAN

1865–1947

IN 1939 the British Academy awarded two Burkitt Medals for Biblical Studies, one to Dr. A. E. Brooke, the other to Dr. N. McLean, joint editors of the larger Cambridge Septuagint.[1] It was a fitting recognition of an academic partnership which had lasted since the early 1890s, and was only broken by the sudden death of Dr. A. E. Brooke on 29 October 1939. An account of Dr. Brooke appeared in the *Proceedings of the British Academy*, xxvi (1940), 439–53, by Professor J. F. Bethune-Baker. After Brooke's death, Dr. McLean was unable to continue the work owing to failing health. He died on 20 August 1947 in Cambridge. He had been elected F.B.A. in 1934. By some oversight no obituary of Dr. McLean ever appeared in the *Proceedings*, though his death was duly recorded. This brief memoir is an attempt to remedy the omission. It is produced under difficulties. Few who remember Dr. McLean well are still alive. But those who knew him at the height of his powers, and who at the same time understood his academic work, are now dead.

Academically Norman McLean belongs in his own undoubted right to an almost legendary race of giants in biblical scholarship. His greatest monument is certainly his part, with A. E. Brooke, and, for a considerable period, with H. St. J. Thackeray, in the larger Cambridge Septuagint. This began to be published with *Genesis* (1906), and he lived to see the first two volumes, (1) the *Octateuch*, and volume (2) *1–4 Kingdoms*, *1–2 Chronicles*, and *1–2 Esdras*, completed. The first fascicule of volume (3) containing *Esther*, *Judith*, and *Tobit* also appeared in 1940. After the war the Cambridge Press eventually decided to discontinue publication, in a new context of rising costs.

The first proposals for the work were made to the Syndics of the Cambridge Press in 1875 by Dr. F. H. Scrivener who was unable to go forward with the work himself. But on 13 March 1883 an announcement was made in the *Cambridge University Reporter* 'that the Syndics of the University Press had undertaken an edition of the Septuagint and Apocrypha, with an ample apparatus criticus, intended to provide materials for the critical determination of the text'. The first fruits of this scheme were

[1] *Proceedings*, xxv (1939), 4.

the three volumes of a 'portable' text, entitled *The Old Testament in Greek according to the Septuagint*, edited by Dr. H. B. Swete. This was completed between 1887 and 1894. In the meantime Dr. F. J. A. Hort drew up a memorandum, in November 1891, concerned with the larger project, echoing the judgement of Swete that this 'must necessarily be the labour of many years and a variety of hands'. This large task was assigned to the Revd. A. E. Brooke and Mr. N. McLean. From those days onwards it became their life work.

A note on the Septuagint work was supplied to Professor Bethune-Baker for his memoir of Dr. Brooke[1] by the present writer, and from that note[2] it will be seen that the object of the huge undertaking was not to determine a critical text of the pre-Hexaplaric text of the Septuagint, but to accumulate and display the evidence upon which such a critical text might one day be attempted. Brooke and McLean were providing a tool for which all subsequent workers in this wide field have every reason to be grateful. The authoritative note, supplied by Sir Frederic Kenyon to Bethune-Baker for the same memoir, should also be consulted.[3] The Cambridge work was eventually to be joined by not a 'rival', but a very different series in the '*Göttingen* Septuagint' which is still being produced. It may suffice here to quote the judgement of Dr. S. Jellicoe in 1968—twenty years after McLean's death, and nearly thirty years after the effective discontinuance of the work—'On the whole, however, it can be said that if and when both [Cambridge and Göttingen] editions are completed their relationship, owing to difference of plan, would be complementary rather than alternative.'[4] We need both.

Independently of his part in this work, and, indeed, one of his notable qualifications for it, Dr. McLean was a Semitic scholar of the first rank. Syriac studies are still in his debt, both for his publication in 1898 of Eusebius, *Ecclesiastical History*, in Syriac (completing work begun by William Wright), and for his masterly survey of *Syriac Literature* in the eleventh edition of the *Encyclopaedia Britannica*.

At this distance of time it has seemed natural to recall first McLean's enduring published work. But it must be remembered that McLean was also a man of large and versatile human sympathies.

[1] *Proceedings*, xxvi (1940), 439–53. [2] Ibid., pp. 444–6.
[3] Ibid., pp. 446 f.
[4] S. Jellicoe, *The Septuagint and Modern Study* (1968), p. 23.

Norman McLean was born at Lanark on 2 October 1865, the eldest son of the late Revd. Daniel McLean of Lanark. He graduated at Edinburgh University in 1885 with Firsts in classics and philosophy. In 1887 he came to Christ's College, Cambridge, as an affiliated student and scholar and was placed in the first class in the Classical Tripos Part I in 1888 and in the Semitic Languages Tripos in 1890. He was awarded the Jeremie Septuagint Prize in 1890, and the first Tyrwhitt Hebrew Scholarship and Mason Hebrew Prize in 1891. He was elected Fellow of Christ's College in 1893, and so was a contemporary there of another famous Scot and polymath—William Robertson Smith (1846–94). McLean married Mary Grace Luce, daughter of Colonel C. R. Luce, J.P., of Malmesbury, in 1896. Sadly his wife died in 1905.

From 1903 to 1931 McLean was University Lecturer in Aramaic, and there is abundant and affectionate testimony to his excellence as a teacher. But perhaps warmest of all is the regard he inspired as tutor of his college from 1911, and Senior Tutor from 1914, and lastly as Master from 1927 to 1936. He is remembered for kindness—especially to students and children. If his own marriage was ended by the early death of his wife and he had no children of his own, the children of his colleagues gratefully found themselves the targets of his generosity.

In Cambridge he is also remembered as chairman of the University Library Syndicate from 1928 to 1932. In committee meetings he was silent, unless he had something to say—a wonderful epitaph.

H. St. J. HART

Note. Apart from oral tradition, slight personal knowledge and the published work, I am indebted to a memoir by Mr. S. C. Grose in the *Christ's College Magazine*, Lent Term 1948; a memoir by the late Dr. W. A. L. Elmslie in the *Cambridge Review*, 11 October 1947; and a slightly larger account by the same in the *Dictionary of National Biography 1941–50*.

PLATE XLVII

SIR JOHN ERNEST NEALE

JOHN ERNEST NEALE

1890–1975

JOHN ERNEST NEALE was born in Liverpool in 1890, one of three sons of a mother who had been widowed early in her marriage; and he enjoyed none of the physical or professional advantages of a comfortable middle-class home. In a retrospective essay on his old master he quoted with approval A. F. Pollard's dictum: 'What a man does depends on what he does without'.[1] It touched a puritan chord in his own mind. He described it as a 'stern creed' but he followed it himself.

He remained throughout his life a systematic worker whose studies (second only to his love of family) enjoyed a primacy throughout the day. His diversions were few: a pleasure in gardening, country walks, and occasional holidays. He had a single-minded devotion to his chosen cause, and from his students he expected that same total commitment to Elizabethan studies. He was once asked to inaugurate with a series of lectures a very distinguished endowment. He was conscious of the honour —and he declined it. He told me that it would have deflected him from the research to which he was committed over the next few years. I can think of few other historians who could have had the stubborn self-denial which the decision required. In any case he would not and could not offer an audience a slipshod, hastily begotten farrago of commonplaces which sometimes passes for a public lecture. His standards were exacting: if he imposed them on his pupils, he imposed them most rigorously on himself.

Yet if there was an austerity in his methods and attitude to life (clearly visible to those who knew him well), there was no less a warmth and a robust humour which was rapidly manifest whatever the occasion. He would roar with laughter at some witty sally by a companion or by himself; and his infectious delight would spread through a whole seminar, whether prompted by an amusing episode of the Elizabethan or any other period or by a new insight into a piece of historical research. He had been an ambitious man, ambitious in the sense that he wanted to prove himself as a scholar and make his department at University College, London one of the greatest in the country,

[1] J. E. Neale, *Essays in Elizabethan History* (1958), 247.

a nursery of professors as he once called it, and which in fact it became. In his early days he could sometimes wound sensitive spirits; but, in his mellow years and the long golden age of his retirement, one saw to the full his sympathy and loving kindness for younger scholars and that generosity of spirit which made possible his equable temperament.

I

Sheer hard work and sacrifice carried Neale through his undergraduate career at the University of Liverpool where he subsequently did some graduate work under Ramsey Muir on William Cobbett. But it was to University College, London that he was drawn and, shortly before the First World War, he was engaged on Tudor research under A. F. Pollard, which he resumed after the war, to be appointed in 1919 to a junior post at the college. His association with University College and the Institute of Historical Research (an institute conceived by Pollard whose drive brought it into being in 1921), lasted for Neale virtually until the end of his life, except for two years at Manchester from 1925 to 1927, as Professor of Modern History. He occupied the Astor Chair of English History at University College for twenty-nine years, from 1927 to 1956, and continued to preside over his famous graduate seminar at the Institute until almost his eightieth birthday. He was especially proud that it attracted as many American graduate students and senior scholars as British. 'To my research students', he once wrote, 'now a goodly company in this and other countries—America in particular—my thanks blend with pride in their work.'[1] His first article, which he published in 1916 in the *English Historical Review*, though extending over no more than nine pages, forecast the character and quality of his later work. In it he printed a hitherto unknown speech by the Lord Keeper accompanied by his own analysis of the text. As ever in his case, it was marked already by a skill in identifying his source and a meticulous examination of its form and content.[2] The same methods were applied in his next article which appeared in 1919[3] and his successive contributions of a like kind over the following decades. But he could not only think like a research scholar, he could

[1] J. E. Neale, *Elizabeth I and her Parliaments*, (1953, 1957), i 12.

[2] 'The Lord Keeper's Speech to the Parliament of 1592/3', *English Historical Review*, 31 (1916), 128–37.

[3] 'Queen Elizabeth's Quashing of Bills in 1597/8', ibid. 34 (1919), 586–8.

write with a fluency and an attractive style on the highly technical problem of the Commons Journals, qualities which were displayed again in his contribution on the Commons' privilege of free speech (a truly seminal article) to the Pollard *Festschrift* of 1924.[1]

The next decade was spent in two major and related occupations: a massive search, already begun before the war, through the public and private materials on the Elizabethan parliaments, the results of which continued to be published in the learned journals; and secondly, the writing of his biography of Elizabeth I. The appearance of the biography in 1934 was in fact something of a literary event.

More than forty years have passed since then and it is almost impossible to recover and describe the state of historical biography at that time. With some important exceptions, studies of both monarchs and their subjects still bore the marks of their nineteenth-century pattern. They tended to fall into the Life and Times . . . category, sometimes extending over three or more volumes, in which the evolution of a man's life was accompanied by a detailed account of the year's events, whether relevant or not. When successful, they were both scholarly and fascinating and brought delight and instruction to a generation more leisured than our own. When they failed—and there were more failures than successes—they could be, or so at least they seem to us, monumentally boring. In one sense, Froude's *A History of England*, from the Fall of Wolsey to the Defeat of the Spanish Armada,[2] was an exemplar of the best of this genre for it included, in effect, a series of biographies of all the Tudor monarchs, except Henry VII, set against the background of the time. Nares's *Life of William Cecil, Lord Burghley*,[3] in three volumes, by contrast was a pedestrian, detailed affair whose weight of paper rather than weight of learning appalled Macaulay, hardly himself a man of few words. It should be added that Pollard never fell into this category. His *Henry VIII*[4] and his *Wolsey*,[5] whatever their faults, were superb in their craftsmanship in placing the man in his times without obscuring focus or losing

[1] *Tudor Studies*, ed. R. W. Seton-Watson (1924), 257–86.

[2] J. A. Froude, *A History of England, from the Fall of Wolsey to the Defeat of the Spanish Armada* (1856–70).

[3] E. Nares, *Memoirs of the Life and Administration of . . . William Cecil, Lord Burghley* (1828–31). Macaulay's review appeared in the *Edinburgh Review* for 1832.

[4] A. F. Pollard, *Henry VIII* (1902).

[5] A. F. Pollard, *Wolsey*, (1929).

proportion. On a much smaller scale, Bishop Creighton's now forgotten short study of Queen Elizabeth[1] was a percipient analysis of her complex character and tortuous ways.

The large-scale historical biography was already beginning to pass out of fashion when Neale began work; but another trend was taking its place. These works were being written, not by academic historians, but by writers who moved in the coteries of the day and whose subjective biographies owed more to their literary qualities than their historical evidence. André Maurois, who said that one important gain from writing a biography of Shelley was that it helped him to understand himself, wrote sensitive and lively biographies which were widely read.[2] Lytton Strachey added to these qualities a scepticism and cynicism which diminished the stature of his central character as was intended and gave his biographies some of the engaging qualities of *chroniques scandaleuses*. In his warmly received short biography in double harness of *Elizabeth and Essex*[3] he used, though with greater restraint than later exponents, some of the psycho-analytical approaches of Sigmund Freud, just beginning to make their impact upon the world of letters.

His volume appeared in 1928 when Neale was already at work on his *Queen Elizabeth*. Strachey's book presented both a challenge and a problem. If Strachey, with no real historical sense of the period, could attract a large readership could the truly professional historian, rejecting sensation and faithful to his sources, succeed as well and, in so doing, win over a large public to serious historical reading? Neale had already dismissed the idea of a Life and Times. . . . He never wrote a textbook or the political history of a period, and never wanted to. But what sacrifice would be called for if he was to reach a readership beyond his colleagues and students?

Here an unresolved question enters into the account. Neale *did* make a sacrifice. When he published his biography in 1934 it carried none of the conventional scholarly apparatus of footnotes and bibliography. At which stage this decision was taken and on whose advice it is impossible now to determine. My own view is that it originated with Jonathan Cape, his publisher, though this is no more than speculative. I met Cape on several occasions. He was a brilliant and dedicated publisher, and a tough business man with a flair for detecting works of high literary standards

1 Mandell Creighton, *Queen Elizabeth* (1896).

2 André Maurois, *Ariel or the Life of Shelley* (1923).

3 Lytton Strachey, *Elizabeth and Essex* (1928).

which would appeal to the educated public. He may also have had good reason to believe that Neale's *Elizabeth* could be selected as a choice of the Book Society (which in fact it was), in those days the accolade for works of acknowledged literary merit. Whether he urged Neale to abandon footnotes or Neale came to that conclusion independently, we do not know.

Neale himself shrewdly grasped what Lytton Strachey had achieved; and, though he spoke of his imitators with contempt, declared himself 'an admirer as well as a critic of his work'. Strachey had tried to understand human beings as human beings, whatever public office they held: the 'historical portraits may have been partly or largely fictional but they lived'. Hence Neale posed the question: 'For our part, as professional historians, our traditions and scholarship ensure that our portraits are factual. May we not learn something from the literary experts and make them also live?'[1]

These were retrospective reflections written long after his *Queen Elizabeth* had appeared but they conform to the belief that he had always held and never abandoned. More than this, Neale envisaged the historian's task as recovering in their full human stature not simply the great figures of the past but the lesser men and women who played some part in the developing society of the time. One of the many remarkable features of his later volumes is that he brought out of the shadows a host of parliamentarians who for the first time since their own day emerged in their strength and weakness of character, with their little foibles and mannerisms, their personal ambitions and their political aims, their intrigues, their courage, their hopes and failures. To read his books or to listen to him talk, made one feel that he was calling to mind men whom he had known intimately. The comparison will seem a strange one, even though I use it in only one particular: but he seemed to me to have the capacity of the novelist Charles Dickens to people his books with a host of lesser men and women as living and individualistic as the most eminent of their generation. Dickens was using the creative imagination of the novelist. Neale was using the re-creative imagination of the historian, for it rested securely on the sources to which he was loyal in every respect.

Neale's faith that there was an educated public eager to read what trained scholars had to say about the past was triumphantly vindicated. His biography of Elizabeth I was widely reviewed in the most laudatory terms, was an immediate best seller, and

[1] *Essays in Elizabethan History*, 226.

was in due course translated into several foreign languages. It was no less remarkable that the book was equally warmly received by the scholars when in due course they came to review it in the learned journals. Even the absence of footnotes received no more than a passing comment of dissent. 'Professional historians will regret', wrote one reviewer, that this decision was taken, but he at once added that 'they will be safe in accepting the author's erudition as a guarantee of the facts presented'.[1] 'Professor Neale has shown us', wrote another reviewer, '. . . how skilfully a garment of literary expression can be woven round the most rigorous historical studies.' It was 'the sort of book, in fact, that only an alert mind, working with patience and insight and fully versed in the documents of the period, could have evolved'.[2] In the United States the reception was equally warm. As one reviewer put it, 'Here is a rare and happy achievement—a book which is a product of careful research, the first fruits of the scholarship of one of the leading authorities on the Elizabethan age, and at the same time a brilliantly written best-seller.'[3]

Did any criticism come from scholarly quarters? On one central theme some of his reviewers joined issue with him. Had he, they asked, in breaking away from the tradition that a biography of a monarch must be a history of the reign, in effect made the queen larger than her context, indeed larger than life? In reversing Froude's judgement of her as a wayward, vacillating creature, dependent on her ministers for their wisdom, and relying on herself for her follies, had Neale restored Gloriana to the pinnacle of a goddess, wise in policy, just in its exercise, the true mistress of her state who guided her ministers rather than depended on their counsel? '. . . It will be obvious to all who read his pages', wrote one critic, 'that the heroine is sometimes judged on a standard different from that applied to her rivals.' The writer was the Scottish historian, J. D. Mackie, who regretted that 'Mary, indeed, gets scant justice all through . . .'. Neale, he had said, was 'reluctant to admit the necessary failings of that supreme egoism whose triumph he acclaims. For him Elizabeth, and with Elizabeth England, are always right. Their success proves it.' '*Real-politik*', he said later in the review,

[1] J. D. Mackie, *History*, N.S. 19 (1935), 343–4.

[2] J. B. Black, *Eng. Hist. Rev.* 100 (1935), 331.

[3] F. C. Dietz, *Journal of Modern History*, 5 (1934), 324–5. Conyers Read in the *American Historical Review*, 39 (1934), 718–19, in the course of a very favourable review, regretted the absence of footnotes.

'has an ugly side which is plainly exposed when the author deals with Elizabeth's contemporaries, but is decently veiled when Gloriana holds the stage. Henry IV of France appears only as a "parasite", and the English heroine becomes too much of a Faerie Queene.'[1] Something comparable was said by the American reviewer, F. C. Dietz, when he wrote, 'Elizabeth comes too close to a new apotheosis'.[2] In other contexts, orally rather than in print, the observation was made that in writing his great biography Neale had fallen in love with the queen. He several times laughingly told me that he was well aware that this was said. Long afterwards he got a full questionnaire from a schoolgirl who told him that as she was doing her 'project' on him as a biographer could he please tell her whether it was true that he had fallen in love with the queen or was there some other explanation? Where would historians be without waste-paper baskets!

But the fundamental question, posed by his critics, as to whether he had depicted Elizabeth as larger than life remained to be answered. Answer it he did in his formidable volumes on the Elizabethan parliaments. For, by the time that Neale's biography was finished, he had already amassed a weight of material (soon to be still further enlarged) which he was convinced revealed Elizabeth as anything but the romantic, headstrong termagant of uncertain principles and faulty judgement. Here was a European statesman of great subtlety and moderation, with a true sense that politics was the art of the possible. She was a ruler who knew where to go for the best advice and use it in the best interest of the nation so that its unity, stability, and strength would be preserved. This was the case he made with a wealth of documentation. Neale was by now satisfied that public taste had changed and the intelligent reader would not be hostile to footnotes, as was confirmed by the reception of the later volumes on *Elizabeth I and her Parliaments*; but almost two decades were to pass before they appeared. Meanwhile he was writing the first historical study ever to have been attempted on the shape and content of the Elizabethan parliamentary system. A contemporary, Sir Thomas Smith, had written such an analysis in 1565 in a book entitled *De Republica*

[1] J. D. Mackie, op. cit. 343–4. F. C. Dietz, by contrast, makes the curious remark that 'idealisation of Elizabeth has one great value in that it enables him to be the complete realist in his handling of Mary, Queen of Scots' (loc. cit.).

[2] F. C. Dietz, loc. cit.

Anglorum.[1] Now Neale brought to bear upon the same problems his deep understanding of the men and the age, and of their constitutional processes. The book was called *The Elizabethan House of Commons*[2] and was published in 1949. It was greeted by the leading Elizabethan scholar in the United States, Conyers Read, a man not given to extravagant praise, with unqualified acclaim: 'This is a very important book, probably the most important book on the politics of Elizabethan England that has ever appeared.'[3] In the quarter of a century which has passed since its publication it has nowhere been significantly challenged in either its detail or its conclusions.

If *The Elizabethan House of Commons* was a major work on constitutional history it also, by its very approach, questioned at its fundamentals the contemporary concept of what constitutional history in fact was about. No one understood better than Neale the minutiae of the institutional processes of the legislature or had devoted so much effort to unravelling its complexities. The second part of the book, and a good deal of the earlier part indeed, reveals for the first time how the constitutional machinery worked. But he had recognized from the early days of his researches that an account of an institution, its law and practice, can be a sterile exercise if it has no regard to the men and society it was meant to serve. Pollard in calling his book *The Evolution of Parliament*[4] had reflected the Darwinian approach now coming into general vogue, but had, in seeking the evolution, found medieval origins which have not stood the test of critical examination. Neale sought part of his answer in the evolution of Elizabethan *society*. Pollard had argued that Parliament was one of the agents for turning Tudor England into a unified nation, though he put this achievement too early in the period. Neale saw the House of Commons as the voice of provincial England with its *diversity* of accents, interests, and personalities. He proved beyond doubt also that the House of Commons was not the instrument of Elizabeth's personal rule but the product of an elaborate patronage system operated by the great men in the capital and the constituencies. He had found and established this pattern by exploring the modes and personalities of provincial life.

L. B. Namier had, before the war, brought out his *Structure of*

[1] Sir Thomas Smith, *De Republica Anglorum*, ed. L. Alston (Camb., 1906).
[2] J. E. Neale, *The Elizabethan House of Commoms* (1949).
[3] Conyers Read, *Journal of Modern History*, 23 (1951), 75.
[4] A. F. Pollard, *The Evolution of Parliament* (1920).

Politics at the Accession of George III[1] which both in its methods and conclusions radically altered the direction of eighteenth-century studies. The questions to which Namier directed his colleagues and students were not questions of constitutional principles or political ideals, though he of course fully recognized their historical importance, but private and family interest, patronage, faction as the power base for political and personal aspiration. Neale's field of study was two centuries earlier when different issues and conditions prevailed. But he paid tribute to the contribution that Namier had made. 'It is a book', he wrote, 'which in retrospect must be regarded in this country as one of the supremely influential historical works.'[2] It is interesting also to recall a passage in the same paragraph, written in 1950, where Neale commented on early signs of what he called the 'biographical' approach:

> I do not know how old this type of historical approach may be. The first modern book in my range of reading to apply it was Charles Beard's *Economic Interpretation of the American Constitution*, the basis of which was a series of biographical studies of the framers of the constitution, keyed into the two rival economic interests of creditor and debtor in the United States. How much of Beard's thesis has survived subsequent critical examination, I am unaware; but clearly, within properly controlled limits his method was a great and promising advance upon what we may call the conventional approach to constitutional history, just as the latter was upon the legal-minded approach of still earlier generations.[3]

The Elizabethan House of Commons is then an analysis of the social foundations of political action. A year after its appearance, when coming to the end of his Creighton Lecture on *The Elizabethan Age*, Neale had directed his mind to the problem that, so soon after the queen's death, there was a marked decline in the quality and character of government. He sought his answer in the generalization: 'Like other societies, the Elizabethan age contained the seeds of its own decay.'[4] In a sense this was a truism though it would require a whole book to examine and explain what exactly the expression may be taken to mean in the Elizabethan/Jacobean historical processes. But we may perhaps see the application of that generalization in much of Neale's later work. In essence, he argued, the Tudors were faced

[1] L. B. Namier, *The Structure of Politics at the Accession of George III* (1929).
[2] J. E. Neale, *Essays in Elizabethan History*, 227.
[3] Ibid. 226–7.
[4] Ibid. 44.

with an institution governed by medieval precedents and procedures but constantly subject to the pressures of a post-medieval society involved in comparatively rapid change. His question was: how far could these pressures express themselves in parliament, indeed how far could they change the institution itself? But first he had to identify the pressures.

The importance of Neale's method (and in this significant respect, as of course in others, it differed from Namier's), was that it did not look down from above on the political and social structure at a given point in time, the accession of a monarch, invaluable though that analysis was. Rather he was concerned with the *dynamics* of social change. What was happening in the provinces and in the capital which was changing Parliament, more specifically the House of Commons, during the forty-five years of Elizabeth's rule?

The answer which Neale reached, and he had come to it independently though concurrently with Tawney's work, was the enlarging influence of the gentry and the bonds they had with the magnates. He was concerned not with conflict between gentry and magnate, an interpretation which was to breed so much controversy in the 1950s, but association, collaboration, dependence, all to be summed up in the one word 'clientage'. Neale, of course, did not invent the term. But it was he who applied it to the conditions of political and social cohesion of the Elizabethan period. Clientage was not feudalism or bastard feudalism, appropriate terms for earlier periods, or patronage and connection, appropriate for later periods though, as is inevitable in the historical process, it had something in common with all of them. Clientage was essentially Elizabethan and it could operate as a force for change as well as with greater flexibility than the feudal relationship.

It is not necessary here to rehearse in detail the themes which Neale developed in his book but simply to draw attention to some of his methods. If a useful phrase had not become a cliché one would say that Neale went back to the grass roots because he believed that the answer to his central question—what made the Elizabethan parliaments different from their medieval predecessors?—must first be sought there. Since four-fifths of the Members of Parliament held borough seats and only one-fifth sat for the shires, he concluded that the answer would be found in the boroughs. So began the exhaustive search by Neale and his students into the borough records (where these had survived) and into every possible biographical source as he began the painstaking processes of counting heads, listing each man's place of birth, family, class, profession, wealth. From it, among much else, there emerged one dominant conclusion. It is now assimilated into Tudor historiography but, when Neale was writing, it was novel enough to make a major impact upon both his readers and on his own approach to the problem: namely the overwhelming majority of the borough representatives were not borough citizens. This was contrary to the constitution but it was a fact of life. It was in the nature of the dialectic: an institution, medieval, monarchical, feudal in origin yet adjusted to represent also the chartered corporations of the later Middle Ages, was now confronted with new and severe pressures to which it was ill adapted. A class of people, which would be called the nobility on the Continent but, in the English context, were gentry, sought a voice in government or, at least, a place in Parliament. True, each shire had already the right to send two knights to Parliament and these were drawn from the gentry. But now their demand for a place had vastly increased. In England, as compared with many continental countries, no urban patriciate had developed. London was in many ways an exception. But elsewhere the city fathers were men of modest means and equally modest ambitions: their comprehension and aims scarcely went beyond the city walls. To incur the costs (even with municipal support) and the inconveniences of going to Westminster in order to approve legislation and commit their fellow citizens to taxation was a delight they could well dispense with. I any case many municipalities were scarcely more than the private franchises of some territorial magnate. He sent them one or two names and, again with some exceptions, they duly sent them forward for election. This was apparently a mutually beneficial arrangement. The boroughs were spared local squabbles and, more important, the expense of sending someone to the capital. The patron gained prestige and confirmation among his dependants of his power and standing. (Conyers Read went further and saw in these arrangements 'a sort of later-day [*sic*] livery and maintenance within the accepted framework of Tudor despotism'.)[1] And what did the gentry gain? To Neale, the 'invasion of the gentry' of the House of Commons was not motivated by a class-conscious desire to change the established order, less still was it motivated by ideological purposes. They went to Westminster because they rated a seat in Parliament as itself a sign of their social standing; because they valued the

[1] C. Read, *Journ. of Mod. Hist.* 23 (1951), 75.

contacts they gained with influential men in the capital; because if they were lawyers or interested in land transactions or commerce—or all three—they were going to the nerve centre of all these activities; and because they and their families could enjoy the social life of the capital with its shops, theatres, fashions, the sight of the great men of the time, and of the queen herself.

But Neale saw, of course, that among these men there were a number, rarely more than a quarter of the total, who had political, religious, economic aims which they wanted to press on the Government. They were not a party or even a consolidated faction of interests and principles but a disparate body of men who could on occasion coalesce to press an agreed purpose. And there was among them a smaller, hard core of committed ideologues, numerous enough in times of tension or danger to carry a much larger part of the House with them, even as far as forcing policy on the Government but more often in frustrating it. It is this element, covered not altogether satisfactorily by the term Puritan, whose membership Neale was to analyse in rich and marvellous detail and whose rise and decline he was to chronicle in his later books.

But before turning from the *Elizabethan House of Commons* we must consider the second important contribution it made. Here for the first time, gleaned from contemporary treatises and a deep familiarity with daily practice, Neale made available a coherent, detailed account of the procedures of the Elizabethan parliaments, from the arrival of Members on through the formalities of the election of the Speaker, the official opening by the queen, the debates, the committees, the defence of privilege, the discipline of Members on to its proroguing or dissolution. Henceforth indispensable to any study of the period it could be said that *The Elizabethan House of Commons* in its double contribution, a social analysis of the politics of provincial society and its elucidation of the processes of Parliament, ensured that students of the age were now able to see the Lower House with an added dimension of depth and a richer variety of colour.

It represented the completion of a task which Neale had set himself as a young man; and now, in his middle age, at the height of his powers and with an unrivalled knowledge of his sources, he moved to the parallel task of revealing and analysing the series of dramatic episodes, as well as the constant development and change, of this community of men who came to share in the government of England. And here attention must be drawn to the title of the two volumes, the first spanning the years 1559–81 which appeared in 1953, and the second, dealing with the latter half of the reign, published in 1957. It is important to notice that he did not call them a *History of the Elizabethan Parliaments* but *Elizabeth I and her Parliaments*. He was quite clear that he was not writing a narrative of the political evolution of the reign—though in the event his is the greatest contribution in the field—but a study of the relationship between queen and Parliament, in conflict and collaboration, which he considered the key to an understanding of the age. If, in the process, he left out important statutes or issues he did so deliberately (though in some cases it was simply that the material did not exist). Where an event, for example the passage of the Statute of Artificers of 1563, did not in his view significantly reflect the queen's relations with her Parliament, it plays no part in his story. It would lengthen the book without developing the argument.

I shall return to this and other questions of Neale's methodology shortly. What, however, are the outstanding contributions of these two volumes must, all too briefly, be summarized under several heads. He was the first scholar to reveal the queen in her relations with Parliament as a statesman of power, subtlety, and with a deep understanding of its processes, its strength and its weakness. Compared with her, some leading parliamentarians of her day, and ours, seem often no more than gifted amateurs. If this appears a large claim to make—the language by the way is not Neale's but mine—we should not forget the obvious point that she served longer in Parliament than any Member of Parliament in the sixteenth century. Neale had closely studied all her speeches which have survived; he had read all the known diaries and discovered others for himself; he had watched her every manoeuvre, drawing together scraps of evidence from a multiplicity of unlikely sources. Even though it may be possible to suggest variants of Neale's interpretation of the 1559 Supremacy and Uniformity Acts, there can be no question that the manner in which he probed into all the sources in the true exercise of the historical imagination was a triumph of craftsmanship. His account of her mastery of the Puritan opposition in Parliament belongs to the same high order.

To have restored the queen to her full parliamentary stature as contemporaries knew her was only one of Neale's achievements. He accomplished the same thing for many of her counsellors and subjects. The name of Peter Wentworth will always be associated with Neale who brought to life that doughty, cantankerous Puritan leader, born before his time. But he also displayed a whole company of men, including Norton, Fleetwood, Arthur Hall, Morrice, Cope, some of them only names to Elizabethan scholars themselves. At the same time he revealed the hitherto unrecognized parliamentary and oratorical talents of leading statesmen such as the Cecils, Walsingham, Knollys, Ralegh, and, most strikingly, Christopher Hatton, for too long dismissed as a political lightweight who owed his high office of Lord Chancellor, of all things, to personal charm. For no earlier period do we possess so rich a series of character studies of its parliamentarians. This may of course in part be attributed to the more limited supply of sources than we possess for the Elizabethan period. But the fact remains that without Neale's work we should still be poorly served in our knowledge and understanding of these men and issues.

The queen, the parliamentarians, the institution of Parliament, have never looked the same since Neale did his work. But there emerged also another uncovenanted benefit. He showed the Privy Council in action through its Members of both Houses; the inner conflicts within its organization, reflected sometimes in the use made of Parliament by individuals; the pressures placed upon the queen through Parliament by her own councillors, for example in attacks on Mary, Queen of Scots. This was, to students of the period, a new facet to the Privy Council and has, incidentally, led to fruitful lines of inquiry into the politics of the early seventeeth century.

It is appropriate also to add, what becomes manifest in any reading of Neale's books and articles, that Neale not only recovered hitherto unused parliamentary documents such as the now famous Cromwell diary in Trinity College, Dublin, but he also taught historians how to extract from both familiar and unfamiliar records information and understanding which no one had hitherto considered within the historian's grasp.

II

I have so far been concerned, in my account of these works by Neale, to survey rather than to critize the pattern and content of his achievement. I want briefly to complete that story. The last of the parliamentary trilogy appeared in 1957, a year after his retirement from his Chair at University College. He continued to write occasional articles and reviews, to read the Elizabethan sources and secondary works, to preside over his seminar, to correspond with and meet scholars from both sides of the Atlantic—he went on attending the Anglo-American conferences until almost the year of his death—and to serve as an editor and member of the Editorial Board of the Official History of Parliament which had been set in motion in 1951. He paid his only visit to the United States in 1958, the fourth centenary of the queen's accession. He had been knighted in 1955.

Long ago Neale had hoped that he would spend his retirement writing a biography of the Earl of Essex. Had he done so it would, as it were, have completed the symmetry of his life's work, beginning and ending with a biography, the second one perhaps measuring up to the first in its knowledge, its insight, and its art. But it was not to be. In accepting the invitation to participate in the 'parliamentary history' he abandoned the other project, which would have been one of the delights of his old age; and we are all the losers. The 'parliamentary history' in which he was now involved, with its committee system, its quasi-Civil Service structure, its machinery for survey and revision irked him; and, as his work began to slow down he found the pressure of date-lines, inevitable in projects involving public funds, as well as some well-intentioned but inapposite detailed revision, irritating and obstructive. As far as Neale was concerned his commitment to the scheme was a mistake and it proved a millstone round his neck. It is necessary, for the record, to add that the final revision of the book was not in his hands nor was it seen by him.

It remains now to attempt a critical assessment of his work though I acknowledge that four decades after the biography and two decades after the completion of his parliamentary studies may be too close in time, and myself too close in friendship, for these conclusions to be anything but interim.

III

I have throughout this paper, except on a few occasions, set forth Neale's approach in his own terms; and because I did not want the coherent pattern of his life's work to be obscured I have largely reserved the critical approaches to his methods and conclusions to my final section. Some at least of these criticisms will be familiar to students of the period and I will therefore present them in summary form.

More than one friendly critic put his finger on two weaknesses to which none of us who work in his field can plead innocence: that the approach was insular in space and time; in short that it had nothing to say about continental developments during the second half of the sixteenth century and little about the medieval parliamentary growth. The first element of this criticism can, I think, be fairly easily countered. Neale was not writing a history of European institutions. He did not possess the necessary equipment to do so and, in any case, the material was not accessible to him. He wrote a delightful short book on the *Age of Catherine de Medici* but it was not designed as a piece of research. If he had attempted this larger survey, or even developed comparable analyses, his major works could never have been written and we should have gained little in the process. The inadequate grasp on medieval developments is a harder criticism to counter. J. S. Roskell,[1] May McKisack,[2] and others have pointed out that the conquest of the boroughs by the gentry can be traced to a process going well back into the fifteenth century. More especially Professor Roskell's article, published in the *Bulletin of the John Rylands Library* in 1964, forms an essential companion piece to the Neale corpus.[3] For in the process of a searching inquiry into the changing fortunes of the House of Commons he challenged Neale's conclusion that the House had made notable strides in legislative influence during the time of Elizabeth.

Professor Roskell fully acknowledged that, as Neale had undoubtedly established, the Commons had gained considerable powers of self-discipline and institutional identity which were to serve it well. But he also pointed out that those M.P.s who spoke up for freedom of speech were few in number and that the most outstanding exponent of this minority opinion, Peter Wentworth, was suppressed by the *Commons themselves*. He underlined, what was being borne in upon some of us from repeated readings of *Elizabeth I and her Parliaments*, how little influence the Commons in effect exercised upon either the legislation or the executive acts of the Government. (I can think of only four occasions when Commons intervention was decisive: in the religious legislation of 1559, though thereafter their intervention in this area was stubbornly resisted by the queen; in ensuring

[1] J. S. Roskell, *The Commons in the Parliament of 1422* (Manchester, 1954).

[2] May McKisack, *The Parliamentary Representation of the English Boroughs during the Middle Ages* (1932).

[3] J. S. Roskell, 'Perspectives in English Parliamentary History', *Bull. of the John Rylands Library*, 46 (1964), 448–75.

the execution of the Duke of Norfolk in 1572 and of Mary, Queen of Scots in 1587; and in the temporary reform in monopolies achieved in 1601. And it must be remembered that the Commons were often supported by at least a section of the Privy Council, otherwise they might not have got away with it.

Professor Roskell also showed the relative maturity of the medieval House of Commons during some phases of its development: that it used the processes of impeachment to gain a degree of control over the king's ministers, a piece of machinery not employed at all under the Tudors; that some late medieval parliaments had greater control over crown revenues than did their Elizabethan successors, both in their grants and in their appropriation; and that it was not until the late seventeenth century that some of the powers and influence of the medieval Commons were restored. A formidable case has been made and I am unaware of any answer which has been offered for this revision of Tudor parliamentary history. It should, however, be said that while Professor Roskell's case is a powerful one, full allowance should be made for the very considerable informal influence which the Commons exercised time and time again on the queen's ministers who had to use every skill of parliamentary management to contain these pressures. When, under the early Stuarts, as Notestein showed, this management became incompetent and weak, the lid was off.[1] It is true that the Commons could usually only exercise a negative force upon government policy, and for that reason it is extremely difficult to measure; but it is perfectly clear that men like Burghley and Robert Cecil were always attentive to these latent powers. Nor, I am sure, would Professor Roskell want to argue that his criticisms in any way diminish the unique and impressive account of a parliamentary institution in action which Neale contributed to Tudor scholarship.

There is another criticism which may be offered to Neale's parliamentary studies: that is that his two volumes are a study of conflict, or at least confrontation, between Crown and Commons and therefore minimize the overwhelming degree of co-operation which existed and which alone could make good legislation and good government possible. This criticism Neale in part anticipated. In the preface to the first of his two volumes on *Elizabeth I and her Parliament* he wrote: 'I have focused the narrative on the relations between the Crown and Parliament:

[1] W. Notestein, 'The Winning of the Initiative by the House of Commons', *Proc. of the Brit. Academy*, 11 (1924–5), 125–75.

partly because the story would have been formless and unreadable if I had attempted to discuss all the business that came before Parliament; and partly because my purpose is to reveal the significance of the Elizabethan period in the constitutional evolution of England, and, more specifically, to banish the old illusion that early Stuart Parliaments had few roots in the sixteenth century.'[1] This is important but I think that the challenge has not been wholly met. Nor indeed can one entirely remove the impression that religion, especially Puritanism, claims so much of the centre of the stage that economic and related issues disappear in the shadows or are banished to the wings. Related to this is the point that Professor R. B. Wernham raised in a review in which he asked whether Neale was right in declaring that 'Elizabethan England, as mirrored in the House of Commons, was overwhelmingly Puritan in its sympathies.'[2] Professor Wernham uses Neale's own evidence to show that throughout the period the Puritans remained a minority in the House and, for a variety of reasons, could carry with them only a diminishing proportion of the parliamentarians and the gentry.

There remain other questions, too complex to raise in a paper of this kind and on this occasion, which could and should be examined at the appropriate time. Central to all this is the role of the queen. Did Neale over-emphasize the power of the queen and was her influence on the preservation of liberty or the welfare of England wholly beneficent? I have indicated elsewhere my growing conviction that her approach during the first three decades of her reign represented statesmanship of the highest order in healing the nation's wounds and in skilfully pursuing a foreign policy which gave full regard to her own precarious position, her limited financial resources, and the defence of the national interests. In the process she skilfully resisted the ideological and other forces which sought to drive her in more adventurous directions. But I have also come to believe that the last third of her reign witnessed a failure in not adapting her policies to changing needs, and in not modernizing her financial methods and organization or preparing her subjects for the changing conditions under her successor. For this failure Burghley shares a good deal of responsibility; and though his son, Robert Cecil, accomplished his first major task of ensuring a peaceful succession,

[1] J. E. Neale, *Elizabeth I and her Parliaments*, i. 11.

[2] R. B. Wernham, *Eng. Hist. Rev.* 69 (1954), 634, citing Neale's *Elizabeth I and her Parliaments*, 1. 418.

the inherited dead weight of outdated principles and organization, and the lack of support from a new and uncomprehending monarch, destroyed the massive scheme of renovation to which Cecil had dedicated himself so late in the day.

Yet none of these observations can affect the basic evaluation of Neale's contributions. In those three major volumes, each a masterpiece in its own right, he portrayed a great institution, in its structure and action, in all the richness of its texture and variety, through his incomparable grasp of its sources and deep, almost uncanny, understanding of its day-by-day handling of its affairs. At the same time he brought to life the queen and her subjects through the creative exercise of his historical imagination of which the Elizabethans themselves would have been proud.

IV

In the Preface to his final volume on the Elizabethan parliaments Neale declared:

> I have now completed a task that was planned when I was young and that has occupied most of my leisure, chiefly in the search for material. I find pleasure in the thought that it has been finished—though I shall miss the deadline in publication—while I still hold the Astor Chair of English History at University College, London. In my mind it is an offering—the discharge of my stewardship—to a College that I have delighted to serve for so many years.[1]

It is perhaps appropriate to leave it to an American, Conyers Read, to pronounce a final word in this context:

> . . . his Tudor seminar then may fairly be regarded as the focal point of nearly everything that has been done in Elizabethan history for the last generation both in England and in America. It will not be extravagant to say that he has done more than any other living English historian to draw English and American scholars into a fellowship in which, without national bias or private envy, they pursue together their common search for the truth.[2]

We who follow Neale count ourselves fortunate in our day and generation that the seeds planted by him have borne such a magnificent harvest for our instruction, sustenance, and delight.

JOEL HURSTFIELD

[1] J. E. Neale, *Elizabeth I and her Parliaments*, ii. 9.
[2] C. Read, *Am. Hist. Rev.* 59 (1954), 610.

PLATE XLVIII

SIR EDWARD STANLEY GOTCH ROBINSON

EDWARD STANLEY GOTCH ROBINSON

1887–1976

STANLEY ROBINSON was born on 4 July 1887 at 23 Westfield Park, Clifton, Bristol, the sixth of the seven children (four sons and three daughters) of Edward Robinson and Katherine Frances, *née* Gotch. His father was one of the eight children of Elisha Smith Robinson, who, coming to Bristol in the earlier 1840s at the age of 27, started business there as a paper merchant and grocers' stationer. In 1875 Elisha visited the United States of America and there acquired the British rights in a new machine which revolutionized the British paper-bag industry, and he introduced the printing of shopkeepers' names on the bags they used. By this means the family fortunes were founded, and Elisha Robinson in due course became Lord Mayor of Bristol and a Justice of the Peace. The Robinsons had in fact been centred around Bristol, Gloucester, and the Forest of Dean for about two centuries; and Nathaniel Robinson (born in 1775) had even thus early been a paper-maker at Winchcombe, while earlier generations had included nail-makers.

Control of the family business passed, in time, from Elisha, under whom the firm became E. S. and A. Robinson, to Edward Robinson. Edward's wife, known as a woman of great sweetness, was the daughter of the Revd. Dr. Gotch, a member of the Old Testament Revision Committee; and both she and her husband were loyal supporters of the Baptist Church. Stanley Robinson (as he was to be known for most of his long life) was thus born into a large, prosperous, nonconformist, West of England family of civic consequence, and, being almost the youngest of that large family, was perhaps of a disposition naturally too gentle to compete easily with the demands of his environment. At all events, after he had attended Miss Cundall's dame-school, he had become a diffident child. He was left-handed by nature, and, whether or not because he was compelled or induced to turn to right-handed usage, he early developed a stammer. This, though cured later in life, left him, even after cure, with a softness—it was not even a noticeable hesitation—in speech. By contrast his handwriting never showed the forced change from left to right hand, developing into a beautiful, free-flowing, but disciplined form which was instantly recognizable.

It was in order to develop him and give him a sense of independence that, at the age of ten or thereabouts, Robinson was sent to London to live for a time with (and receive tuition from) E. J. Seltman, a speech therapist, who was also a numismatic scholar and dealer of note, and the father of that Charles Seltman who was ultimately to become a Fellow of Queens' College, Cambridge, and to make his own name as the author of *Greek Coins* in the Methuen series of *Handbooks of Archaeology*. While he was living with Seltman, Robinson would quite certainly have seen many coins—and principally Greek coins—passing through Seltman's hands, with all the attendant problems of authenticity or doubt; and, as he was being trained in the classics, Robinson doubtless integrated this numismatic knowledge (or rather the beginnings of it) into the general classical education he was receiving. Three elder Robinson brothers—Foster, Percy, and Harold—had all in turn gone to Clifton College at Bristol; and it was to Clifton that Stanley himself went, when he was not much more than eleven, as a day-boy in the college's North Town house. Of the academic details of his time at school nothing is known, save that he was to win a classical scholarship to Christ Church, Oxford, in 1906: this was a step, and a stage, of permanent importance in his life, for it steered him away from the business of the family firm, by now expanding with all success, to a life of scholarship. His time at Clifton was not, however, devoid of other, if minor, distinction, as a player of games: in his last two years there (1905–6) he was a member of the second cricket XI, in which he is recorded as being more successful with the bat than as a bowler. Later on he was to play cricket in the Robinson family XI in the local matches which became a family ritual; and here it was as a bowler that he was remembered: as a boy of only fourteen he had once taken all ten wickets with his cunning googlies, of which the knack afterwards deserted him. He also played rackets at Clifton, being secretary of the Rackets Club.

When Robinson went up to Oxford in 1906, Christ Church, like the University as a whole, was experiencing that renaissance of classical studies which, after the more easy-going days of the nineteenth century, was stimulated by European scholars—philological, historical, and archaeological; and he responded keenly. After a First Class in Honour Moderations, he went on to Greats; and it was from his Greek history tutor, Robin Dundas (or 'D' as the generations of his pupils universally knew him), that he received the personal stimulus which lighted up his mind for the rest of his academic life. Dundas was a terse and laconic Scot. A product of Eton and New College, he had himself only just come as Greek history tutor to Christ Church, and he was afterwards accustomed to say that Robinson, little younger than himself, was his first, as also his best, pupil. Like all succeeding generations of Dundas's pupils, Robinson found in him a tutor who both knew his ancient sources very well (re-reading them, 'D' would say, yearly) and approached them in a constant spirit of inquiring and critical curiosity. He was and remained a first-class tutor, and he left his mark strongly and permanently on Robinson, as well as establishing an intimate friendship for life.

Robinson duly gained his First Class in Greats in 1910; and in the process he had developed his numismatic interests, coming under the influence of Percy Gardner, who, after a period in the British Museum and at Cambridge, had been elected Lincoln Professor of Classical Archaeology at Oxford. Many years later, on the occasion of the presentation, in 1967, of a *Festschrift* for his eightieth birthday, Robinson explained what Gardner had meant to him.

> Gardner was a numismatist by training, and some of his best work lies in this field. He was the first, I imagine, to give regular teaching at Oxford in numismatics in classes as well as to individuals. Wherever possible, he would relate the coins to the history of the time; and, as I well remember, he always insisted on their importance as a primary source for the study of the ancient world in general. . . . He had to content himself with a few casts and photographs for illustration. . . . The coins belonging to the University, such as they then were, were still held *incommunicado* in a strong room in the Bodleian, and similar limitations held for the College collections. In Christ Church, for example, when I first began to catalogue the [Greek] coins, in theory it required the simultaneous presence of two Canons, each with his key, to open the coin cabinet. . . . I think we owe Gardner more than is perhaps realized nowadays.

The year 1910 thus saw Robinson with a First in Mods. and Greats and a clear desire to pursue scholarship, and primarily Greek scholarship, for although he had absorbed Roman history as well, and commanded skill and grace in the composition of Latin prose and verse throughout his life, it was to the culture of ancient Greece that he directed his eager energy. It was natural that he should follow his time at Oxford by a spell at the British School at Athens; and already in 1911 he was to be found embarking on an extended journey of exploration in Lycia with a friend on horseback. This tour occupied about two months, during which the young men lived fairly rough, saw much beautiful scenery, copied a good many inscriptions, verified the sites of certain ancient towns, and survived various crises with tired mounts, flooded streams, flea-ridden beds, and rain-storms. Robinson kept a diary, written in a minutely pencilled hand in a small notebook, and containing some good descriptive passages.

> *April 8th* Found a wedding in full swing . . . about 150 Turks squatting in full dress, blue coat and all, watching a wrestling match . . . as we reached the ground the band marched out to welcome us and when we were established on a carpet laid their drums before us for backsheesh, then the wrestling began. They come out into the middle with great ceremony, then walk round to the weird music in a kind of gawkish dance, then retire, then meet in the middle, rub shoulders and wave their left hands. Suddenly the music stops and they approach, gripping by the arms,—the round lasts 2–8 mins. and is finished by a throw. . . .The preliminaries the most amusing, gone through with grt [*sic*] solemnity and slowness, every gesture and step exaggerated. . . . Didn't like to photo for fear of offence.

Years later, as an old man, Robinson paid a return visit to Anatolia, reviving old memories and creating new ones. It was, he said, the only place to which one could return after sixty years and find it hardly changed.

At this period, possibly, Robinson's inclinations turned away, definitely, from archaeology to historical numismatics. Although his 'Lycian diary' makes many allusions to inscriptions, sarcophagi, carvings, and sites in general, his interests seem to have focused more strongly on the coins which he saw and attempted to buy, often vainly (since prices were above London levels, which he evidently knew), and on scenery and people—'better than archaeology', as he noted in one entry. The diary as a whole, as witnessed by the account of the wrestlers quoted above (did he, perhaps, have in mind the coins of Aspendus in Pamphylia?), shows the development of his inner eye for form and movement; and although in later life he took full advantage of the evidence of archaeology, he preferred it to be impeccably presented and expounded by specialists of the eminence of such great friends as Paul Jacobsthal, Henri Seyrig, and Bernard Ashmole.

In any case, once his spell at Athens was finished, it was to numismatics that he turned for his life's work. In June 1912, he was appointed Assistant Keeper in the Department of Coins and Medals at the British Museum, on provisional tenure that was to be confirmed two years later. At the time of his entry into the British Museum, the Medal Room, as it was then and still is loosely called, had just come under a new Keeper, G. F. Hill, a brilliant Greek scholar (himself the subject of a memoir by Robinson in Vol. 36 of these *Proceedings*) and, like Robinson too, a protégé of Percy Gardner. The two men, one 45 years old, the other 25, formed what turned out to be a close understanding and friendship, based on community of interests and (to quote Robinson's words on Hill) the 'combination of meticulous accuracy with breadth of view'. Hill was not, in the general estimation, a very easy man, but in his young recruit he found a willing disciple, as Dundas had done at Christ Church, and his influence upon him and his work was powerful.

One month after Robinson's confirmation in his post, the First World War interrupted what had seemed to be so promising a pattern of life. Robinson was a first-class scholar, lively and energetic, and his connection with the family business meant that he need not worry about the pittance paid by the British Museum to members of its staff. With the war all this was changed. Robinson joined the Northamptonshire Regiment in 1914 and served in France in 1915–16, until he was very severely wounded in the leg and made a cripple on two sticks for life. Like so many young men of eager spirit, he sought some solace from the horrors of war in poetry, and many of the poems of that time, slight pieces of greatly varied metre, dwelt on love and death. Two in particular illuminate the personal agony that he himself felt after so crippling a physical blow.

I was tall and straight,
Very strong was I,
People turned to look
  When I passed by.

Now my limbs are bowed
O'er ungainly ways.
I must go halting
  All my days.

But inside my thought branching
Like a green beech tree
(Though I go halting,
  Back and knee,

And people turn to look
As they pass me by),
Shoots up straight and strong,
And that's I.

The second, darker and more despondent, recalls the fact that he had been very fond of dancing (he was, incidentally, a great lover of ballet—vicarious movement—in later life):

I shall dance no more.
Never again my feet
Shall move, as the music falls
In urgent beat,
Answering other feet.

I shall ride no more
Nor feel between my knees
Shoulders of a horse
Rippling at ease
As we turn to breast the breeze.

And if round the full-ringed trunk
Though its branches whisper to the sky
Murderous ivies cramp
Green and nigh,
That tree shall surely die.

Having recovered to the extent that he could, Robinson spent a short time in the Home Office, returning thence to the British Museum, to take up again the life work which had been so painfully interrupted. During his convalescence he had married Pamela, daughter of Sir Victor Horsley, C.B., F.R.S., an eminent surgeon. She from this time on, during a remarkably happy married life of nearly sixty years, cherished and cared for him serenely, not so as to fuss over his infirmity, but so as never to forget it, remembering always that his scholastic activities were for him the true half of his existence. They were to have a large and closely united family of six children, two sons and four daughters, in whom (with numerous grandchildren in the years to come) they found and enjoyed a company of never failing stimulus and delight.

Once back in the British Museum, Robinson succeeded automatically to his share in the writing of the British Museum *Catalogue of Greek Coins*. This, begun in 1873 with the volume on Italy, had progressed round the Greek world, clockwise (on the lines first followed by Eckhel in the eighteenth century), reaching the Near East with Hill's successive volumes on Phoenicia, Palestine, Arabia–Persia by 1910, 1914, and 1922 respectively. The sequence now pointed to North Africa, and it was on Cyrenaica that Robinson now worked, the volume being published in 1929. As Dr. Cahn has observed in his academically warm and sensitive obituary remarks (*Schweizer Münzblätter*, Nov. 1976, p. 90), this was more than simply a British Museum catalogue, being in fact a corpus, for it included much material not in the Museum's collection. Robinson was now developing his meticulous and extraordinarily accurate gifts of observation, backed by patient approach, a tenacious memory, and a firm knowledge of his historical sources; and it is interesting to note that his Cyrenaica volume included 275 pages of commentary as compared with only 127 pages of catalogue proper. Every aspect of the coinage of this self-contained area was explored fully—historical, mythological, religious, metrological, and botanical; for the coinage was to be seen in as wide a context as possible. This was always to be his approach, even though it was never again, perhaps, to be quite so abundantly realized.

In the earlier 1930s Robinson began that process which turned him, as Dr. Cahn has emphasized, into *the* authority to be consulted on the authenticity or otherwise of a Greek coin of importance. And so Calouste Gulbenkian, the oil magnate and the Pierpont Morgan of Europe, having bought certain coins from the Prinkipo hoard of 1930, began a long series of consultative visits to the British Museum, adding steadily to a collection of superb quality, in part magnificently catalogued later on by Robinson with M. Castro Hipólito (1971). 'Mr. G.', as Robinson affectionately spoke of Gulbenkian, had a number of standard questions about any coin he fancied buying. Was it certainly genuine? Were its types already known? Was it more, or less, rare? Was its price low or high? Was its condition average, or better than most? Of these questions, authenticity and condition seem to have ranked highest, condition becoming an obsession, so that Robinson found himself virtually charged with the responsibility (Hill having become Director of the British Museum in 1931) of forming Gulbenkian's collection for him on the most exacting standards (see *Colóquio, Revista de Artes e Letras*, Lisbon, Oct. 1966, p. 22). His achievement can be judged from the unique splendour of the collection in the Gulbenkian Museum at Lisbon today.

It seemed that, having catalogued the Greek coins of Cyrenaica, Robinson's attention would now move westward along North Africa to Libya, Carthage, and beyond, for in 1935 he made an extended visit to Tunisia and Algeria, keeping (as previously in Lycia) a minutely detailed record in notebooks, fortunately preserved. He acquired many coins, of which those comprising the El Djem hoard showed that the Punic issues contained in it were not (as previously supposed of parallel issues found elsewhere) of plain bronze, but of silvered bronze. North Africa, however, was to lapse from his programme of work, for his interests were turning in a very different direction. His colleague closest in age at the British Museum was Harold Mattingly, who had already shown the same brilliance in Roman numismatics that Robinson showed in Greek, the first (and revolutionary) volume of the British Museum Roman Imperial Catalogue having appeared in 1923. The two men could never be close personal friends, for they differed too much in temperament and outlook, and Hill, as a Greek scholar, had perhaps smiled the more on Robinson, but they performed a joint exercise of immense importance, by a combination of sheer scholarship and, perhaps, jointly inspired intuition, when in their 'Date of the Roman Denarius' (*Proceedings of the British Academy*, 1932) they dissociated the institution of the denarial coinage of Rome from Pliny's date of 269 B.C. and so opened the way for discussion of other and much later contexts. This was a major, indeed an explosive, change in modern studies of Republican Rome; it is now accepted, in principle, by virtually all scholars. The study involved in this work gave Robinson a deep and permanent interest in the miscellaneous Greek coinages of the Italian peninsula, of which he himself was to collect the coins of certain mints (including Thurii and Velia) on an exhaustive scale. Together with all this, in what must have been a peak period of inventiveness and experiment for a mind of restless activity and criticism, he conceived the project of the *Sylloge Nummorum Graecorum*, long since sponsored by the British Academy, and now uniformly, and flatteringly, followed by other institutions in Europe and America, in which important collections of Greek coins were reproduced, photographically, with a minimum of supporting text. This project, of which he continued to be a primary editior until his death, might in a sense be considered a major monument to him: it communicated to scholars, easily and not expensively, the contents of great collections in a reliably exact form, and it revived, in a manner which achieved universal acceptance in an age of vastly improved reproduction, the format of H. de la Tour's well known but much earlier *Atlas des monnaies gauloises*.

In 1938 Robinson took a step which possibly influenced the directions of his future research work when, after the retirement of J. G. Milne from the Readership in Numismatics at Oxford, he succeeded to that position. It suited him, and he performed it, admirably. He gave no formal lectures, and it is doubtful whether, even if Oxford had followed the example of some European countries by the establishment of a professorship in this now rapidly growing subject of specialist study, he would have been willing to subject his natural hesitancy to such a public ordeal: it had only been by his wife's encouragement that he had consulted and had been greatly helped by an eminent speech therapist. But, coming to Oxford for a night every week or so, and staying at Christ Church with Dundas (with whom he re-established, to his wry amusement, the old pupil–tutor relationship), he could devote the better part of two days a week in the Heberden Coin Room of the Ashmolean to the private instruction of those—undergraduates, graduate pupils, and dons—who wished to learn his views on numismatic points which affected the study of Greek history as such. These tutorials, during which the passage of the hours was disregarded in discussion, were responsible for the grooming of many a student; and for the Coin Room too they were important, as Robinson now became intimately familiar with its university policy and purpose, its Greek collection, and the very great defects in that collection. The effect upon two of his pupils is described a little later; and Bernard Ashmole clearly remembers his great patience and kindness with the young.

Robinson had become Deputy Keeper in his department at the British Museum in 1936, under John Allan, the orientalist, and it was therefore natural that when the coin collection was dispersed for safety during the 1939–45 war—a dispersal abundantly justified when the Medal Room was destroyed, through enemy action, by fire—he should play a primary part in its guardianship in the country, where his time at Compton Wynyates in Warwickshire was perhaps most pleasantly spent. Very possibly, these years, spent quietly away from normal semi-administrative British Museum routine in London, allowed his mind to define and crystallize his views on certain problems of chronology and attribution affecting coinages in their historical context, for a series of fundamentally important papers flowed from him from 1943 onwards. Of these, his study of the coinage of the Libyans (1943; also 1953 and 1956) resulted in the secure attribution of a coinage, hitherto unattributed, to a precise historical context: his study (1946) of the Samians, Rhegium, and Zankle, in similarly elaborating the exact relationship between coinages and recorded history, provided a fixed chronological point for the early issues of Sicily and South Italy: his study (1949) of the Athenian currency decree, which remained without equivalent treatment for two decades, once again demonstrated the close relationship between numismatic and non-numismatic evidence; and his famous paper (1951) on the coins from the Ephesian Artemisium was a total reappraisal of the chronology of early Greek coinage (still unchallenged after a quarter of a century) in which he embraced not only historical evidence but also that of Assyrian sculptural art forms. These notable papers were followed by others in the 1950s and 1960s, of which that (1954) on the 'cistophori' of Eumenes II—by a stroke of genius which he said came to him in his bath—gave them instead to Aristonicus fifty years later, so leading to a complete reassessment of the regal Pergamene coinages. By the same token, his study (1966) of the coinages associated with the second Punic War fixed the vast and varied coinage of the Brettii in a historical framework not likely to be seriously disputed in the future.

Dr. Colin Kraay, himself taught at Oxford by Robinson, and now Keeper of the Heberden Coin Room, has kindly allowed the quotation here of his comments on certain predominant interests and characteristics of Robinson's work.

1. The periphery of the Greek world: Cyrenaica, Sinope, Olbia, North Africa, the Carthaginians in Spain, Persia. One may add from personal knowledge his keen interest in Lycia, South Anatolia, Cyprus, Phoenicia/Palestine.
2. The integration of numismatic with non-numismatic evidence (literature, sculpture, archaeology, etc.).
3. The importance of hoards, overstrikes, die-links, etc. This is worth emphasizing because, though these phenomena were known when Robinson started his numismatic career about 1911, their potential contribution was not yet recognized.

Continuously underlying the 'highlights' listed above was the publication of a vast number of individual coins—such as the components of hoards, in catalogues of collections (Woodward, Locker Lampson, Gulbenkian), in *Sylloge Nummorum Graecorum* (e.g. Lockett), in periodic reviews of British Museum accessions, etc. One cannot here discern trends or influences; these were, as Robinson himself said, the bricks which constituted the edifice of numismatics. Each brick was presented with totally authoritative commentary, founded on his long and intimate knowledge of the great British Museum collection; ideally, he thought every single detail was worthy of record and might one day be useful to someone, but like most of us he did not always achieve this ideal. Sometimes, as in the studies listed above, the bricks were assembled into small, perfectly constructed edifices, but more often they were stacked on one side for future use by himself or others. The completed edifices were in the end rather few because Robinson was a perfectionist; he published only when a problem was completely solved, and when every detail had fallen into place to his own full satisfaction.

Despite the seemingly effortless perfection of his articles, this effect was not obtained easily or without labour. He was not a very systematic worker. Though he assembled a large private library, far from exclusively numismatic, he had no comprehensive system of references or files; notes were written on scraps of paper of varying size and loosely strung together on treasury tags. Articles reached their final form only through a number of drafts in his own hand, each heavily corrected and revised, for his subtle mind tended to see additional complications at each revision.

In the integration of numismatic evidence with that of sculpture and painting, Robinson was closely associated in the British Museum with Professor Bernard Ashmole, then in the Greek and Roman Department, each learning much from the knowledge of the other. Usually they worked together on the trustworthiness of style as a guide to dating, and on the question whether there is any safe chronological comparison to be made between coins, sculpture, and vases. Already by 1936 these two scholars had begun to define certain lines of relationship between coins and sculpture (*Trans. Internat. Num. Congress, London, 1936*, pp. 17 ff.), and their joint studies and discussions were to continue. Professor Ashmole has written in a letter (20 Jan. 1977), 'A few years ago I remember lengthy discussions with Stanley (and argument) over the foundation-deposits at Persepolis, and how the foreign coins there might be dated. Of course it was always Stanley who knew accurately all the historical—and of course numismatic—background, but yet was ready to listen to views from another angle.'

Robinson continued as Deputy Keeper of Coins and Medals from 1936 to 1949, then becoming Keeper until his retirement in 1952, at the age of 65. It was a difficult period in which to hold the Keepership. Destruction of the old and hallowed Medal Room was followed by the re-assembly of the coins in other and temporary parts of the museum, arranged of necessity where they could be, and not as they should be. Perhaps fortunately, his age-seniority limited the span of his Keepership, for although he was able to decide on the rebuilding of the new Medal Room on the site of the old, the actual work involved fell on his successor, Dr. John Walker. Robinson, however, even though he was not by nature inclined to administration, and though his systems of arrangement were sometimes a problem to all but himself, was precise, punctilious, and strictly economical in practical matters. On one occasion, for example, when a visiting scholar wished to work on coins temporarily stored in a room which at that moment lacked the invigilator required by the department's rules, Robinson neatly solved the problem by enrolling the visitor as a kind of special constable. He was, however, looking ahead to his retirement. For some years past he and his family had occupied a charming country house, The Rookery, at Burton Bradstock, in Dorset. Now, in 1951, he took a long lease from the late Lord Crawford of the splendid house known as Stepleton at Iwerne Stepleton, near Blandford Forum, in the same county. To this house, with its little church in the park, its lake, and its gardens (which, after finding them neglected, he helped to restore and re-design, adding a lake and incorporating a swimming pool by the rose garden), he retired in 1952. He had become a Fellow of the Academy in 1948; and he was now made C.B.E.

From this time onward he was able to devote himself to a desired sufficiency of chosen research combined with visits to London (where he also occupied a house, next to the British Museum) and for teaching at Oxford. To both the British Museum and the Ashmolean he now stood forth as a benefactor of the first order. He had been channelling fine and rare Greek coins into the British Museum for a long time past; his gifts there, beginning in 1917 with two Persian sigloi, continued with a wide range of choice or important coins, and with hoard-material, down to the 1960s. At Oxford, continuing as Reader until 1958, and thereafter as Honorary Curator of Greek coins at the Ashmolean, he began to inject great numbers of Greek coins into the collection there, which until then had been very patchy. Of the quality of his teaching and of the purposes of his collecting and his gifts of coins at this time, Dr. Kraay has written as follows:

No comment on Robinson would be complete without some mention of the related aspects of teaching and collecting. His teaching was like, and in some cases no doubt actually was, the preparation of an article. Each tutorial on a given subject was like a new draft of an article—the ground was gone over afresh; newly discovered evidence was evaluated and incorporated; and new ramifications were observed. In these circumstances it is not surprising that he rarely came to definite conclusions; but in compensation, every student could be confident that he was receiving the most thorough and up-to-date treatment of the subject in question. In speaking of collecting, one thinks not only of the coins which Robinson bought for himself but also of those which he gave to the British Museum and to the Ashmolean (over 5,000 to the Ashmolean). This was not collecting in the normal sense nor from the usual motives. The object was to have readily available in this country, whether in London or Oxford, adequate material for teaching and research—and the more complete that material the better. There was no substitute for seeing and handling the coin itself; if it was a unique coin, then its actual local presence was all the more important. In addition to the single coin, there was also the realisation that in some cases the only key to mint history lay in building dense series, as in the cases of Thurii, Velia, Corinth, and Persia. Fortunately in his case both the financial means and the material were readily available at the same time; today such series of coins are probably no longer to be found at any price.

All told, he enriched the Ashmolean collection of Greek coins by some 5,500 specimens, most of them personally approved by himself, for the Ashmolean Coin Room became, in time, the annual beneficiary of a substantial sum for the purchase of Greek coins selected by Robinson himself. And in 1964 he presented his own splendid collection, extraordinarily rich in certain selected series, to the Ashmolean.

Mr. Kenneth Jenkins, until lately Keeper of the Department of Coins and Medals at the British Museum, was also a pupil of Robinson's at Oxford after the 1939–45 war, and he, like Dr. Kraay, was struck by the quality of Robinson's tuition.

Of course I was always deeply impressed by his tutorials, going patiently through details which he knew by heart but which he obviously so enjoyed going through again for the umpteenth time, and it was fascinating when one came to know that there were all sorts of riches waiting in readiness in his head. Never in a hurry to reach conclusions, but letting them grow naturally as far as possible, his discourse could be disconcerting as he would pursue relentlessly any thought that happened to come to him—and with no inhibition about sticking to the point. In my early days with him as his pupil he was still doing early electrum (bewildering detail to a beginner!) and then, in the middle of some knotty point about weight standards he would produce some recherché detail from Assyrian sculpture which unexpectedly made everything fall into place.

In 1955 Oxford conferred an Honorary D.Litt upon him, and Christ Church made him an Honorary Student. He was now retired, more leisured in the sense that he was more free, immensely happy at Stepleton (in which he took to his heart the house and gardens and the many guests who were entertained there), and able to plan his work ahead at a time when many would be laying it down. This consisted, first, of the continuing supervision and editing of the *Sylloge Nummorum Graecorum*; secondly, of work on sundry learned articles and on the Gulbenkian catalogue; and thirdly—and mainly—of the planning and writing, ultimately with collaborators, of what was intended as the first (and pilot) fascicule of a totally revised edition of the *Historia Numorum*, of which the last edition had appeared in 1911. On this he worked unremittingly, contributing a large number of entries, exactly proportioned, carefully documented, and expressed in a lean and lively prose, comparable with that of J. D. Beazley, which made his meaning perfectly clear. In his later years, he was much worried, and his attention was often diverted, by minutiae: should one, for example, write Cumae or Kyme, Caelia or Kailia, and should one's references follow this or that plan? This was, however, perfectionism, and not pedantry, as anyone who knew him as a person could tell. Indeed, his personality at this time flowered into a serene yet acute peak. Although his crippled leg made him steadily less mobile, and although deafness increased (and this alone irritated him), he enjoyed life—leisure and work—to the full. He continued his Oxford visits, staying after Dundas's death with Dr. Sydney Watson, then organist of Christ Church, who has written of him (15 Dec. 1976):

What I would include among my most dominant memories of him is the vivid interest he showed in everybody and everything around him. I remember staying at Stepleton after the filming of certain parts of 'Tom Jones' in the garden, and while filming was still going on in the neighbourhood. Stanley insisted on us driving to Cerne Abbas one afternoon just to see whether anything was happening. We were lucky: filming was happening that day, and Stanley sat on the grass wearing his beret and looking as happy as a schoolboy. We had difficulty in getting him home for tea. . . . On more than one occasion when he was staying with me at Christ Church he came to my rooms and found that I was out. He would go and call on an undergraduate on the same staircase and have a cordial and easy conversation with him, during which he had found out more about the young man than many of that undergraduate's friends. It was impossible, at Stepleton, to think of him as the distinguished academic that he was . . . and equally impossible to imagine him as anything other than the notable scholar whenever he opened his mouth. . . . 'Vivid' is the word that comes to my mind whenever I think of him. He was such a vivid person.

His work at Stepleton was done in a markedly individual way. He would rise late after a frugal breakfast, always of yoghourt, sometimes perhaps with olives. His great bedroom was also his library and his study combined, overlooking the park, and here he could work quietly, clad in winter, if need be, in his own version of a medieval burgher's gown for ease and comfort. Part of the day would be wholly social, or spent in the sunny garden in summer. After dinner in the evening, which he greatly enjoyed, with some good wine, he would sleep for a little before going to his study, about 11, to work in absolute quietness until about 3 a.m. And then to bed.

Oxford claimed two speeches from him on the occasion of his eightieth birthday in 1967, when he and his wife gave a party in Christ Church Hall, and when a volume of essays, dedicated to him by a number of scholars who were friends or former pupils, was presented to him in the Senior Common Room garden. It claimed a third in 1970, when the Vice-Chancellor and the Visitors of the Ashmolean entertained him at dinner at Lincoln College, to his great enjoyment. The crowning mark of distinction, which claimed no public speech, came in 1972 when a Knighthood was conferred upon him 'for services to numismatics and the Ashmolean Museum', an honour which pleased the multitude of the friends of Robinson and his wife.

During his last years, Sir Edward Robinson (as he then became) turned again to writing small poems, some looking back to the First World War, some romantic, some satirical, some epigrammatic, some reflecting his interest in the supernatural, some just to amuse the family. One or two look forward, such as the one written in 1973:

So may no morbid fears
Born of the huge, cavernous, smoke dimmed
past,
Dog these declining years,
Nor linger till the last.

I have made my venture of faith,
The World is seamless, One,
And so, when all is done,
To death.

This was conceived in serenity, when he was 86. And for the most part 'these declining years' were very happy, with his much loved wife and a constantly varying, almost kaleidoscopic pattern of sons and daughters and their wives and husbands and children, and guests, all in the setting of his beloved Stepleton, where the house seemed to have been built expressly for him, and where, increasingly immobile though he was, he seemed to know (by going around in his little electric chariot) every flower that bloomed in the gardens.

One of the chief pleasures in his family circle was his reading aloud—a habit from many years back, founded on his love of English literature. In prose, Dickens was one of his great favourites—with P. G. Wodehouse; in poetry, Bridges, Hardy, and especially Yeats, where he attributed his enjoyment to the influence of his old friend Dame Peggy Ashcroft in re-awakening his poetic interests by her own brilliant reading aloud.

There was much, indeed, to make him repine. He knew that his own capacity for intensive work was slowing down; he could no longer travel with any ease to London or Oxford; the new *Historia Numorum* could hardly be launched in his lifetime; and his deafness could make social conversation difficult for him. And so there came the inevitable contraction, when it was decided to leave Stepleton and move back to the house which he occupied next to the British Museum at 89 Great Russell Street, where he died shortly afterwards, on 13 June 1976. He was buried at Stepleton, in the tiny churchyard of the tiny church (where, though never a member of the Church of England, he had been churchwarden and had regularly chosen and read the lesson from the Bible he knew and loved well), a hundred yards from the house in which he had lived for so long. A memorial service, attended by very many, was later held in Christ Church Cathedral at Oxford.

The dominant personal impression of Robinson that should remain is perhaps that conveyed by the elegant and accomplished portrait, by Devas, which he and his wife generously gave to Christ Church in 1971. This was painted in 1954, when he was in the prime of his powers. It shows him, dressed casually (with a blue neckerchief emphasizing the clear, almost hyacinth blue of his eyes), seated holding a tray of coins at his desk—a study of controlled liveliness, of tightly wound vigour and eagerness held in check, all irradiated by the feeling of gaiety and keen observation. Those who would remember Robinson at that period will remember him also as a dashingly adventurous driver of his Land-Rover through Dorset tracks and fords, a tireless swimmer (he could not dance, alas, but he was a strong swimmer) doing his many lengths in the pool at Stepleton while never ceasing to discuss historical or numismatic details with visiting scholars, and a man of exquisite courtesy and witty conversation and anecdote, always well pointed, but never remotely unkind (even though his scholastic criticism was fearlessly expressed), and totally without complaint at the limitations which his injured leg imposed upon him. 'Massive patience'—the phrase is that of Mr. Jenkins—was a characteristic of his whole life.

As a scholar, he played the part of a deeply skilled and indeed inspired navigator, steering the course of Greek numismatics from the era of Barclay Head (whom he revered) through a great many uncharted areas, in which his superbly acute knowledge and observation were the guarantee of safety, to a new stage in which the comparative study of hoards, the study of die-links, the simplification of metrological questions, and the parallelisms between the art-forms of coins, sculpture, and painting were the essentials. Robinson was easily the greatest Greek numismatic scholar of his day, as was recognized by the distinctions which he received, and the medals and honorary memberships conferred upon him. He took all necessary part in the activities of his profession, being, for example, a Secretary of the Royal Numismatic Society and an Editor of the *Numismatic Chronicle* for many years. But office did not greatly attract him. His restless and richly furnished mind wished to research, reflect, and prove, and—over and above that—to make material available in publication. Hence his long-continuing devotion to the *Sylloge Nummorum Graecorum*, his personal creation, of which he said on one occasion, when its economy of printed detail was being unfavourably criticized by a foreign scholar, 'We give scholars the red meat: it is up to them to prepare it properly'. As a scholar himself he was in the first rank; and in his specialist branch of scholarship, numismatics (which, as it pleased him to recall, Wilamowitz had described as 'the English science'), he was a patient genius of equally matched humanity, charm, wit, and integrity.

C. H. V. SUTHERLAND

Note. This memoir would have been very much the poorer but for the generous help which I have received from Lady Robinson and her daughters, and especially Mrs. Heseltine; from

Miss Fay Gordon Hill; from Dr. Sydney Watson; from Professor Bernard Ashmole, Mr. Kenneth Jenkins, and Dr. Colin Kraay; and from the Head Master of Clifton College. My warm thanks are due to them all.

A bibliography of Sir Edward Robinson's published work down to 1966 is to be found in *Essays in Greek Coinage presented to Stanley Robinson*, ed. G. K. Jenkins and C. M. Kraay (Oxford, 1968). To this should now be added: *Numismatic Chronicle*, 1967, pp. 1 ff. (with M. J. Price), 'An emergency coinage of Timotheos'; *A catalogue of the Calouste Gulbenkian collection of Greek coins*, Part 1, Italy–Carthage (with M. Castro Hipólito), Lisbon, 1971; *Revue Numismatique*, 1973, pp. 229 ff., 'A hoard of Greek coins from southern Anatolia?'

PLATE XLIX

ARNOLD JOSEPH TOYNBEE

ARNOLD JOSEPH TOYNBEE

1889–1975

ARNOLD JOSEPH TOYNBEE was the most famous historian of his time and the most controversial. An abbreviated version of his principal work, *A Study of History*, published in 1946, became a run-away best seller; and during the ensuing fifteen years, Toynbee's ideas about the patterns of universal history, the relation of Western states and civilization to the rest of the world, and mankind's connection with God became a focus of widespread controversy in Great Britain and the United States, and in many other parts of the world where an official Marxism did not inhibit public debate.

Toynbee was born in London, 14 April 1889. His father, Harry V. Toynbee, was a social worker, following the example of his more famous brother, Arnold Toynbee (d. 1884), after whom the future historian was named. His mother had the distinction of having completed the equivalent of a B.A. in English History at Cambridge in an age when higher education for women was unusual, and her enthusiasm for historical studies communicated itself to the young Toynbee at a very tender age. In addition to his parents' influence, Toynbee's childhood was affected by a fiercely evangelical great uncle, who lived with the family and helped to imprint far-ranging familiarity with the King James Bible on the young boy.

At school, Toynbee met a different world. Schoolboy discipline, games, and ritual were generally uncongenial; but Greek and Latin language and literature, which constituted the staple of instruction at Wootton Court and Winchester, proved entrancing. Toynbee exhibited precocious studiousness under the stimulus of having to compete for scholarships, since his father's income was insufficient to pay the full charges at a school such as Winchester. As a result, he mastered Greek and Latin so thoroughly that in later life, whenever personal crises arose, he preferred to express his strongest emotions in Greek and Latin verse, reserving English for more commonplace purposes.

From Winchester he went to Oxford, entering Balliol College as a scholar in 1907. Early in his university career, his father suffered a nervous collapse and had to be institutionalized. Undoubtedly this was a severe shock for the budding scholar, compounded by the financial difficulties into which Toynbee's mother and two sisters were thrust by the catastrophe. Not yet twenty years of age, Toynbee reacted by redoubling his already prodigious academic labours. He capped his First in Mods with a First in Greats.

Toynbee's extraordinary abilities and diligence led to the offer of a Fellowship at Balliol; but before taking up the academic duties this appointment involved, he was able to travel to Italy and Greece, thanks to a special fellowship grant. The academic year 1911–12 was therefore spent making direct acquaintance with the classical landscapes he had hitherto known only through books. In Rome and Italy his experiences were those to be expected of a promising young classicist; but in Greece, in addition to surveying classical remains, he encountered a different sort of world. At the time of his visit, a cluster of British classicists had begun to take lively interest in contemporary Greek folkways and peasant customs, partly because they thought survivals from antiquity might be discerned by suitably sensitized investigation, and partly because Greek rural life was then still exotic in the eyes of a cultivated Englishman, bearing, as it did, strong traces of the Byzantine and Ottoman pasts. Moreover, in the early months of 1912, while Toynbee was still in Greece, public affairs were moving feverishly towards the climax of the First Balkan War; and the young classicist, as soon as he had learned to converse in modern Greek, discovered a preoccupation with international politics and British foreign policy in remote Greek villages which had little analogue in the common rooms of Oxford, where the 'social question', to which his father and uncle had both devoted their principal energies, pre-empted public attention almost to the exclusion of foreign affairs.

By the time Toynbee returned to England and took up his duties as a Fellow at Balliol, 1912–15, he had developed two lasting concerns: an interest in current international affairs, stimulated by his experiences in Greece, and the conviction that Greek and Roman studies belonged together as aspects of a single whole. This viewpoint was unusual in British learning at the time, for a delicate literary taste had banished both the Hellenistic and Byzantine ages from learned attention. German scholarship, on the other hand, had already plunged into these abysses; and in a sense what the young Toynbee set out to do was to supplement the fine flower of traditional classical literary scholarship by combining the growing point of British classical studies (then focused especially around archaeological work and the earliest beginnings of Greek civilization) with Hellenistic and Byzantine expertise ready to be imported from Germany. But the holistic vision of ancient Mediterranean history and culture that Toynbee had begun to nurse was distinctive and personal, and betrayed a synthetic cast of mind he was later to carry to greater and unexampled heights.

His first two publications bore the impress of his training, rather than of his ambitions. A brief note in the *Classical Review*, 'On Herodotus III. 90 and VII. 75, 76', appeared in 1910 when Toynbee was still an undergraduate, and bears the distinction of inaugurating the long series of his published works. It was technical as well as tiny and purely philological; but his second published work, 'The Growth of Sparta', which came out in the *Journal of Hellenic Studies* in 1913, reflected the rapid maturation of his powers. In this lengthy article, Toynbee combined a close criticism of textual evidence with a keen eye for the landscape of Laconia and Messenia and a shrewd sense of the humanly probable.

The Great War of 1914–18 did not at first disturb the academic routines of the young Oxford don, for he had come back from Greece with a bad case of dysentery and was judged physically unfit. As a result, when his friends and contemporaries responded *en masse* to the heroic ideal implicit in classical literature by volunteering for military service and risking their lives for King and Country, the young Toynbee found himself on the sidelines, contemplating the mounting horror that slowly emerged from the strange rapture of August 1914. Teaching Thucydides, as he was doing, aroused uncanny echoes: were not Britons and Germans re-enacting the tragic, classic encounter between Athens and Sparta? Or was the parallel to 1915–16 more truly to be discerned in the ancient agony of the Hannibalic war?

As dismal news from the front continued to pour in, month after month, the conviction that men of old had already experienced shocks similar to those coming from France grew upon him. With this the idea upon which Toynbee was later to construct *A Study of History* began to germinate in his mind, for if the ancients had already trodden the path western European nation states were traversing in the twentieth century, was it not possible that there were rhythms and patterns in civilized history of an even more general kind? Under the stimulus of such thoughts and the distresses of the war, human affairs assumed a tragic form: overweening greed and pride leading to disaster in accordance with an inevitable, though intelligible, pattern. Perhaps the literary form of Greek tragedy, analysed by Aristotle and applied to Athenian affairs by Thucydides, offered a master key to public as well as to private riddles of existence. But the only way to test such a grand hypothesis was to fit the totality of human experience, as recorded in history, into the tragic form; and for that the war years offered no time.

Instead, in 1915, Toynbee gave up his appointment at Oxford in order to assist Lord Bryce, at that time President of the British Academy, in investigating Turkish atrocities against the Armenians. But, characteristically, he supplemented this work by embarking on a general study of nationalities and their rivalries in Europe as a whole. The result was his first important book, *Nationality and the War* (1915). This work discussed how European political frontiers might best be rearranged to take into account the clamant nationalism of the age without undue disregard of economic and strategic considerations. Concepts which were later to find their way into the peace treaties of 1919–20 made an appearance in this book: guarantees for minorities; rights-of-way through alien territories; and an international committee with executive powers to administer such guarantees. The book's tone was liberal and imperial, and at the same time internationalist. Yet Toynbee's capacity to see things from the enemy's side allowed the youthful author to exhibit a quite generous tone towards Germany.

This was, accordingly, a book he never turned his back upon in later years. The same was not true of the propaganda pamphlets and larger treatises he wrote in 1916 and 1917, first on the Armenian atrocities and then on German terrorism in France and Belgium. To be sure, scholarly competence and conscience were both evident in his large tome, *Treatment of the Armenians in the Ottoman Empire* (1916), which documented in minute detail the Turks' systematic effort to uproot Armenians from Anatolia. The tone of his shorter, more popular, propaganda writings is suggested by the title of one of them: *The Murderous Tyranny of the Turks* (1917). In later life Toynbee came to feel profoundly ashamed of his personal part in spreading war propaganda, describing it as 'poisonous', and sinful. Knowing that he had been systematically unfair to the Turks in 1915–17 made him lean over backward in writing about their actions against the Greeks in 1921.

Toynbee's growing knowledge of Ottoman affairs and his skill as a writer and synthesizer of bulky information led to an appointment, in May 1918, in the Political Intelligence Department of the Foreign Office; and from December 1918 to April 1919 he was a member of the British delegation to the Peace Conference in Paris. Toynbee played a very minor part in shaping the Treaty of Sèvres, and had no perceptible part in formulating the other treaties that emerged from the Peace Conference. But his general point of view on international affairs appears to have been in harmony with the prevailing attitudes among the British (and American) delegations. Toynbee subscribed to the right of national self-determination, within limits defined by the economic and strategic self-interest of the great powers. Above all, he pinned high hopes upon the establishment of an institutional means of adjusting international frictions by legal process so that repetition of the diplomatic failures of 1914 would become impossible.

In the Foreign Office and at the Peace Conference he moved among men of affairs, and was one of the circle of experts who felt that on-going 'scientific' study of international relations was needed to create a suitably well-informed public opinion capable of checking and sustaining future governmental foreign policies. International relations had proven themselves more critical to human life than anyone in Britain had suspected before 1914; more critical even than the social question. Men of goodwill were obligated, therefore, to try to repair the ignorance and indifference with which the British and American publics had been accustomed to regard events beyond their respective national borders. The result of such arguments was the establishment of what became the British (later, Royal) Institute of International Affairs in London and a sister organization, the Council on Foreign Relations, in New York.

In 1919, however, Toynbee returned to academic life, accepting the Korais Chair Modern Greek and Byzantine Language, Literature, and History in the University of London. This newly founded chair at King's College depended upon gifts from persons of Greek descent who wished to see the achievements of Byzantine and modern Greece taken more seriously in Great Britain. Such a post suited Toynbee's intellectual ambition for bringing the history of the ancient Mediterranean into a single conspectus running from 900 B.C. to 700 A.D. or beyond. On top of this, study of modern Greece would allow him to maintain his interest in current affairs. What he proposed doing came clear in a remarkable lecture, 'The Tragedy of Greece', which he delivered at Oxford in May 1920. In this he set forth concisely and precisely the pattern of civilizational growth, breakdown, and rout-and-rally leading to eventual dissolution which he later was to use as normative for all civilizations in *A Study of History*. Many of his key terms appeared here for the first time, and the lecture clearly hints how Toynbee had already glimpsed systematic parallels between ancient and modern times. Nevertheless, the notion of a plurality of separate civilizations, equivalent one to another, does not appear in this 1920 lecture. The full scope of his later vision of historical patterning had yet to dawn upon him.

That global vision did take shape in the course of the next year, for it was while returning from a nine months' visit to Greece and Turkey, January–September 1921, that he jotted down the headings that defined the structure of *A Study of History*. What had been added to his earlier understanding was a consciousness of the reality of far-reaching differences between civilizations. From his new vantage point, the Greco-Roman and the subsequent western European experiences were only two exemplars of a larger class of civilizational histories, each of which could be expected to conform to the pattern he had already detected in Greco-Roman and modern European development.

Spengler had something to do with the enlargement of Toynbee's vision from Greco-Roman to global patterning of history. Shortly after delivering his lecture on 'The Tragedy of Greece' he read *Der Untergang des Abendlandes* in the summer of 1920, and, as he later said, 'wondered at first whether my whole inquiry had been disposed of by Spengler before even the questions, not to speak of the answers, had fully taken shape in my own mind'.[1] Spengler had anticipated Toynbee's own discovery of the civilizational unit of study and had likewise treated diverse civilizations as 'philosophically contemporary'. But when it came to explaining how birth and growth of a civilization took place, Toynbee felt he had something new to offer—what he called an 'empirical' approach, as against Spengler's dogmatic determinism.

Toynbee's encounter with Spengler's vision of multiple civilizations moving along parallel tracks was powerfully reinforced by the interpretation he made of events in post-war Turkey. In 1921 he got leave from his new post at the University of London in order to study at first hand what was happening in

[1] 'My View of History', reprinted in Arnold J. Toynbee, *Civilization on Trial* (New York, 1948), p. 9.

Anatolia, where warfare between Greek and Turkish forces had already demonstrated the fragility of the Treaty of Sèvres. To finance the trip, Toynbee became a correspondent for the *Manchester Guardian.* This liberal newspaper, heir to Gladstonian traditions, was predisposed to be anti-Turkish; yet when Toynbee encountered evidences of Greek atrocities wreaked against Turkish inhabitants of Smyrna and adjacent regions of western Anatolia, he did not hesitate to write about what he had seen; and even when his reports aroused criticism in England, the *Guardian*'s editor continued to publish what he sent back. Seeking to observe the struggle also from the Turkish side, Toynbee was grudgingly admitted, but soon won the confidence of Turkish nationalists by the sympathetic tone of his dispatches. Their desperate defence of Anatolia against the invading Greeks appealed to Toynbee's still-undimmed belief in the virtues of national self-determination; and the fact that Lloyd George's government was backing the Greek invaders, at least half-heartedly, meant that Britain was supporting an unjust cause. Such an angle of vision upon events in the Near East gave a cutting edge to his dispatches, and appalled the Greek patriots who had endowed his chair at the University of London.

Undoubtedly, Toynbee was partly inspired by his wish to atone for the unfairness of his wartime anti-Turkish propaganda. But simply to shift from attacking to defending the Turks was unsatisfactory. Toynbee felt a need to understand how ordinary human beings could resort to systematic brutality such as he saw displayed before his eyes in 1921. Observing the behaviour of outwardly civilized (i.e. westernized), men from both sides, he came to the conclusion that a breakdown of older Ottoman patterns of life and manners under the impact of ideas and ideals coming from western Europe was responsible for unleashing the human depravity he saw around him. The 'Eastern Question' that had long plagued the chancelleries of Europe was fundamentally a 'western question' for Greeks and Turks and all other peoples of the former Ottoman empire. The Armenian atrocities he had excoriated so harshly (as well as the more recent Greek and Turkish atrocities) were, from such a point of view, as much the fault of westerners as of Turks. They were the result of civilizational collision, followed by the breakdown and dissolution of the weaker partner; and in this encounter, by and large, westerners had been the aggressors, at least since 1699. What the atrocities registered was the inevitable and natural collapse of effective moral restraints on human behaviour—

restraints which only an intact and growing civilization could exert successfully.

Toynbee's new understanding provoked another book, *The Western Question in Greece and Turkey* (1922). About two-thirds of this work consists of an account of what he had seen as correspondent for the *Manchester Guardian*; but these narrative and descriptive chapters are set in an interpretative framework, expounding his new vision of civilizational encounter and the costs thereof. Turks and Greeks became not wicked offenders against civilized standards of behaviour, as had been the case in his wartime writings. Instead, both peoples were victims of a process far beyond their control, a process in which, if anyone was to blame, it was the restless and aggressive westerners who had intruded so forcefully upon the older Ottoman civilization, disrupting it and depriving the heirs of Ottoman society of any authentic, binding moral code.

Nationalism, which had seemed to him a generally beneficent form of liberation up to this time, now transformed itself into an ugly, destructive force, emanating from the West and creating the moral basis for endless brutality and violence. World War I itself, he had come to feel, was no more than a vast hetacomb to misguided nationalisms; and to see the disease spreading from the West, where it had shown its destructiveness so horribly in 1914–18, seemed simply tragic from Toynbee's transformed angle of vision.

Even when the holder of the Korais Chair supplemented such views with the publication of translations from classical Greek writers designed to illustrate *Greek Civilization and Character* (1924) and *Greek Historical Thought* (1924), the founders of the new chair felt outraged at what Toynbee was saying about the Greek invasion of Anatolia. Instead of defending Hellenism he was attacking it, or so they felt; and they made their displeasure known in such a fashion that Toynbee felt obliged to resign his chair in 1924.

Thus for a second time, Toynbee left academic life. This was a matter of very considerable pecuniary significance for the 35-year-old scholar. He had married Gilbert Murray's daughter, Rosalind, in 1913, and by 1924 they had three sons to look after and educate. In this emergency, Toynbee's friends from the Peace Conference delegation came to the rescue, securing an appointment for him at the British (soon to be retitled Royal) Institute of International Affairs. Toynbee's assignment was to write a survey of international affairs since the Peace Conference.

This was conceived as a continuation of the multi-volume *History of the Peace Conference*, which had been the first substantial piece of scholarly writing sponsored by the new Institute. As a matter of fact, Toynbee had already contributed an essay on events in Turkey since 1918 to Volume 6 of the *History of the Peace Conference*. Moreover, he shared the conviction that a dispassionate and accurate account of international events, kept up to date, could provide the English-speaking public with background information needed for intelligent judgement on matters of current international concern. But to be maximally useful, such volumes had to appear quickly.

Toynbee's initial appointment was for a single year. In that time he organized and wrote a volume surveying international events, 1920–3, published in 1925. Continuation of this effort was assured when the Sir Daniel L. Stevenson Chair in International Studies at the University of London was conferred upon Toynbee in 1925. Initially he planned to combine his duties at the Institute with part-time teaching in the University at the L.S.E.; but this proved impractical. As Director of Studies he became responsible for planning and supervising all research enterprises centred in Chatham House, where the Institute set up headquarters after 1925; but his personal assignment remained the preparation of an annual *Survey of International Affairs*. Thanks to unintermitted diligence and his extraordinary facility in synthesizing vast amounts of data quickly, Toynbee was able to publish an unbroken succession of stout and impressive volumes (in some years two) until 1938. From the beginning, Veronica Boulter assisted him in gathering material, checking details, and compiling indexes; and after 1925 she contributed chapters to the annual volumes. Increasingly, also, Toynbee delegated special topics, such as international finance and economics, in which he had never been much interested, to others.

Nevertheless, the planning and preparation of each annual *Survey* was an enormous task. Successive volumes focused on different parts of the world, depending on the course of events and on how earlier volumes had distributed emphasis. Thus, the *Survey* for 1924 devoted special attention to the U.S.S.R. and the Third International, and Toynbee here developed one of his favourite themes by classifying Communism as a secular religion. For 1925, Toynbee took on the Islamic world since 1920, and this grew to such proportions that it was published as a separate volume, while other authors dealt with the rest of the world in a second, companion volume. For 1926, the *Survey* devoted more than one hundred pages to China; for 1927 attention shifted back to Europe.

From the beginning of the series, publication had lagged two years or more behind events; but in 1929 Toynbee managed to bring out two annual *Survey* volumes, for 1927 and 1928, thus catching up with the calendar as closely as any annual survey could ever hope to do. From that time onward his pattern of work was to decide in the last weeks of the year how to organize the topics to be dealt with in the next volume of the *Survey*, and then write furiously, largely on the basis of newspaper clippings, until about June, when the manuscript had to go off to the printer so as to come out before the end of the twelvemonth succeeding the events with which it dealt. With such a rhythm of work, facing deadlines week by week, the *Survey* might have become a mere catalogue of happenings; but Toynbee's remarkable facility for connecting present with past (and his growing knowledge of the past of each part of the world) gave depth and richness to his chronicle of each year's events. Increasingly, as he gained confidence in his capacity to produce a readable volume of about 500 pages each year, he gave freer rein to his imagination and personal judgements. This sometimes led to friction, particularly when he came down hard against Zionism, seeing it as yet another instance of disruptive, western-inspired nationalism akin to that which had fuelled Greco-Turkish and Turkish-Armenian mutual massacre.

By the summer of 1929, having at last brought the *Survey* up to date, Toynbee felt free to accept an invitation to visit the Far East and take part in a meeting of the newly founded Institute of Pacific Relations. Accordingly, between July 1929 and January 1930, he travelled overland to the Persian Gulf, visited India, China, and Japan for the first time, and returned home via the Trans-Siberian railroad. In this way he began his first-hand acquaintance with Asia and, as was his wont, wrote a book about it, *A Journey to China* (1931). An acute sense of place had long been characteristic of Toynbee's mind. Consequently, this initial encounter with the seat of each of the great Asian civilizations was an important part of his preparation for *A Study of History*, which he began to compose in 1930, as soon as he had dashed off yet another annual *Survey* for 1929.

Ever since 1921, when the plan for his great book had taken definite shape in his mind, Toynbee had been thinking about the project; and, beginning in 1922, he had used whatever spare time he could find to compile notebooks, where he jotted down salient information and ideas derived from his reading. These notebooks became the quarry from which *A Study of History* and all his other scholarly books derived their facts and footnotes. In 1927 he had begun to prepare himself systematically for writing *A Study of History* by reading voraciously about parts of the world that had hitherto escaped his attention. In this way he was able to expand and fill out the original headings he had jotted down in 1921 with an increasing array of exempla; and could wrestle with some of the more refractory passages of world history that did not fit easily into the rhythm of civilizational genesis, growth, breakdown, and disintegration that he had initially applied only to the ancient Mediterranean. Systematic interplay between the annual *Survey* of international affairs and his larger study of human history can be seen in the way Toynbee shifted focus in the *Surveys*, devoting special attention to new regions of the earth year by year. This compelled him in each case to familiarize himself as best he could with the deeper past, geographical conditions, and cultural characteristics of the peoples involved. The resultant richness of context gave his accounts of contemporary events much of their special flavour and value; at the same time, the necessity of covering world events year by year made it impossible for him to cultivate expertise within only one or two civilizational regions of the earth. Globalism became inescapable because he took seriously his professional task of trying to understand current events against the background of the knowable human past—all of it.

This cross-fertilization between work at Chatham House and his private scholarly enterprise achieved a new intensity after 1930, when the actual composition of *A Study of History* got under way. From 1931 Toynbee detected in the course of public affairs a mounting 'world crisis'—a crisis that ominously conformed to patterns of breakdown and dissolution he had discerned in Greco-Roman civilization during World War I. Toynbee's hope that the League of Nations might be able to adjust international rivalries peaceably met its first massive disappointment with the Japanese invasion of Manchuria in 1931: the failure of the League of Nations to do anything effective to check Japan seemed to him a clear enough augury of further disasters to come. This failure coincided, of course, with an economic depression of unexampled severity, and in the *Survey* for 1931 Toynbee interpreted these events as indicative of a general beakdown of Western civilization.

With a growing sense of impending disaster (reinforced in 1933 by Hitler's accession to power in Germany), Toynbee toiled heroically to press ahead with his vast enterprise while simultaneously fulfilling his duties at Chatham House. The quotations with which he adorned the title page of the first three volumes of *A Study of History*, when they appeared in 1934, reflect his mood very clearly:

> 'Work . . . while it is day . . .'
> 'Nox ruit Aenea . . .'
> 'Thought shall be harder
> Heart the keener
> Mood shall be the more
> as our might lessens.'

The three sources—*John* ix, 4, the *Aeneid* vi, 539, and the *Lay of the Battle of Maldon*—also aptly illustrate the primary sources of his inspiration; Biblical, classical, and British.

Of the three, it was the classical thought-world that predominated in the first volumes of *A Study of History*, dealing as they do with the genesis and growth of civilizations. The plot of the whole *Study* was clearly set forth in the Introduction. Toynbee first argued for the reality of 'civilizations' as intelligible units of historical study and then sketched the phenomena of breakdown—a time of troubles, the emergence of a universal state, a universal church, and internal and external proletariats—so as to know what to look for in an 'empirical' survey of the past intended to identify the civilizations which thenceforth were to become the units of study throughout the rest of the book. The measuring rod for this search of the recorded past was Toynbee's vision of ancient Mediterranean history as set forth in his 1920 lecture, 'The Tragedy of Greece'.

By far the most obvious markers, defining deaths and births of civilizations, were universal states, analogous to the Roman Empire, and universal churches, analogous to the Christian Church. Wherever Toynbee found a state comparable to the Roman Empire and a religious organization comparable to the Christian Church, he discerned a transition from an 'apparented' to an 'affiliated' civilization; and when, as in the case of the early caliphate, there seemed to be a succession of empires with no intervening disintegration followed by genesis and growth of a new 'affiliated' civilization, he saved the system by declaring that the caliphate played the role of universal state for a Syriac civilization that had gone underground for a thousand years, being overlaid by an intrusive Hellenism.

Such extravagances strained but did not destroy the credibility of his hypothesis, taken as a whole; and the impressive sweep of Toynbee's erudition, running across all centuries of recorded history and completely around the globe, assured his book of a generally polite reception, and of sufficient sales to require a second edition in 1935. The historical profession paid little attention, but among the general public, as events moved towards the outbreak of World War II, Toynbee's vision of repetitive patterns in history gained ever-enhanced plausibility. The relevance of Thucydides' portrayal of Athens and Sparta to contemporary international confrontations, which had so impressed Toynbee in 1914, came to life again in the late 1930s as Hitler's war drew closer. No one seemed capable of checking international lawlessness, and economic depression at home, persisting both in Britain and the United States until the very eve of the war, intensified the public sense of being caught in vast and irreversible processes. If comparison with what had happened long ago and far away, whether in the ancient Mediterranean or in China, India, or Peru, seemed to cast light on current perplexities and impotence, then a scattered band of thoughtful and troubled readers were willing and eager to accept Toynbee's guidance through realms of historic time and space which traditional educational patterns in English-speaking countries had left almost totally out of account.

Toynbee's role as interpreter of current dilemmas was reinforced by the British Broadcasting Corporation, which from 1929 onwards, invited him to give talks on current events and related themes. In addition to such appearances on the Home Services of the B.B.C., Toynbee did a good deal of broadcasting to foreign countries, through the Overseas Service, and on occasion delivered talks in French, German, Turkish, Greek, and other languages in which he was reasonably fluent. He also was quite prolific as a journalist, writing mainly on current events during the inter-war years for a wide variety of newspapers and journals. Some of his articles were signed; many appeared anonymously and were often undertaken because he needed extra income.

The public professional reputation Toynbee had achieved by the middle and later 1930s was countered by family difficulties, climaxing in the suicide of his eldest son in 1939. In addition, the breakdown of the post-war international order, with Italy's attack on Ethiopia in 1933–4, swiftly followed by Hitler's reassertion of German power, presented Toynbee with sombre themes for his work at Chatham House. Increasingly he came to blame the British government for failing to act resolutely; and in the *Survey* for 1935, he departed from the tone of detachment which had hitherto dominated his writings on current affairs by prefacing Volume II, 'Abyssinia and Italy', with a scathing denunciation of British policy-makers for their lack of courage and sincerity.

Under the impetus of these private and public distresses, Toynbee found his classical mode of thought increasingly inadequate. It was all very well, perhaps, to anatomize the breakdown of human civilizations; but what about action—doing something about it? And what about the pain and suffering—how was that to be borne? His wife became a convert to Roman Catholicism; and in the late 1930s Toynbee himself flirted with the Roman faith but never overcame long-standing doubts and reservations. He had broken away from his Christian upbringing by becoming an agnostic while a student at Oxford; and his subsequent studies of other religious traditions had not made it easier for him to accept the tenets of any Christian creed.

Yet his mind turned achingly away from the secularism that had dominated his thought hitherto. Ever since the war of 1914–18, he had felt himself living on borrowed time, having been so strangely spared by his dysentery from the slaughter that had destroyed so many of his contemporaries. In the post-war years, by dedicating his efforts to spreading knowledge about international affairs, he could hope to contribute to the banishment of war. In that fashion he might in some sense repay a debt owed to those sacrificed in the Great War. But after 1933 such a view of his life-work rang hollow. He might be devoting his energies to the most critical human problem of the twentieth century—how to regulate international affairs. But he now found himself among those urging the British government to resist aggression, even at the risk of war. Repeated failure of that effort brought steadily closer the prospect of a new and more terrible war from which Western civilization might scarcely be expected to emerge intact. Where amidst such futility lay the meaning of human life?

Little by little Toynbee worked his way towards an answer. Perhaps it was a mistake to value civilization as the supreme achievement of human creativity, as he had done hitherto. Perhaps religions were more important than civilizations. Perhaps, even, the personal anguish of his son's suicide and the failure of his life's work for peace had a value and meaning of its own, if only he were wise enough to react creatively. If nothing else, pain taught the vanity of human wishes; acceptance of that insight might eventually breed genuine humility; and true humility in turn might open the soul to awareness of an ultimate spiritual reality, unattainable by mere reason and beyond the realm of ordinary human experience.

In his initial plan for *A Study of History*, each universal religion served as a chrysalis within which a spark of vital continuity passed from a dying civilization to its heir. From his new point of view, values were reversed. Civilizations ceased to be ends in themselves, and served instead as mere vehicles for spirituality and religion. Periods of breakdown acquired special significance, since in such times, when human suffering was unusually intense, men of special spiritual capacity might be stimulated to open their souls to that ultimate reality which Toynbee now confidently came to call God.

Personal mystical experiences helped to define Toynbee's new frame of mind. The first of these occurred not long after the end of World War I, and Toynbee interpreted it as a communion 'with all that had been, and was, and was to come'.[1] A subsequent experience in China in 1929 and a renewed encounter with what he later described in autobiographical writings as a 'transcendent spiritual presence' occurred in 1939.[2] It seems certain that these events moved him deeply, and convinced him of the authenticity of divine revelation, even if the fleeting glimpses of transcendent reality, vouchsafed to him, were devoid of intellectual content.

Toynbee's changing evaluation of the relation between religion and civilization appeared only marginally in Volumes 4–6 of *A Study of History*. These were published in 1939, just two weeks before World War II broke out. They dealt with breakdowns and disintegrations of civilizations, and, as before, Toynbee's erudition and global vision, the aptness of his metaphors, and the persuasiveness of the terms he used to describe recurrent phenomena of human history aroused much awe and admiration, even though most professional historians continued to disregard his book. He was, however, elected a Fellow of the British Academy in 1937. These continuities from his first volumes were supplemented by a number of passages in which Toynbee boldly discussed God's relationship to humankind. Yet on the whole such passages remained subordinate. His original scheme of working out a comparative study of how civilizations broke down and then disintegrated, showing the common

[1] *A Study of History*, x. 139. [2] *Experiences*, p. 176.

features and stages through which they passed *en route* to their final dissolution, continued to dominate the work.

The outbreak of World War II abruptly altered the pattern of Toynbee's life. He interrupted his work on *A Study of History*, dispatching the notes he had made for the remaining portions of the work to New York for safe keeping. His annual surveys of international relations were also suspended; only the first of three volumes describing the events of 1938 came out until after the war had ended. Instead, he accepted official appointment in 1939 as Director of Foreign Research and Press Service; and in 1943 changed titles by becoming Director of the Research Department of the Foreign Office. In 1946 he climaxed his official career by serving as a member of the British delegation to the Peace Conference in Paris; but as in 1919, his role was minor, despite the dignity years and knowledge had by now conferred upon him. Marginality hardly mattered, for by 1946 British weight in international relations had been diminished by the rise of new giant powers east and west; and the hopefulness with which Toynbee had worked at Paris in 1919 was absent from a settlement dominated by mounting distrust between the wartime allies and overshadowed by the destructive power of atomic weapons.

During the war years, the flow of Toynbee's publications almost stopped, except for a lecture, 'Christianity and Civilization' (1940), delivered at Oxford during the week when France collapsed before the Nazis. In this lecture Toynbee sounded like a man ripe for conversion to the Church of Rome; but the crisis passed, and he remained an agnostic to the end of his life as far as religion was concerned. Eventually, his family difficulties were lessened by a separation from his wife in 1942. This eventuated in a divorce in May 1946, followed by remarriage to his long-time assistant, Veronica Boulter, in September of the same year. His second wife thenceforward supported him by bringing a warm, astringent commonsense and brisk practicality to every-day matters, as well as continuing to assist him with all of his literary and scholarly enterprises.

On returning from Paris in 1946, Toynbee left government service and went back to Chatham House. He did not, however, resume the effort to write an annual survey of international affairs. Instead, he delegated that task to others; but as Director of Studies he organized a multi-volumed wartime *Survey* to fill in the gap between 1938 and 1947, when annual volumes were resumed. By the date of his retirement in 1955, at the age of 65, the wartime volumes were complete; but younger experts who had been assigned the task of producing an annual survey found it impossible to keep up with events. Indeed, the extraordinary character of Toynbee's performance between 1924 and 1938 was demonstrated by the way a series of very competent successors foundered in attempting to carry his feat forward into the post-war years. Eventually the enterprise was abandoned with the publication in 1970 of a volume surveying the year 1962—a mere eight years behindhand.

Toynbee's principal concern after the end of the war was to complete *A Study of History*. The first six volumes had dealt with only five of the thirteen headings he had projected in 1921. Yet in writing Volumes 4–6, on the breakdown and disintegration of civilizations, he had already dealt extensively with matter originally reserved for treatment under the headings, 'Universal States', 'Universal Churches', and 'Heroic Ages'. This meant that apart from the difficulty of picking up where he had left off after some seven strenuous years, working from notes, some of which had been compiled initially as far back as the 1920s, Toynbee had to alter the scale of the final sections of *A Study of History* to avoid repeating what he had already said in the earlier parts.

A more important problem was the shift in his point of view which had become firm and fully conscious by 1946, when he resumed work on the great project. He was now prepared to recognize generational differences between civilizations he had once declared to be philosophically contemporary, ranking them according to their relationship to 'higher' religions. The three-generational norm offered by the sequence Minoan–Hellenic–Western European civilizations could be matched elsewhere in the world; and he now believed that slow self-revelation of God through the development of religion and spirituality linked successive civilizations into a grander whole, moving towards some still unascertainable goal of spiritual improvement.

Such a re-evaluation of human experience was profoundly at odds with the framework of his first volumes. Toynbee had, in fact, shifted from a cyclical view of the past, elaborated from classical theories about the cycle of city-state constitutions, towards a linear model for human history, derived from and closely akin to the Judaeo-Christian Providential view of human affairs. The difficulty of reconciling his new point of view with the old framework deprived the task of completing *A Study of History* of much of the *élan* so obvious in the earlier volumes. But with a doggedness perfectly characteristic of him, Toynbee stubbornly stuck to his self-appointed task until it was completed.

Long before he set the last word to the last page of his monumental work, he became suddenly famous. This occurred in 1946–7, with the publication of a condensation of Volumes 1–6 of *A Study of History*. A skilful précis had been prepared during the war by D. C. Somervell, and in 1946 Toynbee approved its publication after making some small alterations. The 617-page volume appeared in Britain in 1946, but the American edition did not come out until mid March, 1947. Its publication, therefore, happened to coincide with the proclamation of the Truman Doctrine, whereby the President of the United States invited Congress to fund the containment of Communism, wherever it might show its hand.

At such a moment, Toynbee's pre-war vision of world history struck a resonant chord among many influential Americans. Were, there, perhaps, forces in human affairs that constrained public behaviour, whether or not men wished it so? Was the American Century, already proclaimed by Henry Luce, publisher of *Time* and *Life* magazines, fore-ordained by ineluctable historical patterns? More specifically, was the United States destined to play the role of Rome or of Carthage in its sudden new confrontation with the Soviet Union? The editors of *Time* decided that such questions were well worth asking, even though neither Toynbee himself nor his book could ever be made to give clear and unambiguous answers. Accordingly, the American publication of Somervell's abridgement of *A Study of History* provided the occasion for a *Time* cover story (17 March 1947). Toynbee became, almost overnight, a public personality to whom prophetic powers were freely imputed. He happened to be in the United States at the time this avalanche of publicity descended upon him; and Toynbee certainly did what he could to damp back the more extravagant vulgarizations to which his ideas were subjected by American journalists. In particular, he refused to say that the Universal State of the future must or ought to be an American empire, and instead insisted that options towards the future remained open, so far as he could see, in spite of any, and all, indications of the imminent onset of a Universal State for western civilization.

Toynbee's unwillingness to prophesy did not prevent the abridgement of *A Study of History* from becoming a best seller. More than 200,000 copies of the book were sold in the United

States alone. The book was translated into fourteen European and six Asian languages, and, for the ensuing fifteen years, Toynbee's ideas about history and religion, as set forth in this book, became matters of widespread debate. Controversy was especially acute in intellectual circles of English-speaking countries and in Germany. At first the French held aloof; Marxian orthodoxy inhibited discussion in all Communist countries; and in Latin America and Japan Toynbee's reputation crested a decade or two later. Amidst all the din, Toynbee kept steadfastly working away at the task of completing his great work according to plan; but in the meanwhile he reinforced his fame and threw fresh fuel on to the fires of controversy surrounding his name by accepting numerous invitations to lecture before college and university audiences, by appearing on radio and television both in Britain and America, and by publishing a continued flow of books largely derived from such public appearances.

A pamphlet, *Can We Know the Pattern of the Past?*, published in 1948, marked the onset of concerted professional criticism of the method and substance of *A Study of History*. It consisted of a recorded B.B.C. debate between Toynbee and the Dutch historian, Pieter Geyl; and the polite tone of their exchange did not really disguise the fundamental discrepancy of viewpoint which made Toynbee uninterested in Geyl's refutation of details. Toynbee's irenic and Olympian detachment may have merely infuriated his professional critics; his current publications, assuredly, paid absolutely no attention to what they had to say.

The first of these, *Civilization on Trial* (1948), announced Toynbee's new religiosity to the world far more conspicuously than before. As he said in the preface:

> The governing idea is the familiar one that the universe becomes intelligible to the extent of our ability to apprehend it as a whole . . . An intelligible field of historical study is not to be found within any national framework; we must expand our historical horizon to think in terms of an entire civilization. But this wider framework is still too narrow, for civilizations, like nations, are plural, not singular; there are different civilizations which meet and, out of their encounters, societies of another species, the higher religions, are born into this world. That is not, however, the end of the historian's quest, for no higher religion is intelligible in terms of this world only. The mundane history of the higher religions is one aspect of the life of a Kingdom of Heaven of which this world is one province. So history passes over into theology. 'To Him return ye every one.'

In addition, the first essay in the book, 'My View of History', inaugurated Toynbee's autobiographical writings by explaining how he had arrived at the plan for *A Study in History* in 1921.

War and Civilization, published in 1950, was no more than a series of extracts from the first six volumes of *A Study of History*; but *The Prospects for Western Civilizations*, published in 1949 on the basis of lectures delivered at Columbia University, and *The World and the West* (1952), based on the Reith lectures for 1952, anticipated and summarized themes to be dealt with at greater length in the final volumes of *A Study of History*. The first of these was relatively uncontroversial. Toynbee, as before, refused to foreclose the future and refrained from predicting the early onset of a Universal State for western civilization. The Reith lectures, however, provoked a storm of criticism. They consisted of a harsh indictment of the West for past aggressions against the other peoples of the world. The tone offended many British listeners, since in large measure it was their empire that was being condemned and at the very moment of its magnanimous surrender!

As he was later to admit, Toynbee was once again leaning over backwards in an effort to see the world through the eyes of non-Western peoples; and in so doing denigrated or disregarded Western achievements. He merely intended to strip away blinkers that an overweening self-esteem had imposed on generations of Europeans and Americans; but the shock he thus deliberately administered proved sharper than he had anticipated. For it was this book, more than anything that had gone before, that provoked a series of bitter, angry denunciations. In particular, Toynbee was accused of betraying western values of freedom and democracy, law and rationality, at a time when, at the onset of the Cold War, the West's liberal and pluralist ways of life seemed hard-pressed to defend themselves against Soviet aggression and the threat of atomic holocaust.

Another factor that embittered the attack on Toynbee's ideas was the way he had dismissed the Jews in *A Study of History* as a 'fossil' of Syriac society. This term rankled; and his additional condemnation of Zionism as a particularly reprehensible example of the modern heresy of nationalism exposed Toynbee to the accusation of being anti-semitic. To be sure, he found one or two defenders among anti-Zionist Jews, but most Jewish opinion resented Toynbee's way of treating post-exilic history and found many spokesmen to express their displeasure.

In 1953 the last four volumes of *A Study of History* finally appeared, thirty-two years from the time the grand structure had been conceived. The new volumes provided fresh ammunition for the chorus of unfriendly critics. Many fastened upon the extraordinary prose poem with which Toynbee ended his vast work. It is a prayer of intercession addressed to gods and prophets, philosophers, poets, and saints selected from all the civilized traditions known to humanity. The sacramental goal Toynbee had ascribed to the study of history in his preface to *Civilization on Trial* here found overt literary expression; and did so in a form that offended believers and unbelievers alike. Hostile critics jumped to the conclusion that Toynbee personally aspired to the prophetic role of interpreting 'ultimate spiritual reality' to ordinary twentieth-century mankind.

As Toynbee was later to confess, the final four volumes of *A Study of History* were less successful in their execution than the first six. The discrepancy between his post-war views and the structure he had laid down in 1921 was too great to overcome; the task of filling out all the corners of his original blueprint simply lost its savour. Hence, for example, the section 'Heroic Ages' received merely perfunctory treatment, since Toynbee had come to feel that these barbarian creations lacked central significance in human history, being far removed from higher religion.

An Historian's Approach to Religion (published in 1956 on the basis of the Gifford lectures delivered at Edinburgh in 1952 and 1953, immediately after the completion of *A Study of History*), was Toynbee's effort to correct the unhappy disproportion between theme and structure that had disfigured the final volumes of his great work. Yet the book remains fragmentary. A first part deals with 'The Dawn of the Higher Religions' by rearranging and condensing material drawn from *A Study of History*. Part II was largely new, and dealt with the theme of 'Religion in a Westernizing World'. Toynbee concentrated attention mainly on the secularization of European thought in the seventeeth century, but in tracing results and consequences of this departure from Christian faith he contented himself with general statements that echoed what he had said already in the later volumes of *A Study of History*. The fact was that he had neither the leisure nor the appetite for reworking and exploring the West's historic record in modern times so as to fit it into his new religious world view; accordingly, the impact of this book was slight.

When he retired from Chatham House in 1955, Toynbee was eager to leave behind all the controversy he had stirred up. In 1956–7 he and his wife travelled around the world, and as usual, he recorded some of his experiences in a graceful travel book, *East to West: A Journey Round the World* (1958). On his return to London, Toynbee started work with renewed vigour on a study of Roman republican history. After eight years' intensive work, his researches resulted in two massive volumes, published in 1965 under the title, *Hannibal's Legacy*. It is hard to escape the impression that in returning to the meticulous detail so characteristic of classical scholarship, Toynbee was seeking to prove himself a fully accredited member of the historical profession and thus rebut, not in words but in deed, the charges so many angry historians had made against *A Study of History*. If so, he succeeded, for *Hannibal's Legacy* triumphantly met the exacting standards of classical scholarship and was well received by professional reviewers, even though, or perhaps rather because, Toynbee's conclusions about the impact of the Hannibalic War on Roman society closely conformed to prevailing ideas. Thus his two stately tomes codified existing scholarship on Roman republican history between 266 and 133 B.C., rather than offering any important new hypotheses.

Yet Toynbee was not content to immerse himself in Roman history to the exclusion of all else. Invitations to lecture continued to pour in, and encounters with his critics could not entirely be avoided. In the ten years 1957–66, no fewer than ten books resulted from these casual sideshows, for Toynbee had now reached an eminence from which anything he said or wrote—indeed in some cases tape recordings of his conversation with an interrogator—could break into print; and since his views on global history and religion were well defined by now, he often repeated himself, or elaborated upon themes already familiar from his other writings. Nevertheless, like an artist who returns again and again to a motif, seeking always to improve upon its former expression, so Toynbee, in reworking old material, always added new touches.

For anyone else the litany of titles his casual labours called into being would be dazzling and incredible: *Mexico e Occidente* (1957), *Christianity among the Religions of the World* (1957), *America and the World Revolution* (1962), *The Present Day Experiment in Western Civilization* (1962), *The Economy of the Western Hemisphere* (1962), and *Comparing Notes: A Dialogue across a Generation*, with his son, Philip Toynbee (1963). The first and penultimate of these books were based on lectures delivered before Latin American audiences, and allowed Toynbee to articulate anew an old theme with which his father and his famous uncle had been identified: to wit, the conflict between economic efficiency and social justice, and the importance of preferring the latter to the former. Thus in addressing Third World audiences, he came back to the 'social question' of his youth. A return to tasks and ideas first conceived in his early years was, indeed, characteristic of Toynbee's old age, and he deployed his time in a remarkably systematic way, addressing himself successively first to one and then to another of the unfinished items left over from his days as a student and young don at Oxford.

Lecture trips to Asia and Africa produced two more travel books in the early 1960s: *Between Oxus and Jumna* (1961) and *Between Niger and Nile* (1965); but the most interesting and significant of his publications before the appearance of *Hannibal's Legacy* was the result of his effort to respond constructively to the criticisms *A Study of History* provoked. Two publications of 1961 conveyed Toynbee's answers to his critics: *L'histoire et ses Interpretations, Entretiens autour de Arnold Toynbee*, edited by Raymond Aron, and a new twelfth volume[1] of *A Study of History*, entitled 'Reconsiderations'.

Aron's colloquy brought Toynbee up against the French intellectual establishment. Pervasive differences of outlook inhibited real exchange of views. The laicism and technocratic cast of most French historical scholarship made it all but impossible for those present to take Toynbee's religiosity seriously; and they remained unimpressed by a great system that left so little room for France, past or future. Nevertheless, in 1968, after Winston Churchill's death, Toynbee was elected to his vacated place in the Academy of Moral and Political Sciences, at the Institut de France. Only one of the innumerable honours he received ranked higher in Toynbee's own estimation, and that was his inscription 'Ad Portes' in his old school at Winchester.

These honours came only later when initial misunderstandings had faded. But in 1961 much the same tone-deafness as between critic and author betrayed itself in Toynbee's own effort to respond to what had been said about him. Nevertheless, his 'Reconsiderations' is a remarkable volume, for Toynbee set out to appraise the strengths and weaknesses of *A Study of History* in the light of his own second thoughts, stimulated by what others had said. He did so in a disarmingly open-minded way. Citing a total of 168 critics, some at length, others only in passing, he freely confessed to his fundamental change of mind between the

[1] Volume XI was an *Historical Atlas and Gazetteer* (1959) prepared by Edward D. Myres.

early and later volumes. He altered the roster of civilizations he had discerned in the first volume radically; and he admitted his fault in systematically undervaluing the West and its achievements. But on essentials he remained firm. The usefulness of civilizational comparisons, the importance of religion and of spiritual forces over all others, the evilness of greed and idolization of collective self-interest, whether national interests or any other: on these and other key points he remained unrepentant; and corrections about details, of a sort that had bulked large in his critics' attacks, he deigned to notice only occasionally.

How much of the grand system of *A Study of History* remained after Toynbee's 'Reconsiderations' was not perfectly clear. He felt that the task now devolved upon other, younger persons to pick up where he had left off and make what sense they could of the world's history. In the remaining years of his life, he preferred to pursue other themes, leaving the anger and notoriety of the years between 1947 and 1961 behind. The modest and gentle tone that pervaded 'Reconsiderations' did much to disarm criticism, as Pieter Geyl confessed, even though he still felt that his original objections had not been really answered. From this time onwards, debate over Toynbee's ideas dropped off in England and the United States almost as sharply as it had burst upon the intellectual scene; but in more distant lands, especially Japan and Latin America, Toynbee's reputation waxed as debate waned in the English-speaking and European countries.

With the publication of *Hannibal's Legacy* in 1965 (together with an earlier book, *Hellenism*, in 1959), Toynbee could justly feel that he had defended his credibility as an historian. During the next ten years of his life, four themes dominated his writing, of which only two were of real importance to him. Fragmentary autobiography and semi-autobiographical travel books continued to break into print, along with discussions of religious and metahistorical matters; but the cutting edge of Toynbee's mind was reserved (1) for reflections on the contemporary world scene (continuing in a more speculative way the work of his mature years on the annual *Survey*), and (2) for continued scholarly examination of critical phases of ancient Mediterranean history.

Age did little to slow the pace of his writing, as a recital of titles will indicate. Autobiographical and travel books included the following: *Acquaintances* (1967), *Between Maule and Amazon* (1967), and *Experiences* (1969). Books dealing with religious and metahistorical matters included: *Change and Habit: The Chal-*

lence of our Time (1966), *Man's Concern with Death* (1968), *Science in Human Affairs* (1968), *Surviving the Future* (1971), *Toynbee on Toynbee: A Conversation between A. J. Toynbee and G. R. Urban* (1974), and a posthumous book, *The Toynbee–Ikeda Dialogue: Man Himself Must Choose* (1976). Generally speaking, Toynbee showed a more relaxed view of ultimate things in these books. In *Surviving the Future*, for instance, which consists of edited and reorganized excerpts from a very lengthy dialogue with a Japanese professor, Toynbee expressed much more optimism than he had in earlier years, when the prospect of atomic war had weighed heavily on his mind. Postponement of Armageddon led him to think that perhaps catastrophe might yet be escaped; and the student unrest and rebellion, so prevalent in the late 1960s, appeared to Toynbee as a healthy sign—proof of a continued upwelling of youthful idealism. Frictions that had been so evident in discourse with Europeans and Americans were absent in his encounters with non-westerners, for whom his vision of the West's unrighteous intrusion upon the rest of the world was welcome. Moreover, his Japanese interrogators were prepared to listen respectfully to Toynbee's religious speculations, since his aspirations matched their own more closely than they matched those of westerners, whether Christian or agnostic.

Gratifying as Toynbee's reception in Japan and other alien lands undoubtedly was, his central intellectual endeavour nevertheless remained elsewhere. With Hannibal behind him, he busily pursued additional lines of inquiry into aspects of classical antiquity that he had dropped when World War I interrupted his first academic career. *Some Problems of Greek History* (1969) was the next fruit of this effort. The longest single essay in this book was an erudite up-dating of his 1913 article on the expansion of Sparta; but he also took up a number of other often highly technical themes connected with the post-Mycenaean Völkerwanderung and the Hellenization of Macedonia and near-by areas. As a final touch, however, he inserted two essays on what might have been if Philip of Macedon had lived to die a natural death, or, alternatively, if his son Alexander had lived a normal life span. The catastrophic reorganization of political history these *jeux d'esprits* conjured up were intended to illustrate the importance he was prepared to attribute to individuals in shaping events—a view of the past Toynbee had been accused of rejecting in favour of some fixed, predetermined pattern.

If *Some Problems of Greek History* explored issues left over from his youthful investigation of the early phases of ancient

Mediterranean history, Toynbee's next scholarly book, *Constantine Porphyrogenitus and his World* (1973) undertook an exploration of the Byzantine postlude to that civilization. This, too, had been an ambition of Toynbee's early career; and rather to his surprise he lived to find the time and energy for the attempt. Nevertheless, while working on *Porphyrogenitus*, Toynbee suffered a serious heart attack, and he never entirely recovered his vigour thereafter. The book betrays a certain incompleteness: themes Toynbee announced at the beginning were not explored, and it seems clear that diminishing physical vigour was what prevented his study of Byzantium from becoming another multi-volumed work comparable to *Hannibal's Legacy*.

Any ordinary man half Toynbee's age might have found his work in Greek and Byzantine history quite enough for ten years; but as was his wont, he continued to maintain a lively interest in current events and never gave up the effort to make sense of the confusion of detail. He did so along two lines: interpreting the manifold political upheavals in the so-called Third World as a peasants' rebellion against their hitherto disadvantaged condition; and viewing the cities into which humanity was crowding as the new, emerging and still-to-be-defined contexts within which future human life was apparently destined to situate itself. If so, some of the inhuman gigantism of the major cities of the twentieth century would have to be overcome; and planning for the future might perhaps benefit by study of the ways in which great cities of the past had been built and maintained.

The theme of a peasant revolution dated back to some of his lectures of the early 1960s. Similarly, his interest in cities and their design attained a new focus after 1962 when he first encountered Constantine Doxiades, a Greek architect and city planner, whose expansive views complemented and stimulated Toynbee's own far-ranging imagination. The upshot, as might be expected, was a number of new books: *Cities of Destiny* (1967), *Cities on the Move* (1970), and *An Ekistical Study of the Hellenic City State* (1971). The first of these is a handsomely illustrated volume, planned by Toynbee but executed by a number of different hands. Toynbee provided a typology of cities in a prefatory chapter, as well as making some remarks on the problem of organizing an emergent world megalopolis on a more nearly human scale. *Cities on the Move* was a full-scale development of these themes, drawing illustrations from the whole range of human history and looking ahead towards the twenty-first century with a confidence and optimism in mankind's capacity to solve problems of the future that contrasted sharply with his sombre tone of the 1950s. *An Ekistical Study of the Hellenic City State* combined Toynbee's classical with his new urban interest and he intended to proceed from this to a large-scale exploration of the ecological encounter between humanity and earth's resources. But the manuscript, published posthumously with the title *Mankind and Mother Earth* (1976), in spite of some programmatic statements at the beginning, does not really succeed in applying the new concepts with which Toynbee had been experimenting to the data of the world's history.

Cities of Destiny had been a commissioned work; and the publishers were so pleased with the result that they persuaded Toynbee to edit two more similar lavishly illustrated works: *Crucible of Christianity* (1969) and *Half the World: The History and Cultures of China and Japan* (1973). For each of these books, Toynbee wrote a prefatory essay. He also designed the chapter headings, and recruited distinguished scholars to write for a semi-popular audience, but left the task of assembling the illustrations to others. Nevertheless, the preparation of these books required careful interweaving of text and illustrations. This experience probably helped to broaden Toynbee's acquaintance with art and sharpen his awareness of the way in which works of art may be used as historical sources. From his earliest years he had been sensitized to literature, and in unusual degree; now in his old age he began to sensitize himself also to visual art in a fashion hitherto unfamiliar to him. This waxing interest found forceful expression in a lecture delivered in 1969 and published as 'Art: Communicative or Esoteric?' in E. F. Fry, ed., *The Future of Art* (1970). A further monument to Toynbee's emerging sensitivity to visual art was the issue of a new illustrated and abbreviated edition of *A Study of History* in 1972.

These new lines of inquiry and sensibility and Toynbee's perpetually renewed literary undertakings were suddenly cut short in August 1974, when he suffered a stroke, and lost the capacity to speak and write. Thereafter he lived in a nursing home until his death on 22 October 1975, at the age of 86.

What is there to say of a man who worked so hard, accomplished so much, suffered greatly, and nevertheless attained a graciousness of spirit that set him apart from ordinary mortals? His fame and the storm of criticism he aroused were both based largely on misunderstanding of his central concerns; but misunderstanding is the normal condition of human efforts at communication. What is historically significant is that his books, articles, and lectures together with innumerable radio and television appearances roused the liveliest responses, whether of adulation or of repudiation, and thus became a powerful element in the general intellectual history of his age. Few men attain such importance; and when they do, it is because their words somehow release thoughts and emotions previously only latent among their readers or listeners. Toynbee's career is extraordinary in this respect in that he aroused such responses not merely among his own countrymen and in the United States, and not merely within the circle of European civilization, but also among peoples of alien cultural traditions, whose encounter with modernity had followed widely differing paths.

There was, throughout Toynbee's career, a consistent intellectual impulse towards synthesis. First he set out to put all ancient Mediterranean history into one whole; then he raised his sights to include all human history; ultimately he added the supernal to the terrestrial realm of universal history. This consistent grasp after wholeness was matched by the extraordinary energy and systematic thoroughness with which he carried through each of his intellectual undertakings. His life was long enough for him to accomplish—or nearly accomplish, since *Constantine Porphyrogenitus* is really only a fragment of his plan—everything he set out to investigate.

In view of the variety and range of his projects, this was an astounding achievement. He paid the price in the form of lifelong discipline of work which gave him time for little else than reading, speaking, and writing. Yet throughout his life, prodigious powers of concentration, phenomenal memory, and sheer physical endurance of a regimen at which most men would have quailed, all were subordinated to his lively, restless imagination. This faculty, raised to the highest pitch by his youthful immersion in literature—Biblical, Classical and European—allowed him to construct hypotheses of the most daring kind with a profusion that only men of genius attain. That some of these hypotheses proved faulty never much bothered Toynbee; he was ready enough to surrender them when evidence showed them inadequate. He proved this over and over again in his 'Reconsiderations'; but the collapse of one hypothesis was for him simply an occasion to struggle after a new and more embracing one within which to organise afresh the tumult of detail.

He was, thus, a literary artist and intellectual in the heroic, Platonic mould. Like Plato, who defined the major questions for Greek and much of modern philosophy, Toynbee opened a series of new questions for historians to wrestle with. Whether worthy successors will emulate his effort at making all human history intelligible remains to be seen; but no more vibrant challenge to professional insulation from the great, perennial questions of human life has issued from an historian's pen in the twentieth century; and whatever the future may do to Toynbee's reputation, it seems sure that his work will stand as a monument of twentieth century thought and feeling, registering for all who care to read, the reaction of a very powerful intellect to the Time of Troubles through which he lived.

William H. McNeill

SIR JACK ALLAN WESTRUP

JACK ALLAN WESTRUP

1904–1975

JACK ALLAN WESTRUP was born at Dulwich on 26 April 1904, the second of the three sons of George Westrup and his wife Harriet (Allan). Although his father was not a clergyman, both his brothers entered the Church and, as the elder, the Revd. Canon Allan Westrup—all three bore 'Allan' as one of their names—has recorded: 'Both our parents were people of deep Christian faith, which was the basis and inspiration of their lives, expressed in regular worship and service for the Church. Although this naturally affected our upbringing, there was no undue compulsion on us as regards religious observance; we just took it for granted.' To which the Revd. Wilfrid Westrup adds: 'After some time at Oxford he shook loose from the orthodox traditions in which he had been brought up although he never lost his sense of ethical values. Of his religious beliefs in later life I know nothing, but I could not fail to be deeply impressed by the beautiful anthem of his, "Nearer my God to thee", that was sung at his memorial service. Perhaps there was an experience here on which we could not intrude.' Indeed this was an area, one of the areas, on which he allowed no one to intrude. His reserve as a boy often puzzled his parents and his father used to say, 'Funny boy, Jack. You never know what he is doing.' His brother adds, 'Even less did we know what he was thinking.' Jack himself wrote in a chapter on 'Problems of Biography' in his book *Sharps and Flats*: 'Each one of us has a secret self which he hides from all but a very few or one alone. . . . A man may live for years, even for his whole life, without betraying his secret mysteries.' However, Canon Westrup believes he had 'a deep if latent faith in God and Christian values'.

They were a happy, close-knit family, sharing seaside holidays each summer and enjoying Bank Holiday outings to the Surrey hills. All three boys went to Alleyn's School, Dulwich. Jack and Allan belonged to a Scout troop and had piano lessons from the music master at Alleyn's, a Mr. Carrick, who lamented Allan's slower progress: 'If only he would practise like his brother!' Actually, writes Wilfrid, who also composed hymn tunes at the piano,

> Allan practised industriously, whereas Jack merely sat down to the

piano and amused himself. Jack enjoyed improvising on the piano, sometimes using irrelevant words such as 'Mr. Barclay Baron, O.B.E.' as a starting point. He also rather shocked my father, who had a harmonium on which he occasionally played hymns, by using the instrument with most unreligious bounce and gusto.

Jack not only improvised; he composed and his boyish compositions—he was no Mozart—were most carefully written out and dated. After winning a scholarship to Dulwich College he was not only trained in the classics but learned, by membership of the O.T.C. band, to play practically every brass instrument. This was an activity he enjoyed much more than rugger; one of his parlour tricks was to play the euphonium while accompanying himself with one hand at the piano, and to the end of his life he would occasionally sing military march tunes to words of the utmost impropriety. His lifelong love of Gilbert and Sullivan—as a young man in the days long before xeroxing he copied out the complete full score of *The Mikado*—probably dates from this period. His tastes were always eclectic; as a boy he enjoyed Debussy as well as Schumann and he widened his knowledge of Bach when, still at school, he had organ lessons from Dr. John Rodgers, organist of St. Saviour's, Denmark Park, for whom after a time he came to deputize. His younger brother says,

> In this he showed his natural resourcefulness. One Sunday he had to cope with a bad cipher on the organ and climbing around in its upper storey he found that a pailful of water poised at a certain spot relieved the trouble. The weight, however, was not quite enough, so at the next service he stationed the large and solidly built sacristan at the same spot.

Given the task of preparing a performance of Stainer's *Crucifixion* with a very inadequate choir

> he was determined to make the performance the best the church had known and boldly announced at the beginning of rehearsals that he did not expect anyone to be singing on the night who had not attended all of these. Inevitably one or two choirmen failed the test and were asked to step down. . . . The Vicar gallantly supported Jack's ruling and the performance was outstanding.

In 1923 Westrup won a music scholarship to Balliol where he read Classical Honour Mods. and Greats, taking his B.A.—a First in Mods. and Second in Greats—and B.Mus. in 1926. (He proceeded to M.A. in 1929.) 'Throughout his life he remained proud of being a Balliol man,' writes one of his friends, Dr. George Rettie, 'but although he gained immensely from his years there he saw little of the social or esoteric side of the university as he was extremely poor.' Naturally he was deeply involved in Oxford music, playing the organ at Pusey House for a time, composing music for the Balliol Players' production of the *Oresteia*—which was performed at, among other places, St. Paul's School, Corfe Castle, and Max Gate (where Hardy left an indelible blot on Jack's memory by the profound remark, 'Ah, if those hills could speak, what a tale they could tell!')—and above all in helping to found the Oxford University Opera Club.

Westrup's performing edition of Monteverdi's *Orfeo*, based on the 1615 edition in the Bodleian, was the origin both of his reputation as a musical scholar and of the Club. In 1925 W. H. Harris (later Sir William Harris), then organist of New College and director of the Sunday night Balliol concerts, conducted a performance of *Orfeo* so outstandingly successful that it was decided to found a club, which began operations with Gluck's *Alceste*, again under Harris. In 1927 Westrup himself conducted his performing edition of Monteverdi's *Coronation of Poppaea*. Then, coming down from Oxford, he was awarded a research grant enabling him to spend a considerable time at Avignon collecting and studying Provençal *noëls*.[1] His work on Provençal song led indirectly to an invitation from Percy Buck to contribute a chapter on 'Song' to the revised second volume (1400–*c.* 1600) of the *Oxford History of Music* which Buck had in hand. It was published in 1932 and was another landmark in his career, but he had found no foothold in the musical world and reckoned himself fortunate in being able to teach classics at his old school from 1928 to 1934.

At Dulwich College he taught at two levels, as a fourth-form master dealing with 13–15-year-olds and at university scholarship level. He told me more than once with what a sinking heart he first confronted the seniors ('But *they* never guessed'). Dr. Rettie, who studied under him at both levels and to whom he later dedicated his book on Purcell, writes that 'his whole

[1] Some of the fruits of his studies were published belatedly in *Music and Letters*, xxi (1940), 'Nicolas Saboly and his *Noëls provençaux*', pp. 34–49. Searching for carols in the Bibliothèque d'Inguimbert at Carpentras, he had the extraordinary luck to come across the composition sketch of Schumann's Piano Quintet, op. 44, which he described in one of his last published writings, his contribution to *Convivium Musicorum: Festschrift Wolfgang Boetticher zum 60sten Geburtstag* (Berlin, 1974), pp. 367–71.

approach to teaching considerably influenced the development of my outlook on life':

Jack Westrup brought a lively, questing, original and often impudent approach to anything he touched. He encouraged his younger pupils to answer him back with wit and confidence, and he would take infinite pains to develop the potential of any promising youngster. As a result, a high proportion of those who had started in his form passed effortlessly into the scholarship stream.

In the sixth form his passion for meticulous accuracy came into its own, and anyone who tried to get away with slovenly work soon got the benefit of his waspish tongue. If the subject was dull he would allow of no concessions, and despite protests would plod on through some obscure point of Greek history or Latin grammar with ferocious thoroughness until it was fully understood.

In a school which was obsessed with every form of game he would have nothing to do with them, saying they were suitable only for blockheads. He assisted in running the school music and played the piano, organ, horn or trombone as the occasion arose. The master in charge was a genial but not very talented amateur and Jack's behaviour was always impeccable in that he never by word or implication criticised what was done, however much grief it may have caused him. He was keenly interested in dramatics and in his last two years at the school directed spirited productions of *Macbeth* and *Henry V*. These were enormous fun, but to some extent all the players walked a tightrope. Jack knew what he wanted from each of them and provided they co-operated and did their best all went well. With those who did not he would never lose his temper—that would have been uncivilised—but he coolly and thoroughly cut them down to size.

Westrup was rescued from schoolmastering by Richard Capell, author of a classic study of *Schubert's Songs*, music critic of the *Daily Mail*, and editor of *The Monthly Musical Record*, a modest but scholarly periodical first edited, sixty years earlier, by the formidable Ebenezer Prout. In 1933 Capell left the *Mail* to become chief music critic of the *Daily Telegraph* and, under the pressure of this new post, decided to give up the *Record*—to which Westrup had been contributing since 1928—and suggested to the proprietors that the 'young schoolmaster' should succeed him. He did—and continued to edit the *Record* until 1945, when I took over from him. Some of his most polished and most stimulating early writing appeared in it anonymously as 'Notes of the Day'. But Capell's help did not end there; in 1934 he invited Westrup to leave Dulwich and join the music staff of the *Telegraph*. The invitation was accepted without hesitation.

Westrup thoroughly enjoyed the round of concert-going and

the occasional interviewing of visiting celebrities such as Kussevitsky, and his readers enjoyed his pungent writing though second-rate performers and composers can hardly have done so. His utter truthfulness did not allow the sparing of friends, though he disliked hurting them. (After a severe, but just, review of a book of mine he at once telephoned, 'But I still want you to be my friend'.) And it forbade false modesty. (A former colleague at Dulwich recalls 'congratulating him on the publication of his book on Purcell, and his reply was "It's definitive" '; it was not a boast but a cold statement of fact.) *Purcell* was published in Dent's 'Master Musicians' series in 1937 and is indeed as definitive biographically and penetrating critically as any book can be; it established him as the most brilliant English musical scholar of his generation.

Not long after its appearance he surprised his friends by marrying. He had been regarded as a confirmed bachelor and I remember that two lively sisters considered it a great triumph when they took him back to their flat after a concert, tied on an apron, and made him help with the washing up. But in 1938 he met a very beautiful girl, Solweig Rösell, daughter of a Swedish musician, was bowled over by her, and married her in Linköping Cathedral—having composed his own wedding march. He soon added Swedish to his languages and she lost little time in bearing him children, four in all. Marriage made him more sociable; our friendship became quadrilateral and was cemented in later years when we became godparents to each others' children. But the outbreak of war soon disturbed happy married life. All London concerts were abandoned, the *Telegraph* cut down its size, and Westrup found himself without a job. However, the leisure gave him an opportunity to make a collection of his essays, nearly all from the *Record* and *Telegraph*, published by the Oxford University Press under the title *Sharps and Flats* in 1940. He and Solweig and their little daughter were given a temporary home by Frank Howes, chief music critic of *The Times*, and his wife Barbara, at Newbridge Mill, near Witney, where he used to invent endless bedtime serial stories for the Howes children. Seeking a scholastic post, since a musical one seemed hopeless, he bethought of him of an old Oxford friend, Walter Oakeshott, then High Master of St. Paul's School, later Rector of Lincoln College and Vice-Chancellor, and of course a Fellow of the British Academy. St. Paul's had been moved out of London to Crowthorne in Berkshire and, Dr. Oakeshott writes,

I jumped at the chance of securing him for the staff. Few men could have been better qualified all round. It happened that at that time we needed more hostels for boys to live in; he and Solweig almost immediately took one over and established it most successfully. He was a great asset.

But he did not stay long at Crowthorne for in 1941 he was offered a Lectureship in Music at King's College, Newcastle upon Tyne, then part of the University of Durham, at 37 his first academic musical post.

At Newcastle he had a chance to conduct again, directing the Bach Choir during 1942–4, and he enjoyed the Northumbrian countryside. Canon Westrup remembers how, when he was staying with them, Jack

had planned a short walking tour for us, which, however, broke down on the second day when we came back home drenched to the skin, having failed to find lodging for the night. The next morning at breakfast I ventured to ask 'What shall we do today?' His answer was 'Walk, of course'. This was a clear glimpse of his character; having once made a decision, he was determined, come what may, to carry it through.

Yet Newcastle was a species of exile. He took as many opportunities as possible to come to London and we became accustomed to his early-morning appearances at our Hampstead house for breakfast after his all-night train journey. Thus his appointment to the Peyton and Barber Chair of Music at Birmingham in 1944 meant much more than promotion; it took him to a much livelier musical centre, with the excellent music library of the Barber Institute, and more congenial friends including an old one, Eric Blom, music critic of the *Birmingham Post* and editor of the quarterly *Music and Letters*, while his brother Wilfrid already had a Birmingham parish. Wilfrid was able to join the University Choral Society which Jack conducted in Brahms's *Requiem* and other works, and relates how 'during rehearsals for Handel's *Saul* he lashed the contraltos at one point with the remark "You sing like a procession of toads down a slippery plank". They loved it!' He appeared particularly happy and relaxed at Birmingham and would romp with his children, enjoying what he called 'elephant races' in which grown-ups on hands and knees would race with children on their backs. But he had never been averse to romping and horseplay; one such bout at home, while an undergraduate, ended in his falling downstairs and spraining an ankle with the result that, by special concession, he had to take one of his examinations at home on the sofa.

In November 1945 Westrup gave the Philip Maurice Deneke Lecture on 'The Meaning of Musical History' at Lady Margaret Hall, Oxford, and the following year his old university gave him a doctorate *honoris causa*, preludes to the offer of the Heather Professorship in 1947 and election to a Fellowship of Wadham. In view of his passionate devotion to Oxford—he once told an assemblage of distinguished foreign scholars that Oxford was the most beautiful city in the world—this was doubly gratifying. Yet Oxford was to present him with perhaps unexpected problems and load him with burdens, some inevitable but some self-imposed, too heavy for any man however tough and determined. To begin with, his appointment was not universally welcomed in Oxford. His predecessor, Sir Hugh Allen, was a very fine all-round musician, an overpowering, magnetic personality who had inspired intense devotion but had no interest in scholarly research; indeed he resigned the emoluments of his Fellowship of New College rather than undertake it. Westrup's personality was not 'magnetic' and he inspired intense devotion only in those who knew him well—and Oxford did not then know him. Moreover, the heir presumptive to the Chair had been passed over. (Many years later he told me that, though disappointed at the time, he had long recognized the rightness of the choice.) Allen had devised a plan for the training of music students within the University and the undergraduate school attracted unexpectedly large numbers for whom there was really no room in those immediately post-war years; welcome in itself, this was one of Westrup's first problems. And although a Faculty of Music had been established under Allen in 1944, with a distinguished scholar (Egon Wellesz) as a member of the Board, it was not until 1950 that music was accepted as a subject for an Arts degree with a curriculum more liberal than that of the B.Mus., which was retained but restructured.

It was only natural that Westrup should be offered the direction of the University Opera Club which had been dormant, save for an isolated production in 1943, during the war period. He led off at once with a performance of *Idomeneo*, followed it in 1948 with *The Beggar's Opera* in E. J. Dent's edition, and in 1949 with Stanford's *Much Ado about Nothing*. Then came a remarkable series of operas, mostly unfamiliar: Gluck's *Iphigenia in Tauris*, Berlioz's *Trojans*, the first performance of Wellesz's *Incognita*, Mozart's *Clemenza di Tito*, Marschner's *Hans Heiling*, Verdi's *Macbeth*, Bizet's *Fair Maid of Perth*, Smetana's *Secret*, Verdi's *Ernani*, Stravinsky's *Oedipus Rex* and Ravel's *L'Enfant et les sortilèges* (as a double bill), Mussorgsky's *Khovanshchina*, the first British performance of Alan Bush's *Men of Blackmore*, Alessandro Scarlatti's *Mitridate Eupatore*, and—the last before he resigned the directorship in 1962—Glinka's *Ruslan and Lyudmila*. This was a wonderful operatic education for Oxford, a revelation to many non-Oxfordians, and a source of continuing pleasure and deep satisfaction to Westrup. But the cost was heavy. His work extended far beyond the subsidiary labour that conscientious conductors undertake, the correction of parts, insertion of phrasing, and so on. In the case of *The Trojans* no full score had yet been published and the score hired from the French publisher was an incredible mess of corrections, alternative versions, and montage from which he had to educe an acceptable reading. He even insisted on translating seven of the foreign libretti himself, basing the Czech and Russian ones on close prose versions supplied by an Oxford friend. If he had had few other calls on his time and energy besides the normal ones on a university professor or if he had handed over after seven instead of seventeen years, this would not have mattered. But there were innumerable other calls—and irresistible temptations. (He always found it difficult to say 'No' and there were times when the need to provide for the education of four children made it hardly possible to do so.) It was not merely that he was in constant demand for lectures, contributions to composite works, reviews: he was the obvious and natural leader in every musicological enterprise in Britain.

First among these was the *New Oxford History of Music*. Soon after the war the University Press had contemplated yet another revision of the old *Oxford History* which, in the wrong hands as seemed likely, would have been disastrous. Wellesz was the first to get wind of this, and he and Westrup persuaded the Press to embark on an entirely new history to be planned by an editorial board with Westrup as chairman. On my suggestion it was decided to give the *New Oxford History* a 'sound companion' of gramophone records, *The History of Music in Sound*, each volume of which—with the accompanying handbook—was to be planned and supervised by the editor of the corresponding volume of the main *History*. Westrup threw himself into all this with his usual zest and his powerful combination of scholarship and practical musicianship but it was symptomatic that, whereas he conducted performances of Orlando Gibbons, Monteverdi, Cesti, Stradella, Alessandro Scarlatti, Logroscino, Blow, Keiser, J. C. Bach, J. S. Bach, Buxtehude, he failed to deliver on time the handbooks to volumes IV, V, and VI for which he was personally responsible and I had to write and edit them.[1] The fate of the main volumes in the *New Oxford History* was even sadder; in the end I had to edit IV, Anthony Lewis and Nigel Fortune V, and he had just begun to write his own chapters for VI when he died.

Another great project in which he was involved from the first was *Musica Britannica*, a collection of the classics of British music published by the Royal Musical Association and initiated on the occasion of the Festival of Britain in 1951. The editorial committee was chaired by Anthony Lewis but Westrup was an active member of it until his death. He was the figurehead (though he was never as passive as a figurehead) of a number of organizations: President of the Galpin Society for research in the history of European instruments from its foundation in 1946 until his death, chairman of the Purcell Society committee from Dent's death in 1957 onwards, President of the Royal Musical Association (1958–63), of the Incorporated Society of Musicians (1963), and of the Royal College of Organists (1964–6). And his eminence was recognized by official honours. In 1954 he was elected a Fellow of the British Academy,[2] only the third musician to be admitted—the first two were Dent and Wellesz in 1953—and when the Academy launched the *Early English Church Music* series he was naturally the chairman of the committee. In 1961 he was knighted. During 1971–2 he was Master of the Worshipful Company of Musicians.

He somehow found time to 'revise'—that is, to produce a greatly expanded edition of—Ernest Walker's *History of Music in England* (1952), as he later did for Edmund Fellowes's *English Cathedral Music* (1969), to write his own *Introduction to Musical History* (1955) for the music series of Hutchinson's University Library, and edit the series, and to organize the Sixth Congress of the International Musicological Society at Oxford in 1955, though not, alas, to edit its Proceedings which remain unpublished.

Some summer holidays were spent with his family on the Isle of Wight where we had a summer home, and there he relaxed, enthusiastically digging sand-castles on the beach at Compton Bay with a former Birmingham colleague Professor Alastair

[1] The information in the bibliography of the memorial volume, *Essays on Opera and English Music* (Basil Blackwell, 1975), pp. 179–80, is incorrect.

[2] On 18 Jan. 1956 he gave the Aspects of Art Lecture, 'The Nature of Recitative', *Proceedings*, xlii. 27–43.

Frazer and his family, and our own, and taking long walks on the downs with me. On one such walk he planned that when we reached the tea place at our goal and the waitress asked, according to precedent as she put the pot on the table, 'Now which of you gentlemen is going to be "mother"?', he would say, 'Neither—unless one of us undergoes an extraordinary physiological change', a typical Westrupian joke. Unfortunately she forgot her cue. But too many long vacations were spent lecturing at American universities, financially rewarding yet exhausting.

Then in 1959, still deeply involved with the Opera Club—and from 1954 to 1963 with the Oxford University Orchestra which he had founded—he embarked on what can only be described as an act of heroic folly. On the death of Eric Blom he took over the editing of both Dent's 'Master Musicians' series of books and the quarterly *Music and Letters*. He did it superbly but he should never have done it, at any rate the editing of *Music and Letters*, at all. He was a real, not nominal, editor of a book or periodical, meticulous in matters of literary and typographical styles, taking endless pains to save his writers from suspected slips or downright blunders. But he was not content with editing *Music and Letters*, which he continued to do across the Atlantic when necessary; he contributed numerous reviews; and, having only occasional secretarial help, deliberately accepted the drudgery of packing and sending out books and music to reviewers and compiling very long and detailed lists of 'Books Received'. He was equally efficient in both roles, editor and office boy, for he did everything, whether intellectual or mechanical, with the utmost care and clarity and precision. These activities worried his friends, who felt that the time given to work which many could do should have been given to the work of scholarship which very few could do, but they were not caprices; they were necessities of his nature.

Yet he went on contributing to encyclopedias and dictionaries, German and American and Italian as well as British, and *Festschriften* for German, American, Danish, and Flemish scholars. In 1966 he edited the *Essays Presented to Egon Wellesz*, which includes his own on Bizet's *Jolie Fille de Perth*. He wrote two admirable little B.B.C. music guides, *Bach Cantatas* (1966) and *Schubert Chamber Music* (1969). And so far as practical music-making was concerned, he ended his Oxford years by taking over the conductorship of the Bach Choir and Orchestral Society in 1970 and giving a fine performance of Elgar's *Kingdom* with them in 1971. He has, incidentally, a permanent monument in

Oxford: the Holywell Music Room. Built in 1748, it had been partially restored and redecorated in the early years of the present century but its genuine restoration to its original form, plus a foyer, was mainly due to the efforts of Westrup, supported by Wellesz and Oakeshott who had found a print of the original plans in a collection in the Lincoln library.

When he left Oxford in 1971 and settled in the east Hampshire countryside near Headley he was quite boyishly excited at possessing a house of his own; hitherto he had lived in university houses. He had never bothered about the scrap of garden in Woodstock Road; now he had a large one and became an enthusiastic gardener, overworking himself at that as at everything else. He continued to write and to attend meetings in London, and of course to edit *Music and Letters* and the 'Master Musicians'. He paid a last visit to the States in 1974, lecturing at Boston. And he continued to play schoolboyish jokes; during the war, an ITMA enthusiast, he would announce himself on the phone in sepulchral tones as 'Funf speaking'; in the 1970s we were haunted by another Germanic voice, 'Professor Stinkenstein'. He was more relaxed, perhaps happier than he had been for thirty years. He knew and made no secret of it that he had *angina pectoris* but appeared not to be worried. And then the end came quite suddenly on 21 April 1975. It was infinitely regrettable that the book which should have been presented to him on his seventieth birthday nine months before, the *Essays on Opera and English Music. In honour of Sir Jack Westrup*, edited by Dr. F. W. Sternfield, Dr. Nigel Fortune, and Dr. Edward Olleson, could be only a tribute to his memory.

In their preface the editors remark, among other things that Westrup 'shunned the tendency of our age toward a proliferation of books that are, in fact, inflated articles'. Dr. Rettie recalls how in his concert notices for the *Telegraph* 'Jack always strove to extract value from every word he wrote. In this respect his devotion to the works and style of Tacitus stood him in good stead.' His brother Wilfrid says the same:

Whatever subject he was dealing with, he showed the same clarity and mastery of language. Picking up a second-hand volume of Pope, he delighted to discover and repeat such lines as:

> The same adust complexion hath impelled
> Charles to the convent, Philip to the field,[1]

[1] *Moral Essays*, Epistle I, ll. 107–8.

and his favourite limerick was that of the old man of Uplyme who married three wives at a time.

> When they said 'Why the third?'
> He replied 'One's absurd
> And bigamy, Sir, is a crime'.

He had an instinctive dislike for all pretentiousness and humbug. A modern prayer ends with the words 'We do not ask that Thou wilt keep us safe but that Thou wilt keep us loyal'. To Jack there was something of a pose in this not asking to be kept safe and he would comment 'It seems a perfectly reasonable request'.

One kind of humbug he particularly despised was the kind of musicology that has lost touch with music.

Condemnatory attitudes were easily suggested by a cold, severe manner which completely deceived strangers and terrified his students in earlier days, much less latterly. They never even suspected the existence of the great warmth and generosity under the cool surface. But the coolness was not a mere mask; it was of his essence which was Apollonian, not Dionysian. In that chapter on 'Problems of Biography' from which I have already quoted, Westrup wrote that biographers

> are often constrained to refuse credence to simple records, on the ground that their evidence conflicts with what may be deduced from other sources. Not so, they say, could such-and-such a man have behaved. . . . We have only to look within ourselves or to study our closest friends to see the truth of the philosophical commonplace that the individual is at the same time one and many.

It was the integrated complex of all his disparate qualities that made Jack Westrup the outstanding personality he was, that compelled so much respect and admiration, and drew to him such deep affection from all who truly knew him.

GERALD ABRAHAM

PLATE LI

SIR MORTIMER WHEELER, C.H., C.I.E., M.C., F.R.S.

ROBERT ERIC MORTIMER WHEELER

1890–1976

'IN a simple direct sense, archaeology is a science that must be lived, must be "seasoned with humanity". Dead archaeology is the driest dust that blows.' These words express one of the mainsprings of Mortimer Wheeler's tireless life. He passionately believed that any young recruit joining the archaeological colours should do so partly for the sake of adventure, and he thought little of those tarnished by the driest dust that blows. This was one of the reasons why his own great contributions to knowledge were made almost entirely through excavations, through excavations carefully selected in order to provide knowledge where it was most needed. Through enterprise and adventure and uniting yourself imaginatively with the peoples whose relics you were discovering, archaeology could be lived.

Imagination was another of the mainsprings of Wheeler's being. 'Reasoned imagination'; 'an informed and informing imagination'; 'a controlled imagination'—the phrases occur again and again, as often as he proclaimed his ideals of what man in general and archaeologists in particular should be. There is no doubt that the ability to visualize the likely intentions or compulsions of the people whose remains he was exploring accounted for his brilliance as a tactician in knowing just where to dig and as a strategist in choosing his sites. But far more than that, was not controlled imagination at the root of the greatest of his gifts, his power of forward planning against all eventualities, the power that brought him his successes not only in archaeology but in his remarkable military career and in his truly extraordinary exercises in galvanizing feeble institutions and creating new ones?

Indeed, imaginative forward planning (wars apart) controlled his whole career. There are few men whose steps through public life, whose choice of jobs and undertakings, owed so little to chance. This is true in spite of the fact that for the greater part of his eighty-five-year journey through this world he was driven by a demonic energy—likened by Sir Max Mallowan in his Memorial address to the 'Seven Devils'.

To these underlying forces in Mortimer Wheeler's life, one more has to be added: his power of command. It is right to put it last, for while adventurousness, imagination, and energy were probably innate and certainly showed themselves early, command developed more slowly and as the product of the deeper qualities. Yet without it, without the sometimes ruthless ability (to quote Sir Max again) by which he 'enlisted the help of lesser mortals and compelled them to bow in his path', he could not have filled the role of Hero that so many of us have assigned to him.

Robert Eric Mortimer Wheeler was born in Glasgow in the year 1890. At that time his father, Mortimer Wheeler, was working for Blackie's *Encyclopaedia*, but before long he moved as a journalist to Edinburgh where his elder daughter Amy was born, and then on to join the staff of the *Yorkshire Daily Observer*. The family was now completed by the arrival of a second daughter, Betty. Mortimer Wheeler was the son of a Bristol tea merchant, a very good-looking man said to have had a diffident manner. He had been an outstanding classical student at Edinburgh and had passed through a phase of Baptist piety to militant free-thinking. For a time he moved in an intellectual circle, including, it should be noticed, Carlow Martin, later director of the Royal Scottish Museum. He himself was quite without ambition, finding happiness in an enjoyment of all the arts and, in his younger days at least, of nature and country pastimes.

Wheeler's mother came from a partly academic background, being the niece and ward of Thomas Spencer Baynes, a Shakespearian scholar at St. Andrews and an occasional welcome visitor in the Wheeler household. She was herself well educated, and taught her children at home until they were seven or eight years old.

All memories, including his own, suggest that Mortimer Wheeler's close relationship with his father was of lasting importance. As soon as the romantically pretty little boy could contrive to keep up with him, his father took him for walks on the surrounding moors that are the boon of all Bradfordians. They studied wild life, but more significantly were always on the look out for antiquities: cup-marked stones, Anglo-Saxon crosses, flints, potsherds, tumuli—anything that came their way. As Wheeler was to recall, 'in these impressionable years the insidious poisons of archaeology were already entering my system'.

His father also taught the young Wheeler to shoot and fish in a purely non-county style that included occasional excursions with a poacher and the enforcement of a rule that the boy must eat everything he killed. Enjoyment in using his skills with rod and gun remained with Wheeler all his life and through all his travels. It brought almost the only sporting relaxation to a man who despised and avoided all organized games.

These out-of-door pleasures learnt from his father were of more than superficial importance in shaping the man. Of more importance still must have been mental companionship with a parent who always spoke and read to him as though he were adult and shared with him his love of the classics, English literature, and, perhaps above all and unexpectedly, his dreams of adventure and the deeds of men of action. There can be little doubt that growing up with these dreams and imaginary heroes helped to inspire Wheeler as a man of action. Immediately, however, living so much in the adult world of his father's mind made him scornful of his very ordinary schoolboy contemporaries. His sister Amy remembers how difficult it always was to induce him to go to parties; he contrived to avoid playing games, and, with the exception of one master, thought of Bradford Grammar School with little admiration, declaring that 'my school was of no great moment to me'. This unintended paternal influence may also have endured, encouraging that impatience sometimes amounting to contempt towards lesser mortals, for which he has often been criticized.

One other activity of this period deserves mention: Wheeler's eager endeavour to train himself as a painter. He spent many half holidays in the Art Room at school, and at home, as Amy recalls, tyrannized over the family through his heedless concentration on poster painting. The two of them united, however, in producing an art magazine, writing all the articles themselves under a variety of names. Although a later oil portrait of Amy shows considerably more ability than has usually been allowed him, this ambition of Wheeler's was probably the only one in his lifetime which he pursued but lacked the talent to sustain. The technical skills that he mastered, such as lettering and elementary drawing, were to be useful to him and a pleasure to the rest of us, in the plans and sections that were to illustrate his archaeological publications.

The formative Bradford years ended when Mortimer Wheeler senior was invited by the *Yorkshire Observer* to take charge of their London office. His son was then fourteen years old, had reached the sixth form, and was confidently expected to win an Oxford scholarship. J. E. Barton, later to be headmaster of Bristol Grammar School, and the only master to have had a considerable influence on the boy, protested vigorously at the

London move, declaring 'You are not taking him away from Bradford, you are taking him away from Oxford'. Neither father nor son was daunted: for both of them the lure of London was too strong. Almost certainly their decision was the right one for Wheeler's future, yet in later years he could feel regret at not having gone to Oxford and was happy to send his own son there.

He never returned to school, his father allowing him something like five shillings a week to gain a freelance education from the great city, its museums, galleries, and buildings, its alleys and thoroughfares. It was part of the bargain, however, that he should also work for his matriculation to the University of London, an examination which he passed when he was sixteen, following it with a classical scholarship that took him to University College in the year 1907.

In those days Gower Street was very much a well-knit college in the academic sense and had distinguished men in most of its faculties. Wheeler was fated to be taught Latin by A. E. Housman—who professed his subject in a 'take it or leave it' style. He often preferred to leave it, for he still cherished his hope of becoming an artist, and had made a private arrangement to study at the Slade. There he greatly admired Tonks, who taught drawing, and made friends with his own contemporary, Paul Nash. Then, quite suddenly, Wheeler took one of those sharp decisions that were to be repeated throughout his career. Realizing that he had no genius and could only be either a penniless rebel modernist or a merely competent professional, he cast out hope and left the Slade on the instant.

He had been earning his keep by coaching and a little journalism, and on taking his first degree was evidently recognized to be a student as promising as he was impoverished, for the Provost offered him a job as his secretary. This enabled Wheeler to work for an M.A. which he gained in 1912. It must have been during these last two years at University College that he turned towards archaeology, for in 1913 he applied for and won an archaeological studentship just established in memory of Wollaston Franks, offering research in Roman-Rhenish pottery. It is well known that as he walked away, jubilant but wondering how to live on £50 a year, Sir Arthur Evans, one of the selection committee, ran after him and said he would like to double the endowment. Such were the advantages of an academe of personal relationships and private fortunes.

Wheeler made his Rhineland study tour, then took a miserably unworthy appointment with the English Royal

Commission of Historical Monuments, at that date almost entirely concerned with buildings. Except that it led him to take a course in architectural drawing, while the pittance he received enabled him to marry the enchanting and gifted Tessa Verney, this was an interlude that might well be forgotten. It was not to last long.

On the outbreak of war, Wheeler immediately volunteered and was commissioned into the Royal Artillery. Although early promoted Captain, his ardent desire to reach the front was frustrated until 1917. In that year he had contrived to use some of his men to excavate the Balkerne Gate of Roman Colchester. Then 'Passchendaele, Italy, the last advance on the Western Front . . . followed in eventful succession'. During that last advance he carried out the crazy exploit of capturing German guns from the castle mound of de Warlencourt that won him the M.C. It is a proof of the present difficulty for even a natural hero to play the heroic role that Wheeler records how, as he led his men into no-man's-land, he had 'a slightly strained feeling about the ribs and a growing sense of the silliness of the whole affair'. It seems clear, however, that the First World War brought out and hardened his power of command. It also gave him the lifelong conviction that he need fear no further experience, for at Passchendaele he had known the worst.

Demobilized in 1919, he had a small son (Michael born in 1915, now a Q.C.) and wife to support. He was obliged to return briefly to the Royal Commission, although this meant that pay and status plummeted from those attained as a Major. He saw this as a year of decision. He was determined to remain in archaeology and had a characteristically clear idea of the part he should play in it. The degree of ignorance of Roman and prehistoric Britain at that time is now often exaggerated, but it is true that excavation was insufficient, without strategic direction, poor in method and techniques. Wheeler had long recognized the greatness of General Pitt-Rivers as an excavator, and saw himself as donning the mantle that had hung neglected on a hook, and returning to the high standards of Cranborne Chase before leading a new advance. In this he was driven on by a deep awareness of himself as an isolated survivor, conscious, as he said, 'of the responsibility which a deadly war had bequeathed to me'. Those other survivors, his friends Cyril Fox and O. G. S. Crawford, were a little ahead of him in their own fields, but he felt himself alone as a leader in purposeful excavation.

He was soon to seize the right opportunity to put this sense of mission into practice on a sufficiently large scale. He won an advertised double post as Keeper of Archaeology in the National Museum of Wales and Lecturer in Archaeology in the University College at Cardiff—making the move in 1920. Here at once was a challenge of the kind he was to meet and overcome several times during his life. There was an enfeebled administration to be energized and an integrated archaeological strategy to be planned and executed.

In 1920 the National Museum in the grandiose new civic centre being built in Cardiff was little more than a façade, construction having come to a standstill in the face of a large debt. As a departmental keeper (his collections were stored) Wheeler could not do much to end this impasse, so set himself instead to get the *idea* of a National Museum recognized throughout the sharply divided principality. He spent much time 'in the hills' (too much, his critics said) lecturing, helping local museums in a practical way. He led them at last into a Welsh Federation of Museums under National Museum chairmanship and with a training school in Cardiff. He also used excavations as a part of this integrating policy and clinched it with his first substantial book, *Prehistoric and Roman Wales*, published in 1925. He refers to it as 'a scrap book' scribbled at odd moments, and it is true that the writing shows only a few touches of his style. Yet it was at once a useful textbook for students and 'served its frankly political purpose, as a primary medium of integration'.

Meanwhile he was not neglecting his lectureship or his avowed aim of winning archaeology a place in the curriculum of the University of Wales. Here again he directed combined operations, for he could train and use his students on his excavations.

In 1924 he was made Director of a museum still sunk in lethargy and debt. Immediately the power was switched on. The grant was increased by a private visit to the Treasury, an inefficient alderman sacked from the treasurership and replaced by a friendly shipping magnate who arrived with a cheque to pay off the entire debt; an appeal was launched, building restarted, collections installed, and a royal opening staged. It can be assumed that the 'private visit to the Treasury' was the very first of many such successful forays—needing no introduction to Fellows of the British Academy.

The main excavations that with Tessa's help Wheeler carried out during his already crowded life at Cardiff were selected to straddle the country and to construct a unified picture of the Roman occupation of Wales. Of the three—the forts of Segontium and Brecon Gaer, and the great legionary fortress of Caerleon—the first is the most significant from a biographical point of view. Here was Wheeler's first chance to test his ability in historical interpretation while at the same time building excavation techniques on solid Pitt-Rivers foundations. He followed his master also in prompt publication—a duty he was always to observe. *Segontium and the Roman Occupation* contains the earliest, still tentative, sections and plans in which Wheeler improved upon the General. At the Gaer the director had the bonus of the 'fishful' Usk; Caerleon (begun only in 1926) was notable as the site of his discovery of the uses of publicity. The *Daily Mail* paid for the digging of the fine amphitheatre, spurred on, he believed, by the spectacularly successful press sponsorship of the opening of Tutankhamun's tomb through which 'archaeology had, almost overnight, acquired a new market value'.

In many ways, then, the achievement of the years in Wales was the Mark I prototype of the greater achievements that lay ahead. One other must be mentioned. In *Still Digging* Wheeler writes movingly of how his Welsh excavations heightened his sense of personal responsibility, as a 'survivor' to gather the young generation about him to share not only skills, but also 'controlled enthusiasm' and a sense of direction. He certainly started well for on these digs he had Ian Richmond, Christopher Hawkes, and Nowell Myres as undergraduates; also Victor Nash-Williams and Aileen Fox.

By 1926 Rik and Tessa Wheeler (the Wheelers as they were now beginning to be called) could feel that their Welsh archaeological mission had been fulfilled in the museum, in the University, and in the field. He feared that if he remained in Cardiff much longer he would inevitably become rooted in the provinces. Already in that year he had been making precise plans for a university Institute of Archaeology where the young could be trained to play an efficient part in the more professional and academically respected archaeology to which he was dedicated. It seems that from boyhood Wheeler had identified himself with London as the heart of power in the land, the place where the High Command could be reached, strategies agreed, and money found. He was therefore convinced that in London his Institute must be, and when through Charles Peers he was offered the directorship of the London Museum he accepted, although the museum was moribund and the pay miserable.

In the same year he was invited to occupy the first chair of Prehistoric Archaeology in the country, the Abercromby Professorship in Edinburgh. That he turned it down was very largely because it was not in London, but perhaps also because Wheeler knew that the life of pure and peaceful scholarship was not for him. These events of 1926 seem to justify a few words about the 'devouringly ambitious temperament' recently attributed to him. At 35 he had turned down the certainties of two positions of considerable prestige in favour of a 'mission' which promised hard work, struggles, and a private life very near to poverty. It seems to the writer that Wheeler was immensely ambitious to incarnate the children of his imagination and therefore to win the power needed to overcome all obstacles and opposition. That purely personal ambition was never paramount is suggested by his attitude to money. The man who raised so much for activities and institutions of all kinds, and who loved panache, style, good food, drink, and other indulgences, never earned a large salary or gave more time to his finances than dashing off a book or two and performing on T.V. He lived against a simple background to the end.

If, as he wrote, Mortimer Wheeler arrived in London his pocket bulging with the blueprints for his Institute, it was to take a long time to build from them. He began to prepare the ground in the learned world and particularly in the University of London (through his fellowship at University College) where hitherto archaeology had hardly been recognized. Meanwhile the London Museum, then in Lancaster House, had to serve as the base for his campaign—and indeed gradually became the Institute in embryo.

The immediate task was to set the London Museum itself in order. That curious establishment with its direct royal patronage had to be cleared of junk, provided with a more adequate staff, and refurbished to make it a worthy shop window to display the best styles in modern archaeology. To attract a wider public a private endowment was found for concerts on the highest level, the music ranging from piano recitals by Harriet Cohen and Schnabel to full-dress performances by the London Symphony Orchestra under Thomas Beecham. Public lectures were delivered and school classes extended. All this was given solidity by the publication of a series of excellent guides, which Wheeler was able later to approve for their 'satisfactory intermingling of *vulgarisation* and scholarship'. The first, *London and the Vikings*, appeared as early as 1927, to be followed by *London in the Roman Times* and *London and the Saxons*. Writing them after a long day, Wheeler could seldom leave the museum before midnight. The useful *Medieval Catalogue*, prepared by his young assistant Ward-Perkins, appeared only in 1940, by which time they were together in the Artillery. *London and the Saxons* led to a vigorous dispute with Nowell Myres concerning the extent of Roman survivals in the city.

Behind all museum work the drive towards an academic Institute was maintained. More students and research workers were attracted to Lancaster House, an Esher studentship was endowed there and Wheeler began to lecture, without fee, to student audiences. An important advance towards the goal was made in 1934 when the University of London gave Wheeler an official, though part-time, appointment as lecturer in British Archaeology and established a post-graduate archaeological diploma.

Side by side with this advance at the centre, the Wheelers were organizing ambitious excavations, as in Wales, where students could be given practical training and, some of them very real responsibilities. The first was not of Wheeler's own selection but the response to an appeal by the Bathurst family to the Society of Antiquaries for an excavator to explore a Roman site in their park at Lydney on the fringes of the Forest of Dean. Here digging was to discover an underlying late Iron Age settlement, the only known Roman iron mine, a temple, bath-house and other buildings associated with a cult of the Celtic god, Nodens, which had lingered on from the fourth into the fifth century. It was Wheeler himself in an idle moment who found the famous Lydney hoard of minute, depreciated fifth-century coins, which, as 'King Arthur's small change' added to the already considerable publicity. It might be said that it was symbolic of the Wheeler partnership that while Rik found the hoard it was Tessa who made the meticulous report on its 1646 coins.

Lydney occupied the seasons of 1928–9. It was to be followed by one of the most extensive and complex excavations of Wheeler's career: that of the Roman Verulamium and the adjacent Belgic settlements and defences. His involvement with Roman London had already convinced him that more knowledge of Roman towns was badly needed and he had recommended Verulamium as the best place to provide it. When, in 1931, the Corporation of St. Albans sought advice on the excavation of that part of the ancient site that they had just acquired for recreation grounds, the undertaking chimed in perfectly with his strategy. Work began that same year and was to last for four seasons.

In his book on methods, *Archaeology from the Earth*, Wheeler chose this excavation as his best example of tactical planning, of the logical advance from the known into the unknown. The walled Roman *municipium* of Verulamium was conspicuous where it lay beside the Ver. It was known that the pre-Roman Belgic capital of Cunobelin's father was in the area and it could be assumed that here, too, was the *oppidum* of his great precursor, Cassivellaunus, stormed by Caesar in 54 B.C. It had also been assumed that the Belgic capital would lie below the municipium. In a campaign of five stages the Wheelers, with their gifted team of assistants, satisfied themselves (though later exploration has proved them to have made some errors) that while the earliest Roman town sacked by Boudicca partly underlay its successor, the post-Caesarean Belgic settlement was behind an embankment above the valley to the west. Also the Cassivellaunian presence could almost certainly be identified with a powerful *oppidum* at Wheathampstead to the north-east adjoining a mighty defensive dyke between Ver and Lea. Meanwhile Tessa directed the uncovering of the Roman city itself.

As his strategy unfolded in this way, Wheeler found himself exploring 'not a site, but a landscape' and had the enjoyment of dashing from digging to digging on horseback—or in the old Lancia in which he also sometimes drove straight from 'the trenches' to address students at Lancaster House.

Taken as a whole, these excavations did much to add substance to the shadowy history of the century before the Roman conquest of Britain, including the characteristics of Belgic tribal centres, and even more in establishing such archaeological foundations as dated pottery types, brooches, and the like. In this they converged with the information being obtained at much the same time at Cunobelin's capital of Camulodunum.

Wheeler's classical education had led him to concentrate his first decade of purposeful excavation on Roman Britain: now Verulamium had led back into the protohistory of late pre-conquest times, and therefore to sites devoid of formal architecture. The great sections cut through the massive Belgic defences were as well suited to his flair for reading history from stratification as they were to the fine draughtsmanship that visualized his findings. This new encounter with prehistory was not disagreeable to him. Indeed, he was later to make the surprising declaration that in 1934

For the moment I suffered from a satiety of Roman things. The mechanical, predictable quality of Roman craftsmanship, the advertised *humanitas* of Roman civilization, which lay always so near to brutality and corruption, fatigued and disgusted me . . .'

So in that year the Wheelers gladly took an opportunity to transfer themselves and their now numerous and experienced staff to the noblest, most spectacular of all our Celtic Iron Age monuments: Maiden Castle in Dorset. Here for the first and only time in his life Wheeler had unexpectedly to deal with important remains from the depths of our prehistoric past—a neolithic enclosure and long-barrow—but the purpose of this remarkable excavation was, of course, to discover the building sequence and history of the famous hillfort itself.

With his usual precision and dispatch, Wheeler followed the development through all its phases from the small fort of the third century B.C. to the last, Belgic-dominated, stronghold that fell to the Romans. With its strong military interest, it was a story that might have been composed for him. The unique tactical ingenuity of the entrance works, the evidence supplied by huge stores of slingstones that the introduction of this weapon accounted for the elaboration of the ramparts, and, far above all, the grim spectacle of the 'war cemetery' appealed to his best interpretative powers.

The cemetery uncovered in the eastern entrance with its battle-hacked skeletons, one with a Roman arrow embedded in the spine, could be identified beyond reasonable doubt with the aftermath of the capture of Maiden Castle by the Second Legion under Vespasian. Wheeler was to reconstruct the events of that day with a brilliance and force that have made them a part of our history. The method of excavation of this east entrance is also of interest. Wheeler had started to explore it with what he called 'substantive' trenching which proved so cumbersome that he switched to the 'grid' system that is still associated with his name, and which he was to employ on a large scale in India. If a choice had to be made of a single site as best representing Mortimer Wheeler as excavator-interpreter, it should probably be the east entrance of Maiden Castle.

Verulamium, so accessible from London, had attracted visitors in large enough numbers to contribute substantially to excavation funds. The romantic fame and dramatic excavation results of Maiden Castle lured them in swarms, and the conduct of parties round the dig laid quite a heavy duty upon assistants and students. One day a week was appointed as a press day. Wheeler was always popular with reporters, for he understood their needs, and, as he freely admitted, enjoyed dealing with them. Inevitably there was criticism from more staid, traditional, or simply envious archaeologists of his use of publicity and what could be seen as the resulting ballyhoo. If there were minor dangers in working under public relation floodlights, it should be remembered that not only was the cash raised from newspapers and visitors much needed in days before the tax-payer met the bills, but Wheeler had always believed that it was part of his mission to rouse the interest of the general public in archaeology and the ancient history it revealed. It is probably true that his success in doing so during the inter-war years, and later through television, did much to prepare opinion for the present generous endowment of archaeology from the public purse.

The Wheelers' two great excavations of the 1930s had a dynamic effect on the now fast-growing science of British archaeology. The writer well remembers the enthusiasm and criticism they generated among its followers everywhere. Moreover, a remarkable group of experienced excavators and specialists was created, many of whom were to become leaders in their turn. That this band was coherent and usually happy, both in the field and back in Lancaster House, in spite of the emotions sometimes aroused by the extra-curricular activities of the Director, was largely due to Tessa's presiding influence. It was therefore a tragedy of many dimensions when in 1936 she died from a totally unexpected medical mishap. Wheeler, who was always to carry the inner scars of this loss, declared that the Maiden Castle dig must be worthily completed as a memorial to her. The last two seasons were carried out in this spirit, with Mrs. Alwyn Cotton gallantly substituting as second in command.

From quite early days of the excavations it was appreciated that the history of the Dorset site could not be fully understood unless it were related to that of the adjacent regions of Gaul—known to have had intercourse with Britain before, during, and after Caesar's campaigns. Preliminary surveys of earthworks in Normandy and Brittany during 1935–6 were succeeded in 1938–9 by further fieldwork and selective excavation by Wheeler and members of his band. This programme, precisely purposeful and well organized as ever, did in fact throw much light into the then dim, uncultivated fields of French archaeology. In particular confirmation was found for cultural connections between Brittany and the Celtic tribesmen of the many-ramparted, sling-using Maiden Castle. Further north, distinctive types of Belgic fortifications were identified for the first time. The results of this bold foray were not fully published until 1957, but they proved of real value when at last French archaeology woke from its slumbers. This was Wheeler's only mature contribution to European studies: in general his interest passed the Continent by, and he probably maintained fewer contacts with European scholars than was usual among his more academic colleagues. His failure to do so may have contributed in a small way to the criticisms from younger men that were the inevitable accompaniment to his rising fame and success during the later thirties.

The Verulamium and Maiden Castle excavations were handsomely published as Reports of the Research Committee of the Society of Antiquaries. *Verulamium, a Belgic and Two Roman Cities*, under the joint authorship of the Wheelers, appeared in 1936, *Maiden Castle, Dorset* not until 1943, when Wheeler, dedicating it to Tessa, apologized for its incompleteness, explaining that it had been prepared 'amidst the watches of the War' and was no more 'than the salvage of the report that should have been'.

Both led to criticism not only of the publications themselves, but of some aspects of the excavation policy they represented. Reduced to essentials, the burden of complaint was twofold. First it was said that Wheeler's highly selective method of digging might miss important features and certainly could not provide the social and economic information that depended upon the total excavation of a site. When Wheeler began his digging the creation of a sound historical framework was the first essential, and it is true that this goal remained paramount for him. The younger generation meanwhile had lent ear to ideas of the economic determinants of history and total excavation was the password of progress. It was to reach its apotheosis a few years later at Little Woodbury where a farmstead was completely excavated by the German archaeologist, Gerhard Bersu. No disciple of General Pitt-Rivers could be unaware of the advantages of uncovering the whole of vestiges of this kind, but it is hard to see how it could have been done at the two enormous sites in question with the limited means of the thirties.

The second line of attack was against the Reports themselves. The main charges were that in his desire for a publication of form and style, Wheeler had provided too little evidence for his interpretations, had given a wrong impression of finality, and even that he had intentionally concealed unanswered questions. There was a further complaint that if excavations were to be published in this elegant way Reports would become literary works rather than serious scientific data banks.

Unquestionably these criticisms marked the beginning of the swing towards a sociological, common-man approach that has dominated the archaeology of the past decade or so. Looking back after suffering the gaseous and insignificant effusions that this has produced at its worst, the virtues of Wheeler's works shine again. The swing also accounts for the great paradox fully recognized by Wheeler: his mission had been to produce the trained personnel for a scientific archaeology, yet for much of his life he found himself passionately defending the humanist values of history.

Science was still very much to the fore when at last the Wheelers' arduous struggle for their Institute was won. During the years of digging and of the development of research and teaching at Lancaster House, efforts were made to raise funds through public appeal. A good beginning had been made when Sir Flinders Petrie handed over a gift he had received for the housing of his important Palestinian collections—on condition that this became the responsibility of the projected Institute. The further money needed came in slowly and there was a long hunt for suitable premises—that is to say a large building at low rent. It was found in St. John's Lodge, Regents Park, the elegant but neglected former town house of the Marquesses of Bute. Refurbished, it was to provide a charming, intimate, if far from glossy, home for the infant Institute.

The opening was in April 1937, when Wheeler shared the platform with the Earl of Athlone, Chancellor of London University, the Vice-Chancellor, and the Colonial Secretary, Lord Harlech. A black marble memorial plaque to Tessa Verney Wheeler made its presence felt. The opening speech from the Chancellor had been carefully prepared by Wheeler to emphasize the Institute as a 'laboratory', a centre of research where humanity could be studied against its natural environments with the aid of 'the geologist, the botanist, the palaeontologist, the climatologist. . . .' A place, too, where students could familiarize themselves with archaeological collections and be trained in techniques needed for excavation and preservation.

The actual provision of the Institute could hardly at first be up to the high status and high aspirations of its opening day. Still, under Wheeler as honorary Director, it had the future Dame Kathleen Kenyon as chief administrator; an environmentalist of repute in Dr. Zeuner; Sidney Smith and Professor Hooke lecturing in Near Eastern and biblical studies; a library, an excellent little photographic studio, and a modest technical laboratory. As well as expanding collections of British antiquities, the Petrie Collection had been reinforced by material from Mesopotamia, Syria, and Cyprus.

Professor Piggott has recently commented on the early weakness of the Institute as a place of academic research, on 'the discrepancy soon to arise 'between promise and performance'. In particular he criticizes Wheeler's failure to relate with other growing points in archaeology, and, despite the brave words put into the Chancellor's mouth, to realize a true collaboration with other sciences.

One explanation is that the Director was an out and out humanist by upbringing, education, and temperament. Another may be that his earlier sense of isolation, of himself as the lone survivor with an obligation for leadership, had not quite left him. Perhaps he did not fully perceive that he was no longer isolated, that a full degree course and scientific projects were going forward in Cambridge, intellectual light emanating from Professor Childe in the Abercromby chair, and potent influences flooding in from the archaeologists of north-west Europe. Shortcomings of the early years of the Institute can also be explained by the pressure of other work on the honorary Director, by acute shortage of funds and the failure of the University of London to welcome a new subject with open arms. At least the place had enough life, ability, and fellowship in it to grow, to survive the war, and to enjoy a post-war period of great distinction under Professor Childe. Professor Mallowan, one of those who then made it a home of Oriental studies, has contrasted the days in St. John's Lodge, 'an exciting place to live in' where everyone was in touch with all that was going on, with those that followed the 1957 move to the expensive 'new box' in Gordon Square, when, in his opinion, the Institute became heartless and impersonal. Whatever judgement is made on such relative merits, there is no question that the Wheelers were the founding parents of what was to grow into the largest, best-endowed centre of archaeological enterprise in our country.

By the middle of August 1939 Rik Wheeler could no longer endure the pursuit of archaeology in the peaceful fields of Normandy and dashed home to press upon the War Office the promise he had extracted during the shameful aftermath of Munich. This was to be commissioned to raise an anti-aircraft battery to defend the citizens of Enfield. Within a day he was in that little-renowned suburb and was soon to recruit his battery —with the assistance of John Ward Perkins, his son Michael and, before long, A. Goodman, solicitor, one of several of his enlisted men who were to achieve eminence.

No one who knew him supposed that Rik would rest content with a battery or with Enfield. The battery grew into a well-trained regiment and its Colonel strove desperately to get an overseas posting. The frustration was severe for it was not until September of 1941 that he sailed for North Africa with three of his batteries. The next year he was in the grim retreat from Tobruk and was commended for the good order in which his regiment accomplished it. Behind the El Alamein line, during rare intervals from dealing with enemy air attacks, he read Gordon Childe's *Man Makes Himself*. In October 1942, in one of the remarkable letters to Cyril Fox published in *Still Digging*, Wheeler wrote 'congratulate me. I'm now in the crack Division of the British Army! This means a seat plumb in the first row of the stalls for anything that is going. . . . I've been able to lead this gang from the suburbs of northern London right into the very middle of the picture'. In the front row he was when the attack started weeks later: with the Armoured Division, Desert Rats, he went through the second battle of Alamein with distinction. Then, beset by characteristic restlessness during the slow advance on Tripoli, he devised and led an advance foray among the retreating Italians and Germans that was a psychological counterpart to the de Warlencourt action of World War I. Once again no men were lost, and if this second escapade was not so completely successful, it did lead to the party entering Tripoli on 23 January. Soon 'the guns were in action on the quays—the first A.A. guns in Tripoli'.

On his first day in Tripoli Wheeler went to the High Command to insist that steps must at once be taken to protect ancient monuments and museums, a duty hitherto totally neglected. The High Command listened. With Major Ward Perkins Wheeler hastened to survey the principal sites, particularly

Lepcis Magna (Sabratha was still in enemy hands) and draw up a forceful report on what must be done. Amazingly, he was able to get Ward Perkins seconded for a month to take charge. At Sabratha the entire staff of the Italian Antiquities service was found sheltering: they offered prompt and valuable collaboration.

After this brief archaeological interlude, Wheeler's military career was resumed. He was given acting command of the Eighth Army's anti-aircraft brigade, and in May, as the advance neared Tunis, he was promoted to brigadier. He was occupied in the strategic planning for the invasion of Italy when his archaeological self was again evoked. It was August and he was in Algiers, when his Corps Commander, General Horrocks, himself dashed up with a signal asking that Wheeler should be released to become Director General of Archaeology in India.

This invitation, originating with Lord Wavell, was a complete surprise, the one turning-point in his work that had nothing to do with his own forward planning. Wheeler accepted, on condition that he would not take up the appointment until after the next battle—which was, of course, Salerno, then only a month ahead. He duly took part in the landings, which he regarded as 'the most absorbing military operation' of his experience and advanced as far as Naples. Once more that lanky, seemingly charmed body came through unscathed. At 53 Wheeler was ready to engage in what was to be the greatest challenge of his civilian career: the virtual creation of an Antiquities Service for a sub-continent together with the filling of vast lacunae in knowledge of its prehistory and ancient history. The appointment was for four years, but already it was possible to foresee that Independence might shorten the time available for a colossal task.

The British had begun to take an official interest in the recording of India's marvellous architectural heritage as early as 1862 and ten years later the Archaeological Survey of India was in being. It flourished for a time, but was moribund by the end of the century when Lord Curzon became Viceroy. With his real interest in Indian art and antiquities, he quickly appointed John Marshall, a classical archaeologist from King's College, Cambridge, to revive the Survey. Wheeler always insisted that Marshall had many notable achievements during his long tenure—including, of course, the discovery of the Indus civilization. He was, however, an amateurish excavator and, even more unfortunately, quite failed to train up a responsible staff or anyone able to succeed him. This failure, together with cuts due to the Depression, ensured that when he left in 1929 the survey sank into a second decline. Just before the war Leonard Woolley had been summoned to prescribe for its revival and had produced a devastating critical report which, among many apt recommendations, asked for the appointment of a European Adviser in Archaeology. It seems that he privily recommended Wheeler for the role, and it is likely that it was this which guided Lord Wavell's choice. In sending his invitation, the Viceroy commented, 'the condition of the department is quite deplorable'.

Wheeler sailed early in 1944, and after a voyage enlivened by a German torpedo-bomb attack, he headed at once for the offices at the top of the Railway Board building in Simla that were the headquarters of the Survey. What happened next has become legendary. Entering his own office over the forms of sleeping peons, and seeing everywhere idle clerks and hangers-on he 'emitted a bull-like roar, and the place leapt to anxious life'. Within an hour he had interviewed all, and sacked many, of his staff. That evening one of the peons moaned 'a terrible thing has happened to us this day . . .'. Rik himself found the right prophetic words, 'The Devil has come down amongst you having great wrath because he knoweth he hath but a short time'.

How true this proved to be. The Survey had vast responsibilities: for the administration of one and a half million square miles stuffed with ancient sites and monuments ranging from megaliths to the Taj Mahal; for the running of many museums; for all excavation, publishing and epigraphy. While vitalizing the whole, immense department, Wheeler deployed most of his own prodigious energies, just as he had in the old days at home, on training young men in the skills of digging and conservation and on a crash campaign of selective excavation. He also set himself the task, against all kinds of opposition, to end the shoddy, shabby standards of Indian publication and produce a journal where all research and excavation could be promptly published. The first issue of *Ancient India* was to appear at the beginning of 1946.

Having reformed his headquarters with ruthless speed, the new Director General set off to reconnoitre his sub-continent—to learn something of its nature, to meet his far-flung staff, and to pick likely sites for excavation. He must have been overjoyed that once again, as in the twenties, wide fields of historical ignorance invited his skill in filling them by purposeful digging. Even before his arrival Wheeler had formed ideas as to where research was most needed. Dividing the country into its two natural parts, he saw the first requirement in the north to be the filling of the gap between the Indus civilization and the Achaemenid empire and in particular to find cultural evidence of the Aryan invaders, while in the south, where there was no archaeology and no fixed dates before the sixth century A.D., the need was to bring some chronological order into a welter of unrelated material. He recognized that the best chance here would be to work from the datum line provided by numerous finds of Roman coins.

Although the first of these propositions had to be modified, they determined the lines of his forward planning and hence, as it proved, the main addition he was to make to 'our knowledge of the components of Indian civilization'. This, he had always believed, was the central purpose of himself and the service he was creating.

With his northern problem in mind, he headed for the Punjab and the North-west Frontier province—a land he was always to love. Quickly selecting Taxila—where Marshall had dug and there were buildings and a site museum—for his projected training school he went on to the eastern Indus capital, Harappa. There Marshall's probings, although they had indeed revealed a new civilization, had failed to discover the essential nature of the ruins. His mistakes had led Professor Childe to identify Indus society as that of a 'peaceful democratic bourgeois economy' with undefended cities and free from the centralized theocracies of Mesopotamia. It seems almost incredible that Wheeler, quite inexperienced in the mudbrick piles of oriental archaeology, instantly spotted that the highest mound at Harappa was in fact a strongly defended citadel. The excavation he was to direct there in 1946, together with his later work at Mohenjodaro, enabled him to portray the Indus civilization as the creation of a highly authoritarian, militaristic, culturally totalitarian state, its urban population fed from huge communal granaries.

This reconstruction of India's earliest high culture, published in *The Indus Civilization*, a supplementary volume to the *Cambridge History of India*, must count as Wheeler's outstanding contribution to the chronicle of northern India. His excavation at Taxila and, much later, at Charsada (*Charsada*, 1962) were to throw light on Achaemenid times, the impact of Alexander the

Great, and later classical influences. It is ironical that while he had such successes, his intention of filling the hiatus between these two periods was almost entirely frustrated. The Aryans were not to be found—unless it was in the remains of a final massacre he uncovered at Mohenjo-daro.

In contrast, when his survey of 1944 was carried into the southern province, all was to go according to plan. His chance discovery of a fragment of Roman amphora in a museum cupboard in Madras led directly to Arretine ware in the public library of Pondicherry and so on to their source—what proved to be a Roman trading port at Arikamedu. Excavations there in the following year made it possible to date native cultures by association with Roman imports, and these correlations were soon carried northward through the peninsula by diggings at Brahmagiri and Chandravali. One result of many was to date the hitherto mysterious megalithic tombs of the region to the last centuries B.C. Ultimately correlations were extended to the cultures of the Ganges.

The important results of Wheeler's historical researches must claim most attention here, but they were, of course, a small part of his labours during those years of 1944–7. His administrative duties were heavy, and made more difficult by the distance between Simla and New Delhi. He had to fight for more money, to improve museums (he helped to establish an All-India Museums Association) and at the same time to deal with hostile intrigues—in some part due to the excessive ruthlessness with which (here as always) he disposed of the idle or incompetent. More important and exacting still was his campaign to train personnel to staff his digs and to carry on when he himself had gone. This began with the unique training school conducted at Taxila over the winter months of 1944–5. Sixty-one students drawn from all parts of the sub-continent were instructed in every technique then demanded by archaeology. Most of them became devoted disciples and colleagues, prepared to toil like mad dogs in the heat of the sun, and the best endured to work in their respective countries after partition. So continuity was assured between the Wheelerian reign and the developments that were to follow in an independent India and (more shakily) Pakistan.

Wheeler's appointment at New Delhi ended in 1948. He had seen something of the horrors and chaos that followed Independence Day. He could do no more than try to protect his staff and trust that he had prepared the Archaeological Survey of India for survival. There was to be some decline in standards and Taxila was never to be published, yet in general that trust was to be deserved.

Some of Wheeler's brightest pupils were Pakistani, but they were few, and the difficulties of maintaining an archaeological department in their country were prodigious. Visiting Karachi to say goodbye to his friends, he was surprised to be officially invited to become a part-time Archaeological Adviser to the Government. Although by now eager to be home, he agreed to go to Pakistan for a few months in each of the next three years. He went in 1949–50, working as usual to train, to dig, to win public support. He succeeded in establishing a National Museum at Karachi and in directing effective excavations at Mohenjo-daro. Yet, as he said, these part-time labours proved Sysyphean and he did not return for the third year. In 1958, however, he was happy to accept the invitation to dig for a season at Charsada.

After the vast sway of India, Britain must have seemed a small place, yet it did not take long to find worthy outlets for his hardly diminished energies. He went straight to a new chair in the Archaeology of the Roman Provinces furnished by the University of London, and he ended a stirring inaugural (see *Alms for Oblivion*) with Ashoka's words, 'Let small and great exert themselves'. Although Wheeler never was, and never wanted to be thought, a true scholar, this chair fitted well to what by now he had made his most valuable scholarly endowment: an exceptionally wide vision of our planetary civilizations, and particularly of the Empire whose relics he had unearthed from Caernarvon to Pondicherry. It was not, however, to be the main outlet for his own exertions. Nor was the presidency of the Society of Antiquaries which came to him in 1949 after a war-time spell as Director. Unerringly, he recognized that his vitalizing powers could best be devoted to the resurrection of the British Academy, to which he had been elected Fellow in a somewhat irregular fashion, as early as 1941.

In these *Proceedings* there is no need to detail the achievements of Wheeler's twenty years as Secretary of the Academy, with their many victories and one failure. He has, moreover, chronicled them with wit and thoroughness in his *British Academy, 1949–1968*.

The Academy, founded to do for the Humanities what the Royal Society had long done for the sciences, had reached its nadir in the post-war years—having fallen there from no great height. Agitation for reform from Sir Charles Webster was largely responsible for Wheeler's appointment as secretary in 1949; when Webster became President the following year they were able to work hand in glove for reform. Wheeler has described with brutal frankness how the gerontocracy was overthrown and the whole arthritic body rejuvenated. As urgent as the retirement of the old men, was the extraction of money from the Treasury—an art and craft in which Wheeler was now adept. He saw that the tedious confusion of the administration of the various British Schools overseas would make an opening. It was not very long before it was agreed that the Academy should be paymaster for them all: the old established Schools at Athens, Rome, and Iraq and the new one at Ankara were found a little more cash; the lapsed School at Jerusalem revived. So the Academy began to mount towards its rightful place as grand patron of the Humanities. Later the Secretary was to play a large part in founding research Institutes in Iran and East Africa, the latter involving him years of scheming, travelling, and hard work.

On the home front there was an urgent need to find funds for struggling learned societies and their publications and for individual research. Happily Trusts and other institutions volunteered or were induced to grant the Academy modest sums that could be used to prime the pump until Government money could be deserved and won. Thus, through the fifties, the Nuffield Foundation, followed by All Souls, helped to rescue societies by subsidizing their periodicals, while the Pilgrim Trust supported a pilot scheme that enabled the Academy to make awards for a wide range of research workers, young and not so young.

All this was admirable, but it became obvious that in contrast with the orderly arrangements for the support of the natural sciences, that for the humanities and social sciences was chaotic: as Sir George Clark said, it was 'a structure which is truly Gothic in its wealth of irregular detail'. A report on that Gothic structure and how it could best be rationalized would be valuable in itself: it was a necessity if a proper case was to be made for substantial Treasury funding. The Rockefeller Foundation agreed to finance the inquiry, and late in 1961, towards the end of Sir Maurice Bowra's presidency, the Report, *Research in the Humanities and Social Sciences*, was published.

In all these matters the Secretary had played an active and often leading part, working closely with successive Presidents.

Now he was to score a personal triumph that marked a great leap forward in the Academy's fortunes. A discussion of the Rockefeller Report with the Financial Secretary had seemed to go well. Although care had been taken not to recommend the Academy as the central authority to administer the proposed grant, no one can have been startled when the Financial Secretary himself made this recommendation, with only the proviso that the Social Sciences were to be provided for elsewhere. Bowra led off his deputation confident of being able to announce the good news in his last Address. Week after week went by without word until in desperate resolve Wheeler went down to the Treasury. 'It was now or never. . . . The dramatic moment had arrived to pin . . . substance to the Financial Secretary's expressed goodwill. I left the Treasury with an initial grant of £25,000 a year' and with a promise that it would soon be doubled.

This undoubtedly was the summit of Wheeler's great services to the British Academy and the humanities. For the rest of his tenure as Secretary, however, there was much to be done in the administration of the new affluence, particularly after 1966 when the Academy began to sustain its own research projects. In all this he maintained fruitful contacts with the Royal Society, particularly in the field of prehistoric archaeology. It was only sad that a project dear to his heart, to found a British Institute of Far Eastern Studies in Tokyo, was killed by the 1967 devaluation crisis just at the moment when success had seemed near. On the other hand, at much the same time his efforts to move the Academy from its poky premises in Burlington Gardens to a part of those vacated by the Royal Society in Burlington House were rewarded. The transfer was made late in 1968, a few months before his retirement.

Wheeler ended his *British Academy* with wry comments on the fact that he, who had once driven the old men from the seats of power, had remained Secretary into his eightieth year. He forgave himself as the last of his kind: the officers of learned societies who worked without a salary—as he had done for twenty years. He most treasured a letter in which Professor David Knowles said, 'I always regard you—along with Webster—as the second founder of the Academy . . . and the move to Burlington House is certainly due entirely to you'.

While the British Academy claimed most of Wheeler's time and thought during the fifties and sixties, he contrived to do much more besides—and the honours came rolling in. In 1951–2, when still holding his professorship, he carried out his last considerable excavation in this country. Stanwick in north Yorkshire, with its extensive earthworks and its association with that most neglected drama of British history, the feud between King Venutius and his pro-Roman Queen, Cartimandua, was almost as well suited to his gifts as Maiden Castle had been. The results were published in his last special Report for the Society of Antiquaries, the slim *Stanwick Frortifications* of 1954. In the same year he published, from the fullness of his experience, the excellent *Rome Beyond the Imperial Frontiers*. In 1968 he was to produce *Flames Over Persepolis* in which, perhaps, he celebrated an inner sympathy with Alexander the Great.

He served as chairman of the Ancient Monuments Board (1964–6) and as Trustee of the British Museum (1963–73). He collected honorary doctorates from the universities of Bristol, Ireland, Wales, Oxford, Liverpool, Bradford, and Delhi. His knighthood came in 1952, his C.H. in 1967; then, in 1968, the honour that probably gave him most pleasure, Fellowship of the Royal Society under Statute 12.

It was in the mid-fifties that he hugely enjoyed his extraordinary success in the T.V. archaeological panel game, Animal, Vegetable, and Mineral. With Glyn Daniel as the perfect foil, his panache, humorous self-display, and fine sense of timing—the delayed recognition—captivated the British Public. Sir Mortimer Wheeler was chosen Television Personality of the Year, wherever he went heads were turned and one London schoolchild out of every three declared in favour of archaeology as a career. After this success Rik Wheeler could always perform for the BBC, and David Collison directed a worthy record of his archaeological life and work.

Even in retirement Wheeler was often to be found at the British Academy, and was still attended by Molly Myers who had done so much to support him in his Secretaryship. He was touched and pleased by the Conference on the *Iron Age and its Hillforts* organized in 1971 by the young members of the Southampton University Archaeological Society 'as a token of respect to mark his eightieth year'. He must also have found much to sustain him when in 1972 a peregrination of India came to resemble a royal triumph. Everywhere those whom he had disciplined, driven, taught, welcomed him with honour and affection. His lifelong restlessness never left him even after he fractured his pelvis during a visit to Rome and suffered a slight stroke in Paris and on the flight home.

A somewhat ill-judged marriage to Mavis de Vere Cole in 1939 did not last long; his third marriage, to Margaret Norfolk, celebrated in 1945 at Simla, was also a failure, although they were never legally separated. Thereafter Wheeler rented a little house in Whitcomb Street close by the National Gallery. Although its frame seemed too small for his own, it made a charming retreat graced by pictures, oriental ceramics, and other treasures.

During his last years he lived very largely in the care of Molly Myers in her Surrey cottage. There, although he still visited London and enjoyed female company, including that of a granddaughter, he raged against the cruel thievings of old age. In their despite he set himself one final challenge: to write *My Archaeological Mission to India and Pakistan.* It was no great thing, but he completed the work. It was good to see an advance copy in his hands shortly before his death. On one side the jacket showed a venerable but still commanding Mortimer Wheeler with Indian disciples, facing, on the other side, that sensuous, provocative bronze dancing girl from Mohenjo-daro.

JACQUETTA HAWKES